THE PLAINS ACROSS

Albert Bierstadt, "The Oregon Trail," ca. 1865. Butler Institute of American Art, Youngstown, Ohio

JOHN D. UNRUH, JR.

THE PLAINS ACROSS

The Overland Emigrants and the
Trans-Mississippi West, 1840–60

UNIVERSITY OF ILLINOIS PRESS

Urbana Chicago London

© 1979 BY THE BOARD OF TRUSTEES OF THE UNIVERSITY OF ILLINOIS
MANUFACTURED IN THE UNITED STATES OF AMERICA

Third Printing, 1979

Library of Congress Cataloging in Publication Data

Unruh, John David, 1937–1976.
  The plains across.

  Bibliography: p.
  Includes index.
  1. Overland journeys to the Pacific.
2. Frontier and pioneer life—The West.   3. The
West—History—1848–1860.   4. The West—History—
To 1848.   I. Title.
F593.U67   1978   978   78-9781
ISBN 0-252-00698-4

For Ellie
and for my Mother and Father

Contents

FOREWORD   xi

PREFACE   xv

INTRODUCTION: THE HISTORIANS AND THE OVERLANDERS   3

Chapter One: PUBLIC OPINION, 1840–48
  "Palpable homicide" or "Merry as a marriage bell"?   28

Chapter Two: PUBLIC OPINION, 1849–60
  Humbugging and Helping   62

Chapter Three: MOTIVATIONS AND BEGINNINGS
  "Life as at a fair"   90

Chapter Four: EMIGRANT INTERACTION
  "Our journey has not been as solitary as we feared"   118

Chapter Five: EMIGRANT-INDIAN INTERACTION
  From "mutual aid" to "massacres"   156

Chapter Six: THE FEDERAL GOVERNMENT
  "Good fellow Uncle Sam is"   201

Chapter Seven: PRIVATE ENTREPRENEURS, 1840–49
  "While others are chasing wealth they are catching it, no dream"   244

Chapter Eight: PRIVATE ENTREPRENEURS, 1850–60
  "Too many cooks spoil the broth"   267

Chapter Nine: THE MORMON "HALFWAY HOUSE"
  "It cost nothing to get in, but a great deal to get out"   302

Chapter Ten: WEST COAST ASSISTANCE
  "Are you men from California, or do you come from Heaven?"   338

Chapter Eleven: THE OVERLANDERS IN HISTORICAL PERSPECTIVE
  "To endure heat like a salamander . . . and labor like a jackass"   379

NOTES   417

BIBLIOGRAPHY   519

INDEX   555

ILLUSTRATIONS

Albert Bierstadt, "The Oregon Trail"   ii
Frank H. Schwarz, "The Great Wagon Train Migration
   at The Dalles"   6
Ezra Meeker, 1906   21
Horace Greeley, 1858   37
James F. Wilkins, "Leaving the Old Homestead"   52
Covered wagon interior   60
William S. Mount, "California News"   63
Independence, Mo., 1853   71
J. Goldsborough Bruff, "Seeing the Elephant, 6: Mining"
   and "7: Going Home with Pile"   76
E. Hall Martin, "Mountain Jack and a Wandering Miner"   82
James F. Wilkins, "Covered Wagons in the Rockies"   95
F. O. C. Darley, "Emigrants Crossing the Plains"   109
St. Joseph, Mo., 1853   113
William Henry Jackson, "Kanesville—Missouri River
   Crossing—1856"   116
William Henry Jackson, "South Pass"   121
"Seeing the Elephant"   125
"Death Scene on the Plains"   138
"End of a Day's March"   142
Charles Nahl, "Crossing the Plains"   144
J. Goldsborough Bruff, "Pilgrim's Progress" and
   "The Rabbit-Hole Springs"   151
Chief Washakie, 1882   161
William Henry Jackson, "Crossing South Platte"   168
"A Chief Forbidding the Passage of a Train through His Country"   174
"An Emigrant Train Attacked by Hostile Indians on the Prairie"   191
Frederick Piercy, "Scott's Bluffs"   199
Frederick Piercy, "Fort Laramie"   204
James F. Wilkins, "Fort Bridger"   211
William Henry Jackson, "Approaching Chimney Rock"   219
William Henry Jackson, "Fort Kearny"   228
J. Goldsborough Bruff, "Fort Hall"   234
Jim Bridger   249
Frederick Piercy, "Elk Horn River Ferry"   255
J. Goldsborough Bruff, "Perilous Crossing of the Missouri"
   and "Ugly Descent & Crossing of Salt"   262
Albert Bierstadt, "Nooning on the Platte"   271
F. R. Grist, "Crossing the Platte, Mouth of Deer Creek"   280
Emigrants fording a river   292
Frederick Piercy, "Great Salt Lake City in 1853"   309

Brigham Young, c. 1850   316
William Henry Jackson, "Devil's Gate"   322
Mormon emigrants at South Pass   331
Oregon City, 1857   346
Elijah Stevens   352
Dr. John McLoughlin   358
William Smith Jewett, "Portrait of General John Sutter"   366
"Are You Men from California, or Do You Come from Heaven?"   371
Sacramento, 1849   376
Emigrant family portrait   384
"California Emigrants—the Last Day on the Plains"   388
"Crossing the Plains"   393
J. Goldsborough Bruff, "A View from the Summit of
    Independence Rock"   399
J. Goldsborough Bruff, "The Fate of Many"   404
J. Goldsborough Bruff, "Descending into Green River Valley"
    and "Accident at Skew Bridge"   411
J. Goldsborough Bruff, "Seeing the Elephant, 1: Leaving Home"
    and "2: Arrival in California"   415

MAPS

1. The Missouri River Frontier, 1840–60   99
2. Locations of Major Indian and White Indian
        Trail Depredations   172
3. Principal Army Forts and Landmarks near the
        Oregon-California Trail   212
4. The Federal Government's Trail Improvements, 1850–60   238
5. Trading Posts, Ferries, and Bridges, 1840–48   246
6. Trading Posts, Ferries, and Bridges, 1849   258
7. Trading Posts, Ferries, Bridges, and Missions, 1850   269
8. The Mormon Kingdom   304
9. Route Improvements Undertaken by Oregon, California,
        and Washington   343

TABLES

1. Overland Emigration to Oregon, California, Utah, 1840–48   119
2. Overland Emigration to Oregon, California, Utah, 1849–60   120
3. Reconstructed Fort Laramie Emigrant Register, 1850   122
4. Estimated Overland Emigrants Killed by Indians, and
        Indians Killed by Overland Emigrants, 1840–60   185

5. Price Ranges at Trading Posts, 1841–48   251
6. Price Ranges at Trading Posts, 1849   265
7. Price Ranges at Trading Posts, 1850   276
8. Price Ranges at Trading Posts, 1852   283
9. Price Ranges at Trading Posts, 1851, 1853–60   290
10. Average Travel Time for the Overland Journey   403

Foreword

THIS MAGISTERIAL STUDY, now an impressive book, was a doctoral dissertation begun under the direction of the late distinguished historian and teacher George L. Anderson at the University of Kansas, and completed after Professor Anderson's death under his colleague Clifford S. Griffin of the same university. The author, John David Unruh, Jr., was admitted to doctoral candidacy at the university in 1967. It was not until October, 1975, that he successfully defended his completed dissertation and was awarded the Ph.D. in history. Eight years of tireless research and writing were invested in completing the dissertation: that it was destined for publication will quickly become evident to the reader.

There is no doubt that it is a superb achievement. The research, both in printed and manuscript sources, is near-exhaustive, as a glance at the extensive bibliography will reveal. Emigrant diaries, journals, and letters, contemporary newspapers, books and articles, theses and dissertations —little escaped John Unruh's attention. What has been fashioned from that prodigious research—the first synthesis on overland travel in the antebellum period—will surely become a classic.

Although a large body of books and articles have touched on some of the subjects included in the narrative—the role played by the federal government, the Indians, and the Mormons in the overland endeavor, ferrying and other entrepreneurial activities, sickness and disease, equipment and costs—this is the first study to present an overall synthesis on overland emigration for the entire 1840–60 period. The Introduction, which ably surveys and critiques the existing body of pertinent literature, makes this point abundantly clear.

Not only has the author structured a comprehensive synthesis, he has also fashioned a hypothesis. He applies "the concept of change through time" in order to increase our understanding and to offer us new perspectives about overland emigration. The fulcrum on which this innovative study balances is found in the focus on "the interaction between the overlanders and other groups in the West—the army, the Indians, the Mormons, the traders and other entrepreneurs—as well as in the interaction of the overlanders with the flora and fauna of the West." Utilizing a broad scope and incorporating new data from the neglected decade of the 1850s, the author traces "the ways in which trails, the West, and the overlanders themselves were changing." By examining such interactions and interfaces we can then discern "the real explanation of how the feat [of overland emigration] was successfully accomplished. . . ." In this endeavor Unruh has succeeded admirably. His study is a major contribution to the history of the American West.

The triumph of this scholarly achievement, a book which will be acclaimed as definitive, indeed a seminal work, is marred by tragedy. On January 18, 1976, two days after undergoing surgery for the removal of a brain tumor which proved malignant, John D. Unruh, Jr., died. The pleasure of seeing his magnificent work in print was thus denied him—though the knowledge that it was to be published was surely a source of deep satisfaction.

Born on a South Dakota farm at Marion, Turner County, on October 4, 1937, John was the descendant of Mennonite pioneers who had settled on nearby Turkey Creek in the spring of 1874. His formative education was completed in Freeman, with the exception of the sixth grade, which was taken by correspondence when his parents were in the service of the Mennonite Central Committee in the Netherlands. In 1957, after completing two years at Freeman Junior College, he transferred to Bethel College in North Newton, Kansas, majoring in history. He took his bachelor's degree with highest academic distinction, and spent the ensuing two years with the Peace Section of the Mennonite Central Committee, serving for a time in Akron, Pennsylvania.

After that church-related duty, John decided to pursue graduate work, no doubt influenced by his father, who holds a doctorate in history and has published several books dealing with the Mennonites. John also had early taken an interest in the history of his faith and family and later joined his father in collaborative research on both subjects as time and circumstance permitted.

Determined on being a historian, John earned his M.A. at the University of Kansas, where he was elected to Phi Beta Kappa. Following the example of his parents, he then decided on a teaching career, accepting an instructorship at Bluffton College in Bluffton, Ohio. Two years later he returned to Kansas to work full time on his doctorate with Professor Anderson. Three arduous years of study culminated in advancement to candidacy. That hurdle behind, on June 11, 1967, John married Elda M. Waltner, whom he had known from high school days in Freeman, and the Unruhs returned to Bluffton, where John resumed his teaching.

Through the intervening years as he labored on his dissertation, he established a solid reputation as a demanding and excellent classroom teacher. His good humor and deep humanitarian qualities won him much admiration as well. His love of nature and his enthusiasm for sports provided him with pleasant diversion, but his dissertation research was all-pervasive: he was a scholar first.

With his premature death, the manuscript had to be steered through publication. In that endeavor three people have played unsung roles. Professor Von Hardesty, a historian colleague of John's at Bluffton College, came to the assistance of Mrs. Unruh, and together the two labored on galleys and related publication details. Elizabeth G. Dulany, managing editor at the University of Illinois Press, prepared the manuscript copy for the printer; her editorial work is a model in all respects—skillful, thorough, restrained.

The results loom large on the pages that follow. It is Unruh's work, perseverance, and dedication that produced it. The reader will find here an exciting narrative clothed in flawless style, exhaustively researched, laced with brilliant insights. There is no question but that it will become required reading for any serious student and scholar of the history of the American West and the westward movement. No historian and scholar could ask for a more fitting epitaph.

University of Southern California   DOYCE B. NUNIS, JR.
Los Angeles
June 16, 1978

Preface

COMPLETING A STUDY ON ANTEBELLUM transcontinental travel at a time when the nation is slowly coming to grips with the travel implications of the energy shortfall of the 1970s is to be reminded anew of the centrality of transportation to the American experience. The overland emigrations of the 1840s and 1850s, which comprise the focus for this study, were enormously significant for western and national history. Ramifications of the overland transit of 250,000 persons to the Pacific Coast before the Civil War were felt in a myriad of diverse realms from international diplomacy to Indian-white relationships and patterns of settlement and economic growth.

The saga of the covered wagon migrations to Oregon and California is a familiar one. The process by which I became convinced that it needed to be retold is admittedly somewhat hazy, for this revisionist study of the overland emigrations commenced ten years ago in Professor George L. Anderson's readings course in the history of the Trans-Mississippi West at the University of Kansas. After I had rashly decided against his recommendation for a dissertation topic, Professor Anderson graciously permitted me to use the last portion of the course to read widely in a search for an appropriate substitute topic.

By the end of the semester I had become enamored of the possibilities of a thorough re-evaluation of the overland emigrations. The more I compared secondary accounts with actual diaries and letters written by travelers of the time, the more I became convinced that previous scholars had paid insufficient attention to certain key factors in interpreting this crucial phase of the westward movement. Specifically, I came to believe that applying the organizing principles of change over time, emigrant cooperation, and interaction between the emigrants and the many temporary and permanent inhabitants of the West was essential to a correct historical understanding of the overland emigration phenomenon.[1]

In choosing the topic and approaching it in the manner I did, I was also influenced by the concerns about the future of western history which were being raised at the time. Among others, Earl Pomeroy, Gene Gressley, Rodman Paul, and W. N. Davis, Jr. (in his provocatively entitled survey report, "Will the West Survive as a Field in American History?") were all stressing the urgent need for more imaginative analysis, interpretation, and synthesis in the writing of western history.[2] Because I had also been much influenced by the thoroughness and comprehensiveness of Dale L. Morgan's historical scholarship, I determined to provide a great deal of supportive evidence for the conclusions I reached, both in the narrative and in the notes. Further, to aid subsequent researchers, wherever possible I have identified specific individuals and locations of importance.

Although I have read widely in the secondary works on antebellum overland travel—and have incorporated facts and insights from those writings wherever appropriate—this project rests primarily upon the actual writings of the overland emigrants themselves. Contemporary newspapers, letters, diaries, and reminiscent accounts have provided the principal resources for this study. As one who has never attempted to keep a personal diary, I am most grateful to the hundreds of overland travelers of the 1840s and 1850s who persisted under the most trying conditions in maintaining their invaluable personal diaries and travel journals. Had it not been for the foresight and perseverance of faithful diarists like Byron McKinstry, this study could not have been written, at least in its present form. McKinstry, an 1850 gold rusher, was admonished by a frustrated companion one evening as he sat painstakingly writing in his diary: "My God, McKinstry, why do you write about this trip so you can remember it? All I hope for is to get home, alive, as soon as possible, so that I can forget it!"[3] Fortunately, McKinstry kept writing.

This study incorporates four principal dimensions. The Introduction is a historiographical survey of the present status of historical writing about the overland emigrants. An investigation of contemporary opinion during the 1840s and 1850s about the overland emigrants and the wisdom and possibilities of their venture is presented in Chapters 1 and 2. The major portion of the work is a systematic analysis of the changing role over time of the major "assistants" to the overland emigrants: the Indians, the federal government, private entrepreneurs, the Mormon settlement in the Salt Lake Valley, and the emerging settlements on the West Coast. Also included are chapters on journey preparation and the motivations for traveling west and on incidences of emigrant cooperation and interaction during the course of the overland journey. Chapter 11 attempts a summary assessment of the overland emigrations.

An earlier draft of the Introduction was published under the title "The Golden History of the Overland Emigrations" in *The Westerners Brand*

Book Number 14, Los Angeles Corral, ed. Doyce B. Nunis, Jr. (Los Angeles, 1974), and a slightly altered version of the first portion of Chapter 4 was published in the Spring, 1973, issue of the *Kansas Quarterly* under the title "Against the Grain: West to East on the Overland Trail."

I am considerably embarrassed to confess that it has taken me a full decade to analyze and interpret two decades of westward migration. During these ten years of research and writing I have benefited from a great many personal and institutional courtesies and favors. Librarians and archivists from coast to coast have put me greatly in their debt, not only in locating and supplying source materials but in permitting me to use my typewriter to expedite note-taking and occasionally assisting in securing lodging.

Anyone who has been privileged, as I was, to spend weeks of concentrated research at such meccas of historical treasures as the Henry E. Huntington Library and Art Gallery, San Marino, California, the Bancroft Library of the University of California, Berkeley, and the Beinecke Rare Book and Manuscript Library, Yale University, New Haven, Connecticut, will appreciate my gratitude to the staffs of those outstanding institutions.

I spent shorter amounts of time, but was no less courteously treated, at the California State Library in Sacramento, the Western History Department of the Denver Public Library, the Western Reserve Historical Society in Cleveland, and at the California, Colorado, Kansas, Missouri, Nebraska, and Ohio state historical societies. While I am indebted to the highly efficient staffs of all these institutions, I wish to express special appreciation to the genial personnel of the Kansas State Historical Society in Topeka, where I spent so many enjoyable research days.

The University of Kansas librarians, particularly Michael J. Brodhead, then director of the Kansas Collection, were most efficient and cooperative. I am likewise indebted to the university for a summer scholarship in 1966 which facilitated research on the West Coast. Ruth K. Salisbury, librarian of the Historical Society of Western Pennsylvania, generously provided me with a copy of an important overland diary, as did Professor Burton J. Williams of Central Washington State College. Elizabeth Anne Johnson of the Library Association of Portland, Oregon, similarly sent me a copy of a crucial government document, and Professor George R. Lee of Culver-Stockton College kindly provided me with a copy of his master's thesis.

Deans Mark Houshower and Elmer Neufeld and Presidents Robert Kreider and Benjamin Sprunger of Bluffton College indulged me in a number of schedule adjustments to hasten my progress. The Title III Faculty Development Grant that Bluffton College accorded me during the spring term of 1970 enabled me to finally complete my research and begin writing. Bluffton College librarians Delbert Gratz and Harvey Hiebert extended to me library privileges far beyond the call of duty. Inter-library loan personnel, especially Julie Brauen Mackey and Susan Headings Gratz, labored creatively and diligently in my behalf.

My departmental colleagues at Bluffton College—Ray Hamman, Von Hardesty, and Rick Hite—provided much encouragement and uncomplainingly shouldered extra burdens to free me for work on a project I am sure they were beginning to suspect might never be completed.

I wish also to acknowledge the special assistance of several individuals. Dale L. Morgan's comments on my initial research proposal induced me to broaden the scope of my coverage to include the entire period between 1840 and 1860. Dr. Jaquelia S. Holliday, then professor of history at San Francisco State College, did me the great honor of inviting me to his private study and turning me loose for an afternoon in some of the source materials for overland travel he had collected. Professor Thomas F. Andrews of Azuza Pacific College generously shared with me much of his vast knowledge of western guidebooks and overland travelers, and, with Professors Doyce B. Nunis, Homer E. Socolofsky, and Von Hardesty, read and helpfully commented on one or more of my chapters, as did Mr. Arman Habegger.

It was my good fortune to have as my dissertation advisers Professors George L. Anderson and Clifford S. Griffin. What unity, preciseness of argument, and elegance of language exist in this work are due in large measure to their perspicacious critiques and wise counsel. They unfailingly accorded me wide latitude in fashioning my organization and approach, enthusiastically gave me a great deal of their time, and bolstered my spirits with kind words of enouragement. But I owe them much more. Treating me always as a colleague in historical inquiry, they extended to me personal courtesies I would never have expected to receive. Above all, their warm friendship and their own excellence as researchers and writers of history were a constant source of inspiration. One of my deepest disappointments is that I was unable to finish this project before Professor Anderson's untimely death. I am especially grateful to Professor Griffin for his unhesitating willingness to serve as my adviser following Professor Anderson's death.

For my wife, Ellie (who typed the final copy of the manuscript and served throughout as an effective stylistic critic), my mother, and my father, no acknowledgment or tribute can ever satisfactorily express my gratitude for their encouragement, their invaluable contributions, and especially for their sacrifices to this project. In many ways this volume is almost as much theirs as it is mine. To them I lovingly dedicate *The Plains Across*. And to them I publicly apologize for its having taken so long.

JOHN D. UNRUH, JR.

THE PLAINS ACROSS

Introduction: The Historians and the Overlanders

In 1855 a distraught father had a special lead coffin made. Filling it with alcohol, he took his recently deceased son's body from Shelby County, Missouri, to Washington Territory, where, six months and nearly 3,000 miles later, the funeral procession ended with the boy's burial beneath the towering western pine trees he had been so anxious to see.[1] A bizarre incident, to be sure, but extreme, strange, and poignant occurrences could constantly be seen along the ruts of the Oregon-California Trail during the several decades it served as the major channel of America's westward movement. Indeed, a panoramic view of the entire human experience was occasionally afforded at a single campground, as on the Sunday in mid-June, 1846, when three companies of overland emigrants all encamped within a two-mile radius. Before their oxen were yoked for the next day's travel, a child had been born, a young couple had been married, and a small boy had been buried.[2]

Similar tales of pathos, of courage and cowardice, of generosity and selfishness, of heroism and grandeur have echoed and re-echoed through American scholarship ever since the interest-kindling overland caravans began to wend their way westward with regularity in 1841. Books and articles concerning the emigrants and the trails they followed continue to appear with astonishing frequency—this has easily been one of the most fascinating topics for writers, folklorists, and historians of the American West. The overlanders' vehicles, their legendary covered wagons, have come to symbolize America's westward movement.[3]

The overland emigrants themselves foreshadowed this interest and productivity by emphasizing the uniqueness and the historic significance of their travels. They took such pains to record their activities for posterity that in the entire American experience probably only the Civil War has called forth a commensurate cornucopia of letters, journals, diaries, memoirs, and reminiscent accounts—a veritable "folk literature" of one of the nations' greatest achievements.[4]

Most of this material falls into several clearly distinguishable categories. First, there are the trail histories, researched in libraries or in the field. Whether scholarly or popular, the authors of such works endeavor to locate accurately the various routes and cutoffs used by the overlanders, often so that the present-day tourist can approximate a similar route over modern highways. Second, there are the hundreds of daily diaries and journals painstakingly kept by individual emigrants. Many of these have since been carefully edited and published, often with lengthy and enlightening introductions explaining various facets of the overland experience. Closely related, if somewhat less trustworthy, are the reminiscent accounts written in the late nineteenth and early twentieth centuries by former overlanders, either to satisfy the curiosity of relatives or their own literary aspirations. These recollections often make for exciting reading since, as 1853 overlander George B. Currey admitted in his 1887 reminiscent address to the Oregon Pioneer Association, "every genuine old pioneer is in honor bound to have had the hardest time on the plains of any other person living or dead."[5] Finally, innumerable articles and books have singled out specific aspects of the overland experience for more concentrated attention.

In analyzing more than a century of scholarship and literature it is at once evident that the record of the overland emigrations has been, with few exceptions, presented in either the narrowly particular or the broadly general. Comprehensive analytical and interpretive accounts are rarely encountered. If they have not been editing an individual diary or assessing some particular phenomenon, most writers have chosen to illustrate the overland story by incorporating a few entertaining quotations and intriguing occurrences as examples from which to generalize about the entire emigrating experience over several decades.

The widely held view that certain emigration years were of critical importance to the history of the nation—1843, 1849, and, to a lesser extent, 1846—has further resulted in the "typical" years. They have become, in their overuse, the framework undergirding most of the writing about the overland emigrations. So many articles and books have concentrated so exclusively on the years of the California gold rush—mainly 1849 and 1850—that this event and these years have become exceptionally "typical," so that writers have tended to depict the entire complex history of the overland migrations with illustrative data of a distinctly golden hue.

This can be seen in the selection of diaries and journals to which scholars have devoted their best and most frequent attention. In 1959 Dale L. Morgan expertly edited James A. Pritchard's 1849 overland diary and

4

appended to it a listing of all the then known diarists of 1849—132—with a tabulation of precisely when each diarist reached over 60 locations upon the route, a monumental task no one has attempted on a similar scale for any other emigration year. More 1849 diaries have since been located, and diaries of that year continue to find their way into print. To be sure, diaries of other emigration years have also been appearing, including many for 1850, but with neither the frequency nor the acclaim of those of 1849. Further confirmation that the most perceptive editorial work has been lavished on 1849 diaries came when a highly respected scholar, himself a sometime laborer in the overland vineyard, recently chose the "best-edited" overland diaries. All had been kept by 1849 overlanders.[6]

In excellence and comprehensiveness of modern coverage only the 1843 and 1846 emigrations compare with the gold rush years. Indeed, 1846 has been termed by one scholar as the "best-documented year" in western travel history.[7] Almost all of the known diaries of 1843 and 1846 have been published, although, at least for those of 1843, not usually in book form. Jesse Applegate's delightful 1900 account of "A Day with the Cow Column in 1843," however, is probably the single most widely quoted overland account.

There is reason, of course, for the fact that these three emigration years have been singled out for special attention. All of these years have at one time or another been heralded as "watershed" years in the history of the West, if not of the nation itself. From such a perspective the approximately 900 persons who reached Oregon in the "Great Migration" of 1843 provided the necessary manpower for the organization of a provisional government, putting the Hudson's Bay Company on the defensive and thereby "saving" or "winning" Oregon from Great Britain. The 1843 overlanders also served history, it has been said, by demonstrating that wagons could be taken successfully to The Dalles, a necessary occurrence if there was to be ever-increasing family emigration and thus eventual American occupation of the Pacific Coast.[8] It is therefore no surprise that one of the four murals adorning the Oregon state capitol building depicts the arrival of the 1843 overlanders.[9] In spite of the fact that in a penetrating article many years ago Frederick Merk established that the 1843 overlanders had only a minimal influence on the outcome of the boundary negotiations,[10] the full-blown theory continues to be used, especially in more popular writings. And even though the yet larger overland contingent of 1844 was preparing to cross the continent with wagons regardless of the results of 1843, there is no denying the far-reaching significance of this first large and successful transcontinental emigration.[11]

To Bernard DeVoto, 1846 was a "turning point in American destiny," and therefore "The Year of Decision." His discerning book by that title, published in 1943, was important in refurbishing the pre-eminence of that year's emigration, even though the approximately 2,700 persons on the

Frank H. Schwarz, "The Great Wagon Train Migration at The Dalles before Departure for the Willamette Valley, 1843" (1938), one of four murals in the Oregon State Capitol rotunda.

trails were of marginal importance to some of the national energies with which DeVoto concerned himself. Incorporated in his analysis of this pivotal year were such matters as the treaty with Great Britain finally dividing the Oregon country, the beginning of the Mormon hegira which would take the Saints the following year to their new refuge in the Salt Lake Valley, the inception of the Mexican War, and the imminent acquisition of California and the Southwest, which, for DeVoto, meant the certainty of civil war. There were also important trail developments in 1846. The Applegates forged a significant new route into the Willamette Valley, the Donner party found its macabre niche in history in the Sierra snows,[12] and from his western trip Francis Parkman fashioned his famous account of the Oregon Trail.

Three years later the hordes of humanity hurtling westward by all possible routes in search of California's gold were caught up in a movement which Dale Morgan has contended "altered the course of history in so many ways that scholars will never trace them all."[13] The forty-niners influenced national and world population movements, economies, finance, politics, transportation, and settlement patterns. The gold seekers traveling on the South Pass overland route also enabled the Salt Lake Saints to insure the success of their Great Basin empire, spawned in their wake fledgling communities, fostered Indian hostility—thereby hastening the ultimate confrontation which would destroy the Indian way of life— and altered the nature of the overland trail and trip in a myriad of ways.[14]

It is now increasingly recognized not only that the legendary forty-niners and their even more numerous followers of 1850 comprised a disproportionate percentage of all the overlanders between 1840 and 1860, but also that they stood against the grain of those overlanders in motivation. Most came not to settle or build but to plunder and, with a stake for the future, to return to their homes and families back in the "civilized States." The gold rush, it has been argued, was thus an interruption of the traditional westward movement, an aberration and not a climactic culmination.[15] Of course, large numbers of gold rushers, lacking the means to return, remained in California. Many eventually found success, and by the time they recorded their reminiscences often believed they had initially come to settle. And many who went home—with or without their pile—soon returned to the Pacific Coast with their families, this time to settle and build. Frequently they again made the journey on the overland trail, enjoying some of the services and conveniences their first momentous expeditions had brought about, and also chancing the increasing dangers which they had likewise accentuated.

These three years thus emerge as exceptionally significant years for western and national history, as well as for the history of the overland migrations. This importance does not, however, automatically make them sufficiently "typical" to illustrate the totality or complexity of the overland emigrations before the Civil War, even though a review of western scholarship indicates that this is precisely what has happened.

The pre-eminent position of the gold-seeking emigrants of 1849 and 1850 can be seen, for example, in the frequent concentration upon the adventures of the members of a single organized company, or of the rushers emanating from a specific community, geographic region, or entire state. Although diaries can be used to good advantage in such studies, principally they have been derived from the pertinent local newspapers, thereby illuminating the manner in which the stay-at-homes vicariously experienced the dangers and excitement their fellow townsmen were encountering. Thus, the Boston-Newton Joint Stock Company of Massachusetts, the "Buckeye Rovers" of Athens County, Ohio, the Connecticut Mining and Trading Company, New Jersey's Newark Overland Company, and the Charlestown, Virginia, Mining Company have all had their chroniclers.[16] Similarly traced in some detail have been the escapades of gold rushers from Ann Arbor and Marshall, Michigan, and Jersey City.[17] The gold seekers from Missouri's "Boonslick" region have been studied, as have the gold rush movements in the states of Missouri, Iowa, Wisconsin, Ohio, Arkansas, West Virginia, New Jersey, and Massachusetts.[18]

An abundance of more particularized surveys of additional phases of the overland experience have appeared, primarily in the journals of western history. Dorothy O. Johansen has written a stimulating treatise on why certain types of Americans chose to go to Oregon and others favored California during the mid-nineteenth-century migrations; Walker D. Wyman has probed the general importance of the Missouri River outfitting posts in several studies; Merrill J. Mattes has endeavored to determine the relative prominence of the several outfitting towns.[19] Several scholars have scrutinized one or more of the guidebooks so hopefully purchased by uncertain emigrants. Under way in this connection, for example, is Thomas F. Andrews's sympathetic re-evaluation of the much-maligned Hastings guidebook of Donner party notoriety. While Lansford Hastings's impact on western travel has always been well known, the significance to the emigration phenomenon of other individual trail travelers, such as Edwin Bryant, has also come under investigation.[20] Dale Morgan has published an exhaustive series on the ferries of the forty-niners, and George Root has authorized numerous studies on the various Kansas ferries, some of which were patronized by overlanders.[21]

Chimney Rock, Independence Rock, Devil's Gate, Ash Hollow, Soda Springs, and the Old Lone Tree are only some of the striking natural phenomena along the trails which have been reviewed in survey articles, generally by a repetitious reprinting of each and every observation about the place by a host of passing overlanders.[22] Forts, especially Kearny and Laramie, and trading posts have been staple topics,[23] as have been geographic studies of the major cutoffs favored by overlanders and the emigrant transit over specific territories and states.[24] Various types of federal aid to the overlanders and the trail, the organizational problems of emigrating companies, the impact of diseases, the numbers and experiences of women and children on the trails, culture among the overlanders, and even the food they ate have generated more or less scholarly attention.[25] As the titles and contents of many of these articles indicate, the focus here again has been largely upon the feverish years of the California gold rush.

It is strange that so little scholarly attention has been given to the relationships between the emigrants and the Indians—a topic which the mass media have so perverted. Robert L. Munkres has recently made a useful beginning in assessing the Indian threat to the overlanders which is doubly welcome because of its coverage of pre- and post–gold rush emigration years. Noting that emigrants were attacked far less than popular folklore would have it—indeed, that many overlanders rarely saw an Indian during the entire trip—Munkres also suggests that the Indians very probably were blamed for many instances of white theft. However, while Munkres properly points out that the Indians were not as potent an inhibiting travel force as has been believed, he somewhat distorts the historical record by restricting his attention to the plains region east of Fort Bridger, for both California- and Oregon-bound overlanders were harassed and killed more frequently west of that point. Munkres might also have paid more attention to the factor of change through time; he has provided no comparative assessment of the decades of the 1840s and 1850s insofar as relative danger was concerned.[26]

While most article-length studies have dealt with restricted considerations, a few writers have adopted a broader thrust and attempted in such limited space something of an overview of the migrations. Surveying in turn the trails on both sides of the Platte River, but only as far as Fort Laramie, Robert W. Richmond sought to evaluate the increasing trading and ferrying facilities available to overlanders before 1854, an extremely useful approach which surprisingly few scholars have attempted.[27] In his article on the Oregon Trail, Gerald Rawling confined his general observations to the period before the Oregon treaty was concluded. Though acknowledging, as few have, the frequent necessity of relief expeditions for incoming overlanders from the small settlements in Oregon and California, Rawling carried to extremes his stress on the trip's difficulties when he stated: "The emigrants commonly arrived at their destination destitute, naked, starving and dispirited, with their nerves frayed to the breaking point.[28] Concentrating mainly on the 1842–47 period, Jonathan Dorris in a much earlier essay also emphasized the hardships of the trek, especially those beyond Fort Laramie, but refrained from praising to excess the bravery and heroism of the pioneers.[29]

Amos William Hartman aspired to even more comprehensiveness in his survey of the migrations during the 1850s, a period scholars have consigned to an obscurity almost but not quite paralleling that of the overland migrations during and after the Civil War. Dividing the period into approximately two halves, he suggested that gold rushers and emigrants dominated travel through 1854, on essentially the traditional routes, while beginning with 1855 new routes were increasingly used and mail carriers, stagecoaches, and freight wagons were nearly as common as the overland caravans. But his article clearly evidenced the difficulties of all writers who have endeavored to generalize from too limited a sampling of overland diaries and journals. Since Hartman's particular meld of sources minimized the Indian threat and the frequency of accidental shootings and drownings, so did his article. At the other extreme, one of his diarists disliked the Mormon guidebook, which led Hartman to the dubious assertion that the Mormon guidebooks were "worthless."[30]

The titles of these articles reveal, as do the titles of virtually all of the books on this topic, another of the intriguing characteristics of the writing about the overlanders: it has almost always been the trails which have been celebrated and not the emigrants. Even though the overlanders have often been the principal focus, very few writers have so suggested by the titles they have chosen.

For F. G. Young, writing in the very first volume of the first western state historical society quarterly, this was a matter of patriotic concern. He reminded his readers that most Americans unfortunately spoke of the "California trail" or the "Mormon trail," which to him was bad history, in spite of the fact that more persons had probably traveled the route destined for California and the Salt Lake region. The Oregon pioneers, Young contended, had been first in time, they had proven the feasibility of the trip, they had decided America's Pacific destiny, they had taken and subdued a home for civilization. Accordingly, Young argued that justice could only be served if the main overland trail was designated "the Oregon Trail," and he so entitled his article. Having honored the trail, Young went on to exalt the heroic pioneers who had wrought these wondrous accomplishments in the face of so many dangers. The very boldness of advancing over four times farther than any Americans had previously dared much impressed Young, as it did other writers during this period, who were doubtless influenced by the reminiscent rhetoric offered by aging pioneers at the annual reunions of the Oregon Pioneer Association.[31]

Jesse Applegate, for example, thirty-three years after his now-famous overland trip, underscored the excellence peculiar to the *American* pioneers: "No other race of men with the means at their command would undertake so great a journey, none save these could successfully perform it, with no previous preparation, relying only on the fertility of their own invention to devise the means to overcome each danger and difficulty as it arose."[32] E. L. Eastham stressed in 1885 that "the bravery and hardihood of the effort was only equalled by the substantial fruits of the achievement," and enumerated the distinguished historical company in which he believed the Oregon pioneers belonged:

Where else in the history of man, civilized or not, do you read the story of a 2,500-mile march through hostile country, over unexplored desert and mountain? The host led by Moses and Aaron wandered for years, but only accomplished a direct journey of a few hundred miles. Xenophon in his famous retreat from the Euphrates had a less distance to go before he reached safe harbor at home. No crusade ever extended over so great a distance, and most of the way through Christian and friendly countries. Napoleon on his disastrous trip to Moscow only essayed a march of 1,500 miles. Truly it was a performance of which all mankind may well be proud. Time is yet too young for the story to be fairly told. The descendants of Oregon pioneers shall yet hear their ancestors' glories sung as we now teach our children to glorify the heroes of the past.[33]

And George H. Himes, an 1853 overlander and longtime secretary of the Oregon Pioneer Association, recalled for his fellow pioneers in 1907 what they had accomplished in their courageous treks across terrain characterized by unfordable rivers, poisonous waters, almost impassable mountains, burning sands, severe storms, and by "wild beasts and by wilder Indians." As if this had not been enough, there had been diseases to survive, usually without benefit of physicians, and even starvation to test their fortitude. All of this, Himes remarked, provided "*a faint idea* . . . of the experiences that the greater proportion of those who came to make homes in Oregon in the Pioneer days had to undergo."[34]

Given enough such pioneer oratory, it is little wonder that scholars sometimes penned similar phrases. The secretary of the Kansas State Historical Society in 1913 proposed a division of this "royal highway" into three distinct eras—the "Romantic" period (to 1834), the "Heroic" period (to the Civil War), and the subsequent "Practical" period, when the trail disappeared in favor of the railroad. A year earlier T. C. Elliott had applied Spencerian terminology in saying that "the development of the 'Oregon Trail' may be otherwise termed an example of 'the fittest to survive.'" And the Federal Writers' Project concluded the more interpretive section of its guidebook-oriented *The Oregon Trail* with the notation: "The biological genes transmitting the characteristics that drained Europe of much of its vitality and made the United States an empire extending from coast to coast have not been bred out."[35] Here again was the explicit assertion that only in America had these glorious extended emigrations been made which somehow proved that Americans were a more "vital" people and served as another way of demonstrating the superiority of Americans and the civilization they were spreading.

These three temptations—regarding 1843, 1846, and/or 1849 as sufficiently typical or representative of all emigration years, generalizing about life on the trail from insufficient research, and intensifying the dangers surmounted and praising the patriotic heroism of the emigrants at the expense of analysis and interpretation—are equally evident in the flood of book-length studies about the overlanders and the trails they followed.

The earliest and probably still the single most widely known volume pertaining to this subject is Francis Parkman's *The Oregon Trail*.[36] The young Harvard graduate and budding historian went west in 1846 for wilderness adventure and to study Indians. But on that trip Parkman never penetrated any farther west than seventy or eighty miles beyond Fort Laramie and then while hunting with newly made Indian friends. Although Parkman encountered overland emigrants with some frequency while traveling to the fort and also in its environs, he seemed to regret every contact. Scholars continue to debate why it was that Parkman viewed the overlanders with such condescension and so completely overlooked their historic significance.[37] Concerned as he was with Indians, in only extremely limited fashion does Parkman's celebrated work provide any enlightenment regarding either the trail or the overlanders who followed it in 1846. The title of this classic book is simply not very germane to its contents and is of little help in appraising the overland emigrations.

John T. Faris succumbed to the temptation of relying on a few "typical examples" to illustrate the experiences of the westward-moving pioneers in his 1920 book, *On the Trail of the Pioneers*. Attempting to cover the westward movement from its earliest days, Faris's assessments of the pioneers trailing to Oregon and California were little more than lengthy quotations drawn from several diarists.

The next year James Christy Bell's *Opening a Highway to the Pacific, 1838–1846* was published. Primarily concerned with the social and economic factors which produced the increasing westward traffic of these years, Bell accorded very little attention to the overland trip itself. In the one chapter centering specifically on the overland journey, Bell was content with a general survey of the 1843–46 emigrations, illustrating some of the difficulties and hardships experienced (several times relying for examples upon diarists who were making the trip as late as 1852) but concluding that these early emigrants had perhaps an easier time on the trails than those who came in later years.

Agnes C. Laut published in 1929 a stridently nationalistic study of the overlanders under the title *The Overland Trail*. Although Laut claimed to have traversed all the trails, her main enthusiasm was really the splendid heroism of the pioneers, who had been fulfilling providential destiny in the triumph of civilization over savagery. Viewing the overland trail as a "racial highway," Laut correlated the emigrants with the Children of Israel in the westward racial march of progress: only the heroic American pioneers had evolved to clear superiority, and the push to Oregon was thus the "culmination of that movement, the Overland Trail stands without parallel in racial history; and that is why it is held in honor today."[38] The scholarly under-pinnings of Laut's work were unimpressive, the chapters a frustrating amalgam of past and present in which the author even found occasion to allocate three pages to a description of the wonderful facilities of a modern Spokane hotel.

Equally unsatisfactory was Maude Applegate Rucker's *The Oregon Trail and Some of Its Blazers.* Appearing in 1930, it brought together in disorganized fashion a number of accounts pertaining to the "Great immigration" of 1843. Almost all of these items—including the ever-present "A Day with the Cow Column"—had been previously printed elsewhere. They were clearly intended to serve as paeans of praise to Rucker's noble forebears, the Applegates, who, with their fellow overlanders of 1843, had overcome hardships and difficulties which made those experienced by New England's Pilgrims pale to insignificance by comparison.

The Great Trek, by Owen C. Coy, was published in 1931. Aimed at treating "as a whole" the overland emigration which revolutionized California in 1849 and 1850, Coy endeavored to trace the progress of the overlanders as they moved along both the South Pass and southern trails to El Dorado. Short on analysis and long on illustrative description, Coy's technique was the not unfamiliar one of quoting at length from various diarists. His chapter "Up the Platte to South Pass," for example, was taken almost entirely from 1850 overlander E. A. Tompkins's diary. After getting the gold rushers to California, Coy concluded with a chapter of vignettes of trail incidents which included everything from mirages to primitive surgery.

Also appearing in 1931 and likewise concerned with the California gold rush was Archer Butler Hulbert's prize-winning *Forty-Niners: The Chronicle of the California Trail,* a strange hybrid of fact and fiction. Based on a reading of many diaries kept during the 1848–53 gold rush period, Hulbert's book was in the form of a synthetic diary in which almost all the factual occurrences of the entire era were experienced on one overland trip by a single forty-niner party. Although the author provided adequate maps of the forty-niners' route, and some interesting gold rush songs and ballads, the simulated conversation he supplied disturbed some readers. While occasionally stimulating and often enlightening, Hulbert's novel-chronicle is ultimately unsatisfying as history.[39]

A. B. Guthrie's exceptional novel *The Way West,* which has since been made into a mediocre Hollywood movie spectacular by the same title, was published in 1949, nearly two decades later, but it nevertheless invites comparison with Hulbert's pseudo-novel. Whereas Hulbert was concerned with the tumultuous gold rush, the setting for Guthrie's narrative was an 1845 trip to Oregon by several families in which the author captured the quintessence of the entire experience, from the debates about going to the exultation upon arrival. For realism Guthrie incorporated the former mountain-man guide, still able to feel only half at home in the civilization the train represented; showed the growth of some men under new responsibilities, shared hardships, and dangers, and the inability of others to rise satisfactorily to the occasion; and emphasized the rankled feelings brought about by months of enforced togetherness. In the novel as in history, the emigrant encounters with the Indians were more often potentially dangerous than actually troublesome. Guthrie's novel was replete with lust, love, sickness, death, the monotonous quality of the trail, the joys of new sights, and the hopes of a new land. Accurate in a historical sense, *The Way West* is one of the few volumes, aside from actual diaries, able to convey the sights, sounds, and smells of the actual emigrating experience. The Pulitzer Prize the book was awarded in 1950 was a fitting tribute to Guthrie's literary skill. However, it remains a striking commentary on the way scholars have dealt with the overland emigrations that the only volume in a century of scholarly output adjudged to have such exceptional merit has been a novel.

One other novel deserving mention, though of lesser accomplishment, is Emerson Hough's fanciful *The Covered Wagon,* published in 1922. Hough had his 1848 overland caravan literally hack its way through virtually all the western Indian tribes massed at different points along the way for a "final stand" against the plow-carrying home seekers. Two major battles are fought, one with nearly 2,000 Sioux warriors, another with over 1,000 Crow and Bannock braves, and the sharpshooting overlanders kill in excess of 100 of these Indians. Four former mountain men—Bill Jackson, Jim Bridger, Kit Carson, and Caleb Greenwood—are prominently featured. Jim Bridger even ends up guiding part of the train nearly all the way to Oregon, free of charge! The romantic love story so central to Hough's plot even necessitated attention to California gold-mining in order for his hero to win the beautiful heroine.

W. J. Ghent, writing in 1934, was obviously correct when he bemoaned the absence of comprehensive and analytical trail studies. But his resultant work, *The Road to Oregon: A Chronicle of the Great Emigrant Trail,* though based on the use of a representative sampling of original sources, fell into the familiar pattern. The year 1873 was the most important one, since "the Great Emigration" then took wagons beyond Fort Hall, thereby saving Oregon for America. Ghent recognized, however, that 1849 was also a turning point of sorts, which separated the true "pioneer" period from the new and varied elements of the 1850s. He even included a chapter on the "Factious Fifties," but in the process of treating all the other western developments affecting the trail during that decade—mail contracts, railroad surveys, handcarts, the "Mormon War," the Colorado gold discovery—he almost completely bypassed the overland emigrants and said nothing whatever about the changing circumstances of the emigration over the passing years.

So it was with another of the standard narrative histories, Jay Monaghan's *The Overland Trail*, issued in 1947, which also completely avoided the decade of the fifties. Monaghan's approach was to select some person or group to demonstrate what he termed the "changing epochs" of the trail. Devoting approximately half his book to the pre-1840 period, Monaghan commenced his treatment of the famed decade with chapters on Pierre-Jean De Smet and John Charles Frémont. Then followed a chapter on the great migration of 1843, and the decade was closed with similar chapters on the Mormon pioneers of 1847 and the fabled forty-niners. In between were chapters on Tamsen Donner and Francis Parkman of the 1846 emigrating year. After the gold-rushing forty-niners, Monaghan leaped across the fifties to treat next the Pony Express.

In 1948, to commemorate the one hundredth anniversary of the recognition of Oregon as a territory, the American Pioneer Trails Association published Walter E. Meacham's *Old Oregon Trail*. A pleasant little treatise, though extremely short, superficial, and inadequate, Meacham principally summarized the experiences and route of the "Great Migration" of 1843, periodically inserting additional data on later developments.

Jacob R. Gregg's strangely organized and somewhat mistitled *History of the Oregon Trail, Santa Fe Trail, and Other Trails* (1955), while extensively treating political and military matters in Oregon following 1849, has little to say about the trails during that period except that cholera was raging. In addition to summarizing the emigration of the 1840s, Gregg places considerable stress on the vicissitudes of trail travel, with chapters entitled "Tragedies of the Trail," "Death Stalks the Trail," and "Mountain Meadow Massacre."

This persistent neglect of the overlanders traversing the plains during the 1850s is puzzling. Apparently these latter-day emigrants have lacked the dramatic interest and importance of their predecessors, even though over four times as many overlanders traveled westward during the 1850s as during the 1840s—200,000 emigrants who proved of incalculable significance to western development. Interestingly enough, the overlanders of the 1850s were also considered far less newsworthy than those of the 1840s by the newspaper editors of their own day. Not to have been involved in a historically significant movement in its earliest years has generally relegated individuals and groups to scholarly oblivion, a fate post–Promontory Point railroaders knew well, and which post-Apollo moon walkers will doubtless share.

The experiences of the overlanders during the 1850s, however, were still extremely challenging. Indeed, in some respects overland travel during the decade of the fifties was more dangerous than it had been in those boisterous earlier years. And certainly the nature of the journey was also much changed. For one thing it could cost considerably more, for another it was potentially faster and less rigorous. But writers, assuming that the emigrations in the fifties were simple repetitions of earlier years of no special historic significance, have bypassed them, as Harry Sinclair Drago did in a 1968 survey, *Roads to Empire: The Dramatic Conquest of the American West.* Aimed at the general reader, and encompassing accounts of the Santa Fe, Oregon, Mormon, and California trails, Drago's work has little value for the serious scholar.

A somewhat different category of volumes is made up of those works which are in fact as trail-oriented as their titles suggest and which endeavor, either solely or in part, to locate geographically the exact routes traveled by the overlanders. Incongruously, some of the best treatments of the overland migrations have been provided in these avowedly "trail books."

Irene D. Paden's intriguing approach to studying the trails is evident in her two helpful books, *The Wake of the Prairie Schooner* (1943), concerning the main overland trail to California and Oregon, and *Prairie Schooner Detours* (1949), covering the Hastings and Lassen cutoffs. Over a number of years the Paden family, with the assistance of other trail devotees, endeavored to locate and follow the exact routes traveled by the antebellum overland emigrants. Mrs. Paden's volumes reveal a broad knowledge of the diaries and journals kept by the overlanders, considerable energy and ingenuity in gaining access to some of the more remote trail regions, persistent questioning of present-day area residents, and much common sense in reconstructing the exact routes from such framentary data a century later. *The Wake of the Prairie Schooner,* especially, has helpful maps of the entire trail. Delightfully written, these two volumes uniquely combine the fieldwork experiences of the Padens as well as selected experiences of the overlanders taken from their diaries. Mrs. Paden's books sparkle with wry humor, and some of her accounts of persons met during the fieldwork ventures are most amusing. Though not providing analysis or interpretation of the overland experience, these trail books are useful to those interested in establishing precisely all the twists and turns of the overland trails, all the streams and springs, every mile of ground, rock, or sand covered on the way west.

Other families have also found the lure of trail-following and book-writing irresistible. Julia Cooley Altrocchi's *The Old California Trail: Traces in Folklore and Furrow* (1945) was the result of a dozen years spent seeking out the wagon ruts. Though the format followed was very similar to the Paden volumes, as a historically important treatise, firmly based upon diaries and journals, the work was clearly inferior. Strongly oriented to culling out trail and town lore from old-timers, Altrocchi even managed to work in two pages of quotations about Wild Bill Hickok's gunslinger exploits. Her vision of the overlanders was romantically heroic. The trail, she wrote, molded the emigrants into giant-like creatures who survived difficulties commensurate with those experienced in Dante's *Inferno* or *Pilgrim's Prog-*

ress. "*Uncommon* clay" she termed them, and bemoaned the fact that no metamorphosis had yet transformed some fabulous trail figure into larger-than-life legendary status. Altrocchi's observation that the trail itself had become and remained the hero is certainly borne out by the titles of the articles and books reviewed in this survey. Unfortunately, Altrocchi's fascination with the Donner party created a serious imbalance in her volume. The Donners are on center stage throughout, and it is the Donner Cutoff which Altrocchi followed and not the regular trail that the over-whelming majority of the Californians took.

Less grandiose than Altrocchi in her assessment of the character of the emigrants is Frederica B. Coons's *Trail to Oregon* (1954). The Coons family used *The Wake of the Prairie Schooner* as a guidebook in their trail-seeking, but Coons's resultant book compares unfavorably with the Paden volume. Eschewing analysis and interpretation, Coons relies mainly on quoting and paraphrasing from a minimal number of primary sources. While she includes examples from emigrants of both the 1840s and 1850s—and on rare occasions even from the 1860s—all are presented in a very haphazard fashion. The book is of no real importance but does contain a suggested itinerary for following the Oregon Trail by car.

Yet another report on family trail-following is Richard Dunlop's *Great Trails of the West* (1971). Dunlop also adopts the usual pattern of combining personal experiences with historical commentary drawn from selected diarists. Although he is most comprehensive in including coverage of a great number of western trails—from the Chisholm to the Chilkoot—his treatment of the Oregon-California Trail and its principal cutoffs is neither as precise nor as scholarly as that found in the Paden volumes.

Ralph Moody in *The Old Trails West* (1963) was clearly more concerned with those who first sought out the trails than with those who made the most use of them. He ends his chapter on the Oregon Trail without even permitting the 1843 overlanders to spill out onto his pages. With respect to California, Moody of necessity devoted more attention to emigrants, for they were more involved in the trail-determining process than were the Oregon overlanders, who followed routes already established by mountain men and fur traders. After erroneously placing the 1844 Stevens-Murphy party into the 1843 emigrating year, Moody mentioned the Donners and the Mormons and had scarcely more than a paragraph left for the forty-niners.

Todd Webb's *The Gold Rush Trail and the Road to Oregon* (1963) is noteworthy mainly for the nearly 100 photographs of the several trails and cutoffs traveled by the author between 1955 and 1962.[40] In one of his opening chapters Webb reprinted Applegate's "Cow Column" in its en-tirety, and then proceeded to progress westward along the trails, relying largely on ten diarists of the 1844–52 period, whose descriptions of scenery and experiences are either quoted or paraphrased. A concluding chapter identified current highways to be followed for the aficionado desiring to approximate the famed trails today.

Similar is Margaret Long's *The Oregon Trail* (1954), which provides automobile logs with specific mileage readings for purposes of trail-following as far as South Pass. Presented in a nonnarrative fashion, Long's volume is essentially a guidebook which reprints all the pertinent historical marker inscriptions but provides virtually no additional information about the overland emigrating experience. Somewhat comparable, although issued in a limited edition and concerned only with the Chimney Rock–to–Pacific Springs section of the overland route, is Paul C. Henderson's pleasantly written *Landmarks on the Oregon Trail* (1953). The short text combines trail lore with an account of a 1951 trail-following journey but is noteworthy primarily for its thirty-two magnificent color photographs of scenic trail sites.

Three volumes in the *American Trails* series deal with the South Pass routes followed by the vast majority of the overland emigrants. David Lavender's *Westward Vision: The Story of the Oregon Trail* (1963), while engagingly written, is really a survey of the geographical penetration of men westward and neither a history of the overland emigrants nor a precise, map-oriented study of the fabled route they traveled. Only 50 of Lavender's 400 pages are concerned with what he terms "true migrants"— families traveling by their own resources without the benefit of large fur caravans as escorts. Fully seven-eighths of the book treats the precursors of the emigrants, from Spanish explorers and French voyageurs to the eager missionaries of the 1830s. And when the author does consider the overlanders, only the 1842, 1843, 1844, and 1845 emigrations receive more than the barest mention, and none are covered in any detail. Lavender's account concludes with the 1847 emigrants and the Whitman massacre of that year.

Beginning in 1847 and continuing throughout the 1850s, thousands of Mormon overlanders were also streaming westward. These Latter-Day Saints were, as Wallace Stegner's judicious and lucidly written *The Gathering of Zion: The Story of the Mormon Trail* (1964) demonstrates, both caught up in and yet decidedly apart from the overland emigrations to the Pacific Coast here under review.[41] The journey of the Mormon emigrants was considerably shorter, normally much less difficult, and marked by far fewer occurrences of fatal disease or Indian attack. The Mormon emigrants sought separation from the Gentile hordes, hence their route followed the north side of the Platte River. This route, which has come to be known as the Mormon Trail, was quickly improved by Mormon pioneers for the benefit of oncoming Saints. By contrast, overlanders on the Oregon-California Trail less frequently made improvements specifically to benefit those in the rear; on rare occasions attempts were even made to hinder those behind. In addition to these contrasting attitudes toward the trail, the Mormons traveled much more consciously as a cooperating community: their emigration was more disciplined, more systematic, better organized. But complete separation was impossible. The Mormon Trail beyond the upper crossing of the North Platte coincided with the regular Oregon-California Trail. Also, during the 1850s—to which decade Stegner devotes considerable attention—more and more Gentile overlanders chose to begin their journey at Council Bluffs on the Mormon Trail. And Salt Lake City was a haven of rest and source of supply for a great many coast-bound overlanders from 1849 on. Unfortunately, Stegner's volume provides very little information on this Saint-Gentile interaction along the trail and in the Salt Lake Valley.

George R. Stewart's substantial contribution, *The California Trail: An Epic with Many Heroes* (1962), is remarkably balanced between trail and emigrants. Easily the best of the trail books and probably also the single most useful account presently available on the overland emigrations (this despite the fact that the entire Oregon migration movement is obviously not treated), Stewart's volume is marked by wisdom and wit. Often drawing helpful parallels between different migration years, Stewart contends that with the 1845 year came a major trail change—henceforth it would be man competitively against man whereas initially it had been man against nature. This interesting comment is at least partially belied by Stewart's own attention to the relief expeditions from California to aid lagging and suffering emigrants as well as his stress on the good-natured, law-abiding qualities of the forty-niners.

Stewart seems inclined to blame the Indians as much as the overlanders for the various conflicts which developed, and he punctures the colorful myth of beleaguered emigrants surrounded by attacking Indians galloping about the encircled wagons.[42] Stewart depicts the American overland emigrations as historically unique. Only the Great Trek of the Boers in South Africa compares with the American transcontinental migrations, but in numbers, distance, and influence Stewart finds the parallel an oblique one. *The California Trail* pays attention to such normally neglected factors as the construction of "prairie schooners," and the mechanics of fording a stream or taking wagons over a Sierra "pass," and Stewart even wryly ponders the diarists' silence on problems of sex and sanitary affairs.[43] Stewart's volume also commendably provides some coverage of the 1850s. Nonetheless, a twenty-three-page chapter for the entire decade, when compared with a chapter for each year between 1841 and 1849, reveals that Stewart's exceptionally fine book has not completely avoided the familiar pattern.

Conspicuously missing in all of this scholarly and literary attention to the overlanders is a well-researched topical study which assesses changing trail developments through both the 1840s and 1850s. Shunning the topical approach, most authors have either progressed chronologically year by year to about 1849, as Stewart has done, or else progressed westward geographically mile by mile, injecting trail occurrences and/or developments from varied years, as Merrill Mattes has mainly done in his encyclopedic *The Great Platte River Road* (1969). For the region covered—to Fort Laramie, the easiest third of the way west—Mattes's book will doubtless long serve as the standard work. Too, it will be long and thankfully used by all future trail and overland researchers for its splendid bibliography. In the preparation of this work Mattes used approximately 700 overland narratives, and he has identified the repositories where they are located. In addition to preparing excellently detailed maps, Mattes has advanced the most reliable statistical estimate thus far tendered of emigrant travel westward between 1841 and 1866. During the quarter-century under his microscopic examination, he suggests that approximately 350,000 overlanders trailed west.

The title is indicative of Mattes's conviction that the Fort Kearny–to–Fort Laramie portion of the overland trails—traveled by everyone virtually without cutoffs over an exceptionally good natural roadway—was the most important route west in America's history. Viewing this route as the trunkline of all the trails, Mattes believes it deserves a more descriptive term than the traditional Oregon-California-Mormon Trail designation, hence his appellation "Great Platte River Road."[44] While Mattes begins with several topically oriented chapters covering in brief fashion the difficulties experienced on this route and the manner and mode of traveling, essentially his technique is to document the "Grand Corridor of Westward Expansion" to Fort Laramie through short quotations from the diaries, letters, and reminiscences of the travelers. Mattes details—frequently at redundant levels—almost all occurrences, developments, and descriptions of the outfitting towns, the different routes to Fort Kearny, the two forts, and the scenic natural sites of Ash Hollow, Court House Rock, Chimney Rock, Scott's Bluff, and Mitchell's Pass. The volume is a vast treasure trove of information from which all future trail scholars will profit.

One of the overlanders whose reminiscences Mattes occasionally quotes is Ezra Meeker, and surely the above-mentioned spate of trail-oriented books owes much to that tireless pioneer's amazing exertions in behalf of marking and memorializing the Oregon Trail. Meeker was born in Ohio in 1830, and the same year that fur trader William L. Sublette led the first wagon train westward along the Platte route, a historic event commemorated a century later by President Herbert Hoover's proclamation designating April 10 to December 29, 1930, as the "covered wagon centennial."[45] During that period more than 1,000 celebrations were held at places like Independence Rock. On December 29 the Oregon Trail Memorial Association, whose existence was a testament both to Meeker's vision and persistence, honored the memory of its first president with a special dinner on the one hundredth anniversary of his birth.[46]

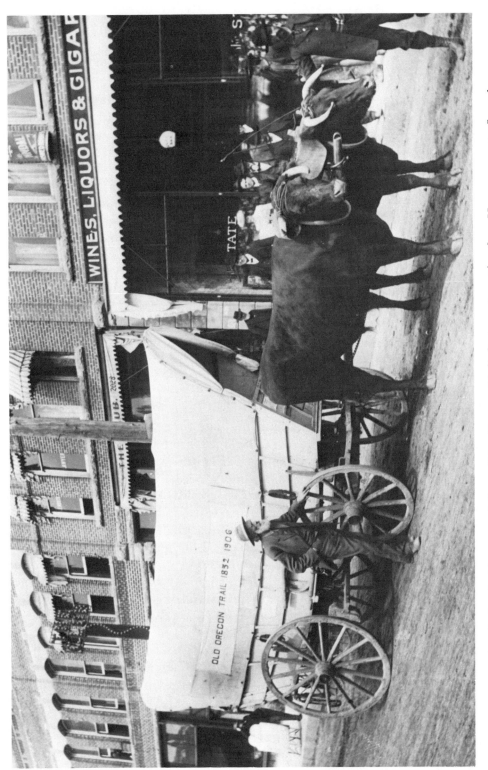

Ezra Meeker, indomitable memorializer of the Oregon Trail, first went west in 1852. He was seventy-five when this photograph was taken at Baker, Ore., on his 1906 eastward trek. Oregon Historical Society, Hazeltine Collection

Meeker had first gone west as an overland emigrant in 1852 and ultimately settled near Puyallup, Washington, where he made and lost a fortune raising hops.[47] Between 1898 and 1900 he made four round trips to the Klondike mines to sell vegetables, but it was in 1906 that Meeker, nearing age seventy-six, began his most famous activity. Against the advice of friends—who counseled against anyone giving contributions to Meeker, for money would only help send him out on the plains to die—Meeker began to trek eastward along the old Oregon Trail in a covered wagon drawn by two oxen. Traveling with one or two assistants and a faithful dog, Meeker gave speeches as he progressed eastward. His exhortations led numerous local communities to raise funds and establish markers along the trail. Meeker himself wrote a book about his life and his effort to eulogize the old pioneers and locate the famous trail they had followed before it was obliterated by the passage of time and progress.

Despite all the dire predictions Meeker did not die, although one of his oxen did. By the time he reached Lincoln, Nebraska, where the first edition of his hastily written *The Ox Team* was printed, Meeker was working an ox and cow together. By now the press was giving Meeker attention, and he claimed that over 20,000 persons had attended dedication ceremonies for markers at various places along the trail.

Meeker wintered in Indianapolis, selling his book and writing letters to newspapers and city officials he planned to visit in spring and summer; for his new goal was to go to the national capital to request government aid in marking the trail. With an unbroken steer now matched to the remaining ox, Meeker took his team and message throughout the East during 1907. He became something of a cause célèbre in New York City, where for over a month there was legal confusion about whether Meeker should be permitted to drive his outfit in the city. He finally reached Washington, where President Theodore Roosevelt viewed Meeker's outfit and pledged his support for the trail-marking plans.

After returning west as far as St. Joseph, Missouri, Meeker then shipped his outfit back to Puyallup in 1908. But there was more to come. In 1910, now nearly eighty, Meeker made a second trip eastward over the trail with his covered wagon, returning to Puyallup in August, 1912. In 1916 he testified before the House Committee on Military Affairs in behalf of a military and post road from St. Louis to Olympia, Washington, to follow as closely as possible the old Oregon Trail, and to be called "Pioneer Way." Also that year he traveled cross country by car in the interests of the trail, as he did in 1924 by plane and in 1926 by train. When Meeker died two years prior to his one hundredth birthday he was busily promoting the sale of Oregon Trail memorial coins.[48]

While caravans, celebrations, and coins have done their part, also of considerable influence in shaping public understandings of the overland emigrations have been the great multivolume histories so popular early in the century. Herbert Howe Bancroft, for example, found many opportunities to comment on the emigrations in his magnificent historical series on the western states. Bancroft, in fact, doubtless bears some responsibility for the interpretations so long in vogue, since as early as 1888 he was emphasizing the strategic importance of "three great emigrations, each three years apart . . . westward to the slope of the Pacific."[49] Moreover, he employed picturesque phrases to depict the hardships endured by the pioneers on the long overland route, and clearly suggested that those who came overland not only braved greater dangers and experienced more of the "romance which danger brings" but were a nobler, stronger, better class of persons.[50] He wrote of the thousands of 1849 overlanders who

might tell a tale more thrilling and more fascinating than any of ancient pilgrimage, trailed over plains and rugged hills of desolation, often with a miserable road, or with no road at all; and exposed to tornadoes fierce enough to demolish a caravan, followed by ravenous wolves and croaking ravens, harassed by savages, keeping watch by night, and sweating and swearing by day; suffering from scurvy and fever engendered by salt[y] unwholesome food, and from cholera brought up the river from New Orleans, and which clung to them until dissipated by the sharp air of the elevated regions 500 miles distant. Over the boundless prairies they straggled, up in to the rarified air that stifled men and beasts, down into waterless, sandy sinks; across sage brush plains efflorescent with alkali, over salty-white flats caked hard as stone, through blinding dust, and into heaps of sand-like drifted ashy earth where the animals sank to their bellies; resting by cooling springs, or thirsting beside fetid and acrid waters; winding along the banks of sluggish water-courses, fording brackish brooks, swimming ice-cold rivers, exposed now to the unbroken rays of a withering sun, and now to chilling hail-storms, hurricanes, and suffocating sandblasts; sometimes miring in mud, sometimes choked in impalpable dust which saturated hair and clothes, filled eyes and nostrils, and made these emigrant trains look like caravans emerging from an ash storm on the plains of Sodom.[51]

Bancroft also clearly sounded the patriotic theme, as in this passage about the Oregon overlanders: "If I have not presented the leaders of the several migrations as heroes, to me they were none the less heroic; while the people were filled with a patriotism as lofty and purposes as pure as any appearing upon the highways of history."[52]

By virtue of the immense amounts of sometimes unrefined source materials included, Bancroft's books differed from other voluminous narrative histories seeking to interpret the entire nation's past. Most of James Schouler's short commentary on the emigrations was confined to the California gold rushers. With Bancroft he found the character of those choosing the overland route to be distinctly superior to that of those going by sea. Schouler's account of the overland journey clearly stressed the privations and hardships the emigrants had endured. A similar emphasis upon hardship and danger characterized the single paragraph James Ford

Rhodes spared for the forty-niners traveling the overland route, and Edward Channing's lone paragraph reiterated this emphasis, finding it "remarkable" that so many safely reached California. Woodrow Wilson likewise confined his overland commentary to the forty-niners and accented their hardships: "The plains were ere long strewn with the bleaching bones of men and beasts."[53]

John Bach McMaster, however, did not restrict himself to the forty-niner epic, nor was he only aware of the difficulties connected with the trip. In his eight-volume *History of the People of the United States* (1929) McMaster avoided comment on only three years from 1842 through 1853, and he took pains to provide statistical estimates of the yearly emigrations. Deriving much of his data from contemporary newspapers, McMaster was well aware of changing trail conditions over the years; of all those writing multivolume national histories he supplied the most comprehensive, balanced, and accurate view of the emigrations.

Neither the *History of American Life* series edited by Arthur M. Schlesinger and Dixon Ryan Fox or *The American Nation* series edited by Albert Bushnell Hart paid much attention to the overland emigrations.[54] Two superficial volumes in the *Chronicles of America* series, however, dealt with aspects of the migrations—Emerson Hough's *The Passing of the Frontier* (1921) and Stewart Edward White's *The Forty-Niners* (1921). Both authors stressed trail difficulties and emigrant heroism, Hough especially giving way to grandiloquent flights of patriotic fancy as in his assertion that as a nation, "in the use of the Oregon Trail we first began to be great." Hough also believed that the female overlander was deserving of far more praise than she had received: "The chief figure of the American West, the figure of the ages, is not the long-haired, fringed-legging man riding a raw-boned pony, but the gaunt and sad-faced woman sitting on the front seat of the wagon. . . . There was the great romance of all America—the woman in the sunbonnet; and not, after all, the hero with the rifle across his saddle horn."[55]

Less romantic and considerably more detailed is Ray Allen Billington's account of the migrations in *The Far Western Frontier, 1830–1860* (1956), a volume in *The New American Nation* series. Billington's narrative focuses entirely on the overlanders of the 1840s, summarizing the principal occurrences of each trail year between 1841 and 1846 and those of 1849. In terms of space allocations, 1843, 1846, and 1849, in that order, stand supreme, with 1841, as in numerous other volumes, being the fourth most frequently cited emigrating year. The overlanders of the 1850s are again conspicuously absent.

Charles and Mary Beard, in their *Rise of American Civilization*, were especially enamored of the Bidwell-Bartleson party of 1841, which departed for California without much idea of how to get there except to travel west. Contending that in comparison the Mayflower voyage was an easy one, the Beards went on to claim that even the imposing hardships surmounted by the Bidwell pioneers were nothing at all when viewed against the harrowing ordeal survived by some of the Donner emigrants in 1846.[56]

The space-plagued historians churning out contemporary textbooks have given the overland emigrations such sparse treatment that rarely are even the emigrations of all three "typical" years mentioned. As might be expected, these brief treatments are quite superficial and tend to emphasize the hardships of the journey. Since the Donner disaster makes excellent copy for such a perspective, it is not surprising that several texts dwell at some length on the gruesome details. The authors of one text accuse "Hansford [sic] W. Hastings" of "an almost criminal negligence" for his role in fomenting the tragedy.[57] While most texts do have their facts straight, the writers of one recent volume aver that the Oregon Trail was "first used by covered wagons in the great migration of 1843."[58]

Somewhat more extensive and sophisticated treatment is provided in the western history textbooks, but the total impact is virtually identical to the stereotype arising from the monographic and periodical literature. Frederic L. Paxson and E. Douglas Branch, in two of the earliest efforts, accorded little more than statistical attention to the overlanders. Cardinal Goodwin supplied considerably more information and came to the conclusion that the sufferings of the 1850 gold rushers "were perhaps unparalleled in the annals of overland emigration in America." Dan Elbert Clark relied on the 1843 emigration—and Jesse Applegate's memorable account—to typify all the trail caravans. Submitting that the death rate was not "abnormally high," Clark felt that especially for the young and strong the trip had been "a long picnic excursion." And with Emerson Hough he had words of praise for the patient heroism of the wives and mothers.[59] LeRoy R. Hafen, W. Eugene Hollon, and Carl Coke Rister's appraisal of the overland emigrations coincided perfectly. After quoting nearly two pages from Applegate's "Cow Column," they contended that Applegate's account of an 1843 trip "might have been any day of 25 other summers, with any of hundreds of other companies bound for California or Utah or other states of the West." Hafen, Hollon, and Rister likewise contended that the trip was "a delightful excursion" for the young and strong, and also praised the pioneer mother as the "heroine of the great trek." Moreover, they concluded, as had Goodwin, that the 1850 overlanders "endured sufferings among the most severe in the annals of overland migration."[60]

Hafen, Hollon, and Rister affirmed that the "great migration" of 1843 saved the fledgling Oregon governmental effort; Thomas D. Clark and Ray Allen Billington offered similar interpretations in their widely used textbooks. To Clark the crucial 1843 emigration was of "major importance" in America's population movement and the "most important" of the mass movements westward. For Billington that year's emigration was a "turning point" in Oregon's history.[61] Both authors chose to stress the hardships involved in the westward journey during the 1840s, which meant devoting some attention to the Donner party. Regarding the perils of the forty-niners, Clark wrote that their route to California was basically a "trail of tears and human tragedy," while Billington maintained that "those who survived to reach the gold fields were indeed well tested."[62]

More prosaic and condensed accounts of the emigrations are provided in Kent L. Steckmesser's *The Westward Movement: A Short History* (1969), Robert E. Riegel and Robert G. Athearn's *America Moves West* (1971), and Robert V. Hine's *The American West: An Interpretive History* (1973). And, though the overland migrations did not loom large in his volume, John A. Hawgood, the 1966 recipient of the Alfred A. Knopf Western History Prize for his *America's Western Frontiers,* also found the traditional interpretations to his liking. Stressing the importance of 1843 for Oregon and 1844 for California—when wheeled vehicles were first forced across the Sierra passes—Hawgood had virtually nothing to say about changing trail conditions other than bare mention of the migrations through 1849.

The use of selections from a "typical" year for purposes of illustrating the overland emigration movement to the Far West is naturally even more standard in the volumes of source materials and readings. Robert V. Hine and Edwin R. Bingham rely on 1843 and a Peter Burnett letter for this, while Clark C. Spence utilizes Jesse Applegate's "Cow Column" and a portion of Francis Parkman's 1846 description of the emigrants at Fort Laramie. Martin Ridge and Ray Allen Billington utilize diary excerpts from 1841, 1843 (Applegate), and 1846 to depict overland travel to the West Coast, and cuttings from 1847 and 1856 diaries and reminiscences to illustrate the Mormon trek to Salt Lake.[63] Only Robert W. Richmond and Robert W. Mardock stand apart from this all-engulfing 1843–1846–1849 tide by using selections from John Hawkins Clark's overland diary of 1852 to depict experiences on the great western trails.[64]

While the scholars must be held accountable for their failure to treat the changing conditions of the 1850s and 1860s, their dilemma has obviously been a real one. With "humanity on the loose," to use Dale Morgan's illuminating phrase,[65] in each and every emigrating year, how can an inclusive and accurate account be prepared that is in any way manageable? The various approaches used have all made distinct contributions to total understandings. From those who have concentrated on the trails or portions of trails—now as well as then—we have gained a clearer understanding of where the overlanders went and how hard it was to go there. Those who have endeavored to treat comprehensively a single year have made evident the awesome complexity of the emigrations. Those who have generalized from the experiences of a few have reminded us of the crucial importance of the 1843 and 1840 movements. And those who have contented themselves with the competent editing of a single diary, or of several diaries kept by members of the same expedition—no mean task—have underscored the particularity of all the westering endeavors. No single writer has been able to do all of this at the same time, and do it well. Therefore, in spite of all the reprinted diaries and reminiscences, all the scholarly and semi-scholarly accounts, poems, and novels, there is still no single volume about the overland emigrations which is widely regarded as "the" treatment of the subject. Perhaps there will never be.

It is clear, though, that most of the foregoing approaches, whatever their considerable merits, have tended to underplay the concept of change through time. Perhaps increased understanding and new perspectives about the overland emigrations can only come with an approach utilizing an even broader scope, one which incorporates the hitherto neglected years and seeks to trace the ways in which the trails, the West, and the overlanders themselves were changing. Such an approach must recognize that while the emigrations called forth sufficient individualism, heroism, and bravado for thousands of television and movie westerns, at base the overland movement was really a cooperative experience, as the Mormons so graphically demonstrated and as Daniel Boorstin so clearly perceived in his stimulating study of America between the Revolution and the Civil War.[66] The new approach must also make clear that it is in the heretofore neglected interaction among the overlanders themselves, in the interaction between the overlanders and other groups in the West—the army, the Indians, the Mormons, the traders and other entrepreneurs—as well as in the interaction of the overlanders with the flora and fauna of the West that the real explanation of how the feat was successfully accomplished will be found. It is such an approach which is attempted in the following pages.

CHAPTER ONE

Public Opinion, 1840–48

"Palpable homicide" or
"Merry as a marriage bell"?

BEFORE SIXTY-FOUR-YEAR-OLD JOSEPH WILLIAMS left his Indiana home in 1841 to make the long trek overland to the Oregon country, his friends sought to dissuade him by emphasizing the many dangers and difficulties surely awaiting him from Indians and wild beasts in the intervening regions.[1] Four years later Benjamin Franklin Bonney left his home in Illinois bound for the same destination. He later recalled the "hullabaloo" his neighbors had created, predicting certain death for the Bonney family, either at the hands of Indians, by drowning, or from starvation in the desert.[2] Both men successfully completed the journey to Oregon, but the pessimistic forecasts of their friends evidenced some of the fears prevalent in America during the decade of the 1840s concerning the wisdom of attempting an overland journey to the Pacific.

These fears persisted despite numerous published assurances that the road to Oregon and California was of no difficulty whatever.[3] Roseate route descriptions had been appearing in the press ever since the St. Louis *Missouri Gazette* had declared in 1813 that wagons could easily be taken to the Columbia River because there was "no obstruction in the whole route that any person would dare to call a mountain" and since "in all probability, they would not meet with an Indian to interrupt their progress."[4] Congressman John Floyd of Virginia, during the course of his abortive endeavors in the 1820s in behalf of the occupation and settlement of Oregon, stated in the House of Representatives, "The route to the mouth of the Columbia is easy, safe, and expeditious." The distance to Oregon, Floyd argued, was the equivalent in time to that which had been required to travel from St. Louis to Philadelphia twenty years before. Indeed, the Rocky Mountains in several places were "so smooth and open" that it would take ten men only twenty days to take a loaded freight wagon from the navigable waters of the Missouri to the Columbia River.[5] In 1826 the St. Louis *Enquirer* relied upon fur trader William Ashley's western experiences to announce that it was so easy to travel from Missouri to the Pacific that thousands could go in safety without ever meeting "any obstruction deserving the name of a MOUNTAIN."[6]

Then in 1830 came a series of newspaper pronouncements celebrating William L. Sublette's safe return with wagons he had taken to the fur traders' rendezvous at South Pass. The St. Louis *Beacon* heralded this notable achievement as proof that " '*scientific*' characters" were propagating "folly and nonsense" when they contended that the Rockies were a barrier to the march of Americans westward. Nearly identical phrasings were used by the Philadelphia *National Gazette* and the Cincinnati *American* to demonstrate that in a few years the trip to the Pacific would be made with complete safety. In 1835 the Washington *Daily National Intelligencer* prophesied that excursions to the mountains would soon be undertaken with the nonchalance displayed by those then flocking to fashionable summer resorts.[7] Sublette himself, with his partners Jedediah S. Smith and David E. Jackson, had written the Secretary of War to report, "This is the first time that wagons ever went to the Rocky mountains; and the ease and safety with which it was done prove the facility of communicating over land with the Pacific ocean."[8]

At approximately the same time, Joshua Pilcher, another presumably knowledgeable fur trader, had written the Secretary of War that the Rockies were no barrier to wagons and carriages and that "nothing is more easily passed than these mountains." In the 1830s, when sometime New England educator Hall J. Kelley began issuing his broadsides promoting emigration to Oregon, he quoted and endorsed Pilcher's confident assurances.[9] Medical missionary Samuel Parker traveled overland to Oregon in 1835, and his *Journal of an Exploring Tour beyond the Rocky Mountains* intimated that if an elderly minister of the gospel could make it to Oregon, anyone could. When reviewing Parker's book, the *American Biblical Repository* rejoiced in the knowledge that there was indeed an easy road to Oregon "excavated by the finger of God."[10] Missouri Senator Lewis F. Linn's 1838 report in behalf of a special Oregon committee waxed eloquent over Oregon's almost "tropical" climate and the ease with which the Rockies could be crossed, even by "delicate females."[11]

These extraordinarily optimistic assertions were quickly challenged by persons less confident of the viability of overland travel. For example, Hall Kelley's propaganda campaigns had called forth at least one book and two magazine articles in opposition.[12] The articles were written by W. J. Snelling of Boston, whose imposing arguments were grounded in such personal frontier experiences as wintering with a band of Sioux Indians.[13] In the first place, Snelling doubted whether half of the potential emigrants would even reach St. Louis, since they would be sorely tempted to purchase the fine, available land over which they would be passing. For those actually persevering onto the prairies Snelling held out little hope. He predicted mass starvation, for overlanders could certainly not take sufficient food with them for the long journey, and as novice frontiersmen they would not possess the Indians' skill in procuring game. Moreover, even Indians perished from periodic famine.

If for some reason the emigrants themselves did not starve, Snelling was convinced that 80 percent of their horses would, since they could not live on prairie grass alone. Even if they could, the Indians burned the prairies "regularly twice a year, from Lake Winipeg to Mexico, and for at least nine months in the twelve, nine tenths of their area is as bare of vegetation as the desert of Zahara." Further, the Indians themselves were certain to attack in retaliation for the pillaging of white hunters. They would also expertly steal the emigrants' horses. Finally, it would be impossible to make the journey in one summer, and Snelling gravely pondered the possibilities of wintering amidst the deep snows of the Rockies. After devouring the horses, the desperate emigrants could, he supposed, try the "nutriment in old shoes," after which they might starve with the wolves. Providence alone would enable them to survive the winter, and Snelling doubted that the easy trails through the Rockies of which Kelley spoke actually existed. After all, Lewis and Clark did not mention them, and they had been there and Kelley had not. Of course neither had Snelling, and these were by no means the only examples of men who claimed to know the West but really did so only at second hand. The upshot of Snelling's arguments was that brave and hardy young men could go overland to Oregon but it was "impossible" for entire families to do so, burdened as they would be with all their possessions and ignorant of western conditions.[14]

These frequently mentioned fears of overland travel derived in large measure from the commonly accepted geographic concept of the so-called "Great American Desert," an area thought to extend westward from approximately the one hundredth meridian to the Rocky Mountains.[15] Until the beginning of the Civil War virtually all maps of these regions in school textbooks and governmental reports were labeled the "Great American Desert."[16] Contemporary literature abounded with analogies to Asiatic Tartars and Arabian Bedouins who could be expected to be reproduced on the American desert because of the pastoral life required by western climate and terrain. Most persons of the time considered the region a totally uninhabitable and undesirable desert. Prompted largely by the reports of the western explorations of Lieutenant Zebulon Pike and Major Stephen H. Long, the myth of the American desert persevered in some quarters until almost 1880, when it was finally replaced with another concept similarly overdrawn—the myth that the western plain was a garden, a veritable agrarian utopia.[17]

It was in such a milieu that thousands of potential emigrants debated the wisdom of traveling to Oregon and California by land. Many, men like Joseph Williams and Benjamin Franklin Bonney, opted for making the attempt. It was little wonder that their neighbors viewed the trek with considerable trepidation. Such schooling as they might have had endorsed the belief that the western regions were inhospitable desert. Even though some men were now claiming that the trip was possible, most reasoned arguments continued to contend that it was not. During the early 1840s, ignorance, unreality, and confusion characterized the status of public opinion concerning the West itself and the likelihood of traversing it to reach the Pacific Ocean.[18] For in this period of pseudo experts who wrote confidently if semi-ignorantly of the actual conditions, the West, and most specifically the overland migrations, were regularly described by the exaggerated phrasings best corroborating the biases of individual writers.[19]

Clearly exemplifying this attitude were the British commentaries concerning the practicability of American overland travel to Oregon. Newspapers and periodicals in Great Britain consistently opposed the American claims to the Oregon territory, though most hoped that arbitration, not war, would eventually settle the dispute.[20] From this perspective they argued, almost without exception, that because it was impossible for Americans ever to settle Oregon by land, and too expensive to do it by sea, it was superfluous for them to desire the territory.

Dr. John McLoughlin, chief Hudson's Bay Company factor at Fort Vancouver, was quoted as having commented to an American minister that American emigrants might as well "undertake to go to the moon" as to travel overland to Oregon.[21] Lord Ashburton had entertained similar notions in 1842 which partially explained his willingness to neglect the Oregon problem temporarily when negotiating the northeastern boundary between the United States and Canada with American Secretary of State Daniel Webster. Ashburton apparently believed that the Indians in the West interposed a barrier between the United States and Oregon which would make the question of ultimate control of that area a problem only for the far distant future.[22] The beliefs of McLoughlin and Ashburton, however, were mild compared with the colorful appraisals appearing in British newspapers and periodicals.

The London *Times* editorialized in 1843 about the American proposals to construct a line of forts to the Columbia in utter disbelief that the usually "acute" Yankees could actually be serious about such nonsense. Quoting liberally from those American congressmen and senators who also thought distance and Indians ruled out such a project, the editors ventured that it would be equally plausible to "expect Lord Ellenborough to establish a line of sentry-boxes from Calcutta to Candahar, or Sir Charles Metcalfe from Montreal to the North Pole." The Manchester *Guardian,* while acknowledging that in another fifty years the Americans could be expected to have passed the Rocky Mountains, saw no danger of war in the current crisis, since better land was available in the United States for which it was not necessary to endure "the toils, the dangers, and the losses of a march of two or three thousand miles, through the barren deserts and rocky defiles" between Missouri and Oregon. That Lewis and Clark's excruciatingly slow and laborious crossing of the continent was a far more accurate indicator of the possibilities of overland travel than the twenty-day "certain, safe, and easy" assessments American enthusiasts boasted about was the conclusion of *Chambers' Edinburgh Journal*.[23]

Also appearing in 1843 was an article in the *Edinburgh Review* which proved so erroneous that American legislators soon quoted it with obvious relish in the halls of Congress. For six months of the year, said the writer, much of the intervening territory between the United States and Oregon was "a howling wilderness of snow and tempests," and during the rest of the year it was a desolate wasteland "of hopeless sterility." It was infested with Indians "of more than Scythian savageness and endurance, who cannot be tracked, overtaken, or conciliated." While the author of the review article noted the "extraordinary energy" of the roving Americans, he concluded with finality "that the world must assume a new face before the American wagons make plain the road to the Columbia, as they have done to the Ohio. . . . Oregon will never be colonized overland from the Eastern States."[24] The year 1843 was, of course, the same year that approximately 1,000 prospective settlers actually reached Oregon by the overland route, demonstrating that wagons could indeed perform the journey.

It would take several more years, however, before the British press would admit that the Americans could reach Oregon overland. In February, 1844, the London *Times* noted that travelers through the western regions of "mountains and barren deserts" could "think themselves well off if they live at all." Including liberal citations from American authorities who also viewed the overland migrations with incredulousness, the editorial writer concluded that if the British were to retain possession of Oregon until thousands of American settlers crossed the plains "to die of hunger and thirst . . . the stability of our empire in those parts can be in no very urgent danger."[25] An article in the *British and Foreign Review* in 1844 similarly maintained that "an almost impassable wilderness extends for several hundred miles east of the Rocky Mountains" which might prohibit overland colonization from the eastern states.[26]

The year 1845 brought a continuing profusion of unbelieving comments on the likelihood of successful overland migration. American occupation of Oregon was viewed by the Manchester *Guardian* as a "chimerical scheme." The London *Times* declared in May that it was time for President Polk to face facts regarding Oregon, namely, that it was "almost inaccessible by sea and land" from America. Besides, it was defended by British agents and wily Indian tribes. A week later the *Times* asserted definitively that Oregon was "inaccessible to any people or any forces but our own." The May 17, 1845, issue of the *Times* contained an extended quotation from John Dunn's *History of the Oregon Territory*. Dunn, who had spent eight years with the Hudson's Bay Company in Oregon, assured his readers that "there is no secure, expeditious, or commodious tract which can ever be used as a highway, so as to afford facilities for an influx of emigrants overland." Dunn admitted that favorable accounts of overland travel had already appeared in America but he discounted them, feeling that their characteristic spirit of bravado and thankfulness was indirect proof of the "utter hopelessness of such a route for general purposes."[27]

British authors joined American writers and congressmen in stressing the difficulty the United States would have in transporting troops overland to Oregon if the contrary claims could not be resolved short of war. This theme had been sounded as early as March, 1843, in a long editorial in the Manchester *Guardian*. Small parties of select men might be able to live off the land, but it was ludicrous to believe that an American armed force encumbered with war materials would ever reach the Columbia overland. Instead, the editor declared that such an expedition faced almost certain destruction even though a few stragglers might eventually arrive to beg for food and assistance from the Hudson's Bay Company hunters and trappers they had been sent to evict. On the other hand, the British armed forces could be supplied by Hudson's Bay Company posts on an easy overland march through Canada, and could also rely on the aid of the Indian tribes, most of which were friendly to Britain.[28]

This theme was reiterated in December in the London *Morning Chronicle*, the Liverpool *Times*, and the Montreal *Gazette*. The London paper felt that all the men the United States could send across the Rocky Mountains "from their squalid mockeries of civilized states on the other side" would quickly "be annihilated by the forces of our Hudson's Bay Company and the friendly Indians, without our Imperial aid." The Liverpool *Times* thought it "passes all conception" that the United States could ever move an army over 3,000 miles of "wilderness"—a task deemed "much more difficult than Hannibal's crossing of the Alps." The Montreal organ thought the American design on Oregon insane, and doubted that much of an army would remain to fight in Oregon after marching 3,000 miles over vast deserts, if they even arrived at all.[29] In 1845 the *Gazette* repeated these arguments, referring also to the "servants of the Hudson's Bay Company and the allied Indians," who would be sufficient to trounce the remnants of any armed force marching overland. The *Economist* also took up this topic in May of 1845 to explain how the Indians would attack the troops, who could only secure ample provisions by hunting—always an unreliable activity in the West.[30] Doubtless it was awareness of such easy references to the Hudson's Bay Company and its Indian "allies" which caused so many incoming overlanders during the early 1840s to be so suspiciously hostile to the company and its officers, especially Dr. John McLoughlin, who did so much to help them.

By mid-1845 the prevailing judgment that the trip was impossible began to give way to the view that the "dangers and toils" of the long journey were simply not worth the potential which Oregon actually had for prospective overland settlers.[31] The Montreal *Gazette* pointed out in July that overlanders who had completed their "difficult and laborious journey" were quite disappointed with what they found and that approximately a fifth of them had already deserted Oregon for California. An editorial in the London *Times* adopted the same philosophy on October 1, arguing that the required 2,000- or 3,000-mile marches "over mountains and sandy deserts, agree rather with the airy temperaments of Khans and Czars than with the sobriety of Yankee calculations." The London *Examiner* contended that Oregon's soil and climate were much inferior to those found in the intervening thousands of miles. Moreover, the United States already possessed far too much territory "for good government or even for civilization" without acquiring Oregon. The *Spectator* editorialized in late November that American journalists and orators were beginning to modify their Oregon claims and demands because they were learning that Oregon was more accessible from Britain than from America and that the easiest access from both countries was by sea.[32]

The year did not pass, however, without the publication of a long discourse on Oregon in the *Foreign Quarterly Review* which contained probably the most unrealistic information regarding the American overlanders that had yet appeared. Asserting that caravans of adventurous Americans who obviously did not value their lives set out for the Rockies, the author claimed that "even the American historians who record these exploits, confess that they have never heard what became of their heroic countrymen. Upwards of a thousand emigrants went off in this way from the United States in the years 1842 and 1843, and more have gone since . . . and all that is known about them is, that a few families are squatted somewhere on farms so small and miserable, that the only wonder is that they should still survive as a warning and example to the rest of their compatriots." The author noted how much easier it was to go to Oregon from Montreal than from anywhere in the United States, quoted Dunn in affirming that no highway could ever be established between the United States and Oregon, and echoed all American and British authorities who claimed that the trip was impossible. The weather was either "piercing cold" or "scorching" hot, west of the Rockies there was no fruit except dangerous berries, travelers either sank into the sand or cut their feet on the jagged rocks, and to assuage the intense thirst occasioned by the scarcity of drinking water it was necessary to suck and swallow leaden bullets and pieces of quartz. It was "unlikely in the last degree" that Americans could ever go overland to Oregon "with the remotest chance of success." Nature had "forever prohibited" the United States from having effortless intercourse with Oregon; to try to contest the superior British legal claim and ease of geographic access was simply "Quixotic."[33]

The Leeds *Mercury* opened 1846 by stressing the "thousands of miles" and the "savage" Rocky Mountains preventing easy access to that wilderness area known as Oregon. But in the main, by 1846 the few references to the overlanders still appearing indicated merely that the migrations were occurring without suggesting that they were either impossible or exceedingly difficult. Such editorials appeared in the *Spectator* and the *Economist,* although the latter journal did note the length of the journey and the "spirit of adventure" which was almost a prerequisite to the undertaking.[34] A new twist to the general interpretation appeared in a book by an Oxford University professor of political economy, Travers Twiss. Dr. Twiss believed that if British settlements had not preceded the American overlanders and furnished them with supplies upon arrival, their "long and perilous journey across the Rocky Mountains" would have resulted in certain death. The London *Times* was also expressing this point of view, inferring that the Americans had all too quickly forgotten these British generosities. If the weary emigrants had not been "liberally and humanely assisted and protected by the British agents," observed the London daily, they would likely have perished.[35] The *Topic,* a London weekly, acknowledged that Americans were making the trip, but reasoned that the perils of the journey drove back, destroyed, dispersed, and crippled others, and that far more protection and security would have to be forthcoming before the overlanders would ever face the risks and privations of the journey with "much enthusiasm."[36]

By 1847 the boundary treaty had been ratified and the British press subsequently lost interest in matters pertaining to Oregon.[37] One of the few post-treaty references to the journey was made in the *Edinburgh Review*'s October issue. Although the writer admired the energy and adventuresome character of the American overland emigrants, he also noted the immense obstacles to successful overland travel, mentioning not only the Indian tribes but the possibility of early snows in the Sierras, which had occasioned such tremendous suffering, cannibalism, and loss of life the previous winter. The same article revealed the widespread acceptance of the "Great American Desert" concept. From about 200 miles west of the Mississippi River to the Rockies the area was judged unsuited for agriculture. Therefore, the author predicted that this territory would eventually encompass great sheep and cattle farms in the pastoral traditions of Australia and Argentina.[38]

The one former British official who had been in the best position to witness exactly what was occurring during the early 1840s—Dr. John McLoughlin—radically altered his initial views. When C. Lancaster reached Oregon City after an 1847 overland trip, he found Dr.

McLoughlin amazed that so many families had, with their possessions, safely traversed the mountains. McLoughlin recalled that years before he had written to friends in England that it was impossible for families to come overland with safety and that any settlers would have to come by sea. Now McLoughlin told Lancaster that "he was ready to aver that the yankees could go right over to China with their ox waggons if they desired to do it."[39]

It was no easier for American commentators to consider the overland emigrations as events unrelated to any ulterior motives.[40] Basically, their view of emigration was dependent on their reaction to a prior question: how urgent was the quick acquisition of Oregon? Those who answered in the affirmative alleged that the trek was quite possible, even easy; those who did not saw it as difficult, or even, as with the British, impossible. Always closely correlated with the attitude toward acquiring Oregon was the estimate of the value of Oregon itself. Those who favored a quick acquisition generally did so because they considered Oregon to be of tremendous worth and potential. Those who saw it as a region of quite a different character saw no reason for braving the dangers they magnified in order to get there.

Horace Greeley is the best example of a consistently negative viewpoint. The editor of the New York *Daily Tribune*, Greeley has usually been depicted as a staunch nationalist whose reasoned advocacy of westbound emigration stood in sharp contrast to the typical provincial eastern opposition.[41] With respect to Oregon, however, Greeley appeared no different from other eastern opponents of westward emigration, except that he offered carefully reasoned arguments rather than simply saying "don't go."

Greeley initially had little use for Oregon and much advice for those who considered going there. He acknowledged the validity of the American claim to part of Oregon, but cautioned against courting trouble with Britain by attempting to occupy the region. Such a course of action would not only be financially prohibitive, but the land itself was not as valuable as the propagandists maintained, and the distance was too great for efficient incorporation into the Union.[42] Again and again Greeley used the pages of his *Tribune* to plead that the United States and Great Britain relinquish their claims to Oregon and permit that territory to be settled as an independent nation.[43]

Greeley's *Tribune* began its campaign against the overland journey in 1843, by chastising the Cincinnati *Chronicle* for asserting that the best trade route from Europe to China led through St. Louis and over the Rockies. Eastern commerce, the *Tribune* predicted, would without question follow a course over the Isthmus of Panama. Later that same year the Greeley organ cautioned against the expenditure of millions of dollars to construct a line of military posts to Oregon, proposing instead that the United States construct a canal across Mexico.[44]

Horace Greeley, photographed by Matthew Brady in 1858. The pages of Greeley's New York *Tribune* reflected his changing attitude toward overland travel.

Greeley was not content merely to suggest alternative water routes to the overland trails. On July 19 he presented a long commentary on the 1,000 emigrants who had just departed from Missouri. Suggesting that the whole enterprise wore "an aspect of insanity," Greeley wondered what the Oregon-bound overlanders could be seeking, leaving behind as they were the best of climate, agricultural lands, schools, churches, markets, bridges, and roads: "For what, then, do they brave the desert, the wilderness, the savage, the snowy precipices of the Rocky Mountains, the weary summer march, the storm-drenched bivouac, and the gnawings of famine? Only to fulfill their destiny! There is probably not one among them whose outward circumstances will be improved by this perilous pilgrimage." Even though the adventurers were confident that they had adequately prepared for all eventualities, Greeley feared that, as with the Santa Fe expedition and that of Francisco Miranda to South America, the overlanders would awake from their "cherished delusion" only when it was too late. He somberly forecast that "we do not believe nine-tenths of them will ever reach the Columbia alive." Food supplies would doubtless be their gravest problem, although Greeley thought the party might subsist on their cattle until they reached the Rocky Mountains. But Greeley maintained— sounding much like Snelling—that the cattle would never be able to cross the Rockies, and this would doom the overlanders for they would have no other supply of food.[45]

The next day the New York *Aurora* published an article which revealed that its editors had completely adopted Greeley's pessimism, his statistics, and his reasoning. Depicting the Rockies as an "eternal barrier" which served as the "half-way house between civilization and despair," the *Aurora* feared most for the children, who were thought to comprise at least half of the 1843 migration. They were simply "tender offerings to the mad ambition of their parents," and not one in ten would ever survive the "ice-ribbed fastnesses of the mountain desert." The sole hope the *Aurora* saw for the "silly" overlanders was the same one the *Tribune* had expressed the previous day—only the benignity of Heaven could get them safely to Oregon. After all, the *Aurora* believed the western wilderness to be a "frightful monster" which, when "suddenly and incautiously encountered, devours up the intruder, and leaves his bones to whiten in solitude and his fate untold forever." The course advocated by the *Aurora* to avert such catastrophes was the more traditional slow push westward into contiguous territory. Approaching the wilderness thus by degrees, "striking at him with one hand while the other holds fast to the world behind, and he loses all his terrors, and meets the stranger with a smiling welcome," was an interesting technique to recommend for the desert land allegedly comprising the western territory. The *Aurora* article was reprinted in the *Maine Farmer and Mechanic's Advocate* the following month in the hope that it would convince Maine residents not to commit the "madness and folly" of traveling overland to Oregon.[46]

The pages of the New York *Daily Tribune* stressed not only starvation as one of the perils the overlanders would face, but also the savage Indian tribes, who could be expected to rain bullets on the emigrants "almost every mile" between Missouri and Oregon. By mid-1843 Greeley's gloomy editorials had aroused other newspaper editors, who called upon Greeley to spell out more clearly his emigration policies. Responding to charges in the Milwaukee *Sentinel and Herald* that the *Tribune* was hostile to all western settlement, Greeley explained that he favored and even encouraged westward emigration but not when it carried beyond the "bounds of civilization." All prudent emigrants should stop "this side of the end of the woods . . . this side of the jumping-off-place."[47]

Slowly progress reports of the 1843 migration drifted eastward. When Greeley learned that eight overlanders had perished before they had even reached the Rockies, he again loosed a salvo against the emigration fever, insisting "that it is palpable homicide to tempt or send women and children over this thousand miles of precipice and volcanic sterility to Oregon." Predicting far greater suffering and loss of life before the group reached their destination, Greeley reiterated his belief that not even fifty military forts would help, because foodstuffs were the primary consideration and food could not be produced by "cannon and bayonets." One week after reporting the eight emigrant deaths, Greeley published a letter he had received from Thomas J. Farnham, author of *Travels in the Great Western Prairies*. Recalling his own "sufferings in those terrible regions," Farnham thought it "remarkable" that not more in the 1843 group had perished even before they reached the Rockies.[48] The New York *American* reprinted the Farnham letter and voiced the accompanying desire that it would cause any potential emigrants to pause before making the hopeless pilgrimage.[49] Though by the end of 1843 Greeley was admitting that men could make the trip if properly outfitted, he continued to encourage everyone to stay at home.[50]

While Greeley himself strongly opposed the overland journey, he apparently did not allow his personal predilections to influence his news coverage. Indeed, the New York *Daily Tribune* probably accorded more space to commentary on and news of Oregon than did any other eastern or southern newspaper. The *Tribune* gave generous space to letters from emigrants to Oregon, written both en route and after arrival, and the majority of those letters encouraged other emigrants to take to the same trails.[51] On one occasion in 1843 Greeley prefaced such a letter with the admonition that his readers should not thereby be influenced to migrate, but the *Tribune* during the early 1840s paradoxically featured an editorial page debunking the overland journey as "palpable homicide," while the rest of the paper frequently contained enthusiastic letters from overlanders who had successfully completed the venture.[52]

Throughout 1844 and the early part of 1845 the *Tribune* had little to say concerning the overland trips. When Oregon was discussed it was only in terms of the claims controversy between the United States and Great Britain. Although it was acknowledged that American settlers were present in Oregon and were increasing in number, nothing was said about how they were getting there.[53] Spring, 1845, found Greeley acquiescing in the feasibility of overland travel, although he continued to denigrate the virtues of Oregon. In one editorial Greeley adopted the tactic that the British were utilizing, emphasizing that the Hudson's Bay Company had kindly saved many of the overlanders from potentially dire consequences. In June the same newspaper which two years earlier had been predicting that nine-tenths of the overlanders were doomed to certain death was arguing that the government "demagogues" were risking disaster with Britain for the sake of excitement, whereas the wise policy would have been to remain inactive, since "our people, who but a few years since had scarcely a footing in Oregon, were pouring over the Rocky Mountains by hundreds" and occupying all the best land.[54]

When by his count nearly 10,000 emigrants took to the trails in 1845, however, Greeley could not resist a few final comments on the "foolhardy" overlanders. With such a multitude invading Oregon he doubted whether the Hudson's Bay Company would continue its assistance, and raised again the questions of securing food, clothing, and shelter, both on the trail and upon arrival in Oregon. Of course it was not at all certain, he wrote, that all would arrive safely, for "inevitably" some "delicate women and children" would die. He noted that one party had gotten lost on the prairies and had been forced to return to Missouri, and Greeley hailed their misfortune as one they ought to "reverently thank Heaven for." The only practice more stupid than the migrations, said Greeley, was suicide.[55]

Again the following summer the *Tribune* stressed the sufferings and privations of overland travel and contended that under the existing circumstances it was "cruelty" to take children on such a journey. Parents ought to await the availability of a "tolerable" road with resting places, depots of provisions, and herds of cattle for trade. Only once did the *Tribune* resort to the tactic so widely used elsewhere in assessing the overlanders and clearly praise their heroic qualities. That was in November, 1845, when it was noted that "indefatigable men" with every difficulty and hardship in their way were establishing a footing beyond the Rockies "at the risk of life and limb."[56]

Though certainly the most prominent anti-emigration newspaper, Greeley's *Tribune* was not alone in inveighing against the overland migrations. The counsel the *Tribune* directed to good citizens, to remain at home where better land was still abundantly available, found expression throughout the United States but primarily in the East, where fears remained current that westward emigration could only impede the manufacturing and financial interest so crucial to New England's well-being. New England anti-expansionists also opposed territorial acquisitions in fear that the United States would then exceed the "natural" size for republics and would of necessity split apart.[57]

Most of the nay-sayers continued to rely upon three basic arguments: that in the event of war the American army could not successfully march overland, that much better land was available at home, and that the trip was too dangerous, especially for women and children. The New York *Journal of Commerce* assumed that Oregon's destiny was to be decided by sea power, since marching an army overland would be a more difficult task than Hannibal had faced when crossing the Alps. To the *Vermont Chronicle* it was "most preposterous" even to think of marching an army overland and then of supporting it, especially when the desert territory in question was of no more usefulness than territory on the moon. The Newport *Herald of the Times* summed up the matter succinctly in early 1846: "We might as well attempt to march an army to the moon, as to march one, over-land, to Oregon."[58]

Potential overlanders, however, were more interested in soil than in armies, so the prophets of gloom portrayed Oregon and California as virtual deserts compared with the good lands so abundantly available in the States. A writer in the *North American Review* asserted that Siberia compared favorably with Oregon and that the route thither was no less difficult than the one to Oregon. The writer chided the American politicians for overplaying the ease of communication with Oregon and indicated that "an Illinois farm of the finest land in the world" could be purchased for less than the cost of the journey to Oregon. The Hartford *Daily Courant* sought to stem the 1843 Oregon enthusiasm by stressing both the dangers of the trip and the vast territories yet available far to the east of Oregon. The Detroit *Advertiser* urged settlers to remain at home, where they were more urgently needed, predicting that because of the difficulty of communicating with Oregon, Canada was far more likely than Oregon to become an integral part of the United States. The Augusta *Age* urged America to secure Oregon before Britain did, but, in another example of viewing the overland migrations from a selfish perspective, contended that the overland passage "over mountains and trackless deserts" was too difficult when compared with the easy communication by sea from Maine and other eastern commercial seaports.[59]

But the most frequently expressed convictions were that if anyone was deranged enough to want to brave such dangers to reach such a worthless territory, let him indulge his insanity—provided he was young, single, and male. Even a few western newspapers took this position. In 1841 the *Western Atlas, and Saturday Evening Gazette,* published in St. Louis, declared its preference for peopling Missouri and not the Pacific Coast. For family men to try to go there overland was "absurd," but for spirited and energetic young men the editor thought it might even be romantic. A correspondent of the St. Louis *Daily Missouri Republican* berated the husband who took his wife and their newly born twins from their bed, placed them in a wagon, and departed for California in 1844. Noting the severe toil involved in getting there, the writer called all who went "ignorant, deluded men" and wished that only men were going out to suffer. The Albany *Atlas* cautioned against elderly persons chancing the overland trip. The influential St. Louis *Daily Missouri Republican,* published near the western frontier, advanced similar arguments. The trip was too treacherous for families, and both California and Oregon were inferior to Missouri; the best advice was "not to move one foot" toward the Pacific Coast. Single men, of course, might go, but it was an "absurdity" for family heads to expose "their wives and children to all degrees of suffering." The *Daily Missouri Republican* as late as 1848 was urging men to remain in the western states and earn an "honest living," since it was an "injustice" to expose families to the hardships of the "long and perilous" journey. The editor maintained that no respect could be accorded anyone who departed for the West planning to settle. Furthermore, it was virtually impossible to return from Oregon and California to the midwestern states (which the editor inferred many wished to do) because it was one thing to cross the Rockies with an almost empty wagon, but to try it with one that was loaded for the long trip eastward was "almost impossible."[60] Even some merchants, bankers, and bystanders in the western outfitting towns voiced sharp disapproval of the initial overland journeys until the 1841 migration revealed that the venture was feasible—and promised profits as well.[61]

In view of the plethora of pessimistic propaganda of this type, one wonders how many prospective overlanders backed out or hesitated uncertainly, as did Ezra Fisher, a Baptist missionary desirous of taking his family overland to Oregon. Both a husband and a father, the Reverend Fisher did not want to expose his young family to the kind of dangers and hardships he was hearing and reading about, so he scrapped his plans of traveling with the 1844 emigration. By the next year, however, Fisher had read convincing comments of a more favorable nature, and he joined the increasing tide of emigrants trekking overland to Oregon.[62]

Those recommending against the land journey to Oregon were, however, mere voices crying in the wilderness compared with the many emigration boosters hailing the heroic qualities of courageous overland travelers. By and large, these enthusiasts viewed Oregon as a desirable acquisition for America. Accordingly, in an attempt to foster emigration to that far distant region, they assured prospective travelers that the overland trip was as practicable as it was easy. It was such writers who finally convinced Ezra Fisher and thousands like him to make the journey. But these Oregon "boomers" were also angling for governmental assistance, in the form of military protection to the overlanders, land grants upon their arrival, and early statehood. Therefore, while many of these writers and orators deemed it appropriate to stress the privations, hardships, and difficulties of the overland trek—frequently in even greater measure than did the pessimists—they did so not to deter emigrants but to encourage and glorify them as worthies deserving governmental largess. Words such as "hardy," "adventurous," and "brave" became staple clichés in most articles and comments emanating from what may be termed the "adventurist school" of overland emigration, a group in which western senators and representatives were particularly prominent.

The tone for much of their rhetoric had been established in the literature disseminated by the Oregon Provisional Emigration Society in 1838 and 1839. This Massachusetts-based association, organized by a group of Methodist ministers and laymen, energetically promoted the emigration of Christian settlers to Oregon, thereby anticipating the early Christianizing of the area Indians. Its short-lived organ, the *Oregonian, and Indian's Advocate,* had a much greater impact than its approximately 500 subscribers would imply, the editor claiming that by August, 1839, at least nine kindred Oregon emigration societies were operating in six states.[63] For 1840 the parent society planned a major overland migration. Two hundred men with their families were to be sent, the society furnishing everything except clothing, blankets, and weaponry for $400 per adult and $30 for each child under sixteen.[64] That this visionary scheme fell through was not as important as the propaganda impact of the supposedly accurate information about the overland journey with which editor F. B. Tracy and others filled the pages of the *Oregonian, and Indian's Advocate.*

The eleven published issues emphasized that "wagons have repeatedly crossed the Rocky Mountains," assured readers that women and children would thrive on the overland journey, which was much safer than an ocean voyage, and confidently predicted that the health of all would improve during the summer crossing.[65] Further, according to Tracy, the Indians never attacked large companies such as theirs would be. Moreover, these Christian settlers would go with the gospel of peace and love to help the Indians, who were certain to recognize such beneficent motives and respond accordingly.[66] The presumptuous clinching argument was that their initial beginnings in Oregon would be pleasant thanks to the princely and compassionate welcome they could count on from the Hudson's Bay Company: "We can go to Oregon with safety, the most perfect safety, and be sure of a reception from Englishmen, every way worthy of the hospitable name of that ancient beef-eating people."[67]

Most Americans were not as confident as the Oregon Provisional Emigration Society that the British in Oregon were trustworthy or that the Oregon boundary dispute would be settled short of war. In fact, the public's fascination with the westbound pioneers fell off sharply after the 1846 treaty with Great Britain was concluded. But during the early 1840s, as national interest in overland travel heightened, a number of themes became distinguishable in the writings of optimistic emigration boosters.

One of the most frequently cited themes was the ease with which the Rocky Mountains could be crossed. To be sure, Senator George McDuffie of South Carolina, who staunchly opposed the colonization of Oregon, had once thanked God "for his mercy in placing the Rocky Mountains there" to prevent Americans from going to the Pacific.[68] For the enthusiasts of overland travel, however, the Rocky Mountains were "mere molehills," a characterization so prevalent that Representative Robert C. Winthrop of Massachusetts wryly offered a literary analogy. In Winthrop's estimation, what was needed in Congress was some Shakespearean Faulconbridge to say to the swaggering braggarts who talked of easy travel over the mountains to the Pacific exactly what had been said in *King John:* "Here's a large mouth indeed. . . . Talks as familiarly of roaring lions as maids of thirteen do of puppy dogs."[69] But neither McDuffie nor Winthrop was able to rebut the glowing testimonials.

Though scattered references to the easy passage over the Rockies had been appearing in newspapers for the previous decade, it was explorer John C. Frémont who ignited the South Pass enthusiasm when he explained how the traveler could go through the pass without any "toilsome ascents," and compared it to the "ascent of the Capitol hill from the avenue, at Washington."[70] From that point on the Rockies stopped few emigrants, at least on the floor of Congress. Senator Lewis F. Linn of Missouri praised the "easy passes" of the Rockies, through which families in wagons passed readily on the "even surface of the inclined plane of the river Platte."[71] In 1844 Representative Robert Dale Owen of Indiana asserted that not even a Chinese wall at the summit of the Rockies would be sufficient to impede the progress of American emigrants.[72] Representative James Thompson of Pennsylvania rephrased Frémont's comments about South Pass being no steeper than the climb from Pennsylvania Avenue to the Capitol, contending that the Rockies could be crossed "without scarcely perceiving the acclivity."[73] Representative Jacob Thompson of Mississippi rejoiced that the "hardy pioneers . . . with their stout hearts and brawny arms" were opening a wagon way through the mountains.[74] Representative James Pollock of Pennsylvania and Senators John M. Niles of Connecticut and Thomas Hart Benton of Missouri also expressed their pleasure that the mountains once considered such a formidable barrier had now been revealed to be so easily passable by the hardy pioneers.[75]

Newspapers and magazines shared in the exuberance. The Cincinnati *Chronicle* held Frémont's passage of the Rockies in the midst of winter to be a feat far superior to any previous crossing of the Alps. A writer in the *United States Magazine, and Democratic Review* accepted Frémont's report as proof that the Rockies were "easily passed" and that the whole route to Oregon was "practicable, even in a state of nature, for carriages and artillery." Now that this joyous fact was known, he confidently assumed that the Oregon emigration would significantly increase. The Boston *Daily Journal* observed that the remarkable pass could be used for a railroad route, since the grade on either side of the pass was so gradual "as to be almost imperceptible." George Wilkes, boosting a transcontinental railroad as early as 1845, contended that in fashioning South Pass for easy passages nature had been more beneficent to the United States than to any other country.[76]

Another theme regularly sounded by the enthusiasts of overland migration was the similarity of the movement to Oregon with that of previous movements westward throughout American history. In this connection the Rocky Mountains were often described as an inferior barrier when compared with the Alleghenies. A writer in a Missouri newspaper explained that there was a good wagon road across the Rockies, whereas the first Virginia emigrants had had none when they penetrated westward over the mountains; another newspaper editor used Frémont as the source for his conclusion that the difficulties posed by the Rockies paled "to insignificance when compared with those once existing in regard to the Alleghenies."[77] Representative David A. Starkweather of Ohio contended that savage men and beasts would still control the western United States if Daniel Boone and other adventurous pioneers had been cautioned not to cross the Alleghenies because of potential dangers in the manner that prospective Oregon emigrants were now being counseled.[78] The Washington *Union* commended the reappearance among the Oregon overlanders of the same "spirit of enterprise" which had previously prompted Boone and other hardy western pioneers beyond the mountains to the forests of Kentucky and the valley of the Mississippi.[79] Iowa territorial delegate A. C. Dodge explained that the initial settlers of any region were always forced to contend with numerous obstacles. Only such "undaunted firmness of mind and constancy of purpose" as that being exhibited by the Oregon emigrants would succeed.[80]

These comments correlated the push to Oregon with the step-by-step process of previous American westward movements when the longest leap had been the 200-mile crossing of the Appalachians.[81] The New York *Evening Mirror*, by contrast, believed that the Oregon migrations were unique. There was simply nothing to compare with them in all recorded history; even "from the time of the Phenicians, the earliest colonizers, there has never been a colony despatched overland for such an immense distance." The romantic nature of the whole undertaking could only be explained, according to the *Mirror*, by understanding the adventurous and resolute western character which within the next fifty years would form a new republic "on the shores of the South sea."[82]

In his book *The History of Oregon and California*, Robert Greenhow, a State Department translator, contended that by their very nature Americans were conditioned to struggle successfully against hardships which Europeans could never overcome. Besides, according to Greenhow, the difficulties on the American overland route to Oregon were insignificant compared with those on the British route of travel.[83] Representative John Reynolds of Illinois endeavored to put the travel hardships in perspective. Recognizing that "delicate females" had already easily passed over the mountains to the Pacific, he predicted that in a few years it would be no more difficult to travel overland to Oregon than it had once been to travel from the Mississippi to Philadelphia. From Missouri the *Western Journal* agreed. Indeed, it went Reynolds one better, forecasting that "a journey from New York to China, by way of Oregon, will be less thought of than it formerly was to St. Louis."[84]

Emigration boosters also frequently adopted biblical analogies. Senator Lewis F. Linn of Missouri, envious of the "wild and strange rapture" Boone must have experienced when he first gazed into Kentucky, believed that identical sensations were motivating the Oregon pioneers as they went forth "to the wilderness like our first parents, when God sent them forth from the garden of Eden to subdue the earth."[85] Representative Orlando B. Ficklin of Illinois compared the overlanders' transcontinental journeys with the travels of Abraham and Lot and with those of Moses and Aaron leading the Children of Israel through the wilderness. Ficklin eagerly anticipated the time when he himself would be able to climb the mountains and see and hear "with wild delight" the roar of the Columbia River as it plunged into the Pacific Ocean.[86] The New Orleans *Daily Picayune* was also impressed with the similarity between the Oregonians and the Boones and Clarks who had opened up Indiana, Illinois, Kentucky, and Ohio for settlement. Moreover, it pictured the overlanders as "pioneers in the great work of spreading republican opinions hard by the waters of the Western Sea, and their children, like those of Israel that followed Moses through the wilderness, will erect temples in the promised land, where generations to come will worship the living God as they alone worship that acknowledge no Lord but him."[87]

Additional themes were mentioned frequently in the newspapers and magazines of the time. Over and over again the overland enthusiasts reminded prospective travelers that the one danger to be feared was the hostility of the Indian tribes. In 1840 Greenhow wrote that all that was needed to insure safe and easy overland passages was the establishment of a few military posts between the Missouri River and the Rocky Mountains. The same conclusion appeared in an article in *Hunt's Merchants' Magazine* in 1842.[88] The New Orleans *Weekly Bulletin* considered the Indian menace to be so severe that it believed no single individual could make the trip and that even large, well-guarded caravans were in "constant jeopardy." The *Bulletin*'s editor therefore joined others in calling for the government to construct promptly a chain of forts for protective purposes. The Iowa City

Iowa Capitol Reporter similarly recommended that emigrants arm themselves well and travel only in large companies, while the Cincinnati *Atlas* assured parties of 500 or more that they need not fear attacks.[89] Although the most popular guidebooks upon which many emigrants relied gave exceedingly little advice on dealing with Indians, they too advised the plains traveler to journey in large and well-guarded companies to avoid molestation.[90]

Requests that the government assume responsibility for protecting overland travelers to Oregon were commonplace. The Weston, Missouri, *Journal* advocated the construction of a series of posts from Missouri to the mountains, and the St. Joseph *Gazette* repeatedly declared that the government was duty-bound to protect the emigrants en route to Oregon.[91] When in July of 1846 the editor of the *Gazette* received information that the Pawnee Indians had killed one overlander, he immediately demanded that the emigrants be protected from the "depredations of these Indians." Again in 1848 the *Gazette* editor, after receiving word that several Mormon parties had been attacked, called for permanent stations of troops to deter the Indians from further attacks. President James Knox Polk's government organ, the Washington *Union,* regarded a line of forts and permanently stationed soldiers as "indispensable"—a project which could no longer be postponed.[92]

The Philadelphia *Ledger* and the St. Louis *Missouri Republican*, probing beyond a mere recital of the Indian danger, concluded that the ominous arm of John Bull lurked behind the trouble. Agents of the Hudson's Bay Company, these papers charged, were responsible for supplying the Indians with weaponry, and would continue to "omit no exertion to inspire the Indians with a hostile spirit towards the Americans." Both papers demanded government protection for the overlanders, and the *Ledger* elaborated on the grand future awaiting a series of military posts. Soldiers stationed at the posts could improve roads between the forts and cultivate gardens and fields so that provisions would be readily available for emigrants. In this manner the military establishments would form the foundation for civilizing towns which would ultimately spring up about them.[93]

These press demands for governmental action to nullify the Indian threat were echoed by a great many congressmen. But a few legislators remained unconvinced that several forts would solve all the overland transit problems of an army march to Oregon in the event of war with Great Britain. These men generally followed the lead of Senator John C. Calhoun of South Carolina. Advocating a policy of "masterly inactivity" on the part of the United States toward the Oregon question, Calhoun contended that if Britain wanted to contest the boundary dispute militarily America was doomed, because it would be inconvenient if not impossible for an armed force to reach Oregon over what Representative Meredith P. Gentry of Tennessee termed the "dreary deserts, and mountains almost inaccessible."[94] Their hope was that if the boundary issue could be permitted to lie dormant for a number of years, enough American settlers would migrate to Oregon to insure its possession by the United States. This was yet another instance in which the overland journey was viewed unrealistically: if it was impossible to march an army overland to Oregon, how could emigrant families be expected to complete the trip?

Most congressmen, however, believing that Indians posed the main problem to transcontinental travel, demanded immediate action. Representatives John Wentworth of Illinois and James B. Bowlin of Missouri maintained that if the United States did not act quickly the British-Indian alliance could prove disastrous, because South Pass was a potential "Thermopylae of the West."[95] Representative Caleb B. Smith of Indiana discoursed as late as 1848 on how perilous the Indians made the route to Oregon,[96] but long before that Leonard H. Sims, representative from Missouri, had put the Indian menace in its proper perspective. Commenting on all the dangers allegedly besetting the route to Oregon, Sims assured his colleagues: "Now, sir, we of Missouri can fit out ten thousand wagon loads of provisions for Oregon at any time, and ten thousand wagon boys to drive them, who, with their wagon whips, can beat and drive off all the British and Indians that they find in their way."[97]

Such braggadocio notwithstanding, President John Tyler utilized two annual messages to call for the establishment of military posts along the route to provide protection from the Indians to the "hardy adventurers" en route to Oregon.[98] President Polk did likewise in his first message to Congress, which refrained from taking positive action in spite of a favorable report on such a bill by the House Committee on Military Affairs.[99] The committee report summed up in the adventurists' best tradition the Indian danger and the other privations the brave overlanders had to face along the Oregon Trail:

Everywhere exposed to the depredations and assaults of treacherous and piratical savages: with no place where supplies of provisions could be obtained in case their original stock were lost or destroyed by any of the casualties to which such a journey is so liable; where the services of a surgeon could be obtained for the wounded, or of a physician for the sick; where damaged vehicles could be repaired; where fresh vegetables could be procured, the enfeebled recruit their strength, or the diseased nursed in security and comfort into a return of health and vigor.

The committee thought that many had probably been deterred from going by such obstacles and argued that the proposed line of forts would solve the problems and "render the journey so secure, easy, and comfortable, that none . . . need be alarmed at its magnitude or its difficulties."[100]

President Polk had no better success with another proposal he often repeated, that of granting tracts of land to arriving Oregon overlanders as a reward for the rigors they had undergone en route and to facilitate their beginnings in the new territory. The President requested such legislation in behalf of the "patriotic pioneers" in his 1845 message to Congress, and continued his public appeals for the "hardy and adventurous citizens" through 1847, but without success.[101]

One theme conspicuously underplayed in the heady propaganda offered by the overland enthusiasts was the incidence of trail tragedies, despite the fact that one of the worst tragedies of the overland trail era befell the Donner emigrant party during the winter of 1846. The nearly ninety overlanders bound for California were trapped in the Sierras by early snows. Nearly half of the party died and the rest survived only by resorting to cannibalism during one of the most heartrending episodes in American history. The New York *Herald*, in one of its most mistaken journalistic predictions, had printed in its columns a letter written en route by Mrs. George Donner with the annotation that Mrs. Donner was a "perfect specimen of our American women—intelligent, educated, brave and spirited. If the rest of the females of the expedition are like Mrs. Donner, there need be no fear of the expedition." For some reason the *Herald* had little to say about the final tragedy. Neither did the New York *Daily Tribune*. In the New Orleans *Daily Picayune* the first mention of the tragedy was buried in the second to last paragraph of a catchall news column on California and was preceded by the printing of a treaty Frémont had concluded with California commissioners. The account noted that the Donner survivors had been compelled to eat the dead bodies of their companions in order to avert starvation, but many readers undoubtedly missed the item.[102]

Most of these newspapers continually stressed sensational events elsewhere in their pages, and this ignoring of an obviously sensational occurrence is puzzling. It may have even represented an attempt to keep the potential dangers of overland travel from public view, although the generally pro-emigration western papers were quite willing to publicize the affair. In the St. Joseph *Gazette,* for example, intimate details of the suffering were recounted. One woman was reported to have eaten parts of the dead bodies of her father and brother; another had seen her husband's heart cooked. The *Gazette* printed the names of both the survivors and the deceased, and on two occasions noted that future emigrants would want to consider whether the new country justified "an exposure to such hardships and sufferings."[103] The editor of the St. Louis *Daily Missouri Republican*, after mentioning the cannibalism, also suggested, "It ought to be a very fine country to justify an exposure to such sufferings and horrors." The St. Louis paper further predicted that news of the tragedy would drastically curtail emigration to California, claiming that it had tried to get the Donners to go to Oregon but that "Hasting's Journal had so inflated their views of that country, that they could not forego their determination to visit it."[104] From San Francisco the *California Star* was likewise predicting that emigration would decline for a few years because of the tragedy. The *Star*'s editor therefore endeavored to demonstrate that the overland journey was perfectly practicable provided the emigrants took normal precautions and did not delay inordinately—as he intimated the Donner party had done.[105]

Elsewhere the use made of the tragedy varied. The Washington *National Intelligencer* asserted flatly that the Hastings Cutoff should not be used, but also informed its readers that the story was full of "thrilling interest."[106] An Ohio editor reflected with wonder that so many continued to hazard so much. *Niles' National Register* suggested that "Napoleon's feat on the Alps was child's play" compared with the Donner survivors crossing the mountains in winter. Representative Willard P. Hall of Missouri covered in gruesome detail the cannibalism and deaths in order to demonstrate the risks and perils the Oregon emigrants encountered, risks which in his estimation justified granting land to the overlanders in Oregon upon their arrival. The *American Review,* in a long analysis of an emigrant journal, noted the sufferings and dangers which the overlanders encountered and quoted a portion of the author's account of the Donner tragedy. The *Review* characterized the chapter as "one of the most terrible in all the history of human sorrow." The *United States Magazine, and Democratic Review*'s analysis of the same volume suggested that the author's account had even been "slightly softened down from the awful truth," and envisioned "a sermon on charity" ensuing from the horror of the event.[107]

Of all the themes utilized by the proponents, undoubtedly the most pervasive was the heroism motif. In the Congress, legislators outdid themselves in finding new ways of depicting the adventurous bravery of the hardy overlanders. A cautionary voice like that of Representative Winthrop of Massachusetts went unheeded. Winthrop had opined that "a march to Oregon . . . would take the courage out of not a few who now believe themselves incapable of fatigue or fear."[108]

Senator Thomas Hart Benton of Missouri contended that the emigrants, inspired by newspapers and encouraged by western congressmen, had won Oregon for the nation despite governmental delay, that these "bold adventurers" had heroically saved Oregon from the British. James Semple of Illinois explained to his fellow senators that the "complete success" of the caravans was due to the "same bold and daring spirits, whose intrepidity has heretofore overcome the western wilderness in the midst of dangers," and predicted that 10,000 emigrants would take to the trails in 1844. Senator Edward A. Hannegan of Indiana refused to admit that the overlanders were "wanton adventurers." Rather, theirs was an honorable spirit seeking to "add to the growing grandeur of their beloved country." Senator David R. Atchison of Missouri agreed, pointing out that the "brave and hardy pioneers" who had risked their lives to "every privation and hardship" crossed the wilderness "with the plough and the pruning hook in one hand, and with defensive weapons in the other."[109]

If anything, the House of Representatives outdid the Senate in praising the valor of the overlanders. The Illinois and Missouri lawmakers again led the eulogies. John Wentworth of Illinois noted that if the adventurous frontiersman could not go to Oregon he would go elsewhere, explaining that in many western regions it was considered "discreditable" and "a lack of manly perseverance" for a young man to settle too close to his parents. He then pictured the heroics of these "dauntless spirits" in all their grandeur:

Only think of it: men, women, and children, forsaking their homes, bidding farewell to all the endearments of society, setting out on a journey of over two thousand miles, upon a route where they have to make their own roads, construct their own bridges, hew out their own boats, and kill their own meat; and undergoing every diversity of pain from agues, chills, sprains and bruises; where twenty miles is an average day's travel, exposed to every variety of weather, and the naked earth their only resting-place! In sickness they have no physician; in death there is no one to perform the last sad offices. Their bodies are buried by the wayside, to be exhumed and defiled by the Indians, or devoured by the wolves.

His fellow Illinoisan, Edward D. Baker, painfully acknowledged that the government might not grant protection to the brave men who took the "arts of civilization" into the wilderness, but demanded that "at least they should be shielded from reproach." James B. Bowlin of Missouri filled his laudation with phrases commending the "noble spirit of enterprise," "hardy sons of the frontier," "noble and patriotic adventure," "gallant spirit," and "fearless character of the western pioneer," triumphantly concluding that no obstacle was too great to be "overcome by a brave heart and stalwart arm." Jefferson Davis of Mississippi shared this high opinion of the "energy and restless spirit of adventure which is characteristic of our people."[110]

While these congressmen were depicting every possible terror and privation which the brave overlanders were heroically overcoming at the risk of life and limb, Secretary of State John C. Calhoun in 1844 was blandly informing Richard Pakenham, the British minister in the Oregon negotiations, that American emigrants were flowing toward Oregon, since "loaded wagons now travel with facility from Missouri to the navigable waters of the Columbia river."[111] This was the same Calhoun who had informed the Senate the previous year that the American army would have extreme difficulty in reaching Oregon by the overland route. As usual, the overland journey could be viewed in whatever manner seemed most appropriate to the circumstances.

In eastern, southern, and western newspapers the pattern of phraseology and argument was strikingly similar. The heroic overland emigrants were the toast of the continent. James Gordon Bennett's New York *Herald,* pro–"Manifest Destiny" and consequently favoring the acquisition of Oregon and California, affords an interesting comparison

"Leaving the Old Homestead," the first painful step, was painted about 1854 by James F. Wilkins, an 1849 overlander.

with its intra-city rival, Horace Greeley's *Daily Tribune*. Not only did the two editors have less than the best relationship personally,[112] their policy of news coverage, their arguments, and their conclusions with respect to the migrations were markedly different. Whereas Greeley began reporting on and editorializing against the migrations in early 1843, Bennett granted them no coverage at all until the summer of 1845. From then on news of Oregon frequently filled the *Herald's* pages, but the commentary was almost always political, and Bennett, unlike Greeley, engaged in very little concrete thinking about the overland journey itself. The initial mention of overland movement to Oregon came on June 1, 1845. Two weeks later Bennett again noted the quantity of "hardy, enterprising settlers" who were proceeding from "almost every town and village in the western and southwestern states." As usual, there was no mention of any travel difficulties.[113]

A month later the *Herald* predicted that the fearless pioneers braving the "hazardous and exhausting journey of the American Desert, and of that waste and wilderness of the Rocky mountains" would certainly have no truck with concessions to Britain. In September the *Herald* stated that there had been too much romantic writing about the route to Oregon and therefore it had great interest in the authoritative letters of emigrant Peter H. Burnett. But having said this, the *Herald* went on to romanticize about how easy the forty-mile-wide South Pass made the contemplated railroad route to Oregon, which could proceed "without any extraordinary natural obstacle."[114]

Throughout 1846 the Bennett organ hummed the heroic tune in its comments on the overland emigrants. On January 19 a long editorial appeared entitled "The Spirit of Emigration." Bennett suggested that thousands of city dwellers, tired of monotonous city ways, were ready to march to California, even though the journey was long and tiresome and filled with hardships for those previously accustomed only to the luxuries of city life. Yet the minor hardship of "sleeping in a tent, and being drenched with rain all night, so that it is almost impossible to prevent being floated off" had never stopped any previous "adventurous American emigrant." Former emigrants had overcome dense forests, howling beasts, mountains, lakes, marshes, rivers, storms, and savages to create a "paradise . . . where only wildness and uncultivation were before." Nothing would stop the continuation of this glorious onward march.[115]

Nonetheless, the *Herald* joined other pro-emigration newspapers in pleading for congressional assistance to facilitate the "hardy Western pioneers" in their migration to Oregon, there to "spread the influences of our happy institutions." Blockhouse forts, troops to protect the travelers, the construction of roads and bridges, the establishment of mail service, grants of Oregon land so that the "hardy emigrants" would cut down trees, scare away wild animals, and thereby drive out the Hudson's Bay

53

Company—the *Herald* championed all these causes. In May of 1846 the *Herald* rejoiced that Frémont's recent discovery of a pass would enable the overlanders to save two months on the route to California, which would increase by "tenfold" the number of "hardy pioneers" who would emigrate to the Pacific.[116]

Editor George Henry Evans of the *Working Man's Advocate,* another New York paper, only infrequently found it possible to mention the journey without linking the comment to the demand that free land for the landless be given in Oregon as throughout America. In 1844 the *Advocate* appealed for the migration to Oregon of some great man who would take the lead in making Oregon a republic based on the equal right of every man to the soil. Such a man "would rank in history as much above George Washington as that great man now ranks above the ideot George the Third." Evans did not favor facilitating emigration by establishing military posts en route to Oregon unless the government agreed to guarantee to every emigrant "his natural right to the free use of land enough for his subsistence." By January of 1845 Evans and others had formed the Oregon Board for the purpose of establishing in that territory a republic dedicated to the recognition of the natural and inalienable right of man to the earth. For that purpose emigration was to be promoted to Oregon, and the *Advocate* indicated that the journey would require 100 days from Fort Leavenworth and would cost a single man only $50 from New York while a family of five could expect to make the journey for $150. The *Advocate* expressed the view that it was unnecessary to go into the details of the journey, although it did caution that the "toils and hardships" should not be forgotten in the "inordinate show of romantic adventure" which frequently accompanied such migrations.[117] Rechristened *Young America!* in 1845, Evans's paper made scarcely any mention of probable hardships in a report it published explaining the route to California, although the "most convenient and safest company" was suggested to be approximately 500 persons. That *Young America!* regarded the overland journey to be little more than a lark, however, was revealed in an 1846 remark. In a long editorial attacking land monopolies, the question the editor most wanted answered was why so many persons in the East were excluded from land so that they were "obliged to stroll away to Oregon or California to get a living."[118]

Also apparently in the "adventurist" tradition was the *American Agriculturist,* a New York publication. The editor prefaced the publication of a letter in which Thomas J. Farnham was less than enthusiastic about Oregon's agricultural potential with the comment that "we might as well undertake to stay the sun and moon in their course over the peaks of the Rocky Mountains, as emigration to the west by the hardy nomadic population of our country." In October of 1844, following a glowing account of Oregon as a boon to the poor man, the editor asked, "Who will not take the risk of being scalped by Indians, or devoured by grisly bears, to say nothing of sustaining innumerable hardships for a succession of years, and living free from all moral and civil restraints, to emigrate to the Ultima Thule or last jumping off place of the El Dorado of the final borders of the great illimitable west!"[119]

Not surprisingly, one of the New York publications lent substance to the view that the "noble . . . migratory legions" moving westward were "leading all the trail of social and civil virtues out into the wilderness, to adorn and beautify its desert places." The myth of the desert remained troublesome for most writers, who, like the one just quoted, occasionally tried to describe the West as both desert and garden. In the same paragraph this enthusiast spoke not only of the desert places the emigrants would civilize but also of "those flowery seas, the Prairies." Four years later in the same journal a writer mentioned again "the deserts said to lie between the two sides of the nation," which might impede the preservation of national unity were it not for the railroad which could span it.[120] To the editor of the *New Genesee Farmer* the myth of the desert also prevailed, and in 1842 he wrote hopefully of the prospects of using camels for transportation on the prairies, which were "likely to remain impenetrable by carriages."[121]

Two other eastern organs were untroubled by any desert myths as they rhapsodized over the adventurous overlanders. The New York *Morning News* envisioned the westbound emigrant tide as soon bringing Oregon into the Union, for "the way is now completely smooth and easy." Even though the travel rigors were inconsequential, the *News* still pictured the overlanders as "hardy, bold, and indomitable" as well as of the highest character. Hearing that the 1843 overlanders had succeeded in progressing past Independence Rock, the *National Intelligencer* assured future emigrants—predicting that there would be many—that the way had now been blazed and lay "clear before them." William E. Cramer of New York, writing in the *Merchant's Magazine,* also contended that access to the West was "so easy and cheap" that even from the farthest corners of the East laborers could "escape from the exactions of capital, and enjoy the fruits of his toil." Not only did he view the West as a safety valve for the hard-pressed eastern laborer, Cramer looked forward to the healthy East-West competition certain to come.[122]

In the South, just as the Whig-inclined New Orleans *Daily Picayune* equivocated on the question of expansionism,[123] so too the tone of its comments on the overland journey fluctuated from bravado to considerable caution. In 1842 the *Daily Picayune* noted that Oregon, like Texas, was quickly becoming an "emigration ground for hundreds of adventurous and bold spirits." After receiving a progress report from the 1843 emigrants, the *Daily Picayune* editor commented that the information made it clear that the overlanders would "make the trip with ease before the bad weather commences." In 1844 word was received that a baby boy had been born en route to a Snooks family and had been named, appropriately enough, "Oregon Snooks." The editor commented that this was "a name which may hereafter be destined to fill the trump of fame, and ring through the Rocky Mountains to the dismay of grizzly bears. Go it, Snooks!"[124]

By 1846, however, the *Daily Picayune* favored the establishment of an overland route across the Isthmus of Panama to "divert the travel to Oregon from the long, dangerous and expensive route across the prairies and Rocky Mountains." The Panama route would be much safer, thought the editor. Moreover, it would make it possible to transport household goods and farm implements with more certainty, and would do away with the time delay necessitated by awaiting the formation of large caravans to cross the American plains. While the *Picayune* was much less interested in the Oregon question than were the New York dailies, this December 18, 1846, comment was one of the very few post–British treaty references to the overland caravans in the eastern and southern newspapers. The July, 1845, issue of the *Southern Quarterly Review* included a long article on the Pacific Coast in which the writer pictured the route as lengthy and difficult but assured "hardy spirits" they would face few dangers.[125]

In western America Oregon enthusiasm was high. As the Madison, Indiana, *Courier and Constitutional Advocate* expressed it, "Everything from this region is looked for and read with breathless anxiety." When Stephen W. Kearny successfully marched dragoons to South Pass and back in 1845, the St. Louis *Daily Missouri Republican* rejoiced that proof was now extant that the American army *could* march to Oregon—and that presumably the British and other negativists would at last accept that fact. In 1845 an Iowa newspaper affirmed that the journey hardships were already acknowledged "to be much less than has heretofore been imagined," and the next year a Missouri paper reported on a gentleman crossing the plains twice in one year, which led the editor to write, "It has almost become a thing amounting to nothing to cross the widespread uncultivated border."[126]

Even when traveling difficulties were described as inconsequential, most western newspapers dwelled on the glorious nature of the overland endeavor, as did the editor of the *Gazette* when a large emigrant party departed from St. Joseph in 1845. Noting that the emigrants could look forward to a new home and fortune and that they were saving American territory as well as extending American laws and institutions, the editor suggested, "The spectacle was of the romantic, but a full view of the size of the company—the length of the journey—and the boundless extent of the prairie on which they entered, made it grand, almost sublime." Even when the *Gazette* reported that a group of Oregon overlanders had lost their way on the prairies, the editor revealed no concern for their welfare, indicating that they were planting buckwheat so as to have sufficient provisions when they continued their journey the following spring. The editor even speculated that the emigrants might well decide to settle permanently in their new location.[127]

Clearly, the overland migrations had caught the nation by surprise. As the foregoing evidence suggests, for a number of years most of the press coverage was both fanciful and overdrawn. However, there were indications by the mid-1840s, primarily in the West, that at least some newspaper editors were beginning to abandon their grandiose romanticizing about the migrations in lieu of providing useful information and advice for departing overlanders. The St. Joseph paper, for example, warned prospective emigrants against changing routes after they had begun their journey unless they were certain of the new route's proven practicality. This cautionary word was apparently prompted by reports of deaths due to Indians and starvation, which the editor blamed on a few "heartless speculators" who endeavored to force the course of emigration to certain portions of Oregon where they held property. Such advices were certainly also advanced in the hope of avoiding any repetitions of the Donner disaster. The St. Louis *Daily Union* and the San Francisco *California Star*, in a *Supplement* to be carried eastbound along the trails in 1848, also cautioned the emigrants to stay on the old route.[128]

The Weston, Missouri, *Journal* urged the careful preparation of company rules and regulations prior to departure to insure orderly and safe travel. Both the St. Joseph *Gazette* and the New Orleans *Picayune* counseled westbound emigrants to employ a good guide—such as mountain man Moses Harris—for a safe trip, while other newspapers recommended the purchase of guidebooks, such as Edwin Bryant's *What I Saw in California*.[129] Still other newspapers provided overlanders with route and outfit information through the many letters they printed from experienced emigrants. The Fayette *Missouri Democrat* requested that its readers furnish whatever letters they might have received from overlanders who had completed the journey so they could be printed, thus providing more accurate route information for the benefit of future emigrants.[130] Some of these letters were widely reprinted, such as those prepared by former Missouri governor Lilburn W. Boggs and Oregon overlander Peter H. Burnett.[131] The *Daily Missouri Republican* even prepared a map of the West with special attention to the routes to Oregon and California, which it furnished to all its subscribers and others who might be interested.[132] The *Oregon Spectator* impartially identified the various routes into Oregon available to the overlanders in an issue that eastbound travelers took with them to give to the oncoming overlanders of 1847.[133]

Perhaps the constant demands for government assistance and protection in behalf of the overlanders should also be evaluated from such a public-service perspective. The *Missouri Democrat* called upon the government to map out the shortest route to Oregon so that the "weary way" of the emigrant might be shortened.[134] Most western newspapers, and some elsewhere in the nation, found occasion to call periodically for construction of military forts along the route and/or military escorts for the emigrants. Pleas for government construction of a practicable wagon route were also frequently expressed.[135]

Nonetheless, despite these hopeful signs, the attitude more typically expressive of the western press was an emphasis upon the adventurous heroism of the overlanders and the grandeur of their emigration caravans. "There is a wild spirit of adventure," wrote the exultant editor of the Louisville *Journal,* "blended with the less romantic spirit of gain, prevailing throughout the United States, and to this spirit the unprecedented expansion of our population over savage territory is attributable." The Cincinnati *Chronicle* viewed the expeditions as "one of the Signs of the Times,— the expression of the SPIRIT OF THE AGE," which was held to be "locomotive commerce" certain to enhance the "genius of civilization" and call forth "vast and rapid developments, both of Society and Nature."[136] This same general theme was reiterated throughout the West as editors gave Godspeed to their heroic fellows and either magnified or minimized the travel difficulties to be encountered, depending on which tactic best suited the writer's goal of illuminating the virtues of America's greatest citizens—the Oregon pioneers.[137]

The Independence, Missouri, *Western Expositor* believed that if only Congress could witness the number of "brave pioneers who are risking their all, and taking their wives and children with them to Oregon," there would be no further delay in bringing Oregon under the American flag. The same organ depicted the 1843 emigrants as having bravely endured "unparalleled dangers and difficulties from savages, from thirst, from hunger, crossing parched treeless plains, fierce angry rivers, and forcing their wagons through a thousand miles of mountains declared impassable by the most experienced guides and voyagers."[138]

It did not take long before these brave pioneers were characterized as America's finest citizens. In the spring of 1845 the Burlington, Iowa, *Hawkeye* suggested that even to start out on such an endeavor revealed "the enterprising character" of the emigrants, and that it was unfortunate that such able men were leaving the community. The editor wished them well in their new homes in the Far West.[139] It was, in fact, very common for western editors to wish departing overlanders a safe journey and much success in their new ventures.[140] Moreover, many editors heaped high praise upon the type of persons going west. The St. Louis *Daily Missouri Republican* utilized typical language in acclaiming the character of the 1845 emigrants: "They are generally men of respectability and good standing in the communities in which they have heretofore lived, and they carry with them not only the necessities, but many of the luxuries of life."[141] The western correspondent of the New York *Gazette* visited a camp of overlanders and found them to exceed in "respectability . . . any of the new frontier settlers." They were well organized, obeyed the laws they had formulated, allowed no whiskey except for medicinal purposes, conversed intelligently, were sensible in their expectations, and were neatly dressed. Also, "Their girls and women are quite tidy, and walk along with an elastic step, which betokens freedom from care and hardship; indeed, hardship scarcely exists." The St. Louis *New Era* applauded the westward-moving caravans with "this is the way to fortify our right to Oregon. Actual possession and occupancy by the right kind of men."[142]

Another visitor to an emigrant camp about to depart was an editor of the Independence *Western Expositor.* Enthralled with the romanticism of the entire enterprise, the journalist watched the "busy multitude" prepare for departure and termed the scene one of "animation, sunshine and excitement." Viewing the wagons drawn up into a circle, he asserted that they were an "impregnable fortress." Should the overlanders ultimately be required to fight against the British in Oregon, the nation could be assured "that truer hearts or better soldiers never primed a rifle or drew a deadlier bead." At approximately the same time the *Western Expositor* was also encouraging prospective emigrants to accompany Lansford Hastings west on his late fall and early winter overland venture, assuring that "none need fear for a moment" concerning the "practicability of the route. . . . it is his intention to show to the world that the plains can be crossed at any and every season of the year."[143] The Independence *Mission Expositor* correlated both these themes by remarking that although the season of the year was already unusually late to begin an overland journey—mid-August—Hastings's party was composed of "men of the right stamp for such an undertaking" who were determined to prove "to the world" that nothing was an obstacle to the crossing of the plains.[144]

Some optimists took the position that even if the overlanders were not the finest men when they started, they certainly would be when their trek was finished, thanks to the healing powers of western nature. The Springfield, Illinois, *Journal* reported on a speech delivered at a local church by an Oregon overlander and explorer who had returned to guide his parents westward. The Oregon enthusiast explained that the journey greatly promoted health, as he had "known feeble men, women and children, in the commencement of the journey unable to take care of themselves, who, before its conclusion, became entirely robust."[145]

But perhaps the most enthusiastic of all the "adventurists" were those who viewed the journey as a kind of honeymoon for newly married couples.[146] The editor of the *Western Expositor,* ecstatic at the prospective overlanders jamming the city, decided that the "pleased expression on every face" meant that " 'all goes merry as a marriage bell.' " As the editor gazed at the long lines of wagons thronging the busy Independence streets, he espied one which appeared especially comfortable, resplendent

Emigrants would later often find it necessary to discard along the trail such treasured family possessions as those photographed in this overloaded wagon.

as it was with an "extremely nice looking lady" serenely sewing inside next to her bureau and mirror. Various ornaments hung from the side: it was, said the editor, "a perfect prairie boudoir." And then there were the handsome team drivers, "not one of them less than six feet two in his stockings. Whoo ha! Go it boys! We're in a perfect *Oregon fever.*" An 1846 issue of the St. Louis *Missouri Republican* affirmed that "a finer looking body of emigrants" had never been seen, all "manly and bold" in their appearance and well prepared for the "long and tedious" journey before them. Some of their wagons were carpeted and furnished with chairs, beds, and even looking glasses. Even more important, there were "numerous young girls just blooming into womanhood, and many of them beautiful, neatly dressed, and bound for Oregon and California. Young men going to these distant countries need no[t] fear of not being able to get a wife, for I assure them that the assortment of girls in the present companies is by no means indifferent."[147]

And so thousands of overlanders streamed west throughout the 1840s. During the period when the national eye had been riveted upon them, their experiences were described in every imaginable way. The doubters called their venture "palpable homicide"; the enthusiasts, stressing mainly the adventure and heroism, termed the journey "merry as a marriage bell." Ezra Fisher and other persons of the time interested in migrating to the Far West via the overland route but first desiring more information about what the journey would entail were unfortunate victims of circumstances. The type and accuracy of the information they received were dependent largely upon the literary organs to which they had access, upon whether their local newspaper editor favored or opposed the national acquisition of Oregon, or upon his willingness to publish favorable and/or unfavorable letters from other overlanders or reports from other newspapers and journals. It seems safe to conclude that most prospective emigrants were faced with a plethora of contradictory testimonials. In view of the prevailing climate of opinion in their locality, it doubtless took much courage for some to set out; for others it may have been necessary to develop the courage after the "easy" task had been begun.

The overland migrations did not remain a favorite topic of the news media for very long. Most of the attention was focused on the overlanders while the future ownership of Oregon territory was in doubt. After the British treaty was concluded in 1846, most of the eastern and southern newspapers neglected the overlanders until interest was rekindled by the discovery of California gold. Only in the western states was continuing coverage given to the overlanders after the forty-ninth parallel became the definite Oregon boundary. Yet overland they still streamed, if not less heroic, apparently less newsworthy.

Public Opinion, 1849–60

Humbugging and helping

THE UNIVERSAL NEWSPAPER HEADLINE IN 1849 was "gold." Phrases such as "from the gold regions," "California gold," and "Ho for the gold regions" were printed over and over again. Editors and other writers marveled at the throngs determined to set out for the new El Dorado, rejoiced in the booming business insured by this quest for the golden grail, and faithfully printed progress reports from their fellow citizens on the seas or trails. Newspaper columns were filled with tempting transportation and merchandise offers—mining machines, health cures, guns and ammunition, wearing apparel, guidebooks. The opportunities for the clever advertiser were unlimited: even tooth wash for good gums was prominently featured, since dentists were scarce in California.[1] This 1849 and 1850 gold mania commanded the nation's attention as not even the Oregon fever had done, but in the years thereafter, consideration of the overland migrations was confined mainly to the western press.[2]

In the midst of this gold rush hysteria it was inevitable that information regarding the trip to California was liberally dispensed. During the 1850s westbound pioneers regularly found reasonably accurate travel information in their newspapers and magazines. Nonetheless, much media coverage continued to be prompted by ulterior motivations. Indeed, with opportunities for financial gain high, these vested-interest viewpoints were even more pronounced than they had been during the 1840s. And, considering the patterns so firmly established in the preceding years, it was not surprising that evidence of the "adventurist" and "palpable homicide" schools of thought continued to appear, although during the decade of the 1850s such attitudes were no longer dominant.

Under the heading "Romantic" the St. Joseph *Gazette* described a young Indiana maiden bound for Fort Hall, where she planned to meet and marry her betrothed, who was trailing east from Oregon. Following the ceremony the newlyweds would honeymoon by traveling on to

The excitement engendered by the gold rush is recorded on the faces of these Easterners as they read the *Tribune*'s "California News"; painted by William S. Mount in 1850.

The Museums at Stony Brook, gift of Mr. and Mrs. Ward Melville

California. Surely such reporting conveyed the desired connotation: the overland journey remained "merry as a marriage bell." The *United States Magazine, and Democratic Review* rejoiced that the brave and fearless pioneers who had been traveling overland during the preceding years would be first on the scene to reap their well-deserved golden rewards.[3] From St. Joseph the New York *Daily Tribune*'s correspondent predicted, quite erroneously as it turned out, that in 1850 and ever afterward overland emigration would be easy, since all the problems had been encountered the previous year and everyone now knew exactly what to do and what not to do.[4] In the same vein were the pleased remarks in a New York newspaper that gold seekers could now ride to California as passengers in cushion-seated spring wagons, and the New York *Herald* editorial characterizing the trip to South Pass as "a holiday journey." The *Herald* editorial writer did admit, however, that once the "half-way house, the happy valley of the Mormons" was passed, the journey became troublesome. In 1851 the *Herald*'s description of the enterprising musket-carrying pioneers who had gone by the tens of thousands to brave "the sufferings of a route through the savage wilds of America" was in the best of the "adventurist" tradition. An editor at an Iowa outfitting point praised the "respectable"-appearing 1851 overlanders, informing his readers that if "Uncle Sam" should come into territory on the moon, "the Yankees would contrive some plan to emigrate to it, and hold it by natural possession. Success to enlargement and enterprize!"[5]

As gold rushers raced across the plains and mountains in unprecedented numbers, it was little wonder that writers were caught up in "adventurist" euphoria. Nor was it surprising that the nay-sayers offered gloomy prophecies about what those overlanders might expect. More persons, after all, ventured out on the overland trip in 1849 alone than had made the continental crossing in all the previous migration years combined. Still greater numbers crowded the trails in 1850 and 1852. No one really knew what might happen.

To judge from his exaggerated report, Etienne Derbec, correspondent for the prestigious French newspaper *Journal des Débats*, never did know what had happened. Derbec believed that the enormous size of the overland caravans accounted for the indescribable suffering, famine, and death which he stressed. In these oversized caravans, according to Derbec's interpretation, travel was slow, provisions were rapidly consumed, forage disappeared, and draft animals had to be killed for food. In such circumstances some emigrants invariably panicked and attempted to find shortcuts to California, only to vanish forever: "Nothing has yet been heard of them; it is only too probable that they perished. As for the emigrants who followed the beaten track, the most fortunate traveled for nine months before reaching the coveted banks of the Sacramento. Eleven or twelve months is the average time for a journey which is sometimes as long as fifteen. Fifteen months, sir, of a slow march which has famine and agony for its escort." In dutifully recording the Donner disaster, Derbec gave the impression that none had survived, writing that "when help arrived, it was all over; they were no longer suffering!" And, like most of those who continued to doubt the safety and wisdom of the overland trek, Derbec portrayed the women and children as suffering the most.[6]

Derbec's extremely pessimistic account was an exception. Most negativists no longer exaggerated the vicissitudes of the overland journey. They did, however, point out that the trip was not an easy one, and directed their cautionary emphases especially to those persons unaccustomed to rigorous activity and privation.

Strangely enough, occasionally even newspapers published in prominent outfitting posts—where the economic stake in the migrations was heavy—counseled potential emigrants to consider seriously the wisdom of attempting an overland journey. In 1852, adopting such a tone, the St. Joseph Gazette suggested that families should remain at home and not risk their lives on the plains. Working men "accustomed to hard work and hard fare" would do well, "but for all others, at this time, we think it folly in the extreme."[7] The Gazette's columns frequently contained such logic. During the 1849 craze the editor expressed fear for the safety of many who had started, and commended those few who went partway and then returned, having had second thoughts about the practicality of the whole endeavor.[8]

It is true that an important element in these arguments was the uncertainty of striking it rich in California. An editorial in the Gazette was one of many in that and other papers that revealed growing disenchantment with the possibilities of success in the mines. Wrote the editor: "We begin to think with Col. Benton that the discovery of gold in California is a subject for regret rather than congratulation, and that the sooner it is used up the better. Within the past two years six persons whom we knew intimately have sought the land of gold, and of these three are dead. The other three would gladly return, but have expended all the money they took with them, and have not the means to bring them back. Truly, fortune-hunting in California is poor sport." Furthermore, the recognition that most would not find many golden nuggets was not the only factor involved: the "hazard and hardships of the trip" and the predictions of suffering and death en route were always clearly articulated.[9] The Kanesville Frontier Guardian and Iowa Sentinel printed two pointed editorials on this aspect in 1852. While the editor wished everyone a safe journey and successful gold-hunting, he predicted, especially for the women, children, and all others unused to hardships, "suffering . . . unparalleled in the annals of history of any previous year." The St. Louis Union anticipated that "terrible sufferings will be the consequence of the rashness and improvidence with which such a formidable journey has been undertaken," and the Lexington, Missouri, Express predicted "trouble and distress" for the legions thronging the trails in 1849. The Liberty, Missouri, *Weekly Tribune*, which had predicted much suffering in 1849, suggested in 1850, "Thousands have in all probability been wrapped in a snowy winding sheet."[10]

From other sections of the nation similar warnings were issued. The editor of the Davenport, Iowa, *Gazette* declared that the man who exposed his family to extensive privation by dragging them to California could not be considered "guiltless" for the ensuing consequences. From Windsor, the *Vermont Chronicle*, fearing that the unprecedented thousands of overlanders would cause a "dearth of forage," forecast hard times for the forty-niners. The Wooster, Ohio, *Democrat* held that the best route to California was to go as far as St. Louis, and then, via Chicago, "make a 'straight wake, for home again.' " A writer in the *North American Review* suggested that wise men would reflect on the dangerous second half of the overland journey before starting (the first half was, after all, "a mere holiday excursion"). He likewise feared, "In all probability, the next autumn will bring us another fearful story of suffering and death on the Sierra Nevada." *De Bow's Review* similarly contended that "the prudent" would admonish their friends to avoid the "arduous and dangerous journey over the plains."[11]

During the peak years of the gold rush, the New York *Daily Tribune* again offered considerable advice on the propriety of journeying overland to California. Always accenting the dangers of the overland trip, although on occasion admitting that it was the healthiest route, the *Tribune* harped especially on the threat of early snows to late-starting emigrants. Contending that any who left St. Louis later than May 10 "would seem virtually to court destruction," the *Tribune* anticipated that at least half of those still east of the Sierra mountain passes when the first snow fell would never "see another spring time or enter the Land of Gold."[12]

Greeley's *Tribune* never enthusiastically endorsed the overland journey, a fact made abundantly evident in the information it provided concerning the "best" route to California. Occasionally the overland route was not even listed among the several possibilities. When the South Pass trail was mentioned it was invariably described as "long," "dangerous," "tedious," and replete with "perils" and "privations." On one occasion the *Tribune* explained that very few ever returned from California overland: "Once crossing the mountains and deserts is a dose for any man. Those who become homesick or from any cause decide to return, take the Isthmus route, if any; if unable to come that way they stay."[13]

For the trip to California the *Tribune* obviously favored the Isthmus of Panama route, perhaps because gold rushers would then utilize New York shipping. Presumably for similar reasons the New Orleans *Daily Picayune* likewise rejected the South Pass route. Instead of the "dangers" and "formidable obstacles" of the Oregon-California Trail, the *Picayune* favored southern land and water routes.[14] The letters and reports filling its pages also presented an enthusiastically favorable view of the Panama route.

With various ocean routes much in vogue, the Missouri River outfitting posts—and the newspapers faithfully reflecting community interests—recognized that one of their first and most crucial tasks was to defend the South Pass overland route. The most vigorous defenses of overland travel were made in the principal newspapers of St. Louis and St. Joseph. In late February, 1849, the *Daily Missouri Republican* printed a letter from a worried old-timer fearing all sorts of disasters for the gold seekers, largely because of his own experiences during an 1832 overland journey to South Pass and beyond. The St. Louis paper took great pains to preface the letter with an updated view. In the intervening seventeen years a trip that was once hazardous had become "little else than a pleasure excursion, requiring scarcely as much preparation as a journey from St. Louis to Philadelphia thirty five years ago." Noting that women and children now feared the overland journey less than had travelers in the 1830s, the *Republican* assured readers that it had no fears about the overland trip, which would be traveled with "ease and facility" by thousands that year.[15]

A favorite and more persuasive technique was to employ endorsements by persons who had previously traveled the overland route and found it excellent, or, even better, by persons who had traveled several routes and pronounced the South Pass route superior in every way—shorter, safer, cheaper, and healthier.[16] For example, Joseph E. Ware's letter to California emigrants termed the southern or Spanish Trail route "the worst that could possibly be thought of," and since Ware's guidebook for the South Pass overland route was being favorably publicized, surely he must know whereof he wrote.[17]

Time and again testimonials of this type were printed, especially in the St. Joseph *Gazette*. In March, 1849, the *Gazette* triumphantly reported that many individuals who had begun traveling west on the Panama route were returning to journey instead across the plains.[18] Relying on reports from such individuals, another Missouri newspaper entreated persons then in California to return overland rather than chancing the unreliable transportation on a Panama trip, which was also characterized as frightfully expensive and feverishly unhealthy.[19] A similar treatise was based upon recommendations by St. Louis residents who had gone to California by the overland route and returned via Panama. Unanimously denouncing the Panama route, they recommended the overland trip instead. Those planning to return to California emphasized that they expected to travel across the plains. These returned gold hunters further stressed good health as an important outgrowth of the overland journey. The western press made much of the health factor:

. . . when the emigrant gets to the gold region, he is fresh, vigorous, inured to exposure, and qualified for all the difficulties and hardships which attend the miner's search after gold. He can do anything—drive a mule, delve in the earth, work the cradle, or walk his forty miles a day, and thrive on it. Take your passenger by the Isthmus, and he is disqualified for the very uses to which he proposes to apply himself in California.—Cooped up in little vessels, ill-ventilated and badly fed—the limbs becoming stiff and indolent, instead of being lithe and elastic, as they are by exercise on the plains—the emigrant when he gets to California, is indisposed to go to work; sick, it may be, for want of bodily and mental employments, and fully prepared to be a loafer, if he was not one before he started.[20]

Extolling the virtues of the South Pass overland route in comparison with all other avenues of westbound travel was, of course, only half the battle. The newspapers published in the Missouri River towns also devoted their energies to enticing overlanders to their particular hamlet for the purchase of traveling outfits. The financial benefits promised to be exceedingly handsome for the town or towns outfitting sizable numbers of overland travelers. Many gold rushers were not farmers as most previous overland emigrants had been, and therefore were in need of purchasing virtually all their traveling supplies. Furthermore, many gold rushers, especially in 1849 and 1850, were quite innocent of any knowledge about reasonable prices for wagons, draft animals, and other equipment and provisions necessary for the overland trip. Equally naive about where the trip was best begun, gold rushers were prime candidates for the hard-sell campaigns conducted by townspeople anxious that their town become the leading supply and jumping-off place. These campaigns were conducted primarily through newspaper editorials and advertisements. Perhaps at few other times did ulterior motivations and vested interests march so conspicuously under the guise of public service. Prudent overlanders were doubtless able to ferret out bits of information useful in making judgments about outfitting and departure points, but could never rely completely on the veracity of what they read.

Geographic considerations dictated the departure point of emigrants who came overland with their wagons directly from their homes, and only infrequently did advertising lead them away from their natural jumping-off place. However, emigrants who came by boat via St. Louis, and who successfully resisted the blandishments of St. Louis merchants to purchase their outfits there, or who chose to have their new outfits transported upriver, tended to purchase their tickets for the outfitting town which had the best or finest reputation.[21] Prior to the gold rush, at least through 1846, that town was Independence, widely known for its involvement with the Santa Fe trade. St. Joseph, Missouri, and Kanesville, Iowa, the latter developing rapidly because Utah-bound Mormons left from there, began vying with Independence for pre-eminence in 1847 and 1848. The situation by early 1849 was obviously a fluid one, and the fact that St. Joseph emerged as the most important gold rush outfitting post was attributable largely to her aggressive advertising.[22]

The main rivalry had been between St. Joseph and Independence. Both cities avidly wooed overlanders with testimonials—from other emigrants, other newspapers, and well-known explorers and guides. The St.

Joseph *Gazette,* in its basic appeal, relied upon a host of prominent western travelers: Commodore Robert F. Stockton and his aides, who had traveled the trail eastbound in 1847 to testify at John C. Frémont's court-martial; General Stephen W. Kearny, who escorted Frémont back over the trail for trial; Missouri congressman Willard P. Hall, who had returned overland with Kearny in 1847; Moses "Black" Harris, famed mountain man and guide who had piloted 1844 emigrants to Oregon and had returned overland in 1847; mountain man Miles Goodyear, who had come east from California with a drove of horses in 1848; and Joseph L. Meek, who came overland from Oregon in 1848 bringing the news of the Whitman massacre and an Oregon memorial to Congress. All of these luminaries, according to the *Gazette,* praised the route commencing at St. Joseph as "the shortest and best."[23] The *Gazette* was even willing to cite the much-maligned Mormons to convince overlanders to depart from St. Joseph, falsely asserting that those frugal and "vigilant" people had purchased all their goods there.[24] Independence, in the name-dropping department, relied principally upon William Gilpin, who had gone overland to Oregon with Frémont in 1843.[25]

The *Gazette's* pages were also filled with letters from lesser-known travelers praising St. Joseph's merchants and the route beginning there. Through such letters and editorial amplifications the *Gazette* endeavored to present factual arguments certain to convince wavering gold seekers. In March, 1850, the *Gazette* printed excerpts from letters sent back by five overlanders who had gone west the previous year. The five, of course, enthusiastically endorsed St. Joseph, citing cheaper supplies and fewer streams and rivers on the St. Joseph route. The *Gazette* repeatedly emphasized these basic points, stressing that the treacherous crossing of the usually flooded Kansas River was avoided on the St. Joseph route, that the trail from St. Joseph to where the roads leading from Independence and St. Joseph converged was at least eighty miles and from six to ten travel days shorter, that goods in St. Joseph were usually up to 20 percent cheaper than at Independence and St. Louis, and that there were more and better ferries for crossing the Missouri River at St. Joseph.[26]

In the contest for supremacy statistics were bandied about loosely. In 1849 the *Gazette* claimed to have fitted out "nearly all" the Oregon and California emigrants for the last three years, an exaggeration equaled by its 1850 claim that for the past four years three-fourths of the Oregon and California emigrants had started from St. Joseph.[27] The *Gazette* happily quoted the St. Louis *Daily Union* assertion that if emigrants were starting late they would "unquestionably" find St. Joseph preferable since it was 100 miles nearer to Fort Laramie, and high waters on streams and rivers were never a problem on the St. Joseph route. Little wonder that the *Gazette* proudly asserted "that the universal testimony of all emigrants is 'that the route from St. Joseph is decidedly the shortest and best.' "[28]

The *Gazette*'s assertions were forcefully repudiated by the Independence press, which advanced its own series of dubious claims. As early as 1847 the Independence *Expositor* had indicated that the road from St. Joseph was "almost impassable" for wagons, while that from Independence was "plain, level and beautiful."[29] The *Gazette*'s response was that twice as many wagons had departed from St. Joseph as from Independence in 1847, proof that Independence's bragging, boasting, and erroneous statements about high prices had been ineffectual.[30] By 1849 and 1850 the controversy had become more acrimonious. The *Expositor* reported that St. Joseph's only ferryboat made merely two crossings of the Missouri per day. Therefore, asserted the Independence editor, emigrants waiting to leave from St. Joseph might still be stranded there as late as July 1. The *Gazette* editor fumed that this was "one of the many thousand lies you have told about St. Joseph and its facilities to accommodate the emigrants."[31]

The *Expositor*'s devotion to news coverage dictated mention of wagons lost in crossing the Missouri at St. Joseph. The dreaded cholera reportedly rampant in St. Joseph in 1849 was similarly highlighted.[32] A circular signed by forty-six Independence merchants promising twelve new ferryboats at the Kansas River crossing in 1850 was printed in the St. Louis press.[33] Independence's vast experience in the Santa Fe trade was carefully emphasized, and it was also claimed that overlanders could depart from Independence two weeks earlier than from St. Joseph because the prairie grasses in the vicinity were suitable for forage that much sooner, an argument certain to appeal to impatient forty-niners.[34] Handbills boosting Independence's virtues were circulated in St. Louis and along the Missouri River—leaflets which the St. Joseph *Adventure* termed "lieing hand-bills and slanderous reports."[35] Independence boomers systematically advertised in St. Louis newspapers, claiming that forty-niners launching out from Independence had reached California earlier than those jumping off from competitor towns. Prospective overlanders were reminded that an Independence agent was stationed in St. Louis at one of the principal hotels "for the purpose of giving information on the subject of outfitting and travelling to California."[36]

These "hard lying" Independence agents and "runners" infuriated the *Gazette* editor, who regularly denounced them and the prejudicial rumors they spread about St. Joseph diseases and prices. While the *Gazette* claimed that Independence stationed agents in Louisville, Cincinnati, and other towns, it was the presumed St. Louis–Independence complicity which was most frustrating to the editor.[37] Charging that St. Louis newspapers encouraged overlanders to procure outfits and supplies in St. Louis by exaggerating St. Joseph prices, and that emigrants were then advised to make Independence their jumping-off point, the *Gazette* editor coupled exposés of this collusion with demands that St. Louis editors switch to truthful reporting.[38] To counter these rumors the *Gazette* frequently

Independence, Mo., a major outfitting post and jumping-off place for westward-bound travelers, as it looked in 1853.

Missouri Historical Society

quoted the prevailing prices for various commodities in St. Joseph, some-times contrasting them in tabular form with those current in other outfit-ting cities.[39]

Occasionally the *Gazette* noted smugly how few overlanders were actually outfitting at Independence in spite of all the devious machinations concocted by that nefarious city. In 1850 the *Gazette* surmised that the meager number of departing overlanders would not even pay the ex-penses of the many agents Independence sent out to boost the city.[40] By 1851 the *Gazette* believed that the truth about the outfitting posts had been sufficiently disseminated so that there would "not be the same opportunity for humbug[g]ing as heretofore."[41] Nonetheless, in 1853 and 1854 the *Gazette* was still aggressively battling for emigrants by pointing out the advantages of the St. Joseph scene. And St. Joseph had also resorted to employing its own paid agents.[42]

By the early 1850s, however, St. Joseph had a serious competitor to the north. Departing overlanders had increasingly pushed northward along the Missouri River until they reached Kanesville, which by 1852 had become the dominant jumping-off point. Surprisingly, the *Gazette* always evidenced more concern with the waning threat from Independence than with the growing assault from Kanesville.

The Kanesville *Frontier Guardian* editor began his public-relations campaign in 1850 by reminding overlanders that there had been very few cholera deaths the previous year among emigrants crossing the Missouri at Kanesville.[43] The lower incidence of severe illness on the north-side Platte River trail was the keystone of Kanesville propaganda. Further, the Kanes-ville paper noted that good ferryboats would be established at the major water crossings on the route along the north side of the Platte River, a route which soon became known as the Mormon Trail.[44] As had the newspaper editors in the other contending outfitting posts, the Kanesville editor also stressed the quantity and quality of stores, gristmills, mechanics, and hotels available to service the overlanders' every need.[45]

Competitors quickly called the Kanesville assertions into question. A Plattesville, Iowa, ferryboat operator, S. Martin, accused the Kanesville vested interests of trying "to gull the people into Kanesville" in boosting the north-side route in early 1851. Obviously anxious for overlanders to cross at his ferry—a task he offered to perform free of charge—Martin pointed out that there were many ferry tolls to be paid on the north route and none on the south side of the Platte.[46] The next week the *Guardian* editor, the redoubtable Mormon Apostle Orson Hyde, struck back. Martin could not charge toll for ferrying persons across the Missouri, Hyde explained, because the southern route was so poor in comparison to the superior trails out of Kanesville and Trader's Point that if toll were charged no one would cross there.[47]

Also in 1851 the *Frontier Guardian* reported that an emigrant had drowned in crossing the Missouri at Trader's Point. Such accidents were not uncommon, but the editor's supplementary comment reflected both the tactics and the virulent anti-Mormon feeling so common during this period: "Wonder if some Kanesville renegade will not forthwith inform the Editor of the St. Joseph Gazette that the Mormons killed him for his money, and decided in Council to keep it a secret! This would be a precious tidbit for the Gazette."[48] Kanesville, the northernmost jumping-off point, also felt the impact of paid agents from other outfitting towns, whose rumors about high prices and smallpox epidemics in Kanesville the *Frontier Guardian* sought to refute.[49]

During 1858 and 1859 the Kanesville community, now known as Council Bluffs, dusted off the old but successful arguments about the superiority of the trail on the north side of the Platte for the benefit of the Pike's Peak gold seekers. By now the local newspaper could boast that a steam ferry plied the Missouri River crossing, that all the rivers were bridged as far west as the Sweetwater, that settlements and farms ranged 200 miles westward, where provisions were always available, that the route west from Council Bluffs was the shortest, and that supplies were as cheap in Council Bluffs as anywhere.[50] And, of course, the route itself was by now, at least according to the newspaper editor, "conceded by all unprejudiced minds" to be the best. Terming it "the great *National* route," the *Weekly Bugle* assured readers, "There is not another road in the United States, of the same length, so nearly straight, level, and without marshes, sloughs, or bad places of any kind."[51]

Although Independence, St. Joseph, and Council Bluffs launched the bulk of the overland emigrants, other Missouri River towns dreaming of becoming great cities also diligently advertised their actual and supposed merits. Liberty, Parkville, Weston, and the future Kansas City, Missouri, all mounted campaigns, as did Atchison, Kansas.[52] The tactics employed were similar to those already described, including frequent newspaper references to the "gentleman" who had always "just arrived" from the rival town with news of disease, exorbitant prices, scarcity of supplies and provisions, or whatever the occasion required.[53] Weston, for example, sought to capitalize on its proximity to Fort Leavenworth, but was hampered in its efforts by tongue-in-cheek endorsements of the type bestowed by the St. Joseph *Gazette* in 1850. Noting the continuing efforts of the Weston press to boost that city as a jumping-off point, the *Gazette* agreed that Weston possessed "great advantages," and to prove it reprinted a paragraph entitled "Horse Thieves" which spotlighted how "midnight marauders" infested that region.[54]

Fortunately, however, the western press did more than boost the overland route and boom certain towns as premier outfitting posts, for it is not at all certain that the overland emigrants were as much benefited by the no-holds-barred competition between the rival towns as the St. Louis *Republican* had buoyantly predicted when the gold rush commenced.[55] Despite occasional lapses into hyperbole, the western press, in its emerging role as public servant, increasingly aided westbound emigrants.

During the peak years of the gold rush, as had been the case in the 1840s, newspapers throughout the nation, but especially those in the West, published thousands of letters and excerpts of letters written by overlanders en route or by those who had already reached their destination. These letters were usually packed with useful information about the trip. In addition to commenting on Indian encounters, points of interest, forts and trading posts, unusual occurrences, and persons from the same community seen along the trails, the gold rushers normally included advice on outfitting, travel routes, and traveling techniques for those planning to make the trip in subsequent years. Such advice from friends and acquaintances actually making the trip was probably heeded more by future emigrants than the counsel of more famous authorities. Many of these letters had been commissioned by the newspaper editors and were printed with regularity as the correspondent progressed westward and his reports filtered back to the frontier settlements. In allotting so much space to informative letters the press perhaps provided its most beneficial service.

One of the most famous western travelers provided valuable information for overlanders in the form of a series of questions and answers concerning the route to take, the specifications for team and wagon, the necessary provisions, arms and ammunition, length of journey, and the proper time for starting. Printed in the Louisville *Courier* and then reprinted in a host of newspapers in late 1848 and early 1849, Edwin Bryant's advice was held in high esteem by prospective overlanders, for many of them had already read his best-selling account of an 1846 westbound journey—*What I Saw in California*—and were preparing to use it as a guidebook.[56] Bryant's overland trip eastward to the States in 1847 with General Kearny lent further credibility to his recommendations.

Suggestions for overland travel prepared by William Gilpin were also widely reprinted, and other veterans of overland trips were likewise induced to prepare instructions which appeared frequently in the press.[57] Some of these reprintings had doubtless been occasioned by requests from potential overlanders scattered throughout the United States. The Kanesville *Frontier Guardian* in late 1851 reported letters from Mormons and Gentiles in "almost every State in the Union" asking for information about making the overland trip.[58] A few newspapers printed tables of distances on the South Pass route, but scarcely with sufficient detail to be of any value.[59] Prospective gold miners also found in their newspapers detailed estimates of the amount and type of provisions and supplies they might need during the course of their march across the continent.[60]

For further route and travel information the newspapers warmly endorsed many of the "instant" guidebooks which appeared with the discovery of gold, usually suggesting in their editorial columns that "every emigrant" ought to purchase one or another of the volumes. Joseph E. Ware's guidebook was the nearly universal recommendation in 1849, although Bryant's book was also endorsed. In later years a number of other volumes were mentioned.[61] On rare occasions editors even pointed out deficiencies in some work, as the *Daily Missouri Republican* editor did with the map accompanying E. Sanford Seymour's guidebook in early 1849.[62] Most newspapers were quite generous in handing out endorsements, so much so that ulterior motives may occasionally have been involved. Specific individuals were recommended as guides or pilots for emigrant caravans, as were many of the commercial passenger trains that the newspapers, especially in St. Louis, reported so enthusiastically.[63] Overlanders were regularly reminded of the fine qualifications of the proprietors, under whose directions emigrants could "rest assured of getting through in good time."[64]

More useful advice appeared as well, such as reminders to emigrants to take certain substances along to neutralize the alkaline water which would be encountered so often during the journey. Eager gold rushers were apprised of the progress of the prairie grasses and warned not to leave the frontier before travel was feasible.[65] Travel and trail techniques were discussed in editorials, such as how important it was to resist taking along unnecessary supplies and provisions since overloaded wagons quickly resulted in jaded teams. Emigrants were also counseled to refrain from traveling too fast at the inception of the journey.[66] Several times overlanders were reminded of the Mormon settlements in the Salt Lake Valley and the Carson Valley, where provisions and supplies could be replenished.[67]

Admonitions regarding treatment of the Indians were certainly not neglected either. The Kanesville *Frontier Guardian* was particularly concerned with this subject. In the spring of 1849 emigrants were warned that since the preceding winter had been a severe one, the majority of Indians were consequently poor and "starving" and that many more wagon-train attacks than usual could be expected. Overlanders were admonished to be on their guard night and day. Two weeks later the editor advised the gold rushers to "treat the Indians with moderation and kindness as long as you can, but never suffer them to come within the circle of your encampment, and not very near the outside." Suggesting fifty firm and watchful well-armed men as the proper number for a traveling company, the *Guardian* editor also counseled that mules and horses would need to be watched with greater care than oxen. Again and again the overlanders were warned to mind their own business, be constantly on their guard, trespass on Indian territory as little as possible, and kill only such buffalo and other game as

Forty-niner J. Goldsborough Bruff corroborated one aspect of public opinion with his sketchbook comments on chances for luck in the gold fields.

they needed. If emigrants did not act accordingly they could expect to be attacked, even though the government had by treaty arranged for transient travelers to cross the Indian domain.[68]

The Kanesville newspaper shifted abruptly from these low-key common-sense instructions in late 1851 after receiving word that the *Guardian*'s own editor and publisher had been attacked and robbed while on a late fall trip with other Mormons to Salt Lake City. Calling now for government action, the *Guardian* warned, "If the emigrant is not to be protected . . . hundreds of Oregon Emigrants have said in our office that emigration will cease for that quarter after this year." Letters were already being sent back to friends not to venture out to Oregon overland unless there was a sufficient armed force on the trails for protection. Several months later Orson Hyde returned, and the *Guardian* now adopted a warlike tone, demanding that mounted riflemen and not infantry be placed at western forts and stationed along the trails. While contending that "treaties are very good," the *Guardian* asserted that "powder and lead are the only effectual treaties that can secure the white man and his property from the rapacity of that people." Hyde urged overlanders to have no confidence in Indians or treaties, "but keep loaded rifles between your property and them; and then your animals may be secure, and yourselves not left on the Plains with wagon and baggage and not an animal to place before it as we were after our four mules were stolen."[69]

From St. Louis the influential *Missouri Republican* was likewise continuing to call for sufficient military might on the plains so that overland emigrants could go to California, Oregon, and New Mexico in safety. The *Republican*, with most other newspapers, demanded that mounted riflemen and not infantrymen be permanently stationed in the West. Believing that approximately 1,000 soldiers would be adequate to protect travelers, the *Republican* editor recommended that this be done no matter what the cost to the national treasury.[70]

Interspersed among the general editorial reflections on the tide of humanity surging to California were extremely favorable comments upon the character of the gold seekers. An Ohio editor, after conversing with many of the argonauts leaving that state, lamented the loss of such a "valuable . . . element of our population." St. Joseph editors stated, "More hardy, enterprising and intelligent companies of men cannot be raised than these," and felt reassured that if California was to be settled by such respectable persons of "high moral character" there need be no fear for its future.[71] The forty-niners appeared to the Kanesville *Frontier Guardian* "to be men of character, wealth, and possess a good share of general intelligence." Noting that he had not yet seen a drunken man among them, the editor felt the future augured well for California if all the emigrants were as honorable, upright, and marked by integrity as those passing through Kanesville. By 1851, when more women and children were numbered among the departing overlanders, the *Guardian* editor again speculated on the glorious future of the West with such paragons of virtue destined to be its citizens.[72]

From the Pacific Coast came complementary judgments: "It is not the drones of society who go out," praised the editor of the San Francisco *Daily Alta California*, "but men of nerve and enterprise, whose absence will be felt, more or less, in any community, and particularly in a new country." In the San Francisco *Daily Herald* the phraseology was similar, the editor observing with pleasure that most of the 1853 emigrants were "of the better class."[73] The editor of Detroit's *Daily Advertiser*, bemoaning that over 6,000 gold seekers had already gone or had made arrangements to leave Michigan, estimated that each departed with $300 to $500 in money and/or outfits—a specie drain with serious implications for the Michigan economy.[74] This impressive composite portrait of the westering movement—good men taking civilization west, on the safest and best possible route, bringing trade and prosperity to the outfitting posts and fortified with the advice, counsel, and good wishes of public-service-minded editors—naturally led some writers to adopt the patriotic phrase "Westward the Star of Empire wends its way" in summing up the magnificent phenomenon.[75]

Yet even in the outfitting towns along the Missouri River the overland emigrations no longer commanded the same interest or press coverage after the gold rush subsided. Although news items from the Far West still appeared with regularity, overland trips to those regions were accomplished in increasingly greater obscurity. Far fewer letters from persons en route were printed, far fewer editorials remarked on departures or offered travel suggestions. By the mid and late 1850s newspaper editors were more concerned with the settlement of the fertile Kansas, Missouri, Iowa, and Nebraska prairies surrounding their expanding towns. The overland emigrations, so indispensable to the growth of these towns before, were treated more and more as matters of incidental interest as they became less and less crucial to the towns' prosperity. Perhaps equally responsible for the reduced press attention to the now-familiar overland caravans was the increased involvement felt by these former frontier outposts in state and national affairs, where the slavery issue loomed ominously.

From the gold rush period on, an important and influential press was also maturing on the Pacific Coast. With minor differences, the far western press coverage of the overland emigrations essentially mirrored that in the older states. Although the public-service functions were even more omnipresent, the migrations were not treated completely apart from ulterior motivations, since a continuing stream of safely arriving overlanders was of utmost importance to the growth and progress of the Far West, and the newspaper editors knew it.

Therefore, one of their greatest contributions was the agitation for organized relief efforts to insure that the thousands of suffering and lagging emigrants might safely cross the Sierra Nevada Mountains before winter snows occasioned ghastly repetitions of the 1846–47 Donner disaster. Not immediately anticipating the potential consequences in 1849, however, California newspapers had little to say beyond warmly reporting the California relief effort, which significantly aided the rear portions of the forty-niner caravans. Indeed, the prestigious San Francisco *Alta California* had even initially contradicted predictions of distress, contending that the emigration was ahead of schedule, that "undue sympathy" was unnecessary, and that suffering was unlikely.[76]

The next year the *Alta* was not caught off guard, and its efforts in behalf of the 1850 emigration were deserving of the highest commendation. The 1850 overlanders, having learned too well from the experiences of the forty-niners, not only avoided overloading but often began with too few provisions. The unanticipated throngs clogging the trails made it impossible for gold rushers to sufficiently replenish their provisions en route.[77] Had not the California newspapers kept the imminent potential disaster before the local citizenry, suffering—which reached major proportions as it was—might have been disastrous.[78]

The *Alta California* conspicuously supervised the campaign, sounding the opening note in the lead editorial in its July 24 issue, under the heading "The Suffering Emigrants." Reporting that San Francisco mayor John W. Geary had called a special meeting for that afternoon in behalf of the distressed overlanders, whose plight had just become known the previous evening, the *Alta* pleaded with citizens to contribute liberally to the cause. Those sympathetic to "the destitute and suffering" were begged to attend the meeting. From that point on the *Alta* editorial staff used every possible tactic to stir Californians to action. Public meetings to discuss the propriety of providing relief were copiously reported. At that first San Francisco meeting, for example, only twelve persons attended and nothing was done. Consequently, the *Alta* endeavored to drum up enthusiasm. Surely California's wealthiest city should be in the forefront of the relief:

Why is it that this apathy exists? Is there no virtue extant? Are those who have traveled thousands of miles over the parched and dreary plains, through a wild country peopled by hostile tribes, who from unfortuitous circumstances are reduced to the most abject state of suffering and distress, to appeal in vain for succor? Are we to hear that the poor wanderers upon the trail are leaving their bones upon the road and yet not send them aid and comfort? . . . It cannot be that our citizens can quietly think of the sufferings their fellow beings may be enduring while they themselves are enjoying all the comforts of civilized life and living in the midst of plenty and not be ready to open their hearts and their purses. We earnestly appeal to them to do something, for the apathetic indifference with which they now treat the subject will be a reproach from which they cannot relieve themselves. Since the public meeting has failed, we would suggest to the Mayor the propriety of collecting a subscription.[79]

Periodically the *Alta* provided harrowing details of the suffering as reported by recently arrived overlanders or by those directing relief efforts. In these accounts the sufferings of "delicate, graceful and fair" women were always conspicuously mentioned. "Only think of women with children at their breast, traveling on foot, without food, dependent upon the charity of the traders, among the cold mountains without even a blanket to shield them from the cold winds of night. Ladies who are in comfort and opulence, think of your sisters in distress, and extend to them the charity of a common humanity."[80] Unburied bodies lying where they had fallen, deaths from actual starvation, men forced to eat the "putrified flesh of the dead animals along the road," subsequent disease epidemics, Indian depredations, predictions of deaths by the hundreds and thousands if redoubled relief efforts were not immediately undertaken— the picture the *Alta* portrayed was of the gloomiest proportions.[81]

A canvass of businessmen and other city residents was enthusiastically promoted by the *Alta*, which cagily introduced into its columns an element of civic pride and competition by dutifully reporting what other communities were doing. Sacramento also played a leading role in the relief movement, and the *Alta* gently asked, "Shall our city, ablest to exercise a noble charity, share in the movement which is winning to a youthful sister city proud renown?"[82] When over $4,000 in cash and pledges and $500 worth of provisions had been collected, the *Alta* optimistically predicted the raising of $15,000 to $20,000 in San Francisco alone with the boastful words, "This will beat Sacramento."[83] Citizens were admonished that "there are none too poor to aid their countrymen in distress," letters from poor persons contributing beyond their means were printed with approbation, and the relief committee was reminded that there were sections of the city yet uncanvassed. The *Alta* editor stressed that "a complete fulfillment of the task which gentlemen of the committee have voluntarily assumed" was expected.[84]

Although the *Alta* protested that the relief movement was undertaken *solely* for the benefit of the "destitute and dying," vested interests did surface.[85] The *Alta* rejected the plan advanced by the Sacramento *Transcript* of sending contributions to Sacramento, where supplies would be purchased and forwarded to the sufferers. After all, admonished the *Alta* editor, supplies purchased with San Francisco contributions should be secured in San Francisco and then forwarded.[86]

The *Alta* also enthusiastically endorsed the benefit performances that San Francisco artists and actors gave for the relief fund.[87] Allusions to the Donner tragedy were made in hopes of making clear the urgency of the situation.[88] There were appeals to patriotism, self-interest, humanitarianism, and Christian charity. Attempts were made to shame citizens into assistance. San Franciscans were informed it was their "duty" to come to assist in this "holy work" and that "the fate of California" depended on their efforts.[89] When reports from the trails in late September continued to be bleak, the *Alta* declared that private philanthropy was no longer equal to the task and demanded quick and generous aid by governmental authorities for this "holiest charity," whether or not prior authorization had been received.[90]

The *Alta* was not alone, in San Francisco or in California, in promoting the 1850 relief movement. The San Francisco *Herald* lent its support, predicting hundreds of deaths in addition to the hundreds who had already died of starvation if speedy action was not forthcoming. The Sacramento *Transcript* held out the noble example of one of the relief directors in asking others to "go and do likewise." The Marysville *Herald* prefaced an editorial on the relief efforts with a quotation from Christ's Sermon on the Mount, and the Sacramento *Placer Times* urged that charity and humanity necessitated providing relief. In Oregon too, when information was received that some of the few 1850 overlanders choosing Oregon as their destination were finding it difficult to complete their journey due to heavy snows, meetings were held and relief parties dispatched. The *Oregon Spectator* summed up the obligations of the residents in this fashion:

Now that the immigrants have got within reach of their assistance, it behooves our people generally to avail themselves of this chance to do good towards their fellow-men. The trials and difficulties of such a journey are known to you all; although you may not have had many favors of this kind shown to you when similarly circumstanced, you had probably the best the country could afford at the time. It is your duty to do the best you can now. The people of Oregon City have done nobly—may we not reasonably expect like good deeds from other quarters.[91]

The overland tides of 1849 and 1850 slowed to a mere trickle in 1851. The following year, however, more overlanders than ever before trailed west. The principal 1852 relief endeavors emanated from Oregon. The Portland *Oregonian* was instrumental in advocating the necessity of relief, explaining that since there was insufficient forage for the large number of draft animals on the trails, many emigrants were arriving on foot after abandoning their wagons and most of their remaining provisions. Moreover, there was much sickness among the incoming overlanders, whose numbers were estimated at from 10,000 to 20,000. Commending the meetings in various Oregon cities which had already raised several thousand dollars for relief, the *Oregonian* urged other cities to do likewise. After reprinting an appeal from the Cascades, where the situation was critical, the editor explained: "Oregonians! let us respond to this call in earnest. Let us all do what *we can* to relieve the distressed, provide for the sick, bury the dead and protect the orphan; and we shall have the approval

Such scenes as E. Hall Martin's "Mountain Jack and a Wandering Miner," painted in 1850, reflected gold rush optimism.

Oakland Museum, gift of Concours d'Antiques

of our own consciences and be the means of bestowing untold good upon our fellow creatures."[92]

By mid-October the suffering was even more serious, with reports circulating that destitute overlanders were dying daily at The Dalles. Incoming overlanders were complaining bitterly that more was not being done for their relief, some apparently contrasting the parsimonious Oregon efforts with the more generous succor California had provided in 1850. While the *Oregonian* acknowledged that Oregon was not as beneficent as California, editor T. J. Dryer maintained that California had known of the vast numbers coming and had been able to plan ahead, whereas this large 1852 emigration to Oregon was entirely unexpected. Many who had started for California had shifted their destination en route due to the scarcity of grass. Thus Dryer felt that when Oregonians realized what was occurring they had "responded nobly to the call of humanity," and he branded as unjust the emigrant charges. On Christmas Day Dryer once more made reference to the recently arrived overlanders, many quite destitute and including many widows and orphans, admonishing that charity and kindness would be in order: "The Lord loveth a cheerful giver."[93]

An even larger emigration streamed toward California in 1852, but the *Alta California,* such a staunch relief advocate in 1850, now vacillated in its attitude, both toward the need for providing relief and toward who should properly be responsible for the relief. The *Alta* opposed a state legislator's proposal that state funds be set aside for the relief of that autumn's needy overlanders, contending that this imprudent action would enlarge the state debt. The more proper response according to the *Alta* would be relying solely upon private charity, which would certainly equal whatever assistance might be needed. This was a rare example of a western newspaper reluctant to accept governmental action; it will be remembered that in 1850 the *Alta* had ultimately called for governmental assistance no matter what the cost. In effect, it did so again in July of 1852, remarking that the relief efforts then in process were beneficial; further:

> Of all the acts of the last Legislature, that passed for the relief of the overland emigration was the most humane and judicious; and no appropriation was better made and to none will the people of our State give a more cheerful acquiescence than to that of $25,000 set apart to succor our distressed fellow citizens who are endeavoring to reach California from the Western States and become a part of us, to share in our toils and reap with us our reward. It cannot but be that they will come among us prepared to be good Californians, citizens strongly attached to the State of their adoption—a State which they now find has, in the hour of their need, risen as one man to extend to them a helping hand and give them a cheering word on their toilsome way.

Yet less than two weeks later the *Alta* was asserting that the traders along the later portions of the route would be able to supply all the needs any emigrants might have and that starvation need not be feared. What the *Alta* did fear was that the destitute new arrivals would suffer in California after their arrival more than they had on the trail.[94]

Meanwhile the Sacramento *Union* lamented the fact that the 25,000-dollar state appropriation was completely inadequate to the enormity of the need and that up to a third of the allocation was being disbursed for administrative salaries and related overhead expenses. Predicting suffering approximating that of 1850, the *Union* called upon the press throughout California to urge extensive contributions for relief, since it seemed clear that government aid would be both insufficient and injudiciously expended. To such appeals the *Alta* was unwilling to respond, until it became convinced the situation was in fact as grave as the *Union* and other newspapers claimed.[95]

In spite of the *Alta California*'s occasional apostasy, the one attribute so clearly characteristic of almost all Pacific Coast newspapers was the constant demand for government action. In both California and Oregon, newspaper editors and politicians based their demands on their conviction that the future of their states was directly linked to a growing population composed of the type of persons who came overland. The *Alta California* editor phrased it this way in an 1851 call for a military highway from the Pacific to the Atlantic: "There is a certain class of population which we need, which cannot and will not reach us by any but an overland route, and we shall utterly fail in our duty to ourselves and to our common country if we do not labor incessantly and perseveringly to accomplish so beneficial an improvement." In 1854 this contention was made more explicit, the *Alta* arguing that 90 percent of those coming overland were "producers"—farmers and mechanics—who came to settle permanently. In contrast, 95 percent of those who came by sea were "consumers"—merchants, speculators, lawyers—who did not produce and remained only temporarily. "The kind of people that California wants now and must have," wrote the editor, "do not and will not come by the steamers. The only really valuable and permanent accession that has been made to the population of the State during the last four years, has come here by land."[96]

The Oregon legislature expressed similar sentiments in an 1851 memorial to Congress phrased in the best "adventurist" tradition. Complaining particularly about the governmental penchant for giving presents to Indian "pirates" (who kept the emigrants in danger every hour), instead of punishing piracy at home as it did on the seas, the memorialists sadly concluded that the brave overlander's only protection was "God in Heaven and his own right arm." The Oregon legislators sounded much like the *Alta* editor in contending that should overland travel cease, "Oregon may write her own epitaph. It is through that channel across the mountains that Oregon is to receive her horses, cattle and sheep, and the supply does not equal the demand made by the immigrations by sea. Oregon requires also the hardy pioneer of the western states, for upon him, and those of like habits of industry and vigor, depend the force necessary to prostrate these mighty forests, and lay bare the hidden treasures of her prolific timbered soil."[97]

Thus convinced of the paramount importance of undiminished overland travel for their future prosperity, both the California and Oregon press missed few opportunities to request government aid. Sometimes the call was for generous land donations to reward overlanders for daring so much to come,[98] but mainly it was for military protection. As the Indian threat to overland travel intensified during the middle 1850s, so also did the newspaper demands.

In response to the increasing reports of Indian depredations, the *Alta* pressed its campaign in a series of long editorials throughout the autumn of 1854. The Indian raids were bad enough, but what most worried the editor of the population-hungry *Alta* was the widespread emigrant refrain that "they would on no account trust their wives and families on the same route again."[99] Repeatedly the *Alta* termed it a "disgrace" that the government had still not provided a series of military posts to protect the "hundreds of thousands" of enterprising settlers anxious to emigrate, overland, to "the promised land."[100] A road protected by troops was so urgently necessary that the *Alta* declared it favored any scheme which might further "the bridge of our salvation."[101] One suggested strategy was to grant free land to persons who would settle on both sides of the Platte River route all the way to California. Coupled with a series of military posts, this plan would in only one year foster contiguous settlement west to Salt Lake.[102] Failing this, the *Alta* called for the state of California to provide a line of depots along the entire route, or for private enterprise to undertake the task.[103] The *Alta* also urged that a forceful memorial be sent to Congress, and called upon other California newspapers to join in stimulating enthusiasm for the project.[104]

On the Missouri River frontier the press had quickly become caught up in political considerations. The same pattern prevailed on the Pacific Coast, where questions of state and national politics periodically influenced the press coverage of the overlanders. Nowhere was this better illustrated than in 1854 in Oregon, where reports of the Indian depredations committed during that difficult travel year caused even more frustrations than had been the case in California. The event triggering a new phase in a continuing political controversy was the so-called Ward massacre, in which nineteen overlanders were killed in late August near Fort Boise. The editor of Portland's *Weekly Oregonian*, T. J. Dryer, who was not very fond of Indians as it was, now demanded that they be severely punished. By the following year Dryer was close to taking the extreme position that dead Indians were the best kind.[105]

Dryer's difficulty, however, was that his political persuasion was not in

favor in Oregon's territorial politics at the time. Acting Governor George
L. Curry, after calling for volunteers and appointing some party
faithful—none from Portland—to lead them, decided that winter was the
wrong time to fight Indians and disbanded the volunteers. Dryer was irate,
and the pages of his *Weekly Oregonian* fairly simmered with epithets ex-
coriating the Democratic clique in Salem. Raging that it was a sin that
nothing had been done, Dryer charged Oregon's federal officers, whom
he termed "mushroom patriots," with "criminal indifference." Dryer, believing that winter was the only time to fight Indians successfully, felt the
sole conclusion to be drawn was that "American citizens may hereafter be
murdered on the plains, their wives and daughters ravished, then tortured
and butchered, innocent children burned, property stolen, and all sorts of
cruelty and inhumanity practiced," but Oregon's territorial officers, too
concerned with the spoils of office, would do nothing.[106] Dryer was therefore instrumental in the convening of an "indignation meeting" in Portland, which voted censure on Acting Governor Currey for not immediately calling up volunteer soldiers, for dismissing them too quickly
after they had been finally mobilized, for choosing incompetent officers to
lead the abortive expedition, and, perhaps most contemptible of all, for
"passing by our city unnoticed."[107]

Overland emigration in 1855 and 1856 declined considerably, an
unhappy fact which Pacific Coast boosters and residents perceived clearly.
The *Alta* dourly predicted that if the government continued its "do nothing" policy, even fewer overlanders would take to the trails in the future.[108] The 1856 petition Californians sent to Congress repeated the
now-familiar themes: California's prosperous future was unlimited if it
received more population, the "best portion" of California's population
regularly came overland, and the intensifying Indian threat now made an
already difficult pilgrimage "nearly impracticable." Actually, the petition
noted, overland travel to California had come to a virtual halt, which was,
of course, causing California "much embarrassment." A wagon road protected by military posts was the only solution.[109]

The impetus for the petition had come from San Francisco, where *Alta*
editorials and news releases publicized the varied techniques used to
arouse enthusiasm for the "Emigrant Road."[110] The important part played
by the press in endeavoring to secure a safer overland route could be seen
most clearly in many smaller communities. Commending California governor John Bigler's Annual Message calling for a line of military posts
every 75 to 100 miles with fifty men stationed at each post, the Marysville
Daily Herald took the position that it was "in the highest degree discreditable" to the government that nothing previously had been done.[111] Then,
when news of the San Francisco petition campaign was received, the *Herald*
editor concurred, noting, "It will not do to rely on the press alone, but
petition, petition till by our importunity if in no other way, our just

demands are heeded." The *Herald* editor pledged 5,000 signatures in Marysville.[112]

Three days later the editor, in announcing a Sacramento meeting on the wagon road subject, pointedly wondered, "When will Marysville move?"[113] Several copies of the proposed memorial were received by the *Herald* editor, who quickly placed them in public places for signatures, printed the petition in the *Herald,* and called also for a committee to solicit signatures.[114] When such a committee had been formed, the *Herald* editor chided them for so noiselessly going about their work, indicating that if 5,000 signatures in Marysville were not procured "we shall have failed in our duty." The *Herald* suggested placing tables at the main Marysville intersections and hiring "a few importunate and reliable men to take these posts of honor, and let them stop everybody that passes, and abuse those who will not sign for not being able to write."[115]

The signatures finally obtained throughout the state were assembled by the San Francisco committee in two 1,000-page volumes of gilded morocco and sent to Washington. The *Herald* editor commented that "Congress ought to think the people of California are in earnest when they ask in such a form."[116] And when Senator John Weller pushed the project in the Senate, the *Herald* editor commended him for finally doing something useful for his state.[117]

Parallels abound between the way western and far western newspaper editors "used" the overland emigrations to advance their own community interests at the same time that they seemed to be impartial champions of the overlanders' cause. The press in the Missouri River outfitting towns had argued long and loudly that the South Pass overland route was the only way to go to the Pacific Coast—and then made certain that prospective overlanders recognized that the best entrance to the Oregon-California Trail was from their individual city. In similar fashion the Pacific Coast press stressed the cruciality of the overland route to their future, bringing as it did the older states' finest citizens, but also endeavored to make certain that the safe wagon route they advocated would terminate in the city of their residence. The controversies among California and Oregon towns over the best arrival point much resembled those among Missouri and Iowa towns over the best departure point.

In California, Sacramento had long held sway as the major terminus of the overland trip. Hopeful that an examination of the rumored new pass through the Sierra Nevadas would demonstrate that the shortest, safest, and easiest mountain crossing would lead to Marysville, the *Herald* quickly pointed out that what the old route had done for Sacramento the projected new one could do for Marysville. If Marysville citizens would open and improve the trail in early 1852 and send out agents with signboards to divert the oncoming overlanders onto the new route, the *Herald* editor predicted Marysville would double in size by fall. Here was a "golden opportunity" which could even lead to Marysville's selection as the terminal point of the Pacific railroad itself.[118] Two and a half years later the *Herald* editor was still dreaming that "we may yet hear the tramp of the Iron Horse through our streets, as he comes and goes over this Highway for the nations, bearing the burden of the world's commerce by our very doors."[119]

While other cities were booming routes through passes terminating at their doorsteps,[120] Marysville waxed enthusiastic about the "incalculable" possibilities the Noble Pass had for its future. The presumed lack of heavy winter snows should insure its choice as the route for the railroad—and it passed through Marysville on its way to the seaboard.[121] But in late 1855 the *Herald* began boosting the nearer Henness Pass route, a survey of which was in process thanks to contributions by residents of Marysville and other towns on the projected route. Much rested on the results of the survey: "If it shall result in securing for us the great immigrant road through Henness pass, its importance cannot be estimated."[122]

What made such surveys and expectations so significant was the California Wagon Road Act of 1855, which provided up to $100,000 for a state wagon road, the most feasible route for which was to be chosen, after surveys, by the road commissioners. Even before Marysville's independently financed survey of Henness Pass was completed, however, the commissioners announced for the El Dorado route along the Johnson Cutoff. This trail, terminating in Placerville and Sacramento, was merely a slight variant of the long-established Carson River route. Upon learning of the choice the *Herald* editor erupted, charging pork-barrel favoritism, indiscretion, and illegality. He concluded his diatribe by threatening the commissioners with injunctions to stop the letting of contracts until *all* possible sites had been surveyed in accordance with the enabling act.[123]

Only when it became apparent that the Henness Pass route was not going to become the state wagon road did the *Herald* begin to press for two or more wagon routes. After all, "the State of California is too great, too rich, to be restricted to one poor wagon road through the Sierra Nevada."[124] As long as it had believed the Henness Pass route to be in the running, the *Herald* had not concerned itself with any inconveniences that improving only one route might make for travelers aiming at a different section of the state, who would be tempted to travel the improved route even if it took them hundreds of miles north or south of where an unimproved pass entered the state near their desired destination. Now, however, the *Herald* was more solicitous of the overlander's possible plight and more unwilling to impose a "vexatious hardship" upon him. The editor therefore used the *Herald*'s pages to champion state wagon roads through every pass, although the Henness and Noble passes were still held to be the finest routes into the state.[125]

The overland emigrations had returned to the national limelight when the 1848 California gold discoveries prompted the turbulent race for riches. The potential gold rushers of 1849 fared better than had the prospective Oregonians of 1843, finding in their newspapers useful and reasonably accurate information about the overland trip. Yet during the gold rush and throughout the 1850s the overland journey was rarely written about with an impartial editorial hand. Because catering to gold rushers promised community prosperity, newspaper editors and other writers were not above taking liberties in describing the overland journey in order to fashion an argument more favorable to their locale. On the West Coast, once the gold rush was under way, the belief gained currency that overland emigrants insured more prosperous states and/or cities; once again the overlanders, their journey, and its particular problems were not completely divorced from ulterior considerations.

But there is no question that during the 1850s, in contrast to the previous decade, the overland emigrations were described less fearfully, less romantically, and much more objectively. Ulterior motivations not-withstanding, the press served as a meritorious public servant. The over-land emigrant did, ultimately, travel with greater understanding of the trip's demands, on partially improved roads, with greater military protec-tion, and with the assurance of relief assistance when necessary. In some measure at least these developments were due to the slowly maturing manner in which the molders and makers of public opinion had re-sponded to the overland emigrations.

CHAPTER THREE

Motivations and Beginnings

"Life as at a fair"

THE OVERLAND JOURNEY WAS ALWAYS BEGUN with a decision. But why considerable numbers of persons suddenly decided to go westward to the Pacific Coast in the early 1840s despite the great quantities of fertile lands still available in the contiguous states has always intrigued scholars. Unfortunately, despite the many speculative answers advanced, the motivational factor has remained almost as elusive as it is popular. While it is tempting to bypass the issue by stating that there were as many reasons for going west as there were emigrants attempting the venture, population movements of the suddenness and magnitude of those in the 1840s and 1850s deserve careful analysis. Surely something of formidable proportions must have sustained men who dared to take their families on a 2,000-mile journey described in some newspapers as "palpable homicide" without even the assurance, in the earliest period, that the emigrants of the preceding year had been successful.

The West, as place, direction, or idea, has fascinated men since time immemorial, men who by their actions have given substance to Henry David Thoreau's poetic phrasings that "eastward I go only by force; but westward I go free" and that "we go westward as into the future, with a spirit of enterprise and adventure."[1] Since American scholarship has virtually enshrined the continent-wide westward movement, it is only natural that much of the speculation concerning the overlanders' motivations has revolved around the so-called "pioneer instinct" of restless frontiersmen.[2] Medorum Crawford recalled, for example, that some of his fellow 1842 overlanders were as unsatisfied in Oregon as they had been everywhere else, and pushed on to California the ensuing year. Among the early departures was one particularly mobile family of whom Crawford remarked, ". . . they had practically lived in the wagon for more than twenty years, only remaining in one locality long enough to make a crop, which they had done in every State and Territory in the Mississippi Valley."[3] To explain such peripatetic pioneers some historians have written of ingrained and instinctive habits, asserting even that westering "was as natural as swimming upstream is to a salmon" or that "the westward surge was a human instinct, like the need to love or to taste spring air and believe again that life is not a dead end after all."[4]

Those overlanders who chose to record the stimuli they believed to be impelling them westward, however, usually mentioned such prosaic factors as financial difficulties, the hope of economic improvement in the Far West, the search for better health, or political and patriotic considerations, before admitting to general restlessness or a desire for adventure.[5] Occasionally noted also was the desire to get away from the increasingly virulent passions surrounding the Negro and slavery, the wish to flee the artificialities and restraints of society, the possibility of evading capture for indiscretions ranging from theft to murder, the willingness to undertake missionary work among the Indians, the attempt to forget a romance gone sour. Some even claimed to be moving because of the better fishing reported in Oregon.[6]

In expressing such sentiments the overlanders were tacitly acknowledging the important impact of promoters and propagandists. It seems abundantly clear that most pre– and post–gold rush overlanders had become convinced that their projected Far West destination was a veritable utopia or Eden in which their long-cherished dreams would be realized more quickly and more easily than if they remained where they were. They viewed the new and fabled lands of Oregon and California as regions of rebirth and hope, where upward mobility was not merely possible but virtually certain.[7] Jessy Quinn Thornton believed desires for status improvement to be motivating the 1846 emigrants with whom he traveled, observing, "They agreed in the one general object—that of bettering their condition; but the particular means by which each proposed to attain this end, were as various as can well be imagined."[8]

Although doubtless there were those in the overland caravans who would have investigated Oregon and California had they known absolutely nothing about those regions, the movement of the vast majority of the overlanders was in response to the extremely favorable ways in which these new "Promised Lands" had been publicized. Paradise was worth a long and dangerous trip, and it was paradise which the promoters were selling in what Ray Billington has termed an extremely successful "public relations campaign."[9]

Beginning as early as 1818, Thomas Hart Benton, Hall Jackson Kelley, and John Floyd, in addition to Jason Lee and other Oregon missionaries, disseminated enthusiastic reports about the Oregon country.[10] Due in large measure to the writings and speeches of these zealous enthusiasts and the work of the Oregon Provisional Emigration Society through its publication, the *Oregonian, and Indian's Advocate,* by 1839 enough Oregon emigrating societies had been organized throughout the United States to afflict thousands of Americans with the "Oregon fever." The harvest began to be reaped with the 1839–40 overland journey to Oregon, over a strange, long, and tortuous route, by Thomas J. Farnham and his small Peoria party. Their trip was a direct result of Lee's eastern speeches and the fabulous stories told of Oregon by some of the Indian lads Lee had brought east with him in 1838.[11]

What Kelley, the missionaries, and the politicians were doing for Oregon, New England merchants and sailors who reached California in the 1820s and 1830s began to do for that region. More persuasive propaganda came from Richard Henry Dana's *Two Years Before the Mast* and in the writings of John Marsh and John A. Sutter, both anxious to entice Americans to settle on lands they owned. The writers of the popular route-oriented guidebooks must also be included among the influential promoters of the far western paradises.[12]

In retrospect, the promotional arguments of these boosters were extraordinarily perceptive. They appealed to man's universal aspirations for wealth, health, and happiness, as well as to his humanitarian and patriotic instincts.[13] In the skillful words of the propagandists, not only was the land fertile beyond measure, it was also available in vast quantities. Much was made of the almost illimitable amount of land available in California and of the bill pending in Congress to permit each American settler in Oregon a 640-acre tract of land.[14] Further, crop yields were held to be fantastic, and the climate was said to be so salubrious that the dreaded ague of the Mississippi Valley was unknown. The promoters not only assured potential travelers that they could expect perennial health in these far western paradises but that the overland trip was itself a virtual cure-all for most illnesses. In 1850 a prominent physician, Dr. Daniel Drake, even published a book to that effect.[15] Additionally, the patriotic argument that emigrants would be taking with them the great American democratic institutions for the benefit of all mankind was held forth as reason enough to go west to aid in securing the Pacific Coast from foreign powers.[16]

Exaggeration was frequently utilized, apparently to good advantage, by these early advertisers of the West. Tongue-in-cheek stories were told and retold about Oregon pigs which roamed about pre-cooked with knives and forks sticking out for the benefit of anyone who might be hungry. Another favorite legend was that of the 250-year-old Californian who discovered he had to move out of that healthy region when he finally wanted to die. But when his body was returned to California for burial the salutary climate immediately restored him to robust health.[17] Certainly the prevalence of such exaggerated depictions of the attributes of Oregon and California must have predisposed the overlanders to their view that much of the wondrous West was bigger than life. Even a casual reading of their diaries reveals how persistently they set down their reflections on the flora and fauna of the West with the aid of numerous superlatives: storms were more severe, the air was clearer, days were hotter, nights cooler, roads straighter, natural phenomena more fantastic, mountains higher, trees larger. The West the overland emigrants were discovering was thus often found to be at least partially as magnificent as the propagandists had promised it would be.[18]

The contention that it was the promotional portrayals of an idyllic Oregon and California which primarily motivated the overlanders of the 1840s is supported by Dorothy O. Johansen's migration hypothesis.[19] In an attempt to determine why some persons chose Oregon and others California when both areas held forth approximately equal opportunities and were also peopled from the same population sources, Johansen theorizes that emigrants were drawn to one locale or the other by the types of value expectations they had come to have for those regions—expectations emanating, of course, mainly from the promotional literature. Further suggesting that the first arrivals communicated their satisfactions and dissatisfactions to those back east, thereby tending to influence similar types of emigrants to follow them, Johansen believes that differences in the character, values, and social orders of the Oregon and California communities are thus explained.

According to this theory the greater risk-takers and gamblers among the overlanders sought out California—which was neither as safely American nor as orderly as Oregon. Moreover, the California farming patterns were not as similar to prevailing stateside customs as were those practiced in Oregon. The emigrants themselves seemed to think the more "respectable" of their number were turning off to Oregon, especially in the years before 1847, and Johansen asserts that by "respectable" they meant emigrants of the Protestant persuasion who possessed a Puritan moral outlook, emphasized thrift and education, and were conservative seekers after law and order. Oregonians during the 1850s believed themselves more "respectable" than their Pacific Coast neighbors to the south, expressing their feelings in an arrogant anecdote: "At Pacific Springs, one of the crossroads of the western trail, a pile of gold-bearing quartz marked the road to California; the other road had a sign bearing the words 'To Oregon.' Those who could read took the trail to Oregon." Even Lansford Hastings, who hoped to ride California's star to fame, praised the respectable character of the Oregonians in his famous guidebook: "And I may add, that the Oregon emigrants are, as a general thing, of a superior order to those of our people, who usually emigrate to our frontier countries. They are not the indolent, dissolute, ignorant and vicious, but they are generally, the enterprising, orderly, intelligent and virtuous."[20]

It is, of course, extremely difficult to analyze accurately the character and nature of large masses of emigrants or communities, even if allowances are made for exceptions and inconsistencies, as Johansen does. But especially significant in her hypothesis is the emphasis that "pull-factors" are of greater importance than "push-factors," especially for migrations spanning long distances. From such a perspective the boundless opportunities the publicists promised in the Far West had even greater causal significance in the overlanders' ultimate decision to make the journey than their contemporaneously felt frustrations.[21]

If the majority of the overlanders trekked westward primarily because they were convinced that their value expectations could be better fulfilled in the Far West than in any intervening region, and if they chose either Oregon or California partially because of their own outlooks and partially because of the reports of those who had preceded them, the key role of those who skillfully molded and then appealed to those value expectations must henceforth be more clearly acknowledged. Of course, the blandishments held out by the propagandists did not appeal to the aspirations of all Americans, or even of all migrating Americans. Most persons were content to stay where they were, or, if they removed themselves farther west, halted before what Horace Greeley had termed the "jumping-off-place." And, since the long overland journey required a certain amount of capital, thousands of poor persons were excluded from the overland emigrations, despite the fact that their value expectations had doubtless also been quickened by the grandiosely favorable accounts about Oregon and California. "Free land" there may have been, but it is clear that it required more than mere desire to go west, especially all the way to the Pacific Coast.[22]

To a large degree, the foregoing observations are applicable also to a motivational understanding of the California gold rush. Certainly the role played by the propagandists was again fundamental: easterners, southerners, and midwesterners did not initially succumb to the reports of the gold discoveries. The mania did not develop until President Polk confirmed the credibility of the gold deposits in his December 5, 1848, Message to Congress and until actual gold samples were placed on display in government buildings.[23] Instant guide and instruction books appeared, as did the familiar exaggerated accounts. Prominent now was the story of the miner who discovered an 839-pound gold nugget. Afraid to leave it even for a moment, he remained perched atop his discovery, offering $27,000 for a plate of pork and beans.[24]

California gold appealed to so many that the "moving panorama" technique was widely used to publicize the delights of that golden paradise and the overland route thither. Artists who had gone west, and some who had not, laboriously filled immense cloth canvases with panoramas of romantic and awe-inspiring scenes of gold rush routes by land and by sea. For several hours enthralled audiences imaginatively went west as thousands of square feet of painted canvas unrolled before them, while

Emigrant wagons are diminished by the grandeur of the landscape in "Covered Wagons in the Rockies," painted about 1854 by James F. Wilkins, the "artist on the overland trail."

commentators, accompanied by appropriate background music, explained the depictions. James Wilkins's "Moving Mirror of the Overland Trail," based upon sketches the artist made during his 1849 overland trip on the South Pass route, was one of the most widely heralded and viewed, but there were many others. These "moving panoramas" strengthened the "pull-factors" for the thousands of spectators who witnessed these early motion-picture spectaculars.[25]

The gold rushers who went to exploit California's natural resources differed in some important respects from the farm-oriented settlers who had gone overland to the Pacific Coast in the pre–1849 period. Those approximately 15,000 persons had traveled largely as family units prepared to stay in their new Eden. The contrasting expectations of the males who thronged the trails during the gold rush, influenced by the propagandists who assured them that California's gold was inexhaustible, were clear—they planned to dig a fast fortune and anticipated an early return to the families and homes they had temporarily left behind. To them California was a short-term golden paradise, since their lasting orientation was presumed to be back east.[26] That for many it did not turn out that way was due to the vagaries of history: they died en route or in the mines; they did not strike it rich and had to remain, for they were too poor to finance a return journey; they found the allurements of California irresistible and stayed, or went east to return quickly with their families.

But such twists of fate were not anticipated in the exuberant beginning days of the rush. For the gold seekers, health, humanitarianism, and patriotism were not much at issue, nor did the propagandists especially stress such factors.[27] The gold rushers sought wealth and they sought it unashamedly, provided, of course, that they commanded sufficient credit to afford the venture, or were able to find employment with someone needing an extra teamster or drover. Elisha Perkins confided to his diary that he was "willing to brave most anything" to get gold, while fellow forty-niner Charles Boyle explained in his very first diary entry that he was bound for California to eradicate "the detested sin of being poor."[28] Sweethearts and pregnant wives were left behind for this once-in-a-lifetime chance at instant riches. At least one prospective bride was stood up at the church when the bridegroom-to-be departed unannounced for California.[29] Another young man rejected an offer of $20,000 from his mother if he would only stay home—what, after all, was a mere $20,000 when 839-pound nuggets awaited in California?[30]

So confident of their success were most forty-niners that they were inordinately gullible and easy prey for sharpies along the way. Bernard Reid, for example, enrolled in gold and silver smelting courses at St. Louis prior to departing. Reid also sacrificed precious dollars for instruction booklets, iron molds for casting gold ingots in 1,000-dollar quantities, copper basins for washing gold dust, and assorted other treasures which eventually contributed to the litter that overburdened gold rushers strewed in their wake.[31] Advertisers were quick to extoll all sorts of devices for gold-seeking in addition to traveling equipment and supplies. Certainly far more fortunes were made by merchants than by miners during the frenetic days of the gold rush. No one was immune to the fever: young men, middle-aged men, old men, women of all ages, supposedly prudent newspaper editors, ministers. Even Notre Dame University sponsored a gold-hunting expedition in 1850.[32]

A recent comparative study of the major "laymen's" gold rushes in American history suggests that in each instance the existence of gold had been fairly well known for some time prior to the actual rush. Effective propaganda coupled with a restless, unusually mobile citizenry was required to produce the rushes.[33] Yet despite the effective propaganda about supposedly limitless gold, a few thousand persons continued to trail to Oregon during the California excitement. This phenomenon further indicates the importance of selective "pull-factors"—not even California's gold was sufficient to deter someone certain that his utopia lay in Oregon.[34] Once the gold rush aberration waned, home seekers again assumed ascendancy in the trail caravans, confident that in one or another of the Far West's storied domains of boundless opportunity their better future was assured. Whether temporary gold rushers or permanent settlers, they had been drawn west by their roseate visions of unprecedented opportunities on the Pacific Coast, visions which had been profoundly nurtured by those who had chosen to publicize those regions in almost supernatural terms.

No matter whether they dreamed of farms, fish, or gold, the overland emigrants all passed through at least one of those communities situated along the banks of the Missouri River which served either as outfitting post or jumping-off point, or, as usually was the case, both. With permanent residence in the Far West in mind, the pre– and post–gold rush overlanders naturally attempted to carry along many of their earthly possessions. Since the vast majority were farmers, they usually already had on hand one or more serviceable wagons and several draft animals, as well as sufficient foodstuffs and other supplies. For many such emigrants it would have been unnecessary to pass through the outfitting towns had they not needed to cross the Missouri River or been desirous of reaching the Oregon-California Trail over a known approach route. The availability of ferryboats and the advertisements about the shortest and most-traveled approaches to the main overland trail therefore channeled these overlanders to the several towns which served as their jumping-off points into what they usually called the "wilderness."

Indeed, the power of precedent and advertising, coupled with the dictates of geography, insured that a number of jumping-off points continued to exist. Since the Oregon Trail followed the Platte River for hundreds of miles westward, the most significant jumping-off point might have been expected to be located at the mouth of the Platte River. A small community appropriately called Plattsmouth did eventually materialize there, but it was never more than a minor departure point.[35] Rather, since Independence, Missouri, had previously gained considerable fame as the outfitting post for Santa Fe traders, most of the overlanders in the early 1840s unquestioningly congregated there to follow the paths of fur traders in a northwesterly direction, to reach the Great Platte River Road near where new Fort Kearny would be located in 1848. Thus, the "great migration" of 1843 routinely departed from Independence, thereby providing the town fathers with impressive advertising arguments for future years.[36]

Yet emigrants coming overland from northern Missouri, Illinois, Indiana, and Ohio, to say nothing of those from Iowa, increasingly recognized the foolishness of making Independence their point of departure. Besides, the Missouri River bore westerly the farther north one went. This furnished the basis for the impressive advertising arguments of the up-river jumping-off points. Overlanders departing from St. Joseph, for example, were already approximately twenty miles west of Independence and considerably closer to the main Platte trail. Those launching out from the northernmost jumping-off point at Council Bluffs, some 200 miles north of Independence, were at least forty miles west of St. Joseph. Given these geographic considerations, overlanders tended to head for the jumping-off point most convenient to their place of origin and also as close as possible to the main overland trail. And those who shipped their outfits upriver by steamboat generally progressed farther and farther north as they learned their geography. By the early 1850s, the overwhelming preponderance of overlanders were launching out onto the plains from the Council Bluffs area.[37]

The gold rushers introduced some new elements into the prevailing patterns. They hailed more frequently from urban centers, rarely brought their families, and only infrequently planned to settle in the Far West. Therefore they tended to utilize commercial transportation to reach the jumping-off points—normally coming up the Missouri River by steamboat from St. Louis—and generally arrived still in need of purchasing most or all of their traveling outfit.[38] Requiring the services of outfitting posts more clearly than most of the overlanders of the previous eight years, and coming in unprecedented numbers, the gold rushers occasioned fierce rivalry as the jumping-off points burgeoned in size and nurtured aspirations that their increased importance as outfitting posts would lead to ultimate metropolitan glory. If the gold rushers coming upriver had not been enticed into outfitting in St. Louis—which is usually not given credit for being the important base it was—they got off at one or another of the five major outfitting post complexes up the river.[39] They made their choices either on the basis of reputation, convincing advertising, or rumors of where the lowest prices, fewest cholera cases, and smallest number of fellow outfitters would be found.

Platte

River

Omaha—
Council Bluffs
area

Plattsmouth

Old Fort
Kearny

IOWA
MISSOURI

Missouri

NEBRASKA
KANSAS

River

St. Joseph
area

Atchison

Missouri River
Frontier

Weston

Ft. Leavenworth

0   20   40
miles

Independence

Kanzas or
Westport Landing   Westport

KANSAS
MISSOURI

Bier

MAP 1

William Rothwell and his traveling companions heard many such rumors as they wended their way toward St. Joseph in 1850. After having been told that men in Lexington were dying daily, when Rothwell's party reached that city they were surprised to learn that there had not been a single case of cholera there all year. Rumors about St. Joseph, then the premier outfitting town, had been even more prevalent, and after arriving there Rothwell wrote his parents:

I never in my life have heard as many false statements, to give them as soft a name as possible, in 17 days as were told us in coming up here. Every man we met tried to tell us some scary tale of cholera, scarcity of feed, starvation, impassable roads, &c. The people in Saline & Lafayette Counties seemed to have a great prejudice against St. Joseph. We were frequently told by persons on the road that at least 15 to 20 cases of cholera were dying daily in St. Joseph, that the emigrants were densely crowded here & that it was impossible to get feed at any price &c, &c.

In St. Joseph Rothwell found that there had not been a case of cholera to date. But the rumors had been effective. Rothwell confirmed that many gold rushers had turned south to Independence and that very few Missourians could be seen in St. Joseph.[40] Farmers in the country east of the outfitting posts also spread rumors about the scarcity of provisions in those towns, rumors which enabled them to sell foodstuffs to unwary overlanders at handsome prices.[41]

Before the gold rush few entrepreneurs had been tempted by the profit potential in devising speedier methods of crossing the plains. There had been little talk in the outfitting posts of anything but whether the traditional covered wagons should be drawn by oxen, mules, or horses. Sparse publicity had been accorded the Independence inventor who in 1846 and 1847 experimented with a "wind-wagon" equipped with mast and sails which he boasted could travel over the prairies at fifteen miles per hour.[42] During one trial run, Wind-Wagon Thomas's crew jumped off as the wagon gained speed, leaving designer and craft to crash in an arroyo. Undaunted, he determinedly exhibited his creation in 1853 and again in 1859 in Westport.[43] A Kansan, Mr. Thompson, constructed a similar "prairie ship" in which he expected to take thirty passengers to the Rocky Mountains in 1856.[44]

The euphoria of 1849, however, resulted in several unique transportation experiments, the most visionary of which was Rufus Porter's "Air Line to California." Porter, the founder of *Scientific American* magazine, advertised widely in eastern cities in early 1849, apparently quickly securing his desired 200 passengers. For $50 they were promised a trip to San Francisco in three days with "wines included."[45] In Boston, Porter advertised that although his air machine might possibly make the 2,400-mile trip in twenty-four hours, the maximum time limit had been set at five days in case heavy head winds were encountered.[46] Porter never built his airship.

However, in New York he demonstrated a model of his proposed 1,000-foot-long propeller-driven balloon to be powered by two steam engines.[47] Western newspapers treated Porter's advertisements and proposals with disdain. The editor of the Liberty, Missouri, *Weekly Tribune* thought the project the capstone of "huge humbugs, and stupendous follies," and promised if the project succeeded to "believe with the Millerites—that the world is coming to an end."[48] In St. Louis and Kanesville the newspaper editors suggested that the projected New York departure date of April 15 would have been better set for April 1 since it was such a foolish project.[49]

While Porter's "Aerial Locomotive" never became airborne, the "passenger trains" organized by various firms enlisted hundreds of gold rushers, most of whom eventually wished that they had been content with more conventional modes of travel. The story of their high expectations and rude awakenings is among the more fascinating aspects of the California gold rush. At least one Independence firm, Hansford and Peacock, and one St. Louis firm, Turner and Allen, planned passenger trains to California in 1849. The Independence-based firm stationed an agent in St. Louis and advertised in St. Louis newspapers. Two trains were planned: an express line which would make the overland trip in forty-five to fifty-five days, with baggage and provisions transported in mule-drawn wagons, and a slower train, presumably drawn by oxen. The announced fare for the express line was $300 per passenger, for which a riding mule, saddle, blanket, and all necessary provisions for the trip would be provided. Each passenger would be permitted up to 200 pounds of baggage.[50]

Whether Hansford and Peacock's train ever departed is not known, but Turner and Allen's venture received such an enthusiastic response that two California-bound trains were dispatched, even though only one had initially been advertised. The favorable public reception was prompted by the enthusiastic endorsements the influential *Daily Missouri Republican* continually accorded this St. Louis enterprise.[51] Thus assured of the reliable character of the proprietors and their previous outfitting experience, eager forty-niners willingly paid the 200-dollar fee. For this they were promised a ride to California in spring wagons carrying six passengers each, food rations for the entire trip, and the transportation of 160 pounds of baggage. The *Daily Missouri Republican* confirmed that the wagons were well constructed, durable, "comfortable and even elegant," and would be drawn by "the finest mules." Further, while the trip was optimistically projected for sixty days, enough provisions would be carried for a hundred days. The train, which came to be known as the Pioneer Line, was scheduled to start from Independence about April 15.[52]

By late March 100 passengers had already paid their fare. Accordingly, Turner and Allen began advertising a second train with a late May departure date. Overlanders were told, "Passengers may depend (unusual obstacles excepted) on arriving out in sixty days. Each passenger will be entitled to one hundred days provisions." The St. Louis newspaper, terming it a "magnificent enterprise," predicted that the innovation would become a permanent fixture of overland communication, since Turner and Allen planned to operate on an even more comprehensive scale in 1850.[53] Indeed, by late April it was announced that the Pioneer Line even intended to send a portion of its first train back from California in the fall, and the St. Louis press predicted Turner and Allen's passengers would make the fastest journey, with the least loss and inconvenience, of any on the plains.[54]

So many emigrants were desirous of traveling in this rapid, easy, and commodious manner that the first train's size was increased to 125 male passengers, and the second train was projected to include at least 75.[55] The first train, numbering twenty passenger carriages and eighteen baggage and supply wagons, with 125 passengers, departed from Independence on May 9.[56] The second train, with between 75 and 100 overlanders, departed approximately June 18, but by the time it reached the California settlements in late October was only three or four days behind, despite experiencing a skirmish with the Sioux near Fort Laramie in which one passenger was reported killed.[57]

The experiment had been an interesting one, but the surviving passengers, especially from the first train, were in anything but a friendly mood after their agonizing trip mercifully ended in long-awaited California. Grumbling began in Independence, when the passengers learned that instead of being able to sit back and enjoy travel comforts while others did the work, they would have to drive the wagons, guard the stock, cook the meals, and perform other incidental chores. The series of unexpected misfortunes which attended the venture, combined with some poor judgment on the part of the proprietors, further sabotaged the project. First, Moses "Black" Harris, former mountain man who had been engaged to guide the train to California, died of cholera shortly before the train's scheduled departure. Then, the Pioneer Line's initial progress was slowed by rainy weather as well as by overloaded wagons and inferior mules. One passenger contended that only one of the approximately 300 mules in the total outfit had ever before been harnessed to a wagon.[58] Moreover, although four mules had apparently been allotted to pull each passenger carriage, only two mules were being used when the train reached Fort Kearny. Some of the animals showed such deterioration that they had to be turned loose.[59] Finally, cholera and other illnesses were frequent visitors to the train, one passenger estimating that more than a sixth of their number died en route.[60]

These misfortunes were compounded by the proprietors' miscalculations. Co-owner Allen, who had journeyed partway with the first train, took several of the wagons and most of the sixty mules being trailed along for replacement purposes back to Independence as the nucleus for the second train. This forced Turner to lighten the overburdened wagons by leaving about a ton of cured meats at the June 2 campsite. Then on June 8, with Fort Kearny finally in view, a sudden hailstorm caused considerable havoc: mules stampeded, wagons were wrecked, and much of the baggage and provisions was thoroughly drenched.[61] It was therefore not surprising that "Pawnee," a *Missouri Republican* correspondent, wrote from the Fort on June 10 that the passengers were irate: only 300 miles on their way and already half of the sixty days projected for the trip had elapsed. "Pawnee" predicted a "general explosion" soon, but also remarked that Turner was energetically doing all that could be expected.[62]

Beyond Fort Kearny almost all who came into contact with the ill-fated Pioneer Line remarked on the dissatisfaction rampant among the passengers.[63] The first desertions—by two teamsters—occurred almost two weeks before Fort Laramie was reached, eliciting the prescient comment from passenger Bernard Reid that "rats are already leaving the sinking ship."[64] Deserting the train, though an increasingly frequent occurrence, was a precarious step. The disgruntled forty-niner then faced the remainder of his journey without provisions or means of hauling his baggage unless he was able to join other groups of overlanders.[65]

The remaining passengers periodically tightened their belts as they slowly progressed westward. On June 13 more provisions were thrown away and it was decided that only sick passengers would henceforth be permitted to ride in the wagons. The few passengers who owned horses and mules could still ride. The majority began walking. At Fort Laramie, on June 27, wagon loads were again lightened. Two weeks later a passenger committee was elected which quickly decreed that each man's baggage must be reduced to seventy-five pounds and that only twelve passenger carriages would be taken any farther. The next day, within sight of Independence Rock, a bizarre free-for-all resulted, with other gold rushers hovering about to snatch choice items, sometimes even before passengers had definitely decided to abandon them!

On July 13 still more was discarded and a major sacrifice made—fifty gallons of liquor was poured into a small stream. Quarrels among the passengers became more frequent as rations were reduced. At Soda Springs on August 2 the last supplies of coffee and sugar were dispensed. By mid-August only flour remained. Morale had long since vanished by the time the Pioneer Line reached the Humboldt Sink. On the ensuing desert crossing the teams broke down and the many sick passengers were left behind to be brought to the Carson River later. More and more passengers departed to forge ahead on their own, usually on foot.[66]

When D. T. McCollum finally reached Sacramento, he calculated that 159 days had passed since the sixty-day train had left Independence.[67] Bernard Reid and seven others forced the unwilling Turner to provide them with passage through to San Francisco as per the original agreement, and these eight men arrived on October 21. By their count they had been 165 days en route. On reaching the mines Reid and other passengers complained so bitterly of Turner's conduct that the rough and ready California miners suggested lynching Turner after appearances had been preserved with a short trial. The threat was not carried out, however, although Reid and other passengers continued to fulminate against the two proprietors, dubbing them "swindlers" and "criminals of the deepest die."[68]

Though Reid leveled other severe accusations at Turner, a fellow passenger, St. Louis merchant Augustus O. Garrett, praised Turner's conscientious efforts throughout the trip. Garrett had been much impressed by Turner's purchase of extra provisions at enormous prices en route. Further, during the journey Turner had labored so long and diligently in behalf of the train that he was at the point of exhaustion and occasionally fell asleep while standing up. This condition probably was due, Garrett thought, to the fact that Turner had been required to stay awake at night to prevent disgruntled passengers from stealing the remaining mules.[69]

The disastrous end result of this novel transportation endeavor was not yet widely known the following spring, when even greater numbers of gold seekers crowded the streets of the various outfitting posts. So once again expectant entrepreneurs organized passenger trains, although Turner and Allen were, significantly, not among the number advertising this inexpensive, safe, and easy manner of transportation. With at least eight trains originating in that city, St. Louis firms were again in the forefront of the passenger-train business.[70] Five of the eight chose St. Joseph as their jumping-off point, two launched out from Independence, while Dr. Reuben Knox's train departed from Old Fort Kearny.[71]

Once again St. Louis newspapers endorsed some of the enterprises, although clearly with less enthusiasm than during the preceding year. On one occasion, however, the *Daily Missouri Republican* suggested that the knowledge gained from the "trials of last year" should facilitate success for the 1850 endeavors.[72] The normally announced fee continued to be $200. The many available trains apparently glutted the market: J. C. Faine and Company on April 1 advertised a "reduced price" of $150 per passenger and one week later announced that they would take additional passengers at the "reduced rates" of $125 each.[73] Wisely, none of the 1850 concerns boasted about how quickly they would make the trip. Alexander and Hall's advertisements came closest, declaring that since both proprietors had successfully crossed the plains in 1849, one in a mere sixty-three days, they were confident theirs would be the first train in California.[74] This was one occasion when advertising could be believed, for an end-of-the-year report from California noted that of all the St. Louis trains only Alexander and Hall's California Mail Line had reached Sacramento with their wagons. All the other passenger trains either disintegrated en route or were forced to abandon their wagons and pack in.[75]

While the exact number of gold rushers choosing this means of reaching El Dorado in 1850 cannot be ascertained, it seems probable that approximately 1,000 overlanders boarded carriages at the trip's inception.[76] One of the new features of the 1850 passenger-train traffic was the presence of several females on the passenger lists. Three, one a Negro girl, traveled in Dr. Reuben Knox's train, at least three more were among Alexander and Hall's passengers, and two of Jerome, Hanson, and Smith's patrons were women.[77]

Another new facet of 1850—potentially disturbing for future proprietors intending to follow the route through Salt Lake City—was the utilization of the courts there to redress grievances. At least two of the trains were involved in judicial proceedings in the Mormon center. McPike and Strother had already dissolved their partnership at Fort Laramie, traveling in two separate companies from then on. When Strother's train shielded a fugitive from Mormon officials beyond Salt Lake, the court did not permit the sheriff to recoup his financial loss by seizing part of McPike's train still in Salt Lake.[78]

It was Glenn and Company's train, however, which most resembled the ill-fated 1849 Pioneer Line. With thirty-nine wagons and 140 passengers, this April Line was probably the year's largest passenger train. Even with a late May start from Independence all was not in readiness, Glenn dallying while the passengers threatened to commandeer the train and go forward themselves. On reaching Independence Rock matters had deteriorated to such a point that one of Glenn's chief aides kept himself "scarce" because some passengers were threatening to shoot him. About twenty-five passengers purchased oxen from a passing government freight train and pushed on alone with carriages the company abandoned, taking thirty-five days' provisions with them. In Salt Lake City in mid-August the remaining passengers divided the train's property, offering notes payable in California for what they planned to take. When the proprietors balked, a few passengers sought legal recourse and others simply took what they wanted and quietly departed. For several days Mormon attorney Hosea Stout was busily engaged in legal suits, most of which were finally concluded to the satisfaction of both passengers and owners. Four of the train's chief officers were eventually arrested and fined from $50 to $100 apiece for refusing to deliver company property pursuant to the court's order.[79] One of the passengers expressed succinctly what surely were the feelings of many—"*Deliver me* from a *passenger train.*"[80] Though the endeavor once had seemed so promising, S. M. E. Goheen probably best summed up the experiences of all concerned when he wrote from California, "Passenger trains have proved a humbug to the passengers and proprietors."[81]

Nonetheless, the temptation of the substantial profits was not easily squelched. In 1852 at least five St. Louis passenger trains were advertised—again, all by conspicuously different companies. Charles A.

and Elias H. Perry, Weston and St. Joseph merchants, also outfitted a
passenger train, as did Blodgett and Company of St. Joseph, while at least
three more trains originated in Ohio. Additional passenger trains were
attempted in 1854 and 1855.[82]

While the results continued generally unsatisfactory, the travails experienced should not overshadow an important ramification of the
passenger-train experience. In an age of inadequate communication and
transportation, the consequences of large numbers of men from diverse
backgrounds being thrown together to live and work for long months in a
difficult joint enterprise were of significance in a union where states' rights
portended possible disruption. McPike and Strother's 1850 train, for
example, had enrolled passengers from Missouri, Indiana, Kentucky,
Iowa, Ohio, Michigan, Tennessee, Wisconsin, Illinois, Pennsylvania, and
Ireland.[83] And within the first week's travel alone cholera struck down in
Perry's 1852 passenger train a man each from New York, Ohio, Massachusetts, Illinois, Canada, and North Ireland, and a woman and her son from
Missouri.[84] Quarrels and harsh feelings there were, but withal there was an
educational process which was an important ongoing feature of the gold
rush movement.

A variant of the passenger-train idea was the individual contractual
agreement. This was employed, often in a rather informal fashion, before,
during, and after the gold rush. Many Oregon- and California-bound
families felt that another young man or two might come in handy to help
drive wagons, herd stock, and fight Indians. Many young men got their
first view of the fabled Far West by working their way across the plains.
Sometimes the employee was asked to pay something in addition, but as
often as not he simply received his meals and transportation in return for
his labor.

During the gold rush the old practice of indentured servitude was also
revived. Speculators offered to pay a man's expenses to California providing he then worked in the mines for a specified period of time, often a year,
with a hefty portion of his proceeds earmarked for the sponsor.[85] The
value of these bargains depended on the character of the individuals
involved. That not all gold rushers were men of integrity is amply revealed
in Hosea Stout's diary. This Mormon lawyer was busily engaged throughout the period when gold rushers streamed through Salt Lake City, and
many of the cases pertained to one or the other of the contracting parties
breaking their agreements—long before California had been reached.[86] S.
M. E. Goheen observed that taking men to California for services to be
rendered there was as much a "humbug" as organizing passenger trains.[87]

Much simpler than the ballyhooed airships, wind-wagons, and "fast"
passenger lines was another novel gold rush transportation experiment—a
few intrepid overlanders endeavored to walk to California, pushing their
entire outfits in wheelbarrows. It appears that there were at least four such

individuals in 1850: Brookmire, who was a Scot from Warren, Pennsylvania, and an Irishman, a German, and a Missourian whose names have not endured.[88] Their progress was reported by various eastbound and westbound travelers, who generally concurred that the men were light-hearted and fearless, and that they out-traveled everything on the trail, including mule teams.[89] The *Missouri Republican*'s correspondent at Fort Laramie reported that one of the wheelbarrow men had reached that point in twenty-five days from St. Joseph, an average daily journey of approximately twenty-three miles.[90] Apparently none of these innovators in prairie travel made the complete trip with their unique outfits: one left his wheelbarrow at Fort Hall and another at Salt Lake City, both to join larger companies, and a third was forced to take such action when the ferryboat transporting his wheelbarrow foundered in the Weber River near Salt Lake City; the fate of the fourth man is unknown.[91] Brookmire returned to Pennsylvania in 1852 with $15,000 in gold dust to discover that his wife had inherited $10,000 from deceased Scottish relatives in the interim—one of the few gold rush stories with a happy ending.[92]

In 1852 there was also a "wheelbarrow train" of sorts when five Irishmen left Independence about May 1 with their supplies in a common handcart. They completed a relatively fast four-month trip.[93] Several other solitary wheelbarrow men were on the plains that summer. One, a Kentucky printer, was found lying by the roadside completely prostrated. Kindly aided by several emigrant companies, he ultimately reached California, where he soon prospered. The 1852 Fort Kearny register listed fifteen overlanders traveling with handcarts.[94]

As mail service from the Missouri River frontier to Salt Lake City and points between became regularized during the later 1850s, stagecoach travel became still another way to go west. Richard Burton, the celebrated British author and explorer, demonstrated how rapidly the plains could be crossed in this fashion in 1860, when he left St. Joseph in a mail coach on August 7 and reached Salt Lake City nineteen days later, having traveled well over fifty miles per day. Such speed was also costly—Burton paid $175 for his ticket.[95] After remaining in Salt Lake approximately one month, he traveled on to California, reaching San Francisco in early November.

These varied methods of travel notwithstanding, the overwhelming majority of overlanders traveled neither by wheelbarrow, stagecoach, or passenger train but by covered wagon. For them the question at issue was not whether to use a covered wagon but what type of draft animal to choose to pull the wagon. The authors of the various guidebooks, most of whom had made the trip themselves, almost unanimously recommended oxen. Whether it was Lansford Hastings's controversial guidebook, which despite its reputation was useful in its advice on outfitting, or the more respected volumes of counsel by Overton Johnson and William H. Winter, Andrew Child, P. L. Platt and Nelson Slater, and Randolph B. Marcy, the litany of virtues attributed to the lowly ox was impressive. Prospective overlanders were advised that oxen were less likely to be stolen by Indians, more valuable on arrival (particularly to Oregon farmers), better able to withstand the fatigues of travel and to subsist on whatever vegetation was available, less likely to stray far from camp, safer, more reliable, almost as fast, and, best of all, least expensive.[96]

The majority of emigrants followed the guidebook writers' advice, although overlanders who spent a great deal of time searching for strayed oxen or whose oxen had been stolen and killed by hungry Indians along the Humboldt River often bemoaned their choice. While no exact statistics can be offered, more than half of all overlanders' wagons were pulled by oxen. Horses and mules, in that order, followed in frequency of use.[97]

Certainly the most systematic approach to this decision was taken by 1852 overlander John Hawkins Clark, who made certain that he would have the best of all possible worlds when he and his partner provided four wagons for the twenty passengers they took with them at $100 per man. One wagon was drawn by oxen, one wagon by mules, and two wagons by horses. At Salt Lake City the oxen were traded for mules, reflecting Clark's growing enthusiasm for the superiority of mules to both oxen and horses.[98] But the question was really unresolvable, for what seemed obvious to Clark was viewed much differently in other quarters. After prevailing on a passing ox team to pull his wagon out of a mudhole from which his mule team could not budge it, 1850 overlander James A. Payne ruefully remarked, "I have found to my sorrow, that an ox team is the way to travel to California."[99] And Henry Coke, soured on the agonies of using pack mules during his 1850 trip, grouched, "What perverse brutes these mules are. . . . Eh, the beasts! How I hate 'em!"[100]

If the choice of draft animals remained a matter of individual preference throughout the emigration years, the question of whether an experienced trail guide was needed had been resolved by the gold rush period. In the early 1840s, however, the outfitting posts had been the scene of numerous bargains between seasoned trail followers—mostly former mountain men—and novice overlanders anxious to provide themselves with some guarantees that they would find their way safely to their far western destinations. Prior to 1840 the few traveling overland to the Pacific Coast who were not themselves trappers and traders always aligned themselves for all or most of the way with mountain men and other fur-trade personnel. The one exception had been Thomas J. Farnham's Peoria company of 1839, which had traveled independently. All the westbound missionaries, however, traveled under the protective umbrellas of fur-trade caravans.[101]

The early overland wagon trains prudently endeavored to follow this precedent. The first family of declared emigrants for Oregon, the Joel P. Walkers, traveling in conjunction with three missionary couples, trailed to

"Emigrants Crossing the Plains," by F. O. C. Darley. The many virtues of the ox made it the overwhelming favorite as a draft animal.

the Green River rendezvous in 1840 with an American Fur Company caravan. At the Green River the Oregonians enlisted the services of Robert Newell and several other mountain men to pilot them to Fort Hall, where they abandoned their wagons.[102] In 1841 the first overland emigrant train, usually known as the Bidwell-Bartleson company, headed west. Having absolutely no knowledge of the route, they were extremely fortunate to join a Jesuit missionary party piloted by experienced mountaineer Thomas Fitzpatrick. Reaching the Fort Hall region safely in this group, the small California contingent was thereafter largely on its own.[103] Newly appointed Oregon Indian subagent Elijah White initially captained the 1842 Oregon-bound caravan which hired James Coates as guide, he having once traveled as far west as the Green River. Also along was mountaineer Stephen H. L. Meek, who would do some piloting; Thomas Fitzpatrick was hired en route. Andrew Sublette, whom White had first engaged as pilot in St. Louis, quit after taking the large motley group to their camp near Independence, despairing of ever preserving order and discipline.[104]

The famous 1843 emigration, by far the largest to that date, contracted with experienced fur trader John Gantt to guide them to Fort Hall for $1 per person. Since Gantt's knowledge of the country ended there, Dr. Marcus Whitman was also given at least $80 to guide the group beyond Fort Hall.[105] Moses "Black" Harris was hired as guide by Nathaniel Ford's Oregon-bound party in 1844, one of the largest of the year; Andrew Sublette was apparently similarly employed by the Cornelius Gilliam party; and Caleb Greenwood was employed to pilot the Stevens-Murphy party of that year as far toward California as he knew the trail—at least to South Pass but presumably to Fort Hall.[106]

By 1845 the felt need for pilots was beginning to diminish. There were, however, two mountaineer candidates for the main overland group rendezvousing at Independence: T. M. Adams and Stephen H. L. Meek. Adams's demand, $500 in advance, was too steep for the parsimonious overlanders, especially when the impeccably qualified Meek asked only $250 to pilot them to Fort Vancouver. Meek was the guide chosen.[107] At least two companies departing from St. Joseph hired John Clark to guide them to where the trails leading from St. Joseph and Independence merged. The fee agreed upon was twenty-five cents per wagon.[108] In 1846 there was virtually no interest in hiring guides. By now the trails were clearly visible, informative letters from previous overlanders had been published and otherwise widely circulated, and guidebooks were also available. Many emigrants that year carried Lansford Hastings's volume. Moreover, a number of Oregon emigrants suspected that a "spirancy of the Pilots," as Elijah Bristow phrased the vested-interest accusation, was responsible for many rumors about hostile Indians and the difficulty of an overland trip. An 1842 Oregon emigrant, Hugh Burns, in an 1844 letter from Oregon which was published on the Missouri frontier, similarly charged, "All this bugbear about Indians is got up by mountain men who are in the States, and want to get back to Oregon or the mountains, and get paid for it."[109]

Another important reason for the demise of guide services began to be clearly evident with the 1847 emigration. Many individuals in that year's caravan were making their second overland trip and were well enough qualified to serve as both guides and leaders. From St. Joseph, for example, William Vaughan and Joel Palmer led companies. Both had gone overland in 1845 and returned east by land in 1846. J. M. Shively, who had gone overland to Oregon in 1843, returned by land in 1845, and published a guidebook in 1846, led a company from Independence. So did William Wiggins and Charles Hopper, both with previous plains experience.[110] By 1848 even more former overlanders were sprinkled throughout the various westbound companies. Joseph Chiles was undoubtedly the most experienced, having previously traveled overland to California in 1841 and 1843 and returned overland to Missouri in 1842 and 1847.[111]

By 1849 trail guides were clearly superfluous, although many greenhorn forty-niners employed mountaineers just the same, finding them helpful in teaching trail savvy and imparting discipline.[112] But during the 1850s there simply were too many experienced overland travelers, in addition to a host of guidebooks and well-established trails, for overlanders to employ mountain man guides. During the early 1840s, however, trail guides had rendered valuable services which contributed to the success of overland travel.

For those who regarded a proper outfit, a guide, or a guidebook as insufficient safeguards against the travails of an overland journey, the outfitting posts also presented a final opportunity for purchasing "protection" in the form of life insurance policies. William Gill, for example, writing from Lexington, Missouri, in March, 1850, informed his wife that he and a colleague were outfitting jointly: "We have had our lives insured at twenty-five hundred dollars apiece; if we die, you will receive one-half of the insurance money."[113]

Numerous overlanders, with decisions about means of conveyance, guides, and insurance long since made, reached the outfitting posts so well prepared that there was no need to stop—except to mail a last letter home. Such travelers jumped off on their journey the same day. But most overlanders stayed at least long enough to develop and record impressions of the various towns and the hundreds or thousands of emigrants temporarily congregating there.

The amount of time spent in the jumping-off places was dependent on climatic conditions, motivation, and extent of prior preparation. If the spring was late and the prairie grasses still too short to sustain forage, as was the case in 1849, a longer than anticipated wait ensued. Men impatient to begin their quest for quick riches also tended to arrive earlier and were less prepared than families moving west to settle permanently. These factors, plus the enormity of numbers involved, combined to make the average overlander's stay considerably longer during the gold rush than was the pattern during the early 1840s and the later 1850s. The typical forty-niner remained in and around one or more jumping-off points about fifteen days. The following year gold rushers lingered, on the average, four days less, and by 1852 the average time spent in the jumping-off points was down to nine days.[114] Spending a month or more at an outfitting post was not uncommon. One 1850 overlander, John T. Williams, although he reached St. Joseph on March 26, did not cross the Missouri River until May 17, fifty-three days later.[115]

Since the main activity for many overlanders was the completion of their traveling outfit, they naturally recorded their reactions to the merchants with whom they dealt. All that 1846 emigrant Jessy Thornton meant to convey when he termed Independence "a great Babel upon the border of the wilderness" cannot be divined, but in general, pre–1849 overlanders did not express negative attitudes toward local entrepreneurs. Gold rushers were much less favorably impressed with outfitting-point business ethics. Many gold seekers were convinced that the merchants were conspiring against them in an attempt to realize a life's fortune in a single year—precisely what the gold rushers themselves had in mind.[116] Several overlanders protested what William Rothwell termed "a general system of extortion": a fixed policy aimed at fleecing overland travelers during what was presumed to be the one time in their life when they would visit the outfitting town.[117] Edwin G. Hall charged that Independence merchants had one set of prices for gold seekers and another, much lower rate for local citizens. Forty-niner William Lorton, who outfitted in St. Joseph, agreed, suggesting that Californians were assessed prices 100 percent higher than those paid by area residents.[118] As late as 1853 emigrants were still complaining that St. Joseph merchants were trying to take advantage of them.[119]

Of course, not all gold rushers viewed the outfitting-post merchants as harshly as Rothwell, who explained that "what I hate in them is a low, trickish, cunning, Jewish disposition."[120] William Stackpole, by contrast, found that in St. Joseph the overlander could procure "*everything* that he needs for the trip at a fair price."[121] Another forty-niner outfitting in St. Joseph termed all prices "cheap," and J. S. Shepherd in 1850 lamented his mistake in purchasing supplies at St. Louis when "comparatively low prices" prevailed in St. Joseph. Shepherd predicted that overlanders could save considerably by buying their complete outfit in St. Joseph and "starting from home with empty wagons."[122]

One reason not all gold rushers carped about inflated prices was because prices did not remain constant during the peak March-May outfit-

An 1853 view of St. Joseph, Mo., which successfully competed with Independence as a principal jumping-off place.

ting season. The price of oxen in Independence offers an instructive example. Over the years prices had been slowly climbing: in 1846 a yoke brought $25, the following year the prevailing range was between $30 and $40. By mid-March, 1849, a yoke of oxen was worth $40; at the end of the month the price apparently peaked within a quoted range of $55 to $65. On April 5 overlanders could expect to pay $50 to $65 per yoke, on the 20th between $45 and $55, and a month later, in late May, prices had increased slightly to range between $45 and $60.[123] A similarly oscillating pattern obtained with the price of mules in Independence, and presumably with foodstuffs and other supplies as well.

Although hard-pressed overlanders believed merchant greed to be the crux of the problem, much of the price fluctuation could be explained by the availability of supplies. The unprecedented numbers of gold rushers thronging the jumping-off places strained supply stocks and drove prices up. During mid-May, 1849, for example, it was reported that the supply of oxen in Independence was completely exhausted.[124] Outfitting in the Missouri River towns was big business. In 1844 a reported $50,000 worth of business had been done in Independence by the overlanders; in 1849 it was estimated that the gold rushers left behind them in that city alone $150,00c—and Independence was not even the pre-eminent outfitting point.[125]

During the peak gold rush years some overlanders outfitted by buying animals, wagons, and supplies at street auctions in the outfitting posts. Significant numbers of would-be gold seekers decided, after seeing the multitudes of competitors and hearing the rumors about grass, Indians, and mountain snows, that they had made a mistake. The ringing of bells announced these bargain-filled auctions, as men now eager to return home endeavored to recoup at least enough of their considerable financial outlay to finance their trip eastward. In Kanesville in early May, 1850, Jerome Dutton witnessed five or six auctions under way at the same time. Not all overlanders turned back voluntarily; due to extravagant purchases, and sometimes to gambling losses, outfits seized by local law officers were also sold at auction.[126]

A few of the auctions were necessitated by the handiwork of the many thieves and desperadoes frequenting the outfitting posts.[127] Observing that there were "thieves enough to steal a man blind" in St. Joseph in 1849, Lucius Fairchild reported one of their brutal crimes. Two overlanders were cutting wood for ox bows in broad daylight only a quarter of a mile from town. When they were momentarily separated one was attacked by two criminals, beaten senseless, and robbed of $55.[128] Another overlander, supposedly robbed for his money, was found three-quarters of a mile from St. Joseph with his throat slit.[129] From Kanesville similar incidents of theft and murder were reported with regularity, tinged occasionally with traces of anti-Mormon prejudice.[130]

Most of the overlanders camped out near the jumping-off places to acquire or refine their camping skills and to train—if possible—their recently purchased animals for yoke or pack. Many overlanders, seeking to prolong the comforts of civilization as long as possible, jammed the hotels and sought accommodations with townspeople. Sometimes messmates joined to secure lodging for a colleague who was dangerously ill.[131] With thousands of overlanders milling about the streets, and campsites spreading out in every direction, it could be maddening to try to find friends during the height of the gold rush. In late April, 1849, emigrant tents reportedly covered a three-square-mile area surrounding Independence. At approximately the same time, forty-niner Henry Tappan scoured St. Joseph for four days before he located his partners, who had preceded him to the city.[132] Since St. Joseph's 1849 population was reported to be approximately 1,800, it is evident that the permanent citizenry was literally engulfed during the outfitting season.[133]

None of the Missouri River outfitting towns was very large. Independence, supposedly named after Andrew Jackson's chief characteristic, numbered 742 residents in 1844; by 1849 its population was variously reported at from 1,500 to 2,000, and the 1860 census counted 3,164.[134] St. Joseph, which supplanted Independence as the principal jumping-off point, had 682 inhabitants in 1845, approximately 1,500 by 1848, something over 3,000 in the early 1850s, and 8,932 by 1860.[135] Westport–Kansas City, which also launched considerable numbers of gold rushers, numbered fewer than 1,000 citizens before the mid-1850s. According to the 1860 census Westport numbered 1,195 and Kansas City 4,418.[136] The population of Weston, Missouri, declined from 1,915 in 1850 to 1,816 in 1860, even though it had reportedly doubled in size during the mid-1850s.[137] The Kanesville/Council Bluffs population also vacillated considerably due to the fact that it had begun as a Mormon way station on the emigration route to the Salt Lake Valley. Most of the remaining Mormons departed for Salt Lake by 1852, after which the town composition became predominantly Gentile. The following year the name was legally changed to Council Bluffs, and by 1860 it had a population of 2,011. During the late 1850s the town of Omaha began to develop across the river from Council Bluffs. By 1860 its population was 1,883.[138]

Despite their relatively small size, these Missouri River frontier towns were crucial to the overland emigration experience. As staging areas, centers of supply, and sources of information, they served both greenhorns and seasoned travelers. Most overlanders filled their days and nights with frenzied activity: seeking out bargains at street auctions, organizing traveling companies, drawing up constitutions, electing officers, writing letters home, warding off criminals and confidence men, visiting the many taverns and grogshops, and getting too little sleep as they pondered whether the motivations impelling them westward were worth

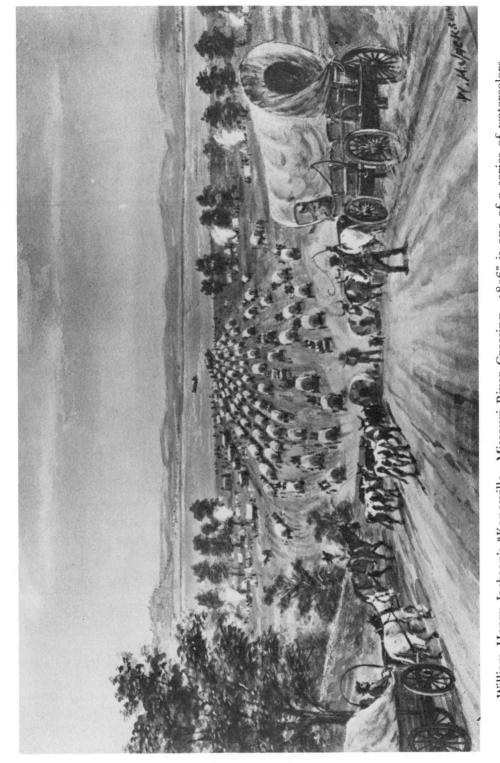

William Henry Jackson's "Kanesville—Missouri River Crossing—1856" is one of a series of watercolors painted in the 1920s and '30s from sketches made when the artist crossed the plains in 1866.

braving all that the rumormongers claimed lay ahead. Greenhorn travelers also experimented—humorously and sometimes painfully—with yoking oxen, packing mules, and cooking over campfires. The art of driving a prairie schooner was not easily learned—wagons overturned easily and wagon tongues were fragile. Even traveling in the right direction did not come automatically. The combination of inexperienced drivers and untrained animals produced resounding collisions with trees and other novice teamsters.[139]

For most overlanders the jumping-off points symbolized an ending and a beginning. The days or weeks spent in these little river towns were savored as the last chance to enjoy "civilization," for looming ahead was the fabled American "wilderness." Westward lay a new start in the paradises of the Pacific Coast. Exuberant emigrants recognized that they were on the brink of a supreme adventure. Most would have agreed with the sentiments forty-niner Wilhelm Hoffman inscribed in his diary at St. Joseph: "In short, it was a great life. . . . It was life as at a fair."[140]

CHAPTER FOUR

Emigrant Interaction

"Our journey has not been as solitary as we feared"

THROUGHOUT THE 1830S SUPPLY CARAVANS related to the flourishing Rocky Mountain fur trade routinely traveled the Platte River road. The advent of Methodist and Presbyterian missionaries in the mid-1830s slowly altered this pattern of fur-trade and hunting expeditions. In 1834 Jason and Daniel Lee, Cyrus Shepard, Philip L. Edwards, and Courtney M. Walker trekked overland to Oregon with a party of fur traders. The next year Samuel Parker and Marcus Whitman inaugurated the Presbyterian missionary effort, with Whitman returning to recruit additional faithful workers after going partway. In 1836 Whitman, with his new bride, Narcissa, H. H. Spalding with his recent bride, Eliza, and W. H. Gray crossed the continent, again under the aegis of a fur-trade caravan. In 1838 the Reverend Gray, with a new bride, went west again, as did three more Oregon missionary couples. Cornelius Rogers, resisting the trend, traveled as a bachelor. The following year two additional couples, the John S. Griffins and Asahel Mungers, accompanied a fur-trade caravan to the Green River rendezvous, from where they followed the increasingly clear trace to Oregon.[1]

Therefore, when Joel Walker took his family overland to Oregon in 1840 in company with yet three more missionary couples, traveling under the protection of the usual fur-trade caravan, he did not seem to be instituting anything new. But once an avowed emigrant had gone, others quickly followed; historians now cite the Walker trip as the beginning of the overland emigration era.[2] The very next year the California-bound Bidwell-Bartleson party became the first emigrant train to travel without experienced rendezvous-bound mountaineers for protection. That small emigrant covered-wagon caravan, accompanied by the Jesuit missionary party of Father Pierre-Jean De Smet, signaled the end of the fur-trade era.

The rapidity with which change now came to the West was illustrated only nine years later, when startled Indians began to speak of emigrating eastward, unable to believe that many whites remained east of the Missouri River.[3] For in the twenty years between the time Joel Walker set his face toward Oregon and Abraham Lincoln was elected President, approximately a quarter of a million overlanders had worn the trails to Oregon and California so deeply that in places the ruts are still visible. In that same period over 40,000 Latter-Day Saints traveled portions of those same trails to their Salt Lake Valley refuge, and by 1860 thousands of expectant gold seekers were penetrating the Pike's Peak region. The magnitude and pattern of this westbound population movement are depicted in Tables 1 and 2. These tables graphically express the enormous South Pass trail traffic engendered by the California gold rush. Throughout the decade of the 1850s this overland movement continued, despite increasing Indian hostility, dwarfing, at least in numbers, the overlanders of the preceding decade.[4]

TABLE 1
OVERLAND EMIGRATION TO OREGON, CALIFORNIA, UTAH, 1840–48

Year	Oregon	California	Yearly West Coast Total	Cumulative West Coast Total	Utah	Cumulative Grand Total
1840	13	—	13	13	—	13
1841	24	34	58	71	—	71
1842	125	—	125	196	—	196
1843	875	38	913	1,109	—	1,109
1844	1,475	53	1,528	2,637	—	2,637
1845	2,500	260	2,760	5,397	—	5,397
1846	1,200	1,500	2,700	8,097	—	8,097
1847	4,000	450	4,450	12,547	2,200	14,747
1848	1,300	400	1,700	14,247	2,400	18,847
Pre–gold rush subtotals	11,512	2,735	14,247	14,247	4,600	18,847

These masses of westering overlanders do not coincide with the popular media image of widely scattered wagon trains traveling in relative isolation. Indeed, particularly between 1849 and 1853, most overlanders longed for privacy instead of the congested trails, crowded campsites, and overgrazed grasses they were experiencing. So many overlanders, for example, set forth from near St. Joseph on the same day in 1852 that teams traveled twelve abreast. Franklin Langworthy reported in 1850, from near South Pass, "The road, from morning till night, is crowded like Pearl Streat or Broadway," noting also that fathers had actually become separated from their sons in the "endless throng" and did not meet again until their arrival in California.[5] Bennett C. Clark's company, in 1849, traveled late into the night near Ash Hollow in a desperate search for a vacant campsite.[6]

TABLE 2
OVERLAND EMIGRATION TO OREGON, CALIFORNIA, UTAH, 1849–60

Year	Oregon	California	Cumulative Yearly West Coast Total	West Coast Total	Utah	Cumulative Grand Total
1849	450	25,000	25,450	39,697	1,500	45,797
1850	6,000	44,000	50,000	89,697	2,500	98,297
1851	3,600	1,100	4,700	94,397	1,500	104,497
1852	10,000	50,000	60,000	154,397	10,000	174,497
1853	7,500	20,000	27,500	181,897	8,000	209,997
1854	6,000	12,000	18,000	199,897	3,167	231,164
1855	500	1,500	2,000	201,897	4,684	237,848
1856	1,000	8,000	9,000	210,897	2,400	249,248
1857	1,500	4,000	5,500	216,397	1,300	256,048
1858	1,500	6,000	7,500	223,897	150	263,698
1859	2,000	17,000	19,000	242,897	1,431	284,129
1860	1,500	9,000	10,500	253,397	1,630	296,259
Grand totals, 1840–60	53,062	200,335	253,397	253,397	42,862	296,259

Statistically inclined emigrants kept track of trail traffic during noon stops, on rare rest days, early in the mornings, and on particularly dusty days. James B. Persinger reported that their company passed 200 wagons early one 1850 morning, were passed by 100 another noon, and passed at least 500 more another day. Joseph Price wrote to his wife from Pacific Springs the same year that the 160 wagons which passed that point on June 27 was a smaller number than usual, a statement to which Reuben Knox's observations lend credence. Knox, writing from near Fort Kearny, reported that 1,000 wagons passed on the last day of May, 1850. On a Sabbath spent resting, one man in Knox's train noted that over 500 wagons trailed past their campsite. James Shields, in the vanguard of the 1850 emigration, climbed Independence Rock early in June and counted 150 wagons in view. Hugh A. Skinner, also in 1850, noticed 50 wagons in the water at the same time crossing the South Fork of the Platte River.[7]

The accuracy of these observations is borne out by a daily analysis of the numbers of men and wagons passing the Fort Laramie station, where the army endeavored to maintain an exact count of westbound travelers. Table 3 demonstrates that during the height of the 1850 emigration it was not unusual for several thousand overlanders to pass the fort on a single day.[8] Such congested trail conditions occasioned frequent comments, such as "we are not at all lonesome" and "there is no lack of company."[9] Indeed, several gold rushers found it so extraordinary when they were able to travel and camp out of sight of other wagons—generally in the later stages of the journey after the migration wave had partially spread out—that they recorded the strange phenomenon in their diaries.[10]

William Henry Jackson, "South Pass." Wagons are here shown traveling three or four abreast, and congestion on the trail could be even heavier, according to emigrant accounts.

Utah State Historical Society

TABLE 3
RECONSTRUCTED FORT LARAMIE EMIGRANT REGISTER, 1850

Date		Men	Wagons	Date		Men	Wagons
May	14	950	215	June	14	23,293	6,345
	22	2,897	845		16	24,930	6,817
	26	5,421	1,509		17	30,964	7,113
	27	5,860	1,630		19	32,037	7,463
	29	6,582	1,849		20	32,740	7,586
	31	8,352	2,266		21	32,760	7,586
June	2	9,972	2,797		22	34,376	8,056
	3	11,443	3,188	July	1	36,615	8,773
	5	12,270	3,436		4	37,171	8,994
	6	14,288	3,986		5	37,171	8,998
	10	16,915	4,672		8	37,570	9,101
	12	18,790	5,122	Aug.	14	39,506	9,927
	13	20,000	5,331				

Not anticipating this trail congestion, emigrants during the gold rush consciously endeavored to travel in companies, formally or informally organized, just as they had in previous years when the trails had not been so crowded. The emigrant goal was always to insure that sufficient manpower would be available for whatever contingencies might arise: bridging or fording a stream, climbing a mountain, rounding up stampeded stock, resisting Indian attack. This vast armada of overlanders swarming together along the trails, especially during the gold rush, often created friction; tempers periodically flared as drivers jockeyed for position on the dusty main trail, and on occasion one traveling company passed another only after an actual race.[11]

Such frustrations, however, were much overshadowed by the omnipresent emigrant interaction, which contributed so significantly to the success of the overland migrations. It is this cooperative quality of the migrations which scholars have so largely overlooked. Two neglected phases of emigrant interchange revolve around travelers who began the westbound journey only to turn back, and overlanders who traveled the trails eastward from the Pacific Coast to the Missouri and Iowa frontiers. For many westbound emigrants, the significant exchanges deriving from interaction with west-to-east trail travelers proved an unexpected bonus.

Although most of the turn-arounds were products of the gold rush years, a few overlanders had reconsidered the wisdom of their proposed venture ever since the overland movement had begun. In 1841, in fact, nearly 10 percent of the departing caravan of California- and Oregon-bound overlanders, Jesuit missionaries heading for the Flathead Indian territory, and other tourists and trappers made their way back to the Missouri settlements. Some had gone as far as the Green River—halfway to

California—before becoming discouraged. Although no subsequent year matched this high percentage of returnees, disconsolate "gobacks" remained a permanent feature of the overland emigrations.[12] In 1842 an Oregon overlander and his sick wife turned back after their baby daughter died. The following year from five to eight overlanders similarly retraced their steps. In 1845 thirteen men had second thoughts; only nine remained with Lansford Hastings on his foolhardy but successful late-season crossing to California. And in 1846 about twenty emigrants returned after Indians had stolen most of their cattle and killed two of their number. At least two other families turned back following deaths in 1846, and one homesick young man pilfered a horse and headed for the settlements.[13]

In these early years, when most of the emigrant companies were bunched closely together and were well prepared, turn-arounds provided little assistance to their more fortunate or more courageous colleagues other than by carrying letters back to Missouri. Much more interaction between westbound overlanders and returnees prevailed during the gold rush, although since the "gobacks" were notorious rumor-spreaders not all of it was useful. Returnees tended to magnify the incidence of cholera fatalities, the insufficiency of grass, or the Indian threat, and frequently encouraged those they met also to turn around and retrace their steps. Apparently their blandishments occasionally met with success. John Wood, for example, was told by a large group of 1850 turn-arounds that his company could "never . . . get through, because there is no grass ahead, and the cholera is getting worse."[14] To companies who had already buried several overlanders, such assertions could prove persuasive enough to produce additional turn-arounds.[15]

Frontier newspaper editors repeatedly cautioned readers that returnee rumors should be taken "with several grains of allowance," since the turn-arounds were most probably attempting to justify their own conduct. The editors pointed out that letters received from overlanders still pursuing the journey—letters which had often been carried by the "gobacks"—revealed that conditions were not nearly as disastrous as the returnees claimed.[16] Major Osborne Cross, traveling to Fort Kearny to catch up with the Oregon-bound Mounted Riflemen in 1849, also suggested that some of the stories he heard about Indian thefts were contrived excuses of men now forced to retrace their steps due to their own carelessness and neglect.[17]

Many returning overlanders needed neither rationalizations nor exaggerated difficulties to justify their actions. For some there had been no alternative. One Ohio company in 1849 lost over thirty cattle in a stampede, and five sorrowful men, unable to purchase replacements, returned. A similar occurrence in 1851 forced the return of the owners of at least ten wagons of a seventeen-wagon train. A company of Irish argonauts, robbed

123

of everything by Indians near Fort Kearny, returned in 1852. So did an 1853 company, only barely under way, after its leader drowned in the Elkhorn River.[18]

Then there was the cholera. One 1850 turn-around, the only surviving member of his entire company, prudently decided to tempt fate no further. The three survivors of a cholera-ravaged seventeen-man group who retraced their steps in 1852 concurred. Ezra Meeker later recalled meeting a train of eleven returning wagons in 1852, all driven by women. Not a single male remained alive in the entire train.[19] Another 1852 company, initially numbering seventy-two men, began to backtrack after more than a third of their number died, but had barely enough men physically capable of driving their teams. The same year a woman—who had probably gone as far west as any turn-around ever did—decided to return after burying her husband beyond Salt Lake City. She had previously watched one of her children die along the Platte River.[20] Others returned because of physical injury, company quarrels, or homesickness. John Edwin Banks was told by one returning forty-niner that he "has money enough; loves his wife more than gold."[21]

Though rumor-spreaders were numerous, many turn-arounds did give clear and unexaggerated information about conditions ahead. Since many of them had gone at least as far as Fort Kearny, and some to Fort Laramie and even beyond, their knowledge and advice were helpful to those pressing on. Indeed, the oncoming hordes so desired information—even if it was slightly exaggerated—that they pestered all returnees they met, unless there was serious sickness among them. A few such harried turn-arounds finally refused to answer any questions, and others even turned off the road to avoid westering overlanders and their never-ending queries, to say nothing of their annoying taunts about whether the returnees had "seen the Elephant."[22]

Through information and mail service (one "goback" forty-niner brought back several letters), the turn-arounds provided their major assistance. But numbers of westbound overlanders who had suffered losses or had discovered outfitting errors or omissions were also much aided by this unexpected opportunity to purchase draft animals, wagons, tents, provisions, and other needed materials, since turn-arounds were usually willing to part with much of their outfit which they would not now be needing. On the other hand, a few returnees, having lost their draft animals, were forced to rely completely upon the charity of westbound emigrants in order to return to the frontier settlements.[23] It is difficult to estimate the actual numbers of overlanders who retraced their steps, but in 1849, 1850, and 1852 there were certainly hundreds, and the yearly total probably approached and may even have surpassed 1,000 in 1850 and 1852.[24]

Hasty conversations on the trail or at noon and evening encampments with eastbound overlanders direct from Oregon or California provided

"Seeing the elephant," a euphemism for the overland experience, was given literal
treatment in this illustration from a gold rush lettersheet. California Historical Society

the most helpful and reliable sources of information to westbound emigrants. Such returning travelers were able to provide accurate—and sometimes disheartening—data on how far it really was to the mines, rumors notwithstanding, and whether the Indians evidenced hostile or friendly intentions. They also furnished advice regarding the various cutoffs, the availability of supplies at forts and trading posts, the presence of ferries at the various river crossings, the prices being charged there, and the location of buffalo herds. On occasion these eastbound parties also served as escorts for turn-arounds.[25]

In the 1840s, before other postal services became available, eastbound overlanders were especially useful as letter carriers. They often stopped for a short time to enable emigrants to pen quick missives to be mailed at the jumping-off points, where newspaper editors frequently reported how many letters had been deposited by recent arrivals from Oregon and California. Dr. Elijah White, for example, brought 541 letters with him in 1845. The following year Wales Bonney carried 125 letters, and Spencer Bulkley reportedly had 840 letters in his possession when he reached St. Joseph.[26] In 1843 and 1845 eastbound overlanders brought letters from Oregonians to specific individuals in the oncoming migration, letters which doubtless contained instructions for the latter portion of the journey. In 1845 a small twelve-man eastbound company even publicly read for the benefit of all the Oregon-bound emigrants some of the letters they were carrying.[27]

Another way in which eastbound overlanders aided in transmitting information was through the Pacific Coast newspapers they made available to westering emigrants. In 1847 and 1848 some of these newspapers contained route information specifically directed to westbound overlanders. In 1852 eastbound travelers sold newspapers—for fifty cents apiece—containing names and addresses of California miners.[28] But probably even more significant to westbound overlanders was the emotional and psychological boost they received when eastbound travelers exhibited gold dust or told stories about the fertile fields of Oregon. Especially encouraging were those who indicated that they were on their way home to bring back their own families; what further proof could anyone need that utopia was just across the mountains, and that those mountains could be crossed?

Because west-to-east travelers were able to answer questions on the two matters of most interest and concern to overland emigrants—conditions on the trail and in California and Oregon—they were plied with questions by oncoming overlanders even more persistently than were the turn-arounds. And since eastbound travelers encountered almost the entire westbound migration this could become extremely frustrating, especially in years when 50,000 overlanders were trailing west. One 1850 party simply kept their mules going at a rapid pace, never stopping to entertain the "hundreds" of queries with which they were peppered, although they did shout back answers until they could no longer be heard. Richard Keen assumed that the "hard looking Customers" in 1852 who refused to answer any of his group's questions were simply tired of being interrogated.[29] In fact, a number of westbound overlanders commented upon the rough, rude, and dangerous appearance of the generally heavily armed eastbound travelers. Francis Parkman described one such Oregonian as "vulgar-looking"; Edwin Bryant, also in 1846, suggested that a small party from Oregon looked "like savages"; Mrs. Benjamin Ferris in 1852 thought the Oregonians she met to have a "dashing look of defiance" about them. She and Bryant both acknowledged, however, that their own appearances were probably not very different.[30]

There was cause for eastbound overlanders being circumspect, especially those coming from California with gold dust in their possession. Enoch Conyers, while riding some distance from the main trail in 1852, encountered a solitary eastbound traveler encamped for the night. Upon first questioning, the man claimed to be a discouraged turn-around. When Conyers recognized him as his uncle, however, the solitary traveler admitted to be returning from California with considerable gold in his possession. He explained that he frequently camped far from the main trail and if seen claimed to be a turn-around. He had adopted this strategy because he feared robbers—especially "white Indians"—although he had barely survived a harrowing attack from real Indians shortly after crossing the Sierra Nevada Mountains.[31]

Conyers's uncle had been more fortunate than a number of eastbound overlanders who fell victim to Indians and "highwaymen." Johannes Dyck and two companions began their return journey from California in, apparently, 1853, with considerable quantities of gold dust. Dyck, thanks to a fast horse, escaped an Indian attack, but his two companions were not so lucky, and all the gold they had been carrying was lost. Dyck accordingly returned to California to begin digging anew.[32] A particularly dangerous year for eastbound travelers was 1856, when the bodies of at least eight returning Californians were found along the Humboldt River after apparent robbery-murders. One, a woman, was known to have had at least $6,000 in gold coin with her, and traders subsequently reported that area Indians suddenly possessed considerable coin and dust. Also in 1856 Mormon handcart emigrants provided assistance to a Californian who had been robbed of all he had by the members of the company with whom he was returning to the eastern states.[33]

Eastbound overlanders were especially lucrative targets for robberies because of the chance that they had considerable gold in their possession. Aside from this special factor, however, their trail experiences paralleled those of the westbound emigrants. The threat of Indian depredations was present along the entire trail, but only rarely were fatalities recorded.

127

Indians were presumably responsible for the death of an 1850 eastbound traveler who was shot with an arrow while standing guard duty along the Humboldt River. Another eastbound group, which made an 1851 west-to-east crossing in sixty-two days, fought five skirmishes with Indians, during one of which a member of their traveling party was killed. In 1853 two men returning from Oregon killed between one and eight Indians who had been harassing them and then quickly joined a larger eastbound party for protection.[34]

Two years later Indians stole a horse along the Humboldt River from an eight-man eastbound company who pursued and killed most of the thieves, appropriating three Indian horses in the process. Also that same year, eastbound overlanders had eight mules stolen near Fort Laramie, while a thirty-two-man group returning from California pursued an Indian who had stolen one of their mules, and on catching the culprit, dispatched him with a fusillade of fourteen bullets. In 1856, near Fort Kearny, Cheyenne Indians killed the wife and child of W. Schoekendick, an eastbound overlander, as well as another man of the company, and stole most of their mules.[35] Brigham Young complained to the Commissioner of Indian Affairs in the fall of 1857 that incidents concerning eastbound travelers were having an unfortunate impact on the safety of overland travel. Writing that a large group of eastbound Californians in the spring of that year had shot at every Indian they saw, Young noted that Indians had begun retaliating in like manner on the westbound overlanders. This explained, Young thought, the many additional depredations of that year.[36]

While fatalities for eastbound travelers were almost exclusively confined to the mid and late 1850s, Indian thievery occurred with regularity throughout the migration period. Dr. Elijah White and his three eastbound companions were captured by Pawnee Indians east of Fort Laramie in late October, 1845. Stripped of some of their clothing, they were bound and beaten before being released minus most of their possessions, including a few of the letters White was carrying east. Wales Bonney, who daringly traveled alone much of the way from Oregon in 1846, was robbed by Sioux Indians of almost all he possessed, and had to be assisted by another eastbound group. In 1847 Pawnee Indians demanded and received various "presents" from an Oregon party, while in 1851 a small California group was similarly forced to divide their provisions with a large band of Pawnees.[37] Indians exacted such "tolls" fairly frequently from overlanders traveling in both directions on the trails.

Eastbound overlanders, just like their westering counterparts, always feared Indians the most, but found that other difficulties occurred more often. When provisions ran low, replenishments could usually be secured from westbound emigrants.[38] There is no evidence that disease was as common or as deadly among the eastbound overlanders, but there remained other sources of injury and death: accidental discharge of the many firearms being carried, falling off mules or horses, crossing dangerous rivers and streams. Since most eastbound travelers were crossing the plains for at least the second time, however, they had sufficient trail savvy to avoid many of the misfortunes so frequent among inexperienced westbound overlanders.

Even previous plains experience, though, was insufficient to prevent attrition among traveling parties; the composition of eastbound overland groups fluctuated almost as much as did that of westbound companies. In 1845, for example, William Winter departed from California in a fifteen-man company. Overton Johnson left Oregon in a twelve-man party, which joined a Hudson's Bay Company group for the trip to Fort Boise. Near Fort Hall, where the two eastbound groups united, two Oregonians chose to remain behind. Adding an additional traveler, the combined party now numbered twenty-six men. That total began diminishing near the Green River, when some felt they could travel faster and pushed ahead. At Fort Laramie the seventeen still traveling together were further reduced when ten men deemed it advisable to rest at the fort before continuing on. Thus only seven remained together until they reached the frontier settlements.[39] One reason it is so difficult to determine how many overlanders traveled the west-to-east route is because the various individuals involved periodically split up, combined, and recombined.[40] Even romance was a factor in eastbound attrition. One of the men returning from Oregon with Joel Palmer in the spring of 1846 was so captivated by a young woman who had wintered at The Dalles with her parents and was now finishing the trip to the Willamette Valley that the smitten youth backtracked with her to the Oregon settlements.[41]

Eastbound overland travel had its own distinctive pattern. There were relatively few women or children who made the trip, presumably because the venture was invariably made with pack mules and pack horses rather than with the traditional covered wagon. While not many women returned overland to the Missouri settlements, some of those who did shocked the sensibilities of conservative westbound overlanders by their practical riding styles. Loren Hastings phrased his reaction this way in 1847: "This day met a returning Co. from Oregon. In the Co. was a Man & his wife & family; they were going back to Adams County, Ill. The woman rode with one foot on one side of her pony & the other foot on the other side. This is the greatest curiosity I have ever seen yet, it knocks everything else into the shade."[42]

Wagons do not seem to have been used by eastbound overlanders before the early 1850s, as one of the earliest references to this development appeared in 1852, when a group of Oregonians eastbound to Iowa were reported to be using one wagon. By 1855 enough eastbound overlanders were traveling with wagons for a San Francisco newspaper editor to comment that only a few years previously such an event had been considered unthinkable. In 1857, too, California-bound overlanders reported seeing five or six eastbound covered wagons.[43]

Additionally, eastbound parties tended to be quite small. There are virtually no references in contemporary documents to more than fifty persons comprising any single traveling group.[44] Returning overlanders generally traveled in parties of less than twenty. Occasionally some bold overlander traveled alone for at least significant portions of the route, as Wales Bonney had done in 1846.

Small eastbound groups made some famous winter crossings. Marcus Whitman's trip east in the winter of 1842–43, much of the way with only one companion, which legend has molded into a heroic venture undertaken to save Oregon for the United States, was concluded in its last stages over the Santa Fe Trail via Bent's Fort. Similar route changes occurred sporadically when eastbound travelers received reports of heavy snows or hostile Indians.[45] Another classic west-to-east late winter crossing was made by former mountain man Joe Meek in 1848. With a small traveling party he carried a memorial from the Oregon legislature to the U.S. Congress requesting protection and other benefits. Meek's group also brought the ominous news that Indians had murdered the Marcus Whitmans and others at their mission. Whitman's 1842–43 crossing had required 136 days, while the Meek party, following the regular Oregon Trail, managed the crossing in only 68.[46]

The number of days required for the crossing varied considerably depending on such factors as the season of the year, the weather, the number of layover days, and the specific route followed. When travelers desired, the trip could be completed with dispatch, and over the years there was a clear reduction in the average number of days required. Most eastbound travelers before the California gold rush consumed at least eighty or more days on the trip, and frequently well over a hundred days were spent en route. During the 1850s, however, trail improvements and easier availability of provisions at trading posts and settlements reduced the average travel time to approximately sixty or seventy days. Occasionally, crossings were completed in less than two months. Apparently the speediest eastbound journey on record was made in 1852 by M. L. Chapen, who journeyed alone from Sacramento to Platteville, Missouri, in thirty-two and a half traveling days. Chapen, an Illinoisan, had stopped for a few days to rest in Salt Lake City, so his total elapsed time may have approached forty days.[47]

The incidence of eastbound overland travelers was not influenced as significantly by the California gold rush as were the numbers of "gobacks" on the trail; throughout the 1840s westbound overlanders had encountered sizable numbers of west-to-east travelers. Nevertheless, with so many men going temporarily to California to dig gold, there naturally were greater numbers of eastbound overlanders in the 1850s. Although hundreds of persons trailed eastward every year, there doubtless would have been many more had not the only season of the year when the plains could be safely crossed coincided with California's best mining period. Thus, as one California correspondent reported, by the time the winter rains came to the gold regions it was too late to return overland, and many who otherwise would have traveled by land were compelled to return to the eastern states by sea.[48] The climatic factor notwithstanding, in 1851 "hundreds" of Californians were reported beginning preparations for the eastbound overland trip. In 1853 returning Californians predicted that approximately 1,200 overlanders would be making the west-to-east journey that year. Californians also estimated that between 600 and 1,000 travelers were planning to return overland to the older states in 1855. Brigham Young noted that a company of 300 to 400 overlanders had been eastbound on the trails in 1857.[49]

These relatively large numbers of overland travelers who flowed against the grain of westbound emigration each year were neither inconspicuous nor insignificant. Through interaction with their westering counterparts they made a significant contribution to the antebellum westward movement. At the very least they enabled westbound emigrants to share the feelings of companionship and anticipation that George Donner expressed in 1846: "Our journey has not been as solitary as we feared, and we have seen several on their return to the States. Several companies are just ahead."[50]

Although the impact of turn-arounds and eastbound overland travelers upon the overland emigrations was significant, the most important cooperation and interaction obviously prevailed among the much greater number of westbound overlanders. Because attrition, traveling company splits, combinations, and recombinations were so common to the overland emigrating experience, the matter of conveying advice, progress reports, and other newsworthy information to relatives, friends, and former traveling companions was extremely important. The "roadside telegraph" which the overlanders devised was a crude but surprisingly effective means of communication. Anyone wishing to leave a message would write a short note and place it conspicuously alongside the trail so that those following behind would be certain not to pass it by. Occasionally strips of cloth were attached as a kind of signal. The notes were usually of two types, those written on paper and those inscribed on such things as trees, pieces of wood, rocks, and animal bones. The cards and pieces of paper were generally inserted into the notched end of a stick located next to the trail, or attached to trees, bushes, or even grave markers. Other messages were carved into trees, painted on rocks beside the trail, or written, often in pencil, on the skulls and bones of buffalo, cattle, elk, and deer. Even human skulls were used. With surfaces which had been smoothed and whitened by the elements, these skulls and bones were strikingly visible, especially when hung on a stick by the side of the trail. The inscriptions, when not purposely rubbed out, lasted a long time. Lodisa Frizzell in 1852 was still able to read penciled messages written in 1849.[51]

Most overlanders were careful not to disturb these precious sources of information. Messages specifically directed to individual emigrants or particular companies were removed, but most others, after having been studiously read, were not otherwise disturbed.[52] However, a few overlanders tampered with the communications, occasionally to good ends, or so they believed. Forty-niner J. Goldsborough Bruff, for example, remarked that on the Lassen Cutoff, "Some of the travellers, among other rascalities, are in the habit of putting up erroneous notices to mislead and distress others. I had the pleasure of correcting some of these statements, and thereby prevented misfortune." William McBride, in 1850, had not detected similar motivations in the Illinois company which marked out other messages on a human skull so friends could be advised to meet them in Salt Lake City.[53]

Some of the additions and deletions seem to have been prompted by the desire to inject wit and humor into the long journey, and some were irately written in denunciation of the original writers' statements. Ansel McCall found such supplementary attempts at rhymes, contradictions, and dubious statements of fact so common that he dismissed the whole operation as the *lying* journals of the plains."[54] Isaac Lord came upon the misspelled but eloquent retort "You ar a Damdid Lyre" appended to a statement that it was only 140 miles to Sacramento. And Helen Carpenter, after noting the periodic advertisements which Dr. J. Noble had been writing in flamboyant red ink on grave markers along the way, wryly observed that some wag had written under the physician's signature the words "Is a Jack Ass." John Clark even discovered that some overlanders occasionally practiced their marksmanship on the prominently placed informative skulls.[55]

While "Bone Express" messages—as George Currey called them— were found all along the trail, at certain places so many notes accumulated that these locations came to be known as "prairie post offices."[56] There had been one in Ash Hollow, in a mountaineer's crude log cabin, as early as 1846. But it was the California gold rush, with its immense numbers and vacillating travel arrangements, which called forth a host of these rudimentary message exchanges where, as forty-niner O. J. Hall phrased it, "Every man was his own postmaster."[57] Someone even carved the words "Post-office" on a rocky ledge near Courthouse Rock, which was serving this function in 1849, but primarily these primitive post offices were found at trail junctions where the road forked and overlanders had a choice of routes to follow. Thus, in 1849 alone, there were additional message exchanges where the Sublette and Hudspeth cutoffs branched off from the main trail, where the California and Oregon routes diverged, where the road to Salt Lake angled to the southwest, where the Lassen Cutoff launched out into the Sierras, and where the emigrants chose between the Carson and Truckee river routes beyond the Sink of the Humboldt River.[58] Groves of trees along the Nemaha and Blue rivers were likewise covered with names, dates, and messages, as were rocks along the Sweetwater. A similar situation prevailed at many river crossings.[59] Invariably, the communicated message named the company and the date of passing that particular trail point, and, when a choice of routes was possible, which trail had been taken. Those in the rear anxious about the safety of relatives and friends were reassured by such messages. If they were trying to catch up, they knew which route to take and approximately how far behind they were. Some forty-niner outfits also made it a point of pride to reach California before those overlanders who had split off from their original company; the notices kept them apprised of how the race was going.[60]

Especially when the road forked and the overlanders had no assurance of the viability of the new cutoff other than the names of some who had chanced it, the roadside telegraph proved an important factor in the final choice. Wilhelm Hoffman explained why his company had decided to follow the Lassen Cutoff into California in 1849: "One of the companies registered there [at the junction post office] had, we knew, very competent leaders, and that decided us to take this way."[61] A host of forty-niners similarly reported that they were much influenced in their decision to follow the Lassen trail when they learned that such respected leaders as Benoni Hudspeth and John J. Myers had taken the cutoff.[62] Since the Lassen Cutoff proved to be one of the biggest "humbugs" of 1849, this was one instance when it would have been just as well had the overlanders really been traveling in the isolation of popular legend.

The roadside messages frequently communicated advice and information reflective of the cooperative concern most overlanders had for each other's safety and progress. The advice was often especially helpful to the many greenhorn travelers of the gold rush period. For example, forty-niner James Wilkins's outfit gratefully followed the recommendation on a trailside notice for avoiding a twenty-mile desert. The notice, according to Wilkins, had been posted "by a philanthropic Kentuckian" who had backtracked specifically to share his discovery of the alternate route for the benefit of those behind. Alonzo Delano found a signboard beyond Fort Laramie which read, "Look at this—look at this! The water here is poison, and we have lost six of our cattle. Do not let your cattle drink on this bottom." At a poisonous waterhole the next year James Evans commented, "Happy is the man who can read!" after observing a myriad of signs warning against tasting the water in phrases such as "He drank of this water and died" and "For God's sake do not taste this water."[63] In addition to cautioning against bad water and grass, overlanders erected signs directing their comrades to fresh-water springs some distance off the road, or admonishing that this was the last available water or the last good grass before a desert stretch was to be crossed. So-called "cutoffs" which saved neither time nor energy were forcefully denounced.[64] Harriet Ward spoke for many grateful overlanders after following a signpost's directions to reach a refreshingly cool spring some distance off the road in 1853: "Oh! what a pleasure to meet with such little mementoes of disinterested benevolence from strangers!"[65]

A great many roadside communications dealt with Indian depredations, warning oncoming overlanders that losses of stock and human life had occurred at a particular location.[66] Such announcements probably served the dual purpose of alerting emigrants to potential dangers as well as reporting the loss of animals, so that if any were subsequently found by other overlanders, the initial owner could claim the animal. Forty-niner John Edwin Banks even saw a notice offering a 200-dollar reward for five stolen horses and the persons who had committed the theft.[67]

In addition to the advertisements posted by physicians, overlanders relied on the roadside telegraph to report camp accidents as well as the convalescent progress of certain injured persons. In fact, William Chandless explained in 1855 that careful study of the roadside telegraph messages was almost akin to reading biographies of the individuals ahead, and that when Chandless chanced to meet some of the note writers along the trail it was like greeting an old friend. The roadside telegraph even flashed the latest national news: in 1850 someone who must have elicited the news from an eastbound traveler tacked up a notice on a Sierra pine tree that President Zachary Taylor had died.[68]

John Lawrence Johnson, in 1851, probably made the most intriguing use of the prairie telegraph. Young Johnson had become enamored of sixteen-year-old Jane Jones, who with her family was traveling in the same train. Johnson's father, a Presbyterian minister, did not approve of the budding love affair and found a pretext to take his family and leave the traveling company. Learning of the plot to keep them apart, the young lovers agreed that whoever was traveling ahead would write love letters on buffalo skulls, using the pseudonym "Laurie." Over a month later they reunited along the trail, and Jane joyously reported that "not a day passed since we parted but what I have found a letter signed by *Laurie* so I knew just where you were and was sure we would overtake you." The two families then traveled together for a time before again separating, but because Johnson's diary ends abruptly before he reached Oregon, whether this plains romance ever blossomed into matrimony remains a mystery.[69]

Everything that the roadside telegraph announced, however, could not be believed, as many overlanders ruefully discovered after confidently launching out on a "time-saving" cutoff on the basis of someone's posted recommendation. Rumors circulated freely on the trails and around campfires, fostered not only by turn-arounds and eastbound travelers but by exaggerated reports posted along the trail and faulty information "packers" brought up from the rear. These were individuals who had abandoned their wagons to travel more speedily by pack mule or horse. Having jumped off from the frontiers later than the wagon trains they were now passing, they brought news—and rumors—from the rear of the migration column.

Most pervasive, of course, were reports of Indian massacres. Because the overlanders could never be absolutely certain whether or not a rumor was false, on innumerable occasions emigrant parties chose campsites with extra care, and intensified their guard after a particularly frightening account of depredations reached their ears. Such rumors often served a useful function, since overlanders did tend to become extremely careless about the Indian threat once they were well into their journey, and an occasional sleepless night was a small price to pay for the reminder that alertness and prudence were constantly required.[70] Forty-niner John H. Benson's observations about Indian rumors illustrate the typical process. Less than two weeks into the journey, rumors of Indian atrocities were so widespread that a large number of overlanders, including Benson's traveling company, gravitated together for protection. For three days they traveled in battle readiness and slept with their guns at hand—only to learn from some army troops that the reports were complete fabrications. Again and again Benson recorded in his diary the ever-circulating rumors. On August 7 he wrote, "Rumors of hostile Indians are floating in the air most of the time, and while we pay little attention to them, we cannot altogether dismiss them from our minds." Several days before Benson finished his journey he summed up his rumor experience in this fashion: "I have traveled about 4 and a half months and probably over 2000 miles, most of the way in what was supposed to be a hostile Indian country. Rumors of depredation were afloat much of the time, but I have not seen a single hostile Indian. All I have met are extremely friendly."[71]

The rumors pertained mainly to alleged conflicts of a relatively minor nature. A few of the reports were more grandiose. After hearing that Indians had killed forty-five men and burned fifteen wagons not far ahead, one forty-niner company immediately held a meeting to refurbish their security measures. Another 1849 outfit heard that the Sioux tribe had murdered approximately 100 emigrants in the Fort Laramie vicinity.[72] The following year Abial Whitman was told that the Indians were going to kill every overlander who passed through South Pass, but shrewdly guessed that the report had originated in the East and not in the West. Prevalent in the Fort Hall region in 1852 was the false report of a massive engagement in which 82 whites and 400 Indians had been killed. In 1852, and again in 1856, large numbers of overlanders bypassed Salt Lake City because of rumors that Indians were particularly troublesome on that route due to Mormon encouragements to attack the overland emigrants.[73] In 1849 some overlanders who had gone via Salt Lake changed their minds and traveled the southern trail to California in lieu of the usual Humboldt River route, having been influenced by rumors that Missouri packers had coldbloodedly killed three Indians and burned the grass for 200 miles to impede the progress of overlanders. As a result the trails were reportedly aswarm with revenge-minded Indians and completely unsafe.[74]

Trail rumors were responsible for numerous such route changes. Many 1852 overlanders who started the trip with California as their announced destination altered their course to trail instead to Oregon because of frightening reports that grass and water were too scarce to chance the California Trail. Imprecise reports about forage conditions were another staple rumor, as Israel Hale discovered in 1849. Near the Bear River he heard that the grass had been burned off on the entire route from Fort Hall to California, but after traveling 400 miles beyond the fort he discovered only a few small areas which had been burned.[75]

Most unplanned route changes, however, stemmed from the favorable accounts about shortcuts and cutoffs which wishful overlanders helped propagate. Emigrant diaries reveal much animated discussion and debate, and occasionally votes, as to whether an unknown cutoff should be attempted. Alonzo Delano, recording the deliberations of his company in 1849 regarding the Lassen Cutoff possibility, noted that emigrants from several traveling companies consulted together and that one man even went out thirty miles on horseback to check the new route. Delano's company, prompted by the urgings of its adventurous young men, took the supposed shortcut.[76] Some of the various cutoff rumors were promulgated by interested parties, but there is ample evidence that many of the stories about how much time and distance cutoffs would save were freely circulated by and among emigrants eager for the trip to end but quite ignorant of any definite facts which would corroborate their roseate assertions.[77]

In addition to rumors about cholera epidemics and severe suffering among emigrants lagging behind, the wildest political and military reports were also heard around overland campfires. In 1849, for example, it was rumored that absolute famine prevailed in California, where provision-stealing guerilla bands were common. Another story had it that Britain and the United States were at war, and that Britain had sent up to 60,000 troops to California and an equal number to Mexico.[78]

Overlanders were unanimous in denouncing the unfounded rumors which were so much a part of their daily plains experience. Charles Hentz lamented that it was nearly impossible to ascertain the truth about anything on the plains, where all accounts of any event differed at least slightly. John A. Johnson, understandably piqued at the rumor that their traveling company had dissolved because Johnson had absconded with the company's funds, claimed, "We cannot rely with any certainty upon the truth of anything we hear as having transpired 5 miles ahead." Particularly concerned about the anxiety that rumors might cause for families and friends at home, gold rushers regularly wrote their wives to treat with caution most of the reports filtering back.[79]

Indeed, the emigrants were uncharacteristically blunt in damning rumor-spreaders. Isaac Lord, toward the end of his 1849 trip, raged, "Almost every man you meet and question proves himself a fool or a liar." Lord complained that any road knowledge secured along the trails was "purely accidental," and concluded that most travelers were "asses, asses all; and but that their hat crowns were shed 'long, long ago,' their ears would thrust their hats off."[80] J. H. Wayman, who believed a tenth of what he heard on the trails, advanced his theory on the origin of rumors: "Such stories are gotten up by some d——d fools, who are fond of gassing, thinking the while, that, perchance their names may appear in print, in conn[e]ction with some act of bravery, or as a witness to some scene of suffering and misery. This seems to be the only incentive for such creatures to lie so basely."[81] It is doubtful that any such theorizing provided much solace for Reuben Knox, who detoured to Salt Lake City in 1850 to meet a stepson while the wagon train he commanded pushed on toward California. While catching up to his train Knox frequently heard the rumor that he himself had died in Salt Lake City. And when Knox reached San Francisco he learned there that he had drowned in the Humboldt River![82]

Bane, blessing in disguise, or merely exasperating, rumors were a significant aspect of emigrant interaction. They seem to have been especially prevalent during the gold rush era because no one could anticipate what the unprecedented number of trail travelers might mean for the emigration experience. That more tragedies did not occur was largely due to the high incidence of cooperation as the emigrating community pushed westward together.

Particularly crucial to the cooperative enterprise were dedicated physicians. Their special significance in the overland caravans began to be recognized in 1843 with Dr. Marcus Whitman's important medical and travel assistance. While westbound emigrants continued to rely upon the professional services of westering physicians throughout the next two decades, it was during the California gold rush that medical doctors made their most significant contribution. A proportionally high percentage of physicians traveled in the 1849 and 1850 overland caravans.[83] All were desperately needed. The gold rush years were marked by the dreaded cholera, carried far out onto the plains from Missouri River towns by unsuspecting overlanders. The sheer immensity of the overland movement sufficiently increased problems of sanitation, so the incidence of other diseases was also high. Further, the many greenhorns on the trail

Cholera, particularly virulent during the gold rush years, may have caused this "Death Scene on the Plains."

during these hectic years were particularly susceptible to accidents. Other demands upon overworked trail physicians ranged from the extraction of teeth to obstetrical work.[84] Emigrant diarists and letter writers frequently commended the valiant and sacrificial efforts of gold rush physicians in stemming the tide of illness and injury.

The pattern of medical services was fairly standard. Physicians often placed signs on their wagons or advertised via the roadside telegraph, although this was hardly necessary since overlanders made certain that they knew approximately where the nearest physician was traveling in the event of emergency.[85] Companies traveling without a physician often endeavored to keep near trains with doctors. At least one traveling company midway through the journey arranged to employ a doctor by promising that each of the approximately fifty company members would pay him $5 to remain with them for the remainder of the journey. The services of New York doctors, highly regarded as "first class" physicians, were particularly sought after. While some physicians invited injured and ill emigrants to join their traveling company temporarily for continuing treatment, the usual procedure was for physicians to respond to requests brought by messengers.[86] It was not at all unusual for overworked doctors to travel fifteen miles or more in order to treat a suffering overlander. In 1845, when fewer physicians were found in the overland columns, trips of sixty or eighty miles to see patients were not unknown.[87]

In the region east of Fort Laramie, where cholera seemed to be most endemic, physicians regularly circulated among the various wagon trains dispensing medicines and advice to thousands of frightened overlanders. They occasionally remained with another train for a day while caring for patients.[88] George W. Davis, who estimated that he had prescribed for some 300 cases during his trip across the plains, indicated that his medical work had so slowed his travel progress that he arrived in California too late to do much prospecting during the 1850 mining season. Another 1850 physician, W. R. Allen, estimated that he had attended over 700 cholera patients on the plains. Dr. Reuben Knox stated that he saw between twenty and forty patients daily.[89] Knox commanded an 1850 passenger train, but the account of a "typical" day on the plains in the cholera regions which he sent to his wife demonstrates that he, like other physicians, spent days on end as a messenger of mercy among all emigrants within riding distance:

... one day started at 3 a.m., rode 3 miles from camp, missed my way in the fog and rode a mile in searching for the place, saw a man from Georgia dying, did not live more than half an hour ... prescribed for 3 more sick in the same camp and some in two other camps on my way back to my own. Breakfasted at 5; got off at 5½ having two men awaiting my departure to conduct me to two camps a mile or two ahead ... prescribed for two sick in one and three in the other, one nearly gone—before I joined the wagons, had another awaiting for me to come up who had a sick wife and child going along in a train ahead of ours, so rode up and administered medicine as the train was moving along. At about 8 called ¼ of a mile off to see a dying man from Arkansas, would not live an hour. The three remaining members of the company had just buried one of their number; gave medicine to them as one of them was quite unwell and the other two almost frightened to death. Kept away from the wagons by constant applications for advice, etc., along the road until 10—found a man there wishing me to go off the road some distance to see a number of sick ones in a train of twenty three or four wagons filled with families from Independence and vicinity—they were burying the sixth—found another dying and 10 or 12 sick. Remained with them until my company had gone so far that I did not reach them until after lunch time and they were about harnessing the mules again. In a mile or so, was called off again. Some distance from the road found a lady from Illinois dying and a young man very sick; ½ a mile from thence and before I reached the road, saw a man dying and his wife quite sick—continued along the road and the river bank among the camps about in the same way constantly trying to relieve the sick and galloping along until 6½ when we camped. Before the mules were harnessed two messengers came post haste for me, one to go two miles back and off the road, the other one mile ahead. In one found 4 sick, one of whom was cold purple and pulseless—but who revived about two hours after and . . . sent more medicine and started off in the morning at 3½, finding some out of danger and the other better.

Knox indicated that on many nights he did not even get one hour's rest.[90]

Not only were physicians generous beyond measure with their time, they frequently did their work gratis. O. W. Nixon praised their company physician, who had charged nothing for all the work he had been called to do during the overland journey; another physician reported that when he charged twenty-five cents for some opium on July 2, it was the first time during the journey that he had requested payment for medicine or advice. Dr. Allen, who had seen 700 cholera patients but only earned $150, stated that he had charged only for medicines since few patients had much money. One physician charged $2 for a cholera call, another received $5 for attending to a fractured arm and dislocated shoulder, while still another made at least $8.75 on a fairly busy day.[91] Whether the professional advice and medicine were benevolently given or rendered for a small sum, it is evident that the physicians were among the heroes of the migrations, especially during the gold rush.

Blacksmiths, wheelwrights, and barbers similarly found their services much in demand. Some were even able to earn considerable amounts of money during the plains crossing.[92] While some overlanders demanded compensation for the trouble involved in taking up strayed animals and keeping them until their owners came for them, most did not expect payment for such neighborly acts. A few even went out of their way to find the rightful owner. In 1853, when large stock droves were a common sight along the trails, Jotham Newton noted that men from virtually every passing train asked for lost stock, and that almost every train had found strays which they were keeping until the owner inquired about them.[93]

There were numerous other ways in which westbound overlanders cooperated to lessen the demands of the journey, almost always in a cheerful spirit of cooperation without seeking personal gain. Seasoned plains travelers advised novice overlanders of safe places to ford rivers so that expensive tolls could be avoided. Emigrant wagons bogged down in mudholes were pulled out by passing overlanders. Ropes, chains, boats, and bridge-building equipment were shared among different traveling groups. Overland companies encamping close together occasionally set out a mutual guard during the night. Following a rainstorm or stampede it was sometimes necessary for several traveling companies to cooperate in sorting out cattle which had milled together.[94]

Also, emigrants on occasion volunteered to help strangers search for stock which had been stolen by Indians. This was emigrant cooperation at its best, for such errands of mercy could be dangerous. In 1857 one group of forty-two men from seven or eight different trains spent two fruitless days seeking sixty-one head of cattle stolen from an Arkansas train along the Humboldt River. Upon their return a second company was mustered from some of the trains which had come up in the interim, and this second group finally recovered thirty-six head of cattle and killed one Indian—seventy miles distant from where they had begun their search.[95] Emigrant hunting parties killing more buffalo, deer, or other prairie game than needed often shared surplus meats with fellow overlanders.[96]

A less joyous cooperative task was the burial of deceased overlanders. Passing emigrants were often asked to assist members of other traveling companies in digging graves and constructing coffins and grave markers. Most overlanders also stopped to rebury any deceased overlander whom they discovered, as Heinrich Leinhard's company did along the Humboldt River in 1846, after finding a man whose body had not only been dug up (presumably by wolves) but stripped of clothing and mutilated as well.[97]

One of the most prevalent forms of interaction among westering overlanders was the inadvertent visit paid to another group of emigrants. Most frequently this was for the night, but it often occurred at mealtimes as well. While traveling westward, overlanders persistently rode ahead, lagged behind, or wandered off from their traveling company to hunt, explore, fix a wagon, read, sketch a picture, visit, and sometimes sleep. Often they did not conclude their activity quickly enough to be able to reach their own outfit that same day, and gladly accepted the hospitality and protection their fellow travelers readily extended in such circumstances.[98] Captains and other traveling luminaries were also periodically invited to share a meal with captains of trains they were passing—Edwin Bryant in 1846 and J. Goldsborough Bruff in 1849 were frequent guests at other campfires during the course of their respective overland trips.[99]

There was always considerable visiting among overlanders who had chosen to halt for a day of rest and recuperation and who were encamped

"End of a Day's March"—emigrants visit with one another as wagon trains prepare for the night in traditional fashion.

in fairly close proximity. When the rest day was on Sunday, as it usually was, emigrants from various companies frequently assembled for a religious service.[100] Gregarious overlanders, of course, needed no excuse to stop, chat, and make new friends. Some occasionally went to great lengths to do so, as with the young 1853 overlander who swam the Platte River to visit a company of emigrants traveling on the other side of that waterway. In addition to the interaction between trains on opposite sides of the Platte, on occasion ladies functioned as nurses among the sick in other trains. And, as proof that the amenities of civilized life were not neglected on the plains, Charlotte Pengra reported in 1853 that she gave her sunbonnet pattern to another lady who had admired it while passing by.[101]

Sunbonnets were peripheral, of course, in comparison with the serious matter of getting one's goods to California or Oregon. Here, too, the overlanders regularly assisted one another. In the first place, there was the problem of replacing lost, broken, or stolen wagon equipment, necessary travel supplies, and all-important draft animals. Some emigrants purchased replacements from turn-arounds or eastbound overlanders; others shopped successfully at the periodic auctions along the trails where the personal effects of deceased overlanders were offered for sale by the remaining members of the traveling group.[102] There was an even greater exchange of animals, wagons, and supplies among westbound emigrants, both within and without their own traveling group. Indeed, some overlanders swapped so much and so often that they arrived at their destination with almost entirely different outfits and personal accoutrements from those with which they had begun the trip. It was only natural that a greater fluidity of personal possessions prevailed during the gold rush, when most overlanders were transient males not attempting to take their most valued belongings with them. The majority of emigrants, however, were only interested in exchanging, replacing, or adding one or more specific items, and there was likewise a greater opportunity to do this following 1848, when so many more emigrants were on the trails.

Opportunities for purchasing additional oxen to pull an overloaded wagon, an extra wagon tongue, a new or extra wagon or riding horse regularly presented themselves somewhere along the trail.[103] Numerous trades of cattle, horses, and mules were also recorded in emigrant diaries. Particularly in 1849, when most overlanders took too much along and had to lighten their loads for the sake of their draft animals, fantastic bargains in clothing, revolvers, ammunition, foodstuffs, and almost everything else were available at many encampments. As the trip stretched out, many overlanders chose to sell their cumbersome wagons and most of their supplies in order to pack in to California by mule or horse. Some gold rushers made this change very early in the journey, retaining just as little in the way of provisions and supplies as they calculated would be necessary to complete the trip. This meant that mules and horses came to be increas-

143

Even the hardy oxen could succumb to exhaustion and thirst. Forty-niner Charles Nahl painted the tragic "Crossing the Plains" around 1856.

ingly valuable in the buying, selling, and trading among the overlanders, while oxen, wagons, and many other supplies and foodstuffs were sold at ridiculously low prices, if they could be sold at all.[104]

An additional problem loomed toward the end of the journey, when overworked animals gave out or fell victim to Indian theft or arrow. Emigrants thus left with no way to transport their belongings sometimes were able to arrange with more fortunate overlanders to have their baggage carried through to the end of the journey, usually for some monetary or equivalent consideration. A few munificent overlanders asked nothing. These were real acts of compassion, since almost everyone's team was considerably worn down toward the journey's end. Along the Humboldt River in 1850, after traveling with his goods on his back for a day, Hugh Skinner secured accommodations in an Illinois wagon, thanks to a lady whose kindness led Skinner to remark, "I have uniformly found the women on the road more alive to the sufferings of their fellow creaturs than the men."[105] The bargain made, the emigrant usually traveled with his benefactor, but on occasion forged ahead on foot or with pack animal, planning to retrieve his goods later in California.[106]

Clothing, blankets, and other personal belongings were important to overlanders, but food was crucial. The most significant assistance overlanders rendered to one another was certainly in sharing and selling provisions. A few gold rushers had even begun the journey with virtually no food supply, frankly planning to "sponge" off their better-prepared colleagues. One such 1849 foot traveler from Maine had reached Fort Kearny by such tactics, and figured that he would continue to find enough "Christians" on the route to supply his needs.[107]

But most overlanders were reduced to begging only if their funds gave out and they were unable to purchase provisions from other emigrants. And once again the gold rush era evidenced far more of this type of interaction than either the pre-1849 period, when emigrants had gone better prepared, or the post-1853 period, when unprepared overlanders found an abundance of commercial establishments where supplies could be replenished. Even within the gold rush itself there was a sharp distinction between 1849, when most had overburdened themselves and were forced to leave many of their supplies along the trails, and 1850, when many gold rushers overreacted and took too little. One of the most difficult of all trail years was 1850, when even the widespread samaritanism of many overlanders was insufficient to stem the starvation tide.[108]

In 1849 emigrants quickly realized their miscalculations and began to lighten their loads. Edward J. Willis, for example, sold 166 pounds of bacon at the Kansas River in early May. With so many overlanders in similar straits, however, it was not a seller's market. Alonzo Delano, who considered himself fortunate to have found a buyer for fifty pounds of his excess coffee, observed, "To sell superfluous articles was quite impos-

sible."[109] Indeed, in their hasty load-lightening many emigrants overreacted and later in the journey were forced to seek replenishments from
other trains. An unforeseen food shortage also developed among many
who took the Lassen Cutoff. Assuming—usually on the basis of rumors—
that the route would greatly reduce the distance still to be traveled to the
gold mines, some traveled the cutoff precisely because their provisions
were low. In actuality the distance to the gold mines was increased on
Lassen's infamous trail.[110]

Probably most of the food which changed emigrant hands in 1849,
however, went to those who had commenced packing and needed to
replenish supplies periodically. Jasper M. Hixson, serving as cook and
commissary for his forty-niner company, offers an amusing example of
how a naive overlander became wise to the pricing of provisions for sale on
the trail. Since Hixson had never known bacon to sell for more than 8 cents
per pound, he was surprised that so many packers willingly paid the 25
cents he arbitrarily asked, assuming that they did so because of "the
superior quality of our bacon." As his company progressed farther west,
Hixson prudently determined that the price should go up, so he began to
ask 37½ cents per pound. He was even more surprised when a packer
unhesitatingly purchased over twenty pounds of bacon at that price. Since
such a price seemed outlandish, Hixson subsequently refrained from
selling surplus bacon, declaring, "I would not commence highway robbery." Later, the astonished Hixson learned that California-based traders
charged and received $1.50 per pound along the Carson River, and that
even in Sacramento bacon wholesaled at 62½ cents per pound. He now
confided to his diary, "I could understand [the packers] buying at the price
without grumbling. Later on I dropped some of those conscientious
scruples about high prices, and gradually fell into the ways of the country."[111]

In 1850 food was at a premium, especially on the later portions of the
overland route. The rapidly increasing number of packers and other gold
rushers running perilously low on rations frantically searched for overlanders well enough supplied to part with some of their provisions. The
rapidly diminishing number of overlanders retaining surplus provisions
happily watched prices skyrocket. Flour commanded up to $2 per pound;
one overlander reported a man going from wagon to wagon unsuccessfully offering $50 for three pounds of flour. Hard bread sold at $1 a
pound. One small group of hungry emigrants immediately slaughtered
the worn-out ox they had chipped in to purchase for $65 from a passing
train.[112]

Overlanders who found available food were the fortunate ones.
Lorenzo Sawyer, in the vanguard of the 1850 migration, commented on
June 23, near Goose Creek, "Not a day passes that we do not have applica-
tions for provisions. Most emigrants are short." By July 6, near the Hum-

boldt Sink, Sawyer indicated that overlanders without provisions were making applications every hour, and commented: "It is hard to turn away a starving man 1500 miles one way, and 300 the other, from any source of supply, but we are obliged to do it. We have already spared every thing we are able to without endangering our own lives, yet the applications are more frequent and more urgent."[113] Byron McKinstry, in mid-August along the Humboldt, estimated that twenty men per day asked for food, and that most of these packers had no money whatever. John Wood was one such packer, and on August 24, also along the Humboldt, he wrote, "I suppose that I have asked to buy of more than one hundred men this forenoon, but with no success." Calculating that half of the overlanders were "literally starving"—some having already died—Wood explained that he and his comrades subsisted in part on worn-out steers other travelers left behind to perish.[114]

In such precarious circumstances, desperate overlanders resorted to tactics both clever and violent to induce their fellows to offer up precious provisions. In 1849 Andrew Orvis, alone and out of supplies, after being refused by one Missouri train, sat down at their breakfast anyway and acted "half craisy." Orvis remained with them through the day until the Missourians promised to sell him some bacon and flour if he would leave.[115] After Oliver Goldsmith had been refused foodstuffs by some southern overlanders, his companion, John Root, who possessed a strong southern accent, managed to get some food from the same group. Root apparently used his accent to good advantage on other occasions.[116]

But ruses seem not to have been as much used as force. Goldsmith and four friends, after being told by one emigrant that they could have all the provisions they wanted, but at the steep price of $2 per pound, "marched up to him and said there were five of us to his one and that we intended to take what we needed at our own price, twenty-five cents a pound, which we did."[117] When 1850 emigrant James Campbell encountered begging over-landers who had eaten nothing but frogs for four days, he prudently began sleeping in his wagon to prevent possible thievery. James Bennett's com-pany also kept a strong guard over their provision wagons every night. Many other 1850 outfits similarly began guarding their draft animals closely after learning that desperate overlanders had stolen considerable numbers of oxen. On the Oregon route too there were thefts and threats on the part of destitute and desperate emigrants.[118] Such conditions, when reported in California and Oregon, prompted the sending of relief expe-ditions from those regions. Before those expeditions began to be effective, however, the shared food among overlanders—voluntary and forced—had been of incalculable significance in enabling many emigrants to reach the Pacific Coast, emigrants who otherwise would have died en route.

Milk and liquor were two additional items of emigrant interchange in almost all travel years. Overlanders were always eager to secure fresh milk from emigrants trailing cows westward. One 1850 overlander reported that for a small price butter was regularly available along the trail.[119] Transactions likewise flourished whenever emigrants discovered an overlander with spiritous beverages for sale. The forty-niners in the Charlestown, Virginia, company were particularly fond of the strong brew. On at least two occasions they sent a delegation to backtrack on the trail, once for a distance of ten miles, after hearing that liquor might be available. The Charlestown gold seekers, like many other emigrants, also made periodic purchases from enterprising overlanders who had stocked up in anticipation of just such thirsty travelers and were operating what amounted to mobile saloons.[120]

Of course not all emigrants were willing to give of their time, skill, money, or materials to aid those in distress. Yet the contemporary records amply demonstrate that no account of emigrant cooperation is complete if the numerous humanitarian acts of kindness and compassion are omitted. Addison Crane remarked in 1852 that since it was considered "out of character" for provisions to be sold among travelers in the same company, anyone's extra foodstuffs were regarded as "common property." And Reuben Shaw remembered that only one person demanded payment for provisions when he and a few colleagues packed in ahead of their train and were forced to rely on handouts: "We never passed a single company without being made welcome to such supplies as could be spared from their scanty stores, which speaks well for the noble, free-hearted souls that crossed the plains in forty-nine."[121]

More serious was the plight of persons actually abandoned by their traveling companions somewhere along the trail. Fortunately, though, some compassionate soul usually took them in for the remainder of the journey, or, as in one 1850 instance, arranged to take them to the nearest settlement. On that occasion, after finding an abandoned woman and her young daughter on the trail about seventy miles west of Salt Lake City, two westbound overlanders escorted them back to the Mormon center and then turned around and retraced their own steps toward California.[122]

Often, too, westering overlanders took up collections to provide unfortunate emigrants with the means to replace stock, wagons, or provisions. Thus, forty-niner Bernard Reid came upon a seventeen-year-old girl all alone save for her younger brother, who lay in their wagon sick with cholera. Both the mother and the father had already died of the dread disease. The oxen were gone, and so was the faithless company with which the family had been traveling. Reid and others immediately took up a collection so that oxen might be purchased, two passing doctors prescribed medicine for the boy, and a Missouri group volunteered to take care of the orphans for the rest of the trip. Another 1850 gold seeker had been left by the trail after having been accidentally shot by one of his company. A passing physician attended to him, and westbound overlanders contrib-

uted money for his continuing care. When overlanders fording Thomas'
Fork of the Bear River witnessed the drowning of one of the two horses an
old man was relying on to take his family to California, they immediately
took up a collection so the father could purchase another horse. And at the
Green River ferry, in 1854, westbound emigrants again contributed funds
to forward on to California the widow of a man who had just drowned.[123]

Another common act of compassion was the attempt to ease the ordeal
of desert crossings with "water wagons" manned and financed by overlanders having just completed the trip. Thirst-crazed overlanders were
known to offer astronomical sums for a single drink of water during desert
crossings. In 1850 on the desert beyond the Humboldt Sink, $5 was
offered for a drink of water, and five gallons of water sold for $50. Henry
Bloom reported that on the Hastings Cutoff desperate 1850 overlanders
offered $10, $20, and up to $500 for a single drink of water.[124] Fortunately
for Bloom and his friends, the water wagon arrived before thirst elicited
similar offers from them. This humane venture was especially prominent
in 1850, when a wagonload of water was sent back every day by the
emigrants who had crossed the preceding day. Not only water for the men
but grass for the draft animals was included, the effort being financed by
contributions from the emigrants encamped at the spring which marked
the welcome end of the treacherous long drive. An 1850 physician noted
that their group had sent two relief loads back at a cost of $25 per wagon,
the funds having been generously subscribed by passing overlanders. The
wagon drivers gave the water free of charge to destitute overlanders, but
those with money were charged from $1 to $5 per gallon.[125] Less organized but similar operations prevailed at other desert crossings. In 1849,
for example, on the crossing to the Truckee River, overlanders sometimes
sent kegs of water back from the river. Apparently in 1852 the emigrants
devised a simple operation at the boiling springs on the same desert
crossing. Each departing overlander would fill water barrels which were
left permanently at the springs so that oncoming sufferers would always
have fairly cool water to drink.[126]

An additional legacy of the gold rush contributing considerably to
emigrant interchange, albeit in a strange manner, was the trail of debris the
greatest "litterbugs" of American history left in the wake of their transit
across the West. Some traces had remained of the westward march of the
overlanders of the 1840s, but since almost twice as many overlanders
trailed westward in 1849 as in the entire previous decade, it was only
natural that their residue would be greater. Further, their leavings were
compounded by the overloaded wagons with which they had begun. They
soon realized that the basic question was what they could do without, since
their draft animals could never survive pulling such heavy loads.[127] Accordingly, they began to seek ways of disposing of their superfluous food,
equipment, and personal belongings. Only a small portion could be sold to

other emigrants, most of whom were in a similar situation. Initially most overlanders could not bring themselves to throw away everything that could be classed as excess; consequently there usually were several trimming sessions. The amount and value of what the overland emigrants left on the plains in 1849 and in the ensuing years of the gold rush border on the incredible.

Many forty-niners began disposal operations as soon as they launched out onto the prairies. In the long run theirs was the wisest decision, providing they did not throw away too much. So much was abandoned within fifty miles of St. Joseph in 1849 that one emigrant indicated he would never go to California if he could have all that had been sacrificed that early in the journey. Persons went out from the outfitting points to collect the usable debris and brought back wagonloads of bacon, ham, flour, bread, beans, stoves, tools, medicines, extra wagon wheels and axle-trees, clothing, and similar items, which were presumably resold or used by the scavengers. After viewing the perfectly good food and other materials along the trail, one forty-niner wrote: "If I was going to start again, I would get a light wagon for mules, and gather up the rest of my outfit along the road."[128]

While debris accumulated everywhere, much of the abandoned merchandise was concentrated in the Fort Laramie vicinity. Many overloaded forty-niners had endeavored to persevere as far as the fort, where they anticipated profitable sales of their excess supplies. Upon discovering that the traders there needed none of their surplus commodities—which could be picked up along the trail for nothing in any case—the overlanders had no alternative but to begin dumping. Joseph Berrien reached the fort on May 30, well in the forefront of the 1849 migration, and dubbed the area "Camp Sacrifice" because of all that had already been left there. More than 20,000 pounds of bacon alone had been abandoned near the fort before June 1, and the great masses of overloaded emigrants were still to come.[129] Howard Stansbury, en route to an exploration of the Great Salt Lake Valley, enumerated some of the debris he saw in the Deer Creek area: "The road has been literally strewn with articles that have been thrown away. Bar-iron and steel, large blacksmiths' anvils and bellows, crow-bars, drills, augers, gold-washers, chisels, axes, lead, trunks, spades, ploughs, large grind-stones, baking-ovens, cooking-stoves without number, kegs, barrels, harness, clothing, bacon, and beans, were found along the road in pretty much the order in which they have been here enumerated."[130] Virtually everything imaginable was found at least once somewhere along the overland trail: weapons, ammunition, tobacco, an iron safe, a Gothic bookcase, law and medical books—even a diving bell and accompanying apparatus.[131]

If anything expendable remained in the wagons, it rarely lasted beyond the desert crossing to either the Carson or Truckee rivers. Here not

Rotting carcasses, broken wagons, and emigrants forced to "pack in" across the litter-strewn desert were among the grimmer realities of the overland experience recorded by J. Goldsborough Bruff in 1849.

Henry E. Huntington Library, San Marino, Cal.

only supplies but wagons and draft animals were left behind in ever-increasing numbers. Estimates of the number of abandoned wagons on the forty-mile desert ranged as high as 2,000 in 1850.[132] Overlanders had already been passing and bemoaning the foul-smelling carcasses of dead animals—the victims of overwork and alkali poisoning—ever since leaving the Upper Platte ferry; what they witnessed on the desert crossings was merely the culmination. Though such tribulations were by no means unique to California gold seekers (Oregon-bound Maria Belshaw counted 190 dead animals along a 321-mile stretch of the Snake River in 1853), the debris, destruction, and stink reached their most astounding proportions on the deserts beyond the Humboldt Sink during the gold rush.[133] One 1850 company found the regular trail so covered with dead and dying stock that they were compelled to forge a new trail. John Clark, crossing in 1852, found that many of the dead animals had been there since 1849 and 1850, having been partially preserved by the desert air. Calvin Taylor, who complained of the "intolerable stink" in the "valley of death," probably came as close as anyone could to describing the desolate scene, which he characterized as having the "appearance of a battlefield."[134]

A few gold rushers attempted a count. One 1850 traveler counted 2,381 horses and mules, 433 oxen, and 787 wagons, estimating the value of this and all other property left on the Carson Desert at $100,000. A subsequent tabulation of 4,960 dead horses, 3,750 dead oxen, and 1,061 dead mules led another observer to appraise the value of the abandoned property at $1 million.[135] Still another 1850 emigrant, who would have been glad to settle for the value of the abandoned guns alone, estimated that millions of dollars worth of stock and thousands of dollars worth of other property had been left on the plains that year. An 1849 overlander similarly assumed that the forty-niners had scattered at least a million dollars worth of property in their wake between Independence and Sacramento.[136]

Crossing a continent littered with so much valuable waste was a trying experience for many overlanders, who could not resist the temptation to appropriate various desirable items. A few choice selections they managed to haul with them to the Pacific Coast, but most acquisitions ultimately had to be thrown away again. Yet this debris was of considerable significance to westering overlanders, who were regularly able to use what others left behind.

Most appreciated, of course, was the discovery of draft animals in good condition. The general principle followed was that any property left behind was no longer claimed by the owner, although with strayed horses, mules, and oxen this was occasionally a difficult determination to make.[137] At times the appropriations were tantamount to theft, as with the 1849 Tennessee company which drove seventy-eight head of stampeded cattle across the Platte River and surrendered them to their rightful owners only with extreme reluctance. And on occasion some travelers hovered like vultures around companies immersed in the painful throwing-away process, absconding with choice items from owners who had not yet decided to discard them.[138] Sometimes, too, objects were simply overlooked when emigrants broke camp. When owners backtracked looking for such material it was generally returned to them. Many overlanders made their charitable intentions very clear by placing signs on piles of goods or attaching placards to lame cattle indicating that emigrants who could use such animals or supplies should take what they needed.[139]

One of the most common tactics, which avoided the error of adding even more weight to already strained teams and wagons, was to substitute superior materials discarded by other emigrants for similar but inferior-grade items already in the overlander's wagon. J. Goldsborough Bruff thus trimmed off all the fat from his own bacon supply at Deer Creek and substituted an equivalent weight of choice bacon from a huge pile discarded there. Bruff also replaced the defective front wheels, axle, and tongue on his wagon with those from an abandoned wagon he found along the Humboldt River. Since axles and wagon tongues were quite susceptible to breakage, the presence of thousands of abandoned wagons was a tremendous aid in making satisfactory repairs quickly, especially in regions nearly devoid of trees. Charles Gray substituted better bacon, flour, and meal for his own mediocre provisions; Elisha Perkins exchanged ninety pounds of his second-rate crackers for a similar amount of "the finest crackers I have seen," which he found near Fort Laramie.[140] When the troubled Pioneer Line reduced its baggage, members of Isaac Lord's company replaced about twenty trunks and boxes from their own train with more valuable material from the Pioneer Line. John Clapp, in 1850, threw away his coat and trousers and put on better garments which he found by the side of the road. Franklin Langworthy, also in 1850, noted that he had exchanged his clothing in such a manner several times en route and also periodically chose a book to read from those in the plains "library." When finished with the volume he tossed it aside and found another.[141]

Other items were used by overlanders for a short time, sometimes only once, and then discarded. Sheet-iron stoves were too heavy to drag along, which is why so many were discarded along the trail. But their weight did not prevent their being used by passing emigrants. Henry Coke encamped near Independence Rock in 1850, where he "found an old stove and baked some bread."[142]

Probably the single most common act, however, was to break up an abandoned wagon and use it for firewood, something which virtually everyone in the gold rush period did at least once, or at least saw being done. Many emigrants also found that when in a pinch for firewood they could make creditable campfires by burning other materials found by the wayside—bacon, ox yokes, abandoned wheelbarrows, the straw inside discarded horse collars, Mormon mileage markers. "What is thrown away one day," Thomas Turnbull appropriately wrote in 1852, "is burnt up the next."[143] Another traveling technique frequently employed was to cut the hide from dead oxen and fashion from it a kind of moccasin which, placed flesh side out and tied securely, provided an excellent remedy for sore-footed oxen.[144]

Sharp-eyed overlanders made all sorts of helpful discoveries along the route. They found log canoes lashed together which were serviceable for fording rivers, as well as usable wells dug by previous overlanders. James Bowen's 1851 traveling group was ecstatic over a rare find: four barrels of good whiskey and twenty gallons of brandy which one of their number found buried in the ground.[145] Emigrants became so conditioned to taking what they found that searching the body of a dead man found floating in the Platte River and dividing his personal effects did not seem to bother a group of 1852 overlanders in any way.[146]

Non-emigrants also benefited from the materials overlanders tossed aside. Indians donned discarded clothing and, especially along the Humboldt River, feasted on the decaying flesh of dead stock. Fur traders found abandoned wagons and oxen useful for hauling furs and hides to the Missouri River towns.[147] And John D. Lee's 1849 venture has become famous as a Mormon scavenging trip from Salt Lake City to pick up abandoned materials of potential value for the fledgling Saint empire.[148]

It was in such manner that the overland emigrants moved westward along the Oregon-California Trail: intersecting with those traveling in the opposite direction, communicating via the "Bone Express," trading and purchasing among themselves, using what others left behind, and cooperating in various humanitarian and occasionally profitable ways to make the journey easier, safer, and more pleasant. While all these interchanges occurred during both of the decades here under review, the California gold rush greatly accelerated the amount of cooperation and interaction. In the 1840s there had been far fewer emigrants and they had remained together somewhat more cohesively in groups large enough to assist and encourage one another. Further, they had been more trail-wise, traveled with less irrational haste, and had, in general, outfitted more judiciously. The vast outpouring of humanity which took to the trails in 1849 invited much more interaction and cooperation *outside* of an emigrant's own immediate traveling group. By the late 1850s the presence of far more trading posts and settlements in the West—themselves a direct result of the gold rush—provided still more ways of achieving what emigrant cooperation and interaction had accomplished during the height of the gold rush.

Probably nothing more clearly evidenced the drastically changed nature of overland emigration by the late 1850s than the use of what others left behind. Whereas previously it had been solely wagons and debris abandoned by fellow overlanders, in 1859 John Favour reported that, in addition to relying on these now-mundane objects for firewood, his company used boards they had torn off an abandoned house along the Platte River. And, when troubled by mosquitoes, they set a haystack on fire.[149] The presence of houses and haystacks in territory which Horace Greeley had not long before characterized as beyond the safe boundaries of civilization emphasized how rapidly the West was changing, and with it the migration experience.

CHAPTER FIVE

Emigrant-Indian Interaction

From "mutual aid" to "massacres"

"T<small>HE DALLES AT PRESENT FORM A KIND</small> of masquerading thoroughfare, where emigrants and Indians meet, it appears, for the purpose of affording mutual aid."[1] Jesuit missionary Pierre-Jean De Smet thus described, in 1846, a scene near the end of the overland route into Oregon's Willamette Valley. He could have written similarly of a multitude of other places along the Oregon-California Trail where overland emigrants and Indians met for purposes of aid and trade. That such beneficial interaction occurred, frequently and with considerable significance, contradicts the widely disseminated myth of incessant warfare between brave overlanders and treacherous Indians. The mass media view is not, of course, completely erroneous: Indians did kill hundreds of overlanders on the trails before the Civil War. The preoccupation with Indian depredations, however, has resulted in radical distortion of the historical record. Moreover, the depredations which did occur can be understood only in the context of the number and nature of Indian-emigrant encounters along the overland trails.

It was quite natural, for example, for overlanders to solicit route information from Indians, especially during the early 1840s and in the initial gold rush period. When the Stevens-Murphy party blazed a trail beyond the Humboldt Sink with their wagons in 1844, they were following the exact directions of a Paiute Indian chief who told them of the route and went ahead with the leaders to show the way. Named in the Indian's honor, the Truckee River route became one of the most frequently traveled overland trails into California and still serves as a modern transportation route.[2] In 1849 an Indian drew a detailed topographical map of the route over the Sierra Nevadas for Ansel McCall's party. Fashioning his diagram in the sand, the native indicated where grass, water, and wood were located and also where hostile Indians might be encountered.[3] Several other emigrants reported route advice given to them by Indians at various places along the trails.[4]

A number of overland groups, beginning with the Bidwell-Bartleson company of 1841, employed and even kidnapped Indians to travel with them as guides, pointing out the trail and identifying good grass and water locations.[5] When Marcus Whitman left the 1843 emigration to push ahead to his mission, he left the overlanders in charge of an Indian guide who, as Peter Burnett recalled, "proved to be both faithful and competent."[6] Some California-bound emigrants in the same year relied upon a succession of Indian guides to show them the route beyond Fort Boise.[7] The Jayhawker party, while struggling across southern trails from Salt Lake City to California in 1849, retained one of the two Paiute Indians they had captured for guide duty. Louis Nusbaumer's 1849 traveling party likewise captured two Indians, who gave helpful route instructions and located a spring. "Unfortunately," Nusbaumer lamented, "the men let the Indians go free, when they could have assisted us as guides and we were left helpless, without food and water—amid the vast hilly plains of California, yet we did not despair."[8] Hugh Skinner, traveling on the Hastings Cutoff in 1850, acknowledged that Shoshoni Indians directed their party to water which they would not otherwise have found. As late as 1854 Indians traveled with a California-bound party along the Humboldt River, pointing out watering places and furnishing fish and pine nuts to hungry emigrants.[9]

While a relatively small number of overlanders relied upon Indians for route information or trail guidance, many overlanders willingly entrusted their stock, wagons, belongings, and even their families to Indian swimmers and boatmen at dangerous river crossings all along the trail. Most of this type of Indian assistance prevailed on the Oregon side of Fort Hall, at crossings of the Snake and Deschutes rivers, and especially in navigating down the Columbia River from The Dalles. The Sioux Indians also attained some renown for successfully swimming stock across the Platte and Laramie rivers, and there are scattered references to comparable Indian aid at other river and stream crossings.[10]

Primarily, however, it was the Oregon overlanders during the 1840s and the early 1850s who relied most extensively on this form of Indian assistance. In doing so they were presumably following the advice of writers such as J. M. Shively, who had explicitly stated in his 1846 guidebook that "you must hire an Indian to pilot you at the crossings of Snake river, it being dangerous if not perfectly understood."[11] Elizabeth Wood secured an Indian pilot after first attempting to ford the Snake River without one, perceiving, "It is best in fording this river to engage a pilot."[12] Amelia Stewart Knight obviously agreed in 1853, remarking that there were many droves of cattle that could not be gotten across the Snake River without Indian help.[13] Emigrant provisions, personal belongings, and wagons were also often put into Indian canoes to be rowed across raging rivers.

Payment was generally made in articles of clothing or in ammunition.

James Longmire discovered on two occasions in 1853 that Indians were by no means devoid of effective bargaining techniques. At the Salmon Falls crossing an Indian, after swimming a few horses over the Snake River, mounted one of the best horses and rode off, while his employers remained helpless on the other side of the river. Later, in crossing horses over the Columbia River, Chinook Indians suddenly halted their exertions in midstream, demanding more money to complete the project. They got it, since any further delay would likely have been disastrous.[14] Usually, however, the bargain, once made, was lived up to by both parties.[15]

Prior to the opening of the several land routes into the Williamette and other Oregon valleys, almost all emigrants took to the Columbia River once they reached The Dalles. In the early 1840s this meant hiring Indians to transport wagons, goods, and families in canoes, as well as hiring Indians to portage belongings around the Cascades. The universal emigrant judgment was that the Columbia was an extremely dangerous river. Overton Johnson and William Winter wrote in their account of an 1843 plains crossing—which later emigrants used as a guidebook—that "it requires the most dexterous management, which these wild navigators are masters of, to pass the dreadful chasm in safety. A single stroke amiss, would be inevitable destruction."[16]

Some of the 1843 overlanders who avoided Indian pilots and boats fared disastrously. The Applegate company constructed their own canoes, which they manned themselves with such lack of skill and luck that three in their party drowned and another was crippled for life. Sarah Cummins praised the Indians who helped their party portage around the Cascades in 1845 as "careful and considerate helpers. Not one deserted the ranks." She also stated that not a single dishonest act had been noticed. Mary Jane Long recalled how the Indians taking their party down the Columbia in 1852 had caught fish, built campfires, and brought up spring water while encamped. Once they even went back to a previous encampment to retrieve a gun which her father had inadvertently left behind but had not yet missed.[17] Of course not everyone who took passage in Indian canoes was ecstatic about the experience. David Maynard, for instance, grumped in 1850, "We had a hard time, in consequence of the Indian being so damned lazy." Most emigrants, however, made the trip safely and with considerable respect for the skill of the native boatmen.[18]

Indians aided overlanders in numerous other ways. Always eager to find ways of getting letters back to family and friends in the States, emigrants periodically negotiated with passing natives to transport letters back to the eastern settlements. At least some of these messengers faithfully fulfilled their trust, since many of the letters reached their destination. Forty-niner William Wells, for example, wrote to his wife from along the Kansas River: "This probably is the last chance I shall have to write to you and I do not know that you will even get this one. We have hired an Indian to take our letters to Independence—he may take them and he may not."[19] One 1849 episode revealed both the shrewdness and trustworthiness of some Indian entrepreneurs. Although some of the forty-niners were dubious about the project, Reuben Shaw's company negotiated with three Sioux braves to carry numerous letters back to Council Bluffs. The Indians sagely refused a package deal for all the letters but instead bargained with each individual sender, thereby securing far more clothing, notions, tobacco, and jewelry. Shaw bartered a calico shirt for his letter and wrote, "The Indians got the shirt, and several months later I had the satisfaction of knowing that my wife received the letter."[20]

Indians were also hired to cut and carry grass for emigrant use while traversing the deserts beyond the Humboldt Sink, to watch and herd emigrant stock during overnight encampments, to bring in wood for campfires, to serve as interpreters and as packers of provisions.[21] In 1851 Cayuse Indians even improved a new travel route out of the Grande Ronde Valley, charging from fifty cents to a dollar per wagon in tolls. The verdict from overlanders who tried it was that it was at least as good as the old road.[22]

Even more astonishing to overlanders normally approaching all Indians with considerable suspicion, at least at the beginning of their overland trek, were the occasional acts of kindness and compassion by the Indians. Seeing William Johnston's difficulty in getting his mule-drawn wagons up the steep banks of Wakarusa Creek, a Shawnee Indian brought his pair of oxen to help pull the wagons up.[23] An Indian with an extra horse overtook John Minto, who was walking ahead of his traveling company to Fort Hall, offered him a ride, and even gave Minto a saddle when he had trouble riding bareback.[24] Another Indian brought wood and kindled a fire for John Zeiber's family at the Elkhorn River crossing in 1851 while Zeiber was occupied with fording wagons.[25]

Indians also shared their knowledge of flora with passing overlanders. From natives near Fort Kearny Micajah Littleton learned which prairie plants were edible. A very hungry Heinrich Lienhard, nearing the end of the Hastings Cutoff in 1846, induced an Indian he encountered to dig some edible roots for him but drew the line at the grasshoppers his new friend also offered. After eating too many roots, Leinhard spent a miserable night suffering from stomachache and diarrhea. The next morning he refused to eat the roots the Indian again brought him for breakfast:

Since I could explain why only by signs, I bent over forward, held my stomach with both hands, and groaned as if I had severe stomach pains. Then I imitated a certain sound with my lips that could come only from another part of the anatomy, and at the same time I made a quick gesture to my behind. The Indians understood completely, and they all burst out in a storm of laughter. My friend laughed loudest of all, and threw his roots at my back. We naturally joined in the laughter and parted as good friends in spite of all.[26]

James Evans was involved in a touching encounter on the Humboldt Desert in 1850. Exhausted and struggling on foot toward the Truckee River, Evans met a nearly naked Indian carrying a little tin bucket filled with water for thirsty emigrants—"When we met he offered me the bucket exclaiming, 'Watty, Watty, Oh! white man—watty!'" Evans declined because he was not in as dire straits as some he had passed, and urged the Indian to minister to them instead. "He went on, and I afterwards learned that he came up to the famishing man and after giving him two or 3 drinks of water brought up an Indian poney, put the white man on him and took him on until he came to Trucky River! Oh! such generosoty! and pray, why do not those Emigrants who are ahead have the same feelings of humanity?"[27] Even the much-despised Digger Indians had their moments: Silas Miller reported a daring 1852 rescue of a drowning emigrant by two Digger braves. The Indians were rewarded for their heroics with suits of clothing and a two-month supply of provisions.[28]

The most consistently praiseworthy Indian assistance was doubtless rendered by Chief Washakie's Shoshoni or Eastern Snake Indians. Frederick Lander, superintendent of the Pacific Wagon Road Expedition, in his 1859 report to the Commissioner of Indian Affairs on trail conditions, stressed the valuable aid given by Washakie's people during that particularly dangerous period of plains travel. Lander pointed out that Washakie's tribe had never committed any recorded "outrages" upon whites; further: "The life of an emigrant was saved by an Indian at 'Green river crossing,' and great assistance rendered at the same dangerous ford in passing trains, by the mounted warriors of the tribe. Lost stock has been driven in, and, by a paper bearing over nine thousand signatures, the emigrants state 'that they have been most kindly treated by the Indians.'"[29]

The Indian aid represented by the preceding examples came as a pleasant surprise to overlanders who had not expected Indians to provide valuable assistance. A considerable number of emigrants, however, fortified particularly by guidebook commentary, embarked on the overland trip anticipating a very profitable type of interchange with plains Indians: trading for Indian goods. J. M. Shively had assured the readers of his 1846 guidebook that even the poorest Indian horse was superior to the finest stateside animal. Joseph Ware, in his much-used gold rush guidebook, likewise advised that only Indian horses were really fit for plains travel, though he was less sanguine than Shively of their easy availability. Shively also informed Oregon emigrants that from Salmon Falls to the end of their journey they would be able to trade with Indians for fish and other foodstuffs. Shively and Lansford Hastings both recommended outfitting with plenty of notions and trinkets for trading purposes.[30]

Because he and many of his forty-niner colleagues were depending on purchasing or trading for Indian horses, James Wilkins even complained about the scarcity of Indians on the route. When Wilkins finally encoun-

Chief Washakie of the Shoshonis, photographed about 1882, counseled peace and friendship with the white man.

tered an Indian and was unable to induce him to give up his horse, he had
to settle for acquiring by trade a pair of moccasins and deerskin pants.[31]
Another forty-niner, Benjamin Gatton, reported similar frustrations at
seeing so few natives, since "a great number of persons are sadly disappointed in not getting horses from them, as they expected."[32] The absence
of trade-minded natives was particularly troublesome to Quincy Adams
Brooks. Since he had anticipated procuring an Indian horse, he had
permitted his sore-footed partner to have their only mount. Brooks, unable to trade for an Indian horse, ended up walking, at least as far as the
Green River.[33]

In spite of such disappointments, during the course of their trip
virtually every overlander met at least a few Indians anxious to "swap."
Most encountered a great many. Though some emigrants did manage to
purchase certain items outright from native entrepreneurs, almost all the
trading was conducted on the barter principle, since specie had little
appeal for most prairie or mountain tribes.[34] Many emigrants quickly
learned, much to their surprise, that Indians were not easy marks in the
bargaining process. Indeed, the traditional stereotype of the easygoing
Indian, victimized in his every dealing with the white man, is simply not
accurate. Finley McDiarmid, for example, found the Snake Indians to be
"very sharp traders not easily cheated"; Cecelia Adams portrayed the Walla
Wallas as "pretty shrewd fellows for money"; William Kelly suggested that
the crafty Sioux compared favorably with wily British merchants; and
Ansel McCall stated that the Sioux "in every case get the best of the
bargain." Cephas Arms admitted his surprise at finding the Indians "much
shrewder" than he had expected.[35] Catherine Haun, one of the few female
forty-niners, incorporated all Indian tribes in asserting: "The Indian is a
financier of no mean ability and invariably comes out AI in a bargain.
Though you may, for the time, congratulate yourself upon your own
sagacity, you'll be apt to realize a little later on that you were not quite equal
to the shrewd redman—had got the 'short end of the deal.' "[36] Such an
instance occurred in 1850, when one of W. S. McBride's acquaintances sold
a very good rifle to an old Snake warrior for what he took to be eight
5-dollar gold pieces. Upon closer examination in better light, however, the
emigrant belatedly discovered he had been given a Cincinnati hardware
merchant's tokens instead. The sly Snake had disappeared into the
mountains as soon as the transaction had been completed.[37]

Especially when it came to the much-desired horses, overlanders
found the natives to be extremely canny bargainers. James Payne put it
succinctly in 1850: "Plenty of indians and pretty ponies today; we tried to
make a trade with them, but you can't cheat them in horses." Payne spoke
from experience, since he had earlier traded horses with the Sioux near
Fort Laramie and "got badly cheated."[38] Amos Steck found that "except in
negotiating for Whiskey they get as much as their Articles usually are

worth—no other article than whiskey will purchase their ponies & then not a good one."[39] Osborne Cross in 1849 and Origen Thomson in 1852 both believed that Indians, when they traded horses, were careful only to offer inferior animals. Although overland diaries are filled with references to Indians eager to trade horses, they are equally replete with accounts of unsuccessful attempts to conclude a horse trade.[40] John Edwin Banks remarked that "some of them are willing to trade anything they possess, except their ponies"; Henry Mann, a fellow forty-niner whose own blandishments had been twice rejected, complained that a Snake Indian tribe "had some beautiful horses but we could get none of them." An 1850 overlander, Abram Krill, unhappily discovered that a Sioux band not only refused to sell their own horses but wanted instead to purchase those of the emigrants.[41]

Then, too, a number of overlanders ruefully discovered that even when a horse trade had been accomplished they could not be absolutely certain that the horse was definitely theirs, since a fellow emigrant, from whom the horse had initially been stolen, occasionally came up to claim his property. This practice was common enough for the Salt Lake City *Deseret News* to warn overlanders about it.[42] Emigrant diaries are dotted with references to such incidents: in 1845 an Indian stole a horse from one overlander and sold it to another traveling to his rear; in 1849 Elijah Farnham purchased a horse from an Indian near Independence which was later claimed by its rightful owner; the next year James Blood learned that horses stolen from their party had been purchased by an emigrant traveling slightly behind them; and an 1855 train which purchased fifteen horses from a group of Indians on the Platte River later encountered the owners of most of the horses and presumably had to give up their newly acquired animals.[43]

There was also a profitable variation to this deceitful tactic. Indians would steal horses or other stock, make an agreement on a certain price for "finding" the animals with the emigrants from whom they had stolen them, and then quickly appear with the animals to claim the reward. Overlanders suspected Indians of employing this stratagem as early as 1843.[44] P. V. Crawford, nearing his Oregon destination in 1851, experienced and commented on this profitable Indian game: "We got ready to start and found that five of our horses were gone, which delayed us till late in the evening, when they were brought back by some Indians, who had agreed to find them for one dollar per head. This we understood."[45] Yet friendly Indians occasionally brought up stock which they had not stolen but had found. And at least once friendly Indians brought back to an emigrant company several mules which had earlier been stolen by hostile Indians.[46] When this happened the Indians always received rewards, which may have prompted some of them to steal stock "temporarily" for the sake of the anticipated compensation.

Despite all these frustrations and difficulties, a large number of over-landers ultimately traded for Indian horses during the trip. Those emigrants who recorded the terms of these transactions make clear that although a wide price fluctuation prevailed, the general trend was upward. Joel Palmer, in 1845, indicated that from $10 to $14 in trade goods (mainly in the form of clothing and blankets) would purchase an Indian horse, or that a cow might be evenly exchanged for a horse. In 1847 a cow was still reported to be worth a good pony, by 1849 mules were being exchanged for Indian ponies, and in 1852 at least one overlander indicated that two cows were now required to secure one pony.[47] Some emigrants swapped their American horses or mules for Indian horses, others plied the natives with blankets, knives, and similar materials. One wagon outfit, preparing to pack in to California from the Sweetwater River, swapped a wagon, its contents, and four yoke of cattle to Snake Indians for five ponies. Forty-niner James Pritchard had to give up a rifle, ammunition, and a blanket for a horse, although three years later Robert Sharp purchased a horse from a Digger Indian for only a rifle.[48] Another forty-niner secured his horse for a gallon of whiskey; in 1850 A. H. Thomasson gave up "2 blankets 1 pistol 1 knife 1 flask of powder 1 box of caps 1 vest 1 shert for a good poney." Charles Boyle, in 1849, calculated that he gave up trade goods worth $10 for a pony whose worth he evaluated at from $40 to $50.[49]

There is also some evidence that prices tended to increase as over-landers pushed westward. Henry Page reported paying $25 for a Sioux pony in 1849, another forty-niner purchased a horse from the Potawatomi Indians for $40, and yet another secured an Indian pony near Fort Boise for $45.[50] In 1850 Madison Moorman reported a 100 to 200 percent price increase in the space of 200 miles. By 1852 the Sioux were reportedly asking $100 to $125 for horses and mules and $65 to $75 for ponies.[51] If, in fact, such price rises were common during the flourishing gold rush period, it obviously reflected the sagacity of the natives in selling more dearly those objects which emigrants particularly desired, an Indian trait respectfully described by forty-niner William Kelly: "[The Sioux] displayed a quickness of discernment, and adroitness of dealing, that would have done credit to a Cheapside apprentice. They saw at a glance where your choice lay, and regulated their estimate accordingly; while in selecting the articles they desiderated, they affected a depreciative indifference, as if there was nothing in the batch that exactly suited them."[52]

Even though horses were the ultimate trading objective for most overlanders, the overwhelming amount of emigrant-Indian trading activity revolved around items of lesser magnitude. Very few overland parties crossed the plains without bartering for assorted Indian goods. Handmade Indian moccasins were probably the most frequently acquired commodity, followed closely by buffalo robes, dressed skins (mainly deer and elk), lariats, ropes, and occasionally bows and arrows.

Though desirable and useful, these articles were not as essential to the success of the migrations as the varied kinds of food also available from the natives. After they passed Fort Boise, Oregon-bound overlanders welcomed the opportunity of obtaining fresh or smoked salmon. Charles Stevens, for example, wrote to his family that at Salmon Falls "we got the first taste of Salmon, and you had better think we feasted." Samuel Francis, another 1852 overlander, thought salmon to be "the best Fish I ever ate."[53] After enduring so long the monotony of their normal fare, the salutary benefits of a dietary change in the form of fish and particularly of fresh vegetables and other produce—corn, peas, potatoes, pumpkins, onions, wheat, camas roots, and even watermelon—were not lost on the emigrants. Peter Burnett traded for Indian corn, peas, and potatoes in 1854, recalling: "I have never tasted a greater luxury than the potatoes we ate on this occasion. We had been so long without fresh vegetables that we were almost famished, and consequently we feasted this day excessively." The entire company was so pleased that they traded enthusiastically, Burnett remarking, "When two parties are both as anxious to barter as were the Indians and ourselves, it is very easy to strike a bargain."[54]

California-bound overlanders were much less fortunate on the later portions of their journey—the destitute Digger Indians living along the barren Humboldt River had little food to trade. During the earlier stages of the journey, however, emigrant trades with Indians for buffalo meat, as well as for choice cuts of deer and antelope, were common. In fact, trailside bartering between Indians and emigrants was often too pervasive, especially beyond Fort Hall, for emigrants trekking to Oregon. They filled their diaries and letters with amazed and sometimes frustrated commentary on the crowds of Indians constantly swarming about for trade purposes—and occasional pilfering on the side. One 1853 emigrant described the normal situation: "Whenever we camp near any Indian village we are no sooner stopped than a whole crowd may be seen coming galloping into our camp, male and female. Some come to swap and others are idle spectators. The squaws do all the swapping except in the pony line. When we will not trade with them they leave with exclamations as no good, NO GOOD."[55]

To fulfill their share of the various transactions concluded, overlanders most frequently offered, in addition to failing oxen and other loose stock, excess or worn-out clothing. Indians particularly relished shirts and wore the strange garments proudly. Mary Burrel noted how their company's Fourth of July had been enlivened by the sale of an old coat to an Indian, who put it on and proceeded to call himself an emigrant.[56] Less exhilarating, at least for some, was the scene in 1847 at Salmon Falls, where an Indian approached one camp proudly adorned in nothing but a tall silk hat and vest, for which he obviously had traded with a preceding company.

At his approach, the camp was alarmed. The more modest hastily retreated to their tents; and some of the men, angry that their wives should be insulted, were for shooting the inconsiderate visitor. A young married man, whose bride was particularly scandalized, was greatly exasperated. But the object of the old Indian was merely peaceable barter. He carried in each hand an immense fish; and Mr. Cosgrove, seeing his inoffensive purpose, bade the boys be moderate, and going out to meet him, hastily sawed a button from his coat, with which he purchased the fish, and sent the old fellow off thoroughly satisfied.[57]

Blankets were almost as popular in the emigrant-Indian bargaining sessions as clothing, and so too were such trinkets as buttons, beads, mirrors, needles, and thread. Guns and ammunition were also staple trade items, although some overlanders were skeptical of the wisdom of providing weapons of war to Indians. Nonetheless, the heavy traffic in these materials continued unabated.[58] Scarcely less desirable were tobacco, foodstuffs—including coffee, sugar, beans, flour, and bread—soap, fish-hooks, knives, medicine, and, according to 1850 overlander James Bennett, umbrellas.[59]

There was also alcohol, and since so much has been made of the Indian propensity for this intoxicant, it is noteworthy that overlanders seemed to be fairly circumspect in dispensing it. Indians approaching emigrant caravans for purposes of trade requested whiskey with regularity. Judging from the number of diary references, the Sioux were among the most persistent seekers. Alonzo Delano, who believed they would have sold their children for whiskey, reported that the first request of Sioux Indians near Ash Hollow in 1849 invariably was for whiskey. In 1850 James Abbey's company was visited by a dozen Indians "the substance of whose remarks was 'how-do-whiske,' that is they want whiskey."[60] At the height of the gold rush the sub-Indian agent for the great Nemaha sub-agency bemoaned the fact that the Iowa Indians had spent more time trying to secure ardent spirits from the passing overlanders than tilling their fields.[61] Overlanders reported that for whiskey the Indians would trade their ponies—or anything they had—but most of the emigrants who recorded these entreaties indicated that they had not provided the natives with firewater. A few did, of course, in order to secure a horse or some other desired article, and Charles Boyle remarked on a typical outcome: "Some of the emigrants traded some whisky to the Indians and this produced its usual effect, brawling and such a noise!"[62]

No summary of emigrant-Indian trading is complete without an assessment of one of the basic components of reminiscent accounts—the attempts of Indians to purchase or trade for emigrant daughters and wives. In their latter-day reminiscences overlanders were fond of magnifying and even inventing such episodes. They have "remembered" astronomical trade offers ranging up to 150 and even 400 horses for a single fair young emigrant girl. More frequently the remembered bids were for less than twenty horses. On one occasion, again in a reminiscent account, three young Sioux women offered six horses for a young emigrant man they fancied.[63] John B. Haas recalled an incident which had occurred during a bargaining session between a Pawnee Indian and an 1853 emigrant. The overlander jokingly offered to trade his wife for the Pawnee's horse and the Indian agreed, immediately endeavoring to possess the woman in question, who took refuge in a covered wagon. The native became quite angry when the overlander refused to follow through with their arrangement, and was pacified only after the emigrant gave him an old blue coat with shiny brass buttons.[64]

Not all such incidents can be relegated to the realm of folklore. Elijah Farnham on June 5, 1849, near the crossing of the South Platte, reported encountering Sioux Indians. "One of these nakedly d[r]essed Indians," Farnham wrote in characteristic overlander spelling, "took quite a fancy to one of the women that was traveling in company with us and offered her husband before her face 3 horses for her. She must of felt herself highly flatterd."[65] Thomas Cramer indicated that a Sioux Indian chief in 1859 responded so favorably to the "Liberality" of Cramer's wife Molly in dispensing trinkets and food that he offered to trade a squaw for her.[66]

While there are further references in contemporary accounts to the trading of persons, almost all of them deal with the reverse procedure— Indians offering to trade their wives or daughters to overlanders. Thus an old Snake woman tried to trade a "young and quite pretty squaw" to Pierson Reading for a horse in 1843. Forty-niner J. Goldsborough Bruff indicated that Bannock Indians offered to trade a middle-aged squaw for a copper powder flask; a Sioux chief offered Edwin Hillyer his prettiest daughter for a pony; and in 1851 Elizabeth Wood reported that Indians frequenting the Grande Ronde Valley were willing to trade a squaw for a pony. In 1852 Richard Keen recounted how an old Indian brought three squaws to their encampment near Fort Laramie hoping to trade them for mules. The next year Celinda E. Hines noted that a Nez Percé woman proposed trading her baby for a skirt, also in the Grande Ronde vicinity.[67]

Trade and aid were extremely significant aspects of the almost infinite variety of emigrant-Indian encounters. But they have been too often bypassed in the usual concentration upon pitched battles, scalps, and massacres. Initially the westbound emigrant wagons were strange curiosities to the natives in the same way that the overlanders were fascinated by the Indian life-style and customs. Accordingly, interaction, trading, and mutual aid prevailed throughout most of these crucial two decades of overland travel.

An analysis of the type and pattern of emigrant-Indian interaction during the antebellum era does suggest, however, that the overland emigrations quickened and perhaps made inevitable the military conquest of the western Indians. Almost from the very first, the perceptive plains Indians had recognized the threat the overland caravans represented to their way of life. Therefore, one of their first responses was to demand tribute of the passing trains. This tactic was employed at least as early as

William Henry Jackson, "Crossing South Platte." Indians, shown here peacefully intermingling with the emigrants, frequently provided friendly and useful assistance on the trail.

Scotts Bluff National Monument, National Park Service

1843.[68] An 1845 overlander, speculating on the origin of this Indian tax, believed the practice to have begun with frightened emigrants willing to promise almost anything to travel safely. But it seems clear that tribute demands, which were most widely experienced by overlanders during the gold rush period, were grounded in more than simple repetition of a previous chance success.[69] Emigrants continually reported that the Indians who came to demand tribute explained also why they were requesting the payments. The natives explicitly emphasized that the throngs of overlanders were killing and scaring away buffalo and other wild game, overgrazing prairie grasses, exhausting the small quantity of available timber, and depleting water resources.[70] The tribute payments, which occasionally were in specie but usually in provisions, were demanded mainly by the Sac and Fox, Kickapoo, Pawnee, and Sioux Indians—the tribes closest to the Missouri River frontier and therefore those feeling most keenly the pressures of white men increasingly impinging upon their domains.

Frequently the Indians presented a document from an Indian agent as proof of the correctness of their demands.[71] Indeed, for many years Indian agents had been reminding the Commissioner of Indian Affairs of the natives' unhappiness at the damage being done by overlanders. Thomas H. Harvey, the Superintendent of Indian Affairs at St. Louis, wrote in 1845, "The Indians say that the whites have no right to be in their country without their consent; and the upper tribes, who subsist on game, complain that the buffalo are wantonly killed and scared off, which renders their only means of subsistence every year more precarious." The next year Harvey returned to the same theme: "No people, probably, are more tenacious of what they consider their rights than the Indians."[72] From the Upper Missouri agency, also in 1846, agent Thomas P. Moore conveyed the bitterness of the Indians frequenting the Platte River at the overlanders' "wanton destruction of game, the firing of the prarie, and other injuries."[73] By 1848 Harvey was predicting "bloody conflicts, if not wars of extermination" if remedial action was not soon taken. He regularly recommended purchasing a right-of-way through the Indian domain.[74]

D. D. Mitchell, who had replaced Harvey as Superintendent of Indian Affairs at St. Louis by 1850, repeated the warnings and the recommendations, noting that the Indians had frequently been promised that their "Great Father" would deal fairly with them and provide compensation for the destruction of game, timber, and grass. From the Upper Platte agency, Thomas Fitzpatrick urged the necessity of coming to an immediate understanding with the Indians regarding a right-of-way through their lands.[75] Agents issued similar pleas in 1851, until the Fort Laramie Treaty that fall, after nearly a decade of fruitless appeals by Indians and their agents, acknowledged the validity of the Indian concern.[76]

In the absence of any official governmental action it was only natural that the Indians endeavored to exact some compensation from the culprits themselves. The overlanders, however, tended to view such demands as unwarranted "black-mail" and were especially perturbed that government employees were sanctioning and even encouraging the Indians in such nonsense.[77] Isaac Lord was particularly incensed when his party was accosted, and his reasoning suggests the core of much of the difficulty between the overlander and the Indian: the assumption that the Indian had no rights whatever. "The whole is a gross imposition. . . . The 'idea' that an old Indian should lay claim to a tract of land as large as all the New England States, and levy black mail on all passers, is sufficiently absurd; but when it is done by the connivance of the U.S. government . . . language becomes useless, and men had better think."[78] Osborne Cross, with the Mounted Riflemen Regiment in 1849, expressed similar sentiments, contending, "If these people really deserved compensation for the wood used, which was of itself too absurd to think of for a moment, it was a proper subject to lay before the Indian department." Cross intimated that the Indian affidavits, which the emigrants came to term "begging papers" or "recommends," had been furnished mainly in an attempt to get rid of pestering Indians and resulted only in considerable frustration for the emigrants.[79]

Overlanders were certainly much annoyed by Indians who swarmed about their wagons and camps, begging for this and that and exhibiting various "documents" purportedly attesting to their good character. Since many of the "begging papers" had been written by fellow emigrants and traders, Cross was undoubtedly correct in his analysis—one overlander would seek to assuage a pestering Indian by writing out a paper with which the Indian felt even more justified in becoming a nuisance to others. Many of the "begging papers" caused considerable merriment among subsequent overlanders, for the words did not always convey the meanings the Indians thought they did. D. A. Shaw, for example, was given a "recommend" by an importuning Indian which read, "This is a bad Indian; he will steal anything he can lay his hands on. Look out for him." John Lawrence Johnson received one which read, "Give this old devil hell if he comes around you he is an old thief." Some of the natives eventually accumulated a large stock of begging papers.[80]

Annoyed by the begging and unconvinced of the justice of the tribute demands, many emigrants simply refused to pay. Sarah Royce noted that the men of her company believed that "the demand was unreasonable! that the country we were traveling over belonged to the United States, and that these red men had no right to stop us." Brandishing their weapons, and threatening to open fire if the Indians annoyed them, this company forged ahead and made no payment.[81]

In addition to making tribute demands, Indians maintained a number of toll bridges at small streams fairly close to the frontier settlements. Here also there were confrontations which similarly fostered ill feelings.[82] Wolf Creek, on the trail leading west from St. Joseph, and Shell Creek, on the north side of the Platte River on the trail originating at Kanesville, were the two locations where westbound emigrants most frequently encountered bands of Indians demanding tolls. In 1849 and 1850 the usual charge for passing over the "rude log bridge" spanning Wolf Creek was twenty-five cents per wagon. In 1850 the Sac and Fox Indians had even hired a white toll keeper, who informed one traveler that by May 13, 2,300 wagons had already crossed that season.[83] In 1852 Indians were collecting the toll, which apparently had been raised to fifty cents per wagon.[84]

As they had with tribute demands, emigrants differed in their responses to this form of native entrepreneurship. John Clark thought it "perfectly right" for the natives to earn money in this manner as reimbursement for the wood and grass overlanders used. But Jay Green, believing the toll bridge to be a speculative enterprise run by the Indian agent, refused to pay.[85] Adopting this course of action was risky, since Indians often followed such companies until nightfall and then drove off or shot their cattle. Indians trailed one company which refused to pay such a bridge toll for two days before finding an opportunity to steal all their stock.[86]

The most serious confrontations seemed to occur at Shell Creek, where Pawnee Indians demanded a twenty-five-cent toll. The Shell Creek bridge had apparently been built and repaired by emigrant companies. When the bridge was swept away in an 1851 flood, the Pawnees refused to permit a group of overlanders to rebridge the stream. While some travelers tried unsuccessfully to bribe the Indians with presents, John Zeiber, a recently arrived emigrant, took charge of the disorganized body of overlanders. Setting all the men of the combined traveling parties to work either building the bridge or standing guard, Zeiber endeavored to assuage the frustrated Indians by showing them maps and claiming that the emigrants had treaty rights and were traveling to Oregon in peace and friendship. After the bridge was finished the emigrants gave some tobacco to the Indians and moved on safely.[87] Overland travelers unsympathetic to the reason for Indian demands for tribute and toll became particularly irate when Indians attempted to levy fees at structures which had been erected by passing overlanders. Although some emigrants paid, many did so grudgingly. In 1852, for example, Dr. Thomas White fulminated about "these hateful wretches" who exacted toll, asserting that he no longer had any sympathy for Indians.[88]

And always there was the temptation to resort to force. Some years after their 1852 confrontation, L. A. Norton proudly reminisced about how he had hit the Indian chief requesting payment at Shell Creek with a

Trail depredation
Post

Locations of Major Indian and
White Indian Trail Depredations

MAP 2

Bier

sword. Imperiously riding among the Indians, Norton had driven them away at sword point while his men, with rifles cocked, crossed the bridge without paying toll.[89] Other 1852 overlanders reported similar incidents.[90] From James Carpenter's company the Indians demanded a bushel of corn per wagon. When another company came up, Carpenter's partner enthusiastically opened the way: "... when we got to the bridge there was a lot of Indians standing there and my Partner made a motion to the right & Left but the Indians did not move he made a dive for the nearest one and with his fist knocked him spralling and with his left fist sent another one down and he had 3 of them down in half the time I have been writing it I had my team close up and the rest of the train was well up behind and the[y] got out of the way and we had no further trouble. ..."

What emigrants like Norton and Carpenter did not acknowledge was the cumulative impact of a series of such arrogant actions. Carpenter himself recalled that "the next day the Indians stoped a train and they undertook to compromise and got into a fight and had several killed."[91] Many of the confrontations over tribute and toll need to be understood in this context. On May 10, 1852, according to the emigrants involved, a large group of Pawnee Indians demanded six head of cattle from an oncoming train. The Indian band had already torn away the bridge. The emigrants rebuilt the bridge, crossed, and gave the Indians nothing. The next day the Indians again demanded tribute from another company. But this time they had cut out the center portion of the bridge. Loose brush had been laid over the hole so as to entrap the lead wagon. Several emigrant companies cooperated to push through, however, engaging the natives in a short battle in which nine Indians were killed and several more wounded. The overlanders suffered no casualties.[92] East Owen mentioned a similar fracas about the same time. A small company refused to pay the twenty-five-cent toll and the Pawnees commenced plundering the wagons. An emigrant then shot at an Indian, and in the ensuing skirmish one overlander was killed. The Indians were pursued with reinforcements from the next train and at least seven natives were killed.[93] Also in 1852 the Pawnees, near Shell Creek, demanded tribute from an emigrant party for crossing their lands. The emigrant group not only refused but launched an immediate attack, following the fleeing Indians to where they endeavored to cross the Platte River and then firing on them, killing four and wounding others.[94]

The bridge tolls and tribute payments demanded by the Indians were insignificant when compared to the ferry and bridge charges asked by mountain men and traders farther west along the trails. Clearly, however, it was not the money as much as the idea that Indians had any "right" to claim payments which infuriated many emigrants. Indignantly refusing compliance, these emigrants willingly instigated skirmishes, which in turn elicited Indian retaliation on subsequent overlanders. As reports of such depredations accumulated, frontier newspaper editors demanded army

"A Chief Forbidding the Passage of a Train through His Country." In the early years of emigration, payment of a tariff could usually resolve the difficulty. New-York Historical Society protection and military reprisals. Within such a milieu, interaction between overlanders and Indians became increasingly volatile. By the mid and late 1850s any Indian encounter along the overland trail was more likely to be violent than at any previous time, one of the more dubious legacies of the California gold rush.

Current misunderstandings of the nature of the Indian threat to the overland emigrants have been molded by oft-repeated images of violent Indian attacks with all the accouterments normally ascribed to them: encircled wagon trains surrounded by mounted Indians emitting blood-curdling war whoops, demonstrating a deadly accuracy with bow and arrow, and mercilessly scalping their victims. Such views, however, are not uniquely the products of the mass media of the twentieth century. Encounters with hostile Indians—often much embellished—are far more conspicuous in latter-day reminiscent accounts than in the journals and diaries in which overland emigrants recorded the actual events of their journey. Even in the letters sent back from California and Oregon summarizing the trip, overlanders tended to give Indian affairs much more prominence than they had in their daily journals and diaries. In both cases this probably was due to the recognition that others would be most interested in the exciting and dangerous aspects of the trip, which were, accordingly, singled out for special emphasis. On occasion they were invented. Indeed, in the daily journals and diaries, eyewitness accounts of depredations are infrequent compared with reports of rapine and slaughter received from someone met upon the trail or circulated via the roadside telegraph. As Caroline Richardson phrased it in 1851, ". . . we are continually hearing of the depredations of the indians but we have not seen one yet."[95]

Since "Madame Rumor," as Madison Moorman termed some of these reports in 1850, was not always to be trusted, the task of scholars in attempting to sift fact from fiction is extremely difficult.[96] Some of the mythical massacres forthrightly reported in the newspapers of the time helped form the milieu in which continuing misunderstandings were nourished. In 1847 the annihilation of approximately 100 overlanders on the Applegate route into Oregon was featured in frontier newspapers. The St. Louis *Daily Missouri Republican,* although printing the story, was properly suspicious, since some of the persons reportedly murdered had already arrived safely in California.[97] In 1849 the *Republican* dubbed as a "hoax" the issuance in St. Louis of a newspaper extra centering on a battle near Fort Hall in which twenty emigrants and many Indians had purportedly been killed.[98] Another imaginary 1849 engagement surfaced in the Louisville *Examiner,* based upon a letter supposedly written from Fort Laramie by a former Louisville resident. This unnamed French gentleman wrote grandly about a battle with Iowa Indians in which he had played the leading role. The incident supposedly took place 200 miles east of Fort Laramie. When all seemed bleakest, the brave Frenchman had taken command to save the women and children by sending them ahead toward the fort under cover of darkness. The next day he led the men in repulsing the Indian attack, which he melodramatically described:

[The Indians] yelled and came directly upon us. You may imagine how I felt. There were some who wished to save themselves, but I obliged them to remain, and gave orders that they should barricade themselves behind the wagons, from which they could fire with their guns, and not to lose courage. The firing commenced on both sides, and every discharge of ours brought down its man. For half an hour we kept them at bay, but notwithstanding, they continued to close in with us more and more, and we could not hold out against their numbers. We were obliged to abandon our ground but not till we had killed some 100 Indians. We had but 13 killed and 9 wounded, of whom 6 so dangerously that they could not follow us. Two fell at my side, and I had my hat pierced by a bullet which only grazed my hair.[99]

In the mid-1850s fictional massacres became even more sensational. An especially creative year was 1855, when the Dixon, Illinois, *Telegraph* expressed its belief that "the reports of the capture and murder of many, if not all, of the emigrants who started to California and Oregon last spring" were true.[100] The most intriguing hoax of the year was the "Doniphan massacre," which was given coverage in at least five different newspapers. According to the several reports, there were only nineteen survivors from a 300-person, ten-wagon train led by "Captain Doniphan" and including also "Col. Gilpin" of Missouri.[101] The train had been attacked by 2,000 Sioux and Cheyenne Indians in the middle of the night while encamped near Devil's Gate on either July 14 or 15. All 3,000 animals which this company had been trailing west were stolen by the Indians. The basic account had been delivered in person to the editor of the *Oregon Argus* by John Wiggins of St. Louis, who claimed to be a survivor of the attack and whose own wife and three children had been killed. Wiggins stated that he and the other survivors managed to walk to Salt Lake City, where Brigham Young provided five teams with which they traveled to Sacramento. From there Wiggins walked to Oregon. One other 1855 overlander, a Mr. Benton, who claimed to have been in a train ahead of the Doniphan one, also reported the alleged tragedy, but indicated that only 150 emigrants had been killed. Yet shortly thereafter another overlander, who had passed Devil's Gate two weeks after the presumed massacre, branded the incident as fraudulent, noting that traders in the Devil's Gate vicinity had not seen a single hostile Indian all year.[102]

Emigrants who were worried about real or imaginary Indians found that the authors of the overland guidebooks allotted frustratingly little space to matters of Indian relationships.[103] Perhaps equally surprising was their lack of emphasis on the danger of violent attacks; instead they agreed that theft of property constituted the major Indian threat. These writers encouraged emigrants to guard their stock and camp carefully every night, to forbid Indians to come into camp, and to form circles with their wagons if an attack seemed imminent. Emigrants were also cautioned not to wander off alone from the train, especially if unarmed, for such action invited robbery. The guidebook writers also made it fairly clear that the most dangerous stretches of the trail, insofar as Indian assaults were concerned, came at the California and Oregon end.[104]

If any general philosophy undergirded their advice it was that the Indians should not be permitted to think the emigrants were afraid. Rather, overlanders were admonished to maintain a clear pattern of discipline at encampments and along the trails, refuse unnecessary concessions, and if Indians became menacing or excessively troublesome, to threaten to shoot, whip, or otherwise punish them. Many overlanders obviously believed that such a policy of separation and harshness was the proper one, recounting proudly in their diaries and reminiscences how they had treated bothersome Indians forcefully, thereby nipping possible depredations in the bud.[105] After all, the renowned Dr. Marcus Whitman had commended 1847 overlanders for roughing up insolent Indians, reportedly stating that "if more men would do likewise, instead of giving them presents for their impudence and theft, it would be better for all concerned."[106]

Reports of depredations, whether accurate or not, combined with the guidebook advice, predisposed overlanders toward treating all Indians with suspicion and distrust. Further, since the major tragedies and mythical massacres occurred almost exclusively during the post-1849 period, it was during the 1850s that overlanders were most uneasy as they launched out onto the plains. For example, on her first day west of the Missouri River in 1850, Margaret Frink acknowledged that for the previous week Indians had been the major conversational topic among emigrants. Printed circulars reminding overlanders of the Indian threat were even circulated.[107]

Thus primed, overlanders were responsible for many incidents which, while often humorous, were sometimes deadly. While these usually occurred at the inception of the journey, all along the trail forty-niners and subsequent overlanders shot at one another, at their own oxen, mules, horses, and sheep, at saddles and blankets, at elk, and even at pelicans. All had been mistaken for marauding Indians.[108] Most of these instances of mistaken identity occurred at night, when nervous guards, seeing shadowy silhouettes and remembering guidebook warnings that Indians sometimes disguised themselves as wolves or other animals, fired first and asked questions later.[109] Indian scares materialized even in broad daylight. Byron McKinstry, whose company had been regularly experiencing false alarms in preceding days, sarcastically greeted another with the words, "An Indian battle! and the whites victorious." His account demonstrated how easy it was in such an atmosphere for frightened overlanders to conjure up an attack out of nothing:

About the middle of the afternoon a brisk firing commenced on the opposite side, and the alarm of Indians—Our Capt. came running into camp from the river and gave orders for every man to load and repair to the scene of action! 'Let's give it to them now we are strong handed' cries the good old capt. I was soon on the river bank with both barrels of Hibbards shot gun, stuffed with Buck Shot—which I put in quicker than I ever loaded it before, for the firing was so rapid, and the screaming of the women and children, and the yelling of the men so incessant that I really believed that an attack was made on the camp while the men were ferrying. We soon ascertained that it was a false alarm. Some young men on that side commenced firing their revolvers, and the women who were alone in the camp really supposed that it was Indians, ran to the river bank screaming as loud as possible, which alarmed their husbands who were ferrying, and all others who saw or heard them. Those that saw them say that they came rushing out of the bushes to the brink of the water swinging their bonnets and screaming that the Indians were killing them all on that side. I don't expect that the poor souls will get over their fright in a month, and I am not sure that all the men will. If there had been Indians within hearing they certainly would have fled![110]

After one or two such humiliating extravaganzas, most travelers shed some of their timidity, realizing that their own fears and imaginations were generally more troublesome than Indians.[111] Indeed, many overlanders became exceedingly careless, so quick were they to conclude that there was no danger whatever. In his 1846 guidebook Lansford Hastings condemned the overlanders' fairly common practice of disposing of their weapons, usually to Indians, when they reached the Green River or Fort Hall. Philip Platt and Nelson Slater similarly decried such foolish tactics in their 1852 guidebook.[112] In 1850 one company, having gone only as far as Ash Hollow, assumed they were out of danger and destroyed their guns to lighten their load. Later, when they experienced an Indian scare on the Lassen Cutoff, their entire outfit could muster only a single rifle plus a few pistols.[113] Benjamin Ferris's traveling party in 1852, when experiencing an Indian alarm some four weeks west of the frontier, discovered that in their entire company there was only one revolver in firing condition. Fortunately the "Indians" turned out to be wolves.[114]

Army officers patrolling western trails during the dangerous late 1850s bemoaned the cavalier lack of concern many overlanders evidenced toward Indian danger. Major Isaac Lynde, for example, disclosed in disbelief, "I have seen many trains on the road during the summer who had plenty of arms, but they carried them in their wagons; and, in many cases, without being loaded. They would laugh at me when I told them of the necessity of always having their arms ready for instant use." And the following year an exasperated Lieutenant Colonel M. S. Howe explained one successful Indian attack by noting, "As usual, with ninety-nine one-hundredths of emigrants, their fire-arms, except revolvers, were in the wagons, some not loaded."[115]

For overlanders who commenced the trip amid depredation rumors—which persisted along the trail—and whose initial overactive imaginations had led to trigger-happy responses, such behavior was indeed strange. It was prompted by several factors. First, a sizable proportion of overlanders in all emigration years had very little contact with the native inhabitants. Infrequent encounters led naturally to a relaxation of travel discipline. The friendly Snake Indians whom William Newby traded with near Soda Springs in 1843 were the first Indians he had seen in two months.[116] Again and again emigrants reported similar experiences. After leaving a Kansas village, Virginia Reed saw no Indians until she reached Fort Laramie; George Curry, also in 1846, saw none for at least 300 miles beyond the fort. In 1847 H. Warren saw almost no natives at all until he met some Sioux at Fort Laramie.[117] John T. Milner, in 1849, who had seen only seven friendly Indians before he reached Fort Kearny, reported that he felt "as safe as I would travelling from Burnside to Columbus [Georgia]."[118] According to a correspondent at Fort Kearny in 1850, seven-eighths of that year's migration had yet to see a single Indian when they reached that point. Travelers in subsequent years found the situation to be similar. In 1856 Mary Powers, from near Fort Laramie, reported, "We have not seen an Indian since we left Omaha nor any signs of any."[119]

Conversely, overlanders who met Indians very frequently, and almost always in friendship and peace, also tended to relax their travel discipline. On at least thirty days in 1843, according to his diary entries, Pierson Reading encountered Indians. Only once, toward the end of the journey, was there any danger. Edward Parrish, the next year, recorded almost as many encounters, as did Joel Palmer in 1845. All were relatively peaceful.[120] In 1846 Edwin Bryant engaged in peaceful interaction with Indians on 32 of the 117 days his overland journey consumed—more than a quarter of the time.[121] The encounters mentioned by Reading, Parrish, Bryant, and other overlanders were varied. Included were visits to Indian villages, Indians traveling with overlanders for a day or more, Indians sleeping overnight in emigrant encampments, frequent smoking of the peace pipe, and the ever-constant trading and presentation of gifts. There were even hints of romance. Henry Coke, who found a party of Cayuse Indians in 1850 to be "pleasant travelling companions," became momentarily enamored of a young squaw in the group. John Hawkins Clark revealed how jealous their entire camp had been of the one fortunate overlander who managed to sit next to a pretty Indian girl when a Sioux band visited their camp to smoke the peace pipe. Clark believed the girl had made a "lasting impression." During this friendly gathering the overlanders even passed around pictures of their sweethearts and wives for their Indian acquaintances to view.[122]

None of this type of interaction fostered much fear of Indians or led overlanders to believe in the necessity of maintaining martial discipline.

Despite the many travelers during the second decade of overland migration who relaxed their military readiness because they saw so many peaceful Indians, emigrants who crossed the plains in the 1840s saw more natives and interacted more frequently with them. Perhaps this was because the traveling caravans were less numerous in the first years and proved such a curiosity to the Indians. The shift to a less frequent and less cordial interaction was not overly abrupt. After all, the vast number of travelers on the trails during the gold rush era insured considerable contact. Throughout the decade there were still many visits to Indian villages, peace pipes were still smoked, and Indians still assisted emigrants and traded with them. On her 1860 overland trip, for example, Mary Guill's traveling company encountered peaceful Indians on nearly twenty days.[123] But throughout the 1850s both emigrants and Indians were more wary. Their interactions were slowly becoming less frequent, less friendly, and more dangerous.

It was, of course, a matter of mere chance that some overlanders saw very few Indians, that others encountered Indians very often, also with no trouble, and that still others suffered mightily, perhaps in the very same month or even week. John R. Tice, for example, wrote to his sister in 1851 that while many depredations had occurred that year, "We were not troubled any but there were some before and behind us that were killed."[124] Some who traveled without difficulty while others did not assumed that it was because they had maintained a strong guard throughout the trip.[125] John L. Johnson's company in 1851 voted on whether they should set out a guard at their evening encampment near Bannock Creek. Since the vote was close, they resolved the issue by establishing two camps about 100 yards apart. One group set out a guard and lost a few oxen, the other did not and had all their oxen stolen. The more vigilant group charitably joined in the search for the missing animals.[126] On the other hand, some overlanders were convinced they escaped unscathed because they were kind and compassionate to all Indians they met. William Keil was of such a mind following the 1855 trip on which he led his communitarian followers west. Despite the many disquieting reports of pillage and plunder, their company did not shun the natives but fed them, traded with them, and exchanged presents with them. Keil concluded, "In short, my only happiness on the plains were the meetings with the Indians."[127]

On one point both overlanders and guidebook writers were agreed: thievery and not murderous attack constituted the major threat posed by Indians. During the course of their long journey, a considerable number of emigrants became so inured to this Indian proclivity that they dismissed it as another of the trip's tribulations—somewhat akin to dusty trails and voracious mosquitoes—a constant not worth worrying about. In summarizing their trip, overlanders frequently used such phrasings as the following: "We have had no trouble with the Indians with the exception of horse and cattle stealing"; "They were very friendly but stole everything they could lay their hands on"; "We have not been troubled by the Indians but very little. They are friendly disposed and no disposition to hostility is shown. They, however, steal all they can but as yet they have not got much from us."[128] Henry Page, endeavoring to reassure his wife, wrote in 1849, "We are & shall not be, in any danger of our lives from the Indians—the only trouble is to keep them, from stealing—but they will not trouble us, so much as they will the mule trains."[129] When Cecelia Adams remarked near Fort Boise that "we do not keep a guard over [our cattle] now, for we are not much afraid of the Indians stealing them," she was likely manifesting sentiments James Payne had earlier expressed in a cavalier manner: "We have lost all fear of the indians and dont notice them any more than so many crows."[130] Payne made his comment shortly after crossing the Green River; A. W. Harlan had been even farther along when he confided to his diary, "The Indians all the way on Carson river shoot all the oxen they can. They also shoot at the emigrants every convenient opportunity but we think so little of it now that I had neglected to mention anything about it."[131]

Harlan, of course, was one of the few who failed to be impressed by bullets or arrows which came his way. But while arrows were infrequent, pilfering was not. After a trading session, or a visit from curious natives, emigrants regularly discovered that some item had disappeared. Byron McKinstry, for example, reported that their company's assistant captain lost considerable money when he had his pockets picked, and that two of his handkerchiefs had also been stolen, one having been taken from around his neck. McKinstry described the technique of these "audacious beggars": ". . . they will put their hands into ones pockets if you are not resolute with them, especially the squaws. They have learned that white men are not so apt to knock down a squaw as they are an Indian, but if they would knock over every one of either kind that came about them it would be much better, but they are a kind of novelty and the whites wish to gain their good graces."[132] An 1845 Oregon-bound company had to drive thieving Kaw Indians away from their encampment every night during the first days of their journey. In exasperation they finally imprisoned one brave and made him promise to refrain from stealing.[133] One company, fearing thievery when many Sioux came to their camp, resorted to a clever ruse to evict the pests. One man wrapped a blanket around himself and lay down in his tent while their company physician told the visiting Indians that the overlander had smallpox. The Indians left and did not return.[134]

But it was the art of stealing horses which, at least according to emigrant testimony, the Indians had absolutely mastered. As S. H. Taylor indicated to his hometown newspaper in 1853, Pawnees would "almost steal a horse from under his rider."[135] Several emigrants, after suffering embarrassing object lessons in the craft of theft, agreed. Mr. Burns, while encamped in Oregon's Grande Ronde Valley in 1852, feared thievery. To prevent any attempts, he tied his horse with a strong rope to the back of his wagon, a few feet from the head of his bed. When he awoke in the morning rope and horse were gone. An 1845 overlander awoke similarly horseless and even more sheepish one morning shortly beyond South Pass. He had retired with his horse's rope tied around his arm.[136] Neither overlander recovered his animal.

Emigrants whose precautions had been insufficient or whose luck had been bad—and there were many—did not regard the Indian threat in the minimal terms their more fortunate colleagues did. If these theft victims were still relatively close to the Missouri River they could turn around and retrace their steps—a task which itself was not easy if most of their draft animals had been stolen.[137] But if the thievery occurred when they were well into their journey their plight was even more precarious. It was to such persons that the humanitarianism of fellow overlanders was especially crucial. Elizabeth Geer illustrated the travail of emigrants in such circumstances when she labeled "a trying time" the three June days in 1847 when their company unsuccessfully searched for thirty missing oxen, presumably stolen by Indians. Having been left with only one yoke, the Geer family was especially endangered. On the fourth day Mrs. Geer plaintively wrote, "So many of us having to get teams, had to hire, borrow, buy, just as we could. Had to take raw cattle, cows, or anything we could get. Some had to apply to other companies for help; at last we moved off."[138]

Analogous examples are numerous. In 1849 Elijah Howell camped near a physician who had not traveled for nearly a week after Indians had stolen all of his cattle along the Humboldt River.[139] Alonzo Delano told of one train on the Lassen route in 1849 from which twenty-seven mules had been stolen during one night. These emigrants had no alternative but to leave their wagons and belongings and start packing in with their few remaining mules. One man walked for three days without food, others fell exhausted in the road and had to be rescued by men who came out from the California settlements.[140] A party of Mormons returning to Salt Lake City from California in 1850 reported that in a canyon stronghold near the head of the Humboldt River Indians were keeping approximately 1,000 head of animals which they had stolen that year from emigrants.[141] Indian agent Garland Hurt, after traveling along the Humboldt River in 1856, believed that property had been stolen from virtually every emigrant train. That year Hurt estimated that at least 300 cattle and 60 to 70 horses and mules had already been stolen or killed along that section of trail.[142]

The loss of all or almost all of a family's or an entire company's draft animals at one fell swoop was disastrous. Overlanders struggling along the Humboldt River with worn-down teams were also more than inconvenienced when Indians shot arrows into oxen and cattle. The native marksmen usually struck at night, but also fired during the day from cover provided by trees and bushes along the river banks. Their goal was to kill or cripple the beasts so that overlanders would have to leave them behind for Indian feasting. Since by this time in their journey many emigrants, especially in 1850, were in a near starving condition, they frequently butchered the cattle themselves and took with them all the meat they could transport—thereby winning a minor victory over the destitute Indian marksmen. Elijah Farnham thus jubilantly explained, "We packed up the cattle that had been killed by the Indians & between us & the hungry packers that came along we used up the flesh of the dead cattle so clean that the diggers did not get a morsel for their pains."[143] The Digger Indians and others who specialized in this practice managed, however, to kill a tremendous amount of stock in this fashion throughout the emigration years. This was certainly the single most common form of Indian depredation California-bound emigrants faced.

Less common but recurring often enough for guidebook writers to warn travelers accordingly was the confrontation risked by overlanders wandering off some distance from their traveling companions. If met by Indians they were entirely at their mercy. On a number of occasions, however, such persons, when mounted, made it safely back to their camps, but not without having been closely pursued and badly frightened.[144] While the Indians were sometimes friendly, they were always cognizant of the choice opportunity to acquire booty. Probably the two most famous such incidents in migration history occurred in 1841 and 1842. Nicholas Dawson, while out hunting, was surrounded by a party of Cheyenne Indians who took his mule, gun, and pistol. Later the Indians returned all but the pistol. Dawson was known thereafter by his comrades as "Cheyenne."[145] The following year Lansford Hastings and Mr. Lovejoy were captured, robbed, and threatened with death when they lingered behind their traveling company to inscribe their names on Independence Rock. Although Hastings's account of the affair exaggerated his own role in their ultimate extrication, their situation had indeed been precarious before the company guide, Thomas Fitzpatrick, convinced the Sioux to give up their prisoners.[146]

During the antebellum era a few overlanders caught in such fashion were killed. The more usual result was as embarrassing as it was frightening. Besides being robbed of all possessions they were carrying at the time, emigrants were stripped of their clothes and had no recourse but to walk back to their encampment stark naked. Loren Hastings, after witnessing a series of unhappy encounters with Pawnee Indians—begging, two attempts to steal horses, and the stripping of two emigrant hunters—was sufficiently infuriated to declare, "The Pawnee Indians are the greatest thieves I ever saw—the best way I think to civilize or Christianize Indians is with powder & lead, & this the way we shall do hereafter."[147] Pawnees caught other hunters in 1847 and the results were identical, except that one group was spared the indignity of losing all their clothes, being permitted to retain their hats and boots. Naked overlanders hiked back to their companies during the years of the gold rush with some regularity, but by then the outcome was not always only humiliating. A small party of seven men, for example, was surrounded near the Humboldt River in 1854. All were stripped of their clothing before three emigrants managed to escape. The Indians killed the remaining four men.[148]

Despite all the aid and trade, and notwithstanding that thievery was the most dangerous depredation to which the vast majority of overlanders were exposed, killings and massacres have remained the favorite manner of characterizing the emigrant-Indian relationship. Yet paradoxically, even though the Indian threat, in *general* terms, has been widely emphasized, nowhere in the voluminous migration literature has much accurate attention been accorded to any of the *specific,* non-mythical trail tragedies of sizable proportions which did occur. Such episodes as the 1854 attack on the Alexander Ward party or the 1860 assault on the Otter–Van Orman train remain virtually unknown despite the large numbers of emigrant deaths, the severity of the accompanying atrocities, and, in the 1860 instance, the cannibalism which capped the gruesome affair.[149] Instead, the most widely publicized trail tragedies—the Donner party's 1846 ordeal in the Sierra snows, or the similar 1856 trial by weather of the Mormon handcarters—are not Indian-related. Indians were involved in the infamous Mountain Meadows massacre of 1857, but at most only as co-conspirators with John D. Lee and other fanatical Mormon zealots and more probably merely as lackeys carrying out Mormon plans.[150]

Influenced by the exaggerated reminiscent accounts, most writers have fostered the impression that the Indians were implacable foes throughout the emigration period. Unfortunately, few have endeavored to lend substance to such generalizations with precise statistical evidence. One of the few numerical estimates made—that 1,800 men, women, and children had been killed by Indians during the emigration years—was offered by an 1852 overlander in a 1904 address to his colleagues in the Oregon Pioneer Association.[151] Table 4, an exploratory attempt to assess the actual number of trail killings between 1840 and 1860, indicates that Charles Moores's 1904 estimate was at least four times too large. These new statistics, however tentative, require new appraisals of this most dreaded aspect of the overland journey.[152]

For example, no one has ever been much concerned about what overlanders were doing to the Indians. Table 4 reveals that the emigrants killed Indians more frequently than they themselves were being killed, in almost every migration year.[153] Indeed, on the basis of this evidence it is no longer possible to argue that the Indians posed an equally hazardous threat in every emigration year, or that the natives had been committed to preventing the emigrations from the very first time they viewed the white-topped wagons.

TABLE 4
ESTIMATED OVERLAND EMIGRANTS KILLED BY INDIANS, AND
INDIANS KILLED BY OVERLAND EMIGRANTS, 1840–60

Year	Emigrants	Indians	Year	Emigrants	Indians
1840	0	0	1851	60	70
1841	0	1	1852	45	70
1842	0	0	1853	7	9
1843	0	0	1854	35	40
1844	0	0	1855	6	10
1845	4	1	1856	20	15
1846	4	20	1857	17 (8)[a]	30
1847	24	2	1858	?	?
1848	2	2	1859	32 (13)[a]	10
1849	33	60	1860	25	10
1850	48	76	Totals	362	426

[a]Emigrants presumably killed by "white Indians"; these twenty-one deaths are not included in the yearly totals.

Apart from 1847, which year's statistics are magnified by the apparent annihilation of an entire train of twenty-three or more persons at Tule Lake on the southern emigrant road to Oregon, the pre–gold rush travel pattern is one of essential safety with only scattered skirmishes and very few deaths. This is especially evident during the important first years of emigration. Had the Indians met the small precedent-setting caravans of 1840–44 with the same hostility they later demonstrated, it is doubtful that overlanders would have subsequently streamed westward in the numbers they did. The new era, which had been foreshadowed in 1847, dawned with the coming of the forty-niners. It is apparent that thereafter a much greater risk prevailed than had been the case during the previous decade.

The impression has long been current that the threat of death was most severe on the Great Plains.[154] Perhaps this is a legacy from the many army-Indian clashes fought in those regions, or maybe it is because the famed Fort Laramie was located there. It may also derive from the bad reputation the Pawnees had among the overlanders, or because this was the territory of the legendary Sioux, who were involved in some of the most-remembered battles of western history. Yet an analysis of the geographic regions where nearly 400 overlanders were killed between 1840 and 1860 indicates that approximately 90 percent of all emigrant killings took place west of South Pass, principally along the Snake and Humboldt rivers and on the Applegate Trail. Clearly, the first half of the overland journey was by far the safest, as well as the easiest. Moreover, in terms of actual deaths as well as percentages of the total numbers involved, it was much safer to travel overland to California—the Digger Indians along the Humboldt River notwithstanding—than to go overland to Oregon. And the southern, or Applegate, route to Oregon was probably the single most dangerous stretch of the overland trail, though by the late 1850s no trails west—or even east—of South Pass were as safe as they once had been.

Knowledge of approximately how many persons were actually killed, and when and where, is incomplete without an understanding of the motivations influencing the killings. Table 4 intimates a pattern of mutual causation or dual responsibility, since in years when Indians killed no overlanders they were also not being killed by the emigrants. Numerous examples from the various migration years demonstrate that the killings and massacres, once begun, influenced and accelerated subsequent atrocities. Yet even though historical responsibility is by no means onesided, the callous attitude of cultural and racial superiority so many overlanders exemplified was of considerable significance in producing the volatile milieu in which more and more tragedies occurred.

Occasionally a few of the semi-permanent residents of the West—traders and trappers—encouraged emigrants to treat every Indian like a mortal foe. An 1843 emigrant hunting party surprised a solitary Sioux Indian. Quickly surrounding him, they proceeded to discuss what was to be done with him. A trader temporarily traveling with them recommended that the Indian be summarily killed. The overlanders, however, reached a more generous decision and permitted the frightened native to depart. But upon returning to their encampment, as Overton Johnson and William Winter related the incident, "all the Traders joined in exclaiming against us, for not killing him . . . and said that as we were among Indians, we must treat them as they treated us; and so the white people, who live in the Mountains, act toward their enemies."[155]

Other ethnocentric overlanders, such as Texan Jim Kinney, needed no prompting from mountain men for their dastardly conduct. Traveling beyond Fort Hall in 1845, Kinney spied an Indian near the trail. Announcing his intention of making the Indian his personal slave, Kinney threatened to kill anyone in his traveling company who interfered. Kinney rode up to the Indian, struck him, and then handcuffed him. Tieing a rope around the Indian's neck, Kinney then fastened the uncomprehending native to the rear of his wagon. While his wife drove the wagon, Kinney rode behind, whipping the Indian. The entire company was so cowed by the blustering Texan that they did nothing. Kinney's reprehensible conduct continued for a week, until he felt the Indian's spirit had been broken. From then on Kinney worked the Indian at various jobs including driving the wagon, confident that if he fled, Kinney's dog would pick up the Indian's trail, just as it had tracked runaway slaves for Kinney in Texas. Kinney repeatedly said, according to a company member, that "if the Indian ran away . . . he could follow him and kill him to show the other Indians the superiority of the white man. He said he had killed plenty of negroes and an Indian was no better than a negro." One windy night the unhappy slave disappeared, taking with him some of Kinney's personal effects, including his hundred-dollar gun. The company members rejoiced—particularly when Kinney's wonder dog was unable to track the vanished Indian—but quietly, in deference to Kinney's temper and threats.[156]

Similar incidents confirmed the total disregard some emigrants had for the natives they encountered. Their insensitive actions helped sour emigrant-Indian relationships. Guide Caleb Greenwood's son shot and killed—and boasted about having done so—an innocent Indian whose only crime had been startling Greenwood's horse. Greenwood had almost been thrown, which caused his companions to laugh at him. Infuriated, he suddenly murdered the Indian.[157] In 1849 emigrants from a Missouri company reportedly ravaged and killed Snake squaws, prompting Snake attacks on subsequent trains. Additional unprovoked murders were also reported in 1849.[158] An 1851 company of emigrants found a peaceful band of Indians already encamped at what was considered the best campsite in that locale along the Snake River. The overlanders summarily ordered the Indians to depart, and speeded the evacuation process by firing shotgun blasts over their heads and pursuing the Indians on horseback to make them run faster. It should not have been surprising that a retaliatory attack occurred the next day in which one emigrant was killed and two wounded.[159]

It was, to be sure, a very small percentage of emigrants whose every action bespoke a blatant assumption of cultural superiority and an arrogant disregard of Indian rights or even humanity. But in the same manner that refusal to pay toll or tribute often elicited reprisals on innocent overlanders, so did despicable actions of this nature. Retaliating overlanders and Indians did not differ much from the army in embracing policies of nonselective reprisal. The next Indians emigrants happened to come across were frequently punished for misdeeds they had not committed; Indians who came in peace to trade and were unsuspectingly fired upon were equally likely to attack subsequent trains, also without warning.[160] It did not require many persons acting in such fashion to generate an aura of ever-widening hostility and violence. And too many did follow such policies, especially during the 1850s, when the tremendous numbers thronging the trails probably emboldened some overlanders to act less circumspectly than might otherwise have been the case. Moreover, it seems likely that since so many westbound emigrants did not anticipate making the trip again, there was correspondingly little concern about what might happen to others the next week, month, or year as a consequence of actions taken.

Chester Ingersoll's 1847 party had four oxen, one cow, and one horse stolen along the Humboldt River. The company's response, according to Ingersoll's concise prose, was, "After that we shot at every Indian we saw—this soon cleared the way."[161] Forty-niner Ansel McCall conversed with three Missourians threatening to shoot the first Indian they saw, since they believed their missing horses had been stolen by Indians. Observed

McCall, "This inconsiderate retaliation upon a whole race for the acts of one of its members, leads to half the conflicts that occur." John Wood reported in 1850 that emigrants traveling on the Hastings Cutoff, after hearing that five overlanders had been "barbarously murdered" by Indians, became very revenge-minded: ". . . every Indian is shot that can be seen." Joseph Francl met a 172-person train along the Humboldt River in 1854 which, having experienced some fatal Indian assaults, "shot and killed every Indian they met on sight, and for that reason the Indians got bad."[162] In attempting to explain the many depredations of 1857 to the Indian commissioner, Brigham Young placed the blame squarely on episodes of a kindred nature:

This is principally owing to a company of some three or four hundred returning Californians who travelled these roads last spring to the eastern States, shooting at every Indian they could see—a practice utterly abhorrent to all good people, yet, I regret to say, one which has been indulged to a great extent by travellers to and from the eastern States and California; hence the Indians regard all white men alike their enemies, and kill and plunder whenever they can do so with impunity, and often the innocent suffer for the deeds of the guilty.

Young further complained, "It is hard to make an Indian believe that the whites are their friends, and the Great Father wishes to do them good, when, perhaps, the very next party which crosses their path shoots them down like wolves."[163] Such reports from Utah were not new. Six years earlier Indian agent Jacob H. Holeman had complained about the inability of emigrants to distinguish between different tribes, and the course of events in which "the innocent suffer for injuries done by others."[164]

Not only large companies practiced indiscriminate retaliation; individual emigrants did too. One 1851 emigrant who was missing a horse, presumably due to Indian thievery, resolved to kill the next Indian he saw. He did—shooting from behind a rock an unsuspecting Indian who was busily spearing salmon in the Snake River.[165] Individual Indians reacted similarly. A Cheyenne brave, after his wife, father, mother, and brother had died of cholera in 1849, vowed to kill the first white man he encountered since he held the whites accountable for the disease. A young St. Joseph emigrant was his victim. The Cheyenne tribe immediately executed the murderer for his crime.[166] An especially grisly story, possibly mythical, appears occasionally in this connection, usually in reminiscent writings. According to the standard version, an overlander had long bragged about how he would shoot the first Indian he saw. When he bravely killed a squaw, her tribe demanded that the murderer be turned over to them. The tribe then proceeded to skin the murderer alive, although refraining from molesting the other company members.[167]

Of course, the aspirations of a few emigrants to kill an Indian, the occasional flagrant disregard of native rights and demands, or the more prevalent notion of indiscriminate retaliation to which both Indian and overlander adhered were not the only factors bringing about trail crises. Young braves seeking battle honors or financial gain could not always be controlled by older chiefs. And some of the assaults, particularly along the Humboldt River, originated with destitute Indians in quest of food and other materials.[168]

Whatever their motivations, Indians began in 1845 to kill overland emigrants. However, the Indian attacks of the 1840s and 1850s did not, as George Stewart has pointed out, follow the normal Hollywood scenario.[169] Since the overland emigrants were least vulnerable when their wagons were encircled, they were only rarely attacked when in such a strong defensive formation. Rather, assaults on entire trains came when the wagons were spread out along the trail. Nor were pack trains immune: near Fort Hall in 1851 a small company of men was fired upon by Indians concealed in bushes alongside the trail. As this company disintegrated, eight men were killed and the Indians appropriated $1,000 in cash, $2,000 in property, and twelve horses.[170] Fatalities usually resulted from short skirmishes and not from long-drawn-out battles or sieges. Most overlanders died individually in isolated incidents; only rarely were emigrants killed in proportions justifying the overused word "massacre." Most overlanders were killed while out hunting or when otherwise absent from their train, when on guard duty, when small emigrant parties tracked Indians in an attempt to retrieve stolen stock, in sudden flare-ups at toll bridges, or when tribute payments were refused. A number of deaths also occurred along the Humboldt River when Indians fired from cover at passing travelers.

Very little is known about the few major antebellum "massacres" occurring along the overland trail, except that they usually took place on the southern Oregon and northern California routes. In 1852, for example, on receiving news of severe Indian depredations in that region, volunteer companies were sent from both Oregon and California. The Oregon rescue party found and buried the mutilated bodies of fourteen emigrants near the Lost River in mid-September, while the California volunteers, commanded by Ben Wright of Yreka, California, buried twenty-two mutilated bodies and such grim reminders of the attendant atrocities as female scalps near "Bloody Point" on Tule Lake. Wright's volunteers, who left Yreka on August 29, arrived at Tule Lake just in time to rescue a beleaguered sixteen-wagon train numbering between forty and sixty persons which was presumably encircled for protection. Wright's men liberated the train while killing between twenty and thirty-five Indians.[171]

More is known about several major tragedies on the main overland trail. At midday on August 20, 1854, approximately thirty Snake River Indians approached a small five-wagon train and attempted to steal a horse. When an overlander shot the thief a deadly battle commenced. The small train was the advance portion of a much larger company which had previously split into three sections. The day before, three men had been killed in the third segment seventy miles behind when eleven Indians had suddenly opened fire after coming up ostensibly to trade. But it was the small advance party which suffered most on that Sunday afternoon only twenty-five miles east of Fort Boise. Only two of the twenty persons in the train escaped: one by feigning death after he had been knocked down, the other after a painful journey of several days to Fort Boise with an arrow in his side, his injury having rendered him unconscious until the day after the attack. These two surviving brothers, Newton and William, were young sons of Alexander Ward of Missouri, apparently the leader of the train, whose large family comprised nearly half the traveling group.

Seven men, traveling east on the trail that day in search of a stray cow, came upon the ghastly scene as the Indians were plundering the wagons and engaged them in battle. Soon one of their number, a seventeen-year-old boy, was killed, bringing the death toll to nineteen in the "Ward massacre." The small party was forced to retreat but did rescue Newton Ward. Two days later eighteen men left Fort Boise in the futile hope of finding additional survivors. The condition of the victims they buried was such that Oregon newspaper editors issued frenzied demands for revenge. The women and young girls had been brutally ravaged. A hot piece of iron had been thrust into the body of one, another had been scalped and her head savagely beaten with clubs, and the pregnant Mrs. Ward had been raped and then virtually cut to pieces. At the site of the tragedy the ground was covered with blood. Later investigations disclosed that Indian squaws had been responsible for much of the tomahawk mutilation on the bodies of the women. The young children had apparently been burned alive. Forty-one cattle, five horses, assorted other goods, and from $2,000 to $3,000 had also been taken. The editor of Portland's *Weekly Oregonian* demanded that Oregon authorities "either exterminate the race of Indians, or prevent further wholesale butcheries by these worthless races resembling the human form," but clearly preferred that the former course be followed—an "EVERLASTING TREATY."[172]

Newspaper editors, particularly T. J. Dryer of Portland's *Weekly Oregonian*, continued in a state of near rage throughout much of the remainder of the decade as they learned of additional depredations. The culmination came with the news of an 1860 episode somewhat paralleling the Donner disaster of fourteen years before. While that earlier tragedy had been prompted by bad weather, the ordeal of the forty-four persons traveling in the eight-wagon Otter–Van Orman train began with an Indian attack on September 9 about fifty miles west of Salmon Falls on the Snake River.[173] For the few survivors the nightmare did not end until their rescue nearly one and a half months later. Although the exact progression of events following the initial attack is not clear, this appears to have been one of the

"An Emigrant Train Attacked by Hostile Indians on the Prairie." Such attacks did occur, but accounts were often exaggerated, inaccurate, or even fictitious.

rare occasions when Indians not only attempted but sustained a prolonged assault on encircled emigrant wagons. The overlanders, who included at least four well-armed soldiers who had been discharged at Fort Hall, withstood the Indians for nearly two days, during which time the defenders suffered several fatal casualties. Finally deciding that their only hope was to abandon the train, most of the emigrants momentarily escaped when the Indians stayed to plunder the wagons. Shortly thereafter Indians killed more of the fleeing overlanders. Evidently as soon as escape seemed possible, the soldiers, mounted on the best horses, took leave of their imperiled colleagues. Before they reached the settlements two were killed by Indians. About the same time Jacob and Joseph Keith also left the dwindling group of survivors, eventually reaching the Umatilla Indian agency on October 2.

Meanwhile, those they had left behind faced a frightening future. In their hasty retreat nothing, not even food, had been salvaged from the wagons. No other trains mercifully appeared to provide succor as so frequently occurred when overlanders found themselves in precarious circumstances. Rescue did not come until after the Keiths brought word of the tragedy to the Oregon settlements. A relief party immediately sent out from the Indian agency was unsuccessful, but an army expedition under Captain F. T. Dent, dispatched from Forts Dalles and Walla Walla, found the destitute survivors.

Their testimony made it possible for the events of the tragedy to be reconstructed. Eighteen emigrants had been killed by the Indians in the several attacks. Mrs. Abigail Van Orman had been ravished before she was killed and the bodies of a few of the other victims had been mutilated. Four of Mrs. Van Orman's children, three girls and one boy, were abducted by the Indians. The girls were never seen again and were presumed killed. The boy, Reuben, according to one account, was finally retrieved in 1862 from his Bannock and Shoshoni captors.[174] The remaining sixteen—later joined, apparently, by one of the four soldiers—endured extraordinary suffering. For over a month they wandered about, slowly progressing to the northwest, living on berries and on salmon which they caught or for which they traded their clothes with friendly Indians. But mainly they starved, and when rescuers reached their destitute encampment near the Owyhee River about ninety miles from the initial attack in late October, only twelve remained alive—twelve naked, emaciated persons who had been subsisting in part on the flesh of the five of their number who had already died of starvation.[175] Dryer's editorial reaction to the tragic affair was of a piece with his earlier suggestions: "We want to see a campaign on the Snake river the present winter, and the savages on the Snake river effectually wiped out."[176]

These trail tragedies instigated by the Indians are sufficient, especially when coupled with the several hundred additional overlanders killed singly or in small groups, to demonstrate that western Indians could be dangerous threats to overland travel. And yet there is a substantial amount of evidence scattered throughout the trail literature which reveals that Indian attacks were not always what they appeared to be; that bands of renegade whites disguised as Indians were responsible for some of the carnage. Overlanders themselves widely assumed that Indians bore the blame for much they did not do. William Rothwell termed these desperadoes "White Indians"; time and again emigrants agreed that impostors were an equal if not more dangerous threat than native tribesmen.[177] Those overlanders who experienced and survived attacks led by suspicious "Indians" were convinced that impersonation was taking place. Their evidence was on occasion bizarre but persuasive, as with the emigrant woman who was raped and then shot by five whites masquerading as Indians in 1859. Before dying she informed her traveling companions that, as the chief justice of the Utah Territory Supreme Court delicately phrased it for the Secretary of the Interior, "they were all white men. They had not taken the precaution to paint the whole body."[178]

Government Indian agents, such as Jacob Holeman, were likewise persuaded that their wards were innocent of many of the depredations of which they were accused. Moreover, Holeman recognized that many of the Indians who committed thefts and murders did so at the conniving behest of white men.[179] Army personnel responsible for guarding the trails in the late 1850s were so certain of the existence of bands of "white Indians" that they even joked about them. Acting Adjutant General L. A. Williams, in directing Lieutenant Colonel M. T. Howe to patrol northern emigration routes during 1860, reminded him: "Judging by the events of last summer, there is a tribe of Indians who have blue eyes and light hair, who wear whiskers, and speak good English. They may always be regarded as so hostile that no terms are to be made with them."[180] Even the Oregon territorial legislature in the 1851 memorial it addressed to Congress matter-of-factly referred to the "bands of marauding and plundering savages led on by out-cast whites, more brutal still than the Indians, and who have fled from civilized communities, and from the justice that awaited their guilty deeds, and whose selfish and reckless natures exact the lion's share of the emigrant's property to enable his escape with his life."[181]

Marcus Whitman, in the early 1840s, had referred to "desperate white men and mongrels" who united in bandit groups and led savage Indian tribes in raids upon the emigration.[182] Nonetheless, "white Indians" were almost exclusively a product of the large migrations of the California gold rush, from which time they continued unabated throughout the decade. While organized bandits disguised as Indians were by far the most formidable adversaries, when emigrants spoke of "white Indians" they also included thieving fellow overlanders who repeatedly stole horses and mules to expedite their westward progress. Considering the publicity the Indian

threat constantly received and the fearful suspicion with which most overlanders approached Indians, it was predictable that virtually all missing
stock was automatically assumed to have been stolen by natives when, in
fact, fellow travelers were periodically responsible.[183] In spite of the high
praise the press had lavished on the character of the gold rushers, many
were not above stealing from their colleagues. Madison Moorman in 1850
and Henry Allyn in 1853 complained that they stood guard not so much
because of Indians but because of thievish whites. At Fort Laramie the
commanding officer daily received complaints about emigrants robbing
one another. Emigrants from one 1850 company took turns registering
their names at the Fort Laramie emigrant register because they were afraid
to leave their wagons unguarded, even momentarily. One 1850 overlander
stated at the fort that "he did'nt mind the wild Indians much, if he could
only get out of the way of the tame ones; he believed he'd turn round and
go back to the States, for there must be a power of honest people there
since so many dishonest ones had left."[184]

Individual thievery occurred everywhere along the trail, but the organized banditry was confined mainly to four fairly extensive regions. The
area adjacent to the Missouri River settlements was prime territory for
robbers specializing in stealing stock and returning it to the outfitting posts
for resale to subsequent emigrants.[185] Sizable numbers of overlanders
suffered stock losses early in their journey, thefts which they were certain
had been committed by bands of white men or by Indians led by white
men. After a raid on their stock, the men of one 1854 train captured an
Indian chief who admitted that whites were allied with the Indians in the
thievery.[186] Some of these thieves, recognizing the salability of Indian
horses, even stole from the Shawnee, Delaware, and Pawnee Indians. The
horses were then sold to overlanders who periodically were forced to
surrender them to their rightful owners.[187] The second region of theft and
banditry was at the California end of the trail, where a number of thefts,
again usually of stock, were attributed to miners as well as to bands of cattle
thieves.[188]

Once they penetrated beyond South Pass, emigrants entered a region
frequented by bands of especially vicious desperadoes. Due to the infamous Mountain Meadows massacre in 1857—when fanatic Mormons and
their Indian allies summarily dispatched about 120 Missouri and Arkansas
overlanders—several additional incidents, and a plethora of rumors, many
overlanders believed these to be Mormon bands. The Mountain Meadows
tragedy was an isolated event, however, perpetrated by zealots fired by
religious revivalism. The other trail incidents seem more probably the
work of apostate Mormons, mountain men, and other outlaws and highwaymen, many of whom were refugees from California justice, than of
officially directed Latter-Day Saints.[189] Indeed, Mormon ferryboat operators returning to Salt Lake City in 1849 with the handsome proceeds of a

194

summer's work were themselves badly enough frightened of a band of robbers preying on the emigration from their base in the Wind Chain Mountains to alter their travel plans.[190] In 1851 Brigham Young placed the blame for many of the depredations upon free traders at the Green River and other places: "I am informed that they have induced Indians to drive off the Stock of emigrants, so as to force them to purchase of the 'Freemen' at exhorbitant prices and after the emigrants have left, make a pretended purchase of the Indians for a mere trifle, and are ready to sell again to the next train that may pass, and who may have been served in the same manner."[191] In 1854 Brigham Young himself warned emigrants in a signed editorial in the *Deseret News* to be careful of "a numerous and well organized band of *white* highwaymen, painted and disguised as Indians," who stole travelers' stock "by wholesale" and committed murders as well. The Mormon leader also denied the accusations made by an 1854 overlander who complained to Young that he had been victimized by Mormon robbers. Young's explanation that "white vagrants" and professional bandits were really at fault satisfied the emigrant.[192]

While the identity of the bandits remains obscure, some of their raids were reasonably well reported.[193] By the end of the decade their assaults incorporated a monstrous savagery. For instance: at midday toward the end of July, 1859, on the Hudspeth Cutoff, while the Shepherd train was traveling through a canyon, a sudden crossfire commenced from the rocks and bushes beside the trail. Four emigrant men were immediately killed and a man and his wife severely abused, wounded, and left for dead. The woman survived but the man died a few days later. The attackers also tossed into the air a small child, who suffered a broken leg upon falling to the ground. The murderers burned the wagons, stole thirty-five horses and mules, assorted valuables, and $1,000 in cash. Train survivors recognized among the leading attackers at least three white men disguised as Indians.[194]

Even bloodier was an attack one month later. Nelson Miltimore was one of nineteen Iowa emigrants traveling together on the Lander Cutoff. On August 31, 1859, approximately twenty-five miles west of Fort Hall, according to Miltimore's later sworn statement, three men disguised as Indians (who had, however, light brown hair, beards, and who spoke perfect English) intercepted them and conversed pleasantly before ordering an attack from both sides of the road by approximately twenty persons. Eight emigrants were killed—all scalped and butchered. Both legs of one little five-year-old girl had been cut off at the knee, both ears were cut off, both eyes gouged out, and she apparently had been forced to walk on her severed stumps before expiring.[195]

Other 1859 travelers reported meeting strange men along the trail who encouraged travel on the Lander Cutoff, saying it was the best and shortest route to California. Another emigrant party apparently encountered the bandits involved in the Miltimore affair at approximately the same time. All spoke good English and knew the value of trade goods in the States perfectly. Some had heavy beards, three had yellow hair, and none had the "long coarse black" hair the overlanders always associated with Indians. Three women were also with the party; the overlanders assumed at most they might have been half-breeds.[196] Lorenzo Suberr, in a sworn affidavit, reported overhearing white men at a mail station rejoicing that the Miltimore train was traveling on the Lander Cutoff. While in Salt Lake City Suberr averred that a Mormon invited him to join their band of some 125 to 135 "Mormons" and 350 Indians who robbed emigrant trains from their Goose Creek hideout.[197] The next year a small four-wagon train of twenty-three persons was attacked September 7 in the City of Rocks vicinity by "Indians" who again spoke English well. Though no emigrants were killed, all their belongings were lost, including 139 cattle and 6 horses.[198]

Similar—or perhaps the same—bandit gangs or joint bandit-Indian groups operated along the Humboldt River and in the Carson Valley area, the fourth region of organized trail banditry. When Indian agent Holeman made a round trip from his Salt Lake City base along the Humboldt to the Carson Valley in 1852, he met oncoming emigrants who testified "that the only difficulties which had occurred—and they were but few—had been the acts of white men." Holeman firmly believed that most of the trouble originated with the proprietors of the numerous trading posts located along the river. In his 1853 report Holeman described the collusion which developed between these unscrupulous traders and certain Indians:

Their stock in trade consists principally of liquors; scarcely an article is found that the emigrants stand most in need of. By unkind treatment to the Indians they make them unfriendly towards the emigrants; schisms arise which they take advantage of, and steal, and commit more depredations than the Indians, all of which they manage to have charged to the Indians. I was told by the Indians that some of these traders had proposed to them to steal stock from emigrants, and run them off into the valleys in the mountains, and after the emigration had ceased passing, they would bring out guns, ammunition, blankets, &c., and trade with them for the stock stolen.[199]

Perhaps T. Turnbull was one of the emigrants met by Holeman in 1852, for he reported that white traders were greater thieves than the Root Digger Indians.[200] Additional emigrants expressed similar beliefs, and in 1853 the Marysville, California, *Daily Evening Herald* demanded an end to the depredations of white men along the Humboldt River and near the Sink of the Carson River, speculating that 150 whites and a large band of Paiute Indians were the main culprits.[201]

The Humboldt River trail was particularly dangerous in 1857. Indians, presumably, attacked the small Holloway party of ten persons while they were arising on the morning of August 13. Six were killed immediately, including a two-year-old child whose head was bashed on the wheels of a wagon. Mrs. Holloway was badly wounded and feigned death while she was scalped. In a hasty departure forced by the arrival of oncoming emigrants the marauders dropped her scalp, from which Mrs. Holloway later fashioned a wig. The other person rescued had also been wounded, two men were missing and perhaps had escaped, and a third of the stock was taken.[202]

One would be tempted to regard this as a bona fide Indian attack if a similar assault nearby at approximately the same time had not been perpetrated by "white Indians." The attack, by approximately twenty bandits, again came in the early morning as a small party of five persons was preparing to travel. The wife and child of an Englishman named Wood were killed as they desperately tried to reach the next train ahead; Mr. Wood was badly wounded. Men returned from the advance train to bury the bodies and discovered that $1,500 in English gold coin was missing from the wagon box where it had been concealed. Three men claiming to be mountaineers afraid of Indians asked to join the rescue train the next day. When Wood, who was being transported in a wagon, saw the men he quickly recognized at least one as an "Indian." The three acted suspiciously, tried to run up a signal flag on their wagon, and ultimately left, denying that they had been involved in the murder and robbery and threatening the injured Wood with death if he made any more "false" accusations. Later, at a roadside tavern near the Humboldt Sink, the man Wood had identified, who gave his name as James Tooly, was overheard boasting that he had "done up" some "Pikers." The men of the train transporting the injured Wood immediately captured Tooly. During the course of the resulting trial $500 in English gold coin was found concealed on Tooly's person, presumably his share of the stolen $1,500. Tooly tried to escape but was shot down and killed.[203] Clearly, "white Indians" had been responsible for the deaths of Mrs. Wood and child. Since the modus operandi had been similar, the likelihood is great that the Holloway tragedy had been their work as well.

Incidents of this nature reveal that many cases of murder and theft usually believed to have been committed by Indians were in fact offenses for which white men were responsible. The far-flung activities of these "white Indians"—men capable of atrocities as revolting as any on record—and the arrogant actions of certain overlanders, when combined with the substantial amount of Indian trade and aid as well as the repeated Indian endeavors to secure redress for the penetration and spoliation of their land, demonstrate the necessity of replacing the old bromides about virtuous overlanders versus treacherous and deceitful Indians with interpretations in accord with the actual events of those troubled years.[204]

To aver that the overland emigrants were almost solely responsible for the increasing hostility Indians evidenced, however, would merely be a further skewing of the historical record. Most westering overlanders were responding to various appeals to travel to the Pacific Coast. Whether these roseate invitations came from publicists or from friends and relatives who had already made the trip, they included no admonitions that the trip was illegal or immoral because proper clearance from the Indian tribes had not yet been received. Precisely the opposite impression was conveyed, that journeying overland to help secure the West Coast Eden was an act of great patriotism. But the fulsomeness of Manifest Destiny at high tide was only one of the factors hastening the final Indian wars. Also influential was a dilatory Congress unwilling or unable to recognize that the migrations posed fundamental threats to Indian rights as embodied in previous treaties. Likewise a contributing factor was the depredation rumors which prejudiced many overlanders, newspaper editors, army personnel, and government officials to a hostile/lethal approach to the western tribes. So, too, was the prevalence of an outlook relegating the Indian to little more than an interesting curiosity—without rights.

Of additional significance were the dominance of the collective responsibility concept among both whites and Indians; the frictions resulting from Mormon travel and that of freighters and postal employees; the dubious contributions of many traders who liquored up and then robbed the Indians throughout the West; the inability of some chiefs to control their braves. In such a milieu it is not surprising that as more and more persons streamed across the continent the situation became more and more abrasive. This despite the fact that beginning with the 1851 Fort Laramie Treaty the federal government finally made a belated effort to treat these problems in a fashion other than by marching troops through the West to overawe the natives. The overlanders were, after all, merely transitory travelers, and many others were involved in what has euphemistically come to be known as "the Indian problem."

Yet however transitory their passage, the emigrations did leave a clear imprint on Indian-white relationships in the West. Not only in the actions of emigrants on the trails but also by the sheer immensity of their numbers, Indians had quickly recognized the overland caravans as the permanent advance of a civilization whose previous record in Indian relationships was deplorable. But even so, the final outcome of the increasingly frequent interaction between the two cultures was not inevitable. Indians and overlanders did not have to be juxtaposed as enemies locked in mortal combat. In fact, most were not, even during the most dangerous periods of overland travel, since firmness and caution, together with a readiness to treat the natives with friendliness and respect, generally elicited reciprocation. Helpful also was an awareness that theft was something of a game with many tribes, although overlanders losing all or most of their stock somewhere along the trail had understandable difficulty in developing much

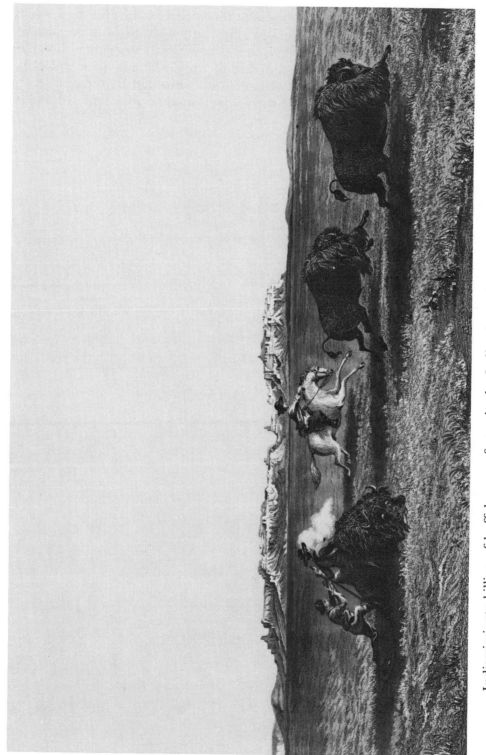

Indiscriminate killing of buffalo was a factor in the Indians' growing hostility toward the white man.

From Piercy, Route from Liverpool to Great Salt Lake Valley (1855) tolerance. Yet in spite of the frequent thefts and scares, almost everyone did complete the trip safely, and this fact needs to be underscored. Nonetheless, it is indisputable that Indians posed a greater threat to overland travel by 1860 than they had in 1840, a situation for which the overland emigrants, especially those lured westward by the gold rush, shared, with their culture and their government, a major responsibility.

CHAPTER SIX

The Federal Government

"Good fellow Uncle Sam is"

The irascible editor of Portland's *Weekly Oregonian* charged in 1860 that Oregon was "cursed" by governmental policies of "imbecility and neglect" which stymied population growth and economic development by failing to furnish adequate protection to overland emigrants.[1] For the previous two decades, newspapermen like Portland's T. J. Dryer, as well as presidents, secretaries of war, army officers, enlisted men, Indian commissioners, Indian agents, congressmen, and overland emigrants had been debating the proper role of the federal government in the westward migrations. Those debates, considering the federal funds ultimately authorized for emigrant-oriented policies and programs, had been decisively determined. For especially by the 1850s, the federal presence in the West was far more important to the success of the overland emigrations than Dryer acknowledged. Most pre–Civil War overlanders found the U.S. government, through its armed forces, military installations, Indian agents, explorers, surveyors, road builders, physicians, and mail carriers, to be an impressively potent and helpful force.

Statistically, frontier soldiers were the most significant dimension of the western federal presence. Throughout the 1850s up to 90 percent of the U.S. Army was deployed at the seventy-nine posts dotting the trans-Mississippi West.[2] In 1860 this meant that 7,090 enlisted men and officers were stationed at the forts and camps of the four army departments whose geographic areas of responsibility incorporated the South Pass overland trails.[3] Primarily, the army was so heavily concentrated in the West because of the "Indian problem"—the central facet of which was the threat to overland travel—and, following 1857, because of the Latter-Day Saints' challenge to national authority and union. And even though Indian agents were at least as influential in pacifying disgruntled and angry Indians, thereby preventing disastrous attacks upon emigrant caravans, overlanders persisted in regarding the frontier army as almost their sole guardian and protector.

Already in 1840, before any emigrant caravans had penetrated beyond the Missouri River, prospective overlanders had been entreating the Congress to provide military protection. The problem then, as in later years, was in agreeing on the kind of military protection that would be most effective. A group of 152 Missouri petitioners requested "the protection of the strong arm of the Government against Indian treachery" but were vague on what that might mean. The demand of twenty-seven Kentuckians had been more specific: that "small garrisons" for protective purposes be established along a federally built road to Oregon.[4] Secretaries of War Joel R. Poinsett in 1840 and John C. Spencer in 1841 recommended that military posts be located along the trail to Oregon to protect overland travelers. Poinsett estimated that three posts would suffice, while Spencer called for a "chain of posts."[5] Presidents John Tyler and James K. Polk agreed and, beginning in 1841, used their annual messages to Congress for similar requests. Tyler emphasized that military posts along the overland route could serve as places of rest as well as security; Polk called not only for a "suitable number of stockades and blockhouse forts" but also for an "adequate force of mounted riflemen . . . to guard and protect them [the emigrants] on their journey."[6] The House Committee on Military Affairs also strongly supported the fixed-post philosophy. Missouri's senators regularly introduced legislation to this effect, the prompt enactment of which was just as regularly demanded by newspaper editors across the nation.[7]

Congress's reluctance to pass such legislation, however, revealed that not everyone was persuaded that permanent bastions of defense were particularly wise. Colonel Stephen W. Kearny, after an 1845 trip along the overland trail as far as South Pass, was confident that powerful military expeditions at periodic intervals would keep the Indians properly respectful of the rapid striking power which the United States could bring against them if depredations were committed. Kearny also prudently reminded his superior officers that such awe-inspiring military expeditions would be less expensive than the establishment and maintenance of a series of posts across the vast western spaces.[8]

And so the issue was drawn: a series of permanent posts from the Missouri River to the Pacific Ocean or periodic campaigns along the trails to impress and, when necessary, chastise the Indians. Sending an occasional military expedition to cow the natives was not a new idea. In 1835 Colonel Henry Dodge traveled to the Rocky Mountains from Fort Leavenworth with 120 mounted dragoons, dispensing presents and admonitions to keep the peace to all Indians encountered.[9] Nine years later Major Clifton Wharton with five companies of dragoons left Fort Leavenworth for the Pawnee villages on the Platte River. Wharton's instructions were to impress the natives with the "Great Father's" military might, to urge peaceful relations between all tribes, and, most important as far as overlanders were concerned, to warn Indians to assist the emigrants and to treat all white persons in the Indian country with friendship. Holding councils not only with the Pawnees but with a number of neighboring tribes, Wharton periodically fired two twelve-pound howitzers to overawe the natives.[10]

Wharton's August expedition was undertaken long after the 1844 overland caravans had departed from the frontiers and thus benefited the overlanders only insofar as the natives abided by their promises. Stephen Kearny's march to South Pass the next year, however, coincided with the westbound 1845 emigration, thereby serving a dual function as emigrant escort and emissary of American power. Kearny's command, numbering close to 300 men, did not leave the frontier until all the emigrant wagons had departed. By rapid traveling Kearny's forces had reached the front of the emigration column upon arrival at Fort Laramie. Leaving a detachment of about 100 men to provide protection for emigrants stopping at that famous trading post, Kearny pushed ahead to South Pass with the remainder of his company. On their return to the fort the dragoons again encountered all the westbound wagons. The overlanders consequently traveled in relatively close proximity to a strong military force for over a third of their journey. The Indians were peaceful. The emigrants, overjoyed with the safety they assumed their military escort had provided, frequently shared fresh milk, antelope meat, and other delicacies with the troops.[11]

That the purpose of Kearny's expedition had not been adequately publicized, however, was evident in a letter one overlander wrote from Fort Laramie. Mentioning that the dragoons were marching nearby, James McMillen indicated that "their business to us is unknown," but correctly surmised it was "probably to protect the Oregon emigrants."[12] In councils with Pawnee, Sioux, and Cheyenne Indians, Kearny made it explicitly clear that "the road opened by the dragoons must not be closed by the Indians, and that the white people travelling upon it must not be disturbed, either in their persons or property." Kearny believed that the Indians would heed his warnings, since they had been much impressed by the number and quality of the soldiers and the power of their weapons (howitzers had again been taken along for demonstration purposes). He was convinced that similar expeditions every two or three years would effectually keep the peace on the plains.[13]

Ultimately, governmental authorities resorted to a number of strategies, often simultaneously, in an attempt to neutralize the Indian threat to overland travel: treaties were negotiated, presents distributed, reservations established, awe-inspiring and/or punitive military expeditions dispatched, roving patrols instituted, military escorts provided. But initially, most persons concerned with this problem shared 1846 overlander Jessy Thornton's outlook that a series of permanent military forts

Fort Laramie grew from a fur-trading post established in 1834 to become the most famous stopover on the Oregon-California Trail.

From Piercy, *Route from Liverpool to Great Salt Lake Valley* (1855) was the best approach. In his book based upon a summer's overland trip to Oregon, Thornton helpfully listed potential fort sites, asserted that "the establishment of a cordon of military posts is important and necessary," and for good measure called for a graded wagon road with ferries and bridges at the major water crossings.[14]

Thornton had barely pushed westward from Independence in 1846 when legislation authorizing the fixed-post concept finally cleared congressional hurdles. The May 19 act provided $76,500 for raising, mounting, and equipping one regiment of mounted riflemen, $3,000 for the establishment of each "military station" on the route to Oregon, and $2,000 to compensate the Indian tribes owning or possessing the land where each station was to be located. Although the act did not specify the exact function of the regiment, most contemporaries shared President Polk's understanding that the Mounted Riflemen were "intended to guard and protect our emigrants to Oregon." Noteworthy too was the nonrestrictive nature of the authorization: as many military posts as the President desired could be established.[15] There would be no more turning back. The federal government had accepted responsibility for overland travel to the Pacific.

Prior to the passage of the 1846 measure, Fort Leavenworth—located on the Missouri River in 1827 primarily as protection for the Santa Fe Trail—had been the only military establishment anywhere near the Oregon-California Trail.[16] After 1846 prospective overlanders were confident that there soon would be more, particularly following an initial flurry of activity. Four days after the act was approved Colonel Stephen W. Kearny formally selected a site at Table Creek, approximately forty miles south of Council Bluffs on the west bank of the Missouri River, for the new army post. Major Clifton Wharton and other officers were directed to supervise the construction of a blockhouse at "Fort Kearny." Kearny chose the location on the twin assumptions that it was necessary for controlling area Indians and that it would quickly become the major origination point for the Oregon emigration—both bad guesses.[17]

The manpower demands of the Mexican War delayed the further implementation of the 1846 enabling legislation. Indeed, even the Table Creek fort was virtually abandoned after 1846, although a battalion of Missouri volunteers did winter there in 1847–48. The Missourians had been requisitioned into service to begin establishing the Oregon Trail military posts, another of which was slated for Grand Island on the Platte River. Located approximately 180 miles west of the Table Creek location where all the trails emanating from the several jumping-off points merged, the site for the new fort had been chosen in the fall of 1847 by Lieutenant Daniel P. Woodbury. In 1848 the Missouri volunteers, commanded by Lieutenant Colonel Ludwell E. Powell, commenced construction. Woodbury named the post Fort Childs, but by December the War Department had renamed it Fort Kearny.[18] Not until late October of 1848 were any Mounted Riflemen ready for trail or post location duty. At that time two companies under Captain Charles F. Ruff relieved the Missouri volunteers still at Fort Kearny, who were subsequently mustered out of the service at Fort Leavenworth in November.[19]

Before the California gold rush, then, little had actually been accomplished. Two expeditions had been sent to overawe the Indians, one of which had escorted the 1845 emigration as far as South Pass. But no chain of army forts yet paved the way to the Pacific, although the second Fort Kearny marked a beginning. American regulars were still a novelty to both Indians and overlanders. After 1849 they were not. In that year the Mounted Riflemen marched the entire length of the trail, establishing additional military installations along the way. At last the long-cherished dream of overland travelers had reached fruition and a new phase in federal policy had been inaugurated—the permanent presence of the army in the West.

The Regiment of Mounted Riflemen included ten companies, of which G and I under Captain Ruff were already stationed at Fort Kearny. The rest moved west in five principal detachments, and several infantry companies designated to garrison the several forts also tramped the trail during that busy summer. Most of Company B under Major John S. Simonson departed from the Table Creek outpost; all other army units apparently started from Fort Leavenworth. The first and fastest was Major Winslow F. Sanderson's Company E, which headed for Fort Laramie with instructions to purchase that famed fur-trading post and turn it into the second military installation along the Oregon Trail. The majority of the Mounted Riflemen—Companies A, D, F, H, and K—traveled as a unit under Brevet Colonel William W. Loring's direction. This large federal force numbered over 600 men, 31 commissioned officers (at least four of whom had their families along), 1,200 mules, 700 horses, numerous oxen, and 171 wagons. Loring's command left Fort Leavenworth on May 10; on June 5 the remaining twenty-five Mounted Riflemen of Company B departed to escort Indian agent John Wilson's small party to California. Company C under Brevet Lieutenant Colonel Benjamin S. Roberts set out about a week later, escorting a number of army officials on an inspection tour to Fort Laramie.[20]

The scattered departures meant, of course, that the various army units interacted with many more overlanders than if the entire regiment had proceeded westward in one concentrated mass. But it was ironic that the army was in the process of providing protection to Oregon-bound emigrants in the very year when the overland tide shifted so dramatically from Oregon to California. In 1846 few had doubted that the Willamette Valley would continue to be the goal for the overwhelming number of overlanders. But the discovery of gold in California immediately made the California region a far more desirable goal for most travelers. Yet the only

Mounted Riflemen who traveled overland to California along the entire length of the trail in 1849 were the twenty-five men from Company B. Since they were nearly the final travelers of the year, they could be of no assistance to the forty-niners.[21] Therefore, although the first two forts established were on the main trail used by all emigrants regardless of final destination, the army in 1849 was of no use to California-bound overlanders during the last third of their journey.

Before branching off to Oregon in late summer, however, Loring's command had numerous encounters with forty-niners, coming to know many of the overlanders so well that fond farewells and handshakings were common where the trails diverged near Fort Hall.[22] The interaction had begun shortly after the departure from Fort Leavenworth and included joint traveling of troops and emigrants, periodic emigrant use of army forges, and army hiring of overlanders for work as teamsters.[23]

Loring's troops reached the new fort at the head of Grand Island on the last day of May. By then the Pawnee Indians had been given $2,000 worth of trade goods as payment for the fort site, and a number of adobe buildings—quarters for the men, stables, a bakery, a storehouse—already overshadowed the many tents. Under construction were a frame hospital and two-story buildings for officers' and soldiers' quarters. Some of the new structures had glass windows and elicited favorable commentary from passing forty-niners.[24] Loring found Brevet Major Robert H. Chilton already on the scene with a company of dragoons after a fast march from Fort Leavenworth. Additional infantry units soon arrived, freeing Ruff and his Mounted Riflemen to accompany Loring on the march to Oregon. Major Osborne Cross of the Quartermaster's Department, with a late-starting party, also reached Fort Kearny on May 31, and by June 2 the Mounted Riflemen had resumed their westward course.[25]

As the soldiers pushed westward, army-emigrant encounters continued, some of a bizarre and others of a charitable nature. For example, Loring discovered a note left for him on the trail by an emigrant company requesting that he capture a "maniac" who had escaped from their train. The Riflemen found the deranged man and escorted him to Fort Laramie, where he was left under an army physician's care. Loring also dispatched army personnel to assist a widow and her family and drive her wagon to Fort Laramie. Arriving there on June 22, Loring learned that Major Sanderson's company had preceded him by a week and was already transforming the trading post into the army's second permanent fort on the Oregon Trail. The formal transfer took place June 26, the "instant" fort costing the United States $4,000. New construction was begun immediately. Sanderson with two companies stayed to command the new army fort, while Loring and the remaining Mounted Riflemen—over seventy of whom died or deserted during the course of the journey—continued westward.[26]

By early June some overlanders had even grown weary of the continued close proximity of the large army contingent. Lucius Fairchild complained that the troops were "always in the way" and were "the most perfect nusance on the whole road." B. R. Biddle found the Mounted Riflemen more than a nuisance. Upon reaching the Mormon ferry across the North Platte, the troops immediately commandeered the ferryboats, thereby separating most of Biddle's company from two wagons which had not yet been rafted across. Biddle grouched, "Dividing a company by an officer of the government sent out to protect the emigrants, is an act too mean and contemptible for the meanest ox-driver on the plains to be guilty of." The sympathetic Mormon ferrymen apparently agreed, for they worked late into the night to cross the two stranded wagons. Biddle's company then moved on some miles from the ferry, "preferring not to be in the neighborhood of the officers whose duty it was to protect us."[27]

While some disagreement and conflict were only natural in the never-ending quest for good grazing grass, quick stream crossings, and speedy traveling, most overlanders appreciated the army's presence. One forty-niner reported that the Riflemen had "rendered valuable assistance in crossing Green River." Moreover, emigrants offered little solace to army deserters, regularly supplying information leading to the apprehension of a number of men who had decided California gold was more appealing than life at a western fort.[28]

In early August Loring established yet another western military outpost. Situated three miles above the Hudson's Bay Company's trading post at Fort Hall, two companies of Mounted Riflemen were left behind to develop the site. Named Cantonment Loring but also referred to as Fort Hall, the post was abandoned the following spring, apparently because of the difficulty of supplying the garrison.[29] Leaving the ill-fated location, Loring pushed on to Oregon City, arriving in early October in company with an emigrant family whose oxen had failed en route.[30] Since Fort Vancouver, which had been established by troops who had arrived by sea in the spring of 1849, was not yet ready for occupancy, the regiment was wintered in homes rented from Oregon City residents who were seeking gold in California. Fort Vancouver was garrisoned in 1850, and Loring ordered two companies under the command of Captain Stephen S. Tucker to backtrack and begin a military fort at The Dalles of the Columbia River. Tucker established Camp Drum on May 21, 1850; by 1853 the outpost had been officially designated Fort Dalles.[31]

The new decade thus dawned with the army firmly situated at three sites adjacent to the Oregon Trail—Forts Kearny, Laramie, and Drum—and in the process of abandoning the temporary Cantonment Loring. This permanent federal presence materially altered the pattern of overland travel during the remainder of the 1850s. Most obvious was a substantial increase in trail traffic, since vast quantities of supplies were constantly freighted to the various forts. Further, with reinforcements, troop rotation, and official inspections a part of the normal routine of military life, there was a great deal of military movement on the trails unrelated to escorts, patrols, or punitive campaigns. The need for swift and reliable communication between military posts virtually guaranteed that a more effective postal service would be forthcoming. Finally, the inevitable "supply" towns quickly appeared near the permanent forts, conveniently providing the soldiers—and all passing travelers—with opportunities to spend their money on such things as liquor, gambling, and carnal pleasures.[32] Overland emigrants welcomed most of these developments, which seemed to imply that the trails would henceforth be safer.

During the 1850s additional military outposts were added to the nuclei of trail forts established by the Mounted Riflemen. Most were located where a skirmish or battle between troops and Indians had occurred or near where Indians were generally troublesome. Some were abandoned almost as quickly as they had appeared; others evolved into significant links in the trail's protective chain.

Perhaps the weakest link was Fort Grattan, a temporary mud fort about equidistant between Forts Kearny and Laramie. Located south of the Platte River on Ash Hollow's south bank, Fort Grattan was erected by General William S. Harney's troops immediately after their decisive triumph of September 3, 1855, over the Sioux Indians in the Battle of Ash Hollow. One company of infantry was left to man the fort and protect mail carriers and emigrant trains, but by mid-December of the same year Captain Wharton had abandoned the breastworks and taken his infantry company to Fort Kearny. Although the fort was never reconstituted, on occasion significant numbers of troops were placed at the Ash Hollow mail station to protect passing emigrants. Maria Norton, for example, found 200 soldiers "stationed" there on June 6 when she passed by en route to California.[33] Somewhat analogous was the temporary installation at the bridge over the North Platte River, some 130 miles west of Fort Laramie. Established by two companies of troops on July 29, 1858, and charged with maintaining communications with Salt Lake City, Fort Payne was operative at least until April 20 of the following year.[34]

Fort Payne derived from the "Mormon War," an event which so accelerated the military presence in the West that thereafter sufficient troops were readily available for patrol and escort duty along the most treacherous portions of the overland trail west of South Pass. The Utah Expedition, an uncertain and poorly organized governmental response to presumed Mormon intransigence, left Fort Leavenworth in July of 1857, much too late for any kind of expedition to the Salt Lake Valley.[35] Harassed by Mormon guerrilla raiders, impeded by initially ineffective leadership, and threatened by inclement weather, the troops wintered in bleak Camp Scott, a precarious encampment in and about Fort Bridger on Black's

Fork. The Mormons had burned most of Jim Bridger's long-standing trading post prior to the arrival of the Gentile forces; rebuilt, the post served as a supply depot and protective bastion through the 1880s.[36]

The major Utah installation, however, was located approximately forty miles south of Salt Lake City. Camp Floyd had been established by expedition commander Colonel Albert Sidney Johnston in June of 1858, after the "war" had been peacefully terminated. An average of 2,400 soldiers were stationed there until 1860, when the garrison's size was considerably reduced prior to its closing in 1861. During 1858 and 1859 more troops were concentrated at Camp Floyd than anywhere else in the United States. Although the post was not located precisely on the main overland trail, to knowledgeable overland emigrants it was easily the most important army establishment during the last years of the decade.[37]

Meanwhile, considerable military activity was also under way in the Pacific Northwest. Following the Whitman massacre, Oregon endured more than a decade of Indian wars. As the various tribes were forced onto reservations, a number of army outposts—such as Forts Lane, Cascades, Yamhill, Hoskins, and Umpqua—were created to control the not yet tranquil Indians. These forts provided some protection, particularly for travelers on southern routes into Oregon.[38] California-bound emigrants of 1860, especially those familiar with the bloody struggles known as the Pyramid Lake or Paiute Indian War occurring during the spring of that year, took comfort in the sight of Fort Churchill, established July 20 along the Carson River and garrisoned by two companies of infantry and one company of dragoons.[39]

A review of developments during the 1850s reveals that the army's permanent western presence—a consequence of the trailside forts—had indeed launched a new era in both government-emigrant and government-Indian relationships. A wider range of responses was now possible, since protecting emigrants and punishing Indians were no longer dependent upon the slow process of troops being marched west from Fort Leavenworth. Overlanders and Indians saw a great many bluecoats during the 1850s; indeed, one calculation has it that between 1848 and 1861 there were 206 battles between soldiers and Indians.[40]

Probably the most common army tactic was the quick relief or punishment foray from the nearest fort. In June, 1849, from the still-uncompleted Fort Kearny, Second Lieutenant Charles H. Ogle with a small force pursued a roving band of Pawnee Indians reportedly molesting emigrants in the vicinity. Unsuccessful at first, Ogle with twenty dragoons attempted another sortie in late October, after Pawnees turned back three mail carriers en route to Fort Leavenworth. The result was a skirmish near the Little Blue River in which at least three Indians were killed and several wounded, while Ogle and six of his men suffered wounds.[41]

James F. Wilkins's 1849 drawing of Fort Bridger, established by mountain man Jim Bridger in 1843.

■ Fort
▲ Landmark

Council Bluffs

(Old) Ft. Kearny

St. Joseph

Ft. Leavenworth

Alcove Springs

Westport

Independence

Kansas R.

Ft. Kearny

North Platte River

Courthouse Rock

Ash Hollow

Platte River

South Platte R.

Ft. Laramie

Scott's Bluff

Chimney Rock

Independence Rock

Devil's Gate

South Pass

Soda Springs

Cantonment Loring

Ft. Bridger

Green River

Missouri R.

Platte River

Great Salt Lake

Camp Floyd

Colorado River

Humboldt R.

Ft. Churchill

Columbia River

Ft. Dalles

Ft. Cascades

Ft. Vancouver

Ft. Yamhill

Ft. Hoskins

Ft. Umpqua

Ft. Lane

Sacramento R.

0   100   200   300
miles

Principal Army Forts and Landmarks
near the Oregon-California Trail

MAP 3

The following year Brevet Major Robert H. Chilton, commanding officer at Fort Kearny, held councils with several bands of Pawnee Indians near the fort. Chilton threatened violent reprisals if the Indians did not leave the trail "clear for emigration."[42] Additionally, two small detachments were sent from Fort Laramie to Fort Kearny, one on April 10, the second about a month later. Both detachments were expected to "remain on the road during the summer."[43] Two major expeditions also headed west from Fort Leavenworth in 1850, but only the first was early enough in the traveling season to mingle with westbound emigrants. This group, which Fort Leavenworth commander Edwin V. Sumner had promised overlanders as a protective escort, included officers, dragoons, and infantrymen bound for Forts Kearny and Laramie. Brevet Colonel Sumner himself led the later contingent of fifty mounted infantry troops, who traveled speedily to Fort Laramie in late June and early July and thence southward to the Santa Fe Trail.[44]

Troops stationed at Forts Kearny and Leavenworth continued active in 1851. In early June a small detail left Fort Kearny to pursue troublesome Pawnees. In mid-month Arapaho Indian thievery along the Little Blue River elicited two reprisal expeditions: Captain Henry W. Wharton escorted a number of emigrant trains and drove a few Indians across the river; Lieutenant Rennselaer W. Foote was also out with a patrol party. From Fort Leavenworth there was again much westbound traffic. Chilton, having been replaced by Wharton as Fort Kearny commander, took fifty men out over 100 miles to hold talks with thievish Kansas Indians in January. In mid-May a small detail escorted the army paymaster to Forts Kearny and Laramie; also departing in May was a detachment of infantry recruits for the same forts. In April and May an army party traveling eastward from Fort Laramie met westbound emigrants daily, while in August Chilton took dragoons west—encountering the eastbound emigration—to keep the peace at the Fort Laramie Treaty Council.[45]

Although 1852 was an exceptionally large emigration year, there was surprisingly little military activity. As usual, the demands upon the troops stationed at Fort Kearny were heaviest. Overlander John Wayman arrived there on May 19 and found virtually no one present, "all having started the day before after a large party of Indians, which had disturbed some emigrants & stole their Mules, Killing one of the party." On May 24 most of the soldiers were still absent; by June 2 one thirty-man company had been out twenty days. In mid-June another squad was ordered onto the trails after an emigrant reported a narrow escape from harassing Indians.[46] The only other major troop activity of the year was the 2000-mile march completed by Major Winslow F. Sanderson with two companies of Mounted Riflemen. Beginning in spring from Fort Leavenworth, they patrolled mainly along the Santa Fe Trail. Finally turning north to Fort Laramie, they returned to Fort Leavenworth in September, escorting at least two wagons of turn-around overlanders.[47]

Prevailing through 1852, then, was a fairly routine pattern of army activity consisting primarily of short missions around Fort Kearny. Nothing resembling a major engagement had yet occurred. In 1853 the scene of action shifted westward to the Fort Laramie vicinity, where a fracas over access to a ferryboat ignited continuing difficulties with the Sioux Indians. A few Sioux braves had commandeered the boat on June 15 after a busy ferryman had refused them passage. When a few soldiers from the nearby fort reclaimed the vessel, they were fired upon by an angered Indian. Fort commander Richard B. Garnett deemed this an act requiring disciplining, which he directed Lieutenant Hugh B. Fleming to administer. With twenty-three men Fleming endeavored to arrest the brave who fired the shot. The result was a skirmish in which three Indians were killed, three wounded, and two taken prisoner—and a host of oncoming overlanders badly frightened. Apparently a small detachment was quickly detailed from the fort to protect the overlanders from possible Sioux reprisals.[48] To the east, two companies of Mounted Riflemen left Fort Leavenworth for three months of protective duty. Unaccountably, however, although their mission was announced in the press as "to protect the emigrants," they did not leave until July, when there were no more westbound emigrants to protect.[49]

The year 1854 began routinely enough with the usual army details from Fort Kearny chasing nettlesome Pawnee Indians and escorting emigrant caravans.[50] Additionally, an impressive army force traveled at the rear of the migration. Going into winter quarters at Salt Lake City on August 31, Brevet Lieutenant Colonel Edward J. Steptoe's command numbered about 175 soldiers, 150 civilian employees, 100 wagons and carriages, and nearly 1,000 horses and mules.[51] Yet only a few weeks after this awe-inspiring aggregation passed Fort Laramie, the army suffered one of its major western disasters—the Grattan massacre.

Sioux Indians, well aware of the previous year's ferryboat incident, were gathering at the fort to claim their annual annuity goods. On August 18 a lame cow wandered away from Mormon emigrants hurrying westward. When the stray cow reached the Sioux encampment it was quickly butchered. From this trivial occurrence ensued a tragic series of errors for which fort commander Hugh B. Fleming and Lieutenant John L. Grattan bore almost complete responsibility. Although the Sioux chief offered generous payment—a horse—for the emigrant animal, somehow the circumstances were utilized to force a major confrontation the next day. Grattan, a firm believer in severely punishing Indians for all their mistakes, demanded the arrest of the offending Miniconjou Sioux brave— who was a guest in the Brulé village. Grattan ineptly attempted a show of force with his contingent of twenty-eight men, refusing a mule as compensation for the now-important cow. A few shots were fired and an Indian was wounded, but still the chiefs cautioned their warriors not to return the fire, evidently hoping the whites had now had their vengeance. But Grattan was not to be denied, and he ordered another volley in which the Sioux chief was killed. Reprisal came swiftly. All twenty-one soldiers and their interpreter were killed; their bodies, especially Grattan's, were badly mutilated. The enraged Sioux raided trading posts around the fort and that fall made a series of attacks on mail carriers, killing at least three.[52]

In August, 1854, tragedy followed tragedy. Just one day after the Grattan debacle, nineteen westbound overland emigrants had been killed near Fort Boise. Acting quickly upon learning of the Ward massacre, Brevet Major Granville O. Haller, with two officers and twenty-six soldiers, left Fort Dalles on August 30. A volunteer force under Nathan Olney was close behind. The rescue parties remained on the trail in the Fort Boise region until all emigrants had passed, killing and capturing several Indians. But army retaliation for the Ward and Grattan massacres awaited the following year.[53]

In 1855 avenging forces moved westward from Fort Leavenworth under Brigadier General William S. Harney and eastward from Forts Vancouver and Dalles under Major Haller. In both regions patrols and escorts for emigrants were instituted. Harney's chastisement of the Sioux did not occur until September 3, long after that year's overlanders had passed Forts Kearny and Laramie. And they had traveled virtually unmolested, perhaps in part because Colonel Philip St. George Cooke was on constant patrol between the two forts with four companies of dragoons throughout the summer.[54] Due to the good behavior of the Sioux during the summer—and the recognition that the Grattan tragedy had not been premeditated by the Indians—the Superintendent of Indian Affairs raised pertinent questions about the wisdom of a punitive campaign.[55] But second thoughts were futile. Far too many, including Harney, were hot for war. The confrontation took place a few miles northwest of Ash Hollow on the north side of the Platte River near Blue Water Creek. Here approximately 250 Indians under Chief Little Thunder were encamped, in violation of the Indian agent's order that peaceful and friendly Indians proceed to Fort Laramie. The battle was a stunning triumph for Harney, whose 600 men suffered only six dead and six wounded while killing at least eighty-six Indians, wounding five, and capturing approximately seventy women and children.[56] Following the engagement Harney marched to Fort Laramie. Holding councils with the Sioux en route, he admonished them to keep the overland trail through their country safe and open for travel. Then Harney headed north to Fort Pierre on the Missouri River, where the following March the Sioux chiefs agreed to a treaty—never ratified by the Senate—which specified, "The Indians must not obstruct or lurk in the vicinity of roads travelled by the whites."[57]

Major Haller's reprisals were less bloody and more selective. Reaching Fort Boise on July 15 with 150 soldiers from Forts Dalles and Vancouver,

Haller immediately held a council with the 200 assembled Indians. Four of the warriors present were seized when Haller learned they had been involved in the Ward massacre. One tried to escape and was killed; the other three were tried by a military commission of three officers, convicted, and sentenced to be hanged over the graves of the emigrant victims. The order was carried out on July 18 some twenty-five miles from Fort Boise. The executed culprits were buried at the foot of the gallows, which were left standing as a warning symbol.[58] This was the extent of the chastisement, and it was insufficient for Portland editor T. J. Dryer, who obviously preferred Harney's tactics—and results. Dryer, while commending Haller for what had been done, wrote that "our only regret is that they did not shoot the whole tribe."[59] Perhaps of more significance for the emigrants, Haller's command then patrolled the Oregon Trail until mid-September, ranging 150 miles east of Fort Boise to await westbound overlanders and escort them to the fort and beyond.[60]

In 1854 a stray cow had triggered a series of events which led to continuing conflict with the Sioux Indians. In April, 1856, a distressingly similar series of events began with the Cheyenne tribe; this time the cause célèbre was a stray horse. A contingent of troops had been stationed at the Platte bridge, evidently on guard duty, when a small band of Cheyenne arrived for purposes of trade. The officer in charge had been informed that the Indians possessed four stray—not stolen—horses belonging to whites. He demanded the animals, promising to reward the Indians for finding and herding them. The natives surrendered three but claimed they had found the fourth animal much earlier and at a different place. The troops were then ordered to arrest three of the Indians. Two tried to escape; one succeeded, the other was killed, and the prisoner ultimately died in captivity. In the course of their precipitate flight the remaining Indian killed an old trapper. In August there were further incidents. Following a misunderstanding between two Cheyenne warriors and the driver of a mail carriage, Fort Kearny troops attacked the peaceful Cheyenne encampment and killed several Indians. But before the attack the Cheyenne chiefs had already disciplined the two braves, who themselves had been fired upon first by the stage driver. The fleeing Cheyenne attacked several parties of travelers they encountered, killed at least eleven persons, and took three captives. One of those killed was Almon Babbitt, Utah Territory's delegate to Congress. The stage had been set for a punitive campaign against the Cheyenne the following year.[61]

That four-month campaign, led by Colonel Edwin V. Sumner, did not result in a victory to rival Harney's triumph at Blue Water Creek. Sumner's command, which traveled slowly to Fort Laramie so as to escort the westbound overlanders of the year, finally engaged a band of 300 Cheyenne approximately sixty miles south of Fort Kearny on July 29. After a short skirmish, in which two soldiers were killed and nine wounded, the Indians fled. Though pursued, they were not overtaken. Sumner had to be content with destroying 171 Cheyenne lodges filled with supplies and with the nine Indians killed and the large number wounded. Sumner pointedly noted, however, that no women or children had been hurt.[62] Harney evidently learned of this comment, for he was soon complaining that only four days after Sumner's engagement 150 of the same Cheyenne attacked a cattle party twenty-eight miles from Fort Kearny, demonstrating that "they not only had no fear for their families from Colonel Sumner's Command, but that his action was not attended by any moral consequences."[63]

While officers sparred for laurels as the most proficient Indian tamers, the massive Utah Expedition toiled westward toward its anticipated rendezvous with the Mormon rebels. The thousands of soldiers and hundreds of supply wagons thronging the trails met only eastbound overlanders, however, due to their late departure from Fort Leavenworth. Also in 1857 a number of soldiers were on the trails in connection with road-surveying parties, information which the Portland *Weekly Oregonian* specifically directed to prospective overlanders in its continuing campaign to make certain that everyone would know that the overland road would be "open this spring and summer for emigrating parties destined for the shores of the Pacific."[64]

Beginning in 1858 most of the army activity along the trails was related in some manner to Camp Floyd. Troops departed from Fort Leavenworth for Utah beginning in March and departures continued through June, thus blanketing the year's westbound emigration.[65] One of the departures was General Harney, who held conferences with Pawnee, Oglala, and Cheyenne Indians en route. Father Pierre-Jean De Smet, traveling along as a conciliator, noted that Harney "strongly advised them to cease molesting the whites who might pass through their borders, adding that on this condition alone could they remain at peace with the United States." Harney returned with his command after receiving word that the Mormons had made peace, having traveled only as far as the ford of the South Platte River.[66] Other detachments continued on to Fort Bridger and Camp Floyd. One regiment of infantry proceeded to California over the regular trail—the first large American army force to travel the entire length of the California Trail during one season. Colonel Johnston also sent 100 dragoons and 50 infantrymen on patrol along the Humboldt River in September after receiving word at his Camp Floyd headquarters that Indians were troubling travelers.[67]

In 1859 troops from Camp Floyd and Fort Bridger fanned out in all directions to patrol the trails and cutoffs throughout the traveling season. On June 12 a small group of disgruntled Mormons left the Salt Lake Valley for California, traveling to within eighty miles of the Humboldt Sink under the protection of Major Isaac Lynde and his companies of infantry and dragoons, who were departing for a summer of escort and patrol duty.[68] Returning along the Humboldt River, Lynde met great numbers of westbound emigrants, many so destitute that he began issuing them provisions. On August 19 he reached the Bear River ford, where a depot had been established a few days earlier by Lieutenant E. Gay, dispatched from Camp Floyd with a dragoon company as soon as word of the brutal attack on the Shepherd emigrant train had been received.[69] First Lieutenant G. A. Gordon also arrived on the 19th with another company of dragoons from Camp Floyd. From this command post Lynde sent scouts and patrols in all directions. Several companies under Captain L. McLaws were dispatched to the Fort Hall region to protect the large number of emigrants in that vicinity.

Both Lynde and Gay had been directed to protect travelers and punish marauders but to avoid unnecessary hostilities with Indians. If punitive measures became necessary, however, their orders specified that the Indians were "to *feel* the power of the government." Yet Gay's detachment was the only contingent to have anything more than a minor skirmish (in which four of Gay's men were seriously injured, approximately twenty Indians killed, and one horse recovered which apparently had been taken from the Shepherd train). Only rarely were Indians even seen. Indeed, since emigrants continued to be attacked and killed in spite of the army patrols and escorts, Mormon observers began suggesting that the army presence was doing more harm than good. They charged that frustrated troops, eager for battle, treated peaceful Indians savagely and violated Indian women, with the result that even normally friendly Indians were vowing revenge.[70]

Oregon-bound overlanders in 1859 thus received at least nominal protection as far as Fort Hall from troops under Lynde's command. Beyond the fort many were able to travel in concert with Major Reynolds, who with 100 soldiers from Camp Floyd escorted the earlier emigrants. Captain H. D. Wallen escorted the later caravans, providing needy overlanders with animals as well as food. Wallen, who had traveled to Camp Floyd from Fort Vancouver in early summer in search of a better route from Fort Dalles to the Salt Lake Valley, believed "that the safety of the emigration has been due entirely to the presence of troops along the route." Wallen recognized, however, that food and draft animals were at least of equal importance. After sending some dragoons sixty miles back along the trail to rescue completely destitute emigrants, he commented, "But for our being out on the road these nine men, four women, and fifteen children, must have perished."[71]

Aside from a second campaign against the Cheyenne, Comanche, and Kiowa Indians, virtually all army trail activity in 1860 was again confined to the far western theater.[72] There was considerable action on all fronts beginning with the Pyramid Lake Indian War in May. The war grew out of

William Henry Jackson, "Approaching Chimney Rock." Knowing Fort Laramie to be but a short distance beyond, overlanders encircle their wagons for the night in view of the towering landmark.

Scotts Bluff National Monument, National Park Service

the murder of five men at a trading post–mail station along the Carson River, an attack which may have been prompted by the abduction of two young Paiute squaws by the men at the station. Under Major William M. Ormsby, a large volunteer punitive force from several Nevada towns was, instead of punishing Indians, itself entrapped and nearly annihilated. Approximately forty-six men were killed, although estimates ranged as high as sixty. Ormsby's defeat thoroughly frightened the Carson Valley. A huge force—numbering more than 800 men, among them several hundred army troops from California—was quickly assembled. Indian resistance was smashed in several ensuing skirmishes in which forty or fifty Paiutes were killed. Captain Joseph Stewart and his troops remained in the area for protection, manning the temporary Fort Haven for a time before constructing Fort Churchill on the Carson River.[73]

Aware of these vicious encounters, emigrants from the Salt Lake Valley planning on traveling to California petitioned both the territorial governor and the commander at Camp Floyd for protection. In response, two separate summer patrols were dispatched. The first, commanded by First Lieutenant Stephen H. Weed, moved out May 26 along the mail route to the Carson Valley that Captain James H. Simpson had laid out the previous year. Weed escorted 186 California-bound emigrants, mostly apostate Mormons, on his westward trek. About 250 miles west of Camp Floyd, in the Ruby Valley, he established a depot from which base his troops patrolled the trail to the east and west during the rest of the summer. Periodically Weed punished Indians for attacks on stage stations and trading posts. Before he returned to Camp Floyd in late September, his men had killed approximately forty Indians.[74]

Lieutenant Colonel M. T. Howe, with responsibility for the main overland trail and the Lander Cutoff, led the second summer patrol. Howe, like Weed, was ordered to warn all Indians not to molest trail travelers, to punish marauders, and to be careful in distinguishing between friendly and hostile Indians. Also, Howe was authorized "to issue to destitute emigrants, who may be without provisions, limited quantities of flour and bacon; and should there be women and children with such parties, coffee and sugar in addition. To emigrants without food, but with the means to purchase it, limited quantities of the same articles may be sold." Howe left Camp Floyd on June 5 with approximately 150 men. He established a depot at the Portneuf River from which he kept patrols active until mid-September, ranging as far west as City Rocks on the California Trail, north to Salmon Falls on the Oregon Trail, and about 100 miles east on the main trail. Howe also dispensed provisions and stock to emigrants who were running low or had been attacked, but evidently engaged in no major skirmishes with either Indians or whites masquerading as Indians.[75]

Finally, there was also considerable patrol and escort activity on the several routes to Oregon in 1860. First Lieutenant Alexander Piper had nearly seventy men from Fort Umpqua on patrol in the Upper Klamath country near the southern emigration trail but reported virtually no emigrant traffic on that route in 1860.[76] There was more action on the main Oregon Trail. Major Grier patrolled southeast to Fort Boise, Captain A. J. Smith, Major E. Steen, and Major George P. Andrews continued Wallen's route explorations, skirmishing intermittently with the natives, and Captain Dent hurried out from Fort Dalles with 110 men to assist the Otter–Van Orman massacre survivors.[77]

The foregoing summary makes clear the steady westward progression of army protective activity as well as the constantly increasing amount of that activity in behalf of the overland emigrants. Yet despite the establishment of the trailside forts, and the relief, punishment, patrol, and escort expeditions, many overlanders were not satisfied, particularly during the early 1850s. Some lamented the inadequate number and injudicious placement of the forts, others wanted more troops garrisoned at each outpost. More forts and more troops were also the incessant refrains of West Coast newspaper editors, who feared that the rising Indian threat during the mid-1850s would drastically curtail overland travel.[78] Other emigrants desired fewer troops stationed at the forts in lieu of an escort squadron of troops every year. Still others stressed their ability to protect themselves and demanded not more military might but more governmental services: guidebooks based upon exhaustive route surveys, government workshops along the trail for wagon repairs, supply stations for provisions, governmental trains to pick up straggling and forsaken emigrants and transport them safely to their destination.[79] All these requests—or demands—were based on the now-common conviction that the federal government carried a clear responsibility to insure safe overland travel.

Overlanders were generally unfamiliar with another important method by which the government endeavored to pacify Indians in the interests of safe plains travel—treaties and agreements negotiated by Indian agents and commissioners. By the time the overland caravans of the early 1840s suggested the nature of future problems, governmental treaty-making with Indian nations was a well-established practice. The Department of Indian Affairs provided the organizational framework within which agents and commissioners struggled with such perennial problems as controlling the Indian trade and stamping out the illicit liquor traffic.[80]

The act organizing the department dated from 1834. Until 1849 the various superintendencies, agencies, and subagencies were located in the War Department, with the St. Louis Superintendency embracing virtually all the Indian tribes with whom overland emigrants came in contact. In 1849 responsibility for Indian affairs was transferred to the new Interior Department, in 1851 the St. Louis Superintendency was renamed the Central Superintendency, and by then there were also superintendencies in Oregon and Utah. Most matters of Indian-emigrant relationships were concentrated within these three areas.[81]

Because in 1787 Congress had combined the office of Territorial Governor with that of Superintendent of Indian Affairs, Brigham Young served as ex-officio Superintendent of Indian Affairs after Utah achieved territorial status in 1850.[82] Most of the difficulties, at least those of policy, procedure, and communication, occurred in the Utah Superintendency. Here the fact that Brigham Young was also the spiritual leader of a people toward whom there was increasing hostility compounded the normal conflict of interest between territorial governors charged with promoting the settlers' welfare and guarding the rights of the natives—simultaneously.[83]

In addition to these serious problems there were commissioners in Washington and agents in the field whose attitudes of white cultural superiority clouded vision and influenced policies. Luke Lea laced his 1852 report as Indian Commissioner with lengthy strictures on why the "enlightened and Christian" whites were justified in seizing the Indians' land:

... much of the injury of which the red man and his friends complain has been the inevitable consequence of his own perverse and vicious nature. In the long and varied conflict between the white man and the red—civilization and barbarism—the former has often been compelled to recede, and be destroyed, or to advance and destroy. ... The embarrassments to which they [Indians] are subjected, in consequence of the onward pressure of the whites, are gradually teaching them the important lesson that they must ere long change their mode of life, or cease to live at all. It is by industry or extinction that the problem of their destiny must be solved.[84]

Of a piece were the 1859 observations that agent Thomas A. Twiss dispatched from his Upper Platte agency—one of the most important along the overland trail:

This great wave of emigration to the prairie west is moving onward with greatly increased velocity. It is beyond human power to retard or control it, nor would it be wise to do so, even were it possible.

This process of development, this law of Anglo-Saxon progress, is a necessity and a consequence of, and flowing directly from, our free institutions, which, in their strength, purity, and beauty, tend to stimulate and bring forth the vast resources of agriculture, mineral and commercial wealth, within the boundaries of our great empire.

Hence, it is that the savage, the wild hunter tribes, must give way to the white man, who requires his prairie hunting grounds for the settlement and homes of millions of human beings, where now only a few thousand of rude barbarians derive a scanty, precarious, and insufficient subsistence; and where, by improved methods in agriculture, and an application of labor-saving machinery, these millions may be fed and clothed, and add, yearly, to our great staples and products of national and individual wealth.[85]

Lea had called for powerful demonstrations of armed strength to frighten the natives into submissiveness and prevent their "natural tendencies . . . to rapine and slaughter" from prevailing. While many officials and agents periodically called for more military posts and troops in their areas, almost all did so on the apparent assumption that the Department of Indian Affairs would have a strong voice in the decisions concerning the use of that military power, especially in the matter of punitive expeditions. That assumption often proved unfounded. Particularly after the 1849 organizational shift to the Interior Department, there obtained considerable controversy over the policies of military deterrence favored by most army personnel and the tactics of negotiation and diplomacy championed by many Indian Department employees.[86]

Within this milieu Indian agents and commissioners labored diligently to entice tribes away from the overland trails through treaties, annuities, and the establishment of reservations. Whether immediate treaty negotiations for the right of overland travel through the Indian country in 1841 or 1842 would have significantly altered the course of western Indian relationships is difficult to determine. It is clear, however, that by 1851, when the first meaningful efforts were made, Indian tribes had accumulated a decade of grievances. Emigrant-Indian and army-Indian skirmishes were increasingly the order of the day.[87]

During the decade of the 1840s only minimal attempts had been made to satisfy accumulating Indian frustrations. To be sure, conventional wisdom recognized the importance of governmental representatives providing Indians with "presents" at every encounter. Senator Thomas H. Benton, for example, urged John C. Frémont to supply himself with ample quantities of suitable presents for his 1843 expedition, since "it is indispensable that the officer who carries the flag of the U. States into these remote regions, should carry presents. All savages expect them: they even demand them; and they feel contempt & resentment if disappointed."[88] In the spring of 1848 Indian agent Thomas Fitzpatrick counseled peace to Arapaho and Sioux Indians along the Platte River, and the 1848 treaty by which the Pawnee Indians received $2,000 for 600 square miles around Grand Island had elicited Pawnee promises to refrain from molesting or injuring American travelers. In April, 1849, Governor Joseph Lane of Oregon Territory met with Cayuse and other Indians at The Dalles, gave them $200 in presents, and had them agree to meet oncoming overlanders in peace. Until 1851, however, this represented, in addition to the admonitions of army officers like Wharton and Kearny, the extent of governmental recognition of Indian distress at emigrant transit over their lands.[89]

The 1850s, beginning with the Fort Laramie Treaty Council of 1851, were different. Agent Fitzpatrick, among others, had long encouraged a general treaty council with the plains tribes. In September Fitzpatrick and Superintendent David D. Mitchell of St. Louis met with over 10,000

Indians—the greatest gathering of plains tribes ever—at Horse Creek, some thirty-five miles east of Fort Laramie. The resultant treaty established tribal boundaries, specified peaceful relations among tribes, authorized the laying out of roads and construction of military posts in Indian territory, and provided for punishment and restitution of any depredations committed—by either Indian or white. For its part the United States promised an annuity of $50,000 of merchandise per year for fifty years. Soon after the signing ceremonies had been concluded, twenty-seven wagons rolled in direct from Fort Leavenworth with the first year's annuity. Additionally, Fitzpatrick escorted a delegation of Indian chiefs east to Washington, already a well-established tradition.[90]

Although the treaty was initially regarded as successful, not all western tribes had been represented, and some that were eventually became troublesome.[91] Therefore, beginning in 1852, Indian agents yearly traveled along the overland trails endeavoring to keep the peace, an activity of considerable importance in averting trail tragedies. Most of this trail peace-making took place west of South Pass—in the most dangerous travel locale—and among tribes which had not been represented at the 1851 Treaty Council.

Jacob H. Holeman, agent from the Utah Superintendency, with a thirty-five-man escort, spent the summer of 1852 traveling from Salt Lake City down the Humboldt River to the Carson Sink and back. In his report he emphasized that the Indians along the Humboldt and Carson rivers had been troublesome only because white emigrants and traders had been troublesome first, murdering Indians without warning or cause and stealing their horses. In the main, Holeman accepted the Indians' defense that they had been merely retaliating in kind. After dispensing presents, counseling peace, and soothing hostile feelings, Holeman concluded that his expedition "has been of service in producing peace and quiet on this road." But Brigham Young, with whom Holeman was already feuding, thought the absence of severe depredations that year had been due instead to the immense numbers of overlanders on the trails. Holeman stressed that the time was ripe for a treaty with these Indians, but suggested too, as agents did from time to time, the need for a few military posts, in this case along the Humboldt River.[92]

Subsequent years revealed a similar pattern. In 1853 Holeman again devoted nearly three months during the height of the emigration season to a pacifying trip along the Humboldt and Carson rivers on the California Trail. Once more he met with various tribal chiefs, received assurances that no depredations would be committed on passing overlanders, and distributed the always welcome gifts. By the time he reached the Carson Valley Holeman had exhausted his supply of Indian goods. After securing an additional shipment from California he began the return journey, on which one of his tasks was to explain to a mournful chief the difference between unscrupulous California traders who had murdered six of his tribe, including his son, and the more peaceful overlanders. Holeman gave all his presents to the aggrieved tribe and returned to Salt Lake confident that "if the emigrants who have to pass the road this season . . . will treat the Indians with any degree of kindness, there will be no further difficulties." Holeman railed especially at the unscrupulous traders infesting the overland trail along the Humboldt River, blaming them for provoking Indian attacks on emigrant trains.[93]

There was also action from the Oregon Superintendency in 1853. Superintendent Joel Palmer dispatched agent Joseph Garrison to treat with Indian tribes between the Willamette Valley and Fort Boise (and if necessary to proceed on as far as Fort Hall). Garrison dispensed presents and reiterated to the chiefs the usual refrain: hostility to overlanders would bring certain punishment from army troops.[94]

Joel Palmer in Oregon and Isaac I. Stevens in Washington were active during 1854 and 1855 in concluding treaties with the several tribes resident in the two territories, agreements by which the Indians accepted reservation status.[95] In 1855 agent Nathaniel Olney accompanied Major Haller's punitive patrol expedition, and Brigham Young sent the new Salt Lake agent, Garland Hurt, to the Humboldt River with Indian gifts to halt the many depredations being reported from that quarter. In August Hurt negotiated a treaty with Shoshonis providing that depredations upon travelers would cease, but the Senate never confirmed the pact, much to Hurt's chagrin, for he greatly preferred permanent treaties to temporary gift-giving.[96]

By 1856 Hurt was as deeply embroiled in disputes with Young and other Mormons as his predecessors, but still made the annual pilgrimage along the Humboldt during the emigration season, meeting with both Indians and overlanders and endeavoring to keep clashes to a minimum.[97] While Hurt was traveling along the Humboldt, Chief Washakie and his Shoshoni band were given approximately $4,500 in gifts. Young explained to the Indian Commissioner that Washakie's people had been given no presents at the Fort Laramie Council but had scrupulously adhered to its provisions and had molested no emigrants even though the Oregon-California Trail passed through the heart of their lands. Their desired and deserved recompense was finally received at Fort Bridger in the fall of 1856.[98]

Meanwhile at the important Upper Platte agency—responsible primarily for the Sioux, Cheyenne, and Arapaho tribes—agent Thomas Twiss labored zealously during the fall to restore peaceful relationships with the Cheyenne following the ominous events of the spring and summer. After a series of councils with the chiefs, Twiss was confident that his efforts had been successful. It was with much unhappiness that he learned of Sumner's punitive expedition.[99]

Endeavors to foster traveling safety continued apace during the last years of the decade. Hurt made one last journey along the Humboldt to the Carson Valley during the summer of 1857; in September, 1858, Jacob Forney, recently appointed as Brigham Young's successor in the Utah Superintendency, likewise followed the Humboldt River trail to the Carson Valley. Frederick W. Lander, supervising the survey and construction of the Fort Kearny, South Pass, and Honey Lake Wagon Road, negotiated with Washakie for the right-of-way between the Sweetwater River and Fort Hall, evidently dispensing merchandise payments to the Shoshoni and other tribes in both 1858 and 1859.[100]

In 1859 Forney again visited the Indians in his superintendency, agent Robert B. Jarvis followed Simpson's route from Salt Lake toward the Carson Valley, instituting Indian farms and trying to prevent depredations, while agent Frederick Dodge from his new post in the Carson Valley enumerated all the tribes within his jurisdiction and distributed the usual presents. Of potential significance for safer plains travel was the 1859 treaty Twiss negotiated at the Upper Platte agency with Sioux, Cheyenne, and Arapaho chiefs, but which the Senate refused to ratify.[101] Dodge continued active in the Carson Valley during 1860, while from Fort Owen Major John Owen, under whose temporary supervision the Shoshoni-Bannock had been placed, pleaded for treaties and presents for those neglected Indians. Owen repeated the oft-expressed explanation for a large share of the Indian hostility:

I do really think that with kind treatment and a prudent Expenditure of a few thousand Dollars Every Year that these Indians could be drawn from their predatory habits and Settled quietly in the Salmon River Country and be taught and induced to cultivate the soil. These Indians twelve years ago were the avowed friends of the White Man.... Their present hostile attitude can in a great Measure be attributed to the treatment they have recd from unprincipled White Men passing through their Country. They have been robed Murdered their Women outraged etc. etc. and in fact outrages have been committed by White Men that the heart would Shudder to record. Those are incontrovertible facts. I do not Wish to see these Indians Shielded from the punishment they so justly deserve. Still these are paliating circumstances that is No More than just should be shown in their favor.[102]

Seven years earlier agent Tom Fitzpatrick, drawing upon his long acquaintance with the natives, had suggested that the governmental approach toward the plains Indians needed to follow one of two courses: "The policy must be either an army or an annuity. Either an inducement must be offered to them greater than the gains of plunder, or a force must be at hand able to restrain and check their depredations. Any compromise between the two systems will only be productive of mischief."[103] But compromise there always was, whether proper or not, thanks to a parsimonious Congress unwilling to provide sufficient funds to compensate the Indians for the loss of their lands and for the damage being done by the emigrations, or sufficient funds for a large enough military force in the West to actually make safe travel a more certain reality.[104] And, as is clear from the reports of many Indian agents and army officers, for real effectiveness such a force would have had to be enormously large. An important phase of its work would have been somehow keeping emigrants, traders, and desperadoes from wantonly insulting, cheating, robbing, and murdering innocent Indians—because many depredations were prompted more by revenge than by desires for plunder. Moreover, all too frequently the very military forces which were supposed to be insuring peace were instead insuring war by the inept and injudicious actions they were committing. The problem, then, was incredibly complex and required far more patience and understanding than most Americans possessed. But despite the failures, and the unfortunate long-range implications of the events occurring between 1840 and 1860, it remains that this considerable federal activity had been called forth by the overland emigrations, was being pursued to protect emigrant travel, and certainly had been responsible for forestalling some trail tragedies.

The desire for protection from marauding Indians prompted most emigrant requests for army troops and forts. Once military outposts had been established, however, it immediately became apparent that "protection" had many dimensions. In fact, for sizable numbers of overlanders the Indian fighting role of the frontier army was its *least* important function. To the chagrin of the commanding officers, emigrants came to depend upon the army outposts—particularly Forts Kearny and Laramie—for a host of services.

Not the least of these ancillary endeavors was dispensing information. Often doubting the accuracy of guidebooks or route information supplied by unknown persons met along the trails, overlanders were more inclined to trust their own government's army. An artist-naturalist who accompanied the Regiment of Mounted Riflemen to Oregon reported on the amusingly chaotic scene at Fort Kearny, where hordes of forty-niners made "thousands of inquiries on every conceivable subject."[105] Troops encountered on the trails were plied with questions as zealously as were fort commanders, beginning with Kearny's dragoon march in 1845. Captain Philip Cooke noted that year that many overlanders "scarcely know where they are going; and these men eagerly question our guide—who has been in Oregon—on the simplest and best known points."[106] In 1850 Major Chilton, Fort Kearny's commanding officer, dispatched an urgent message to all the major jumping-off towns that due to a late spring the prairie grasses were not yet able to support forage. In addition to advising overlanders to postpone their departure, Chilton cautioned them that no supplies or provisions would be available at any of the military forts that season.[107]

William Henry Jackson's "Fort Kearny." This important post, established in 1848, provided a great variety of services to passing emigrants.

Chilton's warning was sobering. Already in Kearny's and Laramie's first year many emigrants were in such dire need of food and other supplies, even though they had not yet traveled far from the jumping-off points, that post commanders and quartermasters felt compelled to assist hardship cases. At Fort Kearny provisions were kept in reserve for distribution to turn-around emigrants forced to forgo the trip and backtrack to their places of departure.[108] Of course, Chilton's warning had fallen on deaf ears. Even though sutlers' stores were available at both forts from 1849 on, post commanders continued to be bombarded throughout the decade with urgent requests from emigrants who did not have the wherewithal to pay the sutlers' handsome prices.[109] In 1850, at least at Fort Laramie, individuals without funds were generously given what they needed gratis. In 1852 a St. Louis editor reminded overlanders that the government furnished needed supplies to emigrants at cost at Fort Laramie, and the next year Laramie's post sutlers, John S. Tutt and Lewis B. Dougherty, themselves advertised in St. Joseph that emigrants in "distress" could purchase flour and pork from the government "at cost and transportation."[110]

Tutt and Dougherty's advertisements, while naturally giving primary emphasis to the vast quantities of high-quality merchandise available from the sutlers, also informed emigrants of another important service available at the fort: "The emigrants will find at Laramie, a large supply of Medicines, and the United States Surgeon stationed there, always ready and willing to render his valuable assistance." As could be expected, the heaviest demands upon the few fort physicians came during the large emigration years of 1849, 1850, and 1852, when a steady stream of ill and injured emigrants sought medical assistance. At Fort Kearny a four-room frame hospital building, under construction throughout the summer of 1849, seems to have been completed by fall. The Fort Laramie hospital was housed in the old adobe fort, although supplementary tents were frequently necessary.[111]

Considering the heavy armament favored by overlanders—fostered in part by the War Department's enticing 1849 offer to sell pistols, rifles, and ammunition at cost to California and Oregon emigrants—it was not surprising that a great many gunshot victims made their way to the fort hospitals.[112] In mid-June, 1849, a passing overlander found four victims of accidental shootings under care at Fort Kearny, as well as a man whose arm had been amputated following a rattlesnake bite. Another four or five emigrant victims of firearm accidents were treated in the Fort Laramie hospital in July of 1849.[113] Cholera also put many patients in fort hospitals and cemeteries, although resident troops remained surprisingly free of the disease.[114] In June, 1850, alone, at least four overlanders died who had been left at Fort Laramie for treatment. In 1852 the hospitals at both Kearny and Laramie were filled with sick emigrants; at Kearny one observer reported the hospital so "crammed" that patients even occupied the soldiers' living quarters.[115] Therefore it is probable that the sickly emigrant one company left in a makeshift tent near Fort Kearny with a fifteen-day supply of provisions because "they would not receive him at the Fort" was refused because the available facilities were so crowded. Doubtless the physician attended him in his tent, although the never-ending demands of diseased and injured overlanders did cause at least one army physician to lose his temper. This doctor, stationed at Fort Laramie, refused to treat some suffering overlanders, grumbling that neither he nor the fort had been placed there for the benefit of emigrants and that it made no difference to him whether the importuning overlanders lived or died.[116] If true, this occurrence was an exception, for the overlanders almost uniformly agreed that the fort physicians were kind and generous. One even rode out from Kearny to administer to emigrants in surrounding camps.[117]

These welcome medical oases, even if primitive by eastern standards, were boons to the overland emigrants. For despite the large number of physicians also trekking westward, many injuries and illnesses required lengthy convalescent periods and the kind of careful, continuing care which was simply not possible in the bustle of daily traveling.[118] Moreover, few companies felt that they could afford the luxury of extended stops for sick comrades. Rather than being bounced along in a lurching wagon, it was far wiser for the seriously ill to remain at the army forts to rest and recuperate. When again able to travel they either joined a subsequent company or returned to the Missouri River frontier, perhaps to try again another year.

The forts were equally welcome oases to emigrants with other needs. While the post blacksmiths normally charged for their services—shoeing animals, repairing wagons and wheels—periodically the work was done free by order of the post commander. Occasionally the emigrants were permitted to use the facilities, especially if there was a smith in their traveling company. At Fort Laramie, Assistant Quartermaster Stewart Van Vliet even requested, evidently without success, $5,000 from the War Department for the construction of an adobe two-forge blacksmith shop and an adobe wagon-making shop. Van Vliet planned to make these facilities available to emigrants so that they could make whatever repairs might be necessary before beginning the roughest two-thirds of their journey.[119] At Fort Kearny there seemed no end to emigrant needs. The commanding officer provided assistance to overlanders whose draft animals had been stolen, sent out search parties to locate emigrants presumably lost on the expansive plains, and in early April, 1852, dispatched wagons to retrieve two Michigan footpackers facing starvation after being robbed by Cheyenne Indians. But when 1852 travelers began to appropriate firewood from the Kearny stockpile, the commandant drew the line rather sharply.[120]

Matters of justice and law also occupied the attention of officers and men stationed at the forts, especially during the peak gold rush period. Since many bored, poorly paid soldiers were no more able to resist the lure of California gold than the thousands of their civilian countrymen thronging the routes west, desertions were common. Deserters often preyed upon the better-prepared emigrants. Four deserting Mounted Riflemen in 1849 robbed an emigrant of $200 and raped the man's wife. Although many soldiers deserted successfully, an army pursuit party caught these four near the Green River with some assistance from overlanders in the vicinity. The culprits were then marched back to Fort Laramie, on foot, to face charges.[121]

Emigrant crime, while infrequent, periodically required the attention of Kearny and Laramie soldiers. Emigrants who stole horses from the army were energetically pursued. Troops were also apparently used to track down emigrants who had stolen possessions from other emigrants.[122] There is fragmentary evidence that in 1849 army troops arrested up to forty emigrants for desecrating Indian graves and attempting to violate Indian women. As many as seven Indians may have been killed by the Pittsburgh emigrants allegedly involved. According to some accounts, the accused emigrants were being escorted to Fort Leavenworth to stand trial for murder.[123] Finally, and certainly of considerable significance to the concerned parties, the Fort Laramie commanding officer adjudicated questions pertaining to traveling contracts. Explaining one such case in 1850, Dr. S. L. Grow commended the decision of an officer who fined and temporarily imprisoned a train captain who had refused to fulfill the terms of the contract he had made with one of his travelers. Grow approvingly concluded, "Good fellow Uncle Sam is."[124]

And a good fellow Uncle Sam was to those overlanders who either began too late in the traveling season or suffered such slowdowns en route that they were obliged to spend the winter at the little military forts along the trail. Since such persons were in a position to get an early start the following year, a fairly large number wintered at Fort Laramie during 1849–50. These "winter soldiers" so severely taxed available supplies that one of the fort's newspaper correspondents, reporting on April 9 that the contingent was about to depart, pleaded, ". . . may Heaven never send us any more, for the winter."[125] Philip L. Platt, who would later write a popular overland guidebook, was one who spent the winter of 1849–50 at Fort Laramie. In subsequent years emigrants wintered at Fort Kearny and Fort Dalles as well.[126] In fact, there were so many overlanders at Fort Laramie during the winter of 1852–53 that all provisions were soon exhausted. By the time the first 1853 emigrants appeared, these "winter soldiers" had been reduced to eating horses, having consumed at least sixteen.[127]

Horse flesh, however, like most food, was more palatable indoors than somewhere along the trail in a raging western blizzard. Now and then a reflective overlander who recognized the many conveniences the trailside forts afforded would gratefully record his appreciation in a letter or diary entry. James Payne in 1850 found Kearny's residents "very kind. . . . Any and everything that could be done to forward us on our trip was ordered done, by the officers." An 1853 traveler reported that Kearny's and Laramie's "highly meritorious" commanders were much praised by the emigrants for their many "favors" to emigrants; overlander J. W. B. Reynolds in 1856 complimented Fort Kearny's Captain Wharton: "To this gentleman we are indebted for many acts of kindness and civility, which I take this opportunity to acknowledge."[128]

Federal assistance to overland emigrants was not limited to protection from Indians or ancillary benefits accruing from permanent trailside forts. Another substantial governmental contribution came through its exploration, survey, and road-building efforts.[129] Although there were important developments during the 1840s—notably Frémont's reports of his explorations—once again it was not until the 1850s that governmental energies began to alter emigration patterns substantially. Those energies, channeled principally through the Army Corps of Topographical Engineers and the Interior Department's Pacific Wagon Road Office, had always been aimed at locating routes which would shorten and ease overland travel to Oregon and California.

Through 1855 the Corps of Topographical Engineers did the most significant work, and John Charles Frémont was by all odds their most illustrious explorer. Yet Frémont's relationship to overland travel is more intangible than that of some of his obscure colleagues. His real impact came not in the discovery of new and better trails, nor even the improvement of existing trails. Further, the intrepid Frémont had relatively little interaction with overlanders during his exploratory ventures. In 1842 his party traveled to the Rocky Mountains several weeks to the rear of the Oregon-bound emigrants; in 1843 there was only infrequent contact, as Frémont's party again spent much time off the main trail until late in the year.[130] Rather, Frémont's importance came through publicity: the national publicity accorded his western heroics; the attention those activities centered on Oregon, enhancing American interest and commitment to that region; and the influence his well-written and generously distributed reports had on potential Oregon overlanders. Though technically a topographical engineer, Frémont always sought, in concert with his expansionist father-in-law, Senator Thomas Hart Benton of Missouri, to go beyond simple surveys or explorations. His expeditions invariably were aimed at the furtherance of broader national goals. For example, in the reports of his 1842 and 1843–44 expeditions he carefully pointed out specific trail locations where American military posts could be situated to protect travelers to Oregon.[131]

Thanks to Frémont's enthusiastic reports, many emigrants launched out for Oregon, and thanks to the excellent accompanying maps prepared by Charles Preuss they felt more comfortable in attempting the venture.[132] Following Frémont's 1843–44 trip there was a hiatus in government activity, although Kearny's 1845 dragoon march had reconnaissance as a secondary objective. Also of momentary usefulness to overlanders were temporary bridges accruing from both Wharton's and Kearny's expeditions.[133]

Not until 1849 did significant exploration near the Oregon-California Trail resume. In that hectic year Captain Howard Stansbury of the Topographical Corps led an eighteen-man party westward, not only to survey the Great Salt Lake, but also to seek out a site near Fort Hall for a military post which would be helpful to overlanders continuing on to California. Stansbury and his men traveled the main trail to Salt Lake, providing protection to a small emigrant party accompanying them. Stansbury's reconnaissance activities in the Salt Lake area were many. Endeavoring to locate better routes from Fort Bridger and Fort Hall to Salt Lake City, Stansbury returned to Fort Leavenworth in search of a more direct route from Fort Bridger than that through South Pass. While later the overland stage, the Pony Express, and the Union Pacific Railroad would follow parts of his new trails, they were not immediately significant for overland travel.[134]

Also in 1849 Captain Langdon C. Easton unsuccessfully attempted to discover a shorter route between Fort Laramie and Fort Leavenworth. In California Captain William H. Warner of the Topographical Engineers followed Peter Lassen's northern California trail in an attempt to find a suitable railroad route through the Sierras to the Humboldt River. Although Warner's party lent provisions and provided information to suffering emigrants entering California on the Lassen Cutoff, their reconnaissance came to an abrupt end when Warner and two of his men were killed by Pit River Indians near Goose Lake.[135]

In 1850 emigrants began using a new military road between Fort Leavenworth and the junction with the St. Joseph trace of the Oregon-California Trail. Laid out in April by Brevet Major Edmund A. Ogden, the road covered slightly more than 100 miles to its termination near the Big Blue River. Emigrants immediately praised the new trail, comparing it favorably with the older, longer, and more circuitous route.[136]

For the next five years most reconnaissance missions pertained to the Pacific Railroad Surveys, an attempt to locate scientifically the best route for the transcontinental railroad. But with at least eight possible routes frequently advocated, and strong political and economic pressures involved, objectivity was hard to come by. The South Pass route, traversed yearly by thousands of overland emigrants, was neither included in the 1853–54 surveys nor given serious consideration. The only reconnaissance

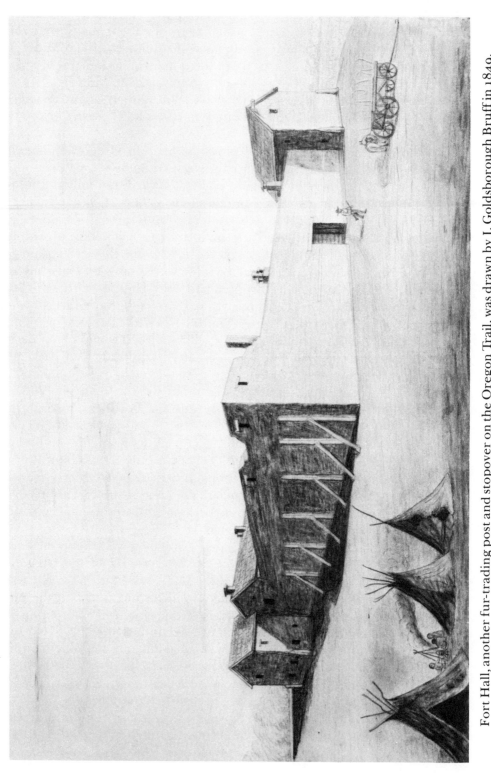

Fort Hall, another fur-trading post and stopover on the Oregon Trail, was drawn by J. Goldsborough Bruff in 1849.

with potential relevance for travelers on the Oregon-California Trail was Frederick Lander's essentially private survey from Puget Sound to Council Bluffs via South Pass in 1854—a route on which Lander reported favorably.[137]

During 1853 and 1854 a military road was built in southern Oregon, parts of which coincided with the southern overland trail into the Willamette Valley. By late 1853 overlanders heading for Washington Territory could also branch northwest from Fort Walla Walla on a newly cleared road to Puget Sound.[138] In 1853 Lieutenant John W. Gunnison and seven of his men were murdered by Utah Indians while surveying a proposed railroad route along the thirty-eighth parallel. His replacement, Lieutenant Edward G. Beckwith, re-explored Stansbury's route between Salt Lake and Fort Bridger in 1854. Lieutenant Colonel Edward J. Steptoe, whose command marched to Salt Lake in 1854 with instructions to capture Gunnison's murderers, was also ordered to supervise the construction of a military road from Salt Lake City southwest to California. Steptoe had little enthusiasm for road construction, however, and after some perfunctory actions marched his troops to California along the main Humboldt River trail.[139] Also in 1855 Lieutenant Robert S. Williamson, who had accompanied William Warner on the disastrous 1849 expedition, went north with Lieutenant Henry L. Abbott to search once more for favorable routes from San Francisco to Oregon and Washington. Parts of these surveys included the overland route through southern Oregon.[140]

By 1856 a great deal of western territory had been thoroughly surveyed, but no decision on a single Pacific railroad route seemed imminent. Since only a few trail improvements had resulted despite all the reconnaissance activity, westerners began to petition Congress zealously for serviceable wagon roads. The Congress responded with a number of appropriations, several relating to the Oregon-California Trail. Thus, during the last four years of the decade the regular trail was markedly improved and several significant cutoffs were appended to it.

In Kansas between 1856 and 1858 roads were constructed from Fort Leavenworth to Fort Riley, 130 miles to the west, and from Fort Riley to Fort Kearny. Another route was surveyed from Kearny west to the Rockies but without immediate impact.[141] Of greater significance for overlanders was the 50,000-dollar congressional appropriation to improve the Mormon Trail from Omaha to Fort Kearny. Lieutenant John H. Dickerson's comprehensive 1856 survey enabled him to shorten the total distance by approximately twenty-six miles. In 1857 the road was improved and six streams between the Missouri and Elkhorn rivers were bridged.[142]

Of comparable importance at the other end of the Oregon Trail were the improvements made between Fort Dalles and Fort Vancouver. Following a careful survey of the inhospitable terrain involved, Lieutenant George H. Derby concluded that an adequate road would cost a million dollars. Since the congressional appropriation was for only $25,000, the initial goals had to be reduced considerably. Remedial efforts were concentrated on the portage road around the Cascades, where the Columbia fell thirty feet in five miles. The road was graded, widened, and timber was cut to brace the mountainsides in an attempt to prevent rockslides. Although not enough funds remained to plank the road as desired, in 1857 planking was put down over the roughest places.[143]

The most massive governmental endeavor in behalf of improving the main emigrant trail to California was the Fort Kearny, South Pass, and Honey Lake Wagon Road. Congress funded this 1857 project with an appropriation of $300,000.[144] The road was divided into three sections: from Kearny to Independence Rock, where it was assumed only minimal work would be required, then to City Rocks over a new and shorter trail than that through South Pass, and finally to Honey Lake on the California border. For the next four years reconnaissance and road-building parties labored on the trail, their progress initially impeded by an incompetent political appointee.[145] William M. F. Magraw, a good friend of President Buchanan, was named to head the eastern and central sections of the project, with Frederick Lander his second-in-command. Magraw was a heavy-drinking, slow-moving, anti-Mormon zealot who accomplished nothing in 1857 but the squandering of time and money. Lander meanwhile competently surveyed the area west of South Pass, locating two possible routes which avoided bridge tolls and desert crossings. Magraw's disillusioned men were begging Lander to assume control by the time they reached South Pass to go into winter quarters. The structure they hastily erected there was officially designated Fort Thompson. Lander returned to Washington promising a full investigation of the charges leveled against Magraw. During the winter Magraw and many of his men joined Colonel Johnston's army.

More progress was made in 1858, with Lander now appointed the supervisor of the entire project.[146] A blockhouse for storage purposes was constructed at South Pass, while road crews worked steadily through the summer on the northernmost of the two routes surveyed the previous year. Lander's employees—bridge builders from Maine, Mormons from the Salt Lake Valley, and army drifters—felled miles of trees, moved thousands of yards of rock and earth, and bridged small streams. Lander indicated that the distance on the route—which soon was known as the Lander Cutoff—was 345.54 miles from Gilbert's Station at South Pass to City Rocks, an estimated saving of five days' travel time over the old trail. Lander again returned to Washington for the winter to keep his political relationships in order as well as to prepare a guide for emigrant use on his road.

Lander had hired a mountaineer to remain at South Pass to direct oncoming overlanders to the new road the following spring. But the employee was killed in a gunfight in early March. When Lander arrived in late June, 1859, area traders were encouraging emigrants to keep to the old road. Lander quickly stationed a former soldier and a blacksmith at Gilbert's Station to praise the new road and distribute the printed guidebooks, while he, hiring Mormons and passing emigrants, further improved the new road and provided assistance and provisions to destitute travelers. Lander claimed that 13,000 emigrants traveled on the new cutoff in 1859.[147] Their principal complaint was the treacherous ford at the Green River. Lander collected 9,000 signatures on a petition requesting governmental funds for a bridge, but the funds were never appropriated. Also in 1859 Lander distributed $5,000 in gifts to area Indians in an endeavor to placate their unhappiness at the heavy emigrant traffic.

In 1860 Lander again went west, this time by sea. Following the Pyramid Lake Indian War, he turned his attention to the final portion of the route. The Honey Lake–to–City Rocks section had been initially surveyed by John Kirk in 1857. Some improvements had been made on the route through the Carson Valley, and protection and supplies given passing overlanders. Little had been done since, for much controversy prevailed about where the route should run, Kirk being prejudiced in favor of the old trail along the Humboldt to the Carson Valley. Lander's principal effort during 1860 was the construction of huge stone reservoir tanks fed by stone culverts at Rabbit Hole Springs and Antelope Springs. The largest reservoir was developed at Rabbit Hole Springs, where an emigrant train of 300 persons and 1,000 animals scarcely depleted the 80,000 gallons in the tank—a tremendous improvement over the previous primitive conditions.

Governmental efforts had thus resulted in a shorter, somewhat improved trail from South Pass to City Rocks, an alternate route to the Humboldt River trail, which included welcome water reservoirs at Rabbit Hole Springs and Antelope Springs, and improvements on the trail in the Carson Valley. In 1858 and 1859 additional important explorations were conducted from Camp Floyd by Captain James H. Simpson of the Topographical Engineers. Simpson first directed a rapid reconnaissance between Camp Floyd and Fort Bridger. He then supervised large work parties which advanced from each end, grading, cutting timber, placing markers and guideposts, and otherwise improving the trail. The new route, while heavily used by government and freighting traffic, was probably not as significant for emigrants as the trail from Camp Floyd to the Carson Valley that Simpson marked out the following spring.[148]

Simpson's new route angled southwest to the Carson Valley, avoiding the long northward trek to City Rocks on the old trail. Indeed, Simpson calculated that his route was 288 miles shorter than the established trail, which could mean a time saving of nearly two weeks for emigrant travel.[149] Simpson's arrival was well received by the pleased residents of Genoa in the

Original trail
Government trail
improvements

Council Bluffs

St. Joseph
1850
Independence

1856-57

1856-58

Ft. Kearny

1857

North Platte River

Platte

South Platte

Missouri River

Ft. Laramie

South Pass

1857-58

Ft. Bridger

1858

Salt Lake City

Great Salt Lake

Camp Floyd

1858-59

Green R.

Colorado

Humboldt R.

1859

Ft. Hall

1860

1853-54

Walla Walla

Columbia River

Ft. Dalles

1856-57

Ft. Vancouver

1853-5

Sacramento R.

0   100   200   300
miles

Federal Government Trail
Improvements, 1850–60

MAP 4

Dyer

Carson Valley, and, following a quick stage trip to Placerville, Simpson was back at Camp Floyd on August 4. A work detail returned some 100 miles to improve and mark the east end of the trail and place wooden troughs at the desert springs to collect water. Shortly thereafter many California-bound overlanders began to follow the new route. They were supplied with hastily prepared itineraries, which were also published in Utah and California newspapers. Simpson's route proved so popular with the overlanders—emigrants passing Camp Floyd daily to follow the trail—that troops were dispatched to guard it in 1860.[150]

With the ordering of Captain Henry D. Wallen to search out a better trail from The Dalles to the Salt Lake Valley in 1859, government survey parties had completely blanketed the Oregon-California Trail, shortening its length by hundreds of miles and much enhancing the ease and safety of travel. Wallen, whose reconnaissance was conducted with perhaps the biggest and best-equipped exploratory unit ever utilized in the West, failed in an attempt to forge a new route but did shave approximately 100 miles from the old trail's length. As with his other western road-building colleagues, Wallen was extremely helpful to the oncoming Oregon overlanders of 1859, providing both protection and provisions on his return trip.[151]

At the heart of the demand for improved wagon roads was the fervent desire for quick and reliable communication between the fast-growing far western communities and the rest of the nation. The inconvenience of an irregular postal service was especially frustrating during the years of the gold rush, when family groups no longer were commonplace but males dominated both the trails and the California mining camps. Overlanders had been anxious for letters from loved ones by the time they reached the jumping-off points.[152] Three or four months later, after a long and tedious overland journey, they were desperate for news of parents, wives, sweethearts, friends, and relatives. They queued up in front of post offices after every sea mail arrived—and sometimes even before.[153] In hopes that letters would await them in California, overlanders instructed correspondents to write frequently. Henry Page directed his wife to adopt "write, write, write" as her motto.[154] David Dewolf was more than insistent when he wrote from the Weaverville mines on December 12, 1849: "Dear Matilda For Gods sake write." He had not heard from his wife since April 20 at Independence, nearly eight months before. Dewolf, who believed his wife had written often but that the letters had gone astray, was beside himself by January 20, 1850: "Oh! Matilda for Gods sake write often for I am very anxious to hear from you." At last in late May in Sacramento he received the letter he had been anticipating for more than a year: "Oh! Matilda you cannot imagine the joy it gave me the tears ran like rain while reading it."[155]

James Bushnell's plight demonstrated that uncertain postal deliveries were occasionally more than inconvenient. Bushnell traveled overland to Oregon in 1852. Finding the prospects there favorable, he wrote to his wife and mother instructing them to come to Oregon. Receiving no responses, and understandably uncertain that his letter had been delivered, Bushnell decided to return to Missouri to get his family. Bushnell left California— where he had subsequently gone to work in the gold fields—and, traveling via the Isthmus of Panama and New York City, returned to Missouri to find that his wife, infant son, mother, sisters, and brothers were en route to Oregon overland. It being too late in the year to chance an overland journey, Bushnell had to return to New York and take a steamer to Panama, and when the joyous reunion finally took place in Oregon, his unnecessary travels had consumed the $400 he had saved from his gold-mining efforts.[156]

Bushnell, Dewolf, and thousands like them were simply not satisfied with the prevailing postal system. Their persistent demand was for a rapid, reliable, and regular overland mail to supplement the sea mail, the various private enterprises which periodically were attempted, and the army couriers, who transported military and emigrant mail between Laramie, Kearny, and the outfitting towns in 1849 and subsequent years.[157] The ultimate result—a governmentally financed but extremely irregular overland service on the South Pass route—was yet another federal development of the 1850s with significant ramifications for overland emigrants. Not only did the new mail service provide more opportunities to communicate with friends and relatives while en route, it meant additional trail traffic and outposts, especially by the later 1850s, when stagecoaches with their attendant service stations for horses and relief drivers came into use.

The initial beginnings were modest.[158] Salt Lake City was the hub of the mail system, a government post office having been established there during the winter of 1849. A "monthly" mail between Independence and Salt Lake commenced on August 1 the following year, when Thomas D. Scroggins left Independence with mule-drawn light wagons to transport the mail.[159] Scroggins was employed by James Brown and Samuel H. Woodson, who had received the government contract specifying departure from Independence and Salt Lake on the first day of every month with stops at Uniontown on the Kansas River and Forts Kearny, Laramie, and Bridger. Yearly remuneration for contractors Brown (who died in December of 1850) and Woodson was $19,500. Scroggins reached Salt Lake over a week late, on September 9, and returned to Independence over three weeks late, on October 24, thereby establishing what would be a recurring pattern.[160] In 1851 Woodson subcontracted the Salt Lake–to–Fort Laramie section with mails scheduled to be exchanged at Laramie on the 15th of each month. That year contracts were also let for a similar system between Salt Lake City and Sacramento, with George Chorpenning and Absolom Woodward receiving $14,000 per year for a monthly mail.

Chorpenning inaugurated the service with his May 1, 1851, departure from the California city.[161]

Although the names of some of the contractors changed, this was the postal system which connected Missouri with California through 1858. The "monthly" service was spotty, especially on the Independence–to–Salt Lake section in winter, when the mails did not always go through. During winters the Salt Lake–to–Sacramento contractors deserted the Humboldt River trail in favor of the route down the "Mormon Corridor" to Los Angeles, with the Carson Valley serviced from Sacramento by the exploits of John A. "Snowshoe" Thompson and others who traversed Sierra snow-drifts on snowshoes.[162] Salt Lake Valley residents, particularly the *Deseret News* editor, frequently complained about the irregular service from Independence and Laramie, especially following 1854, when William M. F. Magraw and John E. Reeside held the contract by virtue of underbidding Woodson. The *News* editor noted that between July, 1854, and August, 1855, only three monthly mails had arrived on time—and some had not arrived at all.[163]

Magraw lost his contract in 1856 for unsatisfactory service and was succeeded by a Mormon, Hiram Kimball, the new low bidder. Brigham Young then took over Kimball's contract, planning a great Mormon commercial enterprise which would carry not only the mails but all goods between the Missouri River and Utah. At least $125,000 had been expended on elaborate forts, way stations, and trailside settlements when the contract was summarily annulled in June of 1857, on the pretext that Kimball was late in fulfilling its terms. The charge was true but only because winter blizzards had, as usual, delayed the mails. In fact, news about the contract had not been received in Salt Lake in time for the Mormon-sponsored Y. X. Carrying Company to begin operations until the spring of 1857. Magraw's unhappiness at losing his contract, and Mormon unhappiness at losing theirs, were contributory causes to the ensuing "war" of 1857–58.[164]

Indian troubles were not uncommon (Absolom Woodward and two of his men were killed in 1851), and mail contractors regularly appealed for and received compensation for their losses. Troop detachments periodically escorted the mail stages or were dispatched to chastise Indians accused of molesting the mailmen. Annual payments to contractors had to be occasionally revised upward.[165] Meanwhile overland emigrants continued to deposit letters at the several locations designated as mail stations, complaining on occasion that they were being charged an illegal fee. And from the mail carriers they encountered on the trails overlanders received the latest trail information, recent newspapers with local and national news, and quick letter service. For their part emigrants occasionally provided the mail carriers with something to eat.[166]

With the awarding of a $190,000 contract for weekly mail service between Independence and Salt Lake to John M. Hockaday in April, 1858, federal mail service on the South Pass route entered an accelerated phase. New post office–stage stations now began to appear.[167] At the other end of the route George Chorpenning received an 1858 contract for $130,000. It likewise specified weekly service between Placerville and Salt Lake. Hockaday's contract committed him to twenty-two-day service, Chorpenning's to sixteen—a mail service from Independence to Placerville of thirty-eight days.[168] Since a semi-weekly overland mail had already been contracted for a southern route, this 1858 upgrading of service on the central route was prompted largely by the War Department's need for swift communication with its large army base near Salt Lake City. The southern-sympathizing postmaster general had awarded a 600,000-dollar yearly contract to John Butterfield in 1857 and essentially forced him to operate on a St. Louis, Memphis, Little Rock, El Paso, Tucson, and Fort Yuma route. Although Butterfield's Overland Mail rendered acceptable service, it did not quell demands for a mail line on the central route.[169]

In 1859 a new postmaster general deemed economy measures to be in order. Cuts were made on the various overland mail operations, Hockaday and Chorpenning being reduced to semi-monthly service. These reductions were a severe financial blow, for by now it was obvious that massive governmental financing was crucial to any enterprise of this scope.[170] Hockaday's and Chorpenning's financially troubled concerns were quickly subsumed by Russell, Majors, and Waddell's Central Overland California and Pike's Peak Express Company, which itself was soon in precarious financial straits. Then the ever-optimistic Russell conceived the Pony Express venture of 1860: a desperate attempt to convince the Congress of the year-round superiority of the central route and thereby secure the large federal stipend for overland mail service which was the last hope for Russell, Majors, and Waddell's financially troubled enterprise.[171]

Russell's Pony Express relay stations strung along the overland trail in a bold attempt to win federal financing graphically demonstrated that within little more than a decade the U.S. government had been responsible for sweeping innovations in the trans-Mississippi West, innovations which much affected the nature and style of overland travel. By 1860 overlanders did not even need to travel in the traditional manner: they could bounce from Missouri to California as passengers in the stagecoaches specified in the government mail contracts. If, as almost all continued to do, they chose to travel in the customary covered wagon or by pack train, they did so on trails which had been surveyed, shortened, graded, and improved by government employees. Overlanders even enjoyed the luxury of crossing bridged streams and watering their stock at large reservoirs. For the injured or ill there were army hospitals along the route, and sutlers, blacksmiths, and generous commanding officers standing ready to distribute provisions to destitute travelers. There were even post offices where letters were mailed *and* received.[172] More important, there were troops to escort overlanders along dangerous portions of the trail, and Indian agents to negotiate with chiefs and buy or bribe native acquiescence to overland travel. The government had transformed the trail into a road.

It is, of course, a moot point whether all these federal services were undivided benefits. The federal presence in the form of permanent forts, patrolling soldiers, and, occasionally, blundering and incompetent officers irritated Indians and sometimes provoked hostilities. It is at least possible that had there been no permanent federal presence along the trails there would have been less need for any. But that was more a question for future historians than for an emigrant of the 1850s.[173] What mattered most to him was that Uncle Sam, that good fellow, had done and was doing much to expedite his overland journey.

CHAPTER SEVEN

Private Entrepreneurs, 1840–49

"While others are chasing wealth they are catching it, no dream"

The success of the overland emigrations was due in large measure to their timely coincidence with the decline of the Rocky Mountain fur trade. Many seasoned western mountaineers, no longer needed for such outmoded ventures as the rendezvous system, were attracted by the related activity of furnishing supportive services to greenhorn overland travelers. Throughout the 1840s and 1850s emigrants benefited immensely from trading outposts adjacent to the trails and from the geographic knowledge and trail savvy of mountain men. The trading forts were vestiges of the cutthroat national and international competition which had characterized the quest for beaver pelts, and most of the canny entrepreneurs who anticipated the profit potential in catering to the many needs of overland travelers were former mountaineers.

The federal government's pattern of implicit but steady acceleration of assistance to overland travel was paralleled by private enterprise. During the 1840s there were relatively few trading posts and river ferries. Then the gold rush so accentuated westward movement that it was impossible to overlook the myriad possibilities for financial windfalls. The gold rush years were marked by a host of varied enterprises, many so successful that overlanders themselves temporarily halted their westward dash to compete for profits at river crossings and beside the trail. By the late 1850s the extensive changes these entrepreneurs had occasioned in the nature of the overland trip were clearly evident.

Most trading forts had been operative for a number of years when emigrant families began trailing westward in the 1840s. Three dated from 1834: Fort William, at the confluence of the Platte and Laramie rivers; Fort Hall, near the junction of the Snake and Portneuf rivers; and Fort Boise, near the mouth of the Boise River. The latter two were outposts of the formidable Hudson's Bay Company. With Fort Walla Walla, established near the convergence of the Walla Walla and Columbia rivers in 1818, they formed a trio of British bastions. In 1840 Fort William, operated by the American Fur Company, was the lone American enterprise near the trails.[1]

The next year there were three. One, Fort Platte, still clearly reflected the fading fur-trade era, having been established by Lancaster P. Lupton to contest the American Fur Company for furs and pelts. Constructed within two miles of Fort William, Lupton and his Fort Platte colleagues specialized in dispensing illicit whiskey to facilitate Indian trading.[2] In response to this challenge, the American Fur Company promptly commenced a new adobe fort to replace deteriorating Fort William. The proprietors designated the new structure Fort John but almost everyone called it Fort Laramie, by which name it became famous.[3] The third post begun in 1841, Fort Bridger, was the first definite response to the emerging era of overland travel. Conducted essentially as a partnership between Louis Vasquez and Jim Bridger, the enterprise was principally geared to supplying the needs of overland travelers, as Bridger made explicit in a letter to his supplier: "I have established a small store with a Black Smith Shop, and a supply of iron in the road of the Emigrants, on Black's Fork, Green River, which promises fairly. They, in coming out are generally well supplied with money, but by the time they get there, are in want of all kinds of supplies. Horses, Provisions, Smith work, &c, brings ready cash from them; and should I receive the goods hereby ordered, will do a considerable business in that way with them!"[4]

Supplementing these stationary posts were transient traders. Frequently from Taos, they began regular pilgrimages to strategic trail sites in 1841, usually with riding or draft animals to trade or sell to passing emigrants. Mountain man Joseph R. Walker thus met the small contingent of 1841 overlanders in the Green River Valley with a drove of California horses and mules.[5]

Since neither Fort Platte nor Fort Bridger was open for business during the 1841 emigration season, the overlanders relied on the limited supplies available at the American Fur Company and Hudson's Bay Company posts. Most trading activity occurred at Fort Hall and Boise. At Fort Hall the Oregonians left their wagons, exchanged their oxen for pack horses, and secured provisions from post commander Francis Ermatinger, who was as helpful and hospitable as his dwindling supplies permitted.[6] The California-bound Bidwell-Bartleson party, traveling without a guide, also dispatched several men to Fort Hall for provisions as well as information on how to get to California.[7]

Twice as many overlanders were on the trails the following year, all destined for Oregon. They found Fort Platte under new ownership— Sybille, Adams, and Company were in control. The emigrant company spent a week near the two forts resting and trading exhausted animals,

Trading Posts, Ferries, and Bridges, 1840–48

MAP 5

repairing outfits, restocking provisions. Already at Fort Laramie mountaineers had advised the 1842 overlanders that it was impossible to take
wagons through to Oregon, and some emigrants began to exchange their
oxen and wagons for horses.[8] Most waited to make the change until Fort
Hall. There area mountaineers joined the new chief trader, Richard Grant,
in convincing the weary travelers that their wagons could not be taken
much farther. A few overlanders managed to secure something in exchange for their wagons; the majority of vehicles were simply abandoned.
At Fort Hall the caravan consumed another week in refitting, resting, and
reprovisioning before beginning the next leg of the journey to Fort Boise.[9]
Earlier, slightly west of Fort Laramie, the emigrants had encountered
eastbound Tom Fitzpatrick. Dr. Elijah White, traveling to Oregon under
appointment as Indian subagent, immediately hired the footloose mountain man for $500 to guide the emigrant party to Fort Hall.[10]

By the close of 1842 the basic pattern of interaction between overlanders and private entrepreneurs which prevailed for the first decade of
overland travel had been established. The emigrants normally divided
their lengthy journey into segments separated by a few days of recuperation at the several trading oases. Mobile traders flocked to the trails,
mountaineers were sought out as guides, and new posts periodically appeared. Since overlanders were not so committed to traveling with the
highest possible speed before 1849, they were less oriented to seeking out
the cutoffs which would ultimately make it possible to avoid both Forts
Bridger and Hall on a California trip. Rather, in the earliest years emigrants gratefully headed for every outpost not ridiculously far afield. As
the decade progressed, however, and more and more travelers took to the
trails, travel routes shifted and shortened at the same time that competition increased. Accordingly, traders became more and more aggressive in
attempts to insure the continuing appearance of creaking wagons at their
service stations.

Sometime after mid-July, 1843, John Cabanne and Bernard Pratte
purchased Fort Platte. However, the more important development that
year was the initial availability of commercial enterprises to expedite the
treacherous and time-consuming water crossings of the overland journey.[11] Joseph and Louis Papin's ferry over the Kansas River, while no
engineering masterpiece, was serviceable enough to be patronized by
overlanders willing to pay the high Papin prices. Due to those prices,
however, most of the year's emigrants crossed the Kansas on rafts of their
own construction.[12] Another of the many rivers overlanders had been
regularly fording was the Laramie. Its crossing began to be facilitated in
1843 by the use of boats from Forts Platte and Laramie, with which a craft
similar to that of the Papins was built.[13]

The 1843 migration, much the largest to date, reoutfitted and reprovisioned so energetically en route west that post resources were severely

strained. The few Spanish traders from Taos who intersected the 1843 overlanders at Fort Laramie with high-priced stocks of flour, sugar, coffee, and whiskey did not materially alter the supply deficiency. Some overlanders talked of forcefully appropriating cattle that Fort Hall traders were reluctant to sell; a few distressed emigrants did employ the threat of force to secure food at the fort. John Boardman, who began the trek California-bound, found at Fort Hall too few provisions, at too high prices, to continue his course. Switching his destination to Oregon in hopes that he could subsist on salmon taken from the Snake River before procuring provisions at Fort Boise, Boardman sadly discovered that purchases by preceding emigrants had virtually bared the Boise shelves.[14]

Enough 1843 overlanders had difficulty in securing needed supplies so that letters began to filter eastward warning prospective emigrants that it could be extremely difficult to acquire necessities en route. Future emigrants were urged to outfit with a comfortable margin for error.[15] Other trail travelers similarly attested to the heavy reliance of 1843 emigrants on post traders. Charles Preuss, Frémont's cartographer, recorded in his diary, "Carson was sent ahead to Fort Hall to secure provisions for us. If the emigrants get ahead of us, we shall not find much there."[16] Missionary Marcus Whitman, who functioned as a guide for many of the year's emigrants, estimated that the overlanders spent upwards of $4,000 at the four principal posts: Forts Laramie, Bridger, Hall, and Boise.[17]

Noteworthy too in 1843 was the decision by most emigrants to push beyond Fort Hall *with* their wagons, despite Richard Grant's usual warning that it was impossible.[18] Not all the route information available at the posts was questionable; at Fort Boise François Payette furnished instructions for finding springs along the trail.[19] Since the most reliable information still came from mountaineers, however, when Joseph B. Chiles's party chanced upon Joseph Walker west of Fort Laramie, they retained him for $300 to guide their party to California.[20]

In 1844 and 1845 there were few new developments. Mountain trappers and traders—with Indian entourages—congregated near Fort Bridger both years to trade with emigrants.[21] Beginning in 1844, overlanders could exchange tired and lame horses for fresh ponies at "Peg-leg" Smith's trading post (occasionally called Smith's Fort or Big Timbers) north of Fort Bridger beside the Bear River. Smith, the celebrated trapper and organizer of infamous horse-stealing raids on Mexican California, maintained his post until 1850 although periodically changing its location.[22]

The appeal of mountaineer guides continued. When Joseph Walker again turned up at Fort Laramie in the summer of 1844, an emigrant party promptly engaged him to guide them to Fort Bridger. At Fort Hall a sizable group of 1845 California-bound emigrants hired Caleb Greenwood and his three sons to lead them the rest of the way for $2.50 per wagon.[23] Jim Bridger, returning to his post in the fall of 1845, guided Lansford Has-

The legendary Jim Bridger, mountain man, fur trader, and guide.

tings's ten-man overland party safely past Indians rumored to be marauding. From Fort Bridger Hastings took his party to Fort Hall, where Grant supplied desperately needed foodstuffs on the promise the men would send money following their arrival in California.[24]

One of the more intriguing examples of trader aid to the overlanders occurred in 1844. As Oregon-bound William Case recalled the incident, a large group of Sioux Indians had gathered near Fort Platte, where they were overheard plotting mischief against the oncoming emigrant caravans. Joseph Bissonette, then apparently serving as chief trader at the fort, called the Indian chiefs together. After reminding them of his past honesty, Bissonette stated that there had already been one smallpox death in the emigrant train. Remembering previous smallpox epidemics, the entire Indian encampment was on the move northward within fifteen minutes. The Sioux did not return to the trail until all overlanders had passed.[25]

Most trader-emigrant activity, however, consisted of tedious bargaining over prices and exchange rates. By 1844 post traders were becoming more precise and inflexible in the terms of their transactions. At Fort Laramie flour was sold only for cash. The following year at Fort Hall, Joel Palmer found: "The price demanded for horses was from fifteen to twenty-five dollars. They [the traders] could not be prevailed upon to receive anything in exchange for their goods or provisions, excepting cattle or money."[26] Indeed, emigrant diarists increasingly used words like "exorbitant" to describe the prices charged by post traders. As Table 5 suggests, there was considerable fluctuation in the rates reported by emigrants, due no doubt to demand, supply, and varying degrees of bargaining prowess.[27]

Following a momentary flurry of competitive activity, the trading rivalry in the Laramie area was resolved, albeit rather suspiciously, in 1846. Cabenne and Pratte had abandoned Fort Platte the previous summer, with assistant Joseph Bissonette acting for them in moving the stock to a new location strategically situated eight miles *east* of Fort Laramie along the Platte River. This meant, of course, that westbound overlanders passed by the new Fort Bernard before reaching Fort Laramie, circumstances the proprietors hoped would redound to their financial advantage. But in December, 1845, Cabenne and Pratte sold their interests in the venture to the American Fur Company. Bissonette now joined John Richard, who had won notoriety for his successful whiskey-running trips from Taos to Fort Platte in previous years, at the helm of the Fort Bernard operation. Determined to make their presence felt, the pair drastically undersold the American Fur Company's Laramie operation and did a prosperous business with 1846 overlanders.[28] After the overlanders had passed, Richard went to New Mexico for more supplies. During his absence the post burned to the ground. Laramie again stood alone.[29]

According to Francis Parkman, who spent considerable time in the

TABLE 5
PRICE RANGES AT TRADING POSTS, 1841–48

		Fort Laramie	Fort Hall	Fort Boise	Fort Platte	Mobile Traders
Flour	1841		.50-1.00[a]			
	1842	.50[a]	.25[a]		1.00-1.50	
	1843	.25- .50[a]	.25- .50[a]			.25
	1844	.40-1.00[a]	.20-1.00			
	1845	.08- .15	.20	.20		
	1846		.20- .40[a]			.50-1.00[a]
	1847		.20			
	1848					
Sugar	1841		.50[a]			
	1842	1.00				
	1843	.50-1.50[a]	.25- .50[a]	.50[a]		2.00
	1844	1.50[a]				
	1845	1.00[a]				
	1846		.50			1.00
	1847					
	1848					
Coffee	1841					
	1842	1.00				
	1843	.50-1.50[a]	.50[a]	.50[a]		1.50
	1844					
	1845	.50-1.00[a]				
	1846					1.00
	1847					
	1848					
Liquor	1841					
	1842				4.00[a]	
	1843	4.00[a]	4.00[a]			2.00[a]
	1844					
	1845					
	1846					1.00[a]
	1847					
	1848					

[a]Price per pint; all other prices given are per pound.

vicinity that summer, emigrant-trader interaction at Fort Laramie occurred under a cloud of suspicion, the overlanders believing the traders to
be "their natural enemies." Parkman acknowledged that the emigrants had
cause for mistrust: "They were plundered and cheated without mercy. In
one bargain, concluded in my presence, I calculated the profits that accrued to the fort, and found that at the lowest estimate they exceeded
eighteen hundred per cent."[30]

Traders up from Taos and Bent's Fort on the Arkansas River added to
the 1846 trading possibilities at Fort Bernard and Fort Bridger. At the
former they marketed mules and flour; at the latter, dressed buckskins in

the form of moccasins, shirts, and pants. Edwin Bryant characterized these transient traders as extremely generous men except when concluding a trade. Then they proved to be "as keen as the shrewdest Yankee that ever peddled clocks or wooden nutmegs . . . [who] whenever they see their advantage, extort money from the emigrants."[31] At Fort Hall, Richard Grant continued to earn praise for services rendered. John McBride recalled that Grant and a colleague, Archibald McDonald, had provided a written document detailing the remainder of the trip. Specifying route, distances, suggested camping locations, and directions for finding grass, water, and wood, McBride found the guidebook "of exceeding value."[32]

At Fort Bridger, however, one of the proprietors had been charged with deceit.[33] In 1844 some California-bound emigrants, acting on information supplied by former mountaineer Isaac Hitchcock, had bypassed the fort by forging what later became known as the Greenwood Cutoff— an ominous portent for the owners' dreams of wealth. Fortunately for Bridger and Vasquez, however, Lansford Hastings's proposed cutoff on the California route launched out from Fort Bridger. Hoping that Hastings's trail would keep emigrant wagons flowing past their post, the proprietors quickly endorsed the unproven route. James Reed in a late July, 1846, letter had praised Bridger and Vasquez as "the only fair traders in these parts." After surviving the Donner disaster, and learning that Edwin Bryant and possibly others had left letters at the fort urging him and other travelers with wagons *not* to take the Hastings route, Reed felt differently: "Vasquez, being interested in having the new route traveled (otherwise the emigration would use the Greenwood Cutoff and miss Fort Bridger), kept these letters."[34]

At the eastern edge of the trail the year 1846 brought continuing progress in river ferriage. Overlanders departing from Independence had to cross the Kansas River, and at a time when it was usually swollen by spring rains. The Papin ferry, begun in 1843, had been ruined by 1844 floods and may not have been re-established until 1847. In any case, others had entered the business. A Shawnee Indian named Toley operated a ferry some eleven miles west of the Kansas-Missouri boundary. Most popular in 1846, though, was Charles Fish's two-boat ferry, situated near the Papin location. Charging $1 per wagon, Fish (also a Shawnee) reported $400 in earnings by late June, virtually all from westbound emigrants.[35] And, as more and more overlanders outfitted and departed from points north of Independence (in 1846 approximately half of the emigrants jumped off from the St. Joseph vicinity), ferries across the Missouri River appeared with increasing frequency.[36]

The nearly 5,000 overlanders trailing west in 1847 made clear that the overland boom was far from ended. Assessing the trends, mountaineer Miles Goodyear endeavored to profit accordingly. Already in late 1845 he had made his plans known on the Missouri frontier: construction of a trading fort and cultivation of enough land to produce vegetables and grains for the emigrant trade. Goodyear, or the Missouri newspaper editor, had spoken of the projected operation as a "*half way house* between this and Oregon and California, where the companies may stop and refresh themselves and obtain . . . supplies." Apparently also banking on the viability of the Hastings Cutoff, Goodyear, with the aid of an Englishman named Wells, located his post in the Great Salt Lake Valley in the fall of 1846. By the following summer he had half an acre enclosed, with log houses at the corners, corrals for animals, and an irrigated garden—this was Fort Buenaventura. But Goodyear ruefully discovered, as did fellow entrepreneur Jim Bridger, that the emergence of trail cutoffs could quickly alter overland travel patterns: most 1847 emigrants took the Greenwood Cutoff, bypassing both Forts Bridger and Buenaventura. Goodyear was an energetic mountaineer, however, whose response was quick. Following his return from California with several hundred horses, Goodyear turned mobile trader. Taking his drove to the cutoff, Goodyear slowly worked eastward, trading fresh horses to the emigrants in exchange for lame and tired animals.[37]

Also mitigating against a long existence for Fort Buenaventura was the 1847 Mormon hegira to the Salt Lake Valley. Intent on solitary settlement, they met Goodyear and investigated his post. Fearing that Buenaventura could become a haven for apostate Saints, they determined to buy him out. Goodyear's willingness to sell was doubtless bolstered by the recognition that the majority of overland travelers might continue to bypass Fort Buenaventura by utilizing the Greenwood Cutoff. In late November Goodyear received $1,950 for his claim and supplies, except for the furs and horses, which he retained.[38]

An additional consequence of the Mormon march to Salt Lake was the establishment of an important ferry over the North Fork of the Platte River.[39] This marked the farthest penetration westward (approximately 130 miles beyond Fort Laramie) of ferry service thus far, at a crossing which was often treacherous. The ferry originated in a chance encounter with a group of mountain traders transporting furs to Missouri who offered the westbound Mormons the use of their buffalo-skin boat to cross the Platte. Aware that the Mormon pioneers were not the earliest westbound travelers of the year, Brigham Young sent ahead an advance company of approximately forty men to secure the "bullboat" from the tree on the river bank where the mountaineers had left it, before other emigrant companies found it and put it into use. Arriving at the site with several Oregon-bound groups, the Mormons were unable to find the mountaineers' craft. But they had with them the "Revenue Cutter," a leather boat which the Oregonians urged them to press into service. So it was that when Brigham and the rest of his band arrived, they discovered the advance company busily ferrying emigrants across the river. The equivalent of $34 in badly needed provisions had already been earned. Recognizing the continuing possibilities of such an endeavor, the astute Young ordered nine men to remain and operate the ferry through the summer, until the second company of Salt Lake–bound Mormons arrived.[40]

The Mormon ferrying group, captained by Thomas Grover, quickly constructed a sturdier boat. They then engaged in a comical competition for supremacy with a few emigrants attempting to turn a fast profit in the same manner.[41] The overlanders (whose enterprise the Mormons termed the "Hill ferry") were located a short distance east of the Mormon operation. Several Mormons were dispatched "to rekanorter the ferry below & see if it could be chartered for laramie post." They found the Hill boat on the opposite side of the river, however, so under cover of darkness a second party proceeded down the north side of the river to cut the boat adrift and let it float to Fort Laramie. They returned at dawn, unsuccessful, "having found it well guarded & a faith ful watch dog." Accordingly, Grover's company packed up their equipment, floated downriver two miles below the Hill site, and re-established the Mormon ferry where the overlanders would reach it first. The Mormons also drastically reduced their prices (to fifty cents per wagon) to insure the early demise of the Hill operation.

Retaliating, the Hill ferrymen sent runners to advertise their ferry a few miles downriver from the new Mormon location. The Mormons, in turn, set up a billboard twenty-eight miles downriver from their initial location announcing the presence of their ferry and blacksmith shop. Finally the Hill group decided that there was insufficient profit in delaying longer. After chopping up their boat they proceeded westward. The battle over, Grover's men returned to their original location. They also returned their fees to the rates Brigham Young had originally decreed—$3 in cash or $1.50 in goods and provisions for each wagon crossed. As the river level fell and fording became easier, however, prices were prudently adjusted downward. In addition to smithwork, the Mormon ferrymen gave emergency dental and medical attention to passing overlanders. Computing the incomplete returns reported by Mormon diarists indicates both the financial success of the operation and its extensive use by overlanders: the North Platte enterprise garnered over $750 in cash and provisions.[42]

In 1848 Brigham Young sent another group of ferrymen east from Salt Lake to the North Fork of the Platte River. By the time the first of the 1848 overlanders arrived, the Mormon ferry was again operational.[43] When the emigrants reached the Green River, an even more dangerous stream, Mormons were also there operating another dugout ferry. Farther east, on the Mormon Trail on the north side of the Platte River, a ferry was established at the Elkhorn River. A bridge was also erected across Papillion Creek. Always concerned about the safe and rapid progress of the large numbers of Latter-Day Saints yearly heading for Salt Lake, the Mormons

The Elkhorn River ferry, established by the Mormons in 1848. From Piercy, *Route from Liverpool to Great Salt Lake Valley* (1855)

regularly made such route improvements. As early as 1844 West Coast–bound overlanders traveled along the north side of the Platte River to Fort Laramie; in 1848 there were many such overlanders; and by the 1850s the trail on the north side was the most popular route. Thus the Mormon Trail improvements eventually accrued to many California- and Oregon-bound overlanders.[44]

Non-Mormon supportive services likewise expanded. At least two more ferries across the Missouri River were begun in 1848,[45] as was a trading fort east of Fort Laramie in the Scott's Bluff region. Operated by members of St. Joseph's Robidoux clan, the post was situated near a spring several hundred yards north of the main trail, which meant it was possible for emigrants to pass by without noticing the establishment. Many apparently did, as the Robidoux post had little impact on the 1848 overlanders.[46]

The patterns of entrepreneur-emigrant interaction changed little in the last years before the California gold seekers accelerated the transformation of the trail into a highway. Arriving at the post oases still meant two or three days of rest, reprovisioning, repair, and, for the women, laundry work.[47] At Fort Laramie some overlanders had taken to renting the blacksmith shop to do their own work—Riley Root's company paid $7.50 for one and a half days of this privilege. Emigrant and Indian business was so good at Laramie that one of the proprietors informed a passing overlander that $25,000 worth of trade goods was being purchased for the fort every year.[48] At Fort Hall the traders again demanded cash for much of their merchandise, but paid emigrants for their surplus supplies only in merchandise.[49] Perhaps it was this tactic which prompted Chester Ingersoll to term the post traders "almost destitute of honesty or human feelings," or Elizabeth Geer to characterize Grant as a "boasting, burlesquing, unfeeling man."[50] Emigrant reaction to the mountaineer traders who continued to haunt the overland trail also revealed increasing frustration with entrepreneurial aggressiveness. Richard May, for example, complained, "The traders follow the train as though their Salvation depended on trade with them there is at this time not less than a dozen of them around Camp and Some of them quite rude in their manners."[51]

Nearly twice as many overlanders traversed South Pass in 1849 as in the nine previous years combined. Such unprecedented numbers proved particularly frustrating at river crossings, where bottlenecks developed despite ferry proliferation. Problems began at the Missouri River crossing, where delays of two or three days were not unusual, even though many ferrymen operated their boats and rafts day and night. River steamboats were even pressed into emergency service.[52] Since impatience was such a characteristic forty-niner trait, violence often erupted at congested crossings. J. Goldsborough Bruff reported that in St. Joseph, where lines of waiting wagons stretched back 300 yards from the river, "Fighting for precedence was quite common, and a day or two since, 2 teamsters, in one of these disputes, killed each other with pistols." At the crowded Kansas River crossing Isaac Wistar's company succeeded in being first in line by having their "best fighters" ring the narrow passageway leading to the ferry landing. Until their own wagons had passed, the pugilists simply permitted no one else to enter.[53]

Just as impatient gold seekers fought for travel advantages in the first hectic year of the gold rush, private entrepreneurs competed energetically for the profits available in servicing large numbers of the passing emigrants. Indeed, aggressive competition between rival entrepreneurs was among the most common themes of 1849. Emigrants departing from Independence found that the Papin or "lower ferry" was contested by Charles Beaubien and Louis Ogee's "upper ferry," located approximately ten miles west at Uniontown. Each enterprise operated two boats; each hired Indian salesmen to roam widely and convince oncoming travelers of the wisdom of using their employer's ferry. Rates fluctuated between $1 and $5 for crossing wagons, with smaller sums assessed for persons and animals.[54] At Fort Laramie the fur company had two ferries in operation: across the Laramie River for those traveling on the south side of the Platte; across the Platte for the north-siders who crossed over at that point.[55]

Farther west, at the North Platte crossing, Salt Lake Mormons held forth again by order of the Latter-Day Saints Council of Fifty. The ten ferrymen, under Charles Shumway's command, reached the ferry site only one day before the westbound gold rushers arrived. They used the same boat as the year before, charged a crossing fee of $3 per wagon— which was rarely altered during the summer in spite of competition ferries—and accommodated at least a quarter of the forty-niners. Total proceeds for the seven weeks of work (including blacksmithing returns) were $6,465 according to one of the ferry operators, although another Mormon who met the ferrymen on their return to Salt Lake reported returns approximating $10,000.[56]

Either figure evidenced that catering to the overland traffic was a highly profitable venture. So profitable, indeed, that many passing forty-niners commented enviously on the gold the Mormons were mining so far from California. Some established competing ferries of their own.[57] Although the profit motive was of course dominant, these developments were also necessitated by circumstances. With the river running high and many hundreds of wagons arriving at the ferry site on the same day, additional crossing points were mandatory if delays of several weeks were not to result. And very few forty-niners were prepared to dally that long on the banks of the Platte less than halfway to California's gold fields.

Consequently, during the latter half of June, when the great mass of overlanders arrived, many emigrants chanced fording the river or patronized the temporary ferries which proliferated along a thirty-mile stretch of the North Platte from the Mormon ferry down to Deer Creek

● Trading post
x Ferry or bridge

Trading Posts, Ferries, and Bridges, 1849

MAP 6

Bier

and below.[58] One added feature of the North Platte crossing in 1849 was the high incidence of overlanders who purchased makeshift scows or boats from the outfit just ahead, ferried themselves, then sold the vessel to the company just behind—invariably for the identical price. This was an ingenious way to secure an "instant" boat and cross the river without paying ferriage fees.[59]

For the difficult Green River crossing beyond South Pass on the Salt Lake road, the Mormon Council of Fifty appointed A. L. Lamoreux to direct a ferry operation. But the Saints did not monopolize the several Green River crossings. In fact, theirs was not even the first ferry to be established there in 1849, that distinction belonging to unnamed mountain men.[60] The mountaineers' profitable venture was located on the heavily traveled Greenwood Cutoff (which forty-niners usually termed the Sublette Cutoff). Soon, however, the energetic Mormons also had a boat in operation on the cutoff, only to face competition themselves on the regular road to Salt Lake from passing Iowa emigrants, who temporarily forced ferriage fees down to $2 per wagon. Several emigrant entrepreneurs also worked temporary ferries at the cutoff crossing, so that at one point in mid-July at least four well-patronized ferries were operative within the space of three miles. Prices for ferrying across the Green River varied widely, in response to competition and changing river depth. The growing expense associated with crossing the plains was most evident on the cutoff, where a number of overlanders reported ferriage fees of $8 per wagon, and a few paid $10.[61]

Argonauts going via Salt Lake City were not yet done with Mormon ferries, there being three more. The first, over the Bear River, was located between Fort Bridger and the Mormon capital; the second navigated the Weber River on the other side of Salt Lake City; and the last crossed the Bear River again near the junction with the regular trail. Conveniences they were, but expensive ones, which is probably why some overlanders were increasingly reluctant to pay the requested fees, usually $4. Samuel Dundass grumbled about "extortion" and "man's inhumanity to man," but James Tolles's company found an effective way to reduce the fee: ". . . when we arrived at the ferry we found the charge for crossing to be $4. per wagon, this we thought to be very high, and by looking a little found a place to . . . ford, and commenced making the road. the ferryman then came down to $2. still we went on with our work he then fell to $1. which offer we accepeted and drove down to the boat and were soon all over and on our way."[62]

At the last crossing of the Bear River, Simon Doyle's outfit employed similar tactics after hearing the announced ferriage fee of $5 per wagon. Uttering expletives about "Blood hounds of iniquity" and "Models of rascality," they began fording preparations. Since the ferry operators did not want a ford established, Doyle's company finally was ferried across for fifty cents per wagon. Doyle later learned that their company had been indirectly responsible for eliminating the ferry enterprise entirely for the remainder of the year: ". . . the next train that came along seeing the banks dug down determined upon fording and dispite the priposition of the ferry Men to Cross them with out charge across the stream they drove and after that the ferry did no more business."[63] Prior to this sudden termination, however, the ferrymen had done good business.

It is evident that forty-niners left tens of thousands of dollars in specie and goods with ferrymen who capitalized on the gold rushers' desire for speed and convenience.[64] Depending on the route taken, it was possible to spend as much as $30 to have one wagon ferried across western rivers after departing from the jumping-off points in 1849. An expensive dimension was being injected into overland travel.

New trade emporiums also appeared from 1848 on, many in conjunction with ferry enterprises. Uniontown, located about a mile south of the Kansas River (near the Beaubien and Ogee ferry), had been established in 1848 as the official trading site for the Potawatomi Indians. A great many forty-niners made last-minute purchases in its half a dozen shops.[65] At the Mormon ferries on the North Platte and Green rivers, trading was also carried on, including the exchange of lame for fresh stock. Overlanders periodically left letters to be sent back to the States by anybody happening by. But the service most in demand at these small outposts was blacksmithing. Resetting wagon tires and reshoeing draft and riding animals kept the Mormon blacksmiths busy. The demand fostered skyrocketing prices. On June 12, for example, the Mormon smiths charged $3 and $6 for shoeing a horse and an ox respectively. By June 18 the fee was $4 and $8; by the 23rd the shoeing charge for a yoke of oxen was $10; and the apex of $12 was reached on June 24. Elisha Perkins was told by the Mormon captain that the blacksmith shop alone had taken in $1,500 by July 15. These profits were enticing enough to cause blacksmiths traveling with other trains to halt momentarily at the ferries spanning the North Platte to ply their trade. Blacksmithing services were also available at Robidoux's Scott's Bluff post and at Fort Bridger—at equally grandiose prices.[66]

The mountaineers encamped at the Green River were more interested in speculative stock-trading and gambling than in smithwork. The high prices they demanded for stock were bad enough, but for some moralistic overlanders the accompanying gambling, drinking, and decadent living were too much. Bernard Reid noted a "monte bank" in one mountaineer's lodge, and John Edwin Banks stated that he had never "seen gambling equal to what I saw in one of their wigwams." Banks went on to proclaim, "I never despised human nature as I now do. I see many having no claim to humanity but form." In the Green River region Niles Searls indicated, "Every few days we come across a canvas lodge occupied by some Canadian Frenchman who dignifies his establishment by the name of a trading post, though the title of 'Gambling Hell' would convey a more correct idea of its uses." The gaming proprietors, thought Searls, were men "destitute of character." P. C. Tiffany was in complete agreement, declaring that the Green River mountaineers were "not half as honourable as the indians."[67]

Not all mountain traders projected such an image, anxious as most were to capitalize on the golden opportunities presented by the overland caravans. And since the emigrants often followed cutoffs to speed their journey to El Dorado, bypassing Forts Bridger and Hall, some traders aggressively brought their wares to the trails being traveled.[68] Vasquez and Bridger did just this, making mobile trading an important feature of the 1849 entrepreneurial effort. For almost a month, from at least June 9 to July 1, Vasquez was encamped near South Pass on the Sweetwater River trading with the gold seekers. Bridger was also present much of the time, and the partners did a flourishing business selling or exchanging draft and riding animals, and hawking dressed animal skins. Charles Tinker, who met the traders on June 19, learned that they had intended trailing their animals to Fort Laramie for sale to overlanders there. But having encountered the first emigrants near South Pass and quickly selling all their animals, they had sent back to Fort Bridger for 130 more, and consequently remained near South Pass. Passing overlanders indicated that sales, at extremely high rates, were frequent: prices for horses ranged from $65 to $150, for mules from $75 to $125, and for oxen up to $125 per yoke.[69] As late as August 6 J. Goldsborough Bruff encountered a Fort Bridger trading party at the Green River that was speculating in horses and demanding the inflationary sum of $300 for most animals. Three days later near Smith's Fork of the Bear River, Bruff met "another detachment of Old Bridger's traders," again with horses for sale. Other itinerant bands of traders from Bent's Fort and other areas were also reported near the trails throughout the summer, some specializing in dispensing liquor to thirsty forty-niners.[70]

There was more to Vasquez's encampment on the Sweetwater than many passing travelers realized, as the shrewd mountaineer not only traded horses but was careful to explain the best route beyond South Pass for all who would listen. Due to his derogatory comments about the Greenwood-Sublette Cutoff, large numbers of forty-niners traveled via Fort Bridger instead. William Johnston's party illustrates the operation perfectly. Johnston's group had intended taking the cutoff—indeed, had been so advised by seasoned plains travelers. But that was before they encountered Vasquez's entrepreneurial persuasiveness. Drawing maps, he stressed the desert and the lack of water on the cutoff. Johnston's party went via Fort Bridger, and when they again returned to the main trail, they ruefully discovered that trains which had previously been behind them

This page from J. Goldsborough Bruff's sketchbook illustrates two ways of getting across rivers—both "perilous." Beinecke Rare Book and Manuscript Library, Yale University were now ahead. Johnston, wiser now, wrote: "The deception practiced by Vasquez, whom it will be recalled we had met at the South Pass, was now painfully apparent, his object doubtless having been to turn the tide of emigration past Fort Bridger, that he might derive profit arising from the sale of supplies."[71]

Although Johnston likely shared Stillman Churchill's conviction that route information received from mountain men was "not to be believed," a good deal of reliable and helpful information about the trails was passed along by mountaineers met on or near the trails. At Fort Laramie a small group about to push on to California received a specially drawn waybill from an old trapper employed there, which listed trail landmarks, mileage estimates, and campsites. Jim Bridger himself laboriously and courteously drew charcoal maps on the floor of his post to explain the route beyond for concerned overlanders. As Vasquez's success suggested, it was hard for greenhorn forty-niners, at least initially, to go counter to the advice of mountaineers seasoned by years of dangerous living in the West. Anthony Ward, for example, had made it all the way to Fort Laramie. But there he listened to veteran mountaineers expound on the disasters sure to occur ahead because less than a quarter of the forty-niners' teams could find sufficient grass in the mountain passes. Ward turned around and backtracked to Kansas immediately.[72]

Mountain traders with wagonloads of furs for the frontier settlements also frequently functioned as letter carriers. Sometimes this service was provided gratuitously, but often a fee of as much as twenty-five or fifty cents per letter was exacted. One such mountaineer party found this to be a highly profitable venture. They collected several thousand letters at their advertised "Post-Office" along the Sweetwater which for fifty cents apiece they promised to return to the States. Henry Mann did not trust them. His instinct apparently was wise, for Alonzo Delano contended it had been "only a pleasant ruse to gull travelers"; none of the letters left by their company ever reached their intended destinations.[73] At least one energetic frontiersman also sought to capitalize on the forty-niners' insatiable thirst for news from home. Having brought out late newspapers and letters from St. Joseph as a speculative venture, he returned to Missouri carrying emigrant letters, charging twenty-five cents per letter.[74]

Transitory traders were not the only active entrepreneurs in 1849. After selling Fort Laramie to the government in June, the American Fur Company did not retire from the field but instead added another post to the impressive number already lining the trails. Their new venture, apparently again called Fort John, was at Scott's Bluff near the Robidoux post. Proximity engendered competition, for which reason the second Fort John was moved three times within three years in futile attempts to pre-empt the emigrant trade. Robidoux had the favored location, however, and the fur company post was more successful in the Indian trade than with passing overlanders, who continued to stop most often at Robidoux's. Perhaps some of the forty-niners favored the Robidoux establishment, because a Robidoux representative intercepted forty-niners in the Ash Hollow region to condemn the fur company traders as "all damned rascals and cheats."[75]

Fort Laramie remained an important oasis for overlanders after it became an army fort in June, 1849, in part because of the post sutler.[76] Post sutlers were civilian merchants whose prerogatives included a monopoly on the sale of provisions and other commodities to post troops. Since sutlerships could prove extraordinarily lucrative, they were often assiduously sought and on occasion even purchased. At Kearny, beginning in 1849, at Laramie in 1850, and subsequently at other western forts, this meant that emigrants could fill their basic or luxury needs in the usually well-stocked sutlers' stores. Sutlers did not, however, account for all sales to emigrants at army installations, the post quartermaster on occasion dispensing bulk items such as sugar and flour.[77]

Many forty-niners launched out on their journey overloaded with foodstuffs and other materials. Soon recognizing their error, but not being wastrels, almost all continued transporting their excess to Fort Kearny, and most to Fort Laramie, in anticipation of selling their surplus to sutler and trader at a small profit. With thousands in similar circumstances, however, this tactic proved chimerical. As Augustus Burbank commented at Fort Laramie (through June still the property of the American Fur Company or, more accurately, Pierre Chouteau, Jr., and Company): "These are sharpers. Say they wish to sell & don't want to buy. They know that the emigrant must throw away, trim down, for they can't well proceed further with heavy loads for the black hills commence here."[78] Throw away the emigrants did, in fantastic amounts, although a few were fortunate to sell a wagon at a fraction of its value, or flour, bacon, or beans at the unrewarding price of two cents per pound.[79]

With such a glutted market it is surprising that the Laramie traders fared as well as they did in 1849. Before the sale of the post, however, company officials maintained that "a profitable business" had been carried on. The following year they regretted selling the post, since it was evident that "by proper management money can be coined there."[80] Nevertheless, as Table 6 reveals, the range of trail prices for most commodities dipped lower at Fort Laramie than elsewhere in 1849.[81]

"Peg-leg" Smith probably prospered as well as any other trailside post proprietor in 1849. Gold rusher Peter Decker indicated that by late June, Smith was making $100 per day from the overland trade, primarily by selling and exchanging horses. A number of passing forty-niners also mentioned a Mormon family evidently associated with Smith's outpost. Likewise engaged in the emigrant traffic, they seemed to specialize in moccasins, food, and liquor.[82] Mormon families keeping a "public house"

TABLE 6
PRICE RANGES AT TRADING POSTS, 1849

	Flour	Sugar	Coffee	Liquor	Bacon	Cheese
Kearny	1.00- 2.00[b]	.25- .64		.19[a]	2.00[b]	
Robidoux's	.10 7.00- 8.00[b]			.62-1.00[a]		
Laramie	.01 .50-12.00[b]	.10- .40	.02- .40	1.00-1.25[a]	.00-.01 1.25[b]	
Mormon ferry, North Platte		.50		.50[a]		
Mobile traders		.25		.50[a]		.30
Bridger				2.00[a]		
"Peg-leg" Smith's	.20			2.00[a]		
Hall	.08- .10	.37½				.25
Lassen's	.40- .60	.50-1.00	1.00	1.25[a]		1.50
Johnson's		.75		1.00[a]		

[a]Price per pint.
[b]Price per 100 pounds. (Numbers without superscripts are per pound prices.)

were also reported at Forts Kearny, Bridger, and Hall, and overlanders at the latter location were particularly appreciative of this opportunity to procure vegetables and dairy products. Slow-moving and/or late-starting forty-niners also wintered at Forts Bridger and Hall in 1849.[83] Amidst all the turmoil and change of 1849 there was at least one constant—kindly Richard Grant. His hospitality led one overlander to remark that of all posts, only at Fort Hall was there "politeness" and "civility."[84]

One added feature of 1849 private enterprise, although very limited in comparison to subsequent years, was the appearance of small, nameless trading posts near the end of the trail. Operated by persons who came out from California to fleece those emigrants so desperate for provisions or animals that they were willing to give up wagons and stock for a song, these outposts fluctuated in location but rarely in intent.[85]

It would have been surprising if men hurrying to California to get rich quick had not also utilized every opportunity to make money en route. These emigrant entrepreneurs—virtually nonexistent in the emigration record before 1849—were not only in evidence at river crossings. Several Missourians made the journey with two wagons heavily loaded with alcoholic beverages. Selling their diluted liquids at fifty cents a pint, they received an enthusiastic reception from many of their fellow travelers. Another profit-minded overlander on the Lassen Cutoff began picking up everything his colleagues were throwing away. With this free merchandise he planned to start a trading post at the California end of the trail.[86]

Yet despite all these developments, perhaps the most significant aspect of 1849 was the widespread knowledge that private entrepreneurs had planted a great many trading posts along the Oregon-California Trail. The

265

dynamics of overland travel had changed so much during the decade that a few forty-niners even planned their entire journey around these establishments, backpacking to California and replenishing their provision packs at each post en route.[87]

CHAPTER EIGHT

Private Entrepreneurs, 1850–60

"Too many cooks spoil the broth"

Dᴜʀɪɴɢ ᴛʜᴇ ꜱᴇᴄᴏɴᴅ ʏᴇᴀʀ ᴏꜰ ᴛʜᴇ ɢᴏʟᴅ ʀᴜꜱʜ, westbound overlanders doubled the 25,000 argonauts of 1849. Trailside entrepreneurial activity continued apace, mirroring this increasingly lucrative market. Yet the second year of the gold rush was no carbon copy of the first. Misapplying the "lessons" of 1849, many overlanders outfitted so skimpily that the result was nearly catastrophic. Had there not been scores of trading posts at the California end of the trail—coupled with numerous acts of humanitarianism by emigrants themselves and a vast relief effort from the West Coast—the starvation deaths among the Donner party four years before would have paled to insignificance by comparison.

By 1850 the river-crossing, postal, and repair services available from the trailside entrepreneurs were so commonplace that they were no longer viewed as traveling luxuries; like food, outfitting supplies, draft animals, and information they had come to be regarded as necessities. Newspapers dutifully reported assurances by returning Californians that taking along extra supplies was unnecessary because of "the forts and settlements on the route." Post-to-post backpackers were familiar sights.[1] But the best means of appreciating the extent and significance of entrepreneurially influenced trail developments at this midpoint in the antebellum overland movement is by retracing the progress of the 1850 gold seekers across the continent.

Ferry service across the Missouri River was virtually limitless, from below St. Joseph to above Kanesville. Owners regularly advertised their "superior" crossing locations and "safe" facilities in local and regional newspapers. Wheeling, Townsend, Clark, and Company of Kanesville advanced the most intriguing advertising claim, asserting that their ferry, "approved by the Indians to whom we make Semi-Annual payments for the privilege of having a road through their country, ensures their good will towards the Emigrants."[2] At the many crossing points emigrants reported ferriage fees ranging from seventy-five cents to $3 per wagon, and usually an additional charge for animals.[3]

Within the first 100 miles of settlements on the several routes leading to Fort Kearny, overlanders passed a number of Indian mission schools. Most of these frontier missions dated from the 1830s and remained active throughout the heyday of overland travel. Though not conducted as traditional business enterprises, stores and blacksmith shops were maintained where emigrants were able to attend to initial travel difficulties. Overlanders following the routes emanating from the Independence vicinity passed the majority of these religious outposts and thus had the most opportunities to fix wagons, reshoe animals, purchase foodstuffs (land was under cultivation at most of the missions), trade with Indians, or even receive medical attention. Approximately three miles west of Westport was the Methodist mission to the Shawnee Indians; several miles to the northwest stood the Baptist mission to the same tribe; and another mile or two beyond was the Quaker Shawnee labor school.[4] Since 1848 the Baptists had also staffed a mission among the Potawatomi Indians, with the manual-labor school located near the upper or Uniontown crossing of the Kansas River. Across the river and some fifteen miles northwest, likewise near the overland trail, was St. Mary's, the Catholic mission to the same tribe.[5]

Contrarily, emigrants launching out from either the St. Joseph or the Council Bluffs area trailed past far fewer religious establishments. The Presbyterian mission to the Iowa and Sac and Fox Indians, located approximately twenty-five miles west of St. Joseph, was the scene of considerable emigrant trading activity during the gold rush years. Less useful because of its close proximity to the settlements was another Presbyterian mission, this one to the Pawnee, Oto, and Omaha Indians. Situated near Bellevue, the landing for travelers crossing the Missouri at Trader's Point, it was only six miles south of Kanesville.[6]

By 1850 the first leg of the journey, to Fort Kearny, caused most travelers little anxiety. Whether they jumped off from Kanesville, St. Joseph, or Independence, overlanders found ferries over most of the principal streams and bridges spanning many of the inconsequential creeks. Those following the route on the north side of the Platte crossed Papillion and other creeks on Mormon or Indian bridges and were ferried across the Elkhorn and Loup Fork rivers on commercial enterprises.[7] Although the crossing vessels usually left a good deal to be desired—at the Loup Fork the boat sank at least twice, and when Thomas Christy crossed he noted that it required three or four men bailing constantly to keep the leaking craft afloat—the ferrymen continued to charge what the market would bear.[8]

On the St. Joseph road the only major river crossing was at the Big Blue, where 1850 overlanders found a ferry in operation at what was

Trading Posts, Ferries, Bridges,
and Missions, 1850

Trading post
x Ferry or bridge
▲ Mission

St. Joseph
Independence
Council
Bluffs
Unionville
Kansas R.
Ft. Kearny
Platte River
North Platte River
South Platte
Bernard
Ft. John
Rebidoux
Ash Point
Ft. Laramie
Deer
Creek
Missouri River
River
Estill's
South
Pass
Sublette
Cutoff
Ft. Bridger
Green R.
Colorado River
Ft.
Owens
Salt Lake
City
Hastings
Cutoff
Great
Salt
Lake
Ft. Hall
Cantonment Loring
Hudspeth Cutoff
Ft.
Boise
Humboldt R.
Ft. Walla
Walla
River
Ft. Dalles
Columbia R.
Oregon City
Lassen
Cutoff
Truckee
route
Ragtown
Mormon Station
Carson route
Johnson's
Sacramento R.
Sacramento

MAP 7

0   100   200   300
miles

apparently called the Independence crossing. This probably was Francis J. Marshall's first combination ferry and trading post.[9] Emigrants departing from Independence likewise contended with the Big Blue, but first they had to navigate the Kansas River, where numerous ferries were operative in 1850. At the Uniontown crossing a fairly substantial Indian settlement of fifty log houses and 300 residents had evolved. More important for overland travelers were the four or five stores offering quality merchandise at reasonable prices—as well as the beer shops.[10] A number of Indian toll bridges also stretched across the smaller creeks on both the Independence and St. Joseph routes, the most mentioned being at Wolf Creek near the Presbyterian mission on the St. Joseph route.[11]

At Fort Kearny, in addition to the sutler (by now comfortably ensconced in a frame dwelling) and blacksmith, 1850 emigrants discovered several "eating houses," where they feasted on such delicacies as cheese, fresh butter, and milk.[12] The next traditional resting site was slightly more than 300 miles away, but before the overlanders reached redoubtable Fort Laramie they had to ford the South Fork of the Platte River. This difficult crossing was a problem only for travelers on the south side of the Platte, who were somewhat compensated by the luxury of finding four trading posts between Ash Hollow and Laramie.

The first encountered was the ubiquitous Chouteau operation, Fort John. Directed by Andrew Drips, in 1850 it was located not on the main trail but in Helvas Canyon, approximately four miles south of the normal route through Robidoux Pass. Most hurrying gold rushers passed it by. Those who stopped found the requisite blacksmith shop flanked by three log cabins and Indian wigwams.[13] The Robidoux concern, situated approximately eight miles northwest beside the trail, was expanding in response to the burgeoning trail traffic. The proprietors now boasted two blacksmith shops, a store, and three or four "seder" cabins. Together with a few Indian wigwams, the place presented a bustling appearance and was one of the most frequently patronized posts along the overland trail during the gold rush era. In 1850 passersby commented that Robidoux's two smiths had "as much work as they can do" and charged "California prices." Later in the traveling season the Robidoux brothers built a second post approximately one mile away.[14] About thirty-five miles past the busy Robidoux location John Richard operated a small one-building post known as Ash Point. During the period of heaviest trail traffic Richard's enterprise, which emigrants associated with the American Fur Company, was without much in the line of provisions. It offered only minimal inducements to emigrant stopovers, especially with well-stocked Fort Laramie only twenty miles beyond.[15] Finally, at or near the site of old Fort Bernard only eight miles from Laramie, James Bordeaux and Joseph Bissonette jointly operated a log hut trading station, again called Fort Bernard.[16]

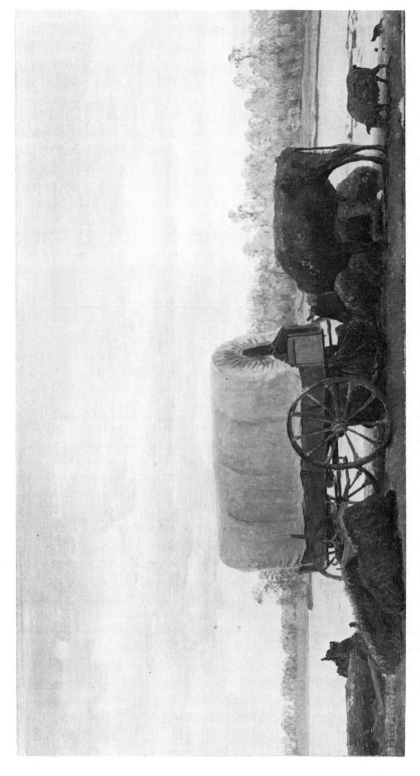

Albert Bierstadt's "Nooning on the Platte" (1858), a scene of peaceful respite on the arduous journey.

St. Louis Art Museum, gift of J. Lionberger Davis

At the Fort Laramie oasis the main emigrant concerns in 1850 were the alleged absence of industry and probity on the part of Uncle Sam's profit-oriented officers who owned the fort ferries over the Laramie and Platte rivers.[17] With ferry service, especially across the Platte, extremely irregular, impatient travelers complained that the soldiers demonstrated insufficient zeal in replacing the frequently lost or ruined boats. On at least three occasions in June, for example, the boat was inoperative for several days: twice after having been mysteriously cut adrift and once following its scuttling by intoxicated overlanders. According to one rumor, emigrants on the south side had cut the boat adrift to prevent north-siders from contributing to trail congestion on the south side.[18] The crossing fee through late June was a nominal $1 per wagon, probably because the emigrants had to do all the work themselves. The fare was upped to $2 after the third replacement craft was launched.[19]

A second source of contention was whether or not an adequate wagon trail existed on the north side of the Platte River, *beyond* the fort. The soldiers claimed there was none, but many emigrants were unconvinced. Before 1850 virtually no one had taken wagons past Fort Laramie on the north side of the Platte River, a profitable pattern the officers obviously hoped to maintain. Thousands of overlanders were now departing from Kanesville each year; if they all continued to cross the Platte at Laramie on the soldiers' ferry, the financial rewards, at either $1 or $2 per wagon, would be immense. Furthermore, if the soldiers were also silent partners in one of the North Platte ferries upriver, as a few overlanders believed, it was important to keep the emigrants traveling on the south side of the Platte so they would patronize those crossing facilities.

Adding to emigrant suspicions were the extravagant scare stories spread by the soldiers. Fort commander Winslow Sanderson was quoted as stating that "a mountain goat cant go up this [north] side of the river."[20] Byron McKinstry filled his diary with some of the assertions he heard: it was nearly impossible; only eight of eighty-four wagons had made it in 1849; the journey could not be finished in a year on the north side because there was an "impassable mountain" which required an 80- or 160-mile detour; anyone traveling on the north side risked his life for no reason. For good measure, mountaineer Kit Carson, at the fort in June, assured questioning emigrants that "the Devil himself could not get through on the N. side."[21] Despite—or perhaps because of—such suspicious pronouncements, McKinstry and others attempted the much-maligned north-side route. McKinstry described it as a pleasurable journey on which two days' travel time had been gained and the expense of twice ferrying the Platte avoided (at Fort Laramie and then again at Deer Creek or the Upper Ferry site). The trail, according to McKinstry, was just as good, the grass better, and the incidence of sickness considerably less than on the regular route. T. W. Hinds's comment that "the officers of Fort Laramie sadly deceive people" seemed increasingly valid.[22]

But the minute number of overlanders remaining on the north side beyond Fort Laramie scarcely alleviated the logjam at the North Platte crossings. There temporary boats operated by emigrant entrepreneurs vied with Mormon ferrymen and a Missouri company for the enormous sums of money nearly 50,000 gold rushers were prepared to spend to speed their trip to the Pacific. The principal profits were garnered by the Salt Lake and Missouri companies. Sharing the preferred Upper Ferry location, they may even have jointly operated one or more boats. The sixteen Mormon ferrymen under Andrew Lytle commenced ferrying operations on May 28, by which time earlybird overlanders had already forded the Platte and were miles beyond. The Missouri ferrymen under David H. Hickman were also under way at least by that time.[23]

The two concerns had from four to six boats in constant operation at the height of the rush, during which time they raised the crossing rate from $4 to $5 per wagon. Well-to-do overlanders who did not relish several days' delay gained precedence over earlier arrivals by paying ferry operators extra. Downriver toward Deer Creek, 3-dollar crossing fees were occasionally assessed. The temporary emigrant enterprises relied on more dangerous crossing contraptions than either the Mormon or Hickman operations. Somewhat handicapped by the appearance of their risky vessels, they competed for business by resorting to what one overlander described as "much meaness & lying."[24] Precarious craft or unscrupulous proprietors notwithstanding, passing emigrants marveled at the money ferrymen were reaping, one estimating $50,000, another $250,000 as the season's take.[25]

Also finding the year's migration a source of considerable profit were mountain traders whose 1850 range encompassed Ash Hollow on the east and the Bear River on the west. Traders up from the Southwest concentrated on the region from Ash Hollow to the Upper Ferry, with almost all putting in an appearance at Fort Laramie at one point or another. Kit Carson, who with Tim Goodale had trailed forty to fifty horses and mules up from Santa Fe, remained at the fort for a pleasant month, imparting both sage and questionable advice to importuning emigrants while selling them his animals "to good advantage." William Bent was also in the vicinity, as were, according to one contemporary, "all the Arkansas men." Taos traders had shrewdly brought a great quantity of corn north to the Ash Hollow area. One such speculator sold 800 bushels at $8 per bushel to early starters whose teams could not yet be sustained on the prairie grasses.[26]

Mountain men were similarly important to the Green River ferrying operations on both the Salt Lake and Sublette routes. Trappers from the Arkansas River worked a two-boat ferry as early as May 26, whereas the Mormon crew from Salt Lake did not get their rope ferry functioning until shortly after June 1. Traffic was heavy on the Salt Lake trail in 1850. At one point in mid-June, approximately 400 wagons were waiting to be crossed. Mormon ferrymen occasionally permitted hard-pressed travelers to pay their ferriage fees ($5 per wagon and $1 per horse) in Salt Lake City.[27] Surprisingly, on the more heavily traveled Sublette route, ferry service was apparently unavailable until a Missouri emigrant fashioned a boat out of a large wagon box on June 10. Soon, however, three distinct enterprises were under way within a five-mile stretch, uniformly charging $7 per wagon. Two mountaineers, Jim Baker and a Pittsburgh man named McDonald, operated, somewhat lackadaisically, one of the ferries; Mormons worked another. The third was a prospering emigrant ferry which James Huddleston had purchased early in the season for $300 from a fellow emigrant entrepreneur. Having constructed two additional boats in the interim, Huddleston sold his enterprise by August 1, $11,500 richer.[28]

Those 1850 overlanders traveling on to Salt Lake City ruefully discovered that the detour via the Mormon oasis required an unprecedented outlay in ferriage fees: $1.50 to $3 at Ham's Fork for a mountaineer ferry when the river was high; $3 or $4 for a ferry over the Weber River; $3 or $4 for a ferry over the Weber River again on exiting from Salt Lake; $2 or $3 to cross Ogden Creek on a ferry; $4 or $5 for a ferry over the Bear River (where an emigrant noticed that the ferryman made $100 before breakfast one morning); and $1 to cross Mud Creek on a ramshackle bridge. This meant an expenditure of $14.50 to $20 to cross one wagon over this motley assortment of rivers and creeks. When added to the $10 to $20 most had spent on ferriage fees even before beginning the Salt Lake detour, the impact of private enterprise on the overland trip was expensively apparent. Since most travelers were well aware that all these supportive services cost considerable money, the purses of the prudent gold rushers, as 1850 argonaut N. A. Cagwin explained, were "full of the bright 5$ Gold Pieces . . . to help them 'O'er the Ferry.' "[29]

Instead of Mormon ferrymen, emigrants bypassing Salt Lake met additional itinerant mountain traders. Near Soda Springs, where the Hudspeth Cutoff veered away from the longer route via Fort Hall, they found the temporary "Owens Trading Post," a combination station and smith shop offering oxen, mules, and horses for sale and exchange at inflated mountain prices. Admirably located for its purpose, to "recommend very strongly the Ft. Hall road," the intent was not to entice potential customers to Fort Hall but to Cantonment Loring, the abortive army installation five miles above the Hudson's Bay Company post. Though already abandoned by the troops, much equipment remained in the care of two men from the quartermaster's department. The sutlers also had considerable material on hand which they hoped to unload on passing overlanders.[30] California-bound emigrants induced to go via Fort Hall, and the small number of Oregon-bound overlanders for whom that outpost was a welcome main route oasis, found Richard Grant short on supplies but as hospitable as ever.[31]

Early in the traveling year the St. Louis *Daily Missouri Republican* correspondent predicted from his Fort Laramie vantage point that backpackers relying on trailside posts for supplies would fare well as far as Fort Hall. "But how," he pondered, "they are to reach California from that point, a distance of over 800 miles, is a problem that only they themselves can solve."[32] The backpackers, and all emigrants who had outfitted too sparingly, solved the problem easily—if they had money. For in 1850 emigrants were able to purchase food at trading posts in the Carson and Truckee valleys and while crossing the Sierras into the California settlements, in some areas finding a post every mile. Emigrants reprovisioned at posts on the desert crossings to the Carson and Truckee rivers; they discovered that a few traders had even inched eastward along the foreboding Humboldt River for purposes of trade; and all the while they encountered mobile traders with pack mules working eastward with food for sale.[33] This sudden appearance of scores of trading posts was eloquent testimony to the profit potential in supplying incoming overlanders with basic necessities. There were, however, so many prospective entrepreneurs swarming about the emigrants that Thomas Christy sagely observed, ". . . they are running that business into the ground as fast as possible as too many cooks spoil the broth . . . there is too many at it to be very profitable."[34]

The few emigrants trekking northwest to Oregon from Fort Hall in 1850 found no comparable facilities, only the long-familiar bulwarks of Fort Boise and Fort Walla Walla, now supplemented by the new army outpost at The Dalles. There simply were insufficient travelers to tempt many traders onto the closing portions of the Oregon Trail.[35] The tens of thousands of gold rushers, however, provided more than enough incentive for entrepreneurs to concentrate on the California Trail.

Although Table 7 indicates comparative prices at these posts, statistics alone are inadequate for an understanding of the interaction occurring between emigrants and California traders. While relieved at the availability of food and drink, most overlanders much resented these trail's-end entrepreneurs, whom they accused of "skinning" incoming travelers. The principal emigrant frustration was, of course, high prices, perhaps best illustrated by the exaggerated cost of eating a single meal. Prices from $11 to a rumored $25 did seem outlandish, despite the fact that weeks of short rations made for hearty appetites.[36]

The outrageous prices affected emigrants in yet another way. Often in precarious circumstances and desperate for food ("lots of elephant tracks," one traveler wrote in his diary), overlanders were easily victimized by unscrupulous stock speculators, who assured them that wagons, harnesses, horses, mules, and oxen were valueless in California. These deceitful entrepreneurs grazed the animals until they were rejuvenated, then trailed them into California, where their value was far higher than the ten or twenty pounds of flour or the $1 to $10 the deluded seller usually

TABLE 7
PRICE RANGES AT TRADING POSTS, 1850

	Flour	Sugar	Coffee	Liquor	Bacon	Beef
Laramie	.12- .50 11.00[b]	.50-2.00	.50	.75[a]	.50	
Mountain traders	18.00[b]	.25		.50[a]		
Hall				.75[a]		
Bridger				2.00[a]		
Humboldt River posts	1.50-2.00	1.00	.50		1.00	.15- .25
Ragtown	1.25-2.50	1.00-2.00	1.00-1.50 .10[a]	1.00[c]	1.00-1.50	.25-1.00
Mormon Station	.50-1.50	.75-1.75		1.50[a]	1.75	
Carson Valley posts	.40-2.50	1.25-1.50	.50- .75	2.00-4.00[a]		.50-2.00
Mobile California traders	1.00-2.00 1.50[b]	1.25 1.50[b]	1.25	1.00-3.00[a]	1.00-2.00	.50

[a]Price per pint.
[b]Price per 100 pounds. (Numbers without superscripts are per pound prices.)
[c]Price per drink.

received. Upon arrival in California, overlanders duped in this manner knew well, as one bemoaned, "how to sympathize with Esau in the sale of his birthright."[37] Even more far-reaching were the accusations 1850 overlander William Wilson leveled at California's trail's-end speculators. In order to entice gold rushers into coming overland to California, Wilson charged, the speculators circulated many of the fanciful stories about gold discoveries so influential in the eastern states: "the moste of the good news is sente to the States by the traders or Speculators   they do it to encourage a large emagration the nexte Sumer   then they will meet them with flour and meat for the lowe price of two dolars per lb and buy thare teams at a low price and if they have an opertunity steel them (they are not all gilty of Steeling but maney of them are)."[38]

The emigrant bill of particulars against California traders further included the firm conviction that many combined theft with speculation, often in concert with area Indians. John Wood was not alone in believing that "men here are doing nothing else but steel horses, cattle and mules." This was no idle suspicion, as Bryon McKinstry explained: "One company lost all their oxen but found three of them in the possession of a trader, and branded, and they had to take them back by force."[39]

Most of the trading stations were either tents or structures hastily thrown together out of boards, brush, and cloth. Most were so temporary as to be nameless, although terms such as "Dale's station" or "Erwin's trading post" occasionally appear in emigrant diaries and letters.[40] A few of the stations were even operated by early-arriving overlanders, who, after a hurried assessment, decided more money was to be made on the trails than in the mines.[41] Virtually all posts had whiskey for sale (incoming overlanders even passed drunken men lying beside the trail), and gambling was such a popular pastime that one post proprietor deeply immersed in a game of eucre did not even bother to inspect the animal he took in trade from an overlander. Emigrants were properly skeptical of most information offered by these post proprietors, who were "such abominable liars for interest sake." William Montgomery's comment doubtless summed up the feelings of many disgusted overlanders: "a rough looking set of christians indeed."[42]

Ragtown, a motley collection of such establishments where the emigrants first struck the Carson River after traversing the dreaded Humboldt Desert (where they invariably "saw the elephant"), was one of the two most important trading stations toward the trail's end. Mormon Station, located in the Carson Valley, was the other. Westbound emigrants noticed construction activity at Mormon Station throughout the first two weeks of July, and by late summer the small group of Mormon pioneers had fashioned log cabins, a corral, and even a bridge over the Carson River. As traders they were sufficiently in tune with prevailing practice to have one overlander term their establishment "a perfect skinning post for emigrants."[43]

As always, mail service was of prime importance to 1850 overlanders, who availed themselves of every communication opportunity private enterprise offered. While many emigrants sent missives, at twenty-five cents per letter, with one of the Robidoux brothers returning to Missouri from the Scott's Bluff station, the year's communication innovation originated in St. Louis.[44] James M. Estill had widely advertised his "Express Mail Line for California" on the Missouri frontier. An express mail from Weston and St. Joseph was sent to California, while the main portion of Estill's caravan halted at Pacific Springs in South Pass to collect letters from the westbound emigration. Estill's wagons then returned to post the letters in Missouri.[45] Additionally, letters collected at eighteen towns from St. Louis to St. Joseph were to be distributed to the addressees as the express wagons passed them en route to South Pass. The express charge per letter was fifty cents, in addition to the regular postage fee. Emigrant enthusiasm was evidenced by the more than 4,000 letters Estill brought back to the frontier in August.[46] Though his venture proved an isolated experiment, Estill had envisioned it as the beginning of a biweekly summer mail and passenger service from Fort Leavenworth to San Francisco. To that end he unsuccessfully tried to interest Brigham Young in cooperating financially in the endeavor and in directing at least the Salt Lake City–to–California portion of the route.[47]

And as in 1849 there again were those entrepreneurially inclined emigrants who stocked their wagons with merchandise to peddle to their trail colleagues. Probably the most intriguing mobile merchant of 1850 was James Philly of West Point, Missouri. Philly shrewdly counted on the inability of travelers to forgo chewing tobacco on the long journey and laid in a large supply at twenty cents per pound. After selling most of his tobacco to emigrants at $1 per pound, Philly disposed of his remaining stock in Salt Lake City for $5 per pound.[48]

Entrepreneurs in outfitting points and beside the overland trail had not anticipated the drastic reduction in overland travel in 1851, when only 5,000 emigrants trekked to Oregon and California. Obviously expecting the boom years of 1849 and 1850 to continue indefinitely, they had expanded and improved old enterprises and inaugurated new ones. When the profitable multitudes did not appear, retrenchment was necessary. John Corby, for example, who had purchased a new steam ferryboat for the St. Joseph Missouri River crossing, used it instead as a packet boat between St. Joseph and Council Bluffs.[49]

Corby's plight was repeated everywhere that entrepreneurs had readied themselves for the expected rush. A Fort Laramie observer reported at the close of the emigrating season, "The bridge and ferry companies, also the traders, have been quite disappointed, having taken but little of their [the emigrants] spare change." Some of the projected—and uncompleted—entrepreneurial undertakings of the year were monumentally optimistic, even in a time of gold rush euphoria: "Even the Great Desert will be removed . . . as a company of men have established a rancho on Salmon Trout River and undertaken to turn the waters of that stream across the fifty-mile Desert; so that, instead of emptying into Pyramid Lake, the Salmon Trout shall fall into the sink of Humboldt or Mary's River, which is some 200 feet lower."[50] Most 1851 developments, however, were considerably less grandiose in scope, though no less important to the overland traveler.

Overlanders making the trip found ferrymen waiting at all the usual crossings. There were the usual complement of Mormon entrepreneurs at the Upper Ferry site, another ferry enterprise equidistant between Deer Creek and the Upper Ferry, and no less than sixteen boats at the Green River crossing.[51] At the Green River ferriage rates stood at new highs: a 10-dollar fee for crossing a single wagon was common, and an 11-dollar charge was assessed at least once on the Sublette route, where both Mormons and mountaineers again worked ferries. Entrepreneurs quickly recognized that in 1851 most emigrants were bound for the Willamette Valley. Hence, on the Oregon leg of their route, beyond Fort Hall, ferry service was available across the Snake River near Fort Boise and across the Deschutes River.[52]

But most clearly expressive of future travel conveniences (as well as of the substantial sums entrepreneurs willingly chanced on the emigrant trade) were at least four bridges spanning major rivers. John Richard and partners had invested $8,000 in structures bridging the Laramie River near the fort and the Platte River near Deer Creek; additional bridges spanned Thomas' Fork of the Bear River and the Portneuf River below Fort Hall. Emigrants seemed leery of these initial spans, however, especially of Richard's Platte bridge. It was little patronized, perhaps because word was out that the bridge sank four feet when one trader crossed his wagons. Richard and his partners either recognized the shortcomings of their bridge or, more likely, endeavored to monopolize crossing operations: they also owned four ferryboats at Deer Creek and two at the Green River.[53]

By 1851 newspaper advertising was increasingly the medium by which trailside entrepreneurs wooed the overland trade. Wheeling, Clark, and Company boosted the north-side trail, where they operated the Elkhorn and Loup Fork ferries. Stressing the speed of travel and absence of cholera on the route, they asserted that only those "who have never seen it" spoke of ferry service over the South Fork of the Platte River, which travelers on the south-side trail had to cross.[54] John Richard and cohorts likewise advertised the joys of travel, but on the south-side trail. Their advertisements emphasized the many trading posts and blacksmith shops, the new bridges, and the ferry service which Richard promised to provide at the South Fork and across the Platte at his Ash Point location. A Langdon, Steele, and Company advertisement of 1851 listed all of nine well-stocked trading stations which rendered the south-side trail such a safe and commodious artery of travel: "Fort Kearny, Ward & Guerry's, Fort John, Robidoux's, Reshoe's, Burdoe's, Bassinett's, Fort Laramie, and Langdon, Steel & Co's."[55]

Although the creative spellings of Langdon and Steele's advertisement camouflaged some well-known posts, it is evident that several additional trailside stations had been established in anticipation of a large 1851 migration. By then Forts Kearny, Laramie, and John were familiar outposts, as were Robidoux's two posts at Scott's Bluff, Richard's post at Ash Point, and the Bordeaux-Bissonette operation at the old Fort Bernard site. Seth E. Ward and William Le Guerrier, probably in April of 1851, purchased and settled themselves at Richard's Ash Point post; thus the advertisement's mention of their association with a post earlier that year suggests a very temporary station somewhere east of Ash Point. James Bordeaux and Joseph Bissonette dissolved their year-old trading partnership sometime in 1850, with Bordeaux remaining at their headquarters eight miles from Fort Laramie and Bissonette moving upriver three miles nearer the fort to institute a competing concern. Finally, the Langdon, Steele, and Company station was doubtless located near the Deer Creek bridge, where a smith shop and extensive stock corrals were maintained.[56]

West of Laramie the new entrepreneurial thrusts were concentrated at the Oregon end of the trail. John Owen, now associated with a man named Wilson, kept a post at Thomas' Fork, presumably in conjunction with the bridge there. A trading station was likewise connected with the

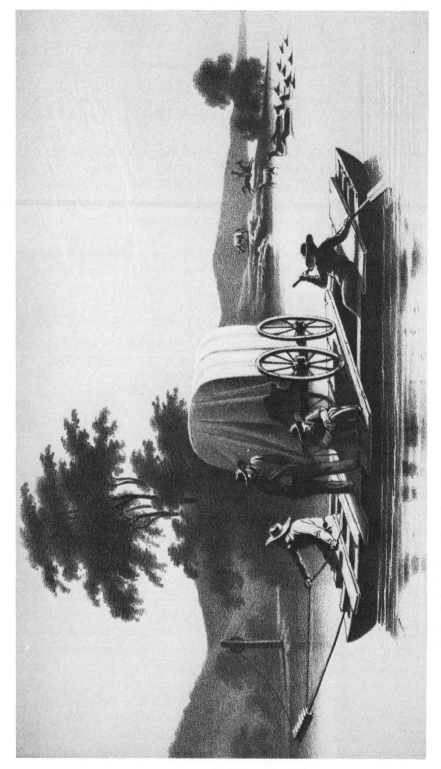

F. R. Grist, "Crossing the Platte, Mouth of Deer Creek"—a calmer crossing than many.
From Stansbury, *Exploration and Survey of the Valley of the Great Salt Lake* (1852)

Portneuf bridge. Richard Grant, on furlough from Fort Hall, traded out of Cantonment Loring with his sons in 1851 and in subsequent years. Other new stations were located on the Oregon Trail. One was a number of miles south of the Umatilla River Indian agency; another was linked with the agency, itself constructed in the summer of 1851; a post was situated at The Dalles; and two additional stations were located east of The Dalles. Moreover, stock speculators—"swindlers," P. V. Crawford called them—again met the overlanders near The Dalles.[57] The few emigrants following the southern route into Oregon were welcomed by the proprietors of a post situated near the Rogue River crossing.[58]

Meanwhile, a far-reaching reaction to the small number of 1851 emigrants occurred in the Carson Valley on the California Trail. Speculators awaiting the overlanders there concluded that it was financially impractical to transport their unsold merchandise stocks back across the Sierras into California. Deeming it wiser to remain, grow vegetables, and await the hopefully larger contingent of 1852 travelers, they thus almost incidentally began the permanent settlement of the Carson Valley.[59] Mormon Station, which became the nucleus of the Nevada settlement of Genoa, had been purchased in April by John and Enoch Reese, Salt Lake merchants. The Reese brothers embellished the establishment, planting corn, wheat, barley, turnips, and watermelons in adjacent fields. A few eastward-drifting prospectors for gold congregated near the future Carson City, and by November the Carson Valley contained a semi-permanent population of approximately 100 persons. Gathering at Mormon Station to organize, the pioneering inhabitants began petitioning for territorial status and actively solicited more settlers.[60]

The year 1852 was a trailside entrepreneur's dream come true: more overlanders trailed to Oregon (10,000) and to California (50,000) than in any other antebellum year.[61] Established entrepreneurs who had persevered through the lean preceding year experienced again the prosperity characteristic of the early gold rush. They were joined by such an armada of newcomers that any attempt to catalogue the supportive facilities available that year is doomed to failure.

Most elusive are the trailside post-blacksmith shops which mushroomed everywhere, not only at the termini of the California and Oregon trails. Trading stations at new locations mentioned with some frequency during the emigration season included Francis J. Marshall's post at what would become the Marysville crossing of the Big Blue River, an unidentified post at the South Fork ford of the Platte River, another in the Black Hills between Laramie and the Platte ferries, several at the Platte ferry sites, several in the Independence Rock vicinity and along the Sweetwater River to South Pass, several in the Soda Springs area, and many along the Humboldt River.[62]

Temporary stations virtually exploded into existence. On the crossing from the Sink to Ragtown on the Carson River, Mrs. Francis H. Sawyer noticed seven or eight trading posts, which made that desert "easier to cross . . . than it has ever been before"; the next day John Wayman counted ten such concerns. Liquids were the chief stock-in-trade of these desert oases, water normally selling at $1 per gallon. Ragtown's growth was similarly explosive: R. H. P. Snodgrass estimated some twenty canvas establishments housing "stock speculators, gamblers and liquor dealers" when he passed through on July 21; two weeks later Wayman tallied over fifty pole-and-canvas tents.[63]

Supplying the posts was big business. Pack trains laden with provisions and liquors left Placerville for the Carson Valley daily. Herds of cattle and horses destined for the same location departed almost as frequently. Insofar as traveling through unsettled country served as a criterion of the overland journey, the California Trail now certainly ended in the Carson Valley, as overlander Robert Sharp's observation confirmed: "There is trading posts every few miles from carson valy to placerville."[64] The absence of carefully identified posts and traders in emigrant diaries and letters further indicates that most overlanders no longer considered trail entrepreneurs much of a novelty. Hundreds of California stock speculators were also on the trails, some meeting oncoming overlanders as far away as 130 miles northeast of the Humboldt Sink.[65]

Beyond Fort Hall on the Oregon Trail a similar plethora of supportive services existed. In addition to Fort Boise, overlanders found principal trading stations on the main trail in the Grande Ronde Valley, at the Umatilla River Indian agency, the Deschutes River crossing, the John Day River crossing, The Dalles, and the Cascades. On variant routes stations were also located near Barlow's Gate in the Cascade Mountains and at Foster's Farm near Oregon City.[66] In their quest for profitable transactions Oregon speculators in stock even ventured east of Fort Boise to meet emigrants. An indication of the rewards they expected is seen in the aspirations of First Lieutenant Ulysses S. Grant, then serving with the Fourth Infantry in Oregon. Grant, as eager an entrepreneur as anyone else, wrote to his wife: "I have been up to the Dalles of the Columbia, where the Immigrants generally first stop upon their arrival in Oregon, comeing by the overland route. I there made arrangements for the purchase of quite a number of oxen and cows, and for having them taken care of during the winter. If I should lose one fourth of my cattle I would then clear at least one hundred per cent."[67]

This greatest migration year brought few changes in the pattern of trader-emigrant interaction, except that former tendencies were fast becoming permanent attributes. Liquor-dispensing at trailside "grogshops," for example, was more common than ever, particularly on the California Trail. The result of excessive imbibing—termed by overlanders getting "Alkalied"—was increasingly seen both during the journey and at its conclusion. By now, too, some of the posts had advanced beyond the rustic, makeshift stage. The sutler at Fort Laramie, according to emigrant testimony, offered "as good an assortment as you will find any where" of "all articles a man wants in civilized countries or on the plains."[68]

TABLE 8
PRICE RANGES AT TRADING POSTS, 1852

	Flour	Sugar	Coffee	Liquor	Bacon	Beef
Before Laramie	.20 15.00[b]	.50- .60	.50	2.00[a]		
Fort Laramie	10.00-10.50[b]	.50- .75	.40		.15	
Between Laramie & Hall	.20 15.00[b]			1.50-2.25[a]		
Between Boise & The Dalles	.30- .75	.40- .75	.50- .75		.30- .75	.20- .75
The Dalles	.15- .40 18.00[b]	.20- .40	.40- .50	.20- .25[a]	.50-1.00	.12½-.25
Cascade City	.25	.30- .35	.30- .35		.40	.20- .25
Humboldt River posts	.25- .35	.75		.25- .50[c]		.25
Ragtown	.20- .25	.50		1.00[a]	.40- .50	.25- .30
Mormon Station	.20				.60	.30
Carson Valley	.25- .40 10.00-20.00[b]	.50 50.00[b]	50.00[b]	1.00 50.00[b]	.25	

[a]Price per pint.
[b]Price per 100 pounds. (Numbers without superscripts are per pound prices.)
[c]Price per drink.

While continuing to rely on traders and their stations for travel needs, many emigrants remained unable to accept either the humaneness or trustworthiness of trailside entrepreneurs. In part this was because so many overlanders were scandalized by the drinking, gambling, and loose living so conspicuous at many trading posts. Addison Crane warned that at the posts "men are generally great liars and very disolute characters." Richard Keen discovered a white American woman in the "possession" of a French trader at a post in South Pass. Her story, at least as recorded in Keen's personal journal, was a bizarre one which in no way endeared post proprietors to this emigrant company: ". . . she wished us to take her on to California. her story was quite affecting She stated that she started to California in 1850 in Company with some young Men who left her here would not take her any farther she had remined with these Frenchmen for 2 years had been bought and sold three times and was used worse than dumb brute notwithstanding all her entreties none of our Company would consent to take her."[69] With other overlanders it was thieving traders, extravagant post prices, and lack of trader generosity to those in need which elicited such comments as "passed another land pirate's post" or "[the traders are] mostly hard cases, though I occasionally find a human man."[70]

The stock speculators aroused practically everyone's ire. Particularly perturbed in 1852 were Oregon-bound overlanders. Mary Long averred that the speculating sharpies were akin to "real estate men on the lookout for men with money." In the Grande Ronde Valley incoming overlanders accused stock speculators of burning the prairie grasses so that the limited forage would force emigrants to sell their animals cheaply. Especially reprehensible was the speculator at Salmon Falls on the Snake River, who induced travelers weary of the trail to sell their teams and float down the Snake River to their destination in their wagon beds. Some who fell victim to him drowned, others ultimately made it back to the trail after harrowing ordeals, minus everything, to finish the journey as charity cases.[71]

Individual responses to the "harder" sort of entrepreneurs differed. Gilbert Cole was so incensed by one roadside salesman's demeanor and prices that after paying $10 in gold for eighty horse nails he "really wanted to be alone with that man for awhile, I loved him so." A radically different but quite understandable response was reported by Enoch Conyers near Barlow's Gate: "At this camp we met with an enterprising emigrant, who was lucky enough to arrive at civilization some two weeks since. He sold his outfit and purchased a supply of the necessaries of life and, returning to this place, had set up a small trading post for the benefit (?) of the poor emigrant. As he said: 'All those traders that we met out here skinned us emigrants for all we were worth, and now I have come back here to skin all the balance of the emigrants.' And I rather think that he made good his word."[72]

Following the entrepreneurial initiatives of 1852, relatively few streams lacked bridge and/or ferry facilities. Crossing improvements existed at approximately twenty-five separate river crossings. Ferriage costs per wagon continued to escalate, ranging from forty cents at the Sweetwater River to $16 at the Green River. Since there were several competing enterprises at the more important streams, at least forty different entrepreneurs, some of them westbound overlanders, must have been active in 1852.[73]

In spite of the intense competition, financial returns were generally high. At the Elkhorn River the ferry operator cleared $500 per day, which was also the reported daily income at one of the Green River ferries. Stephen Gage, at the North Platte crossing near Deer Creek, reported simply that it was "the most money made that I ever saw in one day." Mormon ferrymen at their Upper Ferry on the Platte River reported a *daily* income between $1,500 and $1,800. Two mountaineers at the Green River were reported to have made $65,000 from their ferry operation that summer only to squander it, in part to professional gamblers from the Missouri River settlements.[74]

With such sums involved it is not surprising that ferry owners went to considerable lengths to prevent thrifty emigrants from fording rivers or constructing and manning their own boats. Ezra Meeker encountered difficulty at Kanesville, where his outfit had raised a sunken boat to expedite their crossing of the Missouri. Viewing this makeshift vessel as potential competition, the owners of the established ferry prevailed upon the local sheriff to commandeer the rival boat. The emigrants retaliated with a show of force. With guns at the ready, they forced the constabulary to withdraw and crossed their wagons without further delay. Farther west Henry Bradley's company, after exiting from Salt Lake City, forded the Weber River in lieu of using the toll bridge some six miles from Ogden. The proprietor, presumably James Brown, informed them that they owed him the 3-dollar toll anyway; whether the bridge had been used was immaterial! Brown had understandably little success with this stratagem, although he tried it often. Mormon ferrymen at the Bear River used a different technique. They rendered the ford unusable by digging huge holes, thereby insuring patronage of their ferry—at fees of $3 per wagon.[75] Indeed, ever since Mormon ferrymen had resorted to skulduggery in an attempt to eliminate their North Platte competition in 1847, trailside entrepreneurs aggressively sought monopolies. If Solomon Kingery's report was true, this cutthroat rivalry was the reason John Richard's North Platte bridge was not a factor beyond early June: ". . . it has been Chopped down Soposd to been done by those that own the ferrys above."[76]

On the Missouri River frontier steamboat captains often neglected their regular runs to vie with commercial ferries in setting overlanders across the river for handsome fees ranging up to $5 and $10 per wagon.[77] Despite the speed and capacity of steam-powered vessels, crossing delays were common in 1852. Mrs. Francis H. Sawyer waited a week to cross the Missouri at Old Fort Kearny. John T. Kerns and company crossed nine miles below Kanesville on May 19, having waited impatiently since the 8th.[78] Such frustrated emigrants occasionally resorted to subterfuge or violence to enhance their position among those awaiting passage. Intriguing contests of force and wit between emigrant and entrepreneur were also common, usually prompted by entrepreneur attempts to exact what emigrants considered to be excessive tolls. Elisha Brook's company spent nearly a week assisting two Mormons in the construction and launching of a ferryboat at the North Fork of the Platte River. Preparing then to cross the river, Brooks recalled that "the ferrymen, ignoring our labor on the boat, demanded a price for ferriage which would almost confiscate our outfit. We compromised the matter by posting a guard of our roughs over them with cocked rifles, while we ferried ourselves across as an offset to our work on the boat; then treating those profane ferrymen to a bath in the Platte to cool them off, we drove on."[79]

According to an extensively circulated rumor a more serious altercation had occurred in May, when a company arrived at the Big Blue crossing one evening and bargained to be ferried across on the following morning for $1.50 per wagon. That night the river rose and could no longer be safely forded. Consequently, the ferrymen arbitrarily raised the price to $2 per wagon. In the ensuing fracas two ferrymen and two emigrants were killed.[80] While this particular incident has not been verified, emigrant dissatisfaction with entrepreneurial business ethics was rampant. Dr. Thomas White, for example, after completing an 1852 overland journey in which he paid $65 in ferriage and toll fees, carped about the "Robbers" at the Green River who demanded up to $16 to cross a single wagon. White advised future emigrants to "be willing to pay, a fair compensation for crossing ferries, but pay no outlandish rates. if they will not pass you for a fair compensation then cross yourselves & pay what is just. . . . I payed it always but I would not do it again."[81]

While unbridled free enterprise, featuring ethical unconcern and charging all that the traffic would bear, remained the hallmark of trailside business activity, by 1852 certain legislatures were chartering ferries and bridges, prescribing standard toll rates, and specifying penalties for evading the regulations. On the Missouri River frontier Indian agents threatened legal action if potential entrepreneurs did not procure the licenses necessary to engage in trading and ferrying activities in the Indian territory. At least some entrepreneurs complied: McLaughlin and Middleton's newspaper advertisements emphasized their permits authorizing ferry service at the Elkhorn and Loup Fork rivers.[82] At the other end of the trail the Oregon legislative assembly granted several charters for ferry and road tolls, thereby legalizing Olney's Deschutes River ferry. Toll takers at the three bridges over the Carson River similarly informed incredulous overlanders of their charters (which they never produced) authorizing bridge tolls.[83]

The most intriguing legal developments, however, prevailed in the Salt Lake vicinity. Starting in 1850, the legislature of the Mormon "State of Deseret" had chartered faithful Mormons with exclusive privileges over certain rivers, usually the Bear, Weber, Ogden, and Green. For 1852 such charters had been given to James Brown for toll bridges across the Weber and Ogden rivers; to Joseph Young, David Fulmer, John Young, and William Empey for ferry service over the Bear River and the construction of a substantial toll bridge over Malad Creek; and to Thomas Moor for ferry service anywhere on the Green River.[84]

An 1852 company of Mormons who attempted to bridge the Green River so infuriated area mountaineers and their Indian allies that the bridge builders, but not the ferrymen, withdrew. The traders and Indians claimed prior squatters' rights as it was. When they learned that the Mormon charters contained stipulations that anyone erecting public ferries over certain rivers without the permission of Mormon authorities was liable to fines of up to $1,000 "to be collected for the use of the Territory of Utah," insult was added to injury. Indian agent Jacob H. Holeman sided with the mountaineers and Indians in this continuing conflict. Holeman doubted the constitutionality of the proviso that 10 percent of all ferrying proceeds—most of which came from non-Mormons—were earmarked for the Perpetual Emigrating Fund, an arm of the Church of Jesus Christ of Latter-Day Saints. For their part, in this battle for supremacy in the Green River country, the Mormons blamed mountaineers for instigating Indian attacks on Mormon settlements.[85]

These jurisdictional squabbles did not affect passing overlanders as much as another phase of the charter issue. In awarding the charters the Utah legislature had also specified the rates of toll. At the Green River, for example, Thomas Moor was entitled to charge $3 for each vehicle weighing under 2,000 pounds; $4 for those between 2,000 and 3,000 pounds; $5 for those between 3,000 and 4,000 pounds; and $6 for all vehicles weighing in excess of 4,000 pounds. The fee for each animal ferried over the river was established at twenty-five cents.[86] Moor and his compatriots did not scrupulously follow these standardized rates, however, endeavoring to exact tolls ranging as high as $16 per wagon. John Riker's account of such an occasion illustrates why many emigrants had doubts about Mormon integrity:

They refused to carry us over for a less sum than eleven dollars per team, or eighty-eight dollars for the train. This our captain refused to pay, offering them fifty dollars, which we all considered a sufficient compensation. After a little delay, the teams were all crossed but one, which they refused to bring over until the full amount of ferriage was paid. At this the captain became angry, and immediately the company were ordered a short distance to camp, when nine of the men, well armed, returned to the ferry, determined to bring over the remaining team at all hazards. The captain then demanded their charter, which was reluctantly produced; and upon examination it was found that they were allowed to charge but three dollars per team. Then the captain drew his revolver, and threatened them with instant death if the team was not immediately carried over. They seemed to think the latter preferable, and acceded to his request.[87]

Unhappy emigrants registered complaints so frequently in Salt Lake City that Brigham Young ordered the sheriff to bring in the offending Green River ferrymen so that the allegations could be investigated. Overlanders were advised that following the trial any monies they had been over-charged would be refunded, but most could not afford to delay that long.[88]

The huge emigration prompted another private mail express along the lines of Estill's 1850 enterprise. The 1852 scheme was the creation of George E. Blodget and R. S. Raymond of Milwaukee. They aimed to convey letters back to the States from several points along the trail: "Archambault's Fort" at Devil's Gate, South Pass, and Goose Creek, 200 miles west of the Continental Divide. An "outrider" was scheduled to precede the returning express so that westbound overlanders would have sufficient notice to pen letters. Stamps, stationery, guidebooks, and similar supplies would be available at the several letter-collection points. Blodget's advertising failed to indicate the fee, but overlanders reported paying twenty-five to fifty cents per letter. Following their summer on the plains, Blodget and Raymond returned to St. Joseph in early September. How well they succeeded financially is not known, but there is evidence that the proprietors had cut corners in their operation. Addison Crane discovered at Devil's Gate that instead of returning the letters to the States by fast express as promised,

all they really do with the letters is to keep them until the Salt Lake Mail comes along and then hand them to the driver to be deposited in the nearest P.O. according to law. This I ascertained is the course they take—one of their men unwittingly remarked that they sent of[f] their letters last night, & knowing the Mormon mail must have passed thru then, we having met it early this morning, upon being questioned he admitted he sent by that. Of course they got no letter or half dollar from me as I did not wish to entrust my journal to any such jockeying concern.[89]

Westbound overlanders continued to be as alert to remunerative activity as mountaineer and stateside entrepreneurs. Manning a ferry for a short time, operating a mobile blacksmith shop, or establishing a trading post toward the end of the route remained the favored methods. Some travelers earned extra funds by clearing trail beyond Smith's Fork to avoid a steep hill and then collecting toll for several weeks; an insomniac stood nightly guard for his colleagues for a fifty-cent fee.[90] One innovative group cleared $25 by putting on a musical concert while still in Kanesville. For many enterprising overlanders such activities were necessities and not merely indicative of an avaricious outlook. Lucy Cooke, a performer in the Kanesville musical, noted that the $25 "will pay some ferriages." James Carpenter and his traveling partner worked on Missouri River vessels to earn enough to be able to cross the Missouri and Elkhorn rivers but were out of money by the time they reached the Loup Fork ferry. Avoiding the toll by fording at a new location, Carpenter took to shoeing horses for other travelers so that subsequent ferriage fees could be paid.[91]

Given the presence of so many commercial ferries—and the concerted attempts by their owners to enforce patronage—by the early 1850s cash was of considerable importance to a speedy and successful overland journey. After completing an expensive 1853 overland trip, S. H. Taylor wisely counseled others, "Take nothing for use after getting through—excepting money, of course, tho' I can assure you, you will have much less of that than you expected, when you get there." Taylor had something left on his Oregon arrival; not all did. Amelia Knight's husband ran out of funds and sold his riding horse for more ferriage money; Rebecca Ketcham, whose company experienced similar difficulties, lamented that "one wants a little fortune to start with to cross these toll bridges and ferries."[92]

Approximately 27,500 overlanders thronged the trails in 1853, making it the third largest antebellum migration year, and the fourth since 1849 in which at least 25,000 overlanders trailed west. The service facilities occasioned by this sustained emigration had long since altered the 1840s concept of a segmented journey divided by travel oases. It was difficult for an 1853 traveler, for example, to share the excitement felt by overlanders a decade earlier on reaching Fort Laramie—then a journey milestone and the first chance to reprovision and repair—when he found "within 20 miles of Laramie . . . probably 25 establishments for trade with emigrants." Or to journey unquestioningly to Fort Hall to stock up for the long and lonely final leg of the trip when "the road is lined with trading posts from California to within 150 miles of this city [Salt Lake City]," or, when on the Oregon Trail, he "passed trading posts nearly every day since we left Grande Ronde."[93]

For 1853 proved to be the kind of year Silas Miller had prophesied following his 1852 trek: ". . . if there is much of an emigration you will find enough of traders on the Road selling everything a man wants but at very exorbitant prices."[94] The first to recognize this were overlanders who had wintered in Salt Lake City and finished their journey early in 1853. Trailing into California, they met impressive numbers of pack trains laden with provisions and spiritous beverages en route for Ragtown and the many Humboldt River posts. Those trailing into Oregon witnessed the Hudson's Bay Company augmenting the stocks of Forts Hall and Boise in anticipation of profitable emigrant trading.[95] Tutt and Dougherty, the Fort Laramie sutlers, advertised in frontier newspapers that they had available "every article that is needed on the trip, as well as luxuries, in the eating line that will please the most fastidious taste." But perhaps the clearest indication of the extensiveness of the emigrant and Indian trade at even the less prominent posts was revealed by the disaster which befell R. Archambeault and Company, operators of trading stations at Devil's Gate on the trail and near Old Fort Kearny on the Missouri River. Having completed their purchase of liquors, foodstuffs, and trade goods at St. Louis, the consignment was being loaded onto boats when a wharf fire destroyed almost the entire shipment—which was worth $12,000 to $15,000 in St. Louis and a great deal more on the trail.[96]

Nonetheless, the proliferating entrepreneurs were servicing only half as many emigrants as the previous year. Indications are that entrepreneurial earnings decreased, particularly for stock speculators.[97] As usual, bridge and ferry operators prospered most. Particularly successful were the owners of the new Platte bridge. Though the bridge was rumored to have cost as much as $14,000 or $16,000, it brought in some $40,000 in its first year of existence. The new 300-foot span nearly drove the competing ferries out of business, although the Mormons persevered for the seventh consecutive year in operating a North Platte ferry. The ubiquitous John Richard was a partner in the new bridge, as were Seth Ward, William Guerrier, and "Bissonnette, Kenceleur & Co." Their signed advertisement promising that "the Rates of Toll will be greatly reduced from those of any previous year" first appeared in the St. Joseph *Gazette* on February 23,

TABLE 9
PRICE RANGES AT TRADING POSTS, 1851, 1853-60

		Before Laramie	Fort Laramie	Laramie to Ragtown	Carson Valley	Fort Hall to Oregon
Flour	1851					.15-.20
	1853				.50	.20-.50
	1854		10.50-25.00[b]	.40- .50	.23	
	1855					
	1856			.25		
	1857			.20- .30		
	1858					
	1859			.40		
	1860	.10	16.00[b]			
Sugar	1851					.37½-.75
	1853	.25				
	1854					
	1855					
	1856					
	1857					
	1858					
	1859			75.00[b]		
	1860	.25	.45			
Liquor	1851					
	1853					
	1854	.50[a]				
	1855					
	1856					
	1857					
	1858					
	1859			1.00-1.50[a]		
	1860		.75[a]			
Potatoes	1851					
	1853					
	1854			.12- .25	.10	
	1855					
	1856					
	1857					
	1858					
	1859					
	1860	.50				

[a]Price per pint.
[b]Price per 100 pounds. (Numbers without superscripts are per pound prices.)

1853.[98] Unfortunately, however, crossing fees did not decline: most travelers paid $6 for the privilege of driving their wagon across the once-formidable Platte, plus up to $1 per draft animal. The proprietors' advertising had been more accurate in promising blacksmith and wagonmakers' shops, a grocery and restaurant, and oxen, cows, horses, mules, and Indian goods for sale and trade at the bridge.

Richard was less fortunate with his investment in the Laramie River bridge. Not having been kept in repair, it failed to survive high water early in 1853. Fort Laramie commander Richard Garnett, disgusted with the owners' lack of industry, then awarded the privilege of erecting the next toll bridge on the government reservation to Ward, Guerrier, and Henry Mayer of Illinois. Their sturdy structure was ready by the 1854 traveling season.[99] Yet another travel accommodation, a mountaineer's bridge over the Sweetwater River near Independence Rock, fell victim to high water in late June, thus failing to survive its first season.[100] Most bridges spanned the smaller rivers and streams bisecting the trail west of South Pass. And, by 1853, there were approximately as many bridges as ferries—and more of each than in previous years. Overland travel was steadily becoming easier and more convenient.

Whether for bridge or ferry, most crossing fees were again slightly up in 1853, although the high and low range did not much differ from other years. The most expensive crossings were at Fort Boise, where the operators of the Snake River ferry charged $8 per wagon, and at the Green River, where the usual toll was also $8, though some emigrants paid as much as $12. Overlanders traveling the Salt Lake road paid $6. The Green River was certainly the busiest water crossing in 1853, with large numbers of boats (up to eleven) at three separate locations—on the Salt Lake route, the Kinney Cutoff, and the older Sublette Cutoff. Amidst the bustle of ferrying and trading activity there was also more gambling at the Green River than anywhere else on the overland trail. George Belshaw described the scene in mid-July: "At the ferry is a set of Gamblers they play cards most of the time at 10 & 20 Dollars a game they take in pockets full of gold from the Emigrants they dont value gold any more than you do so much grain, just kick it around any where." A week and a half later the accomplished resident gamblers won $3,000 from an inebriated emigrant.[101]

Though posts specializing in liquor (some proprietors displayed signs stating simply "Beer") were by now common sights, their reputations remained low. Jotham Newton suspected that a gang of thieves associated with such Carson River posts was responsible for his outfit's disappearing cattle; Harriet Ward, in the Independence Rock area, wrote: "There are several trading posts about here the inmates of which I should fear much more than the Indians." Likewise to be feared were the stock speculators, no matter what their disguise. Arriving emigrant Henry Allyn encountered a man pretending to be out meeting his family. Apparently person-

Taking advantage of the low river level, these pioneers have chosen to ford across. Nebraska State Historical Society ally disinterested, the man told all he met of a new road saving 200 miles of travel. Shortly thereafter Allyn talked with some bona fide Oregonians meeting their families. The Oregonians explained that a road company had reported the presumed route impassable *before* the salesman in question went out to sing the virtues of a nonexistent trail to oncoming overlanders, obviously hoping to lure them into a region where their only alternative would be to sell their stock cheap. Incensed, Allyn observed: "Oregon emigrants are in ten times the danger from speculators, ferrymen and traders than the Indians. It is believed that nearly or quite all the thefts that are laid to the Indians are either done or instigated by them. We have proved them to be infernal liars on more than one occasion."[102]

Only in the Mormon domain were service facilities reasonably well regulated. The industrious Utah legislature had awarded a number of licenses for the 1853 year. At the Green River Daniel H. Wells held a three-year charter for ferry service on the Salt Lake and Sublette routes, being authorized to charge from $3 to $6 per vehicle depending on weight, and twenty-five to fifty cents for animals. Joseph Young, David Fullmer, John Young, and William Empey received a three-year charter for the Bear River ferries and a Malad Creek bridge; the prescribed wagon tolls were $3 to $8 for the ferry service and $1.50 for the bridge. Joseph Busby's five-year charter for ferry service over Ham's Fork permitted wagon tolls from $2 to $3.50; James Brown's charter for bridges across the Weber and Ogden rivers authorized tolls of $2 for each vehicle drawn by two animals and fifty cents for every two additional draft animals; and Phineas and Brigham Young's initial ten-year charter for bridges across the East Weber and Bear rivers established tolls of $1 to $2, fees which were quickly amended upward to $3 to $6 per wagon. James Brown's charter specified that a fine of up to $5,000 be assessed against any interloper rash enough to attempt a competing facility without prior approval of Brigham Young and the legislature. Once again 5 to 10 percent of all proceeds were designated for the Perpetual Emigrating Fund. Since bridge specifications were clearly set forth in some of the charters, a further approximation of the substantial quality of some of the crossing facilities is possible: "Said bridges must be made fourteen feet wide in the clear, with a good and substantial hand-railing four feet high, and boarded down to the plank on the bridge; the timbers must be of good mountain pine, and the planking on the stringers must be of good, sound cottonwood, four inches thick, and not over eight inches wide; and at the end of five years from the date hereof, shall be turned over to the Territorial Road Commissioner in good condition, to be thereafter the property of this Territory."[103]

Although the complex and confusing Mormon-mountaineer feud was somewhat subdued at the Green River in 1853, at nearby Fort Bridger another long-standing controversy reached its denouement. While the issues are difficult to sort out, it appears that Mormon authorities not only desired control of Bridger's location but also believed him to be aiding and abetting Indian warfare on the Saint settlements. Moreover, Bridger apparently failed to comply with Brigham Young's order that no trade be conducted with Indians during the so-called Walker War, which pitted Ute Indians against Mormons in the summer of 1853 in areas quite remote from the Fort Bridger area. In late August a large Mormon posse descended on the fort to arrest the formidable mountain man, whose powerful influence with area Indians rankled the Saints. Bridger, forewarned, eluded arrest but apparently never again traded from the fort. In 1855 he and his partner Vasquez agreed to sell the famous outpost to the Mormons for $8,000. After ousting Bridger in 1853, the Mormons established "Fort Supply" a few miles away for use as a Mormon Trail support station, a mission to the Indians, and a base for pressuring mountaineer entrepreneurs at the Green River. To climax Bridger's disastrous year, in May, 1854, Joseph Busby sued Bridger on a matter relating to the ferry they had jointly operated at Ham's Fork in 1853.[104]

While the Mormons were squeezing Jim Bridger out of the Green River region they were also expanding their influence to the southwest in the Carson Valley. John Reese, principal proprietor of Mormon Station, received with Israel Mott the first official Carson Valley charter for toll bridges. Their license, authorizing the three Carson River bridges in the south end of the valley, provided for toll charges of $1 per wagon.[105] The Carson Valley settlement prospered during the 1853 traveling season, with overlanders eagerly snapping up such trail rarities as freshly grown turnips, corn, potatoes, and watermelons. A September estimate indicated a valley population of some forty families who had harvested 600 acres of wheat.[106]

The Carson Valley equivalent on the Oregon Trail was The Dalles region, where most emigrants first reached the Columbia River. By 1853 overlanders found farms in the vicinity, about ten log-and-frame buildings, and approximately thirty canvas grocery and provision stores. The U.S. Army also maintained an installation at the little hamlet. Emigrant Samuel Handsaker identified "The Columbia House" as the main hotel. Farther west along the Columbia, Cascade Falls was similarly booming, already possessing the sine qua non for a bona fide trail town—a combination boarding-gambling emporium.[107]

In some trail locales the number of supportive facilities increased in 1854 instead of diminishing in response to the continuing reduction in the number of overland travelers. Emigrants were thus able to transact business at several trading posts along the trail on the north side of the Platte River. The post at the crossing of the Wood River doubled as a "hospital," at least it was so identified. An overlander traveling on the south side of the river remarked, before even reaching Fort Laramie, "Through this country the French traders are as thick as hasty Puding." Between Fort Laramie and South Pass the same traveler found "plenty of trading Posts through this country," a circumstance familiar both to those utilizing the Fort Hall or Hudspeth Cutoff routes to the headwaters of the Humboldt and those traveling via Salt Lake City and its proliferating satellite towns. New stations also appeared along the Humboldt, while following the Ragtown-to-California road came to be characterized as "a pleasure trip, rather than a toilsome journey" because of the many "houses of entertainment" along the way.[108]

The nature of trailside conveniences was almost as significant as the number. Continuing transitions from hand to steam power on Missouri River ferryboats and from boats to bridges elsewhere en route reflected the steady evolution of the overland journey toward greater comfort, ease, and safety.[109] The presence of sizable numbers of permanent or semi-permanent residents at periodic trail locations was comforting to the long-distance traveler. More and more such communities were materializing: in 1854 approximately twenty families were reported living near the Nemaha bridge on the overland trail spur emanating from St. Joseph; at the Green River at least four women were among the two dozen Mormons operating ferries, groceries, a gambling table, and a "Brewry." Numerous mountaineers added to the size if not the tranquility of the settlement. In the Carson Valley, which was no longer a mere trailside oasis, saw- and gristmills were either operating or under construction, and the population had risen above 1,000. The proprietors of Mormon Station regularly advertised their wares in Salt Lake City newspapers for the benefit of oncoming overlanders.[110]

Entrepreneurial willingness to employ devious tactics in the quest for business and profit continued to be a common feature of trail life. Emigrant speculations about suspicious trader-Indian cooperation in thievery and plunder were rife. One entrepreneur's signboards directing emigrants to his Missouri River ferry were regularly torn down by competitors. A ferry operator near Fort Laramie circulated Indian danger stories to entice river-crossing traffic to his ferry. And the recurring Green River feud achieved new levels of notoriety in 1854. Nine mountaineers led by an inebriated Elisha Ryan forcibly seized one of the Mormon ferries and proceeded to cross emigrants and pocket the fees. Before the arrival of the hastily summoned Mormon sheriff and posse, however, a sobered Ryan surrendered both boat and proceeds and the excitement temporarily waned.[111]

Prices at the various ferries were slightly lower than in earlier years. From the travelers' perspective they remained sufficiently inflated (up to $8 at the Green River) for overlander complaints. William Jones lamented, "I tell you they show no mercy to travelars," while George McCowen moaned, "Considering the amount of these tolls, the amount of provisions on hand and the amount which it will be necessary to purchase to take us through, then counting up the money at our disposal, casts rather a blue streak over our prospects."[112] In a long and vituperative editorial in the *Deseret News,* Brigham Young corroborated these repetitious emigrant dissatisfactions. Mincing no words, the Mormon chieftain warned passing overlanders about the "Land Sharks" infesting the trails:

> While the emigration is passing, these characters line the road from the Sweet Water to the summit of the Nevada; and like the wreckers on the sea-board, lie in wait to prey upon the misfortunes, carelessness, and ignorance of the traveler— having no eye to pity, and, unless at the utmost rates of extortion, no disposition to save.—Like their namesake of the deep, and like the turkey buzzards and prairie wolves upon land, they note their victims afar off, and hang upon their course with a perseverance worthy of a better cause. The main outfit stock in trade is raw whiskey, and vile beer, varied occasionally by a little money, one or more animals, and now and then a few pounds of butter. Thus equipped they bivouac along the line of travel, constantly on the alert to ply their vocation by driving hard bargains for such animals as have become a little jaded, foot sore, or otherwise temporarily unservable. . . .
>
> When slightly unsuccessful in their cut throat trade, or when their inordinate thirst for gain with little labor is not fully gratified, many turn stock drivers and herdsmen, with this peculiarity, that the animals they take such good care of are not their own.

Young likewise attacked those Mormons exhibiting land-shark propensities and called for stern measures to elevate the region's "moral atmosphere."[113]

Between 1855 and 1858 a major western war with the Mormon empire was narrowly averted, Indians became more hostile, and overlanders more scarce. In these changing circumstances many of the entrepreneurs attracted to the overland trails during the prosperous gold rush years departed for more lucrative locales. A few prudently re-established themselves closer to the protective umbrella of army forts. The general exodus of traders occasioned frequent commentary among trail travelers, who routinely dismantled the vacated trading posts to fuel evening fires. In 1855 and 1856 the once-flourishing Ragtown dwindled to three small huts. In those same years two of the oldest and most famous trail outposts were completely abandoned—Fort Boise in 1855 and Fort Hall in 1856.[114] The absence of a few entrepreneurs, however, merely reduced competition; it did not jeopardize the availability of goods and services on which overlanders had come to rely. Trading posts and river-crossing facilities remained abundant. In the course of extolling the trail on the north side of the Platte River in 1858, for example, a Council Bluffs newspaper asserted that every stream was bridged as far west as the Sweetwater River.[115]

Those entrepreneurs persevering during this time of consolidation were usually old-time mountaineers who had never neglected the well-paying Indian trade, even during the heady days of the overland boom.

They were thus still able to prosper when the overland tide dwindled to alarming levels, as it did in 1855, when only 2,000 emigrants trailed to the West Coast. Familiar western fixtures such as Ward and Guerrier, Bordeaux, Richard, Archambeault, Dripps, and Bissonette continued their customary pursuits, and numerous other mountain traders and ferrymen are mentioned in the trail literature.[116] Many did well. Joseph Bissonette, who in 1857 moved his enterprise to Deer Creek to capitalize on the Indian traffic at agent Thomas Twiss's new headquarters, employed fourteen clerks and teamsters. Auguste Archambeault's trading operations along the Sweetwater prospered sufficiently to permit the purchase of two Missouri farms. The Richard brothers reportedly realized over $200,000 apiece from their Platte bridge and trading posts. They would have been wealthy men had not gambling losses cost them their fortune.[117]

Despite the general retrenchment, new enterprises were still being launched. After all, postal developments insured considerable trail traffic, as did overland freighting to Salt Lake City, to army forts, and, beginning in 1857, to the major military complex in Utah. Among the new developments during this period were the way stations in Brigham Young's ambitious design to plant supportive settlements every fifty miles along the trail to Utah. One of the largest of these was the Genoa community. Begun near the Loup Fork crossing approximately 100 miles west of the Missouri River in 1857 by Henry Hudson and others, Genoa's 162 pioneers immediately brought some 400 acres under cultivation. The following year a mill was introduced as well as a ferry at the Loup Fork crossing. Genoa prospered until 1859, when Pawnee Indians were removed to that area and the fledgling community had to be evacuated.

Elsewhere the significant network of Mormon Trail stations ended abruptly in 1857, when the Saints abandoned (and sometimes destroyed) their dwellings in response to Brigham Young's call to gather in Salt Lake to prepare for the impending conflict with the United States. Thus the Brigham Young Express and Carrying Company was terminated, and the controversially acquired Fort Bridger, which Lewis Robinson had since rebuilt, was forsaken. The Carson Valley suffered a severe population loss when the Mormons departed in 1857, although the Mormon exodus did end the valley's long-smoldering Mormon-Gentile dissension.[118]

Many of the trail's new entrepreneurial thrusts occurred immediately west of the Missouri River, where settlers were inching farther onto the prairies. Emigrants regularly commented on the normal indicators of this westward movement: squatters' cabins (which, if not deserted, were prime sources of fresh milk), impressive fields of corn and grain, speculatively surveyed town sites (usually without buildings). While the extent of new settlement varied on the several routes leading west from the jumping-off points, by 1858 emigrants traveled between 100 and 300 miles through territory which could no longer be described as "unsettled"—an extremely significant development insofar as overland travelers were concerned.[119] Indeed, it was doubtless the expectation that such settlement would accelerate which prompted the Florence Bridge Company to announce plans for raising up to $500,000 through sales of stock to finance a bridge across the Missouri. The bridge did not materialize, but since owners of steamboat ferries advertised that they made river crossings in as little as one minute, emigrants and other travelers were certainly not much inconvenienced, especially if they crossed the river at "La Platte Precinct" in Nebraska Territory, where the worthy citizenry advertised a *free* ferry service.[120]

Nearly 20,000 overlanders trailed through South Pass en route to West Coast destinations in 1859; in 1860 approximately 10,000 made the trip. Yet this slight upsurge in overland travel accounted only indirectly for the entrepreneurial achievements of those years. The most striking new developments were prompted by the way station requirements of overland stagecoaching (to Denver and the Pike's Peak country as well as to Salt Lake City and California) and the Pony Express.[121] When coupled with the rapidity of rural and urban settlement west of the Missouri River, east of the traditional California and Oregon destination points, and on all sides of Salt Lake City, the net result was an overland trip which resembled the pioneering ventures of the early 1840s in name only. For in 1859 and 1860 there were, literally, hundreds of supportive facilities en route. Rarely did the emigrant travel more than twenty-five or thirty miles without encountering at least one habitation. Usually there were more. It made no difference whether the overlander began from St. Joseph and traveled via the overland trail on the south side of the Platte River or whether he launched out from Council Bluffs–Omaha on the north side of the Platte— supportive facilities were everywhere.[122]

And they were of all types. One enterprising peddler followed the 1859 emigration with a wagonload of trade goods which featured oysters and pickles. The fare at Joseph Bissonette's Deer Creek post was considerably less sophisticated; at least so thought world traveler Richard Burton: "I wish my enemy no more terrible fate than to drink excessively with M. Bissonette of M. B.'s liquor." Burton's detailed descriptions of the stagecoach stops ably conveyed the drab monotony of most posts and stations as well as the primitive quality of the sleeping accommodations available there: "Upon the bedded floor of the foul 'doggery' lay, in a seemingly promiscuous heap, men, women, children, lambs, and puppies, all fast in the arms of Morpheus, and many under the influence of a much jollier god." At one of the more fashionable "ranches"—fitted out with wallpaper and ornaments—the proprietress set an appetizing table in addition to providing welcome laundry services, still another innovation in overland travel.[123]

Because there were so many posts, gimmickry and advertising came into vogue as tactics necessary for attracting customers. Anyone who has traveled in the modern West and been lured off the highway to a gasoline station and/or restaurant-curio shop by signs advertising the buffalo or rattlesnakes to be seen there will appreciate the cunning of the promoter at Independence Rock who kept a chained grizzly bear at his post, or the one just west of the Green River who exhibited a young grizzly at his trading station.[124] And anyone familiar with the vagaries of neon signs can sympathize with the Ash Point "grocer" of 1859 who specialized, according to his billboard, in "Butte Reggs, Flower & Mele." That eager entrepreneur, however, was unable to blame burned-out bulbs for his eccentric spelling. A miner hastening to Pike's Peak offered an explanation of the grocer's predicament: "At present he does not seem to be overrun with customers; but how can a reasonable man expect the patronage of Pike's Peakers, when he spells flour with a 'w'?"[125] Even mileage markers were appearing. Richard Burton in 1860 at O'Fallon's Bluffs reported, "A sign-board informed us that we were now distant 400 miles from St. Joe., 120 from Fort Kearny, 68 from the upper, and 40 from the lower crossing of the Platte."[126]

Aside from blanketing the trail with service facilities, private enterprise was responsible for few innovations in the closing years of the decade. By then a few traders west of the Green River had accumulated large enough herds of emigrant cattle to occasion commentary by passing travelers, who were particularly intrigued to find that cattle could be wintered in the immediate vicinity.[127] Trail prices, at least at river crossings, had fallen considerably by 1859 and 1860. The continuing duplication of facilities, a phenomenon illustrated perfectly by the second bridging of the Platte River, was finally having an impact upon the cost of an overland journey. In 1859 there were two Platte ferries, one at Deer Creek and the other at the old Mormon ferry site approximately thirty-one miles upriver. John Richard's bridge was situated about six miles below the Upper Ferry location. At bridge or ferry $2 to $2.50 was the assessed fee per wagon. Surprisingly, however, Louis Ganard, flush with some $30,000 earned during the preceding years at his Sweetwater River bridge, also entered the competition in 1859. Ganard's 1,000-foot span, located at the Mormon ferry site within six miles of Richard's enterprise, was completed by the 1860 travel season. The new facility captured, at least that year, the bulk of the emigrant traffic, although one ferry, presumably at Deer Creek, remained in business.[128]

Richard's previous responses to competitors suggest that he was considerably distressed with Ganard's intrusion. The mountaineer had earlier paid one company $300 to discontinue their ferrying activities but neglected to destroy their boat, which remained moored on the north side of the Platte a few miles upriver from his bridge. An 1859 overland contingent reinstituted this ferry after one of their number swam the swollen river with a rope to acquire the vessel. Richard was furious. When this group had refused to cross at his bridge for $2.50 per wagon he had declared that they would pay double when they returned to use the bridge, as he promised they would have to do. When the bridge owner realized, however, that the emigrants would ferry successfully unless stopped, he and three heavily armed cohorts tried to interfere. Following additional warnings, Richard finally announced that he would direct 500 nearby Indians to attack the train and scalp all the travelers. But since one emigrant kept a rifle aimed at Richard throughout the encounter the angered mountaineer could do nothing but threaten and swear—and he did plenty of that.[129]

Tensions between emigrants and trailside entrepreneurs, a pervasive characteristic of overland travel, had clearly not abated by decade's end. Most confrontations continued to be prompted by suspicions of theft, concerns about extortionate charges, or vested interests. It was thus no surprise that John Wilson, after losing an ox near the California end of the trail, assumed that traders from a nearby post were responsible: ". . . these traders on the plains is very hard cases." Or that Thomas Cramer ranked French Canadian entrepreneurs with Indians in their moral, intellectual, and physical attributes. Nor was it surprising that fatalities ultimately resulted from disputes over ferry charges. Cramer provided sketchy details of an encounter at the Marysville crossing of the Big Blue River, where he and other overlanders believed the ferry charge of $2 per wagon to be "enormous": "Some of these men a few days Since, under the influence of . . . whiskey, exasperated at the enormity of the charge, undertook to Seize the boat, which brought on a difficulty—revolvers were used and two of the gold Seekers were killed and one desperately wounded."[130]

Road builder Frederick Lander found it necessary to station a reliable representative at South Pass to provide oncoming overlanders with trustworthy information regarding the newly surveyed government trail. In his reports Lander complained about the "designing parties" (in particular, Mormons and mountaineers) who energetically directed emigrants to travel on the established trail while casting aspersions on the new government route—which bypassed their trading posts and Green River ferries. The agent Lander left at South Pass to observe the winter weather and provide accurate route information was murdered in March, 1859, presumably by the "designing parties."[131]

Overlanders enjoyed a much more amenable relationship with the settlers past whose farms and through whose communities they traveled. In addition to the availability of good water, butter, and milk, there were evening dances to be attended. As Mary Guill learned in 1860 at the small Wood River settlement of Mendota near Fort Kearny, there was even a local newspaper to be purchased—the *Huntsman's Echo*.[132]

The symbols of a changing West which overlanders remarked upon in

1859 and 1860 were varied: newspapers printed in towns beside the trails, a capitol building for the new territory of Nebraska rumored to have cost $100,000 (and situated in Omaha *west* of Council Bluffs across the Missouri River), a liberty pole thirty miles west of Omaha in the new town of Fremont, farmers' sod houses, fledgling settlements (paper towns in some instances) where speculation in land beckoned lawyers who were already prominently displaying their shingles, burgeoning suburbs at Forts Kearny and Laramie, some "thirty small houses" near Richard's Platte bridge, a sixth of the Carson Valley enclosed in fences, and brick buildings at Carson City in Nevada.[133]

Two long-time symbols of overland travel were conspicuous by their absence. In the early 1840s overland emigrants had laboriously forded every river and had eagerly looked forward to reaching the oases of Forts Laramie, Hall, and Boise. In comparison, 1860 overlanders desiring to ford rivers often had to fight off irate ferry and bridge operators. In place of a handful of fur-trading posts there were multitudes of stores, stagecoach stations, grogshops, gambling emporiums, and hotels. Fort Laramie was still there, but for the last eleven years it had been an army fortress. And the Hudson's Bay Company outposts of Forts Hall and Boise, so intimately associated with overland travel from the very first year emigrant wagons rolled west, were no more. Perhaps no other developments so graphically revealed that an epoch had ended. Overland travel had taken on a new form.

CHAPTER NINE

The Mormon "Halfway House"

"It cost nothing to get in, but a great deal to get out"

The BELEAGUERED MORMON FAITHFUL ABANDONING their Nauvoo, Illinois, homes in 1846 yearned for a respite from the Gentile harassment which had forced similar removals from other locations in previous years. Anxious for peace and tranquillity, they hoped that the remote valley of the Great Salt Lake to which Brigham Young led them in 1847 would finally provide the isolation necessary to the development of a kingdom powerful enough to resist future tormentors. But even as the Mormons began their westward hegira, they encountered large numbers of Gentile emigrants likewise trailing west. In 1847 the relationships between Saint and Gentile traveling groups were amicable and mutually beneficial: the overlanders secured safe passage across the Platte River in exchange for goods so desperately needed by the destitute Saints that one of their leaders gratefully wrote, "It looked as much of a miracle to me to see our flour and meal bags replenished in the Black Hills, as it did to have the children of Israel fed with manna in the wilderness."[1]

Thus began the dilemma which bedeviled Mormons for the remainder of the antebellum period. Trading with the Gentile throngs bound for Oregon and California or ferrying them across raging rivers was irresistibly profitable. But it guaranteed continued contact. And as long as the Gentile nation remained hostile to Mormon beliefs and practices, contact insured conflict. Friction was similarly assured by the steady stream of Mormon converts who yearly trekked to the Salt Lake haven on some of the same trails used by Gentile travelers bound for the West Coast. Indeed, the very existence of a sizable settlement relatively close to the Oregon-California Trail virtually precluded isolation, since thousands of overlanders eagerly detoured via the Saint oasis to rest, recuperate, reprovision, reoutfit—and to satisfy their curiosities about Mormon manners and morals. The anti-Mormon reactions of some of the passing emigrants, and particularly the enthusiasm with which they were publicized, contributed significantly to the U.S. Army's 1857 march on the intermontane kingdom to chastise the Saints. Accordingly, an evaluation of the interaction between Mormons and overlanders may be as necessary to an understanding of the causes of the "Mormon War" as it is to proper assessment of the overland emigrating experience.[2]

Brigham Young's plans for the desert mecca were ambitious, extending even to the acquisition of a seaport on the Pacific Coast. Initial explorations into the surrounding area were quickly followed by colonizing missions. Passing emigrants thus found not only an impressive city by the lake but also clusters of small communities presumably located to defend the "inner cordon of settlements" and to sustain the all-weather route to San Diego along the "Mormon Corridor." Within ten years of their arrival at Salt Lake, Mormon pioneer-missionaries under Young's close supervision had established ninety-six separate settlements. Outposts fanned out from the Salt Lake City axis in all directions: southwest along the corridor to San Bernardino, California, southeast to Moab, Utah, northeast to Forts Bridger and Supply, north to the Fort Lemhi mission on Idaho's Salmon River, and westward to Mormon Station in the Carson Valley. An impressive testament both to Young's aspirations and abilities, this extensive domain initially spanned some 1,000 miles from its northernmost to southernmost point and 800 miles from east to west. It incorporated one sixth of the territory of the United States.[3]

Population growth was commensurate with physical expansion, reflecting both a high birthrate and a steady stream of incoming converts, many from Britain, Scandinavia, and other European locations. According to the 1850 census, Salt Lake City residents comprised about half of Utah Territory's total non-Indian population of 11,380. Ten years later Salt Lake City's 8,236 inhabitants represented only a fifth of the territorial settlers. Ogden (located on the site of Miles Goodyear's short-lived Fort Buenaventura), Provo, and Springville all boasted populations ranging between 1,000 and 2,000, and several other towns numbered nearly 1,000 residents. So many farms dotted the landscape that one 1860 traveler described the region north of Salt Lake as "thickly settled."[4]

For this rapid growth the Saints were much indebted to the overland emigrants, whose timely transit had insured the viability of the Salt Lake Valley settlements. Extremely anxious to expedite their California journey in any possible manner, at least 10,000 forty-niners detoured via the Mormon oasis. They anticipated exchanging wagons, lame draft animals, household furniture, tools, clothing, and other excess supplies and provisions for a horse or mule and sufficient flour and vegetables to sustain them during the remainder of their journey.[5] Thousands more traveled via Salt Lake in 1850 and in subsequent years. The impact of the resultant

Ft. Lemhi

Snake River

Ft. Hall

Salt Lake Cutoff

Oregon-California Trail

South Pass

Great Salt Lake

California Trail

Humboldt R.

Ogden

Fts. Bridger and Supply

Golden Pass Road

Hastings Cutoff

Salt Lake City

Provo
Springville

Mormon Station

Moab

Green R.

Mormon Corridor

Death Valley

Colorado R.

Las Vegas

The Mormon Kingdom

San Bernardino

0   100   200

miles

N. Platte R.

Ft. Laramie

Bier

MAP 8

transactions had an extremely salutary effect on the depressed valley economy—as contemporary Mormons clearly comprehended. Through what they believed to be the providential miracle of the gold rush, an inestimable amount of useful material was suddenly made available on extraordinarily favorable terms to a community struggling for survival.[6]

Even that which overloaded overlanders had thrown away before entering the Salt Lake Valley was secured by canny Mormon pioneers whose scavenging parties ranged far out onto the plains. John D. Lee's 1849 gleaning expedition eastward from Salt Lake City was only the best known of many such endeavors. As late as 1856 Mormons collecting debris were encountered along the Sweetwater River. Especially welcome were the tons of iron from abandoned wagons they brought back into the valley, as well as the treasures quarried from pseudo-emigrant graves. Many overlanders unable to bring themselves to throw away especially prized possessions (such as casks of brandy) adopted the tactic of burying the goods in question. The sites were identified with fake grave markers on the assumption that the specter of death would keep the goods safe until they could be retrieved at some future time. Some of these buried treasures were later sold to traders who returned to dig them up. But most were disinterred by Mormon scavenging parties familiar with the stratagem, who, according to Mormon functionary Almon W. Babbitt, "being somewhat inclined to marvellous deeds . . . gave resurrection to many bodies even before dissolution."[7]

Westbound forty-niners recognized so clearly what their passage through the Salt Lake Valley meant for the Mormon economy that they quite naturally assumed the Saints to be following an established policy of luring as many travelers as possible through the valley. Eastbound Mormons, Saints stationed at ferries and trading posts east of the valley, and Mormons circulating among the several outfitting points were all believed to be in league with the Mormon hierarchy to entice emigrants to Salt Lake by whatever means necessary. Suspicious gold seekers thus reported a host of dubious assertions pressed upon them: that the detour via Salt Lake did not lengthen the journey to California, that fire, drought, overgrazing, and/or marauding Indians made the non–Salt Lake City routes extremely precarious, that prudent travelers would not chance the trail beyond Salt Lake with their wagons. J. Goldsborough Bruff, after hearing such tales all along the trail, concluded that they were "Mormon lies" advanced to obtain valuable property cheaply. Bruff did not lead his company via Salt Lake. James Tolles's company, which did detour through the Mormon capital, withstood strong pressures there to sacrifice wagons and baggage in favor of pack animals because "they [did] not fool us for we got too well acquainted with Mormon ways and principles in Nauvoo."[8]

It is doubtful that the Mormon leadership was committed to such a policy in 1849 or any other year. Certainly if there ever had been such a policy it had been repudiated by 1850, as the Saint hierarchy recognized that thousands of passing emigrants were bane as well as blessing.[9] Brigham Young's pronouncements, from the inception of the Salt Lake settlement, candidly revealed his preference that all Gentile travelers bypass the Salt Lake Valley. Within a week after reaching the valley in 1847 Young told the first Mormon arrivals, "We do not intend to have any trade or commerce with the gentile world." In July of 1850 Young publicly encouraged emigrants then in Salt Lake to write their stateside friends to "tell them to bring their supplies, and do not depend on this place for your bread." He also refuted the assertion supposedly advanced by Almon Babbitt that emigrants could secure supplies in Salt Lake, making it clear that Babbitt had been told "positively that we could NOT supply the emigrants with food."[10]

Worried because of the still-precarious status of the Salt Lake experiment, Young particularly feared that valley Mormons would imprudently sacrifice crucial wheat and flour reserves in their enthusiasm to acquire specie and supplies. In 1850 and again in subsequent years, Young warned valley residents that if too much flour was sold or traded to transient overlanders insufficient amounts would remain for the thousands of impoverished Mormon pilgrims arriving each fall. Utilizing speeches and yearly General Epistles, Young reminded the faithful that transforming the Salt Lake Valley into a "Garden of Eden" was a work of more than one or two years, that poor harvests and starvation remained ominously possible, and that misunderstandings were certain to abound if oncoming Saints found flour priced at five or ten cents per pound because Gentile overlanders had secured so much for two or three cents per pound during the summer. The *Deseret News* even threatened to publish the names of those who trafficked to excess with Gentile passersby or who sold flour too cheaply.[11]

Young and other Mormon leaders also complained about such undesirable ramifications of overland traffic as travelers who abandoned sick or injured comrades in Salt Lake City, and those who permitted their stock to run loose through city streets and cultivated fields. In the spring of 1851, rejoicing in the new fencing and quarantine regulations designed to prevent this, Young recommended that overlanders travel via Fort Hall rather than be inconvenienced by these regulations. In 1854 the Mormon leader urged emigrants to utilize every route for travel to the West Coast *except* those winding through the Salt Lake Valley, remarking that it was a real "blessing" so few travelers were choosing to trail through the city. By 1856 Young's anti-emigrant bias was well enough known to have spawned trailside rumors, one emigrant diarist recording the tale that the Mormon mentor excommunicated all Saints who traded with Gentiles.[12]

Despite Young's attempts to keep Saint-Gentile encounters at a minimum, curious overlanders and those in need of various supplies and services flocked to Salt Lake. In the valley energetic trading invariably ensued, since most Mormon residents welcomed the opportunities for profitable trade, Young's strictures notwithstanding. In 1853 the *Deseret News* deplored the great number of Mormons who had literally "run" after emigrants "begging" them to purchase flour at what *News* editor Willard Richards judged the ridiculously low sum of two and a half to three cents per pound. Lamenting the shortsightedness that discounted possible crop failures and starvation, the editor ruefully reported that overlanders were not even bothering to drive their teams to pasture or procure hay since flour could be obtained so cheaply.[13]

Young's aversion to trading with overlanders appeared to lessen during periods of abundant harvest. In 1853 he specifically advised overland travelers that most commodities could be purchased in Salt Lake for less than the cost of hauling them there. Nevertheless, Young and other Saint leaders never wavered in admonishing their brethren to charge high prices for what they sold to Gentile emigrants. That Young was at least partially successful in his exhortations seems clear from the report of an 1856 emigrant group mistakenly thought to be Mormon: "We bought flour at $6 a barrel, if they had supposed us gentiles it would have cost us five times as much."[14]

In 1850 Young suggested that all gold seekers should be made to pay dearly since they were presumably en route to great wealth; three years later editor Richards similarly justified higher prices for overlanders "who have had no toil or expense in the matter [raising foodstuffs in the valley], either by taxes, surveys, roadmaking, bridge or ferry fixins, &c, &c." He predicted that "gentleman travelers" would recognize such a practice as "reasonable." A year earlier Richards had pointedly explained the difference between being kind to strangers by sharing freely with destitute travelers who were penniless (which was encouraged), and selling flour for "nothing" to those who could well afford to pay higher prices (which was denounced). Additional editorials not only recommended charity for indigent travelers but specifically admonished the Saints to treat all passing overlanders with fairness, particularly those who had persecuted the Saints in the States, in the hope that some would be converted and remain permanently in the valley.[15]

Although a few proselytes periodically remained to sojourn permanently with the Saints, a considerable number of overlanders passing through the valley vociferously condemned Mormon business and judicial practices as well as the already notorious religious customs. Before assessing the validity of their bitter complaints, however, a detailed review of the many varieties of Mormon-emigrant interaction in the Salt Lake vicinity is necessary.

Each spring valley observers carefully watched for the first Gentile arrivals of the year. Mormon entrepreneurs ventured far out on the trail to sell vegetables, butter, milk, eggs, and chickens to oncoming emigrants. Usually the earliest overlanders appeared in early June, but in 1850 one speedy company reached Salt Lake City in late May. Emigrant arrivals generally continued unabated through August. During the peak gold rush years of 1849 and 1850 hundreds of weary overlanders rolled into the Mormon mecca daily, with late starters and slow travelers arriving throughout the fall. In 1849 nineteen starving late starters fought their way through snow six feet deep to reach Salt Lake City on December 1.[16] Since the earliest arrivals often jumped off from the frontier before spring grasses could sustain forage, they counted heavily on the Salt Lake oasis for reprovisioning, as they had kept their stock alive on grain and flour. Even more dependent on the Mormon center were destitute travelers whose applications for aid at Fort Laramie had enabled them to secure provisions sufficient only to reach Salt Lake.[17]

For most of these "golden pilgrims," as one Mormon dubbed them, reaching Salt Lake City meant a well-earned rest at what Benjamin Ferris, Secretary of Utah Territory, termed the "half-way house between the eastern and western portions of the continent." Gold rusher Calvin Taylor's comments on reaching the city are illustrative of its significance to overland emigrants: "This was a joyful occasion to us notwithstanding our prospects for the future, as it afforded an opportunity of present relief and of obtaining the rest we all so much needed."[18] With so many gold seekers pouring into Salt Lake City in 1850 the entrepreneurially inclined *Deseret News* editor offered to print their names, home addresses, and Salt Lake arrival and departure dates in the newspaper and to send a copy of that issue to a designated recipient in the States, all for twenty-five cents. An analysis of the more than 600 overlanders who chose this means of communicating their progress to relatives and friends reveals how important the Mormon halfway house was: the average length of stay in Salt Lake City was six and a half days. Virtually no traveler departed from Salt Lake without laying over for at least a day, while some remained nearly five weeks before resuming their westward pilgrimage.[19]

Since most overlanders traveled via Salt Lake for purposes of trade, their week in the city was principally devoted to seeking out the best possible bargains. Initially, these negotiations were conducted only with resident Saints. But alert stateside entrepreneurs were quick to establish stores in Salt Lake City where transient travelers could procure merchandise identical to that available in Missouri and Iowa outfitting points. James M. Livingston and John H. Kinkead of St. Louis opened the first such establishment in the fall of 1849. Despite the eight or ten clerks they employed, the press of business with valley residents and overland emigrants was so great that travelers sometimes found it nearly impossible to complete transactions. According to local rumor the new merchants were able, after only two weeks of business, to pay their bills and send nearly

"Great Salt Lake City in 1853, looking south." Overlanders' impressions of the Mormon mecca varied.

From Piercy, *Route from Liverpool to Great Salt Lake Valley* (1855)

$20,000 back to Missouri. The next year Livingston and Kinkead freighted sixty wagons of merchandise to Salt Lake City. However, their monopoly was shortlived, since other non-Mormon merchants eager to tap the valley and overland trade quickly followed. Among them were Benjamin Holladay and Theodore F. Warner of Weston, Missouri. Opening their Salt Lake emporium in 1850, by the following year they were freighting equally impressive amounts of merchandise to Salt Lake City.[20]

The isolation Brigham Young so desired was further precluded by the aggressive advertising these resourceful merchants conducted in the eastern states. In March, 1852, for example, Livingston and Kinkead, Holladay and Warner, and O. H. Cogswell, three of the many Salt Lake City "merchants and traders," jointly advertised in the St. Joseph *Gazette* that every item the traveler might need was available in Salt Lake City at a fair price. These enterprising advertisers recommended outfitting lightly on the frontier and reprovisioning in Salt Lake City. There was logic—and potential profit—in their suggestion: the most difficult portion of the trip could thus be made with relatively fresh animals whose effectiveness had not been reduced by needlessly pulling heavy loads during the easier half of the journey.[21]

In addition to these commercial emporiums, a plethora of enterprising local merchants and artisans regularly advertised their goods and services in the columns of the Salt Lake City *Deseret News.* Local advertisers sought to incorporate emigrant endorsements into their appeals whenever possible. In 1850 the *Deseret News* carried the advertisements of three surgeon-dentists (one of whom also styled himself an oculist), several merchants, two sellers of fresh beef, the proprietor of an eating house, a hunter of stray stock, and two blacksmiths. One smith, A. L. Lamareaux, ingeniously advertised his "Emigrant's Blacksmith Shop," succeeding in mentioning every possible appealing feature. After referring to his excellent location on the overland trail north of Salt Lake City in the midst of choice grazing land, Lamareaux noted that butter, cheese, milk, and garden vegetables were readily available from surrounding farmers. Indeed, Lamareaux assured, emigrants could even earn money by working on a nearby road then under construction while their cattle were recuperating and smithwork was being done.[22]

Year by year the number and variety of available goods and services increased. In 1851 a tanner, a turning and machine-shop operator, two more dental surgeons, two watchmaker-jewelers, two daguerreotype specialists, a lumber seller, and a grass and hay cutter began advertising in the *Deseret News;* the following year advertisements for bakers, milliners, and barbers appeared. By 1852, according to the *Deseret News* advertising columns, travelers could patronize several eating houses and hotels. In 1853 the United States Hotel owners advertised the only bar in the city, while variety stores and a "Straw Bonnit and Hat Manufactory" had also been added to the many conveniences available in the fast-growing half-way house. By 1856 clothiers, weavers, druggists, sign painters, saddlers, and operators of vegetable markets were also actively engaged in trade.[23]

Hotels and eating houses notwithstanding, a great many overland emigrants boarded with Mormon families during their stay in Salt Lake City. Others rented or even purchased vacant houses. Apparently these arrangements were made quite informally, usually with emigrants stopping at a progressive-looking residence to request board for the duration of their respite in the Salt Lake Valley. For the luxury of sitting down at a table to eat, of dining on such trail rarities as vegetables and milk, and of the reasonable prices charged (fifty cents per meal was common), overlanders were most appreciative. Ansel McCall, in 1849, described his first meal with a Mormon family with obvious enthusiasm: "Our hostess, with dispatch, set before us a sumptuous meal of new potatoes, green peas, bread and butter, with rich, sweet milk. It is needless to say that the hungry wayfarers, who for months had not seen these delicacies, did ample justice to this bountiful repast. The memory of this feast will live with me forever."[24]

The total effect of all this was significant. To be able to interrupt the once-formidable overland journey for an extended sojourn in a large city where an emigrant could feast on memorable cuisine, board in a bona fide hotel, have a likeness made to send back to relatives, have his hair cut, his watch repaired, and even eyeglasses prescribed must have altered the attitudes with which travelers faced the overland journey. Certainly there were no other places on the overland trail where a gold rusher could write, "Tomorrow we leave civilization, pretty girls, and pleasant memories," as James Hutchings did in 1849 when his outfit prepared to depart from Salt Lake City.[25]

Overlanders needing these goods and services soon learned that most Mormons, in keeping with the admonitions of their leaders, bargained shrewdly. During the first years of the Salt Lake settlement the Saints placed highest priority on useful articles, preferring to exchange goods with passing emigrants on a barter basis rather than to sell for cash. Forty-niner Amos Josselyn, who reached Salt Lake City in mid-July, wrote to his wife, "We can trade groceries for anything that they have but they will not sell for money, for they have plenty and cannot buy what they want with it." With many gold seekers so anxious to reach California that they wanted to exchange their oxen, wagons, and surplus supplies for faster-moving horses or mules with pack saddles, considerable trading material was available. The ensuing merchandise exchanges invariably redounded to the benefit of the valley residents, who were able to set prices, as one 1852 emigrant observed, at whatever "their consciences will allow."[26]

The resultant rates of exchange, when compared with stateside prices, reveal that most emigrants traded at a substantial loss. Wagons, for example, quickly glutted the market and brought little, if anything. But emigrants had to pay from $100 to $200 or its trade equivalent for fresh horses, mules, and even cattle. The extremely inexpensive charges for flour the *Deseret News* editor so bemoaned were apparently unknown prior to the summer of 1852, before which time the price for flour fluctuated considerably, ranging up to $25 per 100 pounds in 1850. That year, however, flour was almost equally expensive all along the trail. The Salt Lake prices of other commodities—such as bacon, beef, coffee, and sugar—were actually lower than at other trail trading stations.[27]

Emigrants with an ample supply of desirable merchandise or funds usually had few difficulties in reoutfitting, although in 1850 a scarcity of provisions in the Salt Lake Valley forced many who had gone that way to depart empty-handed. Incoming overlanders who had little to trade and nothing with which to buy faced the greatest difficulties. Unless they arranged to proceed with other emigrants, their only recourse was to obtain employment until they were in a financial position to continue their journey. The existence of the rapidly growing Mormon settlement with its employment opportunities for destitute travelers or for those delaying their journey while traveling companions received necessary medical attention thus proved a boon to the overland emigrant.[28]

Whether or not they compared Mormon prices with those demanded by other trail entrepreneurs, most overlanders were convinced that the Latter-Day Saints were possessed of considerable financial acumen. As the emigrants encountered Mormon outposts on their westward journey they offered a steady stream of comments: at the Mormon ferry on the North Platte River forty-niner William Kelly observed that the Saints were "always on the lookout for gain as well as glory—or salvation, more properly speaking"; after encountering a Mormon trader and his wife near Soda Springs, John Banks indicated that "the Mormons are alive to any means of acquiring wealth"; while another forty-niner asserted that if the traveler was "wily" he could "safely go by the Mormon city" to trade stock, rest, and reprovision. By 1853 some emigrants felt that Mormon prices had become so "exorbitant" that they encouraged oncoming overlanders to bypass the valley settlements completely since there remained "no advantage whatever" in traveling via Salt Lake City for reprovisioning or reoutfitting.[29]

While the overlanders complained even more bitterly about the high prices various private entrepreneurs charged along the trail, doubtless what made Mormon prices seem burdensome to many was their longer stay at the Salt Lake oasis. The tempting assortment of available goods and services also helped loosen emigrant purse strings. John Hawkins Clark, whose company rested for nine days in the Salt Lake vicinity in 1852, probably summed up the reactions of most overlanders when he inscribed in his diary upon leaving the last Mormon settlement: "Visiting Salt Lake valley and city was something like taking in the Irishman's show; it cost nothing to get in, but a great deal to get out."[30]

Although reoutfitting, resting, and recruiting stock were the most important reasons for a pilgrimage via the Salt Lake Valley, the Deseret judiciary was of comparable significance for emigrants with grievances arising from the overland trip. Even though disputes between Latter-Day Saints and some federal judicial appointees for Utah Territory helped bring on the "Mormon War" of 1857-58, it seems clear that the overland emigrants received fair treatment in the Church-administered lower courts, where their travel-oriented difficulties were adjudicated. Army officers Howard Stansbury and John Gunnison, after spending the fall and winter of 1849 and the spring and summer of 1850 in a scientific survey of the Great Salt Lake and surrounding area, both commented on the generosity, fairness, and impartiality with which passing emigrants were treated by the Saints in and out of court. Gunnison, seeking to explain why Mormon justice was receiving such a bad press, explained that over-landers losing cases often made vituperative remarks about the courts and Church leaders—usually the cause of additional fines for contempt of court. According to Gunnison, these dissatisfied litigants then unjustifiably "circulated letters far and near, of the oppression of the Mormons."[31]

For obvious reasons, emigrant reliance on the Mormon judicial apparatus was primarily a feature of the gold rush years.[32] A high percentage of gold seekers had formally organized into companies—complete with constitutions, bylaws, officers, and, most problematic for what transpired, jointly owned property. When the vagaries of human nature prevailed and the companies disintegrated in bickering and frustration—as most of them did—an equitable distribution of property was mandatory. It would not do for someone to be given a wagon without a draft animal or the means to procure one. Since disintegrating joint-stock companies or traveling partnerships were not always able to make these distributions to the satisfaction of all concerned, the presence in Salt Lake City of lawyers, courts, judges, and a police force capable of enforcing legal decisions was fortuitous.

Attorneys Hosea Stout, Henry G. Sherwood, and William Wines Phelps practiced frequently in the courts of William Snow and Aaron F. Farr during the summer of 1850, when emigrant litigation reached its apogee. The tribunals on occasion commenced their work at seven in the morning, often labored late into the night, and at least once remained in session until dawn on a particularly involved emigrant case. Hosea Stout's diary reveals that from early June through late August of 1850 he was almost continuously employed at law by passing emigrants. While court dockets were primarily jammed with property-distribution cases (which even a meticulous diarist like Stout finally found "not very interisting to relate"), there was a great variety of litigation.[33]

The numerous breach-of-contract cases were vitally important to emigrants who had paid an agreed-upon sum to be transported to California only to be unceremoniously abandoned somewhere near Salt Lake

City. While such lawsuits were occasionally dismissed for lack of evidence or false information, the verdict generally favored the plaintiffs. Frequently agreements were also reached out of court after legal proceedings had been instituted. Sometimes the aggrieved party was the entrepreneur, whose passengers had appropriated his outfit or had endeavored to depart without paying anything for their passage to that point. Periodically Salt Lake City police were dispatched to retrieve emigrants who attempted to flee the city without complying with the court's decision. In one instance Mormon constabulary traveled nearly 200 miles westward to apprehend thieves who had taken most of a small emigrant party's outfit. The stolen property was recovered and returned to the emigrants.[34]

Overlanders also sought redress for other journey difficulties. One Iowa traveler was acquitted of the charge that he had abandoned a sick passenger, leaving him to die on the trail; another overlander brought suit against several emigrants operating a temporary ferry over the Weber River. They had guaranteed the crossing, but after accidentally losing the plaintiff's complete outfit in the river they refused to reimburse him for his loss. When the emigrant won his case the ferrymen threatened an appeal, until learning that other unfortunate patrons contemplated similar suits. Quickly paying the 75-dollar judgment, the ferrymen immediately departed for California. Other travelers sought judgments against dishonest emigrants who attempted to sell stock they did not own or requested the court's assistance in distributing the property of deceased emigrants. Stout reported that one overlander was fined $50 and costs "for selling sugar which had been fouled by the excrement of a man dying with something like the Cholera had ran on it & had been thrown away by the owners & geathered up by Def[endan]t and sold for 25 cents pr lb."

Assault-and-battery suits also came before the Salt Lake courts, as did emigrant actions against Jim Bridger and Louis Vasquez for selling horses without "vending the brand" (guaranteeing that the horse was not stolen by certifying that the brand was that of the seller), and against Thomas Moor and other Mormon ferrymen for overcharging emigrants at the Green River. Significant in the Moor case, as in several others, was the fact that Gentile emigrants did win suits against Mormons in Mormon courts. In 1849, for example, a Saint was found guilty of stealing a pair of boots from an overland emigrant, was fined $50, and was ordered to return the boots and pay the emigrant four times their value.[35]

A substantial amount of litigation was also concerned with overland emigrants who ran afoul of local ordinances. Most common in this regard was stock straying into Mormon fields and gardens, an infraction subject to penalty by action of the May, 1849, Deseret legislature. A great many of these "trespass" cases came before the courts, and the fines could be burdensome: one emigrant was assessed $74 for the damage his cattle did in two vegetable gardens one July, 1850, night. On occasion emigrants resisted the enforcement of these regulations. One such objector was the Reverend Alvin Mussett, whose cattle had been impounded after being found in a Saint's grain field. Mussett, threatening to shoot anyone trying to stop him, forcibly retrieved his cattle. He was then haled into court, fined $10 and court costs, and ordered to pay the cost of the destroyed grain. Reflecting the disdain of most Mormons for Missourians, Stout observed that the hot-tempered pastor was "a perfect specimen of the Missouri ministry." Occasionally it was not negligent emigrants but Mormon herdsmen who were fined for illegally pasturing emigrant cattle in community fields. Such entrepreneurs often arranged to herd travelers' draft animals (reported per-animal assessments rose from two cents in 1849 to twenty cents per day ten years later) while the emigrant attended to his reprovisioning and took in the sights.[36]

In 1852 the Saints established a temporary hospital at the mouth of Emigration Canyon and appointed Dr. Jerter Clinton to enforce a quarantine law aimed at preventing oncoming overlanders from introducing diseases into Salt Lake City. That the regulation quickly became a dead letter was obvious from the observations of one of that summer's passing emigrants: ". . . the hospital building is barely large enough to hold the doctor, a barrel of whiskey and a few decanters. . . . The doctor was busily employed in dealing out whiskey and appeared to have a good run of custom in that way, but how many sick emigrants he attended to I did not stop to inquire."[37]

Most emigrants seemed blissfully unaware of Brigham Young's pacifying influence with area Indians, another notable Mormon contribution to overland travel. Perhaps overlanders did not acknowledge Young's important role because his overarching commitment to Mormon interests embroiled him in a great deal of controversy with Gentile Indian agents, or because a number of emigrants suspected that the Mormons occasionally directed Indian depredations against Gentile passersby. Yet Young's maxim that "It is cheaper to feed the Indians than to fight them" is well known and reflected his policies as ex officio superintendent of Indian affairs and governor of Utah Territory. And there is no gainsaying the fact that emigrants trailed through the Mormon domain with greater safety from Indian attack than elsewhere along the overland trail. Lieutenant John Gunnison aptly summed up the situation even before Utah became a territory, remarking that the Mormons were "more than an army against the Indians on the West."[38]

Since Salt Lake City's importance to overlanders as a source of supply, justice, and security derived mainly from its geographical location, it was only natural that westbound emigrants also looked to the Saints for up-to-date information on the journey beyond Salt Lake City. After all, Mormon traffic between Salt Lake City and California had commenced with the settlement of the Salt Lake Valley, and with characteristic thoroughness the

Brigham Young, President of the Church of Jesus Christ of Latter-Day Saints and Governor of Utah Territory, in a photograph taken around 1850.

Saints had quickly familiarized themselves with their surroundings.[39] Since by the early 1850s the ruts of the overland trail were too conspicuous for anyone to require much route information, it was the gold rushers who profited most from Mormon advice and the trails and cutoffs blazed or popularized by Mormon pioneers.

For the edification of overland travelers Mormon writers produced at least four travel guidebooks succinctly summarizing the latest information. The first to appear, William Clayton's *The Latter-Day Saints' Emigrants Guide,* was probably also the most influential. Clayton carefully measured the overland trail on the north side of the Platte River by means of an ingeniously fashioned wheel roadometer while traveling to the Salt Lake Valley with the pioneer Mormon band in 1847 and returning that fall to the Kanesville winter quarters. Clayton's small guidebook, incorporating these mileage figures, was printed in St. Louis the following spring. For the portion of the trail it covered—from Kanesville to Salt Lake City—it proved to be one of the most reliable and highly praised of all gold rush guidebooks. At least two overlanders who traveled by its precepts termed it "perfect."[40]

Ira J. Willis's *Best Guide to the Gold Mines* appeared in 1849. Though considerably less pretentious and precise, it was carefully studied by information-starved emigrants. Willis was also a seasoned western traveler, having marched with the Mormon Battalion in 1846 from Fort Leavenworth to Santa Fe and then to California, where the battalion volunteers were discharged in July, 1847. Willis remained in California another year, even working for a time at John Sutter's sawmill, before traveling to the Salt Lake settlements in the summer of 1848 with a small group of other battalion veterans. Their trip, made with loaded wagons, significantly altered subsequent overland travel since the battalion veterans pioneered two important new wagon routes. The *Best Guide to the Gold Mines* thus contained updated information on the trails between Salt Lake City and California unavailable in other travel guides. Some overlanders, however, found it too sketchy to be of much value. Willis's hand-written guidebook had been hastily prepared and consisted only of two folded sheets of paper sewn together. Apparently different copyists were involved in reproducing the pamphlets, for word spellings varied. The guidebooks were sold, usually for $1, not only in Salt Lake City but along the trail as well.[41]

Considerably more sophisticated were B. H. Young and J. Eagar's *Emigrant's Guide,* available in Salt Lake City in the summer of 1850, and Joseph Cain and Arieh C. Brower's *Mormon Way-Bill, to the Gold Mines,* published by the *Deseret News* in February, 1851. The Young and Eagar guidebook concisely traced the trail from Salt Lake City to San Francisco, while in forty pages Cain and Brower described the last half of the overland journey, from Pacific Springs to the California gold fields, likewise incorporating the most recent trail developments. The Cain and Brower guidebook sold for $1 and apparently was available on the Missouri River frontier for sale to overlanders commencing the long journey.[42]

While thousands of overland travelers used Clayton's guidebook, neither the Willis, Young and Eagar, nor Cain and Brower volumes was disseminated as broadly. All four, however, affected the travel patterns of California gold rushers by publicizing variant trail routes either discovered or improved by Mormon travelers. Clayton's guidebook highlighted the overland trail on the north side of the Platte River, which emerged as the main travel thoroughfare in the 1850s. Cain and Brower were the only guidebook authors to mention the "Golden Pass Road" which served as an alternate trail through the Wasatch Mountains into the Salt Lake Valley during the 1850 traveling season. The Golden Pass Road was surveyed and cleared by Parley P. Pratt. Posting a large signboard to inform travelers of his new toll road, Pratt opened the route for travel about July 4, 1850. While Pratt's road afforded easier travel than the established trail, it was nine miles longer and difficult to keep in repair. Moreover, travelers resented the toll payments. Presumably for these reasons, after Pratt sold his toll rights in the spring of 1851 before departing on a Church mission, the Golden Pass Road lapsed into almost complete disuse and no longer remained a real travel option, despite the guidebook endorsement. During 1850, however, it had been heavily traveled. Perhaps 5,000 or 6,000 overlanders had trailed into the valley on the new road, enabling Pratt to collect $1,500 in tolls.[43]

The major Mormon route innovations, though, occurred west of Salt Lake City, and were explained in the Willis, the Young and Eagar, and the Cain and Brower guidebooks. These travel developments originated in the 1848 eastbound trip of Willis and other battalion veterans. Before that seminal journey overlanders had uniformly trailed into California along the Truckee River route. Despite losing three men to marauding Indians, the battalion explorers pioneered a new route along the Carson River, described that route to westbound overlanders encountered on the trail, and were principally responsible for what became the most popular travel artery into California.[44]

Additionally, the battalion members entered Salt Lake City by a new trail described to them by westbound emigrants with whom they had shared route information. This was the Salt Lake Cutoff, an immediate boon to emigrants who traveled via Salt Lake City. It meant the long journey via Fort Hall or the hazardous trip via the Hastings Cutoff could now be avoided in favor of a shorter, easier route. Indeed, the new route was pioneered in 1848 by a small party of overlanders traveling by pack mule who had tried to exit from Salt Lake City on the Hastings Cutoff but who had returned to Salt Lake City after sudden rains transformed the salt flats into a muddy quagmire. They then blazed a new trail which intersected the main Oregon-California Trail at the City of Rocks. Samuel J.

Hensley, a seasoned overland traveler, was the leader of this pack-mule party. The eastbound Mormons he met traveled over the route, found it acceptable, and publicized its existence as the Salt Lake Cutoff or the Salt Lake Road. From then on it was utilized by most overlanders who traveled via Salt Lake City, although in the vast migration of 1850 possibly 600 or more men still struggled across the Hastings Cutoff.[45]

There was yet another way to reach California from Utah. In 1849 and 1850 more than 1,000 gold rushers followed a southwestern route from Salt Lake City, many employing Mormon guides for the venture. These were overlanders who reached Salt Lake City relatively late in the traveling season, or cautious emigrants who feared that there was insufficient forage for their stock and returned to Salt Lake City after having journeyed two or three days on the Hastings or Salt Lake cutoffs. They were also travelers who had been obliged to spend considerable time in Salt Lake City while receiving medical treatment, or while pregnant wives were delivered of their offspring, or until sufficient funds had been accumulated to reprovision for the later portion of the trip. No matter what the reason for the delay in their progress, however, all were extremely anxious to reach California before the fabled gold deposits had all been discovered. But the Donner disaster had made overland emigrants properly hesitant about attempting the precarious Sierra crossings of the California Trail too late in the travel year. Not looking forward to wintering among the Saints, such persons responded enthusiastically to the blandishments of certain Mormons—some of whom even ran advertisements in the *Deseret News*—that a safe all-weather route to California was at hand along what soon came to be known as the "Mormon Corridor."[46]

Salt Lake City thus also served as a staging area for large numbers of emigrants determined to reach golden California without further postponement. Mormon elder Jefferson Hunt, who had journeyed to California and back over this trail in 1847-48, recommended the route so persuasively in the fall of 1849 that the owners of 100 emigrant wagons agreed to pay him $10 per wagon to pilot them over the southern route. Although a number of Mormon groups had already traveled safely over the trail, they had done so only with pack animals and loose stock. Because of the hardships they endured while inaugurating wagon travel along the corridor, forty-niners came to believe that Brigham Young was responsible for propagandizing the route so that Gentile emigrants would forge a wagon trail to California for Mormon benefit. One forty-niner recollected Brigham Young's persuasive techniques: "The Sunday we were there he stated in his sermon that the Lord had come to him in a vision and told him that no emigrants starting after that time over the northern route to California would arrive there, but would leave their bones to bleach on the plains or in the mountains. Some trains were frightened and went by the southern route, though to their sorrow. We came safely through the northern route, but by a tight squeeze." Whether or not the forty-niners' suspicions about Mormon motivations were true, it remained that most emigrants were desperate to reach California without delay, that the southwestern route was practicable, and that the forty-niners would have experienced a relatively uneventful journey on that trail had not many become captivated by the will-o'-the-wisp hope that a shortcut existed.[47]

Most departing emigrants congregated at Provo, forty-five miles south of Salt Lake City. Here considerable Gentile-Mormon socializing took place, with gold rushers particularly enjoying dances attended by attractive Mormon belles.[48] At least six discernible contingents of over-landers left Provo in 1849 on this southwesterly course, but, characteristically, few arrived in California in the same group with which they began. First to leave was a company of over 100 packers. They reached Los Angeles in late October following a routine journey. The Gruwell-Derr company, composed of twenty-three wagons whose owners refused to pay Hunt's guide fee, moved out just ahead of the Hunt party with a Mexican guide. After splitting into two sections, running out of food, and sending six men ahead to procure supplies in California, they ultimately received additional assistance from the Hunt contingent. The Gruwell-Derr travelers straggled into Los Angeles during December and January. Hunt's "Sand Walking Company" was initially the largest, with slightly over 100 emigrant wagons, at least twenty Mormons (mostly packers), and approximately the same number of Gentile packers. The entire company wasted seven days early in the journey searching for a shortcut of which Hunt had heard but the existence of which he did not guarantee. After this sobering failure, Hunt stuck persistently to the regular trail, but those he was guiding had not yet soured on elusive cutoffs.[49]

One of the emigrant packers, O. K. Smith, had a map, presumably of a direct route westward on which the mines could be reached in a mere twenty days with a saving of 500 miles. Smith had apparently secured this enticing information from mountaineer Elijah Barney Ward, who had traveled extensively in these regions and had been at the Bear River in 1849 encouraging emigration via Salt Lake. Hunt strongly advised against attempting the alleged shortcut. But the prospect of digging gold within twenty days was irresistible for everyone except the sixteen Mormon owners of seven wagons, who remained with Hunt on the regular trail and reached California shortly before Christmas. Eventually most of the emigrants—probably slightly over 300—thought better of their rash trailblazing attempts and returned to follow Hunt's trail to California. The remaining overlanders doggedly persisted on "Walker's Cutoff" in spite of seemingly impassable canyons and inadequate water. They suffered immeasurably as they struggled over rugged terrain to California. A few men died, some were never heard of again, and their ordeal in crossing Death Valley has become legendary.[50]

Three additional 1849 contingents brought up the rear, all prudently remaining on the main trail: the Pomeroy company, a group led by Howard Egan, and one captained by S. D. Huffaker which temporarily joined the Egan group. Probably over 100 emigrants traveled in these last companies, which reached California safely early in 1850.[51] In retrospect, the success of the approximately 750 forty-niners who followed southwestern routes to California fluctuated in relation to their willingness to remain on the regular trail. Those who did fared quite well, some completing the entire journey in as little as fifty days. The 100 or more who stubbornly attempted the variant routes—and scholars have identified at least ten—suffered immensely. The survivors of the Death Valley tribulations spent a full four months in reaching California from the day they hopefully branched off on the twenty-day shortcut.[52]

In 1850 impatient overlanders again launched out from Salt Lake City during the fall and winter on the corridor route, but few again attempted to improve its course. Joseph Cain advertised waybills in the *Deseret News,* while Barney Ward himself, now a baptized Mormon, offered to guide emigrants to Los Angeles for $10 per wagon or per company of five emigrants. The *Deseret News* editor endorsed Ward's proposal, indicating that the "South Route" was "a good road" and that those who had traveled it the preceding year had gone through "safe and are satisfied that it is far pleasanter than the Northern Route." The leaders of one ninety-wagon train sought unsuccessfully to obtain from Brigham Young a detailed report of the route made by a returning Mormon missionary party which reached Salt Lake City in August. This caravan left Salt Lake on October 8 but without Ward, whose interpretive skills had suddenly been needed to help the Saints alleviate an impending Indian conflict. The company made the journey in slightly over two and a half months, relying on a makeshift "memorandum" of the route given them by a friendly Salt Lake resident.[53]

Throughout the 1850s there was considerable traffic along the route. In addition to overland emigrants there were Mormon settlers, missionaries, freighters, and mail carriers. And year by year more Mormon colonists settled along the corridor, so that when Jules Remy and Julius Brenchley traveled along it in 1855, Mormon towns stretched out for over 270 miles from Salt Lake City to Cedar City, Utah. They also found a recently raised Mormon fort at Las Vegas before arriving at the Mormon settlement of San Bernardino, California, one month after leaving Salt Lake City.[54]

But not all overlanders who reached the Salt Lake oasis launched out again the same year to finish their journey to the Pacific Coast. In fact, westbound emigrants had so quickly recognized another of the attractive features of the Mormon halfway house that some forty-niners announced even before leaving the Missouri frontier in spring that they intended to winter in the Mormon settlements if for some reason they were unable to

In this William Henry Jackson painting, emigrants on the road toward the Salt Lake Valley pass the famous Devil's Gate, an important trail landmark.

Denver Public Library, Western History Department

complete their journey during the travel season. John D. Lee, on his 1849 scavenging mission east from Salt Lake, reported that dozens of oncoming emigrants frequently crowded around his wagon asking such questions as "What will be the chance to get fresh animals, Provisions, vegitables, Butter, cheese, &c. & could we winter in the vally? . . . Stop & write us a way bill."[55] A. W. Babbitt, arriving in Kanesville in early September with a load of mail from Salt Lake, reported that when he had left the valley 3,000 forty-niners were planning to winter there. Most of that number, however, ultimately continued on to California, many on the southwestern trail. Although precise statistics are scarce, it is certain that several thousand emigrants wintered in the Salt Lake Valley during the principal years of the gold rush. The peak probably was reached during the winter of 1850-51, when approximately 900 sojourned in the Mormon stronghold. Three years later only 200 "Winter Mormons" or "Winter Saints," as these half-year residents were called, wintered in the valley. The number continued to dwindle, finally consisting largely of overlanders trailing large herds of cattle and sheep to California.[56]

These temporary residents found the Mormon halfway house much superior to army forts or private trading posts, where a few gold rushers also waited out western winters. They were particularly attracted by Salt Lake City's varied opportunities for employment, its medical facilities, its stock-grazing and outfitting services, its religious and cultural activities, and its all-important nearness to California. Yet despite all these advantages, many of the temporarily stranded Gentiles deeply regretted their decision to winter among the Saints. Indeed, the Latter-Day Saints' treatment of the Winter Mormons was so controversial that it became a cause célèbre in the western press, thereby reinforcing the anti-Mormon attitudes already so widespread throughout America.

Nelson Slater and the Reverend J. W. Goodell were the principal publicists of the tribulations endured by the Winter Mormons. Slater, a New York–born schoolteacher, was forty-five years old in 1850 when, with his wife and three children, he interrupted his California trip to winter in the Salt Lake Valley. In 1852 with Philip L. Pratt he would co-author a much-used overland guidebook, but first he compiled a ninety-four-page indictment of the valley Mormons which he entitled, in the prolix fashion of the day, *Fruits of Mormonism; or, A Fair and Candid Statement of Facts Illustrative of Mormon Principles, Mormon Policy, and Mormon Character, by More than Forty Eye-witnesses.* The tract was published in Coloma, California, in 1851, and immediately became an invaluable resource for all newspaper editors, overlanders, and politicians sharing anti-Mormon sentiments. The Reverend Goodell also wintered in the valley in 1850-51 with his family. Becoming the spokesman for those Winter Mormons who trailed to Oregon, Goodell outlined their complaints in nine lengthy letters to the editor of the Portland *Weekly Oregonian* in the spring of 1852. These jeremiads were also widely disseminated by anti-Mormon travelers and newspaper editors, similarly serving to nurture anti-Mormon attitudes.[57]

Both men emphasized that they represented a great many disgruntled emigrants. Slater carefully explained that the California-bound group had initially intended to write individual letters back to the States recommending that no one winter in the Salt Lake Valley except in the most unavoidable of circumstances. However, while gathering in the Carson Valley preparatory to crossing the Sierras in the early spring of 1851, they had decided that the more influential course was to compile a complete and accurate summary of their experiences in pamphlet form which could be mailed to friends and relatives. While assembled in the Carson Valley a set of resolutions and a memorial to Congress describing their grievances were also drafted. Slater claimed that virtually all emigrants remaining in the Carson Valley signed the completed documents: "Nineteen out of every twenty of those to whom they were presented, signed them unhesitatingly, as expressive of their sentiments upon the topics mentioned in them." The resolutions and memorial were appended to *Fruits of Mormonism* and called upon the Congress to abolish Utah's territorial government and to establish in its place a military government "sustained by a strong garrison . . . [to] protect United States citizens, and secure to them their lawful and inalienable rights of life, liberty, and freedom of speech, guaranteed to them by the Constitution of the United States."

According to Goodell, the Oregon-bound emigrants similarly made "a solemn pledge, that if they were ever again permitted to breathe the air of freedom, they would to the utmost of their power expose the corruptions of that [Mormon] people." Indicating that his traveling companions were urging him to write "a faithful history" of their misfortunes, Goodell explained that already in the Salt Lake Valley the Oregon emigrants had appointed him chairman of a committee to draft a memorial to Congress "on the subject of our unjust and cruel treatment." If prepared, Goodell's memorial has to date not been uncovered. However, through the pages of the *Oregonian* he did request that all emigrants who had wintered in the Salt Lake Valley in 1850-51 and 1851-52 supply him with depositions detailing the injustices perpetrated by the Mormons so that he could forward them to Washington.[58] And even though the main focus of Slater and Goodell's fulminations remained on the winter of 1850-51, the western press continued to report "bitter" complaints by subsequent Winter Mormons through the winter of 1853-54.[59]

In addition to the paucity of Mormon evidence on the subject, a principal difficulty in understanding the winter milieu in the Salt Lake Valley is the occasional contradictory testimony of the emigrants themselves. On the one hand, one unidentified forty-niner remarked, "When I first came into the valley there was a large number of emigrants here, that expected to stay till spring, but now all seem determined to go on, which is mainly owing to the uncongeniality of feeling existing between the people here and themselves." On the other hand, most gold rushers were agreed that the Saints treated them with considerable cordiality *until* the traveling season was so far advanced that none but the most foolhardy would still attempt to reach Oregon or California.[60] Further, there is considerable evidence that, at least in 1850, the Saints went out of their way to encourage overlanders to winter in the valley. They had emphasized such inducements as high wages and steady employment, and underscored the lateness of the traveling season and the difficulty of all the trails leading to California.[61]

Recognizing that many of their compatriots who had traveled through the Salt Lake Valley without incident might not believe their assertions, Slater, Goodell, and other disgruntled Winter Mormons maintained that the Saints followed two policies with respect to emigrants: one in the summer, another in the winter. Thus, only in winter could a clear view of the "Mormon elephant" be seen. The discontented emigrants attempted to explain why they had been so strongly encouraged to winter in the valley, speculating that the Mormons had been motivated by the desire for capable artisans and laborers who, being transients, might be willing to work for less than permanent valley residents. Also influential, thought the overlanders, were the funds the Saints expected to raise by levying taxes upon temporary Gentile residents, as well as the concerted attempt to inflate the actual valley population by enumerating Gentile transients in the 1850 census as valley residents, thereby speeding Utah's path to statehood. One disgruntled emigrant complained that the Mormons "followed the emigrants 100 miles to take the census. We contended that they had no right to our names, for we were not citizens of Utah Territory nor never would be. But our arguments availed nothing, and we will therefore be returned to the Government as Mormons, which will be a cheat." Finally, since the Mormons did proselytize among the transient overlanders, it is probable that the missionary emphasis was of at least marginal significance as well.[62]

The anti-Mormon chroniclers cited a host of illustrations to support their wide-ranging charges. One of the most frequently voiced complaints concerned the infringement of personal rights and liberties. Freedom of speech was an especially troublesome area, particularly critical observations about the Mormon religion and its prophets. Friendly Saints tried to warn emigrants of the dangers in speaking freely about religion: "Mr. Thompson, of Great Salt Lake City, warned me to keep my tongue quiet, and I found it best so to do; for, from the many examples I have heard of, there *is* danger of having one of these 'destroying angels' pounce upon one, when one does not know it." Despite such warnings, a number of emigrants were arrested and fined for expressing opinions the Mormons judged to be offensive. Further complicating the situation were Saints who deliberately enticed emigrants into expressing their real feelings about

Mormonism, and then took them to court for doing so. One fiery over-lander was considered fortunate to have escaped with a 50-dollar fine and $30 in court costs after having been provoked to say, as Goodell prudishly explained, " '. . . if a man in the States should get as many wives as Brigham had, he would be called a notorious libertine.' (This was not exactly the word he used, it was of similar import, but a little more offensive.)" Other Mormons represented themselves as returning Californians or apostate Saints in order to tempt Winter Mormons into damaging statements. Thus in fear of informers and reprisals, many emigrants despaired of even meeting publicly to consider their predicament. In fact, those trailing to Oregon had become so accustomed to whispering whenever discussing Mormonism that they found themselves still whispering long after leaving the Salt Lake Valley.[63]

Similarly, Winter Mormons were convinced—as was Indian agent Jacob H. Holeman—that emigrant letters mailed in Salt Lake City were routinely opened and those reflecting negatively on the Mormons de-stroyed. Holeman even took to sending some of his letters by private hands to insure their safe delivery. Several emigrants claimed to have seen torn remnants of their own letters in or near the post office, and Goodell claimed that he had heard Mormons admit that the mails were being monitored in this fashion. A few overlanders who had written critically about the Mormons were subsequently threatened.

Winter Mormons believed that the Salt Lake City anti-swearing statute which appeared in February, 1851, was similarly designed to entrap emigrants—after all, they were virtually the only ones prosecuted. Goodell, who could not countenance swearing, ruefully admitted that many emi-grants paid for their verbal discretions by working on public buildings while encumbered with ball and chain, but still could not quite accept that "the devil [was] punishing sin!" An emigrant correspondent of the Mil-waukee *Sentinel* described this intriguing regulation in more detail in 1852: ". . . a man may commit what *we* call swearing—say hell and the devil, and all that sort of thing, as much as he pleases; but if he should put the usual prefix, and say 'G—d d—n it,' instead of simply 'd—n it,' he is walked before a magistrate and fined five dollars and costs. Several emigrants who have been muleted to this tune think the distinction a very queer one, especially as the faithful all indulge in d—ning to their heart's content, from the head of the Church down."[64]

Most emigrants avoided such fines but few bypassed what they consid-ered an added violation of individual rights—the 2 percent personal property tax.[65] Winter Mormons protested both this "unjust" tax (Slater resurrected the old "taxation without representation" maxim) and the manner in which it was often collected. According to Goodell, heavily armed policemen would appear without warning, evaluate Gentile posses-sions at inflated rates, demand immediate payment, and confiscate emigrant property if payment was not forthcoming. Goodell was taxed $18.80 for his two wagons, four yoke of oxen, four cows, and personal effects, while one Missouri emigrant with five wagons was assessed nearly $60. For those short on cash the tax meant parting with a wagon, precious draft animals, or other possessions. Hard-pressed overlanders particularly resented this tax because it jeopardized the successful completion of their journey.[66]

The property tax was, however, only one among many ways in which the resources of Winter Mormons were exhausted. Indeed, many Winter Mormons were convinced that the Church not only supported but encouraged the use of any tactic—from extortion to murder—which prevented Gentiles from taking cash out of the valley. By midwinter of 1850 emigrants who had contracted for specific wages with Mormon employers in the fall began to receive payment in undervalued produce instead of in cash. Many ultimately received only a small fraction of the agreed-upon salary, if they were paid at all. Ezra Benson, one of the twelve Mormon Apostles, was regarded as an especially notorious offender who provided only partial remuneration and then walked away eschewing explanation and refusing further discussion. Slater's *Fruits of Mormonism* specifically admonished emigrants to "avoid all business transactions" with the unscrupulous Benson.[67]

Another indirect but fruitful means of appropriating emigrant resources was the "nuisance" lawsuit. Winter Mormons, as Slater and Goodell explained the stratagem, invariably lost, even while winning, since Gentile defendants and not the losing Mormon plaintiffs inevitably were assessed the court costs. If the emigrant could not pay, his possessions—usually the all-important draft animals—were attached. According to one disgruntled 1854 traveler, the warped tenets of Mormon justice extended even to the Green River ferry: ". . . there is an organized country here under the jurisdiction of the Mormons and also have officers of justice   I will give an Idea how they Put their laws in force   An emigrant having got drunk there one day shot one of their dogs   they tried him and fined him 80 dollars   he not having the money sold his mothers team to pay the fine." Goodell related an experience of his own to illustrate the pattern. He purchased wheat at the rate of $3 per bushel throughout the winter, some of which local thieves stole from him. One Saint admitted the theft of three bushels of wheat and reimbursed Goodell accordingly. Yet the Saint suddenly demanded the return of his money just when Goodell and the Oregon-bound Winter Mormons were preparing to leave the valley. Accosted by an officer demanding $16 (including $7 for "costs"), Goodell insisted on a trial. The six Mormons comprising the jury surprised him with a verdict of "No cause of action." But before Goodell and his family had returned to the outlying Oregon encampment, the plaintiff, who at the initial trial had admitted taking the wheat, appealed the case to the county court. Officers quickly returned Goodell to Salt Lake City, forcing him to leave his family stranded on the road in a raging blizzard. The jury was unable to agree on a verdict so a third trial was held, where once again a "No cause of action" judgment was rendered. The astonished Goodell then heard the judge assess him, and not the self-confessed thief who had instituted the proceedings, the court costs of $75. His teams and wagons were impounded until Goodell was able to borrow the money from a friend.[68] If the incident occurred precisely as described, it was no wonder that Goodell left the Salt Lake Valley anxious to crusade against the Saints, or that the entire Oregon company halted briefly once beyond the reach of Mormon authorities for a round of speeches, gun salutes, and flag-flying—a "silabracion," as one spelled it, at being "out of mormindam."[69]

Incidents of this nature, and according to Goodell and Slater there were many, underscored another theme stressed by the anti-Mormon publicists—the absence of impartial justice for Winter Mormons. Some overlanders who wished to institute proceedings against Mormons had been prevented from doing so. Prominent Saints like Ezra Benson were assumed to be immune to litigation. Furthermore, emigrants were haled before magistrates (and sometimes so inconvenienced in the process that their departure from the Salt Lake Valley was considerably delayed) on all types of spurious charges. In these circumstances many Gentile sojourners acceded to virtually any Mormon demand, no matter how obnoxious, merely to avoid court proceedings.

Slater also accused Mormon officials of callously administering the estates of emigrants who died in the valley, thereby securing even more emigrant resources and greatly disadvantaging the family or traveling partners of the deceased. Another common allegation was that Mormons implicated in suspicious emigrant deaths were not even brought to trial. In this connection Winter Mormons frequently speculated about "Danites" who killed for the Church, and Indians who were thought to perform similar services for Saint leaders. These accusations were all incorporated in what was certainly the central assertion of Slater and Goodell: that U.S. citizens were systematically victimized in the Salt Lake Valley. Latter-Day Saints could and did, it was argued, cheat, swindle, extort, steal, and murder with impunity.[70]

There was still more in Slater and Goodell's bill of anti-Mormon particulars: the Saints were unpatriotic subversives guilty of treason. It was bad enough to be told the American flag could not be flown in the valley, it was even worse to listen to the profane harangues of Church leaders. Brigham Young, Ezra Benson, other Apostles, judges, sheriffs, and lay persons all were accused of publicly threatening to kill some or all Gentile emigrants, or of verbally abusing the U.S. government. Brigham, at the July 24, 1851, Mormon celebrations even put to a vote the proposition that all overlanders should be beheaded. The assembled Saints passed it unanimously. The anti-emigrant rhetoric, as recorded by outraged over-landers, was indeed ominous:

If I had my way, I would cut your damned throats! [judge]

If I had my way, I would drown you in the Jordan river. [deputy sheriff]

I thank God that the time is not far distant, and I shall rejoice when it comes, that I shall have the authority to pass sentence of life and death upon the Gentiles, and I will have their heads snatched off like chickens in the door yards. [judge at an emigrant's trial]

Hear it ye emigrants! if any of you say ought against the Mormons or their practices we will take off your heads! . . . Yes! we will take off your heads! by the eternal God we will do it, in spite of all the emigrants! and all the United States!! and all hell!!! [Brigham Young][71]

Only rarely did the Saints respond to these wide-ranging allegations, and then the reference was more likely to be tangential rather than a direct attempt at refutation. One such occasion was a *Deseret News* editorial of June 26, 1852, on the California gold worshipers who would soon again be passing through the city. "Know most assuredly," admonished the writer, "that if your enemies speak evil of your good deeds, and write lying, slanderous letters concerning you, and priests and editors publish the same—that you shall be rewarded for all your righteous and benevolent acts toward them, while they shall have part among those who make and love lies."

How justly and benevolently the Saints had in fact treated the overland emigrants—winter and summer—remains the unanswered question. Relatively few contemporaries attempted dispassionate assessments. Two who did were army officers Howard Stansbury and John W. Gunnison. They themselves had wintered in the valley, although a year earlier than Slater and Goodell, whose revelations they found unsatisfying. While among the Mormons they had been warmly received and fairly treated, and so, they disclosed, had all other emigrants in 1849-50. Stansbury's forthright explanation for all the furor was perceptive: "Too many that passed through their settlement were disposed to disregard their claim to the land they occupied, to ridicule the municipal regulations of their city, and to trespass wantonly upon their rights. Such offenders were promptly arrested by the authorities, made to pay a severe fine, and in some instances were imprisoned or made to labour on the public works; a punishment richly merited, and which would have been inflicted upon them in any civilized community."[72]

Benjamin Ferris, who wintered in the valley in 1852–53, was another who did not accept *Fruits of Mormonism* "as conclusive proof upon the subject." While Ferris believed that "more cases of oppression, extortion, and direct plunder have been tolerated among the Saints than could be in any other civilized community on the foot-stool," he assumed that the 1850 sufferers had exaggerated their tribulations for purposes of emphasis. The newly designated Secretary of Utah Territory also believed that even if the Mormons had initially treated the emigrants severely, "a kindlier feeling" was evolving as Mormon memories of stateside persecutions faded.[73]

Even more forcefully on the side of the Saints was the writer of the lead editorial in the May 28, 1851, *Daily Alta California*. Although viewing the Mormons as "great ninnies" in their religious beliefs, their civil and political acumen impressed the writer enough for him to assert that wayfarers living in the valley for half a year, competing with the Saints for jobs and produce, and benefiting from the existence of an orderly community, should expect to pay taxes. Moreover, the editorialist intimated that much of the Gentile-Saint strife was stirred up by the considerable criminal element in the gold rush—men who robbed their fellow emigrants, abused Indians, and no doubt acted similarly while among the Mormons.

These contemporary observers incisively identified both the shortcomings of the anti-Mormon publicists and most of the facts fueling the Winter Mormon controversy. Slater especially had fleshed out his diatribe with anti-Mormon rumors dating to the 1830s, many incapable of proof. Slater and Goodell's emphases were heavy-handed enough for readers to conclude that virtually all Gentiles wintering in the Salt Lake Valley had reason to complain of their treatment, which was not true. And, as both Goodell and Slater admitted, unprincipled overlanders did trail through the valley. Goodell acknowledged his fear that such persons would commit acts which would bring Mormon wrath down upon the innocent as well as the guilty. And Slater's compendium did include references to an emigrant who passed a counterfeit 5-dollar gold piece in the valley and another who struck a local Saint.[74]

Moreover, the impassioned emigrant protests against the property tax suggested an arrogant Gentile assumption that the primary purpose of the Mormon halfway house was to serve overlanders in distress—that the regulations of the Saints need not be taken seriously. There was little appreciation for the difficulties and expense involved in building a wilderness community or providing for the thousands of Saints arriving every autumn. Had more overlanders shared John Udell's conviction that "if travelers would manifest towards them [Mormons] a spirit of kindness, they would receive kind treatment in return, at all times," many unfortunate incidents could have been avoided.[75]

Nonetheless, it would be a mistake to dismiss either the general outlines of the Slater and Goodell fulminations or all their illustrative examples. Many of the specific incidents listed by Goodell and Slater can be corroborated in Mormon sources, although Mormon diarists naturally interpreted the causes and consequences differently. For example, both Slater and Goodell made much of the murder of Dr. J. M. Vaughan in Feb-

Their journey almost over, Mormon emigrants pause for a group photograph at South Pass.

Western History Research Center, University of Wyoming

ruary, 1851, in the settlements to the south of Salt Lake City, by Mormon M. D. Hambleton. The murder had been committed openly as Vaughan came out of a church service, the pretext being that Vaughan had seduced Hambleton's wife. Both Slater and Goodell claimed that Vaughan was a passing emigrant (from Missouri), that no evidence was brought forward to substantiate the seduction charge, that Hambleton was never even arrested, that no trial was held, that Brigham Young had publicly condoned and commended Hambleton's act in a kind of open meeting, and that the Mormon leadership then confiscated Vaughan's $2,000 for their own use. Hosea Stout's diary confirms the substance of the event, but adds interesting detail. Stout explained that he had helped prosecute Vaughan for adultery with the wife of a man named Foote in September and October of the previous year, but unsuccessfully. Further, Stout maintained that in the court of inquiry which investigated Hambleton's actions, Vaughan's seduction of Mrs. Hambleton "was sufficiently proven insomuch that I was well satisfied of his [Hambleton's] justification." Stout confirms that Brigham Young spoke in behalf of Hambleton. There is some additional doubt about whether Vaughan was a Missourian or should be regarded as a Winter Mormon—he having begun to advertise in the July 13, 1850, *Deseret News* as "having located in G. S. L. City for the practice of his profession in its various branches." Whether this meant that he planned to locate permanently in the city or was merely planning to practice through the winter is as uncertain as his guilt in the morals charge. Slater and Goodell, however, were certainly justified in complaining of the informality with which a murderer was treated at law.[76] But there is so much difficulty in ascertaining the truth about any specific incident precisely because of the impassioned prejudice with which Gentile and Saint faced each other throughout the nation as well as in the Great Salt Lake Valley. This religious and social intransigence was the root cause of most of the trouble.

The Latter-Day Saints had not been privileged to begin their desert kingdom tabula rasa, nor had that been their desire. Rumors of impending disasters and memories of previous atrocities colored the outlook of virtually everyone involved. In 1846, a year before the Mormon migration to the Salt Lake Valley even began, overland emigrants completely avoided travel on the north side of the Platte River because of rumors that 5,000 heavily armed Mormons were marching westward on that trail, intent on murdering emigrants and confiscating their property. In 1847 emigrants about to embark on their westward journey heard that the Mormons were out on the plains, had "joined three tribes of Indians, and are going to cut us all off."[77]

Mormon trail tales continued to circulate freely in subsequent years. A favorite emigrant theme was that Mormons could never be trusted to tell the truth. One such mistrustful group of 1848 overlanders refused to believe the reports of the California gold discovery relayed by Mormon ferrymen at the Green River and resolutely trailed on to Oregon. Many overlanders were also convinced that the Mormons cooperated with and/or supervised Indians in thievery all along the trail. "For honesty, purity, truthfulness, trustworthiness and honor, as between the . . . Indian and Mormon, give us the Indian by all odds," reminisced one 1852 traveler.[78] Many emigrants bypassed Salt Lake City in 1852 because of the rumor that it cost $150 in tolls and taxes to take one wagon through the Saints' domain, and that valley residents could be expected to steal everything that remained. In fact, anti-Mormon stories and sentiments were so pervasive that a high percentage of overlanders expressed their surprise at *not* being mistreated, finding that, as one 1853 traveler wrote his brother from Salt Lake City, "These Mormons look and act like human beings." John Clark observed in 1852 that "there are many hard stories related of these strange people that would in any other civilized community be hard to believe," and a man named Radnor, who wintered with the Mormons "on terms of cordiality" in 1854–55, stated, "There is so much prejudice existing in the world against them, I can scarcely expect to remove it from the minds of any, but I consider it due them to assert, that as a community, they are the most peaceable, law abiding, and moral people to be found any where."[79]

Given the prevailing prejudices, it is surprising that so much beneficial interaction between Saints and Gentiles did occur. A great many overlanders concluded, as a result of their encounters with the Saints, that the Mormons were much misunderstood and misrepresented, that they were really an honorable, intelligent, impressive people, perhaps even worthy of emulation. Wrote Edwin Hillyer, "I like the people very much, and should like to live among them." The many letters to friends in the States expressing these favorable sentiments ("I was never in a better country, or among a better people in my life," enthused one Virginian) certainly countered some of the anti-Mormon publicity and perhaps delayed the ultimate national confrontation. Some emigrant companies took it upon themselves to publish resolutions of thanks for assistance rendered them by Mormon travelers en route, others wrote letters of grateful appreciation for their treatment in Salt Lake City. In addition to describing the Saints as Good Samaritans, many emigrants admitted to being much impressed with the fruits of their few years' labor in the valley. "It seems incredible," mused John Benson in July, 1849; "I take off my hat to those who planned and executed it."[80]

Yet Benson was one of the surprisingly few emigrants willing to single out the Mormon leadership for praise. Even those who wrote negatively of Mormonism usually suggested that it was not the general population but the devious, unprincipled leaders who were most at fault. Some observations about polygamy were, of course, a necessity for most emigrant diarists and letter writers—especially the polygamy practiced by the Saint leaders. Emigrants particularly relished repeating rumors about the number of Brigham Young's wives and children, and the requirements for anyone wishing more than one wife.[81]

But it was the pulpit oratory of the principal Saints which most provoked passing travelers. Their bloody threats, foul language, and apparent blasphemy led many Gentile onlookers to conclude that the leading Saints were unmitigated charlatans. Typical was Addison Crane, who, after attending Sunday services at the Salt Lake City Tabernacle, rated the three speakers of the day in his diary: "The first of whom I thought mainly idiotic, the second evidently insane—and the last (Brigham Young) a knave. They preached Mormonism instead of Christianity—and Jo. Smith instead of Christ."[82]

For their part the Saints approached passing overlanders with equally intolerant attitudes nurtured by the survival struggles of the 1830s and 1840s. The rhetoric and incidents so disturbing to overland emigrants during the 1850s had been molded by memories of murderous Missouri and Illinois mobs. This desire to avenge past wrongs was important to most Mormons and is central to an understanding of the difficulties they visited upon the overlanders. William Yates, who sojourned at Salt Lake City during the infamous winter of 1850–51, believed the feeling "that the people of the States treated them like dogs when they were there and now it was their time" undergirded Mormon policy. Deputy Sheriff George Grant made the same point that winter, after arresting three overlanders just embarking on the southern route to California. The charges proved spurious, but the delay and expense forced the innocent men to winter in the valley. No matter, said Grant, as paraphrased by Slater, "the innocent must suffer with the wicked. . . . the mormons had been treated in the same way in the states, having been abused and driven from place to place, when they were innocent."[83]

Subsuming even this general desire for retribution was a vituperative hatred of Missourians and Illinoisans. Gentile emigrants from those states could expect little pity when temporarily stranded in the Salt Lake Valley. Not when prejudices were so intense that one female Saint, while traveling to the valley, made it a special point to trample on the trailside graves of all Missourians. According to 1850 emigrant Calvin Taylor, the Mormons were "invoking curses upon them even to the fourth generation." The San Francisco *Daily Alta California* speculated that Goodell's Oregon-bound company had suffered so much because they were mainly Missourians. Forty-niner Jerome Howard, who did not hail from one of the offending states, had found the Mormons "hospitable and obliging" during his three-week stay in Salt Lake City. But he also wrote, "Perhaps some Illinoions and Missourions who passed through their city would take exception to what I say, and well they might for the Mormons hold towards them a special hatred."[84]

334

Mormon threats against Missouri and Illinois "mobocrats" were legion. Apostle Orson Hyde, for example, publicly asserted that if God would forgive him for having permitted mobocrats to trail through the valley unmolested, "he would have them all killed hereafter." Elder John Taylor also publicly promised that the Saints would send past persecutors daring to enter Salt Lake City "to hell crosslots." Common too was the open and boastful talk that such persons could not get through the valley alive—and that many had not.

Mormons went out of their way to locate overlanders who had participated in the turbulent struggles of the 1830s and 1840s. One 1852 emigrant, for example, who had been active in evicting the Saints from Nauvoo, was recognized in Kanesville by a leading Mormon. The Saint questioned the emigrant closely on his travel plans before speedily traveling to Salt Lake City by horse-drawn carriage. Suspicious at his interest, the Illinois company determined to trail to Oregon so as to avoid the Mormon avengers whom emigrants commonly referred to as "the Destroying Angels." At the Green River crossing, however, several presumed Mormons stopped emigrant trains to inquire after the emigrant in question, W. P. Burns. The investigators even had a photograph of their quarry, but those asked always indicated that Burns would be found in a subsequent train, thus enabling him to slip safely through to Oregon.[85] That others were not always so fortunate, as Slater, Goodell, and others ardently asserted, was partly substantiated by Hosea Stout's August 14, 1854, diary entry:

There has been an Examination going on before the Probate court since friday last against H. B. Taylor for assertions made on the road East and in this place to one Mr Rayney stating that E. T. Benson & others were out there to rob, plunder & kill certain emmegrants   That a plot had been laid to rob Mr Childs & kill him and that it was very common to kill strangers & take their cattle and other property and many other such things. Taylor at first denied the charge in toto but afterwards confessed it. Sunday he was cut off from the church & to day the examination was brought to a close and Taylor was acquitted from the fact there was no law made & provided against any thing charged to him

The emmegrants who had heard Taylor's reports were very much excited and alarmed for their safety.[86]

Well aware of these rabid attitudes, most Illinoisans and Missourians prudently avoided the trails leading through the Salt Lake Valley.[87] More philosophically inclined travelers tried to put this apparent Mormon fanaticism into its proper historical perspective. Forty-niner Charles Gray observed that "there appears to be a tinge of fanaticism as it were about all their actions, their looks & manners. I look upon them as the Puritans of the 19th century, men who had fled from persecution to a remote & distant region to enjoy unmolested their own belief." Nine years later a California-bound freight driver suggested that the Saints "excelled the old-time Puritans in ignorance, but not in fanaticism"; 1850 gold rusher

W. S. McBride ranged further into the past in search of a suitable analogy for the despicable Mormon zealots: "The[y] reminded me of what history relates of the canting Round Heads of Cromwells time."[88]

Newspaper headlines throughout the 1850s made it clear that the intolerant extremism Benjamin Ferris had confidently expected to fade away had been accentuated instead. While the increasing virulence displayed by both Mormons and Gentiles focused on polygamy and Mormon defiance of federal courts and judges in Utah Territory, the travail of the overlanders while in the Mormon mecca was a strong tertiary force in bringing on the Mormon War. The influential report of Territorial Secretary B. D. Harris and Justices Lemuel G. Branderbury and Perry E. Brocchus of the Supreme Court of the United States for Utah Territory not only lamented the unpunished murder of Dr. J. M. Vaughan but discoursed at some length on other forms of Mormon harassment and intimidation experienced by Gentile emigrants trailing through the Salt Lake Valley.[89] As Mormon intransigence grew, irate letters from former overlanders recalling their own sufferings among the Saints began to appear in the pages of prestigious newspapers like the New York *Daily Times*. Western papers had been filled with similar letters during the early 1850s. Newspaper editorials calling for forceful chastisement of the Utah rebels likewise stressed the perils of the overland traveler when among the Mormons.[90] And congressmen such as John Thompson of New York and William W. Boyce of South Carolina not only raged about the "scores" of peaceful emigrants murdered by the nefarious Mormons but invoked the specter of the end of overland emigrant travel to the West Coast if the centrally located Mormon empire was not quickly brought to heel.[91]

Just as in the United States, the furor reached its zenith in the Great Basin kingdom in late 1856 and early 1857, aided by the emotional revivalism of 1856. The following year came the frightening news that a U.S. army was marching on the Saints' desert stronghold. Was it to be Missouri and Illinois all over again? Caught in the vortex of these pressures were the usual westbound emigrant caravans—although not as many as in the past—toiling through the Salt Lake Valley. Tragically, the first train of the year to strike out along the "Mormon Corridor" to California, captained by Charles Fancher, was composed of Missouri and Arkansas overlanders. Their journey south from Salt Lake City was a difficult one: area Indians were hostile, local residents refused to trade, refused even to let them drive through the city of Parowan. The Fancher party was forced to pioneer a new trail around the town. Deprived of trading for desired supplies, some train members took by force what they wanted. The Saints later claimed that some of the Missourians had also boldly vented their anti-Mormon prejudices while in the valley: bragging of having helped kill Joseph Smith, exhibiting what they claimed was the very weapon used, boasting of what the oncoming army would do to the obstreperous Saints. To further insult their longtime adversaries some Missourians had allegedly named oxen for various Mormon leaders so they could whip and damn them while trailing through city streets. The Arkansans in the Fancher train were suspect because word had just reached Utah that the Mormon Apostle Parley Pratt had been murdered in that state.

The combination was volatile. Zealous local Mormons, assuming that they would be fulfilling the desires of the Salt Lake hierarchy, deliberately planned what became the greatest single tragedy of the overland trail. In league with area Indians, who attacked and then besieged the train for five days before the carefully executed massacre of September 11, the vengeful Saints with their Indian cohorts murdered perhaps as many as ninety-six persons, sparing only eighteen young children. This was the Mountain Meadows massacre. The Saints quickly turned their attention to making it appear an Indian responsibility, and, failing that, ultimately foisted the sole blame on John D. Lee so as to spare the Church further embarrassment.[92]

Nelson Slater and the Reverend Goodell, had they penned their anti-Mormon briefs after Mountain Meadows, would have described that infamous event as only a larger-scale version of what the Mormons had been doing for decades, particularly to Gentiles wintering in the Salt Lake Valley. Those overlanders who trailed through the Salt Lake Valley in the summers, dining sumptuously and trading advantageously while admiring Mormon industry and kindness, would have termed it a bizarre and inexplicable aberration. The truth lay somewhere in between. Perhaps the greatest tragedy was that the irrational prejudices of the time prevented so many Saints and Gentiles from fully recognizing how much they both were profiting from the overland emigrant stopovers at the Mormon halfway house.

CHAPTER TEN

West Coast Assistance

*"Are you men from California,
or do you come from heaven?"*

THE CONTINUING EXODUS TO OREGON AND CALIFORNIA attested to the publicists' success in portraying the virtues of those far-away Edens. Westering pioneers anticipated, if not "Paradise" itself, at least the closest version the American continent could offer. Yet those traveling the overland route ruefully discovered that the final segments of the Oregon and California trails were also the most precarious. The most rugged and treacherous terrain of the entire trek confronted the emigrants just when their food supplies were nearly consumed, their draft animals exhausted, their own energies dangerously depleted, and the ominous threat of winter snows daily increasing. This was the great paradox of the overland trail, as the Donner party tragedy so poignantly revealed: the closer the emigrant got to "Paradise," the more unattainable it often seemed.

Fortunately for the oncoming overlanders, however, West Coast residents recognized the catastrophic implications of these late-season end-of-trail dangers. In addition to organizing extensive relief efforts to assist beleaguered travelers, they also marked out a myriad of new and allegedly easier routes of entry into Oregon and California. The development of new trails and the dispatching of guides and supplies to encourage emigrant use of those trails were of course vested interests of communities anxious to become the premier coastal city. To the suffering emigrant, however, it made little difference whether this timely assistance was prompted by ulterior profit-oriented considerations or by Christian and humanitarian compassion. Had it not occurred, the "Paradises" of Oregon and California would indeed have been unattainable for a great many emigrants, and the Donner disaster of 1846–47 would not stand as such an isolated episode.

The initial phase of West Coast emigrant assistance was an outgrowth of the competitive drive for prominence so characteristic of developing regions. Since the international destinies of California and the Oregon country were still uncertain during the first emigration years, pro-American residents there believed that their very survival might depend on how quickly they attracted a large population of hardy American frontiersmen. While relying mainly on publicity through fulsome letters in newspapers, roseate articles in magazines and journals, and the blustering oratory of congressional allies, the Oregon and California boosters did not neglect those emigrants already trailing west.[1] If they could be intercepted at some point en route, perhaps they could be inveigled into altering their destination decision. And Fort Hall, strategically located shortly before the Oregon and California trails diverged, seemed the perfect place for propagandists to ply their trade.

The short flurry of spirited and deceitful inter-regional sparring which began at the fort in 1845 occasionally redounded to the emigrants' advantage.[2] In that first year of competition California was represented by the venerable mountaineer Caleb Greenwood, two of his sons, and a man named McDougal. Whether they were directly in the employ of John Sutter—one of the principal proponents of diverting Oregon-bound emigrants to California—is uncertain, but the intent of their activities at the forts that summer is clear.[3] Joel Palmer, one of the westbound emigrants who remained unmoved by their blandishments, explained their heavy-handed approach:

The most extravagant tales were related respecting the dangers that awaited a trip to Oregon, and of the difficulties and trials to be surmounted. The perils of the way were so magnified as to make us suppose the journey to Oregon almost impossible. For instance, the two crossings of *Snake* river, and the crossing of the Columbia, and other smaller streams, were represented as being attended with great danger; also that no company heretofore attempting the passage of these streams, succeeded, but with the loss of men, from the violence and rapidity of the current; as also that they had never succeeded in getting more than fifteen or twenty head of cattle into the Willamette valley.... it was asserted that three or four tribes of Indians, in the middle region, had combined for the purpose of preventing our passage through their country, and should we attempt it, we would be compelled to contend with these hostile tribes. In case we escaped destruction at the hands of the savages, a more fearful enemy, that of famine, would attend our march; as the distance was so great that winter would overtake us before making the passage of the Cascade Mountains.

On the other hand, as an inducement to pursue the California route, we were informed of the shortness of the route, when compared with that to Oregon; as also of many other superior advantages it possessed.[4]

Perhaps equally persuasive was the assurance that Sutter would send ten Californians to meet those emigrants who agreed to go there; that in

339

addition to aiding the emigrants' passage over the "easy grade" in the mountains these relief agents would provide dried beef, potatoes, and coffee. Tempers flared as the overlanders debated the relative merits of the two regions. Prior to reaching Fort Hall the owners of fifteen wagons in Palmer's division of the 1845 emigration had been committed to California. When the debates were over, a train of fifty wagons headed for California. Others would follow. How influential Sutter's promise of re-provisioning in the mountains had been is unknown, but when the emigrants reached the Sierras, ten Mexicans with a pack train of provisions awaited them.[5]

The admonitions of Greenwood's troupe were echoed by the Fort Hall clerks, particularly by Richard Grant, who oversaw the Hudson's Bay Company's Snake River operations. Many emigrants believed, with some justification, that Grant's recommendations were not impartial because of the company's vested interest in the final destination of the American pioneer caravans. Indeed, at least one 1845 emigrant assumed that the British fur company was the behind-the-scenes financier of all the machinations to entice Oregonians to California.[6]

A number of those thus induced in 1845 to trail to California were so dissatisfied with the region that they made their way north to Oregon the following spring. Knowing that Sutter and the recently arrived Lansford Hastings planned a repeat performance for the 1846 emigration, these disgruntled home seekers forewarned the settlers of the Willamette Valley. An immediate counterattack was planned. Gathering at an Oregon City hotel on June 15 to plot strategy, the concerned Oregonians agreed to send a delegation to intersect the westbound emigrants near Fort Hall. Appointing several committees—one to raise funds for the venture, another to gather depositions from dissatisfied Californians who had recently arrived in Oregon—the Oregon settlers urged their representatives to leave within ten days. The testimonials collected by the committee were circulated among the oncoming overlanders that summer with the intention of preventing the emigrants from "being deceived and led astray by the misrepresentations of L. W. Hastings, who is now on his way from California for that object." The former Californians not only impugned Hastings's veracity and charged him with grandiose revolutionary dreams, but also solemnly denigrated the climate as well as the farming and grazing potential of California.[7]

In early August the contingent of Oregon boosters at Fort Hall was bolstered by the arrival of Jesse Applegate and several members of his exploring party direct from the Willamette Valley over a southerly trail they had just blazed. Applegate's open letter to the emigration, his effective proselytizing at the fort, and the promise of exploring party personnel as guides for the remainder of the journey were enough to turn many overlanders previously committed to California toward Oregon—and

Applegate's new trail. Also spreading the Oregon message that summer were eastbound Oregonians who aggressively accosted westbound travelers all along the trail.[8]

But California enthusiasts were also eastbound in 1846. While those traveling east to the Missouri frontier apparently did some propagandizing, Lansford Hastings was, as Oregonians had anticipated, the most formidable proponent of California's virtues. Hastings, however, did not do the expected and join the other propagandists assembled at Fort Hall. Hastings had pioneered a new route on his eastward trek from California, a route which branched off in a southwesterly direction from Fort Bridger, thereby bypassing Fort Hall completely. Sending letters ahead to the westbound overlanders, Hastings traveled beyond South Pass to Independence Rock in order to turn emigrants toward his allegedly shorter route via Fort Bridger. Impressed by Hastings's credentials—after all, many 1846 emigrants were traveling according to the precepts of his 1845 overland guidebook—a number of those previously inclined toward Oregon altered their courses toward California.[9]

Not everyone bound for California, of course, chose to follow Hastings and his California guides along the new route. Those who did soon learned a harsh lesson about western travel: that no matter how loudly praised by their discoverers and promoters, "cutoffs" usually lengthened the distance to be covered and increased travel hardships. So it was with the several hundred emigrants who followed Hastings into the uncharted region southwest of Fort Bridger. Among the tribulations they endured was the terrifying crossing of an eighty-mile desert. When they finally intersected the main trail along the Humboldt River, after abandoning some of their supplies, livestock, and wagons, they learned to their dismay that those who had traveled via Fort Hall had made much better time. Indeed, those who had remained on the main trail were now far in the lead of the emigration to California, even those who had earlier been at the rear of the migration column.[10] It was this delay which prevented the Donner party, the last group to take the cutoff, from crossing the Sierra Nevadas before winter set in, led to their suffering, death, and cannibalism during that horrible winter in the mountains, and ruined the reputation of Hastings and his so-called "cutoff."[11]

Hastings's enterprising exertions help explain why 1846 was the first year that more overlanders trailed to California than to Oregon. In 1847 and 1848, however, Oregon was again the overwhelming choice of westbound emigrants. The fledgling California press quickly charged the "smooth-tongued hirelings" representing Oregon at Forts Laramie and Hall with responsibility for this alarming drop in California popularity. In their trailside exhortations the Oregon agents had effectively used a printed broadside addressed "To the Oregon Emigrants" by no less than Governor George Abernethy of Oregon Territory. Meanwhile, from San

Francisco the *California Star* editor gamely endeavored to rebut the spreading rumors that widespread famine and bloody warfare were characteristic of California.[12]

California editors always remained alert for similar Oregon "misrepresentations," suspecting dubious machinations whenever the Oregon emigration totals surpassed those of California. After learning that several California-bound companies had been diverted to Oregon in 1851 with rumors of Indian hostility, for example, the *Daily Alta California* editor recalled for his readers the earlier controversies. He concluded his indignant article with the observation that truth would ultimately prevail and California would continue to prosper even if "our sister territory should stand at the back-door and warn the jaded immigrant not to enter the forbidden grounds."[13]

The overland emigrants were indirect beneficiaries of these interregional competitions for settlers. During the mid-1840s they received unanticipated provisions, access to seasoned trail guides, and an abundance of traveling instructions—and somewhat suspect route recommendations. Of even greater significance in easing the rigors of the final segments of the overland journey were the intra-territorial and intra-state competitions for settlers, competitions revolving around variations on the later portions of the Oregon-California Trail. Despite the several trail tragedies directly occasioned by overzealous promoters of new routes, the long-range impact of the vigorous route competition was to the advantage of the overland traveler.

These internal competitions were particularly pronounced in Oregon during the mid-1840s and in California during the early 1850s. In Oregon geographic realities provided the impetus for the development of alternative routes into the Willamette Valley. For all practical purposes the Oregon Trail ended at The Dalles of the Columbia River. From that point it was necessary to travel by water down the treacherous Columbia, portaging around the Cascades, to Fort Vancouver, Portland, or Oregon City. Whether the weary emigrants fashioned their own rafts, hired Indian vessels and boatmen, or traveled via the commercial boats which soon catered to this trade, it was usually necessary to dismantle their wagons for a trip which was rarely accomplished without some loss of possessions, if not of life. Cattle were usually driven along the Columbia across the Cascade mountain range on narrow trails by a few men of each company, but the late fall weather was often disagreeable and the mountain passes occasionally blocked.[14]

Specific examples best convey the anguish which so often characterized this watery terminus of the "overland" journey and undergirded the drive for alternative access routes. On October 27, 1847, Elizabeth Geer and her family reached The Dalles, where they joined a large group of emigrants anxiously endeavoring to arrange for the river passage. The

Route Improvements Undertaken by Oregon, California, and Washington

1 Beckwourth Cutoff
2 El Dorado Cutoff
3 Truckee route
4 Placer County Emigrant Road
5 Johnson Cutoff
6 Pennsylvania Cutoff
7 Carson route
8 Big Trees Cutoff
9 Sonora Cutoff

MAP 9

cold, rainy, and windy weather prevented their little three-family group from launching their hastily constructed raft until November 2. Periodically during the next eleven days they were forced to beach their craft to await calmer water. Meanwhile, their remaining supply of foodstuffs had been almost completely consumed. Sickness, doubtless brought on by the combination of weather, diet, and deteriorating physical condition, made its appearance. On November 8, still short of the Cascade Falls, Elizabeth concluded her daily diary entry with the comment that "my hands are so numb that I can scarcely write." The next day she observed icicles hanging from the wagon beds into the water. Also on that day one of the men on board their makeshift vessel died. On the more positive side, from a better-supplied company Elizabeth's husband purchased fifty pounds of beef. At last, on the 13th they persuaded the operators of a ferry situated above the Cascade Falls to transport their belongings to the Falls. They had made sixty miles in eighteen days.

At the Falls, in a continuing drizzle, they unloaded their belongings, reassembled their wagons, and laboriously completed the five-mile portage over what was euphemistically called a road. On the 18th they joined hundreds of other weary emigrants in waiting for boats to conclude their journey down the Columbia. By now Elizabeth's husband was so ill he could not leave his bed in one of the wagons, and Elizabeth's feet were too swollen from the cold to wear shoes. And always it was raining or snowing. Finally, on November 27, passage was secured on a flatboat, and two days later, at nearly midnight, they docked at Portland. Elizabeth now desperately tried to find accommodations for her family. On the 30th, thirty-five days after they had reached The Dalles, barely 100 miles upriver, they crowded into a ramshackle dwelling with two other families. To get food Elizabeth sold their remaining belongings, but the ordeal had been too much for her husband, who died soon after their arrival.[15]

While the Geers suffered more than most, their experiences were not at all atypical. Even into the 1850s, despite the presence of steamboats, drownings and frustrating delays were commonplace.[16] It was therefore not surprising that the Oregon legislature, in its 1852–53 session, once again addressed itself to the familiar topic—upgrading the transportation facilities to the Oregon settlements. One representative put the matter plainly: "The hardships and losses of immigrants at the latter end of the route, is eminently calculated to make them dissatisfied with our country, and it is a point of public notoriety, that many immigrants on their first arrival here, and while they are vexed and smarting under the stings of an adverse fortune, write back to the states the most severe and discouraging letters about Oregon, not because they dislike the country, for that they have not seen."[17]

What was still needed in 1853, in other words, was what had always been needed: travel improvements on the last portions of the overland journey so that prospective Oregonians would not arrive cursing their new homeland. Initially, in the early 1840s, there had been an additional motive for seeking alternative routes of entry: the fear of war with Great Britain over the Oregon country. Until the 1846 boundary settlement laid their fears to rest, Oregonians had worried about the line of Hudson's Bay Company posts so strategically dotting the Oregon Trail.[18]

In the summer of 1845 Willamette Valley settlers subscribed $2,000 and commissioned Indian subagent Elijah White to seek out a more favorable trail through the Cascade Mountains. White and his eight companions failed, and so reported to the legislature then in session at Oregon City, but White remained convinced that a desirable route could be developed along former fur-trading pathways. While on an eastbound journey to Washington that fall, White apparently shared his convictions with oncoming emigrant parties he met near Fort Boise. One of the westbound travelers with whom White presumably communicated was Stephen H. L. Meek, a former Rocky Mountain trapper now turned emigrant guide. Meek also believed in the desirability of a Malheur River route. It would, he predicted, save at least 200 miles en route to the upper Willamette Valley. At Fort Boise, Meek volunteered to lead a contingent of 1845 overlanders over this route for a fee of $5 per wagon. Meek's reputation and confidence convinced slightly over 1,000 emigrants to follow him into the unmapped interior.[19]

It was not long before the distraught emigrants realized that they were lost. Meek's timesaving "cutoff" soon turned into a nightmare. Low on food and patience, the emigrants expended considerable time seeking sufficient water and forage for their stock. Soon the large caravan began to disintegrate. Mountain fever made its dreaded appearance. The suffering became so intense that some overlanders were reduced to eating berries and dried grasshoppers provided by area Indians. Dissatisfaction with Meek became so prevalent that his life was routinely threatened. Sympathetic overlanders secreted him in a wagon for a time, until finally the guide and his new bride fled in fear.

Meanwhile, a small group forged ahead in an attempt to secure supplies. After a trying journey they finally reached The Dalles. When Meek arrived at The Dalles he was instrumental in organizing the relief expedition which came to the aid of the beleaguered emigrants. Between twenty and twenty-five persons had died while on the "cutoff," and at least that many died shortly after reaching The Dalles, one famished traveler expiring from overeating. Contemporary estimates ranged as high as seventy-five deaths for the ill-advised venture. The Meek escapade is rightly regarded as one of the major tragedies of the overland trail, its place in trail lore further secured by the legendary Blue Bucket gold mine that some of the starving emigrants claimed to have found in their wanderings but which has never been rediscovered.[20]

An 1857 photograph of Oregon City, end of the trail for many weary overlanders.
Oregon Historical Society, photo by Lorenzo Lorain

The second road-building attempt of 1845 was of much greater significance to future emigrants. Illinois overlander Samuel K. Barlow had prudently resisted Stephen Meek's enticing promises about the Malheur cutoffs. But when he reached The Dalles he decided to avoid the long and expensive ordeal of the Columbia passage by forging an overland wagon route across the formidable Cascades.[21] Despite warnings from the missionaries and mountaineers at The Dalles, Barlow led his seven-wagon outfit southwest in the direction of Mount Hood. Joel Palmer, arriving at The Dalles shortly thereafter and learning of the Barlow effort, took twenty-three additional wagons along Barlow's new trail. Barlow and Palmer, reconnoitering the possibilities of a wagon road south of Mount Hood, determined finally that a road was feasible but that it was too late in the year to complete it. Having already sent their cattle to the settlements on the mountain trail along the Columbia, they now cached their wagons and supplies at what they called Fort Deposit, left one of their number on guard through the winter, and pushed ahead via pack animals to the settlements.

Their situation was precarious. Many families were already out of food. At this point those who had gone ahead with the cattle returned with a relief expedition from Oregon City, the settlers there having responded warmly to the news that families were endeavoring to reach the Willamette with wagons over the Cascades and were urgently in need of provisions. Finally, in late December, the last stragglers reached Oregon City. By that time Barlow had already secured a charter from the territorial legislature to open a toll road across the Cascades on the route he and Palmer had located. In early spring Barlow took forty men into the mountains to open the road from the settlements to Fort Deposit, the trail from The Dalles to their cached wagons having been cleared the previous fall. To finance this activity contributions were solicited among the area residents, but apparently little money was ever realized.

Barlow's ninety-mile road, though rough, was an instant success. In 1846 almost all the Oregon Trail emigrants chose it in preference to the Columbia waterway. An 1848 overlander aptly summed up the emigrant reaction to the new road: ". . . as miserable a road as it was, thanks be to Mr. Barlow for his energetic movement in opening a way through so rough a district as the Cascade mountains."[22] After collecting toll (usually $5 per wagon and ten cents per head of stock) during 1846 and 1847, Barlow believed that he had gotten his money back and returned the charter to the territorial government. The road rights were then leased to other entrepreneurs, who continued to collect tolls but did little to keep the road in good repair. In spite of the road's gradual deterioration, however, it continued to be heavily traveled. The 1852 proprietors, for example, recorded that 673 wagons, 3,313 persons, and 7,076 cattle, horses, and mules traversed the road that season. Tolls of $3,660.85 had been collected.[23]

In addition to Barlow, other Oregonians sought road-building charters from the Oregon legislature in 1845. Stephen Meek's petition was denied—his reputation was too besmirched to permit any hint of official sanction. But his idea endured. In the early spring of 1846 mountaineer Moses Harris and six Oregonian colleagues unsuccessfully searched for a pass which would make a road from Fort Boise to the Willamette practicable. Thomas McKay also petitioned to develop a toll road from the Santiam River settlements (the present Albany region) to Fort Boise. With ten other settlers McKay surveyed the area in the summer of 1846, but was likewise unsuccessful in finding a suitable pass across the Cascade mountain range.[24]

More successful was the locally funded endeavor to connect the Rogue and Umpqua river valleys with the main overland trail at Fort Hall, a route which ultimately evolved into a major overland artery. Underwritten by the settlers of Polk County, the first expedition departed in early May under the leadership of Levi Scott. It was aborted when four of the party deserted only seventy miles from home. Scott returned for reinforcements. For the second attempt Jesse and Lindsay Applegate, who had each watched a son drown in the Columbia River in 1843, assumed the leadership. Scott and the energetic Moses Harris, who had also been on the futile first expedition, went again. The fifteen-man exploring party succeeded in linking their southern route with the main California Trail along the Humboldt River near the Black Rock Desert. Jesse Applegate, Harris, and three others proceeded on to Fort Hall, where they persuaded approximately 500 1846 overlanders that the new route was at least 200 miles shorter with far better water and grass than the regular Oregon Trail.[25]

Scott and David Goff remained behind to guide the overlanders, while the Applegates went ahead with the remainder of the exploring party to clear the road, hiring a number of young emigrant men to assist at wages of $1.50 per day. The ensuing trip north into Oregon quickly became controversial. Several of the emigrants, most notably Jessy Quinn Thornton, complained bitterly that the Applegates, acting from selfish motives, had deliberately falsified facts in order to entice emigrants onto the new road. Applegate had certainly misrepresented the length of the new route (the old trail was shorter), but whether willfully or not is unclear. While grass and water were scarce along the trail, many of the emigrants had lagged behind needlessly, perhaps to avoid any road-clearing duties. Even so, the trip had not been easy: there was Indian harassment, with at least one overlander being killed; heavy rains forced some overlanders to wade for a few miles through several feet of water in order to traverse a canyon; some emigrants lost almost all their cattle. Starvation, sickness, and death were widespread. Some emigrants did not reach their destination until February, 1847. They might never have arrived had not the exploring party sent back relief expeditions—one led by the indefatigable Moses Harris—with much-needed food and supplies.[26]

Exhausted by their summer's labor, most of the road crew had returned to their Oregon homes by early October. News of their achievement
traveled quickly, for Applegate's August 10 letter, written at Fort Hall, was
widely reprinted in frontier newspapers, as he had requested. Applegate
assured future emigrants that the road would be opened "at the expense of
the citizens of Oregon, and nothing whatever demanded of the emigrants," that a "way-bill, fully describing the road" would be available at
Fort Hall, and that no guides would be required. Perhaps the waybill had
not yet been completed, for in the spring of 1847 Levi Scott, with approximately twenty other men, backtracked along the Applegate Trail to meet
the oncoming overlanders at Fort Hall. Scott guided between forty-five
and eighty wagons into Oregon over the new route.[27]

Meanwhile, Jessy Thornton had been filling the columns of Oregon
newspapers with diatribes against the Applegates and their trail. The road
builders and their defenders retaliated with denunciations of Thornton.
By the summer of 1847 the dispute had become a major cause célèbre,
culminating when James Nesmith, the champion of the Applegate faction,
came to Oregon City vowing to kill Thornton. Nesmith challenged
Thornton to a duel but the wily judge—who was walking the streets armed
with a revolver and bowie knife—refused to receive any communications
from Nesmith, who then sought vengeance by posting a handbill excoriat-
ing Thornton: "To THE WORLD!! J. Quinn Thornton, Having resorted to
low, cowardly and dishonorable means, for the purpose of injuring my
character and standing, and having refused honorable satisfaction, which
I have demanded; I avail myself of this opportunity of publishing him to
the world as a reclaimless liar, an infamous scoundrel, a blackhearted
villain, an arrant coward, a worthless vagabond, and an imported mis-
creant; a disgrace to the profession and a dishonor to his country."[28]

There was more than met the eye in this Thorton-Applegate/Nesmith
feud. Two basic routes now angled into Oregon: the northern Oregon Trail
with its dual termini of the Columbia River or the Barlow Road, and the
recently established southern Applegate Trail. The northern trail ended in
the Oregon City region of the lower Willamette; the southern trail fed into
the upper Willamette and the Rogue and Umpqua valleys. Thornton, a
Methodist lawyer, was aligned with the so-called "Methodist influence,"
which included, according to Jesse Applegate, missionaries, Oregon City
merchants, Barlow, and the lower Willamette settlers. All were anxious to
promote the northern route. Lindsay Applegate similarly charged that the
Hudson's Bay Company, mindful of its string of posts lining the Oregon
Trail, was collaborating in the attempt to defame the southern route.[29]

It seems apparent that the Applegates lost the first round of this
intra-territorial competition, since the overwhelming number of 1847
overlanders trailed into Oregon on the northern route. The stakes were
high, and the established forces willingly resorted to dubious tactics to
insure this initial triumph, even sending letters to the oncoming emigra-

tion urging them to whip and kill all those advocating the Applegate Trail. The letters were reinforced by a printed circular signed by the governor of Oregon containing an exaggerated version of the disasters befalling the 1846 emigration on the southern route. The governor recommended that travelers use the old Oregon Trail and the Barlow Road.[30]

The advocates of the southern route rebounded rapidly, as evidenced by the legislature's December 20, 1847, passage of an act for the improvement of the southern route. The preamble juxtaposed the "safe and easy" southern road with the "unsafe and perilous" Columbia River route. According to the provisions of the act, Levi Scott was named commissioner and authorized to collect toll. But Scott not only refused the commission, pleading that he had already devoted too many years to opening the trail, he also lambasted the "odious" suggestion that emigrants be forced to pay toll to use the route.[31]

Emigrant travel on the Applegate Trail continued in subsequent years, but the southern route never superseded the Oregon Trail as the pre-eminent Oregon access route. Indeed, the Applegate Trail was most heavily traveled by California emigrants, who traversed portions of the route before branching off on various cutoff routes into northern California. The increasing hostility of the Indians along the southern Oregon route during the early 1850s also contributed to the decrease in travel on the Applegate Trail and underscored the continuing need for a reliable trail from Fort Boise to the upper Willamette Valley.[32]

Since the old dream of a route along the Malheur River died hard, the 1851–52 legislature authorized further exploration. In 1852 a seven-man exploring team expended approximately $3,000 in the continuing search for a feasible route across the interior. After surviving an Indian attack in which three of their number were injured, the explorers intersected the main overland trail near Fort Boise. Their route, which did not closely approximate the Meek "cutoff" except along the Malheur River, seemed promising enough. In the spring of 1853 several public meetings were held to raise additional funds for improving the trail. Although a small crew was sent out, only minimal trail improvements were made. But area enthusiasts resorted to familiar phrases in touting the advantages of the new route: it was ten or fifteen traveling days shorter than all other routes, had no bad mountain or river crossings, had abundant water and grass, and had no ferries or tolls. It was, so the argument proudly went, "an independent, free, emigrant road—built by the enterprize and liberality of the people of Linn and Lane counties."

Meanwhile, Elijah Elliott traveled to Fort Boise from the upper Willamette Valley, via The Dalles, to meet the 1853 emigration. Unfortunately, although nearly 1,500 overlanders were induced to try the new trail, it did not yet qualify as a serviceable road. Worse, Elliott himself had never traveled the route. Thus, much of the 1845 fiasco was repeated. The emigrants got lost and wandered about for weeks near the headwaters of the Deschutes River. There were company disintegration, property loss, sickness, hunger, and death. Elliott's life was threatened, the Portland *Oregonian* even printing a rumor that the irate emigrants had hanged the hapless guide. Ultimately, after much suffering but little loss of life, the emigrants reached their destination. Despite this inauspicious beginning, the route apparently continued to be used throughout the rest of the emigration era.[33]

Washington Territory, though a late entry in the coastal competition for emigrants, followed similar tactics. An initial 1850 flurry of public meetings, subscriptions, exploration, and road-building having come to naught, Washingtonians made a second attempt to connect the Puget Sound area with the Oregon Trail at Fort Walla Walla in 1853. Enthusiastic promoters, led by Edward J. Allen, held public meetings, organized committees, and canvassed the region for funds, laborers, and supplies. A small group of public-spirited men spent the entire summer hewing out a road through dense forests and over the rugged Cascades, perhaps spurred on by rumors that Portland had sent agents to the Oregon Trail to warn emigrants that the overland route to Puget Sound was impassable. The road crew finished its work in time for thirty-five emigrant wagons to inaugurate the new trail to Puget Sound in the fall of 1853. When the laborers returned to Olympia, they were lionized for their impressive contribution to the future growth of the Pacific Northwest. The founder of Steilacoom showed his gratitude by presenting each road worker with a town lot.[34]

A similar congeries of route improvements, proliferating cutoffs, and expeditions to relieve beleaguered travelers characterized the intra-state competition for overland emigrants on the California end of the trail. There had been no California Trail until 1844, when the Stevens-Murphy party succeeded in taking emigrant wagons across the Sierra Nevada into California. Crossing the forty-mile desert beyond the Sink of the Humboldt, these resolute pioneers followed the Truckee River to what would come to be known as Donner Lake, struggled across rugged Donner Pass to the Bear Valley, and then trailed down into the Sacramento Valley. For the next three years this was the route to John Sutter's fort, although the tragic ordeal of the Donner party during the winter of 1846–47 did nothing to endear it to subsequent travelers.

In 1848 a party of Mormons departing from California for Salt Lake City carved out an alternate trail along the Carson River. It was minimally altered, also in 1848, by the Joseph Chiles party. Chiles, already a venerable trail follower, was crossing the plains for the fifth time in eight years. There was relatively little difference between the Truckee and Carson trails into the California settlements. In length they were virtually identical, although the Carson route was slightly less difficult. The Carson Trail soon became, however, the preferred route.[35]

California interests were quick to proffer substitute routings. Rancher

When mountain man Elijah Stevens led the first wagon train over the Sierras in 1844, he blazed a trail that is still in use today.

Peter Lassen was first. His "cutoff" almost immediately rivaled in notoriety those of Stephen Meek and Lansford Hastings. A Danish immigrant to America, Lassen had traveled overland to Oregon in 1839. Dissatisfied there, he journeyed south to California, where he became a Mexican citizen and received a large land grant approximately 100 miles to the north of Sutter's. Lassen went east to Missouri in 1847, returning the next summer at the head of a small group of overlanders he hoped to settle near his Deer Creek ranch. Rather than following the Truckee or Carson routes, however, the confident entrepreneur planned to travel direct to his ranch by using the first portion of the Applegate Trail and then angling south. Unfortunately, Lassen had not himself previously traveled the route; consequently he led his ten-wagon caravan into dead-end valleys and canyons and onto nearly impassable lava beds. This necessitated much backtracking. Progress was so slow that supplies ran short, the wagons had to be cut into carts for better maneuverability, the bickering company split into two groups, and the irate pioneers nearly hanged Lassen. Only the providential appearance of a large company of Oregonians bound for the gold fields prevented total disaster. The 150 well-equipped gold seekers had followed the Applegate Trail southward from Oregon and were now, like Lassen, seeking a wagon route to the California settlements. The Oregonians shared their ample provisions and energetically broke trail— they had forty-six wagons with them—enabling the entire assemblage to finally reach Lassen's Ranch.[36]

Here the wily Dane orchestrated a meeting wherein the emigrants supposedly endorsed him as a guide and warmly praised his cutoffs. This deceptive endorsement was rushed eastward to be printed in newspapers and influence credulous forty-niners hell-bent for the gold fields. Planning carefully, Lassen also dispatched agents to divert forty-niners onto the cutoff and to set up trail advertisements (including a signboard at the Lassen Meadows, where the Applegate Trail branched off from the Humboldt River) with the reassuring message that the diggings were a mere 110 miles ahead.[37] Lassen's efforts, coupled with the power of example, always an important factor in overland travel, induced between 7,000 and 9,000 forty-niners to travel on the cutoff.

The inadvertent example had been provided by two experienced trail guides, J. J. Myers and Benoni Hudspeth. Having already forged the time-saving Hudspeth Cutoff to the east, when these renowned pilots led their large Missouri company onto the Lassen route, virtually the entire remaining emigration trustingly followed their lead, many foolishly discarding surplus provisions on the assumption that only 110 miles remained. The suffering of those choosing the Lassen Cutoff was severe, for it proved to be some 200 miles *longer* than either the Carson or Truckee routes. Had Californians not generously responded to the critical situation with massive relief expeditions, as will subsequently be explained, the end result would have been catastrophic.[38]

Understandably, the Lassen route flourished only in 1849, since many overlanders wrote home to their friends warning against it. Although the next year nearly twice as many emigrants trailed to California, only a handful, perhaps 500, chanced what had come to be known as the "Death Route," "Greenhorn Cutoff," or "Lassen's Horn Route," a satiric comparison of the cutoff with a trip to California around Cape Horn.

Yet it was not only the length and difficulty of the trail which precipitated its immediate fall from favor. The high prices prevailing at Lassen's Ranch led most forty-niners to assume that they had been duped and to charge Lassen with deliberate misrepresentation of his cutoff in order to "make money out of the emigrants."[39] Even more serious were the allegations of J. Goldsborough Bruff:

Found a large coral of wagons, and accumulation of property, by a party of men who were ostensably engaged in felling timber & getting out pine shingles, for Lassen. One of these chaps said that Lassen paid them, (4 men) $10 per diem each. ... They were exceedingly prompt in visiting the newly arrived wagons, and advise the proprietors to abondon or leave them in their charge, &c. And were particularly anxious to take stock to recruit, all of which they branded with an eye-bolt, and sent below, in the Mill-Creek gorge, and with some mysterious assistance, were transferred from one gorge to another, and finally *the indians stole them*.[40]

While the sinister activities described by Bruff may have been carried on without Lassen's knowledge, the emigrant verdict on the whole experience was uniformly negative. If Simon Doyle's spelling was somewhat rusty, his general summary of emigrant attitudes was on target: ". . . some to pore forth Curses and abuse upon Lassin for his rascally deceatfulness in making the northern road in this all hands join and the Old Dutchman is in eminent danger of loosing his life and makes himself as humble as posible."[41]

But neither curses nor warnings from those who had once endured the privations of a mythical "cutoff" nor admonitions by guidebook writers to keep to the main trail at all costs prevented overlanders from continuing to respond to the seductive lure of routes allegedly shortening the California Trail. Even if every overland emigrant had been given a copy of the private letter in which thirteen-year-old Virginia Reed, one of the surviving members of the Donner party, had written, ". . . never take no cutofs and hury along as fast as you can," it is doubtful that the mania for trying what someone claimed was a "better way" would have abated. Once was enough, though, for one close student of overland travel suggests, "No person who had diverged onto Hastings' Cutoff (as far as our knowledge extends) ever committed the imprudence of leaving the main trail again. It was those who had stayed with the circuitous course of the regular route who became impatient."[42]

New cutoffs and alternate trails proliferated during the early 1850s, largely in response to the course of California development. As gold seekers spread across the landscape, new communities evolved. Their leaders were always anxious for additional settlers so as to realize their dreams of transforming a neophyte settlement into California's leading metropolis. The promoters emphasized that it made little sense for incoming emigrants to follow the usual Carson or Truckee routes if their goal was not Placerville or Sacramento, and a new mountain pass had been discovered enabling them to travel more directly toward their intended destination.

The 1849 fiasco on Lassen's route slowed the cutoff enthusiasm until 1851, when the next significant variant appeared—a trail branching off from the Truckee River route through Beckwourth Pass to the mining communities of Bidwell's Bar and Marysville. Jim Beckwourth had discovered the pass accidentally while prospecting. He quickly realized that there might be more profits in promoting emigrant travel than in digging gold, so he began soliciting funds from the citizenry for the improvement of his crude trail. Banking on the substantial compensation promised by enthusiastic townspeople, Beckwourth made minor route refinements that summer. In late August he triumphantly guided the first company of emigrant wagons over the trail into Marysville. The conflagration that leveled Marysville the very night of their arrival, however, burned out the celebration planned in Beckwourth's honor. More important, the disaster deprived the mountaineer of the funds he had been pledged. The next year Beckwourth established a trading post–hotel along his new route. In 1853, still complaining about the lack of compensation for his trailbreaking efforts, he was headquartered at the Humboldt Sink, trying to persuade emigrants to travel past his emporium.[43]

Touting six new shortcuts into the golden state, promoters and entrepreneurs were ready for the deluge of 50,000 overland emigrants hurrying to California in 1852. Two shortcuts angled off from the Truckee River trail: the Placer County Emigrant Road to Auburn and a new, shorter trail to Marysville through Henness Pass, later called the El Dorado route.[44] Three additional trails veered off from the Carson River route: a trail to Sonora, the Pennsylvania Cutoff to Volcano—both serving the southern mining region—and the Johnson Cutoff, which so improved the main Carson Trail to Placerville that it quickly became the favored route. By 1854, however, many emigrants had reverted back to the established Carson Trail in protest at the high bridge tolls and the fee demanded at the Johnson Cutoff summit crossing.[45]

That incoming overlanders still needed to be wary of fast-talking road agents was evidenced by the opening of the Sonora Trail. As part of the 1852 California relief effort the Sonora citizenry had contributed substantial monies and merchandise and dispatched a relief expedition. The leader, Joseph C. Morehead, induced a small train of weary travelers to

355

change course and follow him on the "nearer & better" trail he had apparently identified en route from Sonora. The results were predictable: delays, detours, extreme hardship, loss of stock and wagons, impending starvation. Morehead finally returned to Sonora for additional provisions to relieve the sufferings on his own "cutoff."[46]

Vying in overall importance with the Johnson Cutoff as an 1852 travel contribution was the Nobles Cutoff, yet another product of private enterprise. Marked out by William H. Nobles the previous year, this route connected the Shasta City diggings with the California Trail via portions of the Applegate and Lassen routes. It quickly became the best means of reaching the northern mines. Any emigrants still foolish enough to travel along the meandering Lassen Cutoff ruefully discovered that on one stretch of the trail they might meet travelers on Nobles's route going in the opposite direction—also bound for California but on a shorter route. Shasta residents donated $2,000 for further trail improvements, which were effected by Nobles and other public-spirited citizens during the spring of 1852, preparatory to the customary dispatch of agents to the main trail. Members of the first wagon train enticed into trying the new trail were feted on their arrival in Shasta with a celebration dinner at the principal hotel.[47]

In 1853 a trail to Yreka and the northernmost California mines came into use, relying principally upon the Applegate Trail to Oregon. In 1856 the Big Trees Road, another Carson Trail spur, afforded direct access to Stockton, whose principal citizens had provided $5,000 to open the route and construct eight substantial bridges. Contemporary newspapers during the 1850s contain occasional references to additional passes and trails, but obviously 1852 had marked the pinnacle of community speculation in emigration routes.[48] By the mid-1850s Californians were concentrating their energies on route surveys to prove that the Sierra pass and trail leading to their community was so superior it deserved to be designated *the* state and/or federally funded wagon route into California.[49]

Financing the exploration of mountain passes and hewing out usable wagon roads were of course only the initial steps. Channeling covered wagon caravans onto the appropriate trail was the crucial work. Toward it every conceivable stratagem was employed: promising guides, provisions, and supplies to those utilizing the route; dispatching runners and agents circulating certificates and affidavits extolling the virtues of the route in question; distributing California newspapers containing "objective" editorials recommending a specific route and buttressed with endorsements by emigrants having just traversed it; using Indians to denounce every competing trail. The route agents ("robust liars," an 1852 overlander termed them) met the oncoming emigrants as far away as 400 miles out on the plains. The traders and stock speculators clustering like locusts around the

356

incoming emigrant caravans likewise endeavored to swing the emigrants onto one or another predetermined route.[50]

The lure of profit—for individual, community, region, territory, or state—undergirded this frenetic activity at the western end of the overland trails. Overshadowing even this, however, was a vast outpouring of humanitarian aid by West Coast residents to needy emigrants. Less clearly prompted by ulterior motives and often offered at considerable personal sacrifice, this assistance was of incalculable importance to incoming overlanders in Oregon and California. It was crucial to the success of overland travel.

Compassionate relief was certainly the last thing expected from the Hudson's Bay Company by overlanders nourished on the anti-British diatribes of such pro-Oregon publicists as Hall Kelly, Henry Spalding, Lewis Linn, and Thomas Benton. Linn's and Benton's charges were particularly exaggerated, the Missouri senators being chiefly responsible for the widely repeated rumor that the Hudson's Bay Company had already caused more than 500 American citizens to be murdered.[51] Yet John McLoughlin, chief factor of the Hudson's Bay Company in the Fort Vancouver region, responded to the needs of the early Oregon emigrants with such unanticipated generosity that many of them overcame their anti-British prejudices. Instead of building the forts they had expected to need for protection against the much-ballyhooed company-Indian alliance, grateful overlanders wrote eastern friends about the courtesies they had received from McLoughlin. Guidebook writers Lansford Hastings and John Shively further assured oncoming emigrants of the liberal hospitality the "universally beloved" McLoughlin regularly bestowed upon destitute travelers. The obvious end results of such publicity were the trailside stories of McLoughlin's generosity, which buoyed up discouraged emigrants nearing their Oregon destination.[52]

Oncoming Oregon overlanders most required assistance between 1842 and 1845, and McLoughlin, despite company directives to the contrary, provided it. He furnished Hudson's Bay Company boats, usually free of charge, to transport emigrants down the treacherous Columbia to Fort Vancouver and the Willamette Valley. In the fall of 1842 he launched a large company building program so that prospective settlers could have employment during the winter. To starving emigrants of 1843 who were subsisting on boiled rawhide and hemp seed, the boatloads of free provisions McLoughlin sent upriver were godsends. So were the free clothing, the lodging on arrival, and the Fort Vancouver medical facilities—all of which McLoughlin regularly made available. To enable destitute emigrants to begin more auspiciously in the new country McLoughlin provided tools, seed, wood, cattle, and foodstuffs on generous terms of credit, and occasionally without charge. By the spring of 1844 he had extended

The generosity of Hudson's Bay Company factor John McLoughlin toward hundreds of destitute emigrants was ultimately condemned by his superiors.

over $31,000 of company credit to approximately 400 needy settlers. Apparently a large share of his own personal wealth was also consumed in these humanitarian enterprises. Indeed, so well publicized had been McLoughlin's munificent aid that by 1844 some incoming overlanders complained that the favors being accorded them did not match those provided during preceding years.[53]

Additional ramifications of McLoughlin's prestigious authority were the peaceful relationships the emigrants of the early 1840s enjoyed with the approximately 100,000 Indians inhabiting the territory claimed by the Hudson's Bay Company. This relative freedom from Indian conflict, both on the trails and in the Willamette Valley, was an outgrowth of McLoughlin's long residence in the Oregon country and his ability to convince Indians that white men, whether British or American, should not be attacked. When, for example, some of the Indians in The Dalles region began to talk of killing "the Bostons"—their term for the arriving emigrants of 1843—the influential McLoughlin immediately and thoroughly quashed their designs. He kept the incident quiet, he later explained, so that the volatile Americans would not precipitate a disastrous Indian war.[54]

McLoughlin's puzzled contemporaries, particularly his company colleagues and superiors, could not understand why the chief factor had defied company policy by helping the Americans to establish permanent settlements in the disputed Oregon country. To McLoughlin, however, the need to justify what he had done seemed surprising. From his perspective he had acted clearly, consistently, and in the long-term best interests of the Hudson's Bay Company. His most thorough explanation of his policies was necessitated by the damaging report of British lieutenants Henry J. Warre and Mervin Vavasour. They had charged, following an 1845 investigative survey of the Oregon country, that without McLoughlin's charity there would have been fewer than thirty American families still struggling to survive in the region.[55]

McLoughlin's response to the Warre and Vavasour report was fourfold. First, had he not provided immediate sustenance to the starving Americans in 1842 and 1843, and then loaned them seeds to plant so that food would be available for the fall arrivals, they would have attacked Fort Vancouver in desperation to secure what they needed to survive. The fort would have been destroyed, McLoughlin assumed, which would have either dealt a deathblow to the company's interests in the region or precipitated war between the two nations—or both. After all, McLoughlin reminded his superiors, the emigrations of 1842 and 1843 had brought well over a thousand rugged frontier folk to Oregon who would have proven hardy adversaries. Second, McLoughlin maintained that had he not personally intervened, the Indians would certainly have attacked the American newcomers. The ensuing emigrant charges that the company had instigated the massacres would doubtless also have led to the war

McLoughlin was determined to prevent. Humanitarian compassion, McLoughlin further contended, dictated that starving persons be preserved from death no matter what the political considerations. McLoughlin reminded company officials that world opinion would have mercilessly condemned the company for refusing aid to starving families. Finally, McLoughlin argued that his loans had been good business: most Americans were paying back their debts and the 6 percent return was providing a handsome company income.[56]

Despite these careful justifications, McLoughlin's superiors, and even Fort Vancouver compatriots like James Douglass, felt that at the least he should have been more outspoken in encouraging emigrants to depart from the Oregon country for California. Providing food to keep persons from starving was one thing, but aiding citizens of a rival nation to found permanent settlements was another. Damned by those Americans who blamed the British for anything and everything, and damned by company officials for not more successfully resisting the American overland tide, McLoughlin could not win. Stung by the attacks, he resigned in 1846, to live out his days in Oregon City as a relatively unappreciated American citizen.[57] Yet the assistance he had given to the overland emigrants in the crucial early years of the decade may have been vital to the establishment of the American outpost on the Columbia.

Themselves the earlier recipients of McLoughlin's charity, the Oregon missionaries were similarly in a position to assist their oncoming countrymen.[58] Of the many Indian mission stations dotting the Oregon landscape during the early 1840s, two were situated near the Oregon Trail: a Methodist outpost at The Dalles, and Marcus Whitman's Presbyterian station at Waiilatpu, some twenty-five miles east of Fort Walla Walla. Despite the extra miles required to travel via Whitman's off-trail mission, it figured more prominently as a source of supply and relief than the more strategically located Methodist mission at The Dalles.[59] Perhaps this was because Whitman's name was so intimately associated with the overland emigration experience and therefore acted as a magnet to westbound overlanders. After all, the Presbyterian missionary was already a seasoned trailsman whose eastbound overland trip during the winter of 1842–43 had been much publicized. So had been his trip west with the large 1843 emigration, when he functioned as physician and trail guide, taking many of the emigrants to his station for supplies. Further, Whitman occasionally met arriving overlanders with wagonloads of provisions out on the main trail.[60]

Despite their optimum geographic locations, however, neither the Methodist nor the Presbyterian mission ever rivaled the profit-oriented Hudson's Bay Company in humanitarian relief endeavors. In large measure this was because the missionary enterprises were small and isolated outposts without adequate resources to provision hundreds of importuning emigrants or to launch major relief expeditions. Yet apparently there was also a reluctance on the part of some missionaries to trouble themselves with the bothersome overlanders. The clearest example of this churlishness occurred in 1845. Passing emigrants were aghast when the Methodist missionaries at The Dalles refused to assist in the rescue operation that Stephen Meek was desperately organizing to relieve the hundreds of emigrants he had imprudently led into the unmapped Oregon interior. Fortunately, Meek then encountered a fellow mountaineer, Moses Harris, who agreed to help. Securing relief provisions from area Indians, Harris and several other men located the suffering emigrants and guided them back to the safety of the main trail. Meek's difficulties in securing aid at the mission were not unique. Already the previous year several overlanders caustically noted that The Dalles' missionaries evidenced distressingly little concern with their plight.[61]

At Waiilatpu, though, the reception accorded needy overlanders was invariably hospitable—so hospitable, in fact, that in 1844 long-suffering Narcissa Whitman began complaining openly about her husband's policy of providing wintering overlanders with the best portions of the meager mission fare.[62] Some 1843 emigrants did charge Whitman with deception, claiming that he had induced them to travel out of their way with promises of cheap provisions that he instead sold at exorbitant rates. But setting prices high enough to cover the expenses of raising or freighting the merchandise in question was standard practice at all Oregon missions.[63] Moreover, whenever emigrants claimed to be without funds Whitman provided them with free foodstuffs, even when his mission colleagues were convinced the overlanders were lying. A competent physician, Whitman also provided medical services at his station for the sick and injured and for pregnant emigrant women lingering at Waiilatpu until their babies were born.[64]

But Waiilatpu was probably most important as a winter oasis for those arriving too late in the travel year to complete their journey safely—or those too sick to do so.[65] Year after year the Whitmans struggled to furnish sufficient provender for the needy families descending upon them and for the trail-orphaned children they accepted at the mission. In 1843, for example, a large number of destitute emigrants prevailed upon the Whitman's magnanimity. The next year Marcus and Narcissa adopted seven emigrant children whose parents had died en route. In 1846 six trail-weary families and eight young men wintered at the mission. By late November of 1847, fifty-four of that fall's emigrants had already joined the mission personnel for the winter when Cayuse Indians suddenly murdered the Whitmans, three of their adopted children, an assistant missionary, and seven wintering overlanders. An additional forty-seven emigrants and mission residents were held hostage for several weeks before being ransomed by Hudson's Bay Company employees.[66]

Although the "Whitman massacre" terminated the Presbyterian effort at Waiilatpu, the mission stations and the Hudson's Bay Company had been of fundamental importance to the American colonization of Oregon. Since the fledgling Willamette Valley settlements did not initially possess sufficient resources to accommodate the large numbers of overlanders arriving each fall, the willingness of men like McLoughlin and Whitman to provide needed succor was critical.

While Willamette Valley settlers made isolated attempts to aid emigrants in the earliest years—Robert Shortess led a small relief party in behalf of the 1843 overlanders—it was not until 1845 that Oregon residents demonstrated a readiness to assume continuing responsibility for the relief of needy emigrants.[67] In that year Oregon City residents responded generously to the news that the Barlow-Palmer emigrant party was attempting to carve out a wagon road across the Cascade Mountains but were in need of assistance. The citizenry immediately donated approximately 1,100 pounds of flour, 100 pounds of sugar, and smaller portions of coffee and tea. Eleven pack horses were secured from an Indian chief, and Peter G. Stewart, Matthew Gilmore, and Charles Gilmore hastened eastward to relieve the road party. Reaching them on October 20, they found some families completely without provisions. Other valley residents intercepted the party a week later to assist in clearing the roadway into the settlements.[68]

The following year the main thrust of Oregon relief was directed toward travelers on the southern route reconnoitered that spring and summer by the Applegate exploring party. Several of the road-building crew had returned to the settlements early to secure stock and provisions to take back to the suffering emigrants. In addition to the relief parties sent back at the behest of the exploring party, at least two other rescue teams responded to the crisis: one a six-man outfit with twenty-four horses, the other Thomas Holt's seven-member party with thirty-four horses.[69]

Holt's crew departed from Salem on December 3. Most, including Holt, spent fifty days on their humanitarian mission. They found the overlanders in such difficult circumstances that Holt believed many would have perished had it not been for the relief and assistance provided by valley settlers. Some of the families had been without any food for several days; others had been without bread for over two months. A few of the despairing emigrants had been reduced to eating mice and boiled tallow for sustenance. His relief supplies quickly exhausted in the face of such need, Holt purchased and butchered several head of cattle from the better-equipped overlanders and distributed the beef among the neediest families.

For the last several weeks Holt's party worked in abominable weather: heavy snows, raging rivers, severe cold. Some of the emigrants nearly froze to death. Holt finally led the last of the weary emigrants into the Willamette

Valley in late January. The daily journal he had kept was subsequently published in the Oregon City *Oregon Spectator,* together with the very minimal bill of expenses Holt submitted to his fellow citizens. Although Holt and others of the rescue team expected nothing for their time or the use of their horses, they still had incurred expenses of $426.37. How much compensation Holt ever received is unknown, although the newspaper office opened a subscription fund and encouraged area residents to contribute liberally to reduce the debts accumulated in this errand of mercy.[70]

During the next five years, with the major overland arteries into Oregon completed and California the goal of increasing numbers of travelers, only occasional relief was required by incoming emigrants. In 1847, for example, sickness and heavy rains so slowed a large number of westbound overlanders that worried valley settlers raised funds to rush provisions to the distressed travelers. In 1850 most westbound emigrants outfitted too sparingly. The ensuing reports of famine and suffering prompted liberal contributions for relief expeditions in Portland and Oregon City. In the latter city alone, $5,000 was raised in three hours of solicitation. The following year two Yamhill residents, Benjamin Stuart and Chandler Cooper, met incoming emigrants with fresh cattle and provisions, which they dispensed as liberally to penniless overlanders as to those able to pay.[71]

In 1852, the year of Oregon's largest antebellum overland emigration, a combination of circumstances elicited the territory's largest relief effort. As usual, insufficiently outfitted overlanders were the basic problem, but a scarcity of grass beyond Fort Hall and reports of diseases striking down cattle and humans occasioned fears for the safe arrival of the year's migration. Messages reached the settlements that some families had no food except diseased and decaying beef cut from dead cattle. Other overlanders were subsisting solely on the charity of fellow emigrants. The needs were so obvious that Oregonians traveling eastward on the trail with fresh teams to assist relatives on the last stages of the journey slaughtered their oxen instead to help feed starving overlanders.[72]

Although there was no overall coordinator for the 1852 Oregon relief effort, many groups and individuals had cooperated enthusiastically. The press publicized the need and encouraged contributions. Many communities appointed committees of leading citizens, who raised thousands of dollars, secured supplies, and arranged for their distribution to needy overlanders back on the trails. Commercial establishments as well as individuals contributed large quantities of flour. Conspicuous by the size of his individual donation—1,000 pounds of flour—was the ever-generous John McLoughlin, now living in Oregon retirement. A circus playing in Portland donated the gate receipts—$3,000—from a special benefit performance. At least one of the steamboat companies plying the Columbia River transported relief supplies and those who would distribute them to the

Cascades and The Dalles without charge. Territorial Governor John P. Gaines pledged reimbursement with territorial funds for the considerable quantities of government supplies he requisitioned from the Fort Vancouver military commander.[73] So many sick emigrants congregated at the Cascades that virtually all the residents opened up their own homes, turning the entire town into an emigrant hospital. At The Dalles a house was donated to function as a hospital. In Portland by November 1 yet another emigrant hospital had ministered to eighty-eight overlanders, thirty of whom remained hospitalized.[74]

Relief agents representing the various town committees distributed most provisions to destitute emigrants at the Cascades or The Dalles. In late October at The Dalles, for example, approximately 100 overlanders were stranded without money, provisions, or sufficient clothing. Such persons were given what they needed in order to reach the safety of the valley settlements; those who had money were asked to pay for the relief they received. One of Portland's relief agents, Lot Whitcomb, traveled beyond The Dalles into the Blue Mountains to assist lagging travelers. Whitcomb ultimately drew upon his personal funds in order to provide relief sufficient to the enormous need. I. B. Smith, another relief agent, backtracked along the trail in early December to bring in the last stranded emigrant family of the year.[75]

The following year, when the ever-present will-o'-the-wisp dream of a shorter emigrant road induced nearly 1,500 overlanders to follow Elijah Elliott onto the Malheur River route, Oregonians again rushed relief to endangered travelers. Within twenty-four hours of learning that Elliott's emigrant party was lost and starving (besides slaughtered cattle they had been subsisting on horsemeat, snails, and insects), the citizens of Lane and Linn counties—who had been instrumental in popularizing the trail—dispatched over twenty tons of flour. Within the week a total of twenty-four heavily packed animals, twenty-three wagons, and 290 head of work and beef cattle had been sent. Meanwhile, on the southern Applegate Trail, suffering emigrants joyfully accepted provisions and supplies from three separate relief trains, all under the protective guard of Oregon militiamen.[76]

Indeed, this allocation of territorial volunteers to escort and protect emigrants from warring Indians was an important facet of Oregon relief. Oregon volunteers inaugurated such escort services during the 1848 disturbances following the Whitman massacre. Indian subagent Felix Scott commanded the settler-soldiers along the southern Applegate Trail, while another group of volunteers patrolled the main Oregon Trail. In 1852 a small contingent of Oregon militiamen from Jacksonville, under the command of John E. Ross, and a similar volunteer group from northern California, under Captain Ben Wright, both saw service along the treacherous southern route. Wright's outfit began its fall assignment by rescuing a small emigrant company under siege near Tule Lake and remained to patrol the most dangerous sections of the trail for another three months.[77]

In 1853 and 1854 mounted Oregon volunteers continued patrol duties along the Applegate Trail. Captain Jesse Walker's company of approximately seventy-five mounted volunteers saw service for ninety-six days in 1854, during which time there was no emigrant loss of life, although between thirty and forty Indians were reported killed. Between thirty and forty of Walker's militiamen remained on the Applegate Trail throughout the summer; Walker and the remaining volunteers ranged as far south and east as the Humboldt River. For the sake of safety the soldiers combined small emigrant trains into larger caravans. Walker's company also alleviated emigrant suffering by making available considerable quantities of provisions. Oregon volunteers returned to the southern trail in 1855 following reports that Indians were again molesting overland emigrants.[78]

Meanwhile, Californians launched their first significant relief efforts during the winter of 1846–47 after receiving reports of the Donner party's precarious predicament. Even before reaching the Humboldt River in the late fall of 1846, the nearly ninety emigrants comprising the Donner train had realized their need of assistance. In such circumstances California-bound emigrants thought as quickly of generous John Sutter as Oregon emigrants did of John McLoughlin, and the Donner party dispatched two of their number—C. T. Stanton and William McCutchen—to ride ahead to Sutter's Fort.[79] Sutter's reputation as a benevolent source of assistance to beleaguered travelers was well founded by 1846. His fort on the banks of the Sacramento was the logical terminus of the California Trail, and ever since the first overland emigrants had reached California in 1841 Sutter had provided employment for many newly arrived travelers. Fort Sutter soon became, like Fort Vancouver in Oregon, a center for free medical services. a place of temporary lodging, and a source of free provisions for penniless travelers. Sutter later reminisced about those early years of assisting incoming overlanders: "At times my buildings were filled with immigrants. So much so that I could scarcely find a spot to lay my own head to rest. My farm-houses and store-houses were filled every winter during these immigration times with poor, wet, hungry men, women and children seeking a fortune in a new land. . . . Often it was necessary for me to go with my men and cattle to drag them in to safety out of the snow."[80] Of equal significance to overlanders experiencing difficulty on the trail was Sutter's responsiveness to appeals for assistance. In 1844 he sent aid to those members of the Stevens-Murphy party still encamped in the mountains, barely across the summit; in 1845 he sent two Mexicans with heavily laden pack animals to assist those emigrants who had turned south at Fort Hall for California.[81]

William Smith Jewett, "Portrait of General John Sutter" (1856). The besieged members of the Donner train were among the many recipients of Sutter's beneficent aid.

Oakland Museum, Cal., Kahn Collection

Thus when Sutter received word that the Donner train was short on draft animals and provisions and lagging badly behind the year's emigration, he sent two Indians and seven well-loaded pack mules back with Stanton. Soon another member of the Donner party, James F. Reed, who had been banished from the train following a trail killing, arrived at the fort with further requests for aid. Sutter immediately furnished additional Indian servants and a large train of pack horses loaded with meat, flour, and beans. But Reed and McCutchen's little rescue party found the Sierras already blocked by snow. They reluctantly turned back, after hanging some dried beef in the trees and caching a supply of flour in an abandoned wagon in case the stranded emigrants managed to cross the summit. Until February no further rescue efforts were made, Sutter indicating that until the snow hardened, travel was simply impossible. Besides, the major topic of interest for virtually all Californians that winter was not the emigrants stranded somewhere in the Sierras but the Bear Flag Revolution.[82]

Reed and McCutchen, however, whose families were snowbound in the mountains, continued to publicize the plight of the Donner train in Yerba Buena (the future San Francisco), Sonoma, and Napa. Then, in mid-January, two men and five women emerged from the mountains. They were the only survivors of fifteen persons who had started a month before from the makeshift emigrant camp east of the summit at what would come to be known as Donner Lake. The account the seven gave of their starving comrades encamped near Donner Lake was heart-rending. So was the story of their own flight across the mountains. In order to survive their month-long trek the seven had resorted to eating the bodies of their dead traveling companions.

In response to the critical situation, four rescue parties ultimately departed from Sutter's Fort and Johnson's Ranch, forty miles to the north and the staging area for the relief efforts. Hopeful that the federal government would eventually reimburse them—as ultimately happened— Sutter and three other Californians assumed personal responsibility for financing the various relief endeavors. Individual volunteers were attracted by a promised daily wage. Reed and McCutchen, redoubling their efforts, helped to organize public meetings in the principal California communities, where nearly $2,000 was raised for the purchase of provisions and supplies. Californians, particularly recently arrived emigrants, manned the relief caravans. Reed, McCutchen, and the two men who had succeeded in crossing the summit in December also took part in the rescue operation.[83]

Unaware of these developments, those encamped at Donner Lake faced starvation, illness, death, and, finally, cannibalism. The first relief expedition reached the dwindling group at the lake on February 19; as weather conditions permitted, the three subsequent rescue parties arrived intermittently during the next two months. Each group brought small amounts of foodstuffs and supplies and took back with them as many emigrants as they could. Despite the many acts of individual heroism, in the severe weather conditions several emigrants lost their lives before reaching the safety of Sutter's Fort.[84] All told, including the two Indian servants Sutter had initially dispatched to aid the slow-moving emigrant caravan, forty-two individuals died and forty-seven survived. Had it not been for the four relief expeditions, the only survivors might well have been the two men and five women who managed to escape their snow-bound mountain prison in mid-January. Hence, the tearful comment by the first stranded emigrant to sight the seven members of the first relief party was singularly apropos: "Are you men from California, or do you come from heaven?"[85]

The grisly memories of the ordeal at Donner Lake led Californians to organize relief and rescue operations whenever they feared a repetition of the tragic events of 1846–47. The hordes of inexperienced overlanders jamming the California Trail during the gold rush era elicited many such fears, and prompted the massive relief endeavors of 1849, 1850, and 1852. In 1849 the gravest concern was not with potential starvation, since most of the forty-niners had outfitted with ample quantities of food. Rather, considering the unprecedented number of trail travelers, fears were widespread that forage and water would prove insufficient to sustain the stock of those in the rear of the year's migration.[86] The possible consequence of dying draft animals was obvious: any diminution of locomotive power could so impede the progress of overland travel that winter snows might again close the mountain passes before all emigrants had crossed.

By late August, realizing that something had to be done to prevent a disaster of monumental proportions, California's military governor, Major General Persifer F. Smith, stepped into the breach. Authorizing $100,000 in emergency funds (which was augmented by public subscriptions of approximately $12,000 in San Francisco alone), Smith assigned Brevet Major D. H. Rucker to direct the relief and rescue activity. Although he had few precedents to guide him, and faced the unenviable task of melding civilians—hired at from $150 to $200 per month—and military personnel into a cohesive relief operation, by mid-September the fast-moving Rucker already had several relief teams on the trails. His basic plan was simple: send relief caravans backtracking along each of the three major overland access routes into California with directions to travel far enough east to make certain that even the slowest-moving forty-niners received assistance. Once all travelers had been accounted for, the relief teams would turn around and hasten back to California, dispensing food and animals as needed, and rendering whatever assistance might be necessary to insure that all travelers crossed the Sierras before the onset of winter storms.[87]

A few changes in logistics were necessitated almost immediately. Rucker had earmarked the principal relief emphasis for the Truckee River route since the majority of incoming overlanders normally followed that route. By the time the relief caravans moved out, however, it became obvious that the incoming forty-niners were concentrated much more heavily on the Carson Trail. Since Rucker's contingency orders to John H. Chandler, Charles L. Kilburn, and Ferris Foreman had included directions to switch over to the Carson Trail if they became convinced that the needs were greater on that route, the change was quickly made. Together with Robert W. Hunt, whose initial assignment had been the Carson route, these four relief squadrons were adequate to cover the needs of emigrants arriving by that approach, so that by the first week in November relief activities on both the Carson and Truckee routes had ceased.[88]

It would be late November, however, before relief and rescue operations on Peter Lassen's heavily traveled cutoff could be concluded. John H. Peoples had received the Lassen Trail assignment. His reports of the great suffering on the route and the large numbers of overlanders still to come led Rucker himself to desert his Sacramento base of operations and take to the field with yet another relief caravan. Both Peoples and Rucker, despite temporary incapacitation from severe attacks of mountain fever, labored heroically to get all stragglers in to Lassen's Ranch. Their frantic activity was carried out in increasingly inclement weather; fortunately, however, while both emigrants and rescuers experienced considerable suffering, minimal loss of life occurred.[89]

Certain common themes marked the relief operations on all three routes. The most persistent problem was differentiating between those overlanders who were really in dire straits and those who were merely seeking to supplement reasonably ample supplies by false claims of destitution. Since the problem was insoluble short of searching wagons, most of the relief leaders simply established categories of priority. Rucker, for example, gave first preference to the sick, then to the starving, and then to family groups. Single men packing in on foot were generally not given aid unless they were obviously without the wherewithal to complete their journey safely. J. Goldsborough Bruff, who received some relief provisions for his company from Major Rucker, succinctly described the predicament in which the relief parties found themselves: "[Rucker] was surrounded by begging emmigrants, men, women, & children. . . . The importunity of the begging emigrants, was annoying; some greatly in need, some meanly bent on an increase of stores, and others, who would steal a dying man's shoes. His stores were insufficient to serve those actually in want, but how was he to discriminate?" In one sixteen-day period Rucker indicated that he had received "hourly" requests for food and had provided badly needed foodstuffs to at least 150 impoverished families and 300 footpackers.[90]

Robert Hunt, on the Carson Trail, encountered four German footpackers completely without food. For over a week they had been subsisting on decaying flesh cut from dead mules littering the roadside. Two of the men were carrying approximately ten pounds of carrion around their necks, the smell of which was so offensive that Hunt obliged them to wash thoroughly in the river before he supplied them with a good meal and sufficient provisions to complete their trek.[91] Well aware that some gold rushers applied for relief so they could avoid going on short rations for the remainder of the journey, the relief teams sometimes refused to dispense any foodstuffs. Occasionally such rejected applicants would denounce the relief operations as a sham, but there seems little question that those involved in the relief enterprises strove to deal honorably with all whom they met.[92]

Another common difficulty facing the relief teams originated in Rucker's directive to proceed first to the rear of the emigration so they would know how many sufferers there were before they began to dispense relief supplies. Long before they had completed this preliminary reconnaissance the relief teams found it necessary to distribute aid. Many like the German footpackers might not otherwise have survived. Rucker himself was forced to distribute food at Lassen's Ranch to persons who had theoretically "completed" their journey but who were completely exhausted and without provisions or the funds with which to procure them. The leaders of the several relief squadrons tried to keep lists of those to whom they rendered assistance. As had been expected, one of the most frequent requests was for fresh draft animals. This aid was provided in the form of loaned animals for which the recipients signed, agreeing to return the animals to Smith, Bensley, and Company as soon as they reached Sacramento.[93]

Even with the Donner tragedy such a haunting memory, the relief teams found that one of their major tasks was to convince the oncoming emigrants that speed was of the essence—that in order to beat the winter snows they would have to sacrifice some belongings. Many overlanders initially refused to lessen their loads or to leave their heavy wagons behind. By mid-November the exasperated Rucker wrote the equally worried Peoples, who was still laboring out on the Lassen Trail, "You must tell all the emigrants that they must be more active and get to the valley at once, or they may perish. I cannot conceive what they are thinking of. Their own lives and the lives of their families are certainly worth more than their wagons and effects."[94]

Another of the problems bedeviling the emigrants and relief teams was the Indian propensity to steal and kill draft animals. Peoples's company cooperated with a number of emigrants in killing six Indians in a short skirmish.[95] But the weather remained the primary concern. Peoples's relief caravan, working in deep mud, freezing rain, and finally heavy snow, endured the worst conditions. The difference between life and death on the Lassen Cutoff was measured in miles and hours for those bringing up the rear of the year's migration. Almost all of the rescue-team

"Are you men from California, or do you come from heaven?"—such was the emotional greeting of a Donner party survivor when California rescuers finally arrived at the encampment in the Sierras. Bancroft Library leaders, in their final reports, agreed that their activities had not only been much needed and much appreciated, but that hundreds of forty-niners would have perished had it not been for this West Coast relief.[96]

If anything, the gold mania was worse in 1850. Nearly twice as many overlanders thronged the California Trail as in 1849. Confident that they were learning from the experiences of their predecessors, the 1850 emigrants tended to outfit more sparingly. The ensuing combination of many more travelers with far fewer provisions was disastrous.

John Wood encountered one gold seeker on the Hastings Cutoff who had survived by drinking his own urine. By mid-July fifteen to twenty overlanders were reported to have died of starvation. According to incoming emigrants it was commonplace to find flesh sliced off the thousands of mules, oxen, and horses who had not survived the diminishing grass and water supplies. Decomposing animals and abandoned wagons littered the trail mile after odorous mile—according to one traveler's count seventy dead animals were visible at one time and ninety-two wagons were abandoned within one two-mile stretch.[97] A small emigrant party was known to have lived for six days solely on a few pounds of coffee. One Wisconsin overlander had had only four pounds of bread to sustain him for two weeks; another emigrant claimed to have subsisted for sixteen days on the putrefied flesh of dead mules. Other starving and begging travelers were eating dogs, crows, rose-bush buds, bones, and anything they could salvage from the campsites of more fortunate gold-rushing colleagues. On the desert crossings beyond the Humboldt Sink a nearly naked man too weak to wear shoes begged for a handout; men were also seen "frothing at the mouth for want of water." One incredulous overlander wrote a St. Louis friend about the emigrant who suffered so much from hunger and thirst *"that his tongue became so badly swollen as to completely fill his mouth, and he tore his lips off to obtain relief!!!"*[98]

Such stories, often coupled with dire predictions about the fate of those in the rear of the migration, once again impelled Californians to provide whatever succor they could. Unfortunately, however, the resultant relief activity did not match the high 1849 standards; even if it had, the numbers of the needy were so immense that the suffering could not have been completely alleviated. Absent in 1850 was the careful organization and the overall control which Rucker had exercised the previous year, as well as the substantial governmental funds on which to draw. With the different cities, led by Sacramento, orchestrating their own relief endeavors, communication and coordination were frequently lacking. Not even William Waldo or J. Neely Johnson, who emerged as the most honored practitioners of relief, were able to unify the many strands of relief activity into a cohesive whole.

Despite these drawbacks, the 1850 relief campaign was impressive. Since private contributions and not public funds financed the 1850 relief operations, appeals were made to virtually all segments of the California population. Most cities began with public fund-raising meetings, where street haranguers embellished the accounts of suffering and starvation in order to loosen purse strings. For example, Mendall Jewett, recently arrived from the plains, explained conditions he had seen and experienced at a July 24 evening street meeting in Sacramento. That night $10,000 was pledged for relief.

When the initial turnout for a public meeting was not large, as in San Francisco, where a mere twelve public-spirited citizens showed up, the press could be counted on to drum up enthusiasm (three of the twelve were newspaper reporters). One of the most common techniques was to reprint letters predicting the worst, particularly for women and children. Also widely reprinted were some of William Waldo's reports, portions of which were written with an eye to shaming wealthy Californians into charitable contributions. On one occasion when gold dust was temporarily scarce, Waldo challenged his compatriots to surrender their valuable *"finger-rings and breast-pins"* to benefit the cause.[99]

As in Oregon, most communities quickly resorted to canvassing committees charged with house-to-house solicitation. A few mining districts even assessed miners $3 apiece for the relief campaign. Sacramento theaters turned over receipts from specified performances.[100] With no central collection agency, with so many communities involved, and with contributions coming in both cash and merchandise, it is impossible to estimate how much money was ultimately realized, although the total must have reached at least $40,000 or $50,000.

The logistical patterns of relief differed markedly from those of the preceding year. Instead of relief and rescue caravans plying the major access routes, relief stations or depots were established at strategic locations on the Truckee and Carson routes (the Lassen route's image had been so tarnished in 1849 that no one worried about the handful of travelers who might attempt that trail). Apparently two major stations were located on each route, one on either side of the Sierra crossing. Trail gossip quickly alerted oncoming overlanders to their relief endeavors, and some travelers changed routes so as to benefit from the supposedly heavier concentrations of relief supplies at the Carson Trail depots. While some thought was given to extending operations eastward along the Humboldt River, where suffering was already widespread, the slim resources could not be stretched that far. However, William Waldo, a Missouri forty-niner who donated two months to the relief effort, busied himself at the desert crossing west of the Humboldt Sink, where he hauled water to fatigued overlanders and aided those no longer able to traverse the treacherous sands on their own power. He also worked his way eastward along the Humboldt River ten days' travel from the Sink.[101]

In the main, though, the 1850 relief effort consisted of supplying foodstuffs and medical aid at the relief stations. The bulk of the distribution occurred on the more heavily traveled Carson route, where Sacramento's "Relief Company" was particularly instrumental in furnishing personnel and provisions. J. Neely Johnson was succeeded by Judge James A. Ralston as superviser of the main Carson station at Ragtown (known as Johnson's Station), while Waldo and George R. Elliot directed the major Truckee depot. During his twenty-day stint in command Ralston supplied 1,000 suffering emigrants. Waldo reported that between 500 and 800 pounds of beef per day were being distributed in mid-September at the main Truckee River station.[102]

Johnson, Ralston, Waldo, Elliot, and their associates clearly operated as much on faith as on funds. They were invariably reduced to purchasing supplemental rations from nearby trading-post operators on credit, promising to pay as soon as additional funds were received. To satisfy their creditors they continuously exhorted and implored the Sacramentos, Fremonts, and Yuba Citys to send more funds and supplies. They regularly drew drafts for still-uncollected funds on harried relief committee treasurers. Faced with thousands of penniless and impoverished travelers, the relief station operators were forced to dispense provisions not according to need but according to their dwindling stocks. Johnson had begun at Ragtown by allotting twenty pounds of flour per petitioner; he soon had to reduce the individual ration to five pounds and then to two and a half pounds. He was also obliged to refuse any assistance whatever to travelers possessing property which could be sold or traded for provisions at the numerous trading posts lining the last segments of the California Trail. Fortunately, some of the trading-post proprietors aided the general effort by providing food gratis to the neediest applicants.[103]

William Waldo, the roving goodwill ambassador of the 1850 relief effort, was almost overwhelmed by the enormity of the need. In addition to the usual Indian thievery and stock-killing and the disturbingly early snows in the mountains, there was starvation. For several starving 1850 overlanders the suffering was more than they could endure and they committed suicide, usually by plunging into the Humboldt River. There were also disease epidemics brought on by the unsanitary conditions which felled weakened emigrants by the hundreds. The much-dreaded cholera was in evidence. In one small company Waldo witnessed eight deaths within three hours and reported that seven more were imminent. The overall prognosis appeared so bleak that Waldo appealed to stateside preachers to wield their influence in preventing additional emigrants from starting for California, suggesting "Wo! Wo! Wo! to those that go to California to hunt gold!" as the text for the ministerial message. Dismal though the situation appeared, Waldo's personal generosity never waned. When it appeared that no further relief funds would be forthcoming, he wrote the Sacramento suppliers to send $10,000 worth of flour and meat, pledging all his personal property as payment for these life-preserving provisions.[104] J. Neely Johnson also desperately drew upon his own personal resources to help alleviate the considerable suffering.[105]

After all the surviving stragglers had reached the California communities, a few loose financial ends were tied up. The Sacramento city fathers appealed to the state legislature for reimbursement for the medical assistance provided to sick emigrants in Sacramento and for the expenses involved in burying gold rushers who had not survived the final harrowing days on the trail. The state legislatures of Missouri and California also presented memorials in behalf of William Waldo (aptly termed an "angel of mercy" by one grateful 1850 emigrant). When the national government did not respond, the 1853 California legislature appropriated $27,000 to reimburse that beneficent samaritan for his personal expenditures in behalf of the 1850 emigration.[106]

Because hundreds of gold seekers succumbed without reaching their final destination, the 1850 West Coast relief endeavors seem less successful than those of 1849. Yet had the humanitarian efforts not again been undertaken there is no way of estimating how many might have died.

Proliferating access routes and trading posts, coupled with more carefully prepared overlanders, made the need for relief less urgent in 1852, when the next great wave of gold rushers trailed into California. Reverting to the more centrally organized 1849 pattern, the California state legislature appropriated $25,000 for the relief of incoming overlanders. Governor John Bigler appointed a number of individuals to supervise the distribution of food and provisions.[107] As in 1850 the emphasis was on strategically located depots (which emigrants began terming "government relief stations"), of which there were at least four: one at the Humboldt Meadows shortly before the feared desert crossing, another where the roads to the Carson and Truckee rivers diverged, and one each at the Carson and Truckee rivers beyond the desert crossing. A temporary hospital was also established in the Carson Valley, where over 3,000 sick and injured overlanders received treatment. General Rains, one of Bigler's appointees, announced plans for a small desert oasis, with water, grass, and shade.[108]

Although the suffering was less pronounced than in 1850, the $25,000 financing the relief effort was quickly termed "inadequate" by one Sacramento newspaper. Emigrants relied heavily on the relief stations situated before and after the dreaded desert crossings. The station at the fork in the roads proved particularly beneficial to emigrants traversing the desert, many of whom received water from government employees hauling water supplies from the Truckee River back to the relief station.[109]

The several directors of relief activities were apparently under strict orders to preserve their food supplies solely for destitute travelers. They usually refrained from selling provisions to overlanders merely wishing to

An 1849 view of the bustling river port of Sacramento, destination for many California-bound emigrants.

change or supplement adequate if monotonous daily rations.[110] Allegations that one of the government agents—John Bodley—had departed from these instructions to profiteer in relief provisions caused considerable furor that summer and fall. Bodley was widely accused of refusing to publicize that his "trading station" on the Truckee River was in fact a "government relief station," of selling materials designated for the free relief of impoverished travelers at high prices, and of being coldly indifferent to the needs of destitute travelers. Bodley and his agents allegedly acquired considerable emigrant livestock by making desperately needed food available to impoverished emigrants only if the travelers furnished their draft animals in exchange. "Misapplication of public funds, peculation and extortionate dealings with the emigrants who arrived at his station" were additional charges leveled at the hapless Bodley. To defend himself against the vast outpouring of indignation meetings, depositions, and newspaper testimonials, Bodley published a financial accounting of his relief operations. Claiming that he had even expended $314.70 of his personal funds, Bodley also furnished affidavits from defenders absolving him of any wrongdoing.[111]

At this distance it is impossible to assess guilt or innocence. Although in his defense Bodley acknowledged partnership with Truckee stock speculators—a singularly inappropriate collusion—it seems apparent that the increasing impingement of politics upon what had begun as a humanitarian endeavor contributed to the cause célèbre. Some of the anti-Bodley tirades were as clearly attacks on Democratic governor John Bigler as they were protests against the way his appointee had conducted his affairs. Governor Bigler himself apparently endeavored to gain personal political capital from the relief expeditions. An editorial in the *Daily Alta California,* noting the departure of the first relief train, stressed how ridiculous Bigler had made himself appear by marching proudly on horseback at the head of the departing caravan, the wagons of which bore large placards heralding "The California Relief Train." The only thing missing, the editorial writer sarcastically noted, was an "ear-splitting brass band." A circus atmosphere had unfortunately encroached on something very serious, very necessary, and very commendable—the West Coast relief effort.[112] Analogous attempts to profit at the expense of needy emigrants apparently occurred again in 1853. Mary Sanford later recalled that on the Humboldt Desert crossing government agents instructed to haul water for suffering emigrants instead forced their intended beneficiaries to pay for the desperately needed water and all other provisions.[113]

The most pervasive form of West Coast relief, on both the California and Oregon trails, was dispensed by individuals traveling eastward to meet and assist relatives and personal friends on the closing stages of the overland journey. Usually veterans of the overland trek themselves, these West Coast residents knew that oncoming travelers invariably had questions about alternative route possibilities and usually were in need of additional provisions and/or fresh draft animals. Often backtracking hundreds of miles along the overland trails with their welcome relief, their contribution to the overall success of the overland emigrations was considerable. In addition to providing assistance to the friends and relatives they had come to meet, the Californians or Oregonians frequently aided other needy incoming travelers. Thus, a grateful Hugh Skinner noted in his diary on August 23, 1850, "We are now living on the generosity of persons who are on the road with provisions for their friends who are coming on with their teams either dead or nearly exhausted & themselves out of provisions." When the expected relative or friend had not made the journey after all, or had died en route, the disappointed West Coaster would usually offer his relief materials to those most in need. During the gold rush it was even possible to miss relatives and friends in the masses of westering travelers, an eventuality at least four 1852 Californians sought to avoid by erecting "sign boards" advertising for their wives and families along the Humboldt River trail.[114]

The inability to locate a beloved wife or a long-absent brother on the trail, however, was as isolated a travel phenomenon as the trail tragedies associated with Stephen Meek or the Donners. That there are so few analogies to the Meek and Donner trail disasters is not explained only by the helpful interaction among emigrants, the occasional aid received from Indians, the protective assistance of the federal government, the proliferating trailside presence of private entrepreneurs, or even by good fortune. The trail improvements undertaken by West Coast residents and the substantial quantities of humanitarian relief they provided year after year must also take their honored place on the list of "assistants" to overland travelers.

CHAPTER ELEVEN

The Overlanders
in Historical Perspective

*"To endure heat like a salamander . . .
and labor like a jackass"*

FOR MORE THAN A CENTURY THE REALITY and the significance of the antebellum overland migrations have been distorted by overblown rhetoric. Historians, novelists, poets, artists, screenwriters, politicians, reminiscing overlanders and their descendants—all have contributed to the myths and stereotypes enveloping the story of the westbound pioneers. The end result of this repetitious retelling of the "Old Oregon Trail" saga, as Merrill Mattes has noted in a recent essay, is that almost everyone assumes the overland emigrations to be "a threadbare subject for scholarly investigation."[1] Yet, as this writer has endeavored to demonstrate in the preceding chapters, a comprehensive analysis of the antebellum emigration phenomenon from the fresh perspectives of change through time and cooperative assistance reveals the inadequacy of many of our prevailing assumptions.

Certainly it is time to discard the language of "typicality" in characterizing the migration years. Neither the "great migration" of 1843 nor the trek of the impatient forty-niners encapsulates all that is significant about the antebellum overland movement. No "golden history" of the emigrations will suffice. It is, after all, one thing to acknowledge the stimulating impact of the California gold rushers upon trailside supportive facilities; it is quite another to presume that focusing the historical spotlight on 1849 alone will satisfactorily illuminate twenty emigration years. The felicitous phrase with which Dale Morgan described the 1846 migration year is applicable to each year that overlanders trailed west: ". . . a sense of magnificent spectacle, with human nature on the loose."[2] The emigration experience was ever changing; each travel year evidenced distinctive patterns, unique dramas of triumph and tragedy, new contributions to the mosaic of western development.

For example, it seems axiomatic to distinguish between abnormally wet and abnormally dry years along the trails, since climatic fluctuation had a far-reaching impact upon the overland journey. In 1844 unseasonable rains created such havoc with stream crossings that it took one large company fully two and a half weeks to ford a single swollen creek. Indeed, that traveling group needed sixty-one days to penetrate 200 miles west of the Missouri River. But exceptionally rainy weather had commensurate advantages: 1853 California-bound travelers enjoyed far easier desert crossings because they found grass growing where overlanders had never seen it before.[3]

Differentiation must also be made between years when most emigrants outfitted with considerable care and years such as 1850, when they recklessly took so little that they set the stage for catastrophic starvation.[4] Viewing the overland emigrations in historical perspective similarly requires differentiating between years when disease was infrequent (such as the early 1840s) and the gold rush years, when thousands of emigrants fell victim to cholera epidemics; between years when family groups dominated the trails and the early gold rush years, when the route was thronged with unaccompanied men;[5] between years when the pace of travel was slower and the gold rush years, when the hurry-up atmosphere was so prevalent that many travelers discarded even such standard expressions of compassion as delaying the journey for several days so that a dangerously sick or injured comrade might have a better chance to recover. Thus the 1849 Pioneer Line, which had rashly promised to deliver its passengers to the California gold fields in sixty days, had no time for such niceties. The wagon in which a young Marylander lay at death's door kept bouncing westward. It was ominously followed by two trainmen bearing picks and shovels with which to dig the diseased forty-niner's grave without a moment's delay.[6]

The inexorable growth of supportive facilities, so closely intertwined with the accelerating numbers of westbound pioneers, further negates the usefulness of a "typical year" approach in explaining the westward movement. Overland travel was radically altered by the Mormon hegira to the Salt Lake Valley, by the advent of profit-seeking merchants and entrepreneurs, and by the gradual extension of government services westward to the Pacific. By the early 1850s, for example, the Latter-Day Saints' "halfway house" could furnish the traveler with everything from provisions, wagons, or draft animals to bathhouses, barbershops, and law courts for the adjudication of severed traveling agreements. The optimistic entrepreneurs who bridged rivers and constructed trading posts from one end of the overland trail to the other transformed the character of overland travel at the same time that they made it more expensive. Similarly revolutionizing the nature of the overland journey were the diverse traveler-oriented activities of the federal government: exploration, survey, road construction, postal services, the establishment of forts, the dispatching of punitive military expeditions, the allocation of protective escorts for emigrant caravans, the negotiation of Indian treaties designed to insure the safety of emigrant travel.

The constantly changing pattern of overland travel was evident in many other ways. The California gold rush accelerated the amount of eastbound trail traffic. Trail improvements contributed to significant reductions in the amount of time required to travel the overland route, whether westbound or eastbound. Similarly, it is clear that the Indian "threat" to overlanders was a feature of the 1850s far more than of the 1840s, and that travelers were much more likely to have serious problems west of South Pass than on the early portion of the journey. And it was only a few years before the appearance of reasonably reliable overland guidebooks made the employment of mountaineer guides unnecessary. The need for relying upon a guidebook for route directions, in turn, was quickly rendered superfluous by the heavy trail travel, which indelibly marked the overland route even for the most inept greenhorn—west of St. Joseph the "heavy beaten track" was measured at forty-five paces across in 1852.[7] Not even at the Missouri River jumping-off points did static conditions prevail, since emigrants increasingly gravitated northward toward Council Bluffs–Omaha as their point of departure.

Once the overlanders began traveling westward, they discovered growing settlements initially associated with bridges, trading posts, forts, or stage stations and thus also a direct outgrowth of the overland emigrations.[8] During the 1840s overlanders had regularly remarked that they were leaving "civilization" to launch out into the "wilderness" once they had crossed the Missouri River.[9] By the mid–1850s such phraseology was no longer appropriate, since the westbound emigrant now traveled for hundreds of miles past farms and through towns. The massive amounts of humanitarian relief furnished by Oregon and California in order to ease the travel hardships along the last several hundred miles of the overland trails likewise altered the perceptions with which travelers approached the transcontinental journey. Indeed, the rapidity with which momentous change had come to the Far West was most clearly evidenced by the fact that California had achieved statehood in 1850 and Oregon in 1859. During the early 1840s, in contrast, westbound pioneers did not even know whether they were going to be able to remain citizens of the United States.

Since the overland emigrants themselves paid so little attention to the vicissitudes of overland travel during the antebellum years, perhaps it is not surprising that so many subsequent writers and historians have followed their lead. Only rarely did emigrants acknowledge how different it was to travel "the plains across"—as they occasionally described the cross-continental venture—when they were making the trip than it had been a year or a decade earlier.[10] This is understandable, for the majority of overlanders made the journey only once and were not in a position to make comparisons.

Moreover, the overland trip was unique to each individual traveler, whose perception of it was largely dependent upon his or her expectations, preparations, constitution, traveling companions, luck, and a multitude of related factors. When emigrants did reflect upon the trip, as most of them did at some point during the journey, their comments about the ease or difficulty of the venture were invariably based upon what they themselves were experiencing. Those who were progressing well and were in good health found the trip a veritable pleasure excursion—as they probably would have whether the year had been 1840, 1850, or 1860. But those beset with unanticipated difficulties usually averred that they would never attempt such a horrendous journey again. Such disillusioned travelers, preoccupied with their own difficulties and concerns, cared little about the impact the Mormons, the government, private entrepreneurs, and the states and territories of the Pacific had made upon the nature of overland travel.

In later years, however, when the travails of the trek were no longer a daily burden, veterans of overland travel periodically attempted to assess the nature and meaning of the overland journey. The most intriguing of those evaluations are reported in the transactions of the meetings of the Oregon Pioneer Association. In their annual gatherings these former overlanders, whose reminiscent writings and oratory were so instrumental in apotheosizing the overland movement, inadvertently confirmed that the overland journey had fundamentally changed in character and difficulty during the antebellum period.

The former overlanders had organized in the early 1870s to collect historical material relating to early Oregon and to renew the friendships formed "while making the long, perilous journey of the wide, wild plains, which separated the western boundary of civilization thirty years ago, from the land which they had resolved to reclaim."[11] The constitution they drafted welcomed into membership all former "immigrants," both male and female, who had resided within the boundaries of the future Oregon Territory during the period of joint British-American occupancy and all who had subsequently settled in Oregon Territory prior to January 1, 1853.[12] In 1875, at the third annual reunion of the association, the article on membership was amended to grant eligibility to all territorial residents or descendants of residents prior to January 1, 1854. At the seventh annual reunion in 1879 the cutoff date for recognizing a "pioneer" was set back yet another year, to January 1, 1855.[13] Additional attempts to roll back further the date of eligibility were unsuccessful, culminating in a spirited dispute at the eighteenth annual meeting in 1890, when association members endeavored to clarify whether bona fide pioneers had been obliged to reach Oregon before 1855.

This 1890 Portland assemblage of pioneers and pioneer offspring debated a resolution to establish the membership cutoff date as February 14, 1859—when Oregon had been admitted into the Union. Advocates pragmatically contended both that extending the eligibility date would increase the association's membership and that 1859 marked the clear end of a historical era, pointing out that there was no apparent rationale for the prevailing date of January 1, 1855. Some opponents of adopting the new date obviously wished to keep the association small and elite, but their basic arguments demonstrated an understanding that both the nature of Oregon society and the trip to Oregon had changed dramatically over the years. Curtis C. Strong, an 1849 arrival, advanced this theory:

The word pioneer means foot-soldier, foot-traveler; it properly represents the condition of those who came to this country foot-travelers, and that word prepares the way. . . . I am very much opposed to extending the time beyond 1854. A pioneer is not a pioneer when he can get on a steamship in the port of New York, pay his passage, get three good meals a day, get a berth to sleep in at night, and be landed here with all his bag and baggage without effort on his part; he is not a pioneer in any sense of the word. We have already brought the time down to 1854, and that is far enough; I am opposed to its being continued beyond that time.[14]

The argument of F. V. Holman, whose own arrival in 1854 just barely made him eligible for membership, spoke even more directly to the changing nature of the overland trip:

You cannot call a man a member of the G. A. R. who might have gone to the war and did not, or the man who might have come here in 1842, 1843 and 1845 and did not, a pioneer. You may enlarge the time, you may make it 1859, but the moment you do you have taken away that privilege that is distinctively sacred and honorable, that is due to the hard service, the hard toil, the privations, the fighting, the cutting of the way through the wilderness that was endured by these pioneers, and the pioneers of Oregon are a thing of the past.[15]

Joseph Watt, however, who had come overland in 1844, was more representative of majority opinion in admitting to little change in journey difficulty over the years. It had always been rough:

I do not think that there were any more conveniences in '59 than in '54. Those who came in the former year endured as many privations as those who came in the latter, and I had as lieve take a man by the hand that came in '59 as one that came in '54. We are dying off, thinning out, and in a little time there will be but few left to carry on these meetings. We need new members to keep it up, and I for one hope this meeting will extend the time.[16]

Watt did not get his wish until 1894, at the twenty-second annual reunion, when, after another spirited discussion and two votes, the amendment

The rigors of the trail are evident on the faces of this family, posing for the camera at the end of a long day.

carried 143 to 85. The Oregon Pioneer Association now joined its kindred organization, the Society of California Pioneers, in limiting the pioneer era to the pre-statehood period.[17]

Portraying the overland emigrations in historical perspective further requires an awareness that changing travel conditions must be complemented with an appreciation of the long-neglected factors of cooperation and community. Contrary to prevailing media stereotypes, the overland emigrants did not go west in isolation, each small company alone on the trail with only its ingenuity and heroism to see it through. Even in the early 1840s, before the trails had become so crowded that it was sometimes necessary to stop early to secure a decent campsite, the quantity of trail traffic was astounding: eastbound and westbound emigrants, fur-trapping caravans, traders, hunting and sightseeing parties, missionaries, army units, trade-eager Indians. The overland trip was never as isolated an enterprise as legend would have it. During the California gold rush the trails were transformed into wide and busy highways. Polluted with travel debris, they were often so dusty that overlanders donned goggles to see, and so crowded that traveling partners and relatives became separated in the vast multitudes passing east and west.

Moreover, for too long the antebellum West has been portrayed only negatively as a wilderness barrier of trackless deserts, impassable mountains, bloodthirsty Indians, and savage wild beasts—all of which the courageous little bands of overlanders had to conquer singlehandedly before they reached the paradises on the Pacific. The West, of course, *was* an obstacle to overland travel. But it was also a help, and so too were its inhabitants. Over a quarter of a million successful overland emigrants in a twenty-year time span conclusively attest to the fact that western terrain, climate, and inhabitants posed no insurmountable obstacle to overland travel. The overlander never strayed far from the life-sustaining rivers angling sequentially westward from the Missouri: the Platte, Sweetwater, Snake, Columbia, Humboldt, Carson, and Truckee. If the emigrant outfitted carefully, commenced his journey as soon as the prairie grasses sustained grazing, maintained reasonable hygiene, treated the Indians fairly, respectfully, and strictly, and followed a routine of deliberate daily travel interspersed with regular days of rest, there was little reason to fear the overland trip. Indeed, there was a certain rhythm to successful trail travel. Most emigrants eventually learned that a pell-mell dash westward was a flirtation with disaster. Western weather and landscape could not be bludgeoned into submission, at least not with animal power. Overland travel had to be synchronized with climate and terrain.

The positive contribution of western flora and fauna to successful overland travel is self-evident. Overland emigrants were totally dependent on grass and water for survival, with wood or buffalo chips only slightly less important. Forty-niner Bernard Reid, at an encampment near South Pass where his company found "excellent wood, water and grass," termed these essentials "the emigrant's trinity of good things."[18] Saleratus secured at places like Soda Springs served as an effective substitute for yeast or baking soda during the course of the journey. The West also offered supplemental food. Thousands of hungry overlanders feasted on the buffalo, elk, deer, duck, and other wild game that emigrant marksmen shot, on fish that emigrant anglers took from rivers and streams, on berries and herbs that travelers found near the trails. A great many buffalo, however, were killed not for food but for "sport." It was a rare company of overlanders which did not temporarily forget all trail discipline at their first sighting of a buffalo herd and go racing off in reckless pursuit. The passing overlanders began the senseless assault on the great bison herds which ultimately led to their near extinction. Isaac Foster was one of a handful of diarists who expressed concern at the wanton destruction: ". . . the valley of the Platte for 200 miles presents the aspect of the vicinity of a slaughter yard; dotted all over with skeletons of buffalos; such waste of the creatures that God has made for man seems wicked, but every emigrant seems to wish to signalize himself by killing a buffalo." The ramifications of this non-conservationist outlook on the part of the majority of overlanders were correctly assessed the following year by John Steele after he passed twelve buffalo left to rot: "Such destruction of game doubtless enrages the Indians against the whites."[19]

For virtually all overlanders the western Indians were akin to the buffalo in symbolizing danger and adventure. The first trail encounter with Indians invariably resulted in a long diary entry or a lengthy paragraph in the next letter home, complete with an analysis of Indian character, demeanor, apparel, and customs, and rife with speculation on the nature of future encounters. While fascinated emigrant diarists were not always condemnatory in their attitudes toward the Indians, they rarely acknowledged the positive Indian contribution to overland travel. On examination, however, the much-maligned "savage Indians" of folklore prove to have been of considerable assistance to passing overlanders, particularly during the 1840s before the boom in supportive facilities set in. That Indian begging and thievery were traveling nuisances cannot be denied, but it is also clear that the extent of Indian attacks on overland caravans has been greatly exaggerated. In fact, there is considerable evidence that the fatal trail confrontations which did occur were usually prompted by emigrant insults and disdain for Indian rights, as well as by indiscriminate and injudicious chastisement meted out by the U.S. Army. Notwithstanding the fact that nearly 400 emigrants were killed by Indians in the first twenty years of overland travel, Indian tribes provided overlanders with information, foodstuffs, clothing, equipment, horses, canoeing and swimming skills, traveling materials, and other assistance. Indians, like the West they inhabited, should henceforth be regarded more positively as helpful assistants to overland travelers and not only negatively as barriers.

Just as the overlander who succeeded in the transcontinental trek found it necessary to harmonize his travel with the land and its long-term inhabitants, a successful journey required cooperation with eastbound and westbound colleagues on the trail. Indeed, in describing the overland emigrations it is appropriate to speak of the "traveling community." Emigrants shared information and commiserated about frightening trailside rumors, they forwarded letters, cooperated in erecting rude bridges across streams, and exulted in meeting fellow lodge members. They combined forces to hunt strayed or stolen cattle, to chastise marauding Indians, or to hear and pass judgment upon cases of trailside criminal activity. They sold surplus foodstuffs and traveling supplies, generously aided their less fortunate comrades, and regularly shared meals with those who had temporarily become separated from their traveling company while seeking strayed stock, admiring the landscape, or napping by the side of the trail. Those who still possessed wagons at the end of the journey often transported the baggage of those forced to abandon their conveyances; physicians were on call to those in distress for miles around. When all else failed, there was always someone's debris to fuel a campfire or assuage hunger. On the closing stages of the journey emigrants came to rely so much upon relief and assistance from the settlers of Oregon and California that when it was not forthcoming in the anticipated amounts they occasionally grumbled in dissatisfaction. Forty-niner Elisha Perkins testified to the pervasiveness of this cooperative outlook:

When we left the frontier we were told great stories about the selfishness & want of feeling among the Emigrants that the hardships and uncertainties of the journey had soured what 'milk of human kindness' they might have possessed. I wish to bear my testimony against this slander. Never have I seen so much hospitality & good feeling anywhere exhibited as since I have been on this route. Let any stranger visit a camp no matter who or where, & the best of everything is brought out, he is fed, & caressed almost universally. If at meal time the best pieces are put on his plate & if the train has any luxuries they are placed before him. Nor have I seen any man in trouble, deserted, without all the assistance they could render. There are of course individual exceptions to all this, & such men are known to almost every train following.[20]

That westbound and eastbound travelers, particularly during the gold rush, did not always conclude their journey in company with the companions with whom they had started is less important to an understanding of the emigrations than is this persistence of emigrant interaction. Believing that there was security in numbers, particularly during the 1840s, the emigrants had carefully grouped together prior to starting. Sometimes these were informal traveling associations, while on other occasions constitutions and bylaws were carefully drafted. Once en route it was not unusual for overlanders to switch to another company more congenial to their traveling speed or outlook on life. As new friends were made, old traveling partnerships were scrapped and new ones inaugurated.

"California Emigrants—the Last Day on the Plains." Still enjoying the bounty of the plains and the camaraderie of their shared experience, these pioneers hear the call to move out for the last time. Bancroft Library

The subsequent formation and long history of the California and Oregon pioneer organizations are further evidence of the camaraderie which prevailed among those participating in the great collective adventure of overland travel, an experience which broke down barriers of religion, politics, and place of birth.[21] Perhaps this nationalizing, democratizing quality of overland travel was seen most clearly in the traveling groups of the early 1840s and in the passenger trains of 1849 and 1850, where many total strangers suddenly joined forces with little alternative but to pull together if their journey was to be successful. Traveling in a sixty-man outfit incorporating groups from Mississippi, Tennessee, Illinois, and Ohio, David Dewolf remarked that "we are a mixed up multitude but we all get along fine. Some of them get in a spur now & then but soon get over it. This trip binds us together like a band of brothers."[22]

Another interesting characteristic of the traveling community was the fluidity with which personal possessions changed hands throughout the journey. In 1843, for example, James Nesmith traded guns twice in one day. A horse he had purchased en route from a Snake Indian he subsequently exchanged with a Chinook brave for a canoe. William Chamberlain's 1849 trading activity was considerably more energetic. After beginning by exchanging tents with a Fort Kearny soldier and trading his lantern for butter with some Mormon travelers, he got down to serious swapping at Fort Laramie by exchanging mules with a Cincinnati emigrant. Three days later he traded his new mule for a pony; two weeks later at the Green River he swapped the pony for a mule with a French trader (paying $10 extra); four days later "Peg-leg" Smith, another trader, got the mule and $20 in exchange for an Indian pony. A month later Chamberlain was once again riding a mule. He had owned at least six different riding animals during the course of his overland journey. Other emigrants, growing tired of their wagons or teams (sometimes even before they had begun their journey), would seek out someone willing to swap and move forward with a different vehicle powered by a different type of animal.[23]

Yet another intriguing facet of the traveling community was the unique way in which emigrants came to recognize their fellow travelers by the mottoes emblazoned on their wagon covers. While many overlanders merely affixed their names and place of origin to their canvas tops, countless emigrants revealed their personalities through the slogans they displayed, or at least so some of their traveling colleagues thought. The artistically inclined decorated their wagon covers with huge images of buffalo, eagles, oxen, giraffes, and lions, as well as with the ubiquitous elephant. The more reflective counseled "Patience and Perseverance," "Never Say Die," and "Westward the Tide of Emigration Rolls." In the early 1840s political slogans such as "54° 40' or Fight" and "Oregon, the Whole or None" were much in evidence.

The gold rushers were the most creative sloganeers. Their word plays on gold were to be expected ("Gold Hunters," "Gold or a Grave," and "With my wash bowl on my knee"), as were variations on the trail password *Have You Seen the Elephant?*" Also not unusual were such allusions to song and sweetheart as "Sweet Sallie," "Our Sal," or "Flora." Less predictable were such gems as "Davy Crockett through by day light," "*Bob Tail* Company *East Beat,*" "Be sure you are right and let him rip," and "Brest for doze dat spect noting for dey will not be disappointed." The "Tornado Train," "Prairie Bird," "Albatross," "Merry Suckers," and "Passia Bird" also attracted attention; and surely no one missed the "Hell Greasers," "Red Rover," the "Pirate," or the "Ass." When such a familiarly marked wagon came into view the overlander felt like welcoming an old friend—and was also able to conveniently gauge whether he was keeping up with the flow of travel.[24]

Examples further illustrating the collective nature of the emigrating experience abound, but few are more persuasive than the experience related by Margaret Windsor, a young girl traveling overland in 1852. During the last 500 miles of the journey Margaret cared for a baby whose mother had died en route. At each campground Margaret would seek out a woman to nurse the infant. She was, she later recalled, never once refused. Additional evidence of this collective community can be seen in the many travelers who contributed generously to a fund enabling the victim of an accidental shooting in 1850 to receive continuing treatment and be transported back to his home.[25]

The significantly changing nature of overland travel and the crucial role of cooperative assistance emerge, therefore, as the key factors in understanding the antebellum overland emigrations. Viewing those emigrations in historical perspective, however, requires more than an appreciation of how a 2,000-mile overland journey could be successfully accomplished. What the emigrants took west with them, in matters both tangible and intangible, has had a far-reaching impact upon the nation.

The infusion into West Coast economies of the considerable specie and merchandise many well-to-do overlanders brought with them is only the most obvious example, with the instant impact of the forty-niners on the Mormon economy the most sensational illustration.[26] While the impact of the incoming emigrants upon the diplomacy of the Oregon boundary question was not the dominant factor in the resolution of that controversy, had not the emigrations occurred when they did, proving the viability of overland travel and peopling the Willamette Valley with thousands of staunch American advocates, the history of the Pacific Northwest would certainly have taken a different turn.[27] Similarly, the frequency of emigrant travel through the Salt Lake Valley kept the controversial beliefs and activities of the Latter-Day Saints on the front pages of the nation's newspapers, as did the indignant writings of anti-Mormon zealots who interrupted their overland journeys to winter among the Saints. These factors were instrumental in bringing about the Mormon War of 1857–58, one of the most curious of all American martial endeavors.

Less well known is the contribution of emigrating overlanders to far western horticulture and agriculture. The pioneer coastal horticulturist was an Iowa Quaker, Henderson Luelling, who brought his family overland to Oregon in 1847. As his daughter Eliza later complained, during the journey Luelling was almost more solicitous of the approximately 700 grafted young trees, vines, and shrubs he was taking with him than he was of his family. Luelling's "traveling nursery" occasioned considerable trail interest. It was transported in two large boxes which completely filled his lead wagon. Three yoke of oxen were needed to pull it. The trees ranged in size from twenty inches to four feet and were packed in a composted mixture of charcoal and rich Iowa soil. Included in Luelling's strange trail cargo were such varieties as apple, cherry, pear, plum, black walnut, quince, and shell-bark hickory.[28]

The long-range impact of the safe arrival of this traveling nursery was enormous. Luelling himself made a fortune, as William Barlow ruefully noted in later years, remembering that two years prior to Luelling's journey he himself had departed overland for Oregon with a 300-pound box filled with several varieties of Illinois fruit trees. However, in one of the classic examples of the deleterious influence of trailside information, Barlow dumped his potential gold mine near Independence Rock. He had been convinced by returning Oregonians that he would be unable to get his tree box safely down the Columbia River, and that Oregon was already blessed with good fruit trees anyway. By 1853 Barlow was paying Luelling—who had since combined forces with William Meek, another 1847 Iowa emigrant who had independently transported fruit trees overland to Oregon—$1 apiece for year-old fruit trees. The value of Luelling's wagonload to the Oregon and California economies was estimated by Barlow in 1912 at over a million dollars. Luelling's success influenced another overlander, Illinois dentist James R. Cardwell, to make a similar attempt in 1852. Cardwell's luck held almost until the end of the journey, when on a steep bank of the Snake River his wagon fell into the water and his plants and trees floated away, insuring Cardwell's resumption of the practice of dentistry on his arrival.[29]

While western orchards and nurseries were evolving from Luelling's initial stimulus, overland emigrants were similarly revolutionizing western livestock enterprises. Historians have been far too parochial in dwelling so exclusively on the drama, color, and significance of the "long drives" on the Chisholm and Western cattle trails from Texas to the Kansas railheads. Although such western communities as Salt Lake City, Oregon City, Sacramento, or Yreka are no match for Abilene, Wichita, or Dodge City in American folklore, they likewise functioned as the termini of much earlier,

391

much longer, much more dangerous, and equally significant overland trail drives. Oregon-California Trail "cowboys" trailed virtually everything imaginable westward—cattle, sheep, horses, mules, goats, and even turkeys.[30] Many of the drovers wintered in Utah or Nevada, but many also completed the long drive in one traveling season. And the quantities of livestock trailed westward along the South Pass overland route in the peak years of the early 1850s almost rivaled the numbers of Longhorns trailed northward from Texas nearly a decade and a half later, when the legendary Chisholm Trail first came into use.[31]

Those driving stock on the overland trail never coexisted easily with other overland emigrants. For one thing, they slowed down the rate of progress; for another it usually did not take too many nights of monotonous guard duty before those emigrants without large droves of cattle began to wonder why they should sacrifice needed rest to protect someone else's speculative enterprise. Then, too, a large stock drove meant more noise, dust, smell, and, in the event of stampede, more danger. Already in 1843 the difficulty of meshing cattle-driving with the normal routine of an emigrant caravan was revealed by the split between those trailing surplus cattle west (the "cow column" described in Jesse Applegate's famous essay) and those without such additional retinue.[32]

Perhaps it was for such reasons that relatively few droves of cattle or sheep were trailed to the Pacific Coast during the 1840s. But more probably it was because economically there was no compelling reason for doing so, even though Peter H. Burnett's July 25, 1844, letter from Oregon had called attention to the potential profits to be made in bringing livestock overland.[33] When the 1848 gold discovery attracted such an enormous population to California, however, the price of nearly everything rose so astronomically that shrewd entrepreneurs quickly took to the trails with large droves of cattle and other livestock. The best example of the immediacy with which inflated California market prices influenced trail traffic is the longest trail drive on record—Miles Goodyear's 4,000-mile round-trip endeavor of 1848–49. Goodyear began trailing approximately 230 California horses to Missouri in the spring of 1848, hoping to capitalize on the need for horses occasioned by the Mexican War. After learning, on his Missouri arrival, of the enticing California possibilities, he purchased additional horses and mules. In the spring of 1849 Goodyear hastened westward with his enlarged drove, ultimately selling his surviving stock at good prices in California.[34]

The discrepancy between California prices and those prevailing in Missouri and surrounding states prompted much emulation of the east-to-west portion of Goodyear's long drive. In fact, the endeavor was so potentially lucrative that a number of overlanders made droving trips across the plains their chief business activity during the 1850s. One Oregonian tempted by the potential profits cautioned, however, that such

Indians and buffalo, mealtime on the trail, desolate deserts, droves of livestock were all included along with the familiar landmarks in this 1853 "travel brochure" from a California weekly.

endeavors demanded "a devil daring reckless sort of a fellow."[35] An excellent example of such a daring entrepreneur was Randy Fuller, a forty-niner from Waukesha, Wisconsin. Having returned by sea during the winter of 1851–52 to secure trail stock, Fuller paid $30 for oxen he later sold in California at between $100 and $120 per head; $70 to $100 for horses he eventually sold for $200 to $500 per head; and $12 for cows he sold at between $50 and $150 per head. His venture was so successful he again returned by sea and in 1854 was on the plains with another drove.[36]

At such prices drovers could accept considerable losses en route—a common estimate was between 10 and 20 percent of a trail herd—as well as afford ferriage tolls and still realize enormous profits.[37] One 1853 entrepreneur who purchased 3,300 sheep in Missouri for between $1 and $1.25 per head lost fully a third en route, but still realized over three times his initial investment when he sold the surviving 2,100 sheep in California in October for from $8 to $12 per head. Another Missouri drover who reached California in 1852 with 2,000 of the 2,500 sheep he had started with refused offers of $18 per head because he was convinced he could get more. This canny entrepreneur had earned an additional $2,500 from the sale of wool in Salt Lake City, where he had tarried to shear his sheep. An 1852 speculator who trailed 1,200 sheep to Oregon (losing only fifty head en route) expected to clear $5,000 more on the venture than he could in four years of mining.[38]

In most respects, trailing cattle or sheep to California or Oregon differed little from the normal overland journey, as Thomas Flint's diary of an 1853 sheep drive makes clear. Flint's small crew—between eleven and fifteen men—traveled with two wagons, two cows, eleven yoke of oxen, and 1,880 sheep. Traveling along the north side of the Platte River, they spent $198.80 in ferrying their sheep over the Missouri, Elkhorn, and Loup Fork rivers. They forded the Green River after unsuccessful negotiations with the ferry proprietor. Keeping wolves away from the sheep and the sheep away from poisonous weeds were their major preoccupations during the journey. Indians were not a problem, despite the fact that one of Flint's drovers was killed one night while on guard duty by an unseen assailant presumed to have been an Indian. This incident naturally led those on guard duty to be super-cautious, and the inevitable shooting at shadows occurred. Fortunately only sheep were killed. At Salt Lake City Flint's outfit purchased 210 more sheep from an Illinois drover—the price this far west now stood at $4 per head—plus several additional oxen and cows. From the Salt Lake Valley, like some other drovers, they then followed the Mormon Corridor to Los Angeles. While Flint does not provide a full accounting of the ensuing profits, he does note the sale of 997 wethers for $16,000.[39]

The peak years for stock drives on the overland trail were 1852, 1853, and 1854, although large droves continued throughout the decade. The usual-sized cattle drove varied between 500 and 2,000 head; sheep droves were normally considerably larger, some drovers herding flocks of up to 10,000 sheep. Henry Allyn passed an 1853 cattle drove that was strung out for over a mile; Mary Burrel, a year later, remarked, "This world is all a cattle show, sure enough" after passing an estimated five miles of slow-moving cattle. Also in 1854 an early-starting drover already beyond South Pass was so surprised to see a genuine company of overland emigrants in the midst of all the cattle and sheep on the trails that he recorded the strange phenomenon in his diary.[40]

Estimates of how many sheep and cattle were trailed overland to the West Coast cannot be precise, although the 1853 Fort Kearny emigrant register enumerated 105,792 cattle, 5,477 horses, 2,190 mules, and 48,495 sheep on the south side of the Platte River alone through August 15. Travelers' estimates of the number of cattle and sheep on the overland trails during the 1850s were usually extremely high, 300,000 being the widely mentioned estimate for 1853. There seems little reason to doubt that drovers trailed over half a million cattle and perhaps half a million sheep to the Pacific Coast on the northern overland trails during the antebellum years. Additional herds were brought into California along southern trails. The influx of such numbers not only was significant in meeting the food needs of an increasing population but also had a salutary impact upon the far western livestock industry.[41]

The overlanders' impact upon Indian-white relationships was much less beneficial. Initially most catastrophic were the severely contagious diseases spread among the Indian tribes by the emigrant passage. Some Indians quickly recognized the consequences of these diseases—by 1850 a Fort Laramie observer reported that frightened natives were deserting the trails in hopes of avoiding the deadly peril. But for most tribes Indian-emigrant interaction continued as usual. Accordingly, the demographic impact of cholera alone upon the Osage, Sac and Fox, Kansa, Kickapoo, Potawatomi, Wyandotte, Miami, Delaware, Shawnee, Pawnee, Cheyenne, and Sioux was considerable. These population losses had obvious implications for the ability of western tribes to resist the American expansionist onslaught.[42]

The overlanders' transit through Indian territory was disadvantageous to the native inhabitants in additional ways. Emigrant fears of possible Indian treachery prompted most of the demands for governmental protection and resulted in the onset of punitive expeditions, trailside forts, and army patrols along the South Pass route. These developments, coupled with the legacy of the emigrant passage, probably rendered irrepressible the western Indian wars following the Civil War. The attitudes of blatant superiority exhibited by so many overlanders, together with their reckless actions as they crisscrossed the continent—ignoring Indian claims to tolls or bridge fees, shooting at Indians on sight, nonselective retaliation—occasioned corresponding Indian responses. These widening circles of suspicion and hostility were similarly influenced by the national publicity given to the anti-Indian attitudes held by many overlanders. The prejudices thereby fostered and/or popularized were important in the development of attitudes countenancing excesses against certain or even all Indian tribes. An instructive example of this process is found in the reminiscences of forty-niner Charles D. Ferguson:

Powder, not prayer, is their only civilizer. . . . Nothing will convert an Indian like convincing him that you are his superior, and there is but one process by which even that can be done, and that is to shut off his wind. I never knew but one 'truly good' Indian, and he was dead. I have heard considerable romance, from persons inexperienced, about the brave and noble red man, but I never yet have met one. All I have ever known have been cowardly and treacherous, never attack like men, but crawl upon you, three or four to one, and shoot you down, as they did sixteen of our party in the canon. Then why not attack them, not wait to be attacked by them, and then only in self-defense take, perhaps, one of their worthless lives? . . . The Indian is the emigrant's enemy. If the emigrant gets the advantage, why should he not take it, for most surely the Indian will?[43]

Emigrants often accorded the Sioux and occasionally the Snake Indians grudging compliments. But the Root Diggers and especially the Pawnee were invariably described in such derogatory terms that almost anything done to them was acceptable, if not applauded. Perhaps the clearest example of this anti-Pawnee prejudice (which was not, of course, completely unique to the emigrants, fur traders having already laid some of the groundwork) is in the comment of a forty-niner on board the steamship *Paris* in the Cincinnati vicinity long before any Pawnee had been seen: "Our Rifles are in fine condition and are the admiration of all the passengers—We have amused ourselves all the way down the River shooting at wild ducks; and when no men were around we would shoot at hogs, dogs &c on the shore—thirty or forty rifles, fired all at the same time, would hurry a dog some I reckon—by the time we get among the Pawnees, we will be able to take their eye out without much trouble."[44]

Some of the most significant dimensions of the antebellum emigration experience were these attitudes and impressions developed during the course of the overland journey. The overland pilgrimage itself was nothing less than the discovery of a fantastic new nation. "Come by the plains to see the country" was John Wilson's recommendation to a Missouri friend in 1850. Emigrant diarists and letter writers quickly fashioned a new lexicon with which to describe the wonders they were witnessing, even though, as Addison Crane readily admitted in 1852, no written words could ever describe the "magnificent character" of the West, and anyone who tried would only "make a fool of himself."[45]

But Crane and his colleagues did try. It was a rare diarist or letter writer who did not at least once term some phenomenon "romantic," or "the greatest natural curiosity" ever seen. Most of all, the emigrants viewed the West as larger than life; it was with superlatives that the overlanders reported the West to their countrymen and the world. The scenery was the grandest they had ever seen, the trees the tallest, the natural roads the finest, the water the best, the grass the most luxuriant, the wind the strongest, the rainstorms the heaviest, the hailstones the largest, the lightning the brightest, the thunder the loudest, the rainbows the most brilliant, the mountains the most spectacular, the grasshoppers the biggest, the meat of the buffalo and mountain sheep the juiciest, the Indians the handsomest, the rapid temperature changes the most phenomenal—the list is as endless as there were phenomena to describe.[46]

To be sure, not everything encountered prompted contemplation on the wonderful handiwork of God. Mosquitoes, gnats, dust, deserts, and irritable humans came in for a great deal of special complaint. But even these afflictions were seen as somehow different; they too were more pervasive, more monumental than elsewhere.[47] John Lewis, who thought the sun to be hotter on the plains than anywhere else, suggested that in the West even sexual intercourse took on a new dimension: ". . . love is hotter her[e] than anywhare that I have seen when they love here they love with all thare mite & some times a little harder."[48]

Mesmerized emigrants exulted at the beautiful wild flowers they discovered (and the seeds of which they mailed home); they marveled at the many butterflies, animals, birds, and trees they had never seen before; they amazedly threw snowballs and dug for ice beneath the grass near South Pass in midsummer; they waxed eloquent over such natural wonders as Chimney Rock, Independence Rock, Devil's Gate, and Soda Springs, and unashamedly carved their names or initials in the stone as proof of their presence.[49] One awed 1853 emigrant opined that American tourists should "be more desirous of seeing their own country before going to Europe." After all, where else could anything so moving be experienced? Edwin Bryant's panegyric to Truckee Lake in 1846 is typical of this use of superlative imagery in portraying the West: "The Alps, so celebrated in history and by all travelers and admirers of mountain landscape, cannot, I am satisfied, present scenery more wild, more rugged, more grand, more romantic, and more enchantingly pictureque and beautiful, than that which surrounds this lake, of which the lake itself composes a part."[50] These conceptions of the boundlessness, the grandeur, the vast proportions of the seemingly inexhaustible West have never been completely discarded. Certainly the oral reports as well as the letters, diaries, and later reminiscent publications of the overland emigrants were instrumental in the development of this larger-than-life imagery.

At the same time that the emigrants were emotionally responding to the wonders of the West they were also formulating realistic calculations about its future. Like other Americans in an age of optimistic expansion,

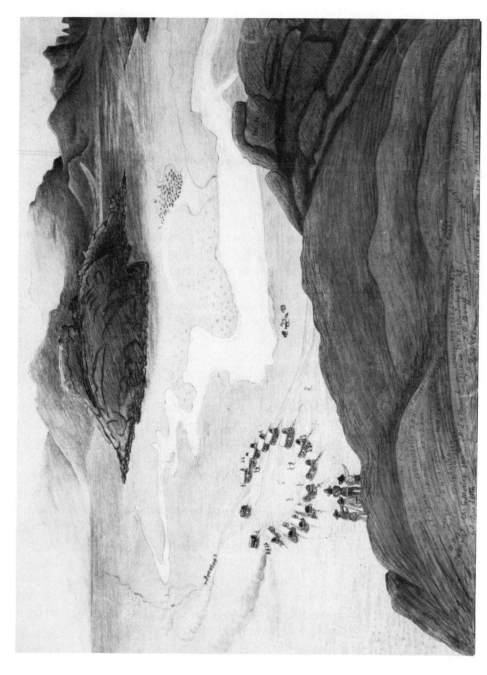

The J. Goldsborough Bruff party at Independence Rock, where thousands paused to scratch their names on the famous landmark.

the overlanders were always alert to prospects for entrepreneurial opportunity. In their diaries and letters they carefully identified regions where cattle could be grazed the year round, where coal might be mined, where summer health resorts could be established, and particularly where high-yield agriculture was feasible. Again and again the passing emigrants remarked on the fertility of the lands they were traversing, although often bemoaning the scarcity of timber for fencing. Edwin Bryant's lament was typical: "The strongest objection to the territory we have passed through, since we left the Missouri line, is the sparseness of timber. With this single objection, the country appears to be the most desirable, in an agricultural point of view, of any which I have ever seen. It possesses such natural wealth and beauties, that at some future day it will be the Eden of America."[51] Emigrant diarists regularly singled out specific western localities as potential centers for dense settlement: the Grande Ronde, Bear River, and Carson valleys, the territory around Soda Springs, regions along the Kansas, Big Blue, Platte, Sweetwater, and Humboldt rivers.[52]

This precise geographic appraisal of the trans-Mississippi West is readily apparent in any perusal of emigrant diaries and letters. Even though many of the textbooks and maps of the day characterized most of the western regions as the "Great American Desert," very few of the passing emigrants were prepared to generalize so broadly. Forty-niner Jasper Hixson's prescient evaluation is representative of the manner in which most overlanders reflected upon the potential of the land they were crossing. Shortly after beginning the journey, while about to cross the Kansas River, Hixson observed: "The land is too fertile and it possesses too many inducements for settlement to remain in the possession of the Indians forever. Now that so many from the older States begin traveling over this fine land, and comparing it with the soil they have to scratch so hard to get a living from they must write to their friends to 'Go West.'" Nearly two months later, now in the Great Basin area, Hixson returned to the same theme:

In the best map we can get hold of, this is all marked the Great American Desert, and while much of the land would not be considered desirable to people of the Western States, who still had plenty of room, this is better than much of the country we have traveled over. At the same time, we had seen a great deal that would make desirable homes. There were millions of acres better than some of our older States, and tens of millions that would be called a paradise by those living in the north of Europe.[53]

Hixson was not alone in anticipating the glorious future of western development. The majority of overland emigrants were disinclined to link the "Great American Desert" concept to anything more than specific and clearly demarcated sections such as the desert beyond the Humboldt Sink or Utah's Great Basin. Instead, their letters and journals suggested that the appropriate appellation for the American West was either "the plains" or "the prairies." And the descriptive image many emigrants meant to evoke was reflected in their widespread use of terms like "the Garden of Eden" or "the garden of the world." While the breakdown of the "Great American Desert" concept resulted from many factors, the crucial significance of hundreds of thousands of overlanders who crossed the trans-Mississippi West in the two decades before the Civil War and saw at first hand that most of the West was habitable and cultivable has been too long neglected. Many emigrants looked forward to the day when much of the region would blossom like a rose. Some were among those returning to particularly desirable locales to begin the settlement process.[54]

One widely discussed project which many assumed would accelerate western development was the Pacific railroad.[55] The enthusiastic agitation in behalf of a railroad to the Pacific was but a further extension of a doctrine the overland emigrants and their congressional supporters had been espousing since the early 1840s: that the federal government carried basic responsibility for the safety of overland travel. Stereotypes about hardy frontier individualism and self-sufficiency notwithstanding, the common emigrant request was bluntly phrased by T. H. Jefferson in his 1849 guidebook: "Why don't the government do something immediately that will be of practical utility to the emigrant or traveller across our own territory?" The following year overlander Abial Whitman similarly pleaded, "*Uncle Sam* ought to do Something to protect the emigration."[56] The emigrants and their allies appealed persistently—and with marked success—for forts, troops, escort squadrons, guidebooks based upon careful route surveys, trail improvements, workshops and supply stations, relief trains, wagon roads, and regular transcontinental postal services. These impressive government services should be recognized both as a significant nationalizing force and as an important factor in the growth and justification of federal power.

Such far-reaching ramifications of the antebellum overland emigrations underscore the historical significance of the quarter of a million pioneers who journeyed over the Oregon-California Trail. Hundreds of thousands of their compatriots also arrived on the Pacific Coast during these two decades, using a myriad of competing land and sea routes. Therefore, in order to place the South Pass overland emigrations in their proper perspective, it is also necessary to compare these alternative antebellum options for reaching the Pacific Coast.

Prior to 1849 those few westbound travelers who did not travel on the Oregon-California Trail reached the Pacific Coast either by sailing around Cape Horn or by following the Santa Fe Trail from Independence and then striking a northwesterly course from Santa Fe. In the wake of the race for California's riches, however, a profusion of alternate routes materialized. The additional routes appeared because most fortune seekers suspected that California's gold was not inexhaustible, the stories of fabulous gold deposits notwithstanding, and that it was therefore imperative to arrive in the mining regions before everything was taken. Consequently, the frustration of waiting several months until the prairie grasses could support draft animals, coupled with recurring fears of the Indians, deserts, mountains, and potentially insufficient forage on the South Pass route, led many hopeful prospectors to seek out any conceivable route "guaranteed" by some "authority" to be faster or easier. Some of the routes thus attempted and improved, such as that across the Isthmus of Panama, soon joined the Oregon-California Trail as important arteries of travel to and from the Pacific Coast.

From 1849 through 1860 approximately two-thirds of all travelers bound for the Pacific Coast chose some other route than that through South Pass. Some 9,000 forty-niners and lesser numbers in subsequent years traveled over the so-called southwestern trails to California, a term incorporating such routes as the Santa Fe, Gila, and Spanish trails. Farther south were several gold rush routes across Mexico. Approximately 15,000 argonauts toiled across these trails in 1849 and again in 1850; by then the hardships of the route had been sufficiently publicized so that relatively few followed in later years. Still farther south were the well-traveled isthmian crossings of Nicaragua and Panama. In the mid–1850s, the Nicaraguan route almost superseded the Panamanian route in popularity, but entrepreneurial competitions and William Walker's ill-advised filibustering expedition closed the route in 1857 after 56,811 westbound travelers had crossed since its 1851 opening. A mere 335 travelers inaugurated the Panama crossing in 1848, but by 1860, 195,639 had traveled to San Francisco via Panama, only a few thousand less than had traveled over the California Trail during the same period. The other major route option—in 1849 the most popular choice next to the South Pass overland trail—was the long sea voyage around Cape Horn. Nearly 16,000 gold seekers reached San Francisco by this route in 1849, almost 12,000 in 1850, and declining numbers in subsequent years.[57]

For the first two years of the gold rush, the only years that a few of the marginal routes were much used, most competing routes shared several shortcomings: grossly inadequate conveyances and support facilities, wildly fluctuating prices, and, on routes where sea and land transportation had to be coordinated, total unreliability. For example, virtually every imaginable craft was pressed into service for either the Cape Horn route or for shuttling passengers to San Francisco from all Pacific seaports north of Panama City. Some of these vessels were completely unsafe, they were often poorly manned, and they were invariably overloaded. The result was a large number of recorded and unrecorded tragedies. Moreover, the thousands of sweltering gold rushers congregating on the Pacific after feverish journeys across Mexico, Panama, and Nicaragua never knew how soon a connecting vessel might appear. When a ship did stop, frantic gold rushers were still not assured of passage. Would the vessel accept more passengers was the all-important question, and if so, how much would a coveted ticket cost? In these desperate early months of the gold rush, payments of up to $500 and even $1,000 for completion of the passage to San Francisco were not unknown. And until 1851, when travel arrangements became reasonably regularized over the isthmian routes, the gold seeker was almost always impatiently waiting. The necessity of waiting weeks and even months in a squalid Pacific seaport where illness was rampant, sanitation nonexistent, food expensive, and tempers volatile must have led many to regret their choice of route.[58]

In such unpredictable circumstances some travelers proceeded expeditiously at reasonable rates and others did not; it is almost impossible to arrive at comparative averages. Sailing time for vessels leaving eastern ports for the voyage around Cape Horn to San Francisco in 1849 ranged between 117 and 355 days. One random survey of twenty-three vessels revealed an average elapsed time from coast to coast of 199 days, while the sailing time of all American ships docking at San Francisco before August 1, 1849, averaged 168 days.[59] The cheapest passage for the trip around the Horn might be managed for as little as $150; many paid at least twice as much and more. In 1849 the cost in joint-stock company sailing vessels has been estimated at $500. Gold rushers crossing the Isthmus experienced similar fluctuations, although normally the trip was faster and cheaper. Aggressive entrepreneurs soon lowered rates and improved travel facilities, making this route an ever more attractive option. During the first years of the gold rush it required at least six weeks to complete a passage from New York to San Francisco via Panama. By the early 1850s this time had been reduced to between three and four weeks. Prices likewise plummeted from highs of $450 to $500 in 1849 to less than $100 during the cutthroat competition of the mid-1850s.[60]

Even this brief summary of the major alternative routes to the Pacific Coast indicates that the South Pass overland trail compared very favorably with all other routes on the all-important factor of cost, and with all except the isthmian passages in speed. Table 10, based upon a comparative study of over 250 trail diarists between 1841 and 1860, demonstrates that an overland journey from the Missouri River jumping-off points to a California or Oregon destination averaged approximately 125 days, or just about four months.[61] Throughout the antebellum emigration era the trip to California could almost always be made more expeditiously than the trip to Oregon. During the 1840s overland travel to California required, on the average, approximately one month less time; during the 1850s, approximately two weeks less time. Table 10 also corroborates the importance of change over time: on both the Oregon and California routes, trail improvements and increasing traveler expertise considerably reduced aver-

TABLE 10
AVERAGE TRAVEL TIME FOR THE OVERLAND JOURNEY (in days)

	California	Oregon	Combined Totals[a]
1841–48	157.7	169.1	164.5
1849	131.6	129.0	131.6
1841–49	134.6	166.2	139.5
1850	107.9	125.0	108.6
1850–60	112.7	128.5	116.3
1841–60	121.0	138.6	124.6

[a]In order to be able to suggest average travel times for an overland journey to the Pacific Coast—to either California or Oregon—the average travel times for trips to California and Oregon were combined in this column.

age travel time in the 1850s. The striking disparity between the first and second years of the gold rush further evidences the futility of advancing 1849 as a "typical" travel year. Forty-niners consumed, on the average, approximately 132 days for the California venture. The next year average travel time had been markedly reduced to 108 days. This average reduction of three and a half weeks in travel time reflected the plethora of trail improvements as well as the wisdom of avoiding the Lassen Cutoff.

Averages, of course, do little more than suggest general trends and relationships. The range of travel times differed enormously in every travel year. Some travelers in the 1840s, to both California and Oregon, consumed up to and over 200 days for the westering enterprise—more than half a year. At the other extreme, lawyer Lorenzo Sawyer, who would ultimately become chief justice of California's Supreme Court, sped overland in a mere seventy-six days in 1850.[62]

To further keep these average travel times in perspective, it is necessary to add the days, weeks, or even months consumed in traveling to the outfitting towns from the emigrant's place of residence, as well as the time spent at the jumping-off points completing the travel outfit or waiting out a late spring. Indeed, a high geographic correlation usually existed between the route followed and the section of the nation from which the traveler hailed. Southerners were most likely to travel southwestern routes, to cross Mexico, or to board vessels at New Orleans for Panama and Nicaragua. Residents of the eastern seaboard, however, appear as disproportionately on the rosters of vessels rounding the Cape or stopping at isthmian ports as do residents of Missouri, Iowa, Illinois, Wisconsin, Michigan, Indiana, and Ohio on the newspaper listings of those launching out on the Oregon-California Trail.

Since geographic proximity dictated that the overwhelming number of midwesterners chose the overland route, the abundant evidence that residents of Missouri comprised by far the greatest percentage of all overland emigrants is not surprising. Overlanders themselves periodically commented, sometimes in apparent disbelief, on the disproportionate

Bruff gave a realistic title to this graphic sketch.

number of Missourians on the trails and in graves beside the trail.[63] Gold rushers who counted fresh graves and dutifully recorded the home states of the deceased, like J. Goldsborough Bruff in 1849 and Micajah Littleton in 1850, afford the emigration historian the rare opportunity of statistical evaluation. Bruff and Littleton both traveled toward the rear of their year's migration and both maintained their count for the entire trip. Their statistical data coincides amazingly. According to Bruff's listing, 53 percent of all deceased emigrants were Missourians in 1849. Littleton's 1850 survey placed the Missourian percentage at 54. Upon arriving at Fort Laramie many emigrants reported the number of deaths to that point; Missourians comprised 48 percent of the 1850 count. In 1852 the proprietors of the Barlow Toll Road in Oregon kept track of emigrant deaths reported by those patronizing the road. Once again Missourians predominated with 37 percent, as they did with 40 percent on a list kept by a California emigrant between Independence and Fort Laramie. Scattered data collected by other travelers usually yields similar statistics.[64]

An additional source of data is found in frontier newspapers recording home states of departing overlanders. Since relatively few Missourians, for obvious geographic reasons, departed from Kanesville, Iowa, it is unfortunate that Kanesville's *Frontier Guardian* editor was the most zealous in recording (for a small fee) the home states of departing overlanders. Illinoisans led in Kanesville gold rush departures, with Iowa, Michigan, and Wisconsin residents grouped closely in a somewhat distant second. A listing of 1844 emigrants in the St. Louis *Missouri Republican,* however, indicated that 60 percent of 237 departing overlanders were Missourians.[65]

The most conclusive data derives from census reports which reveal that native Missourians ranked first in the Oregon population and second to New Yorkers in California's population in both 1850 and 1860. A careful analysis of the 1850 census returns further reveals this Missouri preponderance in the westward migration. Of the nearly 25 percent of Oregon residents born in Missouri, 75 percent were dependents—children born in Missouri to parents recorded in the census as born elsewhere but who had, in the classic frontier pattern, finally reached Missouri in their westward progression before emigrating to Oregon. The percentage of previous Missouri residents in Oregon was thus somewhat higher than even the census findings indicate.[66]

How much it cost an emigrant, whether from Missouri or elsewhere, to make the overland journey depended on such important variables as individual taste, present circumstances, and traveling distance to the Missouri River. Many farm families, for example, already owning draft animals, wagons, and most other necessary traveling accouterments, made virtually no cash outlay for an overland trip. Most city residents had to purchase almost everything. Further, most overlanders, if they were so inclined, could regain substantial portions of their initial expenditures, or even turn a profit, by selling part or all of their traveling outfit upon arrival—an option unavailable to those having traveled by sea.

Additionally complicating the matter of costs was the fact that overlanders did not usually travel as individuals. In the pre- and post–gold rush era the migration was primarily composed of family units, but in the gold rush era primarily of men. They pooled resources in some agreed-upon ratio to form small traveling groups, or else purchased shares in one of the countless joint-stock companies which, other than for personal effects, endeavored to provide everything individual members might require.[67] The pricing of these shares, although usually based upon careful preliminary research, varied widely. Between $200 and $300 seems to have been the normal rate, though some joint-stock companies demanded as much as $500 for an individual travel share. Writers of overland guidebooks and of the travel advice inundating the newspapers generally agreed that the individual cost for the trip ranged between $100 and $200.[68]

One final cost figure—expenditures en route—also has to be taken into consideration. Prevailing early in the emigration era had been the common-sense assumption that once the traveling outfit had been assembled the overlander would need to make no additional monetary expenditures. According to Lansford Hastings's guidebook the only requirement for the journey was time, since the "barbarous" Indians understood neither money nor its value.[69] This erroneous idea was quickly discarded as word spread that the coin of the realm was not only useful but on occasion essential, whether for the ferry, bridge, and trading-post entrepreneurs, or for the purchase of surplus foodstuffs from other travelers. In fact, some emigrants even had to sell livestock or other possessions in order to secure sufficient money for expenses on the plains. By 1850 many gold rushers were reminding friends and neighbors back home to come fortified with considerable sums of money specifically for the trip itself; their recommendations normally ranged from $50 to $200.[70]

A few travelers kept precise records of their complete expenditures for the overland journey. While conclusive generalizations from these scattered accounts are impossible, they confirm the contemporary cost estimates. Jacob Snyder's 1845 list of expenditures, $274.62, is noteworthy in that he indicated no disbursements en route, a phenomenon which would not long prevail. D. Jagger, the secretary-treasurer of a six-man 1849 outfit, totaled its expenses at $954.04. This included fare to Independence, provisions, one wagon, six mules, one riding horse, and $47.85 en route for travel tolls, food, and periodic alcoholic refreshments. On arrival in Sacramento they sold their wagon and team for $250 and estimated they had $100 in supplies remaining. Thus the five surviving men (one had died at Independence of cholera) had actually spent only a little more than $100 apiece to cross the continent. William Renfro

Rothwell, in 1850, paid, as his share of a four-man outfit, $118.15, to which he added personal expenditures of $93 for clothing, blankets, a rifle, and medicines. Rothwell also took along what proved to be a barely adequate $40 in cash for the trip. Horace Pomroy's account book revealed 1850 expenses of $691.94 before even beginning the journey and another $178.27 after crossing the Missouri River for tolls, foodstuffs, supplies, whiskey, and equipment repair. Most striking in the Pomroy records is the tremendous number of individual transactions of both purchase and sale, many with other emigrants—further evidence of the importance of cooperative assistance.[71]

Other emigrant ledgers yield similar statistics. Thomas Lewis's careful records of the travel expenses of two Ohio gold rushers in 1852 total $438.48, which sum was reduced by $155.35 through sales of supplies and equipment en route and upon arrival in California. John Grindell's personal share of his outfit's 1850 expenses *after* launching out from St. Joseph was $45.78; the costs for John Wayman, a physician, while on the plains in 1852 were $72.30; and when 1850 gold rusher E. A. Tompkins arrived at the figure of $432.75 by adding the $80 he expended en route for tolls, foodstuffs, and incidentals to his beginning expenses (including travel to Independence), he groused that "this is by far the most expensive mode of travelling to California." Perhaps in initial agreement was Clarence Bagley's father, whose two wagons, two mules, and four horses had cost $550 in 1852 but brought over $1,000 in Oregon, just about covering the other expenses of the trip.[72]

John Smith, an 1853 Oregon-bound overlander, kept even more detailed accounts. They revealed how expensive the long-distance family move to the Pacific Coast could be. There were eleven in the Smith party: his wife, three daughters, one grandson, a friend, and four employees. (The four paid workers, of course, had found the cheapest way to go west—hiring out for "room and board" as employees to those in need of extra hands for driving wagons, herding stock, and standing guard duty.) Smith began with three wagons and one carriage, five horses, seven yoke of oxen, thirteen cows, and one bull. An additional expense was the possessions which had been shipped by sea to Portland. Unfortunately, Smith did not specify what his wagons, stock, and provisions had cost him, but he did record expenses of $342.43 from his Pittsburgh, Indiana, home to Council Bluffs as well as $233.54 in Council Bluffs, presumably for the completion of the traveling outfit. Between Council Bluffs and Oregon City Smith spent $202.28 in bridge and ferry tolls and for having his stock swum across rivers, at least $16.37 in supplemental food and clothing purchases, and $440.50 for replacing worn-out oxen and related purchases. These astronomical expenditures of over $650 on the plains were partially offset by income of $388.80 from sales of surplus foodstuffs to other emigrants and traders and from the sale of eight worn-down oxen to a Blue Mountain entrepreneur. At that, Smith's total expenses west of Council Bluffs alone amounted to $270.35. Thus, it cost this 1853 over-lander $846.32 to take his family from Indiana to Oregon, a sum which neither included all of his foodstuffs and provisions nor the value of his wagons and livestock. Even conservative estimates for the cost of the total venture must run to at least $1,500 plus the shipping charges for the materials sent by sea.[73]

Finally, viewing the overland emigrations in historical perspective requires a reconsideration of the dangers attendant to the journey. While there was a great deal of potential disaster associated with an overland trip during the antebellum era, it remains a moot point whether the mortality rate on "the plains across" much exceeded the average death rate among Americans resisting the call of the frontier to remain at home.[74] Estimates of trail mortality have varied widely, ranging as high as 30,000 emigrant deaths for the 1842–59 period. Although overall estimates rarely fall below 6 percent of those starting west (a figure accepted by Mattes in the most recent assessment of mortality on the overland trail), this writer believes that a 4 percent rate of trail mortality comports more closely with the available evidence.[75]

Whatever the actual percentage, one fact is clear: the actual dangers of the overland venture have been considerably misrepresented by the myth-makers' overemphasis on Indian treachery. The less than 400 emigrants killed by Indians during the antebellum era represent a mere 4 percent of the estimated 10,000 or more emigrant deaths. It follows that disease and trail accidents were far more to be feared by the prospective overlander than were the native inhabitants of the West.

Disease was far and away the number one killer, accounting for nearly nine out of every ten deaths. Although the emigrant was never completely safe from the scourge of epidemic disease, the initial portion of the trail to Fort Laramie, otherwise the easiest segment of the journey, occasioned the most disease-induced deaths. During her trip to Oregon in 1852, for example, Cecelia Adams carefully recorded in her diary the locations of 401 new graves, speculating that she had seen only one-fifth of the fresh graves. Slightly over half of the burials had occurred east of Fort Laramie, nearly three-fourths prior to Fort Hall, and the last 21 percent beyond Fort Boise. Considering the hasty burials so characteristic on the trip, grave-counting was often a doubly depressing task, as John Clark, an 1852 tabulator, explained: "The Sign for a new grave was to See their feet with old Shoes or boots on Sticking up through the Sand at other places you Saw the old hat & dusty garments that had been thrown away & quite a number had been So lightly Covered with Sand or Sod the Kiotes had drawn them partly out & Eat of the Carcase this is a coman occurance on the plain."[76]

Diarrhea, tuberculosis, smallpox, mumps, and a host of other illnesses downed travelers, but the chief afflictions were cholera, mountain fever, and scurvy. In 1850 and again in 1852, at least 2,000 overlanders died of the dreaded cholera, most before reaching Fort Laramie. Raging epidemically in the American West between 1848 and 1855, Asiatic cholera killed with exceeding quickness. It felled entire families, decimated large caravans, and lined the trail with individual and mass graves. One 1852 traveler enumerated fifty-two graves at a single encampment. Perilous as cholera was on the trail, the emigrant was scarcely any more susceptible than he would have been back in the settlements. In St. Louis alone more than 4,000 citizens fell victim to cholera during 1849. John H. McBride was not entirely in error in reassuring his wife in an 1850 letter from Fort Laramie, "There is less sickness probably among the emigrants en route for California than among the same number of men at their homes East."[77]

Once beyond Fort Laramie the overlanders entered the zone where they encountered what was commonly termed "mountain fever." Either Rocky Mountain spotted fever or Colorado tick fever, the disease was less virulent than cholera but deadly enough. If the travelers shook off mountain fever, as most ultimately did, the last portion of the journey found them most susceptible to scurvy as months without sufficient fruits and vegetables began to take their toll. Again, deaths were infrequent but suffering was widespread. These major trail diseases were all so inadequately understood that even the presence of many physicians and pseudo-physicians in the emigrations was of little consequence in prompting greater concern with sanitation, hygiene, and diet. The Mormons, by contrast, whose passages to Salt Lake City were invariably better organized and included a higher percentage of females, succumbed less frequently to diseases on their north side of the Platte River trail.[78]

Since no section of the overland trail was accident-free, prudent emigrants never relaxed their vigilance, for carelessness was second only to disease as a hazard of cross-country travel. Perhaps one of the most persuasive factors in convincing overlanders that the prevailing notion of the Great American Desert needed considerable refinement was the extraordinarily high incidence of drownings and near drownings during the course of the trip. One of the most unexpected facets of the "overland" journey was that death by water claimed almost as many victims during the antebellum era as did the much-feared Indians—perhaps as many as 300, at least 90 in 1850 alone. Drownings commenced at the crossing of the Missouri River even before the trip had fairly begun, and continued at virtually every stream and river crossing on the entire length of the Oregon-California Trail. Most drownings occurred in the Platte River, particularly at the Fort Laramie crossing, where approximately nineteen overlanders drowned in 1850, and at the North Fork some 130 miles beyond the fort, where at least twenty-eight were lost in 1849 and twenty-one in 1850. The Green River crossing was another particularly treacherous stretch of water which claimed at least thirty-seven victims in 1850. In the mid-1840s the notoriously dangerous Columbia River had provided the motivation for several of the attempts to fashion ancillary routes into the Willamette Valley. Even the seemingly tame Humboldt River reaped its share of careless travelers—at least nine in 1850.[79]

Drownings continued year after year, reaching their apex during the crowded conditions of the gold rush, when, despite the presence of bridges and semi-safe ferries, impatience, poverty, and/or parsimony led many travelers to attempt their own crossings, often with disastrous results. But men—and drowning victims were almost exclusively male—were lost also while patronizing ferryboats, while swimming and bathing, while crossing stock over a river to forage on better grass. One inebriated 1853 emigrant misjudged rain-swollen Buffalo Creek for a slough, drove his wagon in, and was never seen again. While accidental drownings usually claimed men in individual mishaps, small groups were also lost, invariably following the capsizing of a raft. On one such 1850 occasion at the Green River, nine out of the ten men aboard drowned.[80]

Almost every emigrant diarist records either a drowning witnessed personally, a report of one or more drownings shortly before or after their own successful passage of a river, or one or more narrow escapes. Even when an emigrant barely escaped while attempting to ford a river, the outcome was often catastrophic. Orange Gaylord witnessed an 1850 mishap at the Green River, where an emigrant lost his wagon, provisions, and belongings. Obviously, the impact of the many "near misses" upon the traveling community was significant, as were the family tragedies occasioned by many of the drownings. In the space of less than twenty-four hours in 1847, for example, two women were widowed and nine children rendered fatherless by drownings at a Snake River crossing.[81]

After drownings the commonest cause of fatal accidents was careless handling of the fantastic arsenal of firearms the overlanders carried west with them.[82] Jacob Snyder's largest single expenditure in 1845 was for armaments: more than he spent on his wagon, or his mule, or his cattle, or even his food for the entire journey. Jessy Thornton reported in 1846 that their seventy-two-wagon train of 130 men, 65 women, and 125 children possessed 104 pistols, 155 guns, 1,672 pounds of lead, and 1,100 pounds of powder. William Kelly's description of their twenty-five-man company's weaponry characterized men marching off as to war—which is what some emigrants expected the journey to be: ". . . but we were well equipped, each man carrying in his belt a revolver, a sword, and bowie-knife; the mounted men having besides a pair of holster-pistols and a rifle slung from the horn of their saddles, over and above which there were several double and single-shot guns and rifles suspended in the waggons, in loops, near the forepart, where they would be easily accessible in case of attack."[83]

"Pawnee," writing from his Fort Kearny vantage point, witnessed so many companies like Kelly's that he appropriately termed the forty-niners

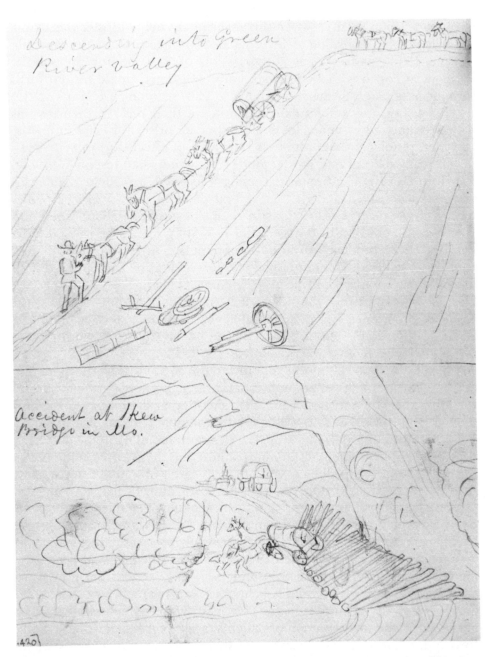

In this page from the Bruff sketchbook it is evident that going down could be just as dangerous as going across. Beinecke Rare Book and Manuscript Library, Yale University "walking arsenals," and wryly suggested that "arms of all kinds must certainly be scarce in the States, after such a drain as the emigrants must have made upon them."[84] Even the government helped foster this mania for armaments. According to Texas senator Thomas S. Rusk, the rationale for the 1849 congressional authorization of $50,000 for the sale of weapons at cost was that the westbound emigrants should not go forth without adequate "means of defence." The Secretary of War's notice specifying how the emigrants could procure their desired firearms was widely publicized in newspapers. The cut-rate prices for rifles, muskets, carbines, pistols, and ammunition remained in effect during 1850.[85]

It really did not matter that guidebook writers like Joseph Ware and Lansford Hastings admonished emigrants to treat their dangerous weapons with care; or even that several prudent joint-stock companies incorporated careful restrictions in their constitutions about when and where guns could be discharged and how they should be carried. The overlanders had to learn from bitter experience, as Hastings's own 1842 company had done. Their guns had been carried capped and primed until one of their number had been accidentally killed. The correctness of Hastings's analysis that they had been "mere sophomores in the great school of experience" was demonstrated yearly on the plains, beginning in 1841 with the fatal shooting of emigrant James Shotwell, who tried to remove his gun from a wagon—muzzle first.[86]

The bloodshed was most pronounced in 1849 and 1850. Forty-niners reaching the jumping-off points by boat from St. Louis had been recklessly spending their days in target practice, shooting at deer, hogs, dogs, and most anything else they saw. William Kelly noted that only at mealtimes did the "unintermitting fusilade" stop. Careless gun handling in the outfitting posts resulted in accidental shootings almost daily. Once out on the plains the mayhem quickly peaked.[87] William Kelly's well-prepared company lost their first man while fording the Big Blue River, after he had attempted to draw his loaded gun from his wagon—muzzle first. The thirteen buckshot passing through his body killed him instantly. Andrew Orvis, after himself having been accidentally shot in the hip and seeing several men killed and maimed, commented that "hundreds of guns and pistols" had been accidentally discharged. Several overlanders acknowledged that they were much more frightened of carelessly handled guns in their own trains than they were of any hostile Indians. The validity of their observations was borne out by the steady stream of patients treated for bullet wounds at the Kearny and Laramie army hospitals, as well as by the grave markers beside the trail.[88]

Once the emigrants had gotten over their sophomoritis, however, greater care began to be exercised, and the number of accidental shootings and killings declined drastically. Indeed, an analysis of fatalities from accidental shootings through 1850 indicates that fully nine-tenths of all mishaps occurred east of South Pass. Alonzo Delano, cognizant of this remarkable turnabout, opined that it was basically because the Indians proved to be so peaceful: "When we first crossed into the Indian territory above St. Joseph, every man displayed his arms in the most approved desperado style, and rarely thought of stirring from the train without his trusty rifle. But no enemies were seen. By degrees the arms were laid aside, and by the time we reached Fort Laramie all were abandoned except a knife, and sometimes a pistol, which might be seen peeping from a pocket."[89]

Hundreds of additional emigrants were injured and at least several dozen killed in the almost infinite variety of other accidents endemic to the overland journey. A great many casualties derived from wagon mishaps and accidents in which draft animals were involved. Children and adults alike fell under moving wheels, were dragged to death after becoming entangled in ropes, and fell off or were kicked by riding animals.[90] At least six emigrants were killed by lightning; four overlanders were crushed to death by a falling oak tree on Lassen's jinxed trail in 1849; one died from overdrinking after a tedious desert crossing; another from an overdose of preventive medicine; and a five-year-old child succumbed after inadvertently swallowing a bottle of laudanum. One traveler was even scalded to death in the boiling springs on the Truckee Desert crossing.[91]

Overland diaries also contain a number of references to caravan members who wandered away onto the prairies never to be seen again. Although most of these individuals doubtless ultimately linked up with another company, it seems likely that some of the missing-person cases culminated in eventual death from either starvation, overexposure, or at the hands of Indians or highwaymen.[92] Other emigrants survived painful injuries incurred in stampedes and from fires and hailstorms. While emigrants killed many rattlesnakes, there were extraordinarily few incidences of snakebite. Ravenous wolves also only rarely nipped an unwary emigrant, once causing rabies, another time ripping open the nose of a luckless sleeping traveler.[93]

Beset by the ravages of cholera and other diseases, by a countless variety of traveling accidents, by occasional Indian harassment, and by peculiar difficulties imposed by climate and terrain, the typical overland emigrant glimpsed more of the "elephant" than the westbound sea traveler did of the "shark." The steadily accelerating trail improvements and the cooperative assistance among the emigrating community mitigated but did not end either the dangers or the frustrations of an arduous four-month overland journey. There was, after all, little that anyone could do if your clothes, including your good woolen dress, fell out of the wagon one night, as happened to Cecelia Adams in 1852, and the oxen "ate them up." Jonathan Moore—an extremely deficient speller who was wiser than he knew—titled his 1852 travel diary "Journal of Travails on the Roade to

Oregon."[94] That the "travails" were coterminous with overland "travel" is self-evident, as an anonymous 1852 overlander lyricized:

To enjoy such a trip along with such a crowd of emigration, a man must be able to endure heat like a Salamander, mud and water like a muskrat, dust like a toad, and labor like a jackass. He must learn to eat with his unwashed fingers, drink out of the same vessel with his mules, sleep on the ground when it rains, and share his blanket with vermin, and have patience with musketoes, who don't know any difference between the face of a man and the face of a mule, but dash without ceremony from one into the other. He must cease to think, except as to where he may find grass and water and a good camping place. It is a hardship without glory, to be sick without a home, to die and be buried like a dog.[95]

Acutely conscious of such tribulations, most emigrants reflectively writing about the overland trip expressed considerable impatience and unhappiness with a venture they vowed never to repeat. Most of the negative appraisals of the overland journey originated with travelers during the gold rush years, particularly among the overlanders of 1849 and 1850, who waxed especially eloquent about the agonies of an overland passage. Forty-niner William Wells, who believed he had "undergone more hardship than I ever thought possible to live through," wrote his wife, "Tell Green McDowell TO THANK his God hourly that he did not start on this trip—if he had he would have wished himself in HELL, at home or any where else but here ten thousand times." While Wells could conclude, "But never mind Gold is ahead," James Evans in 1850 declared that not even $25,000 would induce him to face again the agonies of plains travel. He admonished his brother to come by sea: "Be it known throughout the world, to remotest nations, from the shivering Laplanders to the rude Hottentots, that if any man hereafter should take a notion to come to California—not to cross the Plains for the Lord sake!!!!"[96]

Part of the explanation for this dissatisfaction with plains travel doubtless lay with the human propensity toward overreaction. Less than one year after he had counseled his friends to avoid the distasteful overland trip, George Hall blissfully wrote his stateside relatives, "I believe that the rout across the Plains is the most pleasant way to return to the states   All except Bob Payne of us expect to return across the plains next summer."[97] The "grass is greener" syndrome, the tendency to assume that any alternative must be superior to the route on which one was experiencing difficulty, also came into play. Complaining overlanders would have been surprised to know that some sea voyagers were so dismayed with their situation that they were strongly encouraging their friends to travel overland instead.[98]

The explanation for the high incidence of dissatisfaction with the overland journey among gold rushers may also be linked to the urban occupations of many of the argonauts. The farm families predominating during the emigrations of the 1840s and then again during the later 1850s

Before and after "seeing the elephant." Bruff's sense of humor also apparently survived.

were more capable of taking the inconveniences of overland travel in stride. An 1845 emigrant endeavoring to place the trip in perspective sagely compared it to a typical summer's labor on the farm, contending that crossing the plains required no more toil than that expended by the average farmer. Persons inured to such activity ordinarily did not find the overland passage particularly burdensome. Those not used to strenuous physical exertion were more inclined to react negatively when hardships were encountered. Even the complainers, however, recognized that those reaching California by the overland route were invariably better prepared to withstand the strenuous activity associated with prospecting for gold than those arriving by sea. One 1850 gold seeker, for example, who immediately following his own cross-country trip had condemned the overland journey, within several years was singing its praises as the only way to cure tubercular afflictions.[99]

If the health-giving qualities of the overland journey are difficult to measure, the important ramifications of the overland transit of a quarter of a million antebellum pioneers are not. But because this epic westering experience has become so enveloped in myth and stereotype, the reality of how it was accomplished remains historically elusive. An appreciation of the changing nature of the overland venture, and an awareness that the emigration phenomenon was made possible by emigrant cooperation and by interaction between the emigrants and the many temporary and permanent inhabitants of the West, are fundamental to attaining historical perspective.

But a revisionist emphasis upon these understandings need not detract from the color, the drama, or the poignancy of the experiences overlanders shared along the Oregon-California Trail. The energy, perseverance, and courage of the overland emigrants are as impressive today as they were in the 1840s and 1850s. It is no wonder that those who completed the adventure wrote and spoke about it often in subsequent years. It *was* something to be proud of: to have traveled "the plains across."

Notes

PREFACE

1. I was further convinced of the validity of my approach when soon afterward I came across Dale Morgan's perceptive article, "The Significance and Value of the Overland Journal" (1962). Morgan, in addition to reflecting upon the unique virtues of the overland journal for historical scholarship, also called attention to the significance of the matter of change over time along the overland trails.

2. Pomeroy, "Toward a Reorientation of Western History" (1955), 579–600; Davis, "Will the West Survive as a Field in American History?" (1964), 672–85; Gressley, ed., *The American West* (1966), v–xiv; Paul, "The Mormons as a Theme in Western Historical Writing" (1967), 511.

3. Bruce L. McKinstry's Foreword to Byron McKinstry, Diary (microfilm of typescript).

INTRODUCTION

1. "From Bethel, Missouri, to Aurora, Oregon," trans. Bek (1953), 23–24; "Boy's Funeral Followed Oregon Trail" (1930), 194–95.

2. Bryant, *What I Saw in California* (1849), 85–91; Thornton, "Occasional Address" (1879), 44–45.

3. Stewart, "The Prairie Schooner Got Them There" (1962), 5, 7; Zenor, "By Covered Wagon to the Promised Land" (1974), 30–41.

4. Winther, "Immigrant Trains" (1969), 163; Holliday, "Some Notable Views of the Elephant" (1967), 12.

5. Currey, "Occasional Address" (1887), 39.

6. Winther, "Immigrant Trains," 166–67. Winther's triumvirate included Read and Gaines, eds., *Gold Rush* (1944); Potter, ed., *Trail to California* (1945); Giffen, ed., *The Diaries of Peter Decker* (1966). This writer would add Morgan's *Overland Diary of James A. Pritchard* and Clark, ed., *Gold Rush Diary* (1967) to the list of exceptional editing achievements.

7. Parkman, *The Oregon Trail*, ed. Feltskog (1969), 11a. Morgan's *Overland in 1846* (1963) merits mention as an extraordinarily useful endeavor which reprints many diaries of that year as well as all the references in newspapers to the emigrants of 1846 which Morgan, an indefatigable scholar, was able to locate over a number of years of zealous searching.

8. See Penrose, "The Wagon Train of 1843" (1943), 361–69, for the clearest statement of this outlook. Also see Schafer, "Notes on the Colonization of Oregon" (1905), 386, for the contention that the "Cow Column" of 1843 was as important to the Pacific Northwest as the Massachusetts Bay Puritans of 1630 were to New England. Scott, in "Influence of American Settlement upon the Oregon Boundary Treaty of 1846" (1928), 1–19, arrived at an essentially similar conclusion. See also Husband, "To Oregon in 1843" (1973), 7–16. Marcus Whitman has been singled out as the individual savior of Oregon by some writers who believe his winter ride from Oregon in 1842–43 influenced diplomacy, and also that Whitman was primarily responsible for recruiting the large 1843 migration as well as for guiding it to Oregon. See Nixon, *How Marcus Whitman Saved Oregon* (1895) for a grandiose expression of such a view.

9. Barry, "The Murals in the State Capitol" (1939), 149–50, 159. The other murals note the arrival of the ship *Columbia*, Lewis and Clark at Celilo Falls, and Dr. John McLoughlin welcoming missionary wives Eliza Spalding and Narcissa Whitman at Fort Vancouver.

10. Merk, "The Oregon Pioneers and the Boundary" (1924), 681–99. Bell also argued against the theory that Marcus Whitman and/or the pioneers had "saved" Oregon in his *Opening a Highway to the Pacific* (1921), 193–202; as did Bourne, "The Legend of Marcus Whitman" (1901), 276–300. See also Husband, "William I. Marshall and the Legend of Marcus Whitman" (1973), 57–69. Jacobs, however, in his *Winning Oregon* (1938), was much more receptive to the idea that the pioneers had been of extreme importance in forcing the issue and in the way the boundary dispute was finally settled. See pp. 219, 223, 229–31, 233–34.

11. Ramsdell, "Reminiscences" (1897), 108, recalled that when the 1844 emigration left Missouri they had not yet heard whether the 1843 overlanders had gotten safely through. See also Stewart, *The California Trail* (1962), 53–54. The "Safe Arrival of the Oregon Emigrants," however, was announced in the St. Louis *Daily Missouri Republican* on Apr. 2, 1844, and also in other newspapers, and since the 1844 band did not depart until early May, the knowledge was doubtless widespread by that time, although the planning for the journey had been done long before.

12. The best modern study of the Donner tragedy is Stewart, *Ordeal by Hunger* (1960). Poets, novelists, and presumably readers continue to be mesmerized by the drama of the Donner party. For the two most recent endeavors to recapture the experience in fictional fashion see Keithley, *The Donner Party* (1972) and Rhodes, *The Ungodly* (1973).

13. Morgan, ed., *Overland Diary of James A. Pritchard*, 11. A very brief preliminary attempt at evaluating the gold rush in history is Bieber, "The Gold Rush and Its Historians" (1949), 370–74.

14. Roske, "The World Impact of the California Gold Rush" (1963), 187–232; Holliday, "The California Gold Rush in Myth and Reality" (1959), 399; Arrington, *Great Basin Kingdom* (1958), 64–69. One of the most obvious results of the tumultuous surge to El Dorado in 1849 was the way in which national attention and interest veered abruptly away from the previously pre-eminent Oregon country.

15. Holliday, "The California Gold Rush in Myth and Reality," 2–13; Holliday, "The California Gold Rush Reconsidered" (1962), 35–41. Historians have delimited the boundaries of the "gold rush" differently. Paul has suggested the 1848–53 period, while Morgan asserted that "the Gold Rush proper ended in 1850." Paul, "An Interpretation of California's Golden Era" (1949), 30; McCollum, *California as I Saw It*, ed. Morgan (1960), 15.

16. Hannon, *The Boston-Newton Company Venture* (1969); Scamehorn, ed., *The Buckeye Rovers in the Gold Rush* (1965); Kihn, "Connecticut and the California Gold Rush" (1963), 1–13; Marshall, "The Newark Overland Company" (1952), 173–87; Potter, ed., *Trail to California*.

17. Bidlack, *Letters Home* (1960); Epstein, "The California Gold Rush as Reported by the Marshall Statesman" (1950), 19–28; Richardson, "The Argonauts of Jersey City" (1926), 170–86, 369–77, 525–31.

18. Gregg, "Boonslickers in the Gold Rush to California" (1947), 345–60; Gregg, "Missourians in the Gold Rush" (1945), 137–54; Wyman, ed., *California Emigrant Letters* (1952); Lorch, "Iowa and the California Gold Rush of 1849" (1932), 307–76; Gara, "Gold Fever in Wisconsin" (1954–55), 106–8; Thomas, "Buckeye Argonauts" (1950), 256–69; Oakley, "Arkansas' Golden Army of '49" (1947), 1–85; Ambler, "West Virginia Forty-Niners" (1941), 59–75; Marshall, "New Jersey Expeditions to California in 1849" (1952), 17–36; Howe, *Argonauts of '49* (1923).

19. Johansen, "A Working Hypothesis for the Study of Migrations" (1967), 1–12; Wyman, "Council Bluffs and the Westward Movement" (1949), 99–118; Wyman, "Omaha: Frontier Depot" (1936), 143–55; Wyman, "The Outfitting Posts" (1949), 14–23; Mattes, "The Jumping-off Places on the Overland Trail" (1967), 27–39.

20. Billington, "Books That Won the West" (1967), 25–32, 72–75; Kroll, "The Books That Enlightened the Emigrants" (1944), 103–23; Andrews, "The Controversial Hastings Overland Guide" (1968), 21–34; Andrews, "The Ambitions of Lansford W. Hastings" (1970), 473–91; Andrews, "Lansford W. Hastings and the Promotion of the Salt Lake Desert Cutoff" (1973), 133–50; Andrews, "Satire and the Overland Guide" (1969), 99–111. Andrews also has under preparation a full-scale biography of Hastings. For an assessment of Bryant's role in the westward movement see Clark, "Edwin Bryant and the Opening of the Road to California" (1971), 29–43.

21. Morgan, "The Ferries of the Forty-Niners . . ." (1959–60); Root, "Ferries in Kansas . . ." (1933–37).

22. Mattes, "Chimney Rock on the Oregon Trail" (1955), 1–26; Munkres, "Independence Rock and Devil's Gate" (1968), 23–40; Munkres, "Ash Hollow: Gateway to the High Plains" (1970), 5–43; Munkres, "Soda Springs: Curiosity of the Trail" (1971), 215–35; Heaton, "The Old Lone Tree" (1950), 147–52.

23. Holtz, "Old Fort Kearny—1846–1848" (1972), 44–55; Mantor, "Fort Kearny and

the Westward Movement" (1948), 175–207; Hafen and Young, *Fort Laramie and the Pageant of the West* (1938); Mattes, "Fort Laramie, Guardian of the Oregon Trail" (1945), 3–20; Mattes, "Robidoux's Trading Post at 'Scott's Bluffs' " (1949), 95–138; "Fort Hall, 1834–1856" (1968), 28–31; Davis, "The Sutler at Fort Bridger" (1971), 37–54; Gowans, "Fort Bridger and the Mormons" (1974), 49–67.

24. Harstad, "The Lander Trail" (1968), 14–28; Kelly, "Gold Seekers on the Hastings Cutoff" (1952), 3–30; Kelly, "The Hastings Cutoff" (1930), 67–82; Kelly, "The Salt Desert Trail" (1930), 35–52; Korns, "West from Fort Bridger" (1951), 1–297; Helfrich, "The Applegate Trail" (1971), 1–106; McNary, "Route of Meek Cut-off, 1845" (1934), 1–9; Miller, "The Parting of the Ways on the Oregon Trail" (1973), 47–52; Caughey, "The Transit of the Forty-Niners" (1971), 17–27.

25. Dorris, "Federal Aid to Oregon Trail prior to 1850" (1929), 305–25; Dale, "The Organization of the Oregon Emigrating Companies" (1915), 205–27; Shaffer, "The Management of Organized Wagon Trains" (1961), 355–65; Read, "Diseases, Drugs, and Doctors on the Oregon-California Trail" (1944), 260–76; Groh, *Gold Fever* (1966); Read, "Women and Children on the Oregon-California Trail" (1944), 1–23; Munkres, "Wives, Mothers, Daughters" (1970), 191–224; Manning, "Literacy on the Oregon Trail" (1940), 189–94; Troxel, "Food of the Overland Emigrants" (1955), 12–26.

26. Munkres, "The Plains Indian Threat" (1968), 193–221. Even though the full title promises coverage to 1860, the author has used no diaries or other sources for either 1859 or 1860—an important and especially dangerous period of plains travel.

27. Richmond, "Developments along the Overland Trail" (1952), 154–79, 237–47.

28. Rawling, "The Oregon Trail" (1961), 751.

29. Dorris, "The Oregon Trail" (1918), 473–547.

30. Hartman, "The California and Oregon Trail" (1924), 1–35. On the Mormon guidebooks see p. 5.

31. Young, "The Oregon Trail" (1900), 339–45.

32. Applegate, "A Day with the Cow Column in 1843," 377. Applegate first read this now-famous essay in 1876 at the fourth annual reunion of the Oregon Pioneer Association, from whose *Transactions* the Oregon Historical Society *Quarterly* reprinted it.

33. Eastham, "The Occasional Address" (1886), 9.

34. Himes, "Annual Address" (1908), 135–36, italics mine.

35. Connelley, "National Aspects of the Old Oregon Trail" (1915), 415, 417–18; Elliott, "The Earliest Travelers on the Oregon Trail" (1912), 83; Federal Writers' Project, *The Oregon Trail* (1939), 33.

36. The edition by E. N. Feltskog (1969) is by all accounts the best available.

37. DeVoto, *Year of Decision*, 116, 141, 171–73; Parkman, *Oregon Trail*, 31a–43a; Jacobs, ed., *Letters of Francis Parkman* (1960), 1:xxxix.

38. Laut, *The Overland Trail* (1920), esp. xxi, 3–4, 98–99, 211, 352–53.

39. Shortly before he died, Frederick Jackson Turner sent Hulbert, a former student, a congratulatory letter upon learning that *Forty-Niners* had been awarded the *Atlantic*'s literary prize. But Turner also wrote: "The combination of fiction and history, even in skilful hands like yours, finds me somewhat unconvinced." Turner to Hulbert, Feb. 2, 1932, in Jacobs, ed., *The Historical World of Frederick Jackson Turner* (1968), 249.

40. Instead of photographs Glen Rounds utilizes numerous pen-and-ink sketches of trail life to decorate his short and superficial *The Prairie Schooners* (1968), which is focused almost completely on the route to Oregon.

41. Another volume focusing on this trail, at least according to its title, was Inman and Cody's *The Great Salt Lake Trail* (1910). As might be expected, however, this lengthy volume stressed the exploits of Buffalo Bill, Indian lore, and famous Indian battles. Packed with various reminiscent accounts and ranging from the earliest explorations to the building of the transcontinental railroad and Custer's last stand, almost no attention was paid to the overland emigrants, and none at all to the Oregon migrations. In addition to the Buffalo Bill stories, the volume is noteworthy mainly for the authors' preference for the "Great Salt Lake Trail" nomenclature—and it was the initial appearance of this volume among others which had caused Young to begin his campaign for the "Oregon Trail" designation. See Young, "The Oregon Trail," 343–44.

42. See pp. 97–99, 189, 322–24. The Indians, Stewart points out, were too smart to make an attack in a manner which was least likely to be successful and most likely to be dangerous. More usual were attacks on trains spread out while traveling.

43. Dale Morgan has provided some information about those "unmentionable" latrine arrangements: "Once I discussed this particular silence in the overland journals with a well-known authority on Mormon history and Mormon folkways. She had some answers, but not from any written source; rather, from conversation with her grandmother. When the Mormon trains set out, she told me, the captain immediately established the rule: women to go to this side, men to that. And on the flat and treeless Plains, Mormon women solved the problem of privacy when privacy is peculiarly desired by walking out in a group, several standing with skirts spread wide to provide a screen for their sisters. We may assume that something of the sort held for all family migrations in the West." Morgan, "The Significance and Value of the Overland Journal," 31. The entire essay underscores the need that all scholarly work on any phase of western history during this period be firmly grounded in the journals and letters written by the overlanders.

44. In a 1973 essay, "New Horizons on the Old Oregon Trail," Mattes reviews his principal conclusions in *Great Platte River Road* in addition to suggesting further avenues for exploration in overland emigration history.

45. Presumably William H. Ashley had taken the first wagon west of the Missouri River any distance in the fall of 1824, and in 1827 he transported a four-pound cannon to the Great Salt Lake on a two-mule carriage—the first wagon through South Pass. Korns, "West from Fort Bridger," 3–4; W. H. Ashley to A. Macomb, Mar., 1829, in *Message from the President of the United States* (1831), 7; Morgan, ed., *The West of William H. Ashley* (1964), 100, 166. For Hoover's proclamation see New York *Times*, Feb. 23, 1930.

46. Hawkins, "Centennial of the Covered Wagon" (1930), 115–24; New York *Times*, July 4, Dec. 30, 1930. In an Apr. 10, 1930, editorial the *Times* praised Meeker's efforts in behalf of marking the trails. Then in 1952 occurred the Centennial Celebration of the Covered Wagon, which included a caravan driving west from St. Joseph to Oregon commemorating both the large migration of 1852 and Meeker's trip west as an overland emigrant. There had also been, in 1949, appropriate ceremonies commemorating the California gold rush. See Haines, "Baker's Covered Wagon Centennial" (1952), 209–13, and Vail, "Gold Fever" (1949), 237–71.

47. The best of several reminiscent books Meeker wrote is *The Busy Life of Eighty-five Years* (1916), on which most of the following account is based. See also Shafer, "Eastward Ho! Ezra Meeker Memorializes the Oregon Trail" (1968), 42–49.

48. Galbreath, "Ezra Meeker: Ohio's Illustrious Pioneer" (1927), 38–42; Shafer, "Eastward Ho!," 42, 48.

49. Bancroft, *California Inter Pocula* (1888), 92. The three years were, of course, 1843, 1846, and 1849.

50. Ibid., 119–20; Bancroft, *History of California* (1886–90), 6:148, 160–61.

51. Bancroft, *California Inter Pocula*, 113–14.

52. Bancroft, *History of Oregon* (1886–88), 1:783.

53. Schouler, *History of the United States of America* (1904), 5:135–36; Rhodes, *History of the United States* (1920), 1:112–113; Channing, *A History of the United States* (1925), 6:43–45; Wilson, *A History of the American People* (1902), 4:135.

54. Fish, *The Rise of the Common Man, 1830–1850* (1937) is the only volume in either series which makes even passing mention of the overlanders, noting the 1843 and 1849 migrations. See pp. 301, 309.

55. Hough, *Passing of the Frontier*, 93–94.

56. Beard and Beard, *The Rise of American Civilization* (1929), 1:600–601.

57. Morris and Greenleaf, *U.S.A.: The History of a Nation* (1969), 1:558.

58. Graebner, Fite, and White, *A History of the United States* (1970), 1:652. The foregoing observations are based on a survey of the following additional textbooks: Bailey, *The American Pageant* (1971); Blum *et al.*, *The National Experience* (1973); Carman, Syrett, and Wishy, *A History of the American People* (1967); Handlin, *America: A History* (1968); Handlin, *The History of the United States* (1967); Hicks, Mowry, and Burke, *A History of American*

Democracy (1966); Malone and Rauch, *Crisis of the Union* (1960); Morison, *The Oxford History of the American People* (1965); Parkes, *The United States of America* (1968); Perkins and Van Deusen, *The United States of America* (1968); Current, Williams, and Freidel, *American History* (1971); Williams, Current, and Freidel, *A History of the United States* (1969); Garraty, *The American Nation* (1971); Miller and Ward, *History of America* (1971).

59. Paxson, *History of the American Frontier* (1924); Branch, *Westward* (1930); Goodwin, *The Trans-Mississippi West* (1922), 464; Clark, *The West in American History* (1937), 467, 472–73, 475, 485.

60. Hafen, Hollon, and Rister, *Western America* (1970), 181, 182, 240.

61. Ibid., 179; Clark, *Frontier America* (1969), 497, 500; Billington, *Westward Expansion* (1967), 528.

62. Clark, *Frontier America*, 573; Billington, *Westward Expansion*, 591.

63. Hine and Bingham, eds., *The American Frontier* (1972), 155–57; Spence, ed., *The American West* (1966), 91–102; Ridge and Billington, eds., *America's Frontier Story* (1969), chaps. 19, 20, 22.

64. Richmond and Mardock, eds., *A Nation Moving West* (1966), 169–78. A short selection from an 1844 diarist bound for Oregon is also included, pp. 179–80.

65. Morgan, *Overland in 1846*, 1:115.

66. Boorstin's emphasis on community as the key to understanding the westward movement is developed in Part Two of *The Americans: The National Experience* (1965).

Chapter One: Public Opinion, 1840–48

1. Williams, "Narrative of a Tour" (1955), 211, 215.

2. Lockley, ed., "Recollections of Benjamin Franklin Bonney" (1923), 37.

3. See pp. 42–61 below for an analysis of the arguments of those portraying the overland trip as easy and safe.

4. St. Louis *Missouri Gazette*, May 15, 1813, quoted in Morgan, ed., *The West of William H. Ashley* (1964), xl.

5. *Annals of Congress*, 17 Cong., 2 Sess., 407 (Dec. 17, 1822); 16 Cong., 2 Sess., 954 (Jan. 25, 1821).

6. *Missouri Advocate, and St. Louis Enquirer*, Mar. 11, 1826, reprinted in Morgan, ed., *The West of William H. Ashley*, 140–41.

7. St. Louis *Beacon*, Nov. 4, 1830, in Morgan, The Mormons and the Far West (typescripts); Cincinnati *American*, Nov. 22, 1830, in ibid.; Philadelphia *National Gazette*, Nov. 26, 1830, quoted in Nunis, "The Enigma of the Sublette Overland Party" (1959), 334–35; Washington *Daily National Intelligencer*, Aug. 3, 1835, in Morgan, The Mormons and the Far West.

8. Smith, Jackson, and Sublette to John H. Eaton, Oct. 29, 1830, in *Message from the President of the United States* (1831), 22.

9. Pilcher to Eaton, n.d., in ibid., 19; Kelley, "A General Circular to All Persons of Good Character Who Wish to Emigrate to the Oregon Territory," in Powell, ed., *Hall J. Kelley on Oregon* (1932), 84–86.

10. Van Every, *The Final Challenge* (1964), 313–14; "Article X. Critical Notices" (1838), 251.

11. Quoted in Husband, "Senator Lewis F. Linn and the Oregon Question" (1971), 6–7.

12. Powell, ed., *Hall J. Kelley on Oregon*, xiii.

13. Lavender, *Westward Vision* (1963), 227–28; Hulbert, ed., *The Call of the Columbia* (1934), 70.

14. Snelling, "Oregon Territory" (1832), reprinted in Hulbert, ed., *Call of the Columbia*, 73–76, 77–84, 89.

15. Morris, "The Notion of a Great American Desert East of the Rockies" (1926), 190. For further treatment of the "Great American Desert" concept see Chap. 11 below. See also Bowden, "The Great American Desert and the American Frontier" (1971), 48–79.

16. Webb, *The Great Plains* (1931), 152–53, 159; Smith, *Virgin Land* (1950), 207.

17. Ibid., 205, 202, 213; Bowden, "The Great American Desert and the American Frontier," 51–52; Goetzmann, *Exploration and Empire* (1966), 51, 62.

18. Merk, *Manifest Destiny and Mission in American History* (1963), 18–19.

19. The same type of approach was used by writers describing Oregon itself, who characterized it as either an "Eden" or a "most appalling" place, depending on their predilections. Meinig, *The Great Columbia Plain* (1968), 102.

20. Cramer, "British Magazines and the Oregon Question" (1963), 382.

21. Quoted by Driver, "Annual Address" (1887), 26.

22. Merk, "The Oregon Question in the Webster-Ashburton Negotiations" (1956), 402–3. That Ashburton was not alone in holding such views was evidenced by a writer in the *Westminster Review* whose appraisal of the 1842 treaty led him to agree that the Indians and the "sterile" and inhospitable regions they inhabited insured that the Oregon questions could be "left untouched awhile." "Art. VIII—North American Boundary" (1843), 200.

23. London *Times*, Mar. 7, 1843; Manchester *Guardian*, Feb. 22, Dec. 30, 1843; "Oregon" (1843), 62.

24. "Art. VI" (1843), 192.

25. London *Times*, Feb. 20, 1844.

26. Reprinted in "The Oregon Territory" (1844), 467.

27. Manchester *Guardian*, Jan. 15, 1845; London *Times*, May 9, 16, 1845; Van Every, *The Final Challenge*, 330; London *Times*, May 17, 1845.

28. Manchester *Guardian*, Mar. 8, 1843. See also the issues of Feb. 15 and Apr. 9, 1845, for similar assertions.

29. London *Morning Chronicle*, Nov. 3, 1843, reprinted in Montreal *Gazette*, Dec. 23, 1843; Liverpool *Times*, n.d., reprinted in *Supplement to the Leeds Mercury*, Dec. 13, 1845; Montreal *Gazette*, Dec. 23, 1843.

30. Ibid., May 1, 1845; "The Oregon Dispute—the Last News from America" (1845), 453.

31. "Art. VIII. The Oregon Question" (1845), 245, 260; "The Oregon Question" (1845), 495.

32. Montreal *Gazette*, July 25, 1845; London *Times*, Oct. 1, 1845; London *Examiner*, Apr. 25, 1845, reprinted in Washington *Daily National Intelligencer*, June 12, 1845; "Oregon" (1845), 1116.

33. "Art. VIII. The Oregon Territory" (1845), 491–92, 493–95, 516.

34. Leeds *Mercury*, Jan. 3, 1846; "Settlement of the Oregon Controversy by Arbitration" (1846), 35; "The Oregon Territory" (1846), 733.

35. Twiss, *The Oregon Question Examined* (1846), 380; London *Times*, Mar. 16, 1846.

36. "Oregon," *Topic*, Apr. 18, 1846, reprinted in Carey, intro., "British Side of Oregon Question, 1846" (1935), 273.

37. Cramer, "British Magazines and the Oregon Question," 382.

38. "Art. IV" (1847), 392–94. Ten years later the same *Edinburgh Review* smugly referred to this earlier article, asserting that the passing years had shown the accuracy of its earlier predictions that there was "little probability" of much overland travel to the Pacific. Since the distances were too great and the attendant hardships too severe for all but "occasional recruits from the boldest class of pioneers," even the California gold mania had not altered the situation. The *Review* believed that most who had reached California had gone by sea and that only about a sixth of California's white inhabitants had braved the overland route, although "many thousands" had died on the way and their bones now lay bleaching on the prairies and in the Rocky Mountain canyons. Plainly, it was difficult for some writers to give up the idea that you could not get from Missouri to Oregon or California by land. "Art. I—Annals of California" (1858), 297–98.

39. Lancaster went on to write, with tongue in cheek, that on McLoughlin's authority, "if I conclude to go to China I shall go with an ox team by the way of the sandwich Islands, at which place I will write you a full description of the general pasturage of the route." Lancaster to Elisha Whittlesey, Dec. 9, 1850 (MS).

40. The French, who were advancing no claims, could afford more objectivity. Eugene Duflot de Mofras came to Oregon in October, 1841, on a commercial mission in behalf of the French government, and predicted that a wave of immigrants would soon come over the Rockies. In commenting on those who had already taken wagons through South Pass, he mentioned no outstanding difficulties. Pipes, trans., "Extract from Exploration of the Oregon Territory, the Californias, and the Gulf of California . . . by Eugene Duflot de Mofras" (1925), 151, 189–90. The official French representative in Washington, Alphonse Joseph Yves Pageot, in a dispatch of Nov. 27, 1843, likened the willingness of adventurous Americans to expose themselves to "certain privations, terminated, for the first pioneers, by a premature death" to a "chimera" which nevertheless had validity and reality because of the ardor of those who traveled. Blue, "France and the Oregon Question" (1933), 39, 46. And a French reviewer in *La Revue des Deux Mondes* in 1845 contended that it was not as easy to travel to Oregon as some of the enthusiasts allowed. *Littell's Living Age*, 4 (Feb. 1, 1845), 284.

41. Ross, "Horace Greeley and the West" (1933), 64–66.

42. New York *Daily Tribune*, Feb. 2, 1843.

43. Ibid., Feb. 2, 15, July 19, 1843, Feb. 3, 1845.

44. Ibid., Feb. 15, Dec. 19, 1843.

45. Ibid., July 19, 1843.

46. New York *Aurora*, July 20, 1843; Augusta *Maine Farmer and Mechanic's Advocate*, Aug. 5, 1843.

47. New York *Daily Tribune*, Mar. 9, July 21, 1843.

48. Ibid., Dec. 18, 25, 1843.

49. Reprinted in London *Times*, Jan. 17, 1844.

50. New York *Daily Tribune*, Dec. 18, 28, 1843.

51. Greeley outlined this policy in ibid., Apr. 22, 1844.

52. Ibid., Dec. 28, 1843.

53. In one 1844 reference to the emigrants Greeley did note that the emigration continued "to force itself across the Great Western Desert" in its movement toward the Pacific. Ibid., Apr. 22, 1844.

54. Ibid., May 28, June 6, 1845.

55. Ibid., July 26, 1845.

56. Ibid., July 28, 1846; ibid., Nov. 15, 1845.

57. Hulbert, ed., *Call of the Columbia,* 69–70; Fowler, "Territorial Expansion—a Threat to the Republic?" (1962), 34–42.

58. New York *Journal of Commerce,* Oct. 30, 1845, reprinted in Washington *National Intelligencer,* Nov. 8, 1845; Windsor *Vermont Chronicle,* Feb. 25, 1846; Newport *Herald of the Times,* Jan. 15, 1846.

59. "The Oregon Question" (1846), 228–29, 217; Hartford *Daily Courant,* July 21, 1843; Detroit *Advertiser,* n.d., reprinted in Augusta *Maine Farmer,* Feb. 8, 1844; Augusta *Age,* n.d., reprinted in New York *Working Man's Advocate,* Feb. 8, 1845.

60. St. Louis *Western Atlas, and Saturday Evening Gazette,* May 1, 1841, in Morgan, The Mormons and the Far West; St. Louis *Daily Missouri Republican,* June 11, 1844; Albany *Atlas,* Oct. 21, 1845; St. Louis *Daily Missouri Republican,* Sept. 22, 1847, Feb. 8, 1848.

61. Tobie, "From the Missouri to the Columbia, 1841" (1937), 138, 159; Bancroft, *History of California* (1886–90), 4:266.

62. Fisher to Benjamin M. Hill, Jan. 22, June 15, 1844, in Henderson, Latourette, and Latourette, eds., "Correspondence of the Reverend Ezra Fisher" (1915), 95–96, 103–4.

63. "Associations of Emigrants to Oregon" (1839), 349. Drury, "The Oregonian and Indian's Advocate" (1965), 159–67, provides a brief overview of the society's goals and work; a number of additional societies subsequently formed are identified in Dale, "The Organization of the Oregon Emigrating Companies" (1915), 205–27.

64. "Editorial" (June, 1839), 286. See also Drury, "The Oregonian and Indian's Advocate," 165–67.

65. "Editorial" (June, 1839), 287–88; "Difficulties of Emigration to Oregon" (Jan., 1839), 123–25; "Editorial" (July, 1839), 313–14.

66. "Difficulties of Emigration to Oregon," 125; "Editorial. Our Society, and Emigration to Oregon" (1839), 346–49.

67. "Disposition of the Hudson's Bay Company" (1839), 314–15.

68. *Congressional Globe,* 27 Cong., 3 Sess., 200 (Jan. 25, 1843).

69. Ibid., 28 Cong., 2 Sess., App., 294, 292 (Feb. 1, 1845).

70. John Charles Frémont, *"Report* of the First Expedition, 1843," in Jackson and Spence, eds., *The Expeditions of John Charles Frémont* (1970–73), 1:253–54.

71. *Congressional Globe,* 27 Cong., 3 Sess., App., 78–79 (Jan. 9, 1843), 153 (Jan. 26, 1843).

72. Ibid., 28 Cong., 1 Sess., 186 (Jan. 24, 1844).

73. Ibid., 29 Cong., 1 Sess., App., 162 (Jan. 28, 1846).

74. Ibid., 202 (Feb. 2, 1846).

75. Ibid., 121 (Jan. 16, 1846), 555 (Mar. 19, 1846); Benton, *Thirty Years' View* (1856), 2:721.

76. Cincinnati *Chronicle,* n.d., reprinted in "Lieut. Fremont's Expedition to Oregon and California" (1845), 339; "Fremont's Expeditions" (1845), 71, 77; Boston *Daily Journal,* Sept. 8, 1845; Wilkes, *The History of Oregon* (1845), reprinted in *Washington Historical Quarterly* (1907), 2:88.

77. Jefferson City *Jeffersonian Republican,* Apr. 25, 1840, in Morgan, The Mormons and the Far West; "Oregon" (1843), 138.

78. *Congressional Globe,* 29 Cong., 1 Sess., App., 388–89 (Feb. 6, 1846).

79. Washington *Union,* n.d., reprinted in Springfield, Mo., *Advertiser,* Oct. 11, 1845.

80. *Congressional Globe,* 29 Cong., 1 Sess., App., 346 (Feb. 7, 1846).

81. Van Every, *The Final Challenge,* 297.

82. New York *Evening Mirror,* n.d., reprinted in London *Times,* Dec. 2, 1844.

83. Greenhow, *The History of Oregon and California* (1845), 404.

84. *Congressional Globe,* 27 Cong., 3 Sess., App., 112 (Jan. 30, 1843); [probably] Liberty *Western Journal,* Jan. 4, 1845, reprinted in *Working Man's Advocate,* Jan. 25, 1845, and in Albany *Atlas,* Jan. 28, 1845.

85. *Congressional Globe,* 27 Cong., 3 Sess., App., 152 (Jan. 26, 1843).

86. Ibid., 29 Cong., 1 Sess., App., 175 (Feb. 6, 1846).

87. New Orleans *Daily Picayune,* June 12, 1845.

88. Greenhow, *Memoir . . . on the Northwest Coast* (1840), 199; Sherman, "The Oregon Territory" (1842), 319.

89. [Probably] New Orleans *Weekly Bulletin,* n.d., reprinted in New York *Daily Tribune,* Aug. 4, 1842; [probably] Iowa City *Iowa Capitol Reporter,* n.d., reprinted in *Niles' National Register,* 64 (May 27, 1843), 196; Cincinnati *Atlas,* n.d., reprinted in Augusta *Maine Farmer,* May 29, 1845.

90. Kroll, "The Books That Enlightened the Emigrants" (1944), 108.

91. Weston *Journal,* Jan. 4, 1845, reprinted in "Documents" (1903), 273; St. Joseph *Gazette,* June 6, 1845, May 1, 1846.

92. St. Joseph *Gazette,* July 10, 1846, May 19, June 16, 1848; Washington *Union,* Nov. 17, 1845, reprinted in New York *Herald,* Nov. 20, 1845.

93. Philadelphia *Ledger,* n.d., reprinted in Springfield, Mo., *Advertiser,* Jan. 7, 1845; St. Louis *Missouri Republican,* Dec. 14, 1843, reprinted in "Documents," 405.

94. *Congressional Globe,* 29 Cong., 1 Sess., App., 183 (Feb. 5, 1846); ibid., 27 Cong., 3 Sess., App., 139 (Jan. 24, 1843); ibid., 29 Cong., 1 Sess., App., 87 (Jan. 7, 1846), 368 (Feb. 7, 1846).

95. Ibid., 28 Cong., 2 Sess., App., 136, 167 (Jan. 27, 29, 1845).

96. Ibid., 30 Cong., 1 Sess., App., 1067 (July 31, 1848).

97. Ibid., 29 Cong., 1 Sess., App., 84 (Jan. 5, 1846).

98. Tyler, "Third Annual Message," Dec., 1843, and "Fourth Annual Message," Dec. 3, 1844, in Richardson, comp., *A Compilation of the Messages and Papers of the Presidents* (1903), 4:258, 337–38.

99. Polk, "Annual Message to Congress," Dec. 2, 1845, in ibid., 4:396.

100. U.S. Congress, Committee on Military Affairs, *Military Posts on the Route to Oregon* (1845), 3.

101. Polk, "Annual Message to Congress," Dec. 2, 1845, "To the Senate and House of Representatives of the United States," Aug. 5, 1846, "Second Annual Message," Dec. 8, 1846, "Third Annual Message," Dec. 7, 1847, all in Richardson, comp., *Messages and Papers,* 4:397, 458, 504, 559.

102. New York *Herald,* Aug. 3, 1846; New Orleans *Daily Picayune,* May 27, 1847.

103. St. Joseph *Gazette,* Aug. 20, July 30, 1847.

104. St. Louis *Daily Missouri Republican,* July 20, Aug. 28, Oct. 2, 1847.

105. San Francisco *California Star,* May 22, Mar. 13, 1847. By 1847 the two San Francisco newspapers, the *California Star* and the *Californian,* were locked in a heated circulation struggle. One manifestation of the scramble for subscribers was manufactured news, including imaginary tales of emigrant cannibalism on the "Mormon Corridor" route from Salt Lake City to San Bernardino. See Hall, "Journalism in California: The Pioneer Period" (1971), 632–33.

106. Washington *National Intelligencer,* May 29, Sept. 7, 1847. The *California Star* had also spoken of "thrilling scenes" and the "thrilling event" in its coverage of the Donner disaster (May 22, 1847).

107. Wooster *Democrat,* Aug. 5, 1847; "From California" (1847), 330; *Congressional Globe,* 30 Cong., 1 Sess., App., 804 (July 28, 1848); "The Route to California" (1848), 211; "California" (1848), 172.

108. *Congressional Globe,* 28 Cong., 1 Sess., App., 318 (Mar. 18, 1844).

109. Benton, *Thirty Years' View,* 2:469; *Congressional Globe,* 28 Cong., 1 Sess., App., 186–87 (Jan. 25, 1844); ibid., 28 Cong., 1 Sess., 313 (Feb. 23, 1844); ibid., 29 Cong., 1 Sess., App., 349 (Mar. 12, 1846).

110. Ibid., 28 Cong., 2 Sess., App., 136 (Jan. 27, 1845); ibid., 29 Cong., 1 Sess., App., 153 (Jan. 29, 1846); ibid., 28 Cong., 2 Sess., App., 162 (Jan. 29, 1845); ibid., 29 Cong., 1 Sess., App., 215 (Feb. 6, 1846).

111. Calhoun to Pakenham, Sept. 3, 1844, in *Message from the President of the United States* (1845), 153.

112. On one occasion Bennett wrote, "Did we not see Greeley & McElrath [co-editor of the *Tribune*] like consummate blockheads as they are." New York *Herald*, Feb. 16, 1845.

113. Ibid., June 1, 15, 1845.

114. Ibid., July 15, Sept. 18, 1845. The attitude of the *Herald* on the feasibility of building a railroad overland to Oregon is fascinating. Again on October 1, 1845, the *Herald* emphasized the ease of construction; on March 3, 1846, an editorial commented that "there is not a region of country in the world that offers less obstruction to such a project." On July 17, 1846, the *Herald* took to task an unfavorable congressional committee report on the continental railroad, believing that the committee conjured up absurdities in stressing difficulties of construction. And then, on August 10, 1848, the *Herald*'s attitude changed completely. Though acknowledgment was made that it had earlier been enthusiastic about the project, the *Herald* now concluded that "it is perfect insanity, or the next step to it, for any one to indulge in further discussion about the feasibility of a railroad from the Mississippi to the Pacific, at the present time." Perhaps a century later, when the West had been filled with population, the project could be revived, but for now, "If Congress had common sense, they would not discuss such a subject . . . but those men in Washington, seem to be more disposed to make fools of themselves, at the price of eight dollars per day to the people, than to go to work and do their duty to their constituents."

115. Ibid., Jan. 19, 1846.

116. Ibid., Mar. 22, Apr. 3, Aug. 10, May 2, 1846.

117. New York *Working Man's Advocate*, Apr. 27, Dec. 7, 1844, Jan. 11, 1845.

118. New York *Young America!*, July 19, 1845, Jan. 10, 1846.

119. *American Agriculturist*, 2 (Nov., 1843), 273; "The Oregon" (1844), 325–26.

120. Review of Josiah T. Marshall's *The Farmer and Emigrant's Hand Book* (1845), 326; "California" (1849), 332.

121. *New Genesee Farmer*, n.d., reprinted in Boston *Evening Mercantile Journal*, Aug. 26, 1842.

122. New York *Morning News*, n.d., reprinted in "Oregon" (1845), 228–29; Washington *National Intelligencer*, Nov. 8, 1843; Cramer, "The March of Our Republic" (1845), 547, 550.

123. Merk, *Manifest Destiny and Mission in American History*, 154.

124. New Orleans *Daily Picayune*, June 2, 1842, Sept. 16, 1843, June 30, 1844.

125. Ibid., Dec. 18, 1846; "Art. VI—the Northern Pacific" (1845), 215.

126. Madison *Courier and Constitutional Advocate*, Dec. 9, 1843, quoted in Jacobs, *Winning Oregon* (1938), 161; St. Louis *Daily Missouri Republican*, Sept. 1, 1845; Burlington *Iowa Territorial Gazette and Advertiser*, May 3, 1845, and Jefferson City *Inquirer*, Oct. 20, 1846, in Morgan, The Mormons and the Far West.

127. St. Joseph *Gazette*, May 2, July 18, 1845.

128. Ibid., Aug. 27, 1847; St. Louis *Daily Union*, Sept. 9, 1847, in Morgan, The Mormons and the Far West; San Francisco *California Star, Supplement*, Apr. 1, 1848.

129. Weston *Journal*, Mar. 15, 1845, reprinted in "Documents," 278; St. Joseph *Gazette*, Dec. 3, 1847, and New Orleans *Daily Picayune*, Mar. 13, 1844, reprinted in "Documentary" (1901), 200; Weston *Journal*, Jan. 18, 1845, reprinted in "Documents," 276; Louisville *Examiner*, Sept. 30, 1848.

130. Fayette *Missouri Democrat*, Sept. 15, 1845. See also Washington *National Intelligencer*, Oct. 29, 1846.

131. St. Louis *Daily Missouri Republican*, Nov. 17, 1842, Sept. 22, 1847; Louisville *Examiner*, Oct. 9, 1847; Liberty, Mo., *Weekly Tribune*, Aug. 15, 1846.

132. St. Louis *Daily Missouri Republican*, Sept. 18, 1847.

133. Oregon City *Oregon Spectator*, May 13, 1847, reprinted in Morgan, ed., *Overland in 1846* (1963), 2:729–31.

134. Fayette *Missouri Democrat*, Sept. 15, 1845.

135. St. Joseph *Gazette*, Oct. 3, 10, 1845, Jan. 16, 1846; St. Louis *Daily Missouri Republican*, June 16, 1847; Albany *Atlas*, Feb. 4, 1845; San Francisco *California Star*, Apr. 10,

May 22, 1847; St. Louis *Daily Union,* June 19, 21, 30, 1847; Springfield *Illinois State Register,* Jan. 23, 1846—all in Morgan, The Mormons and the Far West. See also pp. 47–49 above.

136. Louisville *Journal,* [probably] May 18, 1848, reprinted in St. Joseph *Gazette,* June 2, 1848; Cincinnati *Chronicle,* n.d., reprinted in Wooster *Democrat,* June 5, 1845.

137. The focus in Chap. 1 has been primarily upon the overland emigrations to Oregon, since the sources used by this writer were much more concerned with Oregon than with California. Graebner has, however, argued for a rather strong California orientation among at least some newspapers in 1845 in his "American Interest in California, 1845" (1953), 13–27.

138. Independence *Western Expositor,* n.d., reprinted in New Orleans *Daily Picayune,* May 9, 1844; Independence *Western Expositor,* Oct. 26, 1844, reprinted in Washington *National Intelligencer,* Nov. 12, 1844. As an example of the manner in which every scrap of Oregon information was eagerly seized upon by the nation's media, I have found this same quotation reprinted in at least four other newspapers—Springfield *Advertiser,* Nov. 19, 1844; Albany *Atlas,* Nov. 14, 1844; Philadelphia *United States Gazette,* Nov. 12, 1844; St. Louis *Reveille,* Nov. 4, 1844, in "Documents," 406.

139. Burlington *Hawkeye,* Apr. 17, 1845, reprinted in New York *Daily Tribune,* May 17, 1845.

140. For a sampling of such expressions see Springfield *Illinois State Register,* Apr. 4, May 16, 1845, and Jefferson City *Inquirer,* May 1, 1847, in Morgan, The Mormons and the Far West. Also see St. Louis *Daily Missouri Republican,* Apr. 14, 1846; Independence *Expositor,* n.d., reprinted in Liberty *Weekly Tribune,* Apr. 17, 1847; Liberty *Weekly Tribune,* May 15, 1847.

141. St. Louis *Daily Missouri Republican,* May 12, 1845. See also Painesville, Ohio, *Telegraph,* May 24, 1843, St. Louis *Daily Union,* Apr. 20, 1847, St. Joseph *Gazette,* Apr. 30, 1847, and St. Louis *Missouri Reporter,* Mar. 20, 1846, all in Morgan, The Mormons and the Far West, for laudations of the "pillar of the community" types comprising the bulk of the overlanders. Pomeroy, *The Pacific Slope: A History* (1965), 34–36, has contended that the overlanders of the 1840s were above the average in educational background and financial status.

142. New York *Gazette,* n.d., reprinted in "The Emigrants" (1845), 341; St. Louis *New Era,* June 4, 1845, reprinted in "Oregon" (1845), [240].

143. Independence *Western Expositor,* n.d., reprinted in "Oregon Emigrants" (1845), 246; Independence *Western Expositor,* n.d., reprinted in Fayette *Missouri Democrat,* Aug. 20, 1845.

144. Independence *Mission Expositor,* July 6, 1845, reprinted in "Emigrants for California" (1845), 7. Hastings and nine other men left Independence about August 17 on this daring fall and winter journey and reached Sutter's Fort on Christmas Day, having crossed the plains and Sierras uneventfully and just ahead of the snows, which came unseasonably late. The Donners would not be so fortunate the following year. Barry, *The Beginning of the West* (1972), 560–61.

145. Springfield, Ill., *Journal,* Oct. 22, 1846, reprinted in New York *Daily Tribune,* Nov. 4, 1846.

146. Bright, "The Folklore and History of the 'Oregon Fever'" (1951), 253.

147. Independence *Western Expositor,* May 3, 1845, reprinted in "The Oregon Fever" (1845), 203; St. Louis *Missouri Republican,* [probably] May 11, 1846, reprinted in "Oregon and California" (1846), 281.

CHAPTER TWO: PUBLIC OPINION, 1849–60

1. New York *Daily Tribune*, Jan. 31, 1849.

2. See Epstein, "The California Gold Rush as Reported by the Marshall Statesman" (1950), 19–28, for a case study of one Michigan newspaper's coverage.

3. St. Joseph *Gazette*, Apr. 5, 1850; "The Wedding in the Gate of the Rocky Mountains" (1849), 124.

4. New York *Daily Tribune*, Apr. 4, 1850. Similar sentiments were expressed in the St. Louis *Daily Missouri Republican*, Jan. 31, 1850. The Sacramento *Placer Times*, June 12, 1850, also expected the 1850 overlanders to have less difficulty thanks to the knowledge gained the previous year (reprinted in New York *Herald*, July 22, 1850).

5. New York *Commercial Advertiser*, n.d., in Washington *National Intelligencer*, May 4, 1850; New York *Herald*, Nov. 7, 1850, Mar. 10, 1851; Kanesville *Frontier Guardian*, May 16, 1851.

6. Derbec to Editor, May 16, 1850, in *Journal des Débats*, Sept. 24, 1850, reprinted in Nasatir, ed., *A French Journalist in the California Gold Rush* (1964), 95–96.

7. St. Joseph *Gazette*, Aug. 18, 1852.

8. Ibid., May 4, June 1, 1849.

9. Ibid., Dec. 25, Nov. 27, 1850.

10. Kanesville *Frontier Guardian and Iowa Sentinel*, May 28, June 4, 1852; St. Louis *Union*, [probably] May 25, 1849, quoted in Washington *National Intelligencer*, June 5, 1849; Lexington, Mo., *Express*, [probably] June 1, 1849, quoted in Windsor *Vermont Chronicle*, June 6, 1849; Liberty, Mo., *Weekly Tribune*, May 18, 1849, Dec. 13, 1850.

11. Davenport *Gazette*, Apr. 12, 1849, quoted in Lorch, "Iowa and the California Gold Rush of 1849" (1932), 325; Windsor *Vermont Chronicle*, May 16, 1849; Wooster *Democrat*, Mar. 15, 1849; "Art VIII. Adventures on the Prairies" (1849), 180–81; "Art. IX—Oregon and the Territory of Washington" (1853), 604–5.

12. New York *Daily Tribune*, Feb. 13, 1849, Mar. 3, 1852; ibid., Apr. 28, 1849.

13. Ibid., Dec. 16, 21, 1848, Nov. 20, 1849, May 1, Dec. 9, 1850.

14. New Orleans *Daily Picayune*, Apr. 5, 1849.

15. St. Louis *Daily Missouri Republican*, Feb. 27, 1849.

16. Ibid., Mar. 2, 1849, Feb. 14, 1850.

17. Springfield, Mo., *Advertiser*, Feb. 17, 1849, reprinted in "Missouri History Not Found in Textbooks" (1960), 94.

18. St. Joseph *Gazette*, Mar. 9, 1849. The St. Joseph *Adventure*, n.d., also reported on California-bound gold seekers who returned from Panama to travel instead across the plains (reprinted in Kanesville *Frontier Guardian*, Jan. 23, 1850). This argument worked both ways. Arkansas newspaper editors, who were staunch advocates of the Canadian-Gila overland trail and constantly denigrated the South Pass route to the north, eagerly publicized the few overland companies who turned back after a few days' journey on the South Pass route to make the trip instead on the Arkansas route. See Oakley, "Arkansas' Golden Army of '49" (1947), 17–22.

19. Columbia *Missouri Statesman*, n.d., reprinted in St. Joseph *Gazette*, Apr. 9, 1851. See also ibid., Mar. 9, Dec. 14, 21, 1849, Jan. 28, 1852, Apr. 13, 1853. See also Gregg, "Missourians in the Gold Rush" (1945), 146; St. Louis *Daily Missouri Republican*, Feb. 7, 1849; Liberty *Weekly Tribune*, Dec. 7, 1849.

20. St. Louis *Daily Missouri Republican*, Feb. 14, 1850. See also St. Joseph *Gazette*, Jan. 11, 1850, and Liberty *Weekly Tribune*, Jan. 11, 1850.

21. Wyman, "The Outfitting Posts" (1949), 23.

22. Mattes, "The Jumping-off Places on the Overland Trail" (1967), 38.

23. St. Joseph *Gazette*, Feb. 16, 1849, also printed under the same heading in the St. Louis *Sunday Morning Republican*, Feb. 18, 1849. Interestingly, Goodyear took his horse drove back to California in 1849, but even advertised in the *Gazette* that he was starting from Old Fort Kearny (present Nebraska City, Neb., approximately eighty miles to the north) and would take others with him. See Barry, *The Beginning of the West* (1972), 806. Some of the background data on the travels of the above dignitaries has been drawn from Barry's immensely useful volume.

24. St. Joseph *Gazette*, Feb. 16, 1849.

25. Louisville *Examiner*, Mar. 3, 1849; St. Louis *Daily Union*, Mar. 21, 1849, and subsequent issues, cited in Barry, *Beginning of the West*, 799–800. The files of the Independence *Expositor* were lost to history in a fire, so it is impossible to be as precise about the Independence advertising campaigns as one would wish. Gregg, "Missourians in the Gold Rush," 148.

26. St. Joseph *Gazette*, Mar. 1, 1850; ibid., Nov. 2, 1849, Jan. 11, 1850.

27. Ibid., Feb. 16, 1849, Jan. 11, 1850. The *Gazette* editorial staff strangely allowed an inconsistency to creep into these assertions of outfitting supremacy when two years later, in 1852, they were still only arguing that for four years the overlanders had chosen St. Joseph as the best and major starting point. See ibid., Jan. 28, 1852.

28. St. Louis *Daily Union*, Feb. 14, 1849, in Morgan, The Mormons and the Far West (typescripts); St. Joseph *Gazette*, Mar. 9, 1849, Jan. 11, 1850.

29. St. Louis *Daily Union*, May 15, 1847, in Morgan, The Mormons and the Far West.

30. St. Joseph *Gazette*, June 25, 1847, in ibid.

31. Ibid., May 4, 1849.

32. Gregg, "Missourians in the Gold Rush," 148. The *Gazette* was especially resentful of inferences that emigrants valuing their health would not go to St. Joseph because of the cholera raging there, and in 1850 accused the Platte City, Mo., *Argus* of slandering St. Joseph by talking about nonexistent cholera cases. St. Joseph *Gazette*, Apr. 12, 1850.

33. Barry, *Beginning of the West*, 903.

34. St. Louis *Daily Missouri Republican*, Mar. 21, 1850; Wells, "The Growth of Independence" (1959), 44.

35. St. Joseph *Adventure*, n.d., reprinted in Kanesville *Frontier Guardian*, Jan. 23, 1850; Wyman, "The Outfitting Posts," 17.

36. St. Louis *Daily Missouri Republican*, Mar. 21, 1850. Also see the St. Louis *Daily Union*, Mar. 20, 21, 1849, in Morgan, The Mormons and the Far West.

37. St. Joseph *Gazette*, Mar. 29, Apr. 12, 1850.

38. Ibid., Apr. 20, 1849, Apr. 5, 1850, Apr. 21, 1852.

39. See, e.g., ibid., Feb. 16, 1849, Apr. 12, 1850, Apr. 21, 1852.

40. Ibid., Apr. 12, May 3, 1850.

41. Ibid., Dec. 31, 1851.

42. Ibid., Apr. 20, 1853, Jan. 18, 1854; Kanesville *Frontier Guardian and Iowa Sentinel*, Apr. 29, 1852.

43. Ibid., Jan. 23, 1850.

44. Ibid., Feb. 20, 1850.

45. Ibid., Feb. 7, 1851.

46. Martin to Editor, Feb. 15, 1851, in ibid., Mar. 7, 1851. "Platteville" was presumably Plattsmouth, approximately twenty miles south of Kanesville and a feeder into the trail on the south side of the Platte River.

47. Ibid., Mar. 21, 1851.

48. Ibid., May 2, 1851.

49. Kanesville *Frontier Guardian and Iowa Sentinel*, Mar. 25, Apr. 29, 1852.

50. Council Bluffs *Weekly Bugle*, Mar. 17, 24, Oct. 13, Dec. 1, 1858, Jan. 19, 1859.

51. Ibid., Jan. 19, Feb. 9, 1859. Willard, "Sidelights on the Pike's Peak Gold Rush" (1935), 3–13, provides some general information on the various newspaper campaigns by the rival towns. See esp. p. 7.

52. St. Louis *Daily Missouri Republican*, Apr. 9, 1850; St. Louis *Daily Union*, Mar. 15, 1848, in Morgan, The Mormons and the Far West; St. Louis *Daily Missouri Republican*, Feb. 6, 1850; St. Joseph *Gazette*, Apr. 5, 1850, Nov. 10, 1852; Wyman, "Atchison, a Great Frontier Depot" (1942), 297–308; Liberty *Weekly Tribune*, Mar. 9, Dec. 7, 1849, Apr. 19, 1850, Apr. 9, 1852; Barry, *Beginning of the West*, 1076.

53. Weston *Reporter*, n.d., reprinted in St. Joseph *Gazette*, Nov. 10, 1852.

54. Ibid., Apr. 5, 1850.

55. St. Louis *Sunday Morning Republican*, Feb. 18, 1849. On January 31, 1850, the *Republican* had again predicted that prices of "every thing" would be reduced by the competition for emigrants.

56. New Orleans *Daily Picayune,* Dec. 18, 1848; Albany *Atlas,* Dec. 29, 1848; Hartford *Daily Courant,* Jan. 9, 1849; Gregg, "Missourians in the Gold Rush," 143.

57. Ibid., 143–44; Albany *Atlas,* Feb. 9, 1849.

58. Kanesville *Frontier Guardian,* Oct. 3, 1851.

59. Louisville *Examiner,* Mar. 3, 1849.

60. Albany *Atlas,* Feb. 6, 1849.

61. St. Louis *Daily Missouri Republican,* Feb. 14, 1849; Liberty *Weekly Tribune,* Feb. 16, 1849; St. Louis *Daily Union,* Feb. 15, Mar. 23, 1849, in Morgan, The Mormons and the Far West; Gregg, "Boonslickers in the Gold Rush to California" (1947), 347; St. Joseph *Gazette,* Apr. 5, 1850; *Kanesville Frontier Guardian,* Feb. 7, 1851, Apr. 22, 1852; Kanesville *Western Bugle,* Sept. 7, 1852.

62. St. Louis *Daily Missouri Republican,* Apr. 14, 1849.

63. Kanesville *Frontier Guardian,* Apr. 3, 17, 1850; Gregg, "Missourians in the Gold Rush," 144–45; St. Louis *Daily Missouri Republican,* Feb. 6, 7, Mar. 8, 1849; St. Joseph *Gazette,* Mar. 10, 1852; St. Louis *Daily Missouri Republican,* Feb. 28, 1850.

64. St. Joseph *Gazette,* Mar. 10, 1852.

65. Ibid., Apr. 14, 1852; Kanesville *Frontier Guardian,* May 15, 1850.

66. St. Joseph *Gazette,* May 5, 1852.

67. St. Louis *Daily Missouri Republican,* n.d., reprinted in New York *Daily Tribune,* Mar. 20, 1849; New York *Herald,* Nov. 12, 1849, Aug. 22, 1850; Washington *National Intelligencer,* Nov. 12, 1850; Albany *Atlas,* Feb. 9, 1849.

68. Kanesville *Frontier Guardian,* May 2, May 16, 1849, May 15, 1850, May 16, 1851. The *Frontier Guardian* editor did not identify the treaty to which he alluded.

69. Ibid., Aug. 22, Nov. 14, 1851.

70. St. Louis *Daily Missouri Republican,* Dec. 11, 1849. The Liberty *Weekly Tribune,* Dec. 21, 1849, similarly called for a large dragoon force to be "kept constantly in motion between Fort Leavenworth and Oregon and California" for protective purposes.

71. Cincinnati *Cist's Weekly Advertiser,* Mar. 14, 1849; St. Joseph *Adventure,* n.d., reprinted in Kanesville *Frontier Guardian,* Apr. 18, 1849; St. Joseph *Gazette,* n.d., reprinted in Jefferson City *Inquirer,* Apr. 28, 1849. See also Liberty *Weekly Tribune,* Apr. 6, 1849.

72. Kanesville *Frontier Guardian,* May 16, 1849, June 13, 1851.

73. San Francisco *Daily Alta California,* May 17, 1850; San Francisco *Daily Herald,* May 25, 1853, in Cohen, Scrapbooks (typescripts), 104-5.

74. San Francisco *Daily Alta California,* July 3, 1850.

75. Kanesville *Frontier Guardian,* June 13, 1851; Liberty *Weekly Tribune,* Jan. 12, 1849.

76. San Francisco *Alta California,* Sept. 13, 1849.

77. Marysville, Cal., *Herald,* Sept. 3, 1850.

78. For a more comprehensive account of the actual mechanics of the relief operations see Chap. 10 below.

79. San Francisco *Daily Alta California,* July 26, 1850.

80. Ibid., July 29, Sept. 24, 28, 1850.

81. Ibid., Aug. 21, 23, Sept. 24, 27, 1850.

82. Ibid., Aug. 21, 26, 1850.

83. Ibid., Aug. 22, 1850.

84. Ibid., Aug. 25, Sept. 1, 27, 1850.

85. Ibid., Aug. 25, 1850.

86. Ibid., Aug. 26, 1850.

87. Ibid., Aug. 25, 29, 1850.

88. Ibid., Aug. 21, Sept. 1, 1850.

89. Ibid., July 31, 1850.

90. Ibid., Sept. 27, 1850.

91. San Francisco *Daily Herald,* n.d., reprinted in Washington *National Intelligencer,* Oct. 10, 1850; Sacramento *Transcript,* Aug. 19, 1850, reprinted in New York *Herald,* Oct. 7, 1850; Marysville *Herald,* Aug. 23, 1850; Sacramento *Placer Times,* n.d., reprinted in New York *Herald,* Aug. 22, 1850; Oregon City *Oregon Spectator,* Oct. 27, 1850, reprinted in New York *Herald,* Jan. 29, 1851.

92. Portland *Oregonian,* Sept. 4, Oct. 2, 1852.

93. Ibid., Oct. 16, Dec. 25, 1852.

94. San Francisco *Daily Alta California*, Mar. 30, July 19, 28, 1852.

95. Sacramento *Union*, n.d., reprinted in San Francisco *Daily Alta California*, July 23, 1852; ibid., July 28, 1852.

96. Ibid., Nov. 30, 1851, Dec. 26, 1854.

97. Portland *Oregonian*, Dec. 27, 1851.

98. Oregon City *Oregon Spectator*, Feb. 22, 1849, reprinted in Knuth and Gates, eds., "Oregon Territory in 1849–1850" (1949), 11.

99. San Francisco *Daily Alta California*, Nov. 10, 1854.

100. Ibid., and also Oct. 9, 18, 22, 1854.

101. Ibid., Oct. 22, Dec. 1, 1854.

102. Ibid., Aug. 4, 1854.

103. Ibid., Oct. 9, 18, Nov. 7, Dec. 1, 29, 1854.

104. Ibid., Nov. 16, 1854.

105. Portland *Weekly Oregonian*, June 16, 1855, and also other issues.

106. Ibid., Sept. 16, 30, Oct. 7, 1854, Feb. 24, 1855.

107. Ibid., Oct. 7, 1854.

108. San Francisco *Daily Alta California*, Nov. 19, 1855.

109. Marysville *Daily Herald*, Apr. 2, 1856. See also "The California Wagon Road" (1856), 58–63.

110. See, e.g., the San Francisco *Daily Alta California*, Jan. 3, 22, Aug. 11, 1855.

111. Marysville *Daily Herald*, Jan. 13, 1856.

112. Ibid., Mar. 27, 1856.

113. Ibid., Mar. 30, 1856.

114. Ibid., Apr. 2, 1856.

115. Ibid., Apr. 9, 1856.

116. Ibid., Apr. 23, 1856.

117. Ibid., July 8, 1856.

118. Ibid., Mar. 8, 1851.

119. Ibid., Sept. 15, 1853.

120. Sonora, Cal., *Herald*, Apr. 30, 1853, and San Francisco *Daily Herald*, Oct. 12, 1854, in Cohen, Scrapbooks, 104E, 146, 19.

121. Marysville *Daily Evening Herald*, Sept. 15, Nov. 15, 1853.

122. Ibid., Sept. 25, 1855.

123. Ibid., Sept. 29, Oct. 6, 30, 1855. The *Herald* accused the road commissioners of surveying only the trail which they initially favored, the El Dorado route.

124. Ibid., Oct. 25, 1855.

125. Ibid., and also Oct. 30, Dec. 7, 1855.

CHAPTER THREE: MOTIVATIONS AND BEGINNINGS

1. Baritz, "The Idea of the West" (1961), 618–19; Thoreau, "Walking," in *Works* (1908–13), 5:168–69.

2. Bright, "The Folklore and History of the 'Oregon Fever'" (1951), 251; Ellison, "The Covered Wagon Centennial" (1930), 164.

3. Crawford, "Occasional Address" (1882), 17–18.

4. Stewart, "The Prairie Schooner Got Them There" (1962), 8; Lavender, *Westward Vision* (1963), 26.

5. Thornton, *Oregon and California in 1848* (1849), 1:25–26; Burnett, "'Recollections and Opinions of an Old Pioneer'" (1904), 64–65; James Williams to Sarah Ann Staley, June 16, 1850, in Williams, Papers (MSS and typescripts); Carleton, *The Prairie Logbooks*, ed. Pelzer (1943), 264; Wade, ed., *The Journals of Francis Parkman* (1947), 2:442.

6. Currey, "Occasional Address" (1887), 34–35; May 7 [6], July 23, 1849, entries, in Kirkpatrick, Journal (copy of MS); "Reminiscences of Honorable John Minto" (1901), 130; Lienhard, *From St. Louis to Sutter's Fort, 1846*, trans. and ed. Gudde and Gudde (1961), 13–14, 18; Williams, "Diary of a Trip across the Plains in 1853" (1922), 180, 203–4; McIlhany, *Recollections of a '49er* (1908), 9. See also Billington, *America's Frontier Heritage* (1966), chap. 2, for additional treatment of "Why and How Pioneers Moved Westward," and Husband, "To Oregon in 1843" (1973), 7–9.

7. Billington, *America's Frontier Heritage*, 27–28; Bell, *Opening a Highway to the Pacific* (1921), 188–89.

8. Thornton, *Oregon and California in 1848*, 1:26.

9. Billington, *Words That Won the West* (1964), 8, 18–19.

10. Hansen, "Thomas Hart Benton and the Oregon Question" (1969), 491–93, 497; Powell, ed., *Hall J. Kelley on Oregon* (1932), vii–xiii; Schroeder, "Rep. John Floyd, 1817–1829" (1969), 339–46; Ambler, "The Oregon Country, 1810–1830" (1943), 3–24; Blue, "The Oregon Question—1818–1828" (1922), 193–219; Wardell, "Oregon Immigration prior to 1846" (1926), 63; Billington, *Words That Won the West*, 7–8; Bell, *Opening a Highway to the Pacific*, 81, 85, 91.

11. Hafen and Hafen, eds., *To the Rockies and Oregon* (1965), 19–23.

12. Billington, *Words That Won the West*, 7; Billington, "Books That Won the West" (1967), 25–32, 72–75; Kroll, "The Books That Enlightened the Emigrants" (1944), 103–23; Starr, *Americans and the California Dream* (1973), 46–47.

13. Billington, *Words That Won the West*, 8; Starr, *Americans and the California Dream*, 68.

14. Billington, *Words That Won the West*, 7–9; Becker, "Diseños" (1967), 55–56, 59.

15. Billington, *Words That Won the West*, 10; Baur, "The Health Seeker in the Westward Movement" (1959), 93–101. Groups of health seekers were occasionally seen on the trails, often burying their dead, as an 1844 party did with some frequency. See Barry, *The Beginning of the West* (1972), 513.

16. Billington, *Words That Won the West*, 11–14.

17. Ibid., 9, 11; Baur, "The Health Seeker in the Westward Movement," 98–99.

18. See Chap. 11 below for a further elaboration of the overlanders' reactions to the West.

19. Johansen, "A Working Hypothesis for the Study of Migrations" (1967), 1–12.

20. Ibid., 8; Hastings, *The Emigrants' Guide to Oregon and California*, ed. Carey (1932), 58.

21. Billington, who refers to and accepts the Johansen hypothesis in his *America's Frontier Heritage*, 28–29, writes of abundancy and deficiency motivation in attempting to explain the migrating process, concepts which apparently mean much the same as Johansen's push and pull factors. See p. 26.

22. Billington, *America's Frontier Heritage*, 190; see also Condon, "The Process of Selection in Oregon Pioneer Settlement" (1900), 63–64, for a similar emphasis. See Chap. 11 below for further data on the expenses of an overland journey.

23. Bieber, "California Gold Mania" (1948), 16–20; Billington, *Words That Won the West*, 15–17.

24. Ibid., 18.

25. See esp. McDermott, "Gold Rush Movies" (1954), 29–38; McDermott, ed., *An Artist on the Overland Trail* (1968), 3–19, 80–82; St. Louis *Daily Missouri Republican,* Oct. 8, 1850, Feb. 1, 1851; Marysville, Cal., *Herald,* June 3, 1851; Arrington, "Skirving's Moving Panorama" (1964), 133–72.

26. Holliday, "The California Gold Rush in Myth and Reality" (1959), 2–13; Holliday, "The California Gold Rush Reconsidered" (1962), 35–41.

27. Billington, *Words That Won the West,* 17–18.

28. May 30, 1849, entry of Elisha Douglass Perkins, in Clark, ed., *Gold Rush Diary* (1967), 13; Apr. 2, 1849, diary entry of Charles Elisha Boyle, in Columbus, Ohio, *Sunday Dispatch,* Oct. 2, 1949.

29. Liberty, Mo., *Weekly Tribune,* Dec. 27, 1850.

30. Albany *Atlas,* Feb. 6, 1849.

31. The Diary of Bernard J. Reid, Esq. (typescript), 4. See also Kelly, *An Excursion to California* (1851), 1:33.

32. Gordon, "The Influence of River Transportation on St. Joseph and Elkhart Counties" (1950), 291–92. Under the heading "California Adventurers," the St. Louis *Daily Missouri Republican* of Mar. 22, 1849, commented in some amazement on the passing through of an old man and woman whom the editor guessed to be approximately seventy years old—optimistically preparing to go to California in search of their fortune in the mines.

33. Parker, "The Causes of American Gold Rushes" (1969), 337–45.

34. Johansen, "A Working Hypothesis for the Study of Migrations," 11.

35. Mattes, *The Great Platte River Road* (1969), 103; Potter, ed., *Trail to California* (1945), 75.

36. Mattes, "The Jumping-off Places on the Overland Trail" (1967), 36.

37. Mattes, *Great Platte River Road,* 104, and maps following p. 140. Based on his comprehensive survey of diaries and reminiscent accounts, Mattes asserts that Independence and the Kansas City area were dominant through 1846 as the overlanders' jumping-off points, after which St. Joseph attained the prominence it enjoyed through 1851, although Kansas City, Council Bluffs, Weston, and Old Fort Kearny also launched sizable numbers. From 1852 on, Council Bluffs was the most important outfitting point for all overlanders, as it had been for the Mormon departures since 1847. See also Mattes, "The Jumping-off Places on the Overland Trail," 36–39.

38. Wyman, "The Outfitting Posts" (1949), 15. Given the high incidence of steamboat mishaps (explosions, fires, and sinkings), many emigrants also lost their effects and were forced to reoutfit completely. See, e.g., Apr. 23–May 8, 1850, entries, in Kelly, ed., "The Journal of Robert Chalmers" (1952), 30, 33–36.

39. Mattes, *Great Platte River Road,* 103–4. The five complexes Mattes discusses are those corresponding to present-day Kansas City, Weston-Leavenworth, St. Joseph, Nebraska City, and Council Bluffs–Omaha.

40. Rothwell to his parents, Apr. 18, 29, May 5, Apr. 25, 27, 1850, entries, in Rothwell, Journal and Letters (mss and typescripts).

41. S. H. Taylor to "Friend Hadley," May 24, 1853, in "Letters of S. H. Taylor to the Watertown [Wis.] Chronicle" (1921), 127. See also Marshall, "The Newark Overland Company" (1952), 177.

42. Liberty *Weekly Tribune,* Oct. 17, 1846; Barry, *Beginning of the West,* 650–51.

43. Walker, *The Wagonmasters* (1966), 113.

44. St. Louis *Daily Missouri Republican,* Oct. 18, 1855; San Francisco *Daily Alta California,* Dec. 11, 1855.

45. St. Louis *Daily Missouri Republican,* Mar. 23, 1849; Gilman, "Pioneer Aeronaut: William Markoe and His Balloon" (1962), 168.

46. Hartford *Daily Courant,* Mar. 15, 1849.

47. St. Louis *Daily Missouri Republican,* Mar. 3, 1849; Watkins, "The Revoloidal Spindle and the Wondrous Avitor" (1967), 25.

48. Liberty *Weekly Tribune,* Mar. 23, 1849.

49. St. Louis *Daily Missouri Republican,* Mar. 23, 1849; Kanesville *Frontier Guardian,* Apr. 18, 1849. Porter in January, 1851, and John Wise of Lancaster, Pennsylvania, in

December, 1850, petitioned Congress to support their research in this field financially. Stupefied congressmen, uncertain as to which committee should consider the petitions, made sport of these proposals. *Congressional Globe*, 31 Cong., 2 Sess., 132, 316, 369 (Dec. 30, 1850, Jan. 23, 29, 1851). In 1855 a Californian also advanced a proposal for three-day balloon trips between San Francisco and St. Louis, but again apparently few took the matter seriously. Wilmington, Ohio, *Clinton Republican*, Apr. 18, 1855.

50. Advertisement, St. Louis *Daily Missouri Republican*, Feb. 22, 1849; ibid., Feb. 28, Mar. 19, 1849.

51. See, e.g., ibid., Feb. 6, 1849, in which the editor stated, regarding Turner and Allen, ". . . whatever they undertake they will perform." The project had even been favorably mentioned in the New Orleans *Daily Picayune*, Feb. 12, 1849.

52. St. Louis *Daily Missouri Republican*, Mar. 8, 1849; advertisements in ibid., Feb. 6, Apr. 15, 1849.

53. Advertisement, St. Louis *Daily Missouri Republican*, Mar. 24, 1849; ibid., Mar. 21, 1849.

54. Ibid., Apr. 23, 1849. "California," writing from Independence under date of Apr. 17, indicated that the Pioneer Line was the only passenger train of the year to his knowledge—and that it was a fine one. Ibid., Apr. 23, 1849.

55. Ibid., May 17, 1849.

56. Ibid. One passenger, however, gave May 8 as the starting date. See Diary of Bernard J. Reid, 5, 6. Reid also stated that twenty-two freight and baggage wagons accompanied the first train.

57. St. Louis *Missouri Republican*, June 21, 1849; Barry, *Beginning of the West*, 875–76. The second train's wagons were less heavily loaded and reached Fort Kearny, according to one report, on July 11, "fourteen days from Independence," which would mean, if accurate, that it departed June 28 instead of June 18. Mr. Allen was in charge of the train which reached Fort Laramie on August 1. See also St. Louis *Sunday Republican*, Aug. 5, 1849; Cincinnati *Daily Gazette*, Sept. 13, 1849.

58. D. to Editor, June 15, 1849, in Cincinnati *Morning Chronicle*, June 25, 1849; Diary of Bernard J. Reid, 5, 6; Barry, *Beginning of the West*, 861–62.

59. St. Louis *Missouri Republican*, July 6, 1849; Diary of Bernard J. Reid, 6.

60. David T. McCollum to J. H. Lund, Oct. 20, 1849, in Bidlack, *Letters Home* (1960), 35. Since the Pioneer Line started with 161 passengers, teamsters, and other employees (Diary of Bernard J. Reid, 7), such a percentage would mean that over twenty-five died. The St. Louis *Daily Missouri Republican* listed the deaths of fifteen passengers and teamsters in its Dec. 24, 1849, issue. One overlander who passed the first train en route, however, indicated that over 200 men were traveling in the company. James Lyne to Henry Lyne, May 22, 1849, in Lyne, Letters (MSS and typescripts). A Mississippi traveler indicated that the deaths were "numerous" and that "the bodies of the dead were thrown out on the prairie without burial." D. to Editor, June 15, 1849, in Cincinnati *Morning Chronicle*, June 25, 1849.

61. Diary of Bernard J. Reid, 7, 14, 17–18. Reid also appreciatively noted that the officers and men at the fort had provided assistance in repairing wagons and refitting outfits.

62. St. Louis *Missouri Republican*, July 6, 1849.

63. A. W. Babbitt to Editor of St. Louis *Union*, n.d., reprinted in St. Joseph *Gazette*, Oct. 19, 1849; "Joaquin" to Editor, July 21, 1849, in St. Louis *Daily Missouri Republican*, Aug. 29, 1849; June 26, 1849, entry of James F. Wilkins, in McDermott, ed., *Artist on the Overland Trail*, 48.

64. June 15, 1849, entry, in Diary of Bernard J. Reid, 23.

65. Alonzo Delano's company, for example, on July 26, shortly before reaching the Humboldt River, met and fed a lone footman with a small knapsack on his back, who had left the train when rations had been reduced. He planned to rely on handouts and luck to survive the remaining 1,000 miles. Delano, *Across the Plains and among the Diggings* (1853, 1936 reprint), 68. Another passenger purchased a horse and, leaving everything else behind but several blankets, left the train shortly before Fort Laramie to catch up with some relatives in an ox train some 100 miles ahead. June 26, 1849, entry of James F. Wilkins, in McDermott, ed., *Artist on the Overland Trail*, 48.

66. The foregoing summary is drawn from the Diary of Bernard J. Reid, 21–62.

67. McCollum to Lund, Oct. 20, 1849, in Bidlack, *Letters Home,* 34.

68. Diary of Bernard J. Reid, 69–70; Reid to his sisters, Oct. 24, 1849, in Van Trump and Reid, eds., "A California Gold Rush Letter from Bernard J. Reid" (1961), 225–32. Reid especially stressed Turner's increasing reliance on strong drink.

69. Sept. 19, 1849, entry of James F. Wilkins, in McDermott, ed., *Artist on the Overland Trail,* 74. Elisha Douglass Perkins, who in his Sept. 3, 1849, diary entry congratulated himself for not having purchased a ticket on the Pioneer Line as he had been tempted to do, remarked that Turner had been very active in procuring additional supplies en route, indicated that the spring coaches were "very neat & comfortable," and speculated that if the mules had held out the passengers would have traveled comfortably. Clark, ed., *Gold Rush Diary,* 116. Even the discontented Reid had remarked that the passengers had dined well early in the journey. Diary of Bernard J. Reid, 8.

70. One additional St. Louis passenger train was advertised, by a Judge James Brown, who claimed much freighting experience, charged $175 per person, and intended starting from either St. Joseph or Independence, but there is no indication that Brown's train materialized. St. Louis *Daily Missouri Republican,* Apr. 9,1850. S. Roundy and Company planned to start a train from Council Bluffs with passenger fare set at $300 per individual, but again there is no evidence that this train ever departed. Barry, *Beginning of the West,* 899. One wild scheme also failed—Sands and Howes, circus proprietors, announced an early June departure from Independence of an overland line to San Francisco with camels as the beasts of burden. St. Louis *Daily Missouri Republican,* Apr. 17, 1850.

71. The trains were: J. C. Faine & Co.'s Southwestern Company for California, via Independence; W. D. Harrington's train, via Independence; Glenn & Co.'s April Line for California, via St. Joseph; Alexander & Hall's California Mail Line, via St. Joseph; Jerome, Hanson & Smith's Mississippi and Pacific Line, via St. Joseph; McPike & Strother's Express Line for California, via St. Joseph; Wiles & Bennett's train, via St. Joseph; and Dr. Reuben Knox's train, via Old Fort Kearny. St. Louis *Daily Missouri Republican,* Feb. 28, Apr. 9, Nov. 18, 1850; Barry, *Beginning of the West,* 925–27, 942–43; first and Sept. 10, 1850, entries, in Montgomery, Diary (MS), 1–5, 76.

72. St. Louis *Daily Missouri Republican,* Jan. 28, Apr. 9, 16, 1850.

73. Ibid., Apr. 1, 9, 1850.

74. Ibid., Feb. 28, 1850.

75. C. to Editor, Sept. 22, 1850, in ibid., Nov. 18, 1850. C. also conjectured that only the Alexander and Hall expedition would turn a profit.

76. The smallest train was likely Wiles and Bennett's, with twelve wagons and forty passengers, most others numbering a hundred or more passengers. Barry, *Beginning of the West,* 926–27, 942–43.

77. St. Louis *Daily Missouri Republican,* May 18, July 30, 1850; Montgomery, Diary, 1–5.

78. July 20, 1850, entry of Hosea Stout, in Brooks, ed., *On the Mormon Frontier* (1964), 2:374.

79. Henry A. Stine to his mother, June 3, 1850, and journal entries of July 23, 27, 30, Aug. 18, 1850, in Stine, Letters and Journal (typescripts); Aug. 17, 19, 22, 1850, entries of Stout, in Brooks, ed., *On the Mormon Frontier,* 2:378.

80. July 27, 1850, entry, in Stine, Letters and Journal.

81. Goheen to Editor, Nov. 27, 1850, in St. Louis *Daily Missouri Republican,* Jan. 23, 1851.

82. Barry, *Beginning of the West,* 1070–72; St. Joseph *Gazette,* Mar. 10, May 5, 1852. For the Ohio trains see "A Historic Document" (1932), 34, pertaining to a Cincinnati train, Joseph and L. Dana, proprietors; Robert L. Sharp and James Garden's agreement in Sharp, Agreement and Diary (MS), pertaining to the John Coulter and Company train from Columbus; Barry, ed., "Overland to the Gold Fields of California in 1852" (1942), 227–28, pertaining to a Cincinnati train organized by John Hawkins Clark and Andrew Brown. Also see Barry, *Beginning of the West,* 1206; Council Bluffs *Bugle,* Apr. 3, 1855.

83. Barry, *Beginning of the West,* 926.

84. Ibid., 1070–71.

85. See, e.g., Berry and Berry, Contract (duplicate copy), in which Williams and Thomas Berry contracted to work for J. C. Hays for twelve months in California, agreeing to give him half of all they made during that time. For these considerations Hays paid their way to California, except for clothing and guns, all their expenses in California, except doctor bills, and agreed also to pay their way back to Missouri at the end of the year if the Berrys so desired.

86. Brooks, ed., *On the Mormon Frontier*, 2:*passim*. To judge how widespread this practice was during the gold rush these examples must be somewhat extrapolated, for only a minority of overlanders traveled through Salt Lake City, which was not the most direct route to California—and during the gold rush overlanders invariably preferred the most direct route, even if it had not yet been adequately explored.

87. Goheen to Editor, Nov. 27, 1850, in St. Louis *Daily Missouri Republican*, Jan. 23, 1851.

88. Ibid., June 20, 1850; Liberty *Weekly Tribune*, Mar. 26, 1852; Apr., 1850, journal entry of Adam Mercer Brown, in Kiefer, ed., "Over Barren Plains and Rock-bound Mountains" (1972), 18.

89. Kanesville *Frontier Guardian*, July 24, 1850; Liberty *Weekly Tribune*, June 21, 1850; St. Louis *Daily Missouri Republican*, June 15, 16, 1850.

90. "Cheyenne" to Editor, May 14, 1850, in St. Louis *Sunday Republican*, June 10, 1850.

91. St. Louis *Daily Missouri Republican*, Oct. 3, 1850; Liberty *Weekly Tribune*, Nov. 8, 1850; Gunnison, *The Mormons* (1856), 66.

92. Liberty *Weekly Tribune*, Mar. 26, 1852. The happy result was also reported in the St. Joseph *Gazette*, Mar. 24, 1852, and the San Francisco *Alta California*, per *Steamer Northerner*, Apr. 16, 1852.

93. May 20, 30, 1852, entries of Richard Owen Hickman, in Phillips, ed., "'Dick's Works'" (1929), 245, 247; San Francisco *Daily Alta California*, Aug. 29, 1852. This experiment antedated by several years the celebrated Mormon handcart expeditions to the Salt Lake Valley which commenced in 1856.

94. June 18, 1852, entry, in Kingery, Letters (MSS and typescripts); June 26, 1852, entry, in Paxson, ed., "T. Turnbull's Travels" (1914), 182; Johnson, A Trip to the Gold Fields of California in 1852 (photocopy of typescript), 10; Barry, *Beginning of the West*, 1084.

95. Burton, *The City of the Saints*, ed. Brodie (1963), 12.

96. Andrews, "The Controversial Hastings Overland Guide" (1968), 29–30, 32, 34; Hastings, *Emigrants' Guide to Oregon and California*, 145; Johnson and Winter, *Route across the Rocky Mountains*, ed. Cannon (1932), 180; Child, *Overland Route to California* (1852, 1946 reprint), iv–vi; Platt and Slater, *Travelers' Guide across the Plains* (1852, 1963 reprint), xvii; Marcy, *The Prairie Traveler* (1859), 27–28; Kroll, "The Books That Enlightened the Emigrants," 108.

97. It will be noted that this ordering differs from the 60/20/20 percent ratio Merrill Mattes suggests in his *Great Platte River Road*, 37. From the various available statistics and estimates of overland travel between 1840 and 1860, it appears that while oxen were far in the lead, horses were more frequently utilized than mules, although it is true that more horses than mules were on the trails for use as riding animals, which helped to swell horse totals. The one year with the most useful statistics is 1850, when the Fort Laramie register—which was by no means complete—listed as of August 14: 9,927 wagons, 36,116 oxen (and also 7,233 cows), 23,172 horses, and 7,548 mules. While the 1850 horse/mule ratio (35/11 percent) was wider than usual, in most emigration years statistics given for horses were higher than those for mules. Perhaps one reason for the significant 1850 ratio disparity was explained by the May 3 St. Joseph *Gazette*, which indicated that so many emigrants had horse teams because there was a scarcity of oxen and mules in Michigan, Iowa, Wisconsin, Illinois, and Indiana, the states from which many emigrants came who used St. Joseph as their jumping-off point. Barry, *Beginning of the West*, 919–20. For the Fort Laramie statistics see "Laramie" to Editor, Aug. 26, 1850, in St. Louis *Daily Missouri Republican*, Oct. 3, 1850.

98. Barry, ed., "Overland to the Gold Fields of California," 227–28, and entries of May 8, July 22, Aug. 31 (pp. 234, 275, 295).

99. July 13, 1850, entry, in Payne, Saint Louis to San Francisco (typescript), 71–72.

100. Sept. 27, 1850, entry, in Coke, *A Ride over the Rocky Mountains* (1852), 281–82.

101. Dale, "The Organization of the Oregon Emigrating Companies" (1915), 206. A useful account of the Peoria company's trip by one of its members is Shortess, "First Emigrants to Oregon" (1897), 92–107. Other documents pertaining to this journey are collected in Hafen and Hafen, eds., *To the Rockies and Oregon* (1965).

102. Barry, *Beginning of the West*, 392, 409; Haines, "Pioneer Portrait: Robert Newell" (1965), 5–6; Lavender, *Westward Vision*, 341–42. Newell, at the rendezvous, had agreed to pilot the overlanders for less than the figure Moses "Black" Harris had wanted. The enraged Harris then unsuccessfully attempted to murder Newell for this price-cutting, foreshadowing the competition which developed among mountaineers for this type of employment.

103. Barry, *Beginning of the West*, 428–30; Stewart, *The California Trail* (1962), 11–12, 17–18. Accounts of route information secured in the West, and guides met and hired while on the trails, will be treated in subsequent chapters. Here we are only concerned with arrangements concluded in or near the outfitting–jumping-off points.

104. Allen, comp., *Ten Years in Oregon* (1850), 143–45, 153–54; Crawford, "Occasional Address," 10; Barry, *Beginning of the West*, 447–48; Tobie, "Stephen Hall Meek," in Hafen, ed., *The Mountain Men and the Fur Trade* (1965–72), 2:232; Clark and Tiller, *Terrible Trail* (1967), 17–18.

105. Lenox, *Overland to Oregon*, ed. Whitaker (1904), 17–18; "Document" (1900), 398–402; Carter, "John Gantt," in Hafen, ed., *The Mountain Men and the Fur Trade*, 5:113.

106. Peltier, "Moses 'Black' Harris," in ibid., 4:112; "Reminiscences of Washington Smith Gilliam" (1904), 204; Barry, *Beginning of the West*, 509–11; Stewart, ed., *The Opening of the California Trail* (1953), 34–37, 64.

107. Palmer, *Journal of Travels over the Rocky Mountains*, ed. Thwaites (1906), 39–40, 42–43; Tobie, "Stephen Hall Meek," 234–35. Meek had only asked $30 in advance and the balance on arrival. A treasurer was appointed who collected at least $190 of the remainder, although some families refused to pay. Meek's services, for some reason, ended at Fort Hall, though beyond the fort he did guide a small number onto a disastrous "cutoff." In 1846 he sued Presley Welch, train captain, for $130 of his pilot's fee and was awarded $66. See Clark and Tiller, *Terrible Trail*, 34–37. An 1845 emigrant from Ohio wrote his brother that they gave Meek $275 but that he was a "loafer." Letter printed in Albany *Atlas*, July 11, 1845.

108. Barry, *Beginning of the West*, 539; Lockley, *Captain Sol. Tetherow, Wagon Train Master* (n.d.), 24, 26.

109. Stewart, *The California Trail*, 146; Elijah Bristow to Susanna Bristow, June 18, 1845, in Bristow, Letters (reproduced); Hugh Burns to Allen McLane, Oct. 29, 1844, printed in Jefferson City *Inquirer*, Oct. 9, 1845, in Morgan, The Mormons and the Far West (typescripts).

110. Barry, *Beginning of the West*, 677–79.

111. Stewart, *The California Trail*, 324; Barry, *Beginning of the West*, 747.

112. Potter, ed., *Trail to California*, 35, 53–54; Apr. 21, 1849, entry, in Johnston, *Overland to California* (1948), 22–23. J. Goldsborough Bruff's company paid $75 to a guide whom they dismissed at Fort Hall; Antoine Robidoux charged $1.50 per emigrant for the caravan he guided to California; Joseph Thing, who first went west with Nathaniel Wyeth in 1834 and remained to command Fort Hall until he sold it to the Hudson's Bay Company in 1837, charged $5 per emigrant to pilot the Granite State and California Mining and Trading Company to California—and got the company temporarily lost; and George Wood Ebbert received $72 to pilot a few overlanders to Oregon. May 2, 1849, entry, in Read and Gaines, eds., *Gold Rush* (1944), 2:7; May 2, 15, 1849, entries, in McCall, *The Great California Trail* (1882), 10, 19–20; Austin, "Joseph Thing," in Hafen, ed., *The Mountain Men and the Fur Trade*, 9:366–76; Tobie, "George Wood Ebbert," in ibid., 4:92. The most convenient listing of some of the former overlanders involved in the 1849 rush is Barry, *Beginning of the West*, 833–40.

113. William Gill to Harriet Tarleton Gill, Mar. 14, 1850, in Clark, ed., *California Letters of William Gill* (1922), 10. Insurance could work both ways, as Hugh Skinner observed in his diary entry of May 7, 1850, on board the steamboat *St. Paul*. As the boat neared Independence an elderly gold rusher died and Skinner commented: "... it is rumoured on the boat

that his family had his life insured and sent him to california to die." The life insurance business was in its infancy when the gold fever erupted, prior to which time contracts generally specified that written permission was required in order to travel west of the Mississippi River, among other places. Most gold rushers were able to purchase insurance, however, but were charged higher premiums, and some route restrictions were also stipulated. The risks for the companies were high. One company discovered that half of the California risks it took became losses during the gold rush. See Brayer, "Insurance against the Hazards of Western Life" (1947), 223, 225–26, 229–31. Also see Newport *Herald of the Times,* Jan. 25, 1849, and Albany *Atlas,* Jan. 12, 1849.

114. These estimates are based on a statistical analysis of approximately 200 overlanders whose diaries clearly specify the length of time spent in and about a particular town from the day of arrival until the day the Missouri River was crossed, or, in the case of Independence, the only one of the jumping-off points located on the west side of the Missouri River, serious traveling was begun.

115. See "Journal of John T. Williams" (1936), 393–409. The actual river crossing was made somewhat to the north of St. Joseph.

116. Thornton, *Oregon and California in 1848* (1849), 1:14.

117. Rothwell to his parents, May 5, 1850, in Rothwell, Journal and Letters. See also the Apr. 11, 1849, entry of Joseph Waring Berrien, in Hinckley and Hinckley, eds., "Overland from St. Louis to the California Gold Field" (1960), 285–86; Apr. 30, 1850, entry, in Ingalls, *Journal of a Trip to California* (1852), 10–11.

118. Hall to his father, May 11, 1849, in Hall, Letters (typescripts); letter of William B. Lorton, May 9, 1849, printed in New York *Sun,* June 8, 1849, in Lorton, Diary and Letters (microfilm of typescripts).

119. Apr. 5, 1853, entry, in Agnes Stewart, Diary (reproduced), 1. Kanesville did not escape such charges either. See Kerns, "Journal of Crossing the Plains to Oregon" (1917), 156.

120. William R. Rothwell to Thomas P. Rothwell, May 3, 1850, in Rothwell, Journal and Letters,

121. Apr. 29, 1849, entry, in Stackpole, Journal (MS), italics his.

122. Lucius Fairchild to J. C. Fairchild and family, Apr. 23, 1849, in Schafer, ed., *California Letters of Lucius Fairchild* (1931), 11; Shepherd, *Journal of Travel across the Plains* (1851, 1945 reprint), 1.

123. May 21, 1846, entry, in "Diary of George McKinstry," in Morgan, ed., *Overland in 1846* (1963), 1:205; George W. Buchanan to Col. William M. King, Mar. 2, 1847, in "Letter and Circular of Information" (1910), 307; St. Louis *Daily Missouri Republican,* Mar. 17, Apr. 7, 10, 30, June 3, 1849.

124. Ibid., May 17, 1849.

125. Wells, "The Growth of Independence" (1959), 38; St. Louis *Sunday Republican,* June 3, 1849.

126. Piercy, *Route from Liverpool to Great Salt Lake Valley,* ed. Brodie (1962), 97; Jerome Dutton to LeRoy Dutton, May 7, 16, 1850, in Dutton, "Across the Plains in 1850" (1910), 455; Louisville *Examiner,* June 2, 1849; Lucius Fairchild to J. C. Fairchild and family, Apr. 24, 1849, in Schafer, ed., *California Letters of Lucius Fairchild,* 14; Baydo, "Overland from Missouri to Washington Territory in 1854" (1971), 68.

127. Kanesville *Frontier Guardian,* May 1, 1850; Apr. 19, 1849, entry, in Giffen, ed., *The Diaries of Peter Decker* (1966), 55.

128. The victim, though seriously injured, survived. Lucius Fairchild to J. C. Fairchild and family, May 5, 1849, in Schafer, ed., *California Letters of Lucius Fairchild,* 17–18. F. D. Everts, in his journal entry of May 4 (MS and typescript), reported the same incident, changing only the detail that the men had been cutting whip stalks and upping the monetary figure to $60. William T. Stackpole added that the victim, who he said lost $50, had also been stabbed, and located the affair one mile from town. May 2, 1849, entry, in Stackpole, Journal.

129. May 4, 1849, entry, in Everts, Journal.

130. See Randall Fuller's 1849 journal on Kanesville (typescript); May 11, 12, 14, 19,

1853, entries, in "Journal of Henry Allyn" (1924), 384–85, 389; Kanesville *Frontier Guardian,* May 1, 1850; Wyman, "Council Bluffs and the Westward Movement" (1949), 106.

131. Apr. 18, 20, 1849, entries, in Giffen, ed., *Diaries of Peter Decker,* 54, 55. John T. Williams boarded at $2 per week in St. Joseph prior to his 1850 overland trip. Mar. 27, 1850, entry, in "Journal of John T. Williams," 395.

132. Edmund B. C. Park to Susan Maria Park, Apr. 22, 1849, in Park, Letters (typescripts); Apr. 27–30, 1849, entries, in Walters and Strother, eds., "The Gold Rush Diary of Henry Tappan" (1953), 116–17.

133. Barry, *Beginning of the West,* 794; Apr. 22, 1849, diary entry of Charles Elisha Boyle, in Columbus *Evening Dispatch,* Oct. 7, 1849. These huge throngs preparing to embark on the South Pass overland route frightened a number of overlanders into switching their route to the Santa Fe Trail. See Edmund B. C. Park to Susan Maria Park, Apr. 22, 1849, in Park, Letters; May 12 [11], 1849, entry of James F. Wilkins, in McDermott, ed., *Artist on the Overland Trail,* 30.

134. Webb, "Independence, Missouri, a Century Old" (1927), 31; Wells, "The Growth of Independence," 40; Apr. 19, 1849, entry of Elijah Bryan Farnham, in Mattes and Kirk, eds., "From Ohio to California in 1849" (1950), 300; Barry, "Charles Robinson—Yankee '49er" (1968), 180; Apr. 16, 1849, entry, in Spooner, Diary (microfilm copy); *Population of the United States in 1860* (1864), 292.

135. Barry, *Beginning of the West,* 538, 791, 992; *Population of the United States in 1860,* 289.

136. Apr. 15, 1849, entry, in Shombre, Diary (MS and typescript); Barry, "Charles Robinson—Yankee '49er," 182; May 3, 1852, entry, in Sharp, Diary; Hart, "James Redpath, Missouri Correspondent" (1962), 72; "Our City Is No Speculative Bubble" (1942), 115; *Population of the United States in 1860,* 292.

137. Barry, *Beginning of the West,* 917, 993, 1226; *The Seventh Census of the United States: 1850* (1853), 661; *Population of the United States in 1860,* 296.

138. Aitchison, "The Mormon Settlements in the Missouri Valley" (1907), 287–88; Wyman, "Council Bluffs and the Westward Movement," 99–118, esp. 109; Wyman, "Omaha: Frontier Depot" (1936), 143–55; *Population of the United States in 1860,* 151, 559.

139. Apr. 24, 1849, entry, in *Journal of Samuel Rutherford Dundass* (1857), 8.

140. Hoffman, Journal (MS and typescript translation).

CHAPTER FOUR: EMIGRANT INTERACTION

1. A convenient summary of missionary travel to Oregon in the 1830s is contained in the first volume of Bancroft's *History of Oregon* (1886–88). For a brief but precise account of the missionaries and the caravans with which they traveled consult Barry, *The Beginning of the West* (1972).

2. Morgan, ed., *Overland in 1846* (1963), 1:14.

3. Reported in a letter signed "Cheyenne," dated at Fort Laramie May 4, 1850, and printed in the St. Louis *Daily Missouri Republican*, June 15, 1850.

4. This table is based primarily upon contemporary statistics provided in Oregon, California, Utah, Missouri, and Iowa newspapers, upon estimates made by both westbound and eastbound overlanders, upon government sources, especially the emigrant registers kept at Forts Kearny and Laramie during the peak gold rush years, upon the statistical information provided in Barry, *Beginning of the West*, and upon assorted other articles and books. For most of the statistics concerning Mormon emigration to Utah I am indebted to Stegner, *The Gathering of Zion* (1964), and for many of the California emigration figures I have been much influenced by Stewart, *The California Trail* (1962). The migration estimates given by Mattes in *The Great Platte River Road* (1969), while the most comprehensive offered to date, are hampered because Mattes has combined the Mormon emigrant totals with the totals for overlanders bound for the West Coast. His estimates are also not as precise as might be wished, the author having chosen to render them in round numbers. While I disagree with some of Mattes's estimates, no one attempting to provide statistics for the overland emigrations can offer more than educated estimates for most years, especially for the later 1850s, when the estimates of necessity become almost pure guesswork, and the estimates in Table 1 will doubtless be revised as more information comes to light.

5. Barry, *Beginning of the West*, 1089; Langworthy, *Scenery of the Plains, Mountains and Mines,* ed. Phillips (1932), 62, 4–5.

6. June 2, 1849, entry, in Bieber, ed., "Diary of a Journey from Missouri to California" (1928), 17.

7. May 16, 24, 25, 26, 1850, entries, in A Chapter from the Diary of the Late Judge James B. Persinger (typescript); Joseph Price to Elizabeth Price, June 27, 1850, in Marshall, ed., "The Road to California" (1924), 255; Reuben Knox to Eliza Knox, June 1, 1850, plus undated next letter, in Turner, ed., "Reuben Knox Letters, Part II" (1960), 252, 256; June 10, 1850, entry, in Shields, Journal (MS); June 3, 1850, entry, in Skinner, Diary (MS).

8. These figures are derived from the emigrant register kept at Fort Laramie, as reported in emigrant diaries and letters and by newspaper correspondents, especially for the St. Louis *Daily Missouri Republican,* but statistics were also reprinted in the Salt Lake City *Deseret News,* Kanesville *Frontier Guardian,* St. Joseph *Gazette,* Liberty *Weekly Tribune,* and San Francisco *Daily Alta California.* See also Becker, ed., *Thomas Christy's Road across the Plains* (1969), 6–7. For one of the days—June 3—I have found the same statistics cited by four different contemporary authorities, for several days by two and three. Occasionally the figures cited vary slightly, but in the absence of the emigrant register itself, which apparently has not survived, there is no more accurate information available. Statistics for the numbers of women, children, and draft animals have not been included in this table.

9. Letter of N. P., June 17, 1849, in New York *Herald,* July 31, 1849; June 2, 1849, entry, in Tolles, Diary (typescript), 14; Sept. 3, 1850, entry of Calvin Taylor, in Williams, ed., "Overland to California in 1850" (1970), 338.

10. July 30, 1852, entry, in Dale, ed., *The Journal of James Akin Jr.* (1919), 20; July 27, 1853, entry, in "Journal of Henry Allyn" (1924), 420.

11. See, e.g., the June 30, 1853, entry, in ibid., 407–8; May 15, 1850, entry, in Rothwell, Journal and Letters (MSS).

12. St. Louis *Daily Missouri Republican,* Sept. 28, 1841; Tobie, "From the Missouri to the Columbia, 1841" (1937), 146, 148, 150; Nunis, ed., *Josiah Belden: California Overland Pioneer* (1962), 128, 130, 135; Barry, *Beginning of the West,* 436. Horace Greeley reported in 1859 that William H. Byers called the returnees "gobacks." Greeley, *An Overland Journey from New York to San Francisco,* ed. Duncan (1964), 90.

13. Hastings, *The Emigrants' Guide to Oregon and California,* ed. Carey (1932), xxv, 7;

Barry, *Beginning of the West*, 448, 477; Burnett, "'Recollections and Opinions of an Old Pioneer'" (1904), 92; Nesmith, "The Occasional Address" (1876), 53; St. Louis *Daily Missouri Republican*, Aug. 21, 1845; Morgan, ed., *Overland in 1846*, 1:29–30; Jefferson City *Inquirer*, July 21, 1846, in ibid., 2:597; May 13, 14, 1846, entries, in "Diary of Nicholas Carriger," in ibid., 1:150; John R. McBride's 1846 reminiscences quoted in ibid., 1:93.

14. June 14, 1850, entry, in *Journal of John Wood* (1852), 19.

15. June 10, 1849, entry, in Webster, *The Gold Seekers of '49* (1917), 44–45; May 12, 1852, entry of John Hawkins Clark, in Barry, ed., "Overland to the Gold Fields of California" (1942), 236.

16. See, e.g., St. Louis *Missouri Republican*, June 15, 1849; St. Joseph *Gazette*, June 15, 1849, June 28, 1850. The Liberty *Weekly Tribune* reprinted the St. Joseph items on June 22, 1849, and July 5, 1850. The Council Bluffs *Bugle* of June 5, 1855, gave short shrift to one particularly sensational rumor of that year: "Rumor Says, that the emigrants on the plains have been met and massacred, all to a man. We have not the least confidence whatever in the report." With many uneasy about increasing Indian hostility, 1855 was a premium rumor year. The St. Louis *Daily Missouri Republican* of July 3, 1855, under the heading "From Kansas Territory," printed its correspondent's report exposing a rumor being spread by a frightened returnee that Fort Laramie had been captured by Indians.

17. May 23, 1849, entry, in "The Journal of Major Osborne Cross," in Settle, ed., *The March of the Mounted Riflemen* (1940), 42.

18. May 23, 1849, entry, in [Granville Overland Company, Ohio], Journal (MS and typescript); Liberty *Weekly Tribune*, Aug. 1, 1851; Mattes, *Great Platte River Road*, 101; May 6, 1853, entry, in "Diary of Mrs. Amelia Stewart Knight" (1933), 40.

19. Liberty *Weekly Tribune*, Sept. 13, 1850; June 7, 1852, entry of John Hawkins Clark, in Barry, ed., "Overland to the Gold Fields of California," 248–49; Meeker, *The Busy Life of Eighty-five Years* (1916), 46.

20. Barry, *Beginning of the West*, 1083; letter of Sept. 27, 1852, in Ferris, *The Mormons at Home* (1856), 55.

21. June 9, 1849, entry, in Scamehorn, ed., *The Buckeye Rovers in the Gold Rush* (1965), 17.

22. William R. Rothwell to his parents, May 17, 1850, in Rothwell, Journal and Letters, 58; San Francisco *Daily Alta California*, Sept. 29, 1850; May 14, 1850, entry, in Read, ed., *A Pioneer of 1850* (1927), 31; June 9, 1852, entry, in Adams, "Crossing the Plains in 1852" (1905), 290; James M. Woods to Mrs. M. C. Woods, May 6–22, 1850, in Woods, Letters (typescripts). "Seeing the Elephant," though it had pre- and post–gold rush currency, was an immensely popular expression among the overlanders (and those who went by sea as well—although they sometimes spoke of "seeing the Shark"—see the Windsor *Vermont Chronicle*, Nov. 21, 1849) connoting, in the main, experiencing hardship and difficulty and somehow surviving. Emigrant diaries and letters are filled with humorous references to that ubiquitous animal. For short treatments of the history of the phrase see Tamony, "'To See the Elephant'" (1968), 23–29; Rea, "Seeing the Elephant" (1969), 21–26.

23. St. Joseph *Gazette*, July 20, 1849; Everts, Journal (MS and typescript); May 31, 1849, entry, in Benson, Diary (typescript), 12; June 5, 1849, entry, in Stansbury, *Exploration and Survey of the Valley of the Great Salt Lake* (1853), 18; June 11, 1850, entry of Calvin Taylor, in Williams, ed., "Overland to the Gold Fields of California" (1969), 136; June 14, 1850, entry, in *Journal of John Wood*, 19; June 4, 1849, entry, in Delano, *Across the Plains and among the Diggings* (1853, 1936 reprint), 24.

24. One 1849 estimate from St. Joseph that 2,000 emigrants had "become dissatisfied with the trip to California, and have turned their faces toward home" may have referred to gold seekers who gave up the journey in that outfitting town and never started. An 1850 estimate, again from St. Joseph, suggested that 5 percent of the prospective argonauts returned home without ever commencing the overland trip. See letter of June 18, 1849, in New York *Herald*, June 26, 1849, and Washington *National Intelligencer*, May 18, 1850. In 1859 there were many more turn-arounds, but they were turning back from journeys to the Colorado gold fields and not the Pacific Coast. See May 6, 7, 1859, entries, in Wilson, A Trip across the Plains (MS); Hiram W. Studley to Lydia M. Trego, Oct. 16, 1859, in "Letter Describing a March to Utah in 1859" (1923), 614–15.

25. Morgan, ed., *Overland in 1846*, 1:68.

26. St. Louis *Daily Missouri Republican*, Oct. 11, 1845, Oct. 8, 1846; Washington *Daily Union*, Dec. 4, 1845; Morgan, ed., *Overland in 1846*, 2:759, n. 99. Eastbound travelers continued to serve as letter carriers into the 1850s. See John H. Fresh to Mary Fresh, July 6, 1851 (MS).

27. July 20, 1843, entry, in Nesmith, "Diary of the Emigration of 1843" (1906), 342; June 25, July 8, 1845, entries, in "Diary of Jesse Harritt" (1914), 512, 514.

28. Yerba Buena *California Star, Supplement*, Apr. 1, 1848; Oregon City *Oregon Spectator*, May 13, 1847, in Morgan, ed., *Overland in 1846*, 2:729–31; June 23, 1852, entry, in Paxson, ed., "T. Turnbull's Travels" (1914), 180; June 29, 1852, entry, in Egbert, Diary (photocopy of typescript), 28.

29. July 23, 1850, entry, in Frink, *Journal of the Adventures of a Party of California Gold-Seekers* (1897), 79; June 15, 1852, entry, in Keen, Journal (typescript), 47. Cecelia Adams, also in 1852, encountered a group of Oregon men who refused to stop and talk. July 22, 1852, entry, in Adams, "Crossing the Plains in 1852," 301.

30. June 12, 1846, entry, in Wade, ed., *The Journals of Francis Parkman* (1947), 2:437; Edwin Bryant to a friend, June 16, 1846, in Morgan, ed., *Overland in 1846*, 2:559; letter of Mrs. B. G. Ferris, Sept. 10, 1852, in Ferris, *Mormons at Home*, 42. See also the July 4, 1848, entry, in May, Journal (MS); Aug. 16, 1850, entry, in Coke, *A Ride over the Rocky Mountains* (1852), 185.

31. June 29, 1852, entry, in "Diary of E. W. Conyers" (1906), 447–52.

32. Dyck, "In the California Gold Rush" (1956), 27–28.

33. Portland *Weekly Oregonian*, Sept. 20, Nov. 1, 1856; "Captain McArthur's Report on the Second Handcart Company," in Hafen and Hafen, eds., *Handcarts to Zion* (1960), 216–17.

34. Aug. 8, 1850, entry, in Kelly, ed., "The Journal of Robert Chalmers" (1952), 51; St. Louis *Daily Missouri Republican*, Sept. 25, 1851; St. Joseph *Gazette*, Sept. 17, 1851; July 18, 22, 1853, entries, in "Diary of Celinda E. Hines" (1921), 103–5.

35. Council Bluffs *Chronotype*, July 25, 1855, Nov. 12, 1856; St. Louis *Daily Missouri Republican*, July 26, Oct. 24, 1855.

36. Young to James W. Denver, Sept. 12, 1857, in Denver, *Report of the Commissioner of Indian Affairs*, Nov. 30, 1857, 35 Cong., 1 Sess., House Ex. Doc. 2, Ser. 942 (1858), 598.

37. Allen, comp., *Ten Years in Oregon* (1850), 302–8; Washington *Daily Union*, Dec. 4, 1845; St. Louis *Weekly American*, Oct. 9, 1846, in Morgan, ed., *Overland in 1846*, 2:655; Barry, *Beginning of the West*, 647; St. Louis *Daily Missouri Republican*, Aug. 5, 1847, Aug. 26, 1851.

38. July 13, 1857, entry of Granville Stuart, in Phillips, ed., *Forty Years on the Frontier* (1925, 1957), 117.

39. Johnson and Winter, *Route across the Rocky Mountains*, ed. Cannon (1932), 122–65.

40. Morgan, ed., "The Mormon Ferry on the North Platte" (1949), 159, n. 87.

41. Palmer, *Journal of Travels over the Rocky Mountains*, ed. Thwaites (1906), 226.

42. July 17, 1847, entry, in Hastings, Journal (typescript), 13. The next day Hastings was probably equally dumbfounded when the wife of a returning Oregon missionary passed, also riding astraddle! When Richard Owen Hickman in 1852 saw two eastbound Oregon women riding mules in this fashion, he predicted that "they would see the old elephant before getting to Missouri, if they had not already seen it." June 14, 1852, entry, in Phillips, ed., " 'Dick's Works' " (1929), 248.

43. June 24, 1852, entry, in Adams, "Crossing the Plains in 1852," 295; San Francisco *Daily Alta California*, Sept. 8, 1855. The Salt Lake City *Deseret News* made the same comment in its July 11, 1855, issue. See also Portland *Weekly Oregonian*, June 13, 1857. Doubtless once also considered unlikely was Miles Goodyear's 1848 eastbound trip *from* California via South Pass with a drove of over 100 California horses the mountaineer intended to sell in the States. Barry, *Beginning of the West*, 785.

44. In his July 11, 1850, diary entry, S. M. Jamison reported meeting fifty eastbound packers, and Theodore Potter encountered fifty returning California miners along the Humboldt River in 1852, all colorfully dressed and proceeding eastward at the rate of fifty miles a day. "Diary of S. M. Jamison" (1967), 22; *The Autobiography of Theodore Edgar Potter* (1913), 83.

45. Barry, *Beginning of the West*, 466. See also Bourne, "The Legend of Marcus Whitman" (1901), 276–300; Nixon, *How Marcus Whitman Saved Oregon* (1895).

46. Tobie, "Joseph L. Meek," in Hafen, ed., *The Mountain Men and the Fur Trade* (1965–72), 1:330; Bancroft, *History of Oregon*, 1:676–77, 717; Barry, *Beginning of the West*, 466.

47. St. Joseph *Adventure*, n.d., in Jefferson City *Inquirer*, Nov. 13, 1852, reprinted in "A Record Trip from California to Missouri" (1930), 608. The estimates for average travel time between 1840 and 1860 are based on available statistics for approximately forty eastbound companies.

48. New York *Herald*, Feb. 12, 1852.

49. St. Louis *Daily Missouri Republican*, June 4, 1851; Barry, *Beginning of the West*, 1175; Salt Lake City *Deseret News*, June 6, 1855; Young to Denver, Sept. 12, 1857, in Denver, *Report of the Commissioner of Indian Affairs*, 598.

50. Donner to a friend, June 27, 1846, in Springfield, Ill., *Sangamo Journal*, Aug. 13, 1846, reprinted in Morgan, ed., *Overland in 1846*, 2:576.

51. July 12, 1849, entry of J. Goldsborough Bruff, in Read and Gaines, eds., *Gold Rush* (1944), 1:40; June 22, 1852, entry, in Frizzell, *Across the Plains to California in 1852*, ed. Paltsits (1915), 28.

52. Elisha Douglass Perkins commented in 1849 that "I have never known an instance of any note or scrap of paper being disturbed or misplaced." July 25, 1849, entry, in Clark, ed., *Gold Rush Diary* (1967), 78.

53. Sept. 23, 1849, entry of Bruff, in Read and Gaines, eds., *Gold Rush*, 1:188; June 24, 1850, entry, in McBride, Journal (MS).

54. May 19, 1849, entry, in McCall, *The Great California Trail* (1882), 22, italics his.

55. Sept. 24, 1849, entry, in Lord, Diary (MS and clippings); June 24, 1856, entry, in Carpenter, Diary (typescript), 32; May 29, 1852, entry of Clark, in Barry, ed., "Overland to the Gold Fields of California," 245.

56. Currey, "Occasional Address" (1887), 43; May 9, 1849, diary entry of Charles Elisha Boyle, in Columbus *Evening Dispatch*, Oct. 13, 1849.

57. June 19, 1846, entry, in Bryant, *What I Saw in California* (1849), 98; June 20, 1846, entry, in "Diary of George McKinstry," in Morgan, ed., *Overland in 1846*, 1:213. John F. Dodson on June 24, 1852, noted that he drove to the Ash Hollow "Post Office." Weisel, ed., "Dodson's Death: The Diary of John F. Dodson" (1953), 28; Sept. 29, 1849, entry, in Hall, Diary (typescript), 16.

58. June 7, 1849, entry, in Delano, *Across the Plains and among the Diggings*, 26; July 17, 28, Aug. 25, 1849, entries, in Sedgley, *Overland to California in 1849* (1877), 39, 44, 52; July 26, 1849, entry, in Lorton, Diary and Letters (microfilm of typescripts), 156; June 17, 1849, entry, in Giffen, ed., *The Diaries of Peter Decker* (1966), 100; Aug. 17, 1849, entry, in Mann, Diary (typescript), 42; Sept. 3, 1849, entry, in The Diary of Bernard J. Reid, Esq. (typescript), 56. J. Goldsborough Bruff described the post office at the junction of the main trail with the Lassen Cutoff, noting that there was a large red barrel, with "Post Office" printed in black, which was half filled with letters and notices. Nearby a billboard was also covered with notes. Bruff left a note himself. Sept. 19, 1849, entry, in Read and Gaines, eds., *Gold Rush*, 1:179.

59. May 17, 1849, entry, in McCall, *The Great California Trail*, 21; Benjamin H. Gatton to Geo. H. Camlbell [*sic*], July 1, 1849, in Springfield *Illinois Journal*, Oct. 3, 1849, in Morgan, The Mormons and the Far West (typescripts).

60. June 10, 1849, entry, in Gray, Diary (MS), 41.

61. Hoffman, Journal (MS and typescript translation), 24.

62. See, e.g., the Aug. 24, 1849, entry, in Howell, Diary (MS); Sept. 11, 12, 1849, entries of Elijah Bryan Farnham, in Mattes and Kirk, eds., "From Ohio to California in 1849" (1950), 417–18; Aug. 30, 1849, entry in [Granville Overland Company], Journal; Campbell, "Benoni Morgan Hudspeth" (1968), 13.

63. Sept. 19, 1849, entry of Wilkins, in McDermott, ed., *An Artist on the Overland Trail* (1968), 74; June 18, 1849, entry, in Delano, *Across the Plains and among the Diggings*, 34; June 22, 1850, entry, in Evans, Journal (MS), 93–94.

64. June 24, 1849, entry of Wakeman Bryarly, in Potter, ed., *Trail to California* (1945),

116; Aug. 8, 1849, entry of James F. Wilkins, in McDermott, ed., *Artist on the Overland Trail*, 62; Sept. 14, 1849, entry, in Austin, Diary (typescript), 77; July 7, 1850, entry, in Jewett, Journal (typescript), 34; Baydo, "Overland from Missouri to Washington Territory in 1854" (1971), 77.

65. June 22, 1853, entry, in De Witt and De Witt, eds., *Prairie Schooner Lady* (1959), 76.

66. See, e.g., the Aug. 27, 1849, entry, in "The Diary of Dr. Jonathan Clark" (Aug. 8, 1925), 3; July 11, 18, 1850, entries of William H. Kilgore, in Muench, ed., *The Kilgore Journal* (1949), 43, 46; Aug. 21, 1850, entry, in McDiarmid, Journal and Letters (microfilm of MSS and typescripts); Aug. 17, 30, 1850, entries, in Bennett, *Overland Journey to California* (1906), 36, 40; Waters, "Account of a Trip across the Plains in 1855" (1929), 65, 72.

67. Aug. 14, 1849, entry, in Scamehorn, ed., *The Buckeye Rovers in the Gold Rush*, 65.

68. June 24, July 1, 1856, entries, in Carpenter, Diary, 32, 41; May 7, 1850, entry, in Sawyer, *Way Sketches*, ed. Eberstadt (1926), 20; July 26, 1849, entry, in Lorton, Diary, 156; Chandless, *A Visit to Salt Lake* (1857), 67; Aug. 29, 1850, entry, in Newcomb, Journal (photocopy of MS), 170.

69. June 6–7, July 21, 1851, entries, in Johnson, Diary (MS), 47, 75.

70. Major Isaac Lynde, commanding army troops protecting overlanders along the Humboldt River in 1859, reported that emigrants often laughed at him when he admonished them to have their weapons ready for instant use. Lynde to F. J. Porter, Oct. 24, 1859, in *Report of the Secretary of War*, 1859, 36 Cong., 1 Sess., Sen. Ex. Doc. 2, Ser. 1024 (1860), 243.

71. May 21, 24, July 29, Aug. 7, Sept. 16, 1849, entries, in Benson, Diary, 7, 9, 44–46, 49–50, 66.

72. May 19, 1849, entry, in Hinman, Diary (MS); June 5, 1849, entry, in Stitzel, Diary (microfilm of MS), 107. Both reports were false.

73. June 10, 1850, entry, in Whitman, Diary (MS); July 27, 1852, entry, in Kerns, "Journal of Crossing the Plains to Oregon" (1917), 174; Cole, *In the Early Days along the Overland Trail*, comp. Hardy (1905), 75; July 27, 1856, entry, in Carpenter, Diary, 62.

74. Aug. 8, 1849, entry, in Arms, Diary, in Knoxville, Ill., *Journal*, Jan. 30, 1850. The typescript of letters containing Arms's diary was kindly made available to me by Dale Morgan of the Bancroft Library, who was preparing the diary for publication prior to his death.

75. A. I. Davis to William B. Hazen, Jan. 9, 1853 (MS and typescript); San Francisco *Daily Alta California*, July 27, 1852; Aug. 14, 1849, entry, in Hale, "Diary of a Trip to California" (1925), 107–8.

76. Aug. 10, 15, 16, 18, 20, 1849, entries, in Delano, *Across the Plains and among the Diggings*, 75–84.

77. See, e.g., Aug. 31, Sept. 4, 1849, entries, in Castleman, Diary (microfilm of typescript), 70, 72.

78. Henry A. Stine to his mother, June 17, 1850, in Stine, Letters and Journal (typescripts); June 24, 1854, entry, in McCowen, Diary (typescript); Richard J. Oglesby to Editors, Aug. 12, 1849, in *Illinois Daily Journal*, Oct. 23, 1849, reprinted in Eversole, ed., "Richard J. Oglesby: Forty-Niner" (1939), 162; July 30, 1849, entry of Bennett C. Clark, in Bieber, ed., "Diary of a Journey from Missouri to California," 36–37; Sept. 25, 1849, entry, in Arms, Diary, in Knoxville *Journal*, Feb. 6, 1850.

79. Charles Hentz to his mother, June 1, 1849, in Hentz, Letters (photocopies of typescripts); John A. Johnson to his wife, May 10, 1849, in Johnson, *Pioneering on the Plains* (1924); William Wilson to Lovina Wilson, June 18, 1850, in Wilson, Letters and Day Books (MSS and typescripts).

80. Sept. 18, 1849, entry, in Lord, Diary.

81. J. H. Wayman to J. V. Wayman, June 5, 1852, in Wayman, Journal and Letters (photocopies of MSS).

82. Knox to his wife, Sept. 20, 1850, in Turner, ed., "Reuben Knox Letters, Part II," 269.

83. Applegate, "A Day with the Cow Column in 1843" (1900), 379–81; Carleton, *The Prairie Logbooks*, ed. Pelzer (1943), 251; June 7, 1847, entry, in Hastings, Journal. Henry Page and William Rothwell, in 1849 and 1850 respectively, both asserted that there was a very high proportion of physicians in the overland caravans—Page thinking every com-

pany had one and Rothwell suggesting each train had two or three and that every tenth man was a "professional character." Henry Page to Mary A. Page, May 2, 1849, in Page, *Wagons West* (1930), 108; May 11, 1850, entry, in Rothwell, Journal and Letters, 47. A contrary view was printed in the St. Joseph *Gazette*, July 31, 1850, wherein a correspondent indicated that "not 1 train in 100 has a physician or medicine this year."

84. May 5, 15, 1850, entries, in Thomasson, Diary (typescript), 3, 6; June 2, 1850, entry, in Grow, Journal (MS); Dr. Thomas White to Samuel Porter Williams, Apr. 19, 1853, in Winther and Thornbrough, eds., *To Oregon in 1852* (1964), 11, 14, 19.

85. Cole, *In the Early Days along the Overland Trail*, 48; *Autobiography of Theodore Edgar Potter*, 36; John Nelson to his sister Mary, Apr. 2, 1851, in Nelson, Letters (photocopies of MSS).

86. May 23, June 21, July 18, 1849, entries, in McCall, *The Great California Trail*, 24, 40, 53; Reuben Knox to his wife and daughter, June 16, 1850, in Turner, ed., "Reuben Knox Letters, Part II," 259; Aug. 6, 8, 1850, entries, in Wright, ed., "The Journal of John Lowery Brown" (1934), 201.

87. June 30, 1850, entry, in Shepherd, *Journal of Travel across the Plains* (1851, 1945 reprint), 18; Aug. 10, 1852, entry, in Wayman, Journal and Letters; Carleton, *Prairie Logbooks*, 251.

88. July 1, 1849, entry, in Lord, Diary.

89. Dr. George W. Davis to Walters [*sic*] Watkins, Dec. 6, 1850 (MS and typescript); Dr. William R. Allen to Washington Franklin Allen, May 4, 1851 (typescript); Reuben Knox to his wife and daughter, June 16, 1850, in Turner, ed., "Reuben Knox Letters, Part II," 259.

90. Ibid.

91. Letter of O. W. Nixon, Sept. 7, 1850, in Wilmington, Ohio, *Clinton Republican*, Nov. 1, 1850; July 2, 1849, entry, in Caldwell, "Notes of a Journey to California by Fort Hall Route," in Read and Gaines, eds., *Gold Rush*, 2:1256; Dr. William R. Allen to Washington Franklin Allen, May 4, 1851; June 1, 1850, entry, in Frush, Diary (MS and typescript); *Autobiography of Theodore Edgar Potter*, 37; June 7, 1850, entry, in Prosch, ed., "Diary of Dr. David S. Maynard" (1906), 52.

92. May 19, June 10, 1850, entries, in Cagwin, Diary (typescript); July 2, 1850, entry, in McDiarmid, Journal and Letters; Carpenter, I Crossed the Plains in the 50's (microfilm of MS); Sept. 26, 1847, entry, in Gray, Diary, 147. For barbering see June 14, 15, 26, 1859, entries, in Hays, ed., "Diary of Taylor N. Snow" (1932), 200–201.

93. July 14, 1850, entry, in "Diary of S. M. Jamison," 22; May 22, 1849, entry, in Morgan, ed., *The Overland Diary of James A. Pritchard* (1959), 67–68; May 31, 1853, entry, in Newton, Diary (MS).

94. Carpenter, I Crossed the Plains in the 50's; May 15, 1849, entry of Vincent Geiger, in Potter, ed., *Trail to California*, 79; July 3, 1843, entry, in Nesmith, "Diary of the Emigration of 1843," 337; June 6, 1850, entry, in "Journal of A. W. Harlan" (1913), 39; Aug. 20, 1850, entry, in Wheeler, Diary (MS).

95. T. J. Ables to his parents, Oct. 12, 1857 (typescript), 14–17. See also the Aug. 2, 1849, entry of Wakeman Bryarly, in Potter, ed., *Trail to California*, 176; July 7, 1850, entry, in Gorgas, Diary and Letters (MSS).

96. Aug. 7, 1850, entry, in Payne, Saint Louis to San Francisco (typescript), 95; June 14, 1851, entry, in Cranston, Journal (MS and typescript); June 17, 1852, entry, in Richardson, Journal (MS), 68.

97. July 21, 1849, entry, in Howell, Diary; May 11, 14, 1852, entry of John Hawkins Clark, in Barry, ed., "Overland to the Gold Fields of California," 235–37; Sept. 20, 1846, entry, in Lienhard, *From St. Louis to Sutter's Fort*, trans. and ed. Gudde and Gudde (1961), 152.

98. See, e.g., the June 5, 1849, entry, in Tiffany, Journal (MS and typescript); May 31, June 1, 17, July 3, 1849, entries, in Chamberlain, Diary (typescript), 5, 10, 16; July 23, Sept. 12, 13, 14, 16, 1849, entries, in Diary of Bernard J. Reid, 43, 60–63.

99. Bryant, *What I Saw in California, passim;* Read and Gaines, eds., *Gold Rush, passim.*

100. See, e.g., the Aug. 14, 1853, entry, in *Diary of Basil Nelson Longsworth* (1927), 27.

101. June 18, July 21, 1853, entries of Harriet Ward, in De Witt and De Witt, eds., *Prairie Schooner Lady*, 72; June 24, 1853, entry, in Pengra, Diary (reproduced), 31.

102. May 31, 1849, entry, in Burbank, Diary (microfilm of MS), 33; May 27, 1849,

entry, in Shombre, Diary (MS and typescript); Sept. 24, 1849, entry, in Stuart, *My Roving Life* (1895), 1:69.

103. June 15, 1849, entry, in Morgan, ed., *Overland Diary of James A. Pritchard*, 91; May 8, 1849, entry, in Spooner, Diary (microfilm of MS); July 10, 1849, entry of Bennett C. Clark, in Bieber, ed., "Diary of a Journey from Missouri to California," 27; July 28, 1852, entry, in Thomson, *Crossing the Plains* (1896), 73; May 7, 1852, entry, in Lobenstine, ed., *Extracts from the Diary of William C. Lobenstine* (1920), 18; June 30, 1852, entry, in Bailey, Journal (MS and typescript).

104. David T. McCollum to J. H. Lund, June 27, 1849, in Ann Arbor *Michigan Argus*, Sept. 5, 1849, reprinted in Bidlack, *Letters Home* (1960), 20; unidentified letter, June 23, 1849, in New York *Herald*, Sept. 11, 1849.

105. July 7, 1849, entry, in *Journal of Samuel Rutherford Dundass* (1857), 51; Aug. 3, 1849, entry of Edwin Hillyer, in Holzhueter, ed., "From Waupun to Sacramento in 1849" (1966), 240; Aug. 13, 1850, entry, in Steele, *Across the Plains in 1850*, ed. Schafer (1930), 150; Aug. 3, 1850, entry, in Skinner, Diary.

106. July 13, 1849, entry, in Castleman, Diary, 41.

107. Letter of "Pawnee," May 18, 1849, in New Orleans *Daily Picayune*, June 12, 1849. Leander Loomis also noted encountering such a "spunging" footman in 1850. Loomis, *A Journal of the Birmingham Emigrating Company*, ed. Ledyard (1928), 40. See also Robert James to Editor, May 18, 1850, in Liberty *Weekly Tribune*, June 21, 1850; July 9, 1852, entry of John Hawkins Clark, in Barry, ed., "Overland to the Gold Fields of California," 270.

108. See the July 14, 1849, entry of Elijah Bryan Farnham, in Mattes and Kirk, eds., "From Ohio to California in 1849," 404–5; Aug. 18, 1849, entry, in Hale, "Diary of a Trip to California in 1849," 111; S. M. E. Goheen to Editor, Nov. 27, 1850, in St. Louis *Daily Missouri Republican*, Jan. 23, 1851; also numerous letters in Wyman, ed., *California Emigrant Letters* (1952).

109. May 13, 1849, entry, in Willis, Journal (MS and typescript); June 3, 1849, entry, in Delano, *Across the Plains and among the Diggings*, 23.

110. Aug. 30, 1849, entry of Elisha Douglass Perkins, in Clark, ed., *Gold Rush Diary*, 111–12; Edwin G. Hall to his father, Oct. 26, 1849, in Hall, Letters (typescripts).

111. Aug. 2, 1849, entry, in Hixson, Diary (photocopy of typescript), 41–42.

112. Aug. 29, 1850, entry, in Whitman, Diary; Fawkes, ed., *The Journal of Walter Griffith Pigman* (1942), 30; July 4, 1850, entry, in Jewett, Journal, 32; July 17, 1850, entry, in "The Memoirs of Lemuel Clarke McKeeby" (1924), 64.

113. June 23, July 6, 12, 1850, entries, in Sawyer, *Way Sketches*, 69, 85–86, 93.

114. Aug. 18, 1850, entry, in McKinstry, Diary (microfilm of typescript), 111; Aug. 24, 25, 31, 1850, entries, in *Journal of John Wood*, 57, 59, 61.

115. Orvis, Journal (MS and typescript).

116. Goldsmith, *Overland in Forty-Nine* (1896), 81.

117. Ibid., 68–69.

118. Campbell to his wife and brother, Sept. 8, 1850, in California Gold Rush Letters (MSS and typescripts); Aug. 25, 1850, entry, in Bennett, *Overland Journey to California*, 39; Dr. George W. Davis to Walters [*sic*] Watkins, Dec. 6, 1850; Dr. William R. Allen to Washington Franklin Allen, May 4, 1851; unidentified letter, Aug. 14, 1851, in St. Joseph *Gazette*, Nov. 5, 1851.

119. May 27, June 5, 30, 1849, entries, in Chamberlain, Diary, 5, 6, 15; June 8, 13, 1849, entries, in Sedgley, *Overland to California in 1849*, 22, 24; June 7, July 18, 1853, entries, in "Journal of Henry Allyn," 397, 416; July 14, 1850, entry, in Stine, Letters and Journal.

120. July 14, 1849, entry of John Edwin Banks, in Scamehorn, ed., *The Buckeye Rovers in the Gold Rush*, 41; May 26, 1852, entry of John Hawkins Clark, in Barry, ed., "Overland to the Gold Fields of California," 243; May 24, June 18, July 23, Aug. 1, 1849, entries of Vincent Geiger and Wakeman Bryarly, in Potter, ed., *Trail to California*, 84, 110, 163, 175.

121. June 13, 1852, entry, in Crane, Journal (MS); Shaw, *Across the Plains in Forty-Nine*, ed. Quaife (1896, 1948 reprint), 139–40.

122. Aug. 20, 1850, entry, in "Journal of John T. Williams" (1936), 406; Aug. 13, 1850, entry, in "Diary Kept by William Edmundson" (1908), 528; June 28, 1852, entry of John Hawkins Clark, in Barry, ed., "Overland to the Gold Fields of California," 264.

123. July 20, 1849, entry, in Diary of Bernard J. Reid, 40–41; May 19, 1850, entry, in A Chapter from the Diary of the Late Judge James B. Persinger, 7; June 17, 1850, entry, in Clapp, *A Journal of Travels to and from California* (1851), 30; June 27, 1854, entry, in McCowen, Diary, 35.

124. July 16, 1850, entry, in Clapp, *Journal of Travels*, 40; July 13, 1850, entry, in Ellis, Diary (photocopy of MS); Aug. 2, 1850, entry, in Bloom, Diary (typescript), 38.

125. July 30, 31, 1850, entries, in Paden, ed., *The Journal of Madison Berryman Moorman* (1948), 57; letter of J. W. B. Reynolds, Dec. 1, 1850, in St. Louis *Daily Missouri Republican*, Mar. 20, 1851; Aug. 10, 1850, entry, in Wright, ed., "The Journal of John Lowery Brown," 202; Aug. 7, 1850, entry, in McDiarmid, Journal and Letters.

126. Aug. 5, 1849, entry of Bennett C. Clark, in Bieber, ed., "Diary of a Journey from Missouri to California," 40–41; Phillips, ed., *Forty Years on the Frontier*, 52.

127. New Orleans *Daily Picayune*, Nov. 21, 1843, in Field, *Prairie and Mountain Sketches*, ed. Gregg and McDermott (1957), 28; Chenoweth, "Occasional Address" (1883), 32; Aug. 1, 1856, entry, in Carpenter, Diary, 65.

128. May 22, 1849, entry of Elisha Douglass Perkins, in Clark, ed., *Gold Rush Diary*, 6; May 11, 1849, entry, in Wood, Diary (MS); New Orleans *Daily Picayune*, June 1, 1849; Wooster, Ohio, *Democrat*, June 7, 1849; Jos. Henderson to "Dear Bill," May 29, 1849, in Pittsburgh *Post*, July 9, 1849, reprinted in New York *Herald*, July 12, 1849.

129. June 13, 14, 1849, entries, in Spooner, Diary; St. Louis *Daily Missouri Republican*, Oct. 25, 1849; May 30, 31, 1849, entries of Berrien, in Hinckley and Hinckley, eds., "Overland from St. Louis to the California Gold Field" (1960), 310–11.

130. July 27, 1849, entry, in Stansbury, *Exploration and Survey*, 63.

131. Ibid.; Aug. 26, 1850, entry, in Dutton, "Across the Plains in 1850" (1910), 474; June 19, 1849, entry of Elijah Bryan Farnham, in Mattes and Kirk, eds., "From Ohio to California in 1849," 312; July 12, 1849, entry, in Searls, *The Diary of a Pioneer* (1940), 48; July 17, 22, 1849, entries of J. Goldsborough Bruff, in Read and Gaines, eds., *Gold Rush*, 1:17, 51.

132. Aug. 23, 1850, entry, in "Journal of John T. Williams," 407; A. M. Williams to his father, Nov. 10, 1850, in Wyman, ed., *California Emigrant Letters*, 123.

133. July 13, 1849, entry, in Diary of Bernard J. Reid, 38; Aug. 25–Sept. 15, 1853, entries, in Ellison, ed., "Diary of Maria Parsons Belshaw" (1932), 321–27.

134. Aug. 27, 1850, entry of Adam Mercer Brown, in Kiefer, ed., "Over Barren Plains and Rock-bound Mountains" (1972), 27; Aug. 18, 1852, entry of Clark, in Barry, ed., "Overland to the Gold Fields of California," 289; Sept. 11, 15, 1850, entries of Taylor, in Williams, ed., "Overland to California in 1850," 340–42.

135. C. to Editor, Sept. 22, 1850, in St. Louis *Daily Missouri Republican*, Nov. 18, 1850; Mack, *Nevada: A History of the State* (1936), 132.

136. Dr. James Williams to his wife, Aug. 20, 1850, in Williams, Papers (MSS and typescripts); David T. McCollum to J. H. Lund, Oct. 20, 1849, in Ann Arbor *Washtenaw Whig*, Dec. 26, 1849, reprinted in Bidlack, *Letters Home*, 34.

137. Riley Senter to Ordelia Alverson, July 24, 1849, in Senter, *Crossing the Continent to California Gold Fields* (1938); May 28 [29], 1849, entry of James F. Wilkins, in McDermott, ed., *Artist on the Overland Trail*, 36; Sept. 9, 1849, entry of John Edwin Banks, in Scamehorn, ed., *The Buckeye Rovers in the Gold Rush*, 83.

138. June 10, 1849, entry, in Arms, Diary, in Knoxville *Journal*, Oct. 24, 1849; July 12, 1849, entry, in Diary of Bernard J. Reid, 37.

139. Sept. 7, 1849, entry, in Stuart, *My Roving Life*, 1:60; Oct. 3, 1849, entry, in Hutchings, Diary (microfilm of MS); Pearson, *Overland in 1849*, ed. Goodman (1961), 17; May 26, 1852, entry, in Paxson, ed., "T. Turnbull's Travels," 165; Aug. 11, 1850, entry, in Frink, *Journal of the Adventures of a Party of California Gold-Seekers*, 89–90.

140. July 17, Aug. 3, 1849, entries of Bruff, in Read and Gaines, eds., *Gold Rush*, 1:47, 163; June 8, 1849, entry, in Gray, Diary, 39; July 1, 1849, entry of Perkins, in Clark, ed., *Gold Rush Diary*, 49. See also New York *Daily Tribune*, Aug. 14, 1849.

141. July 12, 1849, entry, in Lord, Diary; May 25, 1850, entry, in Clapp, *Journal of Travels*, 20; Sept. 21, 1850, entry, in Langworthy, *Scenery of the Plains*, 119.

142. Aug. 11, 1850, entry, in Coke, *Ride over the Rocky Mountains*, 168. See also the June

27, 1850, entry, in Evans, Journal, 105–6; May 16, 1852, entry, in Frizzell, *Across the Plains to California in 1852*, 15.

143. July 13, 1849, entry, in Merrill, Journal (typescript); Charles Hentz to his mother, Nov. 20, 1849, in Hentz, Letters; May 30, 1850, entry, in Millington, Diary (microfilm of MS); Aug. 15, 1850, entry, in Skinner, Diary; June 10, 1849, entry, in Johnston, *Overland to California* (1948), 96–97; July 26, 1852, entry, in Paxson, ed., "T. Turnbull's Travels," 203.

144. June 30, 1852, entry, in "Diary of E. W. Conyers," 453. See also the June 6, 1850, entry, in Kelly, ed., "The Journal of Robert Chalmers," 40.

145. July 10, 1849, entry, in Starr, Diary (microfilm of MS); June 5, 1849, entry, in Castleman, Diary, 13; Aug. 28, 1851, entry, in Bowen, Diary (microfilm of copy).

146. July 3, 1852, entry, in Gee, Journal (MS and typescript).

147. Joseph Price to Elizabeth Price, June 26, 1850, in Marshall, ed., "The Road to California," 254. In the starvation year of 1850 desperate emigrants also ate meat from oxen which had been dead for several days. See the Aug. 22, 1850, entry, in Olson, ed., "The Diary of James Mason" (1952), 119; Lowe, *Five Years a Dragoon*, ed. Russell (1965), 44.

148. July 17–Aug. 17, 1849, entries, in Cleland and Brooks, eds., *A Mormon Chronicle* (1955), 1:111–13.

149. June 3, 5, 1859, entries, in Favour, Diary (MS).

CHAPTER FIVE: EMIGRANT-INDIAN INTERACTION

1. Father Pierre-Jean De Smet to Father Provincial, July 18, 1846, in Chittenden and Richardson, eds., *Life, Letters and Travels of Father Pierre-Jean De Smet* (1905), 2:557.

2. Stewart, ed., *The Opening of the California Trail* (1953), 26, 64–65, 98, n. 23.

3. Sept. 1, 1849, entry, in McCall, *The Great California Trail* (1882), 77.

4. Aug. 8, 1849, entry, in McCoy, *Pioneering on the Plains* (1924); May 7, 1853, entry, in "Diary of Celinda E. Hines" (1921), 88.

5. Oct. 6, 7, 9, 12, 15, 16, 24, 25, 27, 1841, entries, in Bidwell, *A Journey to California* (1842, 1937 reprint), 23–24, 26, 27.

6. Burnett, " 'Recollections and Opinions of an Old Pioneer' " (1904), 76–77; Oct. 5, 1843, entry, in Nesmith, "Diary of the Emigration of 1843" (1906), 354.

7. Oct. 10, 11, 14, 17, 1843, entries, in Bekeart, ed., "Journal of Pierson Barton Reading" (1930), 183–84.

8. Nov. 26, 1849, entry, in Young, Diary (typescript), 14; Nusbaumer, Diary (typescript translation).

9. July 31, 1850, entry, in Skinner, Diary (MS); San Francisco *Daily Alta California,* Nov. 15, 1854. See also the June 27, 1850, entry, in Lane, Diary (photocopy of MS), and the Aug. 8, 1852, entry, in Kingery, Letters (MSS and typescripts), for additional accounts of Indians used as guides by overland parties.

10. See, e.g., the June 14, 1852, entry, in Thomson, *Crossing the Plains* (1896), 47; Aug. 7, 1853, entry, in McClure, Diary, 84; May 14, 1849, entry of Edwin Hillyer, in Holzhueter, ed., "From Waupun to Sacramento in 1849" (1966), 222; July 3, 1850, entry, in Newcomb, Journal (photocopy of MS), 102.

11. "The Shively Guide," in Morgan, ed., *Overland in 1846* (1963), 2:739.

12. Aug. 21, 1851, entry, in Wood, "Journal of a Trip to Oregon" (1926), 200.

13. Aug. 5, 1853, entry, in "Diary of Mrs. Amelia Stewart Knight" (1933), 48–49. Proficient Indian swimmers accomplished this by swimming one animal across the river. The other draft animals generally followed in its wake.

14. "Narrative of James Longmire" (1932), 55–57. See also the Sept. 28, 1845, entry, in Palmer, *Journal of Travels over the Rocky Mountains,* ed. Thwaites (1906), 119.

15. See, e.g., the Sept. 28, 1845, entry of John Ewing Howell, in "Diary of an Emigrant of 1845" (1907), 152; Aug. 3, 27, 1847, entries, in Pettijohn, Diary (MS); Aug. 25, 1849, entry, in Pease, Diary (typescript), 31–32.

16. Johnson and Winter, *Route across the Rocky Mountains,* ed. Cannon (1932), 35–36.

17. Bancroft, *History of Oregon* (1886–88), 2:408; Cummins, *Autobiography and Reminiscences* (1914), 50–51; Long, *A True Story* ([1915]), 12–14.

18. Sept. 20, 1850, entry, in Prosch, ed., "Diary of Dr. David S. Maynard" (1906), 61.

19. William Wells to Virginia E. Wells, May 15, 1849, in Wells, Letters (typescripts). See also the June 2, 1846, entry, in "Diary of George McKinstry," in Morgan, ed., *Overland in 1846,* 1:210; St. Louis *Weekly American,* July 17, 1846, in ibid., 2:551; New Orleans *Picayune,* Sept. 16, 1843, in "Documentary" (1901), 192.

20. Shaw, *Across the Plains in Forty-Nine,* ed. Quaife (1896, 1948 reprint), 30–33.

21. Aug. 21, 1849, entry, in Kirkpatrick, Journal (copy of MS), 28; Price, ed., "From Hannibal to the Gold Fields in 1849" (1961), 9; Aug. 17, 1853, entry, in Miller, Journal (MS), 64; Aug. 3, 1859, entry, in Casler, *A Journal Giving the Incidents of a Journey to California* (1863, 1969 reprint), 40–42; Sept. 24, 1850, entry, in Coke, *A Ride over the Rocky Mountains* (1852), 270; July 17, 1849, entry, in *Journal of Samuel Rutherford Dundass* (1857), 38; Sept. 9, 1859, entry, in Cummings, Journal (MS and typescript); Tabitha Brown to her brother and sister, Aug., 1854, in "A Brimfield Heroine" (1904), 203.

22. Crawford, *Scenes of Earlier Days* (1898, 1962 reprint), 54; Aug. 11, 1851, entry, in "Robert Robe's Diary while Crossing the Plains" (1928), 63.

23. Apr. 30, 1849, entry, in Johnston, *Overland to California* (1948), 33.

24. "Reminiscences of Experiences on the Oregon Trail" (1901), 214–15.

25. June 6, 1851, entry, in "Diary of John S. Zeiber" (1923), 311.

26. June 12, 1850, entry, in Littleton, Diary (typescript), 8; Sept. 6, 1846, entry, in Lienhard, *From St. Louis to Sutter's Fort,* trans. and ed. Gudde and Gudde (1961), 132–34.

27. James W. Evans to Ellis G. Evans, Oct. 27, 1850, in Evans, ed., "A Missouri Forty-Niner's Trip across the Plains" (1948), 43–44.

28. Miller to his brother, Nov. 24, 1852 (photocopy of MS), 18–19.

29. "Report of F. W. Lander, Superintendent, &c., to the Commissioner of Indian Affairs," Feb. 18, 1860, in U.S. President, *Massacre at Mountain Meadows* (1860), 121. See also Reynolds, "The Redskin Who Saved the White Man's Hide" (1960), 54–55; Trenholm and Carley, *The Shoshonis* (1964), 166–67.

30. "The Shively Guide," 734, 736, 739–40; Ware, *The Emigrants' Guide to California,* ed. Caughey (1932), 9; Hastings, *The Emigrants' Guide to Oregon and California,* ed. Carey (1932), 146.

31. July 1, Aug. 5, 1849, entries, in McDermott, ed., *An Artist on the Overland Trail* (1968), 50, 61–62.

32. Benjamin H. Gatton to Geo. H. Camlbell [*sic*], July 1, 1849, in Springfield *Illinois Journal,* Oct. 3, 1849, in Morgan, The Mormons and the Far West (typescripts).

33. Brooks to "Dear Ruter," Nov. 7, 1851, in "Letters of Quincy Adams Brooks" (1914), 211.

34. Aug. 16, 1849, entry, in "The Journal of Major Osborne Cross," in Settle, ed., *The March of the Mounted Riflemen* (1940), 189; Sept. 21, 1850, entry, in Langworthy, *Scenery of the Plains, Mountains and Mines,* ed. Phillips (1932), 119; Pearson, *Overland in 1849,* ed. Goodman (1961), 19; June 5, 1849, entry, in [Granville Overland Company, Ohio], Journal (MS and typescript).

35. July 21, 1850, entry, in McDiarmid, Journal and Letters (microfilm of MSS and typescripts); Oct. 23, 1851, entry, in Adams, "Crossing the Plains in 1852" (1905), 327; Kelly, *An Excursion to California* (1851), 1:133; June 5, 1849, entry, in McCall, *The Great California Trail,* 31; Aug. 1, 1849, entry, in Arms, Diary, in Knoxville, Ill., *Journal,* Jan. 23, 1850 (typescript). See also the May 29, 1849, entry, in Churchill, Diary (microfilm of typescript), 19; Aug. 23, 1853, entry, in McClure, Diary, 99.

36. Haun, A Woman's Trip across the Plains in 1849 (MS), 23.

37. June 22, 1850, entry, in McBride, Journal (MS).

38. June 5, July 2, 1850, entries, in Payne, Saint Louis to San Francisco (typescript), 39, 62.

39. June 5, 1849, entry, in Steck, Diary (MS and typescript). Various overlanders commented on what shrewd judges of horses Indians were. See the July 2, 1849, entry, in Tiffany, Journal (MS and typescript); Hale, *California as It Is,* eds. Hunter and Wellington (1851, 1954 reprint), 14.

40. Sept. 9, 1849, entry, in "Journal of Major Osborne Cross," 223; Aug. 27, 1852, entry, in Thomson, *Crossing the Plains,* 87.

41. Aug. 4, 1849, entry of Banks, in Scamehorn, ed., *The Buckeye Rovers in the Gold Rush* (1965), 57; July 11, 13, 1849, entries, in Mann, Diary (typescript), 17, 19; June 17, 1850, entry, in Krill, Diary (MS). See also the Aug. 5, 6, 1849, entries, in Castleman, Diary (microfilm of typescript), 56; July 13, 1853, entry, in Ward, Diary (MS), 62.

42. Salt Lake City *Deseret News,* July 13, 1850.

43. Aug. 24, 1845, entry, in Palmer, *Journal of Travels,* 96; May 8, 1849, entry of Farnham, in Mattes and Kirk, eds., "From Ohio to California in 1849" (1950), 300; July 2, 1850, entry, in Blood, Diary (typescript), 37; San Francisco *Daily Herald,* Sept. 3, 1855, in Cohen, Scrapbooks (typescripts). See also Haun, A Woman's Trip across the Plains in 1849, 23; William Keil to "Dear Brothers and Sisters," June [July] 12, 1855, in "From Bethel, Missouri, to Aurora, Oregon," trans. Bek (1953), 30.

44. Jesse Looney to Maj. John C. Bond, Oct. 27, 1843, in Looney, "From the Far West" (1929), 356.

45. Aug. 25, 1851, entry, in Crawford, "Journal of a Trip across the Plains" (1924), 163. See also July 13, 14, 1847, entries, in "Diary of Mrs. Elizabeth Dixon Smith Geer" (1908), 159, for an account of Indians being paid for unsuccessfully hunting cattle. For successful Indian searches, see the May 7, 1853, entry, in "Diary of Celinda E. Hines," 88; May 22, 1853, entry of Rebecca Ketcham, in Kaiser and Knuth, eds., "From Ithaca to Clatsop Plains" (1962), 255.

46. May 11, 1849, entry, in Josselyn, Diary (microfilm of typescript), 4. See also the July 30, 1853, entry, in Miller, Journal, 56; Marysville, Cal., *Daily Herald,* Dec. 17, 1856.

47. Aug. 30, 1845, entry, in Palmer, *Journal of Travels*, 98, 235; Aug. 20, 1847, entry, in Pettijohn, Diary; June 5, 1849, entry of Vincent Geiger, in Potter, ed., *Trail to California* (1945), 99; May 21, 1849, entry, in Johnston, *Overland to California*, 67; July 21, 1852, entry, in Hanna, Journal (typescript), 26.

48. July 6, 1849, entry, in Benson, Diary (typescript), 30; July 2, 1849, entry, in Morgan, ed., *The Overland Diary of James A. Pritchard* (1959), 104; Aug. 1, 1852, entry, in Sharp, Diary (MS).

49. May 26, 1849, entry, in Dr. T., Diary (copy of MS); June 23, 1850, entry, in Thomasson, Diary (typescript), 24; June 23, 1849, diary entry of Charles Elisha Boyle, in Columbus, Ohio, *Evening Dispatch*, Nov. 1, 1949.

50. Henry Page to Mary A. Page, May 8, 1849, in Page, *Wagons West* (1930), 115; May 24, 1849, entry, in Searls, *The Diary of a Pioneer and Other Papers* (1940), 20; Aug. 9, 1849, entry, in Watson, *Journal of an Overland Journey to Oregon* (1851), 36. On August 20 Watson reported that near Grande Ronde, Oregon, Indians were asking from $50 to $150 for some of the best ponies he had ever seen.

51. May 29, 1850, entry, in Paden, ed., *The Journal of Madison Berryman Moorman* (1948), 16; May 29, 1852, entry, in Ashley, Diary (typescript), 1.

52. Kelly, *An Excursion to California*, 1:133.

53. Stevens to his brother and family, Oct. 31, 1852, in Rockwood, ed., "Letters of Charles Stevens" (1936), 144; Aug. 14, 1852, entry, in Francis, Diary (MS and typescript).

54. Burnett, "'Recollections and Opinions of an Old Pioneer,'" 82.

55. Sept. 17, 1853, entry, in Handsaker, Diary (reproduced), 30. See also, for examples of trading for fresh meats, the June 3, 1850, entry, in Frink, *Journal of the Adventures of a Party of California Gold-Seekers* (1897), 46; May 31, 1850, entry, in Read, ed., *A Pioneer of 1850* (1927), 52.

56. July 4, 1854, entry, in Burrel, Diary and Letter (MSS and typescripts).

57. Lyman, ed., "Reminiscences of Hugh Cosgrove" (1900), 263–64.

58. Bagley, "Crossing the Plains" (1922), 176.

59. July 28, 1850, entry, in Bennett, *Overland Journey to California* (1906), 29. "The Upper Missouri Fur Trade" (1961), 1–28, lists the type of Indian trade goods the fur traders relied upon in their operations and is useful for comparative purposes.

60. June 4, 1849, entry, in Delano, *Across the Plains and among the Diggings* (1853, 1936 reprint), 24; May 25, 1850, entry, in Abbey, *A Trip across the Plains* (1850), 22.

61. William P. Richardson to D. D. Mitchell, Oct. 21, 1850, in *Report of the Commissioner of Indian Affairs, 1850*, 31 Cong., 2 Sess., House Ex. Doc. 1, Ser. 595 (1850), 61–62.

62. John R. McBride's 1846 reminiscences, quoted in Morgan, ed., *Overland in 1846*, 1:96; June 1, 1849, entry, in Mattes, ed., "Alexander Ramsay's Gold Rush Diary" (1949), 446; May 26, 1849, entry, in Dr. T., Diary; May 23, 1849, diary entry of Charles Elisha Boyle, in Columbus *Evening Dispatch*, Oct. 20, 1949.

63. See Haines, "Goldilocks on the Oregon Trail" (1965–66), 26–30; Lyman, ed., "Reminiscences of F. X. Matthieu" (1900), 82–83; Staats, "The Occasional Address" (1878), 49–50; Andrew J. Chambers, "Crossing the Plains in 1845," quoted in Munkres, "Wives, Mothers, Daughters" (1970), 213; Parker, "Early Recollections of Oregon Pioneer Life" (1933), 18. The offer to purchase the emigrant man is recalled in "Reminiscences of Honorable John Minto," 157–58.

64. Haas, "Pioneer Autobiography" (Oct., 1938), 7.

65. Mattes and Kirk, eds., "From Ohio to California in 1849," 307.

66. June 10, 1859, entry, in Cramer, Journal (MS and typescript). See also Harriet S. Ward's 1853 account of an Indian offering two ponies for a seventeen-year-old emigrant girl, in Haines, "Goldilocks on the Oregon Trail," 29.

67. Aug. 31, 1843, entry, in Bekeart, ed., "Journal of Pierson Barton Reading," 175; Aug. 12, 1849, entry of Bruff, in Read and Gaines, eds., *Gold Rush* (1944), 1:89; Holzhueter, ed., "From Waupun to Sacramento in 1849," 230; Sept. 8, 1851, entry, in Wood, "Journal of a Trip to Oregon," 203; May 26, 1852, entry, in Keen, Journal (typescript), 32; Sept. 5, 1853, entry, in "Diary of Celinda E. Hines," 118.

68. Oliphant, ed., "Passing of an Immigrant of 1843" (1924), 206–7.

69. May 21, 1845, entry, in "The Diary of Jacob R. Snyder" (1931), 226.

70. Caughey, ed., "The Jacob Y. Stover Narrative" (1937), 167–68; May 15, 1849, entry

of Vincent Geiger, in Potter, ed., *Trail to California,* 78; June 9, 1849, entry, in Howell, Diary (MS), 8; Lucius Fairchild to J. C. Fairchild and family, June 5, 1849, in Schafer, ed., *California Letters of Lucius Fairchild* (1931), 25; May 24, 1850, entry, in "Journal of John T. Williams" (1936), 397.

71. May 27, 1849, letter, in Lord, Diary (MS and clippings); Charles Hentz to his mother, May 21, 1849, in Hentz, Letters (photocopies of typescripts); Washington *National Intelligencer,* June 5, 1849; May 22, 1849, entry, in "Journal of Major Osborne Cross," 41; May 1, 1852, entry, in Lewis, Memorandum or Notes (MSS and typescripts).

72. Harvey to T. Hartley Crawford, Sept. 10, 1845, in *Report of the Commissioner of Indian Affairs,* 1845, 29 Cong., 1 Sess., Sen. Doc. 1, Ser. 470 (1846), 535–36; Harvey to William Medill, Sept. 5, 1846, in *Report of the Commissioner of Indian Affairs,* 1846, 29 Cong., 2 Sess., Sen. Doc. 1, Ser. 493 (1847), 286.

73. Moore to Harvey, Sept. 21, 1846, in ibid., 292–93.

74. Harvey to Medill, Oct. 4, 1848, in *Report of the Commissioner of Indian Affairs,* 1848, 30 Cong., 2 Sess., House Ex. Doc. 1, Ser. 537 (1848), 441–42.

75. Mitchell to L. Lea, Sept. 14, 1850, in *Report of the Commissioner of Indian Affairs,* 1850, 47–48; Fitzpatrick to Mitchell, Sept. 24, 1850, in ibid., 55.

76. Mitchell to Lea, Nov. 11, 1851, in *Report of the Commissioner of Indian Affairs,* 1851, 32 Cong., 1 Sess., Sen. Ex. Doc. 1, Ser. 613 (1851), 289–90; John E. Barrow to Mitchell, Oct. 1, 1851, in ibid., 357; John H. Holeman to Lea, Sept. 21, 1851, in ibid., 445. Thomas S. Twiss, agent at the Upper Platte agency, wrote A. B. Greenwood, the Commissioner of Indian Affairs, on Aug. 16, 1859, to report on the great concern Indians were demonstrating by that time about the diminishing number of buffalo. See U.S. Interior, *Indian Councils* (1860), 3.

77. May 17, 1849, entry, in Breyfogle, Diary (mimeographed copy), 5. James Hutchings, an 1849 overlander, was one of the few who admitted that such claims were just, and paid willingly. June 9, 1849, entry, in Hutchings, Diary (microfilm of MS).

78. May 27, 1849, letter, in Lord, Diary.

79. May 22, 1849, entry, in "Journal of Major Osborne Cross," 41; May 17, 1850, entry, in McKinstry, Diary (microfilm of typescript); Shaw, *Eldorado, or California as Seen by a Pioneer* (1900), 25.

80. Ibid., 25; Aug. 2, 1851, entry, in Johnson, Diary (MS), 85. See also Miller, "Early Oregon Scenes" (1930), 63. For an indication of how important a document signed by a famous white man could be to an Indian who trusted the whites, see Sarah Winnemucca Hopkins's references to her grandfather Truckee in *Life among the Paiutes,* ed. Mann (1883), 18–19, 22, 25–26, 28, 69.

81. Royce, *A Frontier Lady,* ed. Gabriel (1932), 13.

82. James Payne, who ferried the Kansas River on May 10, crossed three small Indian toll bridges the next day. May 11, 1850, entry, in Payne, Saint Louis to San Francisco, 20. It seems evident that Indians felt the bridge tolls to be another way of procuring tribute payments for crossing Indian territory. See the May 23, 1849, entry, in Castleman, Diary, 5; Munkres, "The Plains Indian Threat" (1968), 210–11.

83. May 5, 1850, entry, in "Diary of Thomas Woodward" (1934), 348. Woodward was one of the exceptions who paid fifty cents for crossing the stream. See also the May 13, 1850, journal entry of H., in San Francisco *Daily Alta California,* Sept. 24, 1850.

84. Bushnell, Autobiography (reproduced), 11. Several 1852 overlanders indicated that Indians also kept another toll bridge seven or eight miles beyond, at Buffalo Creek, where the toll was twenty-five cents. See the May 6, 1852, entry, in Andrews, Journal (MS and typescript); May 10, 1852, entry, in Clark, The California Guide (MS and typescript).

85. May 10, 1852, entry, in ibid.; May 2, 1852, entry, in *Diary of Jay Green* (1955), 7.

86. May 10, 1852, entry, in Laird, Book (MS and typescript); May 14, 1853, entry, in Helen Stewart, Diary (reproduced), 3.

87. June 7, 8, 9, 1851, entries, in "Diary of John S. Zeiber," 311–14.

88. May 12, 1853, entry of Nathaniel Mayer, in Ham, ed., "Journey into Southern Oregon" (1959), 389; White to Samuel Porter Williams, Apr. 19, 1853, in Winther and Thornbrough, eds., *To Oregon in 1852* (1964), 12.

89. Norton, "My Overland Trip to California in 1852" (Sept., 1934), 10.

90. See the Ezra Meeker account, which may have pertained to the Shell Creek crossing, in Meeker, *The Busy Life of Eight-five Years* (1916), 39. E. W. Conyers noted that their company, which refused to give the Pawnees either tribute or toll, had traveled with arms at the ready in case the "red devils" tried anything, and had been somewhat eager to "make a small starting for a good-sized Indian graveyard." May 26, 1852, entry, in "Diary of E. W. Conyers" (1906), 435–37.

91. Carpenter, I Crossed the Plains in the 50's (microfilm of MS).

92. May 10, 12, 1852, entries, in Kingery, Letters; Kanesville *Frontier Guardian and Iowa Sentinel*, June 11, 1852.

93. May 19, 1852, entry, in Owen, Journal (MS).

94. St. Joseph *Gazette*, May 26, 1852.

95. May 24, 1852, entry, in Richardson, Journal (MS), 37. For a perfunctory comparison of reminiscent and contemporary accounts regarding Indian encounters, see Crow, "A Comparison of Stereotypes of Pioneer Travel" (1967), 91, 93–94.

96. May 23, 27, 1850, entries, in Paden, ed., *Journal of Madison Berryman Moorman*, 13, 15.

97. St. Louis *Daily Missouri Republican*, Sept. 9, 1847; Liberty, Mo., *Weekly Tribune*, Sept. 10, 1847.

98. St. Louis *Daily Missouri Republican*, Aug. 20, 1849.

99. Louisville *Examiner*, Aug. 18, 1849.

100. Dixon *Telegraph*, July 4, 1855, in Morgan, The Mormons and the Far West.

101. The usual ratio was from three to five persons per wagon, not thirty as in this case, one of the first clues to the mythical nature of this attack. Another mythical massacre, in 1857, went to the opposite statistical extreme, seventeen wagons and only twenty persons, all of whom were reportedly murdered by Sioux and Cheyenne Indians 100 miles west of Fort Kearny. See Portland *Weekly Oregonian*, Aug. 15, 1857.

102. Marysville *Herald*, Sept. 18, Oct. 2, 1855; Council Bluffs *Chronotype*, Oct. 31, 1855; Council Bluffs *Bugle*, Nov. 6, 1855; San Francisco *Daily Alta California*, Aug. 31, Sept. 17, Oct. 1, 1855; St. Louis *Daily Missouri Republican*, June 29, 1855. A similar conclusion apparently applies to a supposed 1859 affair in which an encircled sixty-wagon train numbering 300 persons was attacked for three consecutive days on the Oregon Trail in present Idaho by Indians who killed all but five persons, who managed after considerable hardship to reach the settlements and report the tragedy. See Sam Clay, "Few Histories Mention Story of Almo Tragedy," *Idaho Statesman*, Oct. 24, 1937, in Masters, Papers. Stewart, *The California Trail* (1962), 323–24, indicates that the "Massacre of Almo Creek" actually occurred in 1861.

103. Kroll, "The Books That Enlightened the Emigrants" (1944), 108.

104. Hastings, *Emigrants' Guide*, 58–59, 148–50; "The Shively Guide," 735–41; "The Map of T. H. Jefferson," in Morgan, ed., *Overland in 1846*, 1:242; Ware, *Emigrants' Guide*, 13, 15, 32–33; Child, *Overland Route to California* (1852, 1946 reprint), 46; Platt and Slater, *Travelers' Guide across the Plains* (1852, 1963 reprint), xviii, 3; Marcy, *The Prairie Traveler* (1859), 198, 207–8, 210–11, 213–14.

105. See, e.g., Carpenter, I Crossed the Plains in the 50's.

106. Geer, "Occasional Address" (1880), 38.

107. May 14, 1850, entry, in Frink, *Journal of the Adventures of a Party of California Gold-Seekers*, 28. See also the Apr. 23, 1849, entry, in Giffen, ed., *The Diaries of Peter Decker* (1966), 57–58.

108. May 26, 1849, entry, in The Diary of Bernard J. Reid, Esq. (typescript), 12–13; Aug. 18, 1849, entry, in Mattes, ed., "Alexander Ramsay's Gold Rush Diary," 460; June 1, 1849, entry of Vincent Geiger, in Potter, ed., *Trail to California*, 93; June 24, 1849, entry, in Austin, Diary (typescript), 24; July 7, 1850, entry of Adam Mercer Brown, in Kiefer, ed., "Over Barren Plains and Rock-bound Mountains" (1972), 23; July 22, 1852, entry, in Gage, Diary (typescript), 15; Munkres, "The Plains Indian Threat," 213–14.

109. Hastings, *Emigrants' Guide*, 149; Ware, *Emigrants' Guide*, 13.

110. May 20, 21, 23, 25, 27, 1850, entries, in McKinstry, Diary, 20–27.

111. May 9, 1850, entry, in McBride, Journal, 17.

112. Hastings, *Emigrants' Guide*, 150; Platt and Slater, *Travelers' Guide*, xviii.

113. Keller, *A Trip across the Plains* (1851, 1955 reprint), 4, 20–22.

114. Ferris, *Utah and the Mormons* (1854), 13–14.

115. Lynde to Maj. F. J. Porter, Oct. 24, 1859, in *Report of the Secretary of War*, 1859, 36 Cong., 1 Sess., Sen. Ex. Doc. 2, Ser. 1024 (1860), 243; Howe to Acting Assistant Adjutant General, Hdqrs., Dept. of Utah, Aug. 22, 1860, in *Report of the Secretary of War*, 1860, 36 Cong., 2 Sess., Sen. Ex. Doc. 1, Ser. 1079 (1860), 101.

116. June 17, Aug. 23, 1843, entries, in Winton, ed., "William T. Newby's Diary" (1939), 223, 231.

117. Reed to Mary C. Keyes, July 12, 1846, in "The Miller-Reed Diary," in Morgan, ed., *Overland in 1846*, 1:278; [Curry] to St. Louis *Reveille*, July 12, 1846, reprinted in Morgan, Overland in 1846, 2:610; letter of H. Warren, July 4, 1847, in St. Louis *Daily Union*, Aug. 17, 1847, in Morgan, The Mormons and the Far West.

118. John T. Milner to Lilly E. Milner, May 18, 1849, in "John T. Milner's Trip to California" (1958), 523. One apparent reason why forty-niners met as few Indians as they did was because the traders reportedly spread the rumor among Indian tribes that overlanders were fleeing from the smallpox and that many had it—which caused many natives to absent themselves from the trails. June 14, 1849, entry of Joseph Waring Berrien, in Hinckley and Hinckley, eds., "Overland from St. Louis to the California Gold Field" (1960), 318; Henry Page to Mary A. Page, July 2, 1849, in Page, *Wagons West*, 159.

119. Letter of "Observer," May 21, 1850, in St. Louis *Daily Missouri Republican*, June 15, 1850; Powers, "A Woman's Overland Journal to California" (Oct., 1950), 2. See also Jackman, ed., "After the Covered Wagons" (1962), 10; Sacramento *Union*, n.d., in San Francisco *Daily Alta California*, Aug. 7, 1854.

120. Bekeart, ed., "Journal of Pierson Barton Reading," *passim;* Parrish, "Crossing the Plains in 1844" (1899), *passim;* Palmer, *Journal of Travels, passim.*

121. Bryant, *What I Saw in California* (1849), *passim.*

122. Sept. 27, 1850, entry, in Coke, *A Ride over the Rocky Mountains*, 282; June 14, 1852, entry, in Barry, ed., "Overland to the Gold Fields of California" (1942), 252–53.

123. Guill, Diary (typescript), *passim.*

124. Tice to his sister Ann, Oct. 5, 1851, in Santee, ed., "Letters of John R. Tice" (1936), 25–26. See also John Coleman to his brother, Oct. 15, 1854, in Coleman-Hayter Letters (MSS and typescripts).

125. Letter of S. M. Gilmore, Nov. 11, 1843, in *Western Journal*, Mar. 15, 1845, reprinted in "Documents" (1903), 283.

126. July 8, 1851, entry, in Johnson, Diary, 65–66.

127. Keil to Henry Conrad Finck, June 25, 1855, Keil to his brothers and sisters, June [July] 12, 1855, Keil to brothers and sisters in Christ, Oct. 13, 1855, in "From Bethel, Missouri, to Aurora, Oregon," 26–36; Simon, "Wilhelm Keil and Communist Colonies" (1935), 130–32, 134.

128. Letter of M. M. M., June 10, 1843, in St. Louis *Daily Missouri Republican*, Aug. 7, 1843; B. F. E. Kellogg to Preston G. Gesford, July 5, 1846, in Morgan, ed., *Overland in 1846*, 2:580; June 7, 1850, entry, in Kelly, ed., "The Journal of Robert Chalmers" (1952), 40.

129. Henry Page to Mary A. Page, May 8, 1849, in Page, *Wagons West*, 116.

130. Sept. 21, 1852, entry, in Adams, "Crossing the Plains in 1852," 318; June 28, 1850, entry, in Payne, Saint Louis to San Francisco, 59.

131. Sept. 8, 1850, entry, in "Journal of A. W. Harlan" (1913), 60.

132. May 17, 1850, entry, in McKinstry, Diary, 19. Occasionally an unscrupulous emigrant retaliated in kind. See July 24, Aug. 3, 1859, entries of Melyer Casler, in *Journal Giving the Incidents of a Journey to California*, 35–36, 39–41, for the account of an emigrant who stole a pair of new moccasins from an Indian who had come to trade for them.

133. Albany *Atlas*, July 11, 1845.

134. May 15, 1850, entry, in "The Shoemaker Diary of 1850" ([1961]), 5.

135. Taylor to "Friend Hadley," June 4, 1853, in Watertown, Wis., *Chronicle*, July 13, 1853, reprinted in "Letters of S. H. Taylor to the Watertown Chronicle" (1921), 128.

136. Aug. 29, 1852, entry, in "Diary of E. W. Conyers," 493; Smith, ed., *The Narrative of Samuel Hancock* (1927), 22.

137. See, e.g., St. Louis *Daily Missouri Republican*, July 28, 1851.

138. June 29–July 2, 1847, entries, in "Diary of Mrs. Elizabeth Dixon Smith Geer," 157–58. It should be pointed out that animals often strayed or stampeded in foul weather or because of wild animals and that Indians were sometimes unfairly blamed for such losses.

139. Aug. 12, 1849, entry, in Howell, Diary, 39. Presumably this was the same man seen by the writer of the [Granville Overland Company] Journal on Aug. 13, 1849.

140. Delano, *Across the Plains and among the Diggings,* 105.

141. Joseph Cain to Dr. Willard Richards, Oct. 2, 1850, in Salt Lake City *Deseret News,* Oct. 5, 1850.

142. Garland Hurt to Brigham Young, Sept., 1856, in *Report of the Commissioner of Indian Affairs,* Nov. 22, 1856, 34 Cong., 3 Sess., House Ex. Doc. 98, Ser. 893 (1857), 781.

143. Sept. 6, 1849, entry, in Mattes and Kirk, eds., "From Ohio to California in 1849," 416.

144. See, e.g., the June 12, 1850, entry, in Steele, *Across the Plains in 1850,* ed. Schafer (1930), 62.

145. June 5, 1841, entry, in Bidwell, *Journey to California,* 4–5; Nunis, ed., *Josiah Belden: California Overland Pioneer* (1962), 38–39.

146. Hastings, *Emigrants' Guide,* xxvi, 11–17; Allen, comp., *Ten Years in Oregon* (1850), 155–57; Crawford, "Occasional Address" (1882), 13; Bancroft, *History of Nevada, Colorado, and Wyoming* (1890), 706–7.

147. June 10, 13, 1847, entries, in Hastings, Journal (typescript), 6–7.

148. Hockett, Experiences along the Oregon Trail in 1847 (MS and typescript), 5–6; Lyman, ed., "Reminiscences of Hugh Cosgrove," 259–60; Delano, *Across the Plains and among the Diggings,* 20; July 10, 1850, entry, in Grindell, Overland Narrative (typescript); July 8, 1850, entry, in "The Memoirs of Lemuel Clarke McKeeby" (1924), 62; May 7, July 13, 1850, entries, in Loomis, *A Journal of the Birmingham Emigrating Company,* ed. Ledyard (1928), 9–10, 85; San Francisco *Daily Alta California,* Nov. 30, 1854.

149. The only particularized treatment of either of these disasters of which the writer is aware is Peltier's "The Ward Massacre" (1965), 12–16.

150. See Brooks, *The Mountain Meadows Massacre* (1962), for a detailed and judicious examination of this sordid episode.

151. Moores, "Annual Address" (1905), 271. Russell, in his argumentative statistical analysis of the result of several centuries of white-Indian conflict—"How Many Indians Were Killed?" (1973), 42–47, 61–63—offers no estimates for the antebellum overland emigrations, although he intimates that there were few deaths. His apparent acceptance of the statement that "there were no Indian attacks along the Oregon Trail in 1849," however, is as erroneous as his inference that few Indians were killed by civilian travelers.

152. These are very tentative statistics based almost solely on contemporary sources, which are far too voluminous to list. The tabulation has been closely restricted to reasonably definite reports of deaths and eschews most of the rumored massacres and killings. Therefore it seems apparent that these are minimum figures subject only to upward revision, which the writer is certain will be necessary as additional data are discovered. Further, only overland emigrants as defined in this study are represented in this table—not Mormons, mail carriers, government teamsters, army troops, or West Coast residents who came out either as volunteers to patrol trails or simply to meet relatives and friends. A few specific annotations are necessary. The 1847 figure does not include those emigrants killed in the Whitman massacre, their overland trip having concluded when they opted to winter at Whitman's mission. Nor does the 1857 figure include the approximately 120 emigrants killed in the Mountain Meadows massacre, since the Indians, though very much involved, were not primarily responsible for the tragedy. The 1860 figure does not include those in the Otter–Van Orman massacre (see below) who died of starvation subsequent to the Indian attack, or were lost or kidnapped. And the writer has decided not to include the forty or more overlanders killed at Massacre Lake on the southern route to Oregon in 1850 mentioned by Mack in her *Nevada: A History of the State* (1936), 322–23. This because neither of the two very valuable contemporary government documents which endeavored to include every possible person killed, overlander or otherwise, on the trails into Oregon mentioned such an incident. See *Report of the Committee on Military Affairs* of the Oregon

Legislative Assembly, submitted by Nathaniel Ford, Jan. 14, 1859 (copy kindly provided me by Elizabeth Anne Johnson of the Library Association of Portland), and Maj. C. S. Drew to Brig. Gen. George Wright, Feb. 20, 1863, in *Report of the Commissioner of Indian Affairs, 1863*, 38 Cong., 1 Sess., House Ex. Doc. 1, Ser. 1182 (1863), 175–77. Finally, for those years where emigrant deaths seem clearly to have resulted from attacks by "white Indians," the number presumably dispatched by non-Indians is given in parentheses following the total yearly estimate. See pp. 193–97 below for a consideration of the "white Indian" problem.

153. It is probable that the Indian statistics given in Table 4 need to be revised upward. This because overlanders frequently were uncertain whether they had killed or only wounded fleeing Indians, and diarists were never as precise in recording numbers of Indian deaths as they were with those of their fellow travelers. Of course, it is quite possible that on occasion overlanders inflated certain battle statistics to better credit their courage and marksmanship. After all, persons capable of bragging that they had killed already deceased Indians whom they found "buried" in trees according to the custom of the plains tribes were certainly capable of inflating statistics, and one 1847 overlander had done just that, in what Hastings termed the "Battle of the Dead Indian in a Tree." See the June 20, 1847, entry in his Journal, 9.

154. That the only scholarly attempt to investigate the Indian danger on the Oregon Trail before the Civil War was confined to the region *east* of Fort Bridger is a perfect illustration of this prevalent opinion. See Munkres, "The Plains Indian Threat," 193–221.

155. Johnson and Winter, *Route across the Rocky Mountains*, 21–22.

156. Lockley, ed., "Recollections of Benjamin Franklin Bonney" (1923), 41–43.

157. Ibid., 43–44; Bancroft, *History of Nevada, Colorado, and Wyoming*, 60–61.

158. St. Louis *Daily Missouri Republican*, June 12, 1849, Jan. 18, 1850; Stansbury, *Exploration and Survey of the Valley of the Great Salt Lake* (1853), 97; Liberty *Weekly Tribune*, June 22, 1849.

159. Madsen, *The Bannock of Idaho* (1958), 73–74.

160. See Hopkins, *Life among the Paiutes*, 20–21, for an interesting account of the temptation of indiscriminate retaliation to the Paiute tribe. Passing emigrants, apparently during the gold rush era, shot at Paiutes fishing in the Humboldt River, killing six and wounding five. The tribe repeatedly pressed its chief, Truckee, for permission to attack the emigrants at the Humboldt Sink, but Truckee persistently refused to exact retribution from those innocent of the initial attack.

161. Ingersoll to Editor of Joliet, Ill., *Signal*, Sept. 10, 1847, in Ingersoll, *Overland to California in 1847*, ed. McMurtrie (1937), 38–39.

162. Aug. 14, 1849, entry, in McCall, *The Great California Trail*, 68; Aug. 16, 1850, entry, in *Journal of John Wood* (1852), 49; *The Overland Journey of Joseph Francl* (1968), 47. Sarah Winnemucca Hopkins was so frightened of passing emigrants who shot at Indians on sight that her mother once buried her during the day, protecting her face from the sun with sage bushes. Her Northern Paiute tribe endeavored to avoid the overland trail during the summer, crossing only during the night. Hopkins, *Life among the Paiutes*, 11–15; Josephy, "Indians in History" (1970), 70–71.

163. Young to James W. Denver, Sept. 12, 1857, in Denver, *Report of the Commissioner of Indian Affairs*, Nov. 30, 1857, 35 Cong., 1 Sess., House Ex. Doc. 2, Ser. 942 (1858), 598–99.

164. Holeman to L. Lea, Sept. 21, 1851, in *Report of the Commissioner of Indian Affairs, 1851*, 445.

165. Crawford, *Scenes of Earlier Days*, 44–46.

166. Liberty *Weekly Tribune*, Sept. 14, 1849.

167. Harrington, "Pioneer Reminiscences" (1936), 13; Stuart and Stuart, eds., "Calvin B. West of the Umpqua" (1960), 56–57; Liberty *Weekly Tribune*, Mar. 8, 1850.

168. Madsen, *The Bannock of Idaho*, 120–21; Paden, *The Wake of the Prairie Schooner* (1943), 23, 60.

169. Stewart, "The Prairie Schooner Got Them There" (1962), 101; Stewart, *The California Trail*, 322–24.

170. St. Louis *Daily Missouri Republican*, Oct. 7, 1851.

171. Col. John E. Ross to George L. Curry, Nov. 10, 1854, "Statement of W. T. Kershaw," Nov. 21, 1857, Joel Palmer to B. F. Dowell, Dec. 17, 1857, L. F. Grover, "Memo-

rial," all in U.S. Congress, *Protection Afforded by Volunteers of Oregon and Washington Territories* (1859), 15, 30, 41–42, 55–56.

172. The foregoing account is based principally on the following sources: R. R. Thompson to Joel Palmer, Sept. 3, 6, 1854, in George W. Manypenny, *Report of the Commissioner of Indian Affairs*, Nov. 25, 1854, 33 Cong., 2 Sess., House Ex. Doc. 1, Ser. 777 (1854), 486–88; U.S. President, *Indian Disturbances in California* (1856), 12–19; Portland *Weekly Oregonian*, Sept. 2, 23, Oct. 21, 1854; Frost, "Experience of a Pioneer" (1916), 123–24; Peltier, "The Ward Massacre," 12–16; Baydo, "Overland from Missouri to Washington Territory in 1854" (1971), 81.

173. In some accounts the date of the initial attack is given as September 13, and there is also some uncertainty as to the number of persons traveling with the train, forty-four being the most frequently mentioned figure in the reports of Indian agents and of army officers involved in the rescue. Other totals mentioned include forty-two and forty-six. Bancroft, *History of Oregon*, 2:69, specifies fifty-four, the highest estimate the writer has seen. Bancroft further contends that thirty-nine persons died, but both figures are inflated. In addition to Bancroft's account, the following sources have been most helpful in reconstructing the record of this tragedy: Edward R. Geary to A. B. Greenwood, Nov. 7, 1860, and G. W. Abbott to Edward R. Geary, Oct. 30, 1860, in U.S. Interior, *Depredations and Massacre by the Snake River Indians* (1861), 1–16; Capt. F. T. Dent to Capt. A. J. Hardie, Oct. 28, Nov. 8, 1860, and Col. G. Wright to Lt. Col. L. Thomas, Nov. 22, 1860, all in U.S. War Dept., *Indian Depredations in Oregon and Washington* (1861), 84–90; Col. G. Wright to Lt. Col. L. Thomas, Oct. 10, 1860, and Byron N. Davis to Capt. A. J. Smith, Oct. 3, 1860, in *Report of the Secretary of War*, 1860, 36 Cong., 2 Sess., Sen. Ex. Doc. 1, Ser. 1079 (1860), 126, 143–44; New York *Times*, Oct. 23, 1860; Portland *Weekly Oregonian*, Oct. 6, Nov. 10, 17, 1860.

174. Ibid., Dec. 22, 1860; Hart, "Rescue of a Frontier Boy" (1965), 51–52; Lt. Col. Reuben F. Maury to Gen. Benjamin Alvord, Sept. 22, 1862, and Col. P. Edward Connor to Lt. Col. R. C. Drum, Dec. 2, 1862, in *The War of the Rebellion* (1897), 167, 182–83. Major John Owen, who spent some time seeking the captives, believed that the hostility being demonstrated by the Bannock and Shoshoni tribes, who twelve years earlier had been friendly, was in retaliation for outrages perpetrated upon them by the white man. Madsen, *The Bannock of Idaho*, 123–25.

175. Thus it is presumed that the Indians were directly responsible for the deaths of twenty-three, while five more died of starvation.

176. Portland *Weekly Oregonian*, Oct. 27, 1860.

177. May 20, 1850, entry, in Rothwell, Journal and Letters (MSS and typescripts), 61. For examples of testimony that Indians were no more dangerous than renegade whites, see the May 11, 1850, entry, in Kelly, ed., "Journal of Robert Chalmers," 36; Byers, Journal (MS), 168; May 20, 1853, entry, in "Journal of Henry Allyn" (1924), 389, 424; May 31, 1853, entry, in Handsaker, Diary, 7. One 1852 emigrant suggested that there were so many "white Indians" infesting the route and that since "all the blacklegs in the universe" seemed to be trailing west, crime in the eastern states must surely be at low ebb. Lem. Newell Doty to Editors, June 29, 1852, in New York *Daily Tribune*, Oct. 14, 1852.

178. D. R. Eckels to J. Thompson, Sept. 23, 1859, in U.S. President, *Massacre at Mountain Meadows* (1860), 111.

179. Holeman to L. Lea, Sept. 21, 1851, in *Report of the Commissioner of Indian Affairs*, 1851, 445–46; Holeman to Brigham Young, Sept. 25, 1852, in *Report of the Commissioner of Indian Affairs*, 1852, 32 Cong., 2 Sess., House Ex. Doc. 1, Ser. 673 (1852), 442–43; Holeman to Young, Sept. 30, 1853, in *Report of the Commissioner of Indian Affairs*, 1853, 33 Cong., 1 Sess., Sen. Ex. Doc. 1, Ser. 690 (1854), 446–47.

180. Williams to Howe, May 22, 1860, in *Report of the Secretary of War*, 1860, 80.

181. Portland *Oregonian*, Dec. 27, 1851.

182. Whitman to James M. Porter, n.d., rec'd June 22, 1844, in Nixon, *How Marcus Whitman Saved Oregon* (1895), 320–21.

183. See, e.g., the May 13, 1850, entry, and William Renfro Rothwell to his parents, May 17, 1850, in Rothwell, Journal and Letters, 51, 58; Aug. 6, 1849, entry, in John F. Lewis, Diary (MS and typescript); May 22, Aug. 16, 1849, entries of John Edwin Banks, in Scamehorn, ed., *The Buckeye Rovers in the Gold Rush*, 9, 67; July 21, 1849, entry, in Delano,

Across the Plains and among the Diggings, 62; Aug. 8, 1850, entry, in Skinner, Diary. W. R. R. wrote Col. W. F. Switzler on May 21, 1850, from the Little Blue River, that one such thief had been caught and was undergoing trial. The letter was printed in *Weekly Statesman,* June 14, 1850, reprinted in Wyman, ed., *California Emigrant Letters* (1952), 101. Father Maurice Gailland at the Potawatomi mission in 1849 noted that many westbound gold rushers were passing "counterfeit money" as well as stealing horses. Burke, ed., "Early Years at St. Mary's Potawatomie Mission" (1953), 520.

184. Aug. 27, 1850, entry, in Paden, ed., *Journal of Madison Berryman Moorman,* 76; May 20, 1853, entry, in "Journal of Henry Allyn," 389; letter of "Cheyenne," June 5, 1850, in St. Louis *Daily Missouri Republican,* July 20, 1850; May 29, 1850, entry, in Clapp, *A Journal of Travels to and from California* (1851), 21.

185. May 11, 1850, entry, in Kelly, ed., "Journal of Robert Chalmers," 36.

186. See, e.g., Shaw, *Across the Plains in Forty-Nine,* 22; May 6, 1850, entry, in Payne, *Saint Louis to San Francisco,* 16–17; May 22, 1852, entry of John Hawkins Clark, in Barry, ed., "Overland to the Gold Fields of California," 239; Sacramento *Union,* n.d., in San Francisco *Daily Alta California,* Nov. 9, 1854.

187. Thomas Moseley, Jr., to Col. D. D. Mitchell, Sept. 1, 1852, in *Report of the Commissioner of Indian Affairs,* 1852, 369; J. L. Gillis to A. M. Robinson, Oct., 1860, in *Report of the Commissioner of Indian Affairs,* 1860, 36 Cong., 2 Sess., Sen. Ex. Doc. 1, Ser. 1078 (1861), 317.

188. Sept. 14, 1850, entry, in *Journal of John Wood,* 71; San Francisco *Daily Alta California,* Aug. 6, 1854.

189. One scrap of contrary evidence is found in the San Francisco *Daily Alta California,* Sept. 10, 1854, under the heading "Justice on the Plains," which reports on a trailside trial of a horse thief who "confessed that he was one of the many sent out by the Mormons, instructed to join with the Indians in the stealing of horses and stock."

190. Aug. 5, 1849, entry of John D. Lee, in Cleland and Brooks, eds., *A Mormon Chronicle* (1955), 1:112.

191. Young to Luke Lea, May 28, 1852, in Morgan, ed., "Washakie and the Shoshoni, Part II" (1954), 73–75. See also Anderson, *Desert Saints* (1942), 127–28.

192. Young, "Emigration," in Salt Lake City *Deseret News,* July 13, 1854; San Francisco *Daily Alta California,* Oct. 29, 1854.

193. A man named Hetherly was identified in 1852 as a member of a "systematically organized band of thieves" operating between Salt Lake City and the Carson Valley. See San Francisco *Daily Alta California,* June 27, 1852.

194. Portland *Weekly Oregonian,* Oct. 15, 1859; Col. A. S. Johnston to Lt. Col. Alonzo Thomas, Nov. 2, 1859, and Maj. J. Lynde to Maj. F. J. Porter, Oct. 24, Aug. 20, 1859, in *Report of the Secretary of War,* 1859, 231, 236, 242–43; Anton W. Tjader, M.D., James R. Shepherd, Oscar F. D. Fairbanks, and George Everett, "Statement," in U.S. President, *Massacre at Mountain Meadows,* 108–9; July 28, 29, 1859, entries, in Hays, ed., "Diary of Taylor N. Snow" (1932), 205–6.

195. Nelson Miltimore, "Statement," Sept. 20, 1859, and Thomas Wright and William Jones, "Statement," Oct. 21, 1859, in U.S. President, *Massacre at Mountain Meadows,* 113–14, 119; Salt Lake City *Deseret News,* Sept. 21, 1859, quoted in Madsen, "Shoshoni-Bannock Marauders on the Oregon Trail" (1967), 8–9.

196. Wright and Jones, "Statement," 119–20.

197. Lorenzo Suberr, "Statement," Sept. 19, 1859, in U.S. President, *Massacre at Mountain Meadows,* 113.

198. Lt. Col. M. S. Howe to 1st Lt. B. H. Robertson, Sept. 29, 1860, in *Report of the Secretary of War,* 1860, 103–4.

199. Holeman to Young, Sept. 25, 1852, in *Report of the Commissioner of Indian Affairs,* 1852, 442; Holeman to Young, Sept. 30, 1853, in *Report of the Commissioner of Indian Affairs,* 1853, 446–47; Morgan, *The Humboldt* (1943), 213–14. For an account of an 1855 visit to one of these establishments operated by unscrupulous "traders," see Remy and Brenchley, *A Journey to Great-Salt-Lake City* (1861), 1:70.

200. July 26, 1852, entry, in Paxson, ed., "T. Turnbull's Travels" (1914), 203.

201. Aug. 29, 1849, entry, in "The Diary of Dr. Jonathan Clark" (Aug. 8, 1925), 3; Aug.

6, 7, 1849, entries, in Hale, "Diary of a Trip to California" (1925), 101–3, 109; St. Joseph *Gazette,* Jan. 11, 1850; Marysville *Daily Evening Herald,* Aug. 13, Sept. 5, 1853.

202. Maxwell, *Crossing the Plains* (1915), 55, 62–72; Stewart, *The California Trail,* 314–15.

203. Maxwell, *Crossing the Plains,* 116–59; Stewart, *The California Trail,* 315–17.

204. Other reconsiderations of these traditional stereotypes are certain to accrue from the burgeoning popular and scholarly interest in Indian history. See Munkres, "Indian-White Contact before 1870" (1971), 439–73, for one such recent assessment.

CHAPTER SIX: THE FEDERAL GOVERNMENT

1. Portland *Weekly Oregonian*, Nov. 24, 1860. See also ibid., Nov. 10, 1860.

2. Bender, "The Soldier in the Far West" (1939), 161. See also Utley, *Frontiersmen in Blue* (1967), 19.

3. *Report of the Secretary of War*, 1860, 36 Cong., 2 Sess., Sen. Ex. Doc. 1, Ser. 1079 (1860), 216–17, 224–29. The four were the Department of the West, hdqrs. St. Louis; Department of Utah, hdqrs. Camp Floyd; Department of Oregon, hdqrs. Fort Vancouver; Department of California, hdqrs. San Francisco.

4. U.S. Congress, *Petition of a Number of the Citizens of the State of Missouri* (1840), 1–2; U.S. Congress, *Petition of a Number of Citizens of Kentucky* (1840), 1.

5. *Report from the Secretary of War . . . in Relation to the Establishment of a Line of Military Posts* (1840), 1–3; *Report of the Secretary of War*, 1841, 27 Cong., 2 Sess., Sen. Doc. 1, Ser. 395 (1841), 61–62.

6. Tyler, "First Annual Message," Dec. 7, 1841, "Second Annual Message," Dec. 6, 1842, "Third Annual Message," Dec., 1843, "Fourth Annual Message," Dec. 3, 1844, all in Richardson, comp., *A Compilation of the Messages and Papers of the Presidents* (1903), 4:87, 202, 258, 337–38; Polk, "First Annual Message," Dec. 2, 1845, in ibid., 396.

7. U.S. Congress, Committee on Military Affairs, *Military Posts on the Route to Oregon* (1845), 3; Dorris, "Federal Aid to Oregon Trail prior to 1850" (1929), 317–18. See Chap. 1 above, p. 47, for mention of a number of newspaper editorials demanding speedy action.

8. Kearny, "Report of a Summer Campaign to the Rocky Mountains, &c., in 1845," in *Report of the Secretary of War*, 1845, 29 Cong., 1 Sess., Sen. Pub. Doc. 1, Ser. 470 (1846), 212.

9. Beers, "The Army and the Oregon Trail to 1846" (1937), 351–52; Hughes, "The First Dragoons on the Western Frontier" (1970), 124–25.

10. "The Expedition of Major Clifton Wharton in 1844" (1925), 272–305; Carleton, *The Prairie Logbooks*, ed. Pelzer (1943), 87–89.

11. Prucha, *The Sword of the Republic* (1969), 381; Hughes, "The First Dragoons on the Western Frontier," 135; St. Louis *Daily Missouri Republican*, July 3, 1845; Carleton, *Prairie Logbooks*, 180–81, 200, 226, 242, 245–52, 260; Kearny, "Report of a Summer Campaign to the Rocky Mountains," 210–13; June 5, July 1, 1845, entries, in "Diary of Jesse Harritt" (1914), 509, 513.

12. McMillen to John Wentworth, June 27, 1845, in Wooster, Ohio, *Democrat*, Sept. 25, 1845.

13. Kearny, "Report of a Summer Campaign to the Rocky Mountains," 211. See also St. Louis *Daily Missouri Republican*, Sept. 1, 1845.

14. Thornton, *Oregon and California in 1848* (1849), 1:67–68.

15. *The Statutes at Large and Treaties of the United States* (1851), 9:13–14; May 21, 1846, entry, in Quaife, ed., *The Diary of James K. Polk* (1910), 1:412.

16. Frazer, *Forts of the West* (1965), 56. The passage of the 1846 legislation by no means terminated the army's continuing reassessment of the most appropriate military protective policies. See Smith, "The Army and Western Transportation" (1960), 301–2.

17. Barry, *The Beginning of the West* (1972), 586–87; Watkins, "History of Fort Kearny" (1911), 231–32; Mattes, *The Great Platte River Road* (1969), 118; Holtz, "Old Fort Kearny—1846–1848" (1972), 44–55.

18. The correct spelling of either fort is *Kearny*—although overlanders, army officials, historians, and residents of Kearney, Nebraska, have tended to believe otherwise! Watkins, "History of Fort Kearny," 231–32, 241–43; Mattes, *Great Platte River Road*, 118, 167–69; Barry, *Beginning of the West*, 708, 712–13, 755–56.

19. Ibid., 782, 785–86.

20. The movements of these various companies have been pieced together from several sources, the most helpful being Barry, *Beginning of the West*, 851–53, 872, 874. Also useful was Settle, ed., *The March of the Mounted Riflemen* (1940), 34–35, nn. 36, 38; Mattes, *Great Platte River Road*, 171–73; Victor, "The First Oregon Cavalry" (1902), 124.

21. Lockley, ed., "Reminiscences of William H. Packwood" (1915), 42–50.

22. May 18, 1849, entry, in "The Diary of George Gibbs," in Settle, ed., *March of the Mounted Riflemen*, 286; Aug. 2, 1849, entry, in "The Journal of Major Osborne Cross," in ibid., 160.

23. May 20, 1849, entry, in "Diary of George Gibbs," 290; May 24, 26, 1849, entries, in "Journal of Major Osborne Cross," 44, 48; Dorris, "Federal Aid to Oregon Trail prior to 1850," 324–25.

24. Frazer, *Forts of the West*, 87; U.S. Interior, *Report of the Chief Engineer* (1849), 225; May 28, 1849, entry of Elijah Bryan Farnham, in Mattes and Kirk, eds., "From Ohio to California in 1849" (1950), 305; June 19, 1849, entry, in Stansbury, *Exploration and Survey of the Valley of the Great Salt Lake* (1853), 30; May 24, 1849, entry, in Hale, "Diary of a Trip to California" (1925), 65; May 31, 1849, entry, in Murphy, Diary (MS).

25. Barry, *Beginning of the West*, 865–66; Mattes, *Great Platte River Road*, 173.

26. June 25, 1849, entry, in "Diary of George Gibbs," 317; June 9, 16, 1849, entries, in "Journal of Major Osborne Cross," 75, 90; Hafen and Young, *Fort Laramie and the Pageant of the West* (1938), 140–43, 155–56; Barry, *Beginning of the West*, 851–53; Victor, "The First Oregon Cavalry," 125. See also Hoffman, Journal (MS and typescript translation), 11–12.

27. Lucius Fairchild to J. C. Fairchild and family, June 5, 1849, in Schafer, ed., *California Letters of Lucius Fairchild* (1931), 31. Biddle's comments are quoted by Morgan, "The Ferries of the Forty-Niners" (1959), 22–23.

28. James Lyne to Henry Lyne, July 23, 1849, in Lyne, Letters (MSS and typescripts); July 10, 1849, entry, in "Journal of Major Osborne Cross," 130. See also Dorris, "Federal Aid to Oregon Trail prior to 1850," 324–25. The 200-dollar reward the army offered for each deserter captured by emigrants doubtless was an important factor in the apprehension of many deserters. See the July 10, 1849, entry of James F. Wilkins, in McDermott, ed., *An Artist on the Overland Trail* (1968), 54; Aug. 3, 1849, entry, in Mann, Diary (typescript of MS), 34.

29. Frazer, *Forts of the West*, 44–45.

30. Aug. 13, 1849, entry, in "Journal of Major Osborne Cross," 181; Barry, *Beginning of the West*, 853.

31. Utley, *Frontiersmen in Blue*, 98; Frazer, *Forts of the West*, 127, 176; Knuth, " 'Picturesque' Frontier: The Army's Fort Dalles" (1966), 297–98. The site chosen was where Oregon volunteers had earlier constructed a stockade following the tragedy at the Whitman mission in 1847.

32. Fort Kearny boasted two ancillary towns, both dating from 1858. Valley City or Dogtown was eight miles east of the fort but never amounted to much more than a few shacks; Kearny City or Dobytown was two miles west and apparently became quite a swinging city. Both locations served also as stage stations and outfitting and supply posts but dealt liberally in grogshops and gambling dens (Mattes, *Great Platte River Road*, 216–20). "Laramie City" was one of several trading-post enclaves which appeared adjacent to that famous fort (Burton, *The City of the Saints*, ed. Brodie [1963], 97), while by 1856 Dalles City encompassed fifty-two houses, of which, surprisingly, only two were billiard saloons. By 1859 there were approximately 1,000 residents (Knuth, " 'Picturesque' Frontier," 22–27). Most notorious was probably Fairfield's "Frogtown" or "Dobieville" section adjacent to Utah's Camp Floyd (see p. 210 below). Almost immediately after the post was established in 1858, seventeen saloons complete with thieves, gamblers, and prostitutes were open for business. Shootings and murders were not infrequent (Alexander and Arrington, "Camp in the Sagebrush" [1966], 6–10). In spite of their racy reputations, however, supplies, equipment, and honest citizenry were also found in these towns.

33. Frazer, *Forts of the West*, 86; Mattes, *Great Platte River Road*, 329–35; St. Louis *Daily Missouri Republican*, Dec. 15, 1855; June 6, 1859, entry, in Norton, Diary (photocopy of typescript), 28.

34. Sept. 12, 1858, entry, in Lowe, *Five Years a Dragoon*, ed. Russell (1965), 250; Coutant, *The History of Wyoming* (1899), 367–68.

35. An excellent study of the entire episode is Furniss, *The Mormon Conflict, 1850–1859* (1960).

36. Frazer, *Forts of the West*, 178; Furniss, *The Mormon Conflict*, 148–49. Overlander John W. Powell estimated on July 11, 1859, that 400 troops were located at Fort Bridger. Powell, Diary (typescript), 20.

37. Furniss, *The Mormon Conflict*, 202–5; Alexander and Arrington, "Camp in the Sagebrush," 3–21; Horace Greeley's dispatch of July 21, 1859, in Greeley, *An Overland Journey from New York to San Francisco*, ed. Duncan (1964), 207–9. For six months prior to its July 27, 1861, demise, Camp Floyd was called Fort Crittenden, since its namesake, Secretary of War John B. Floyd, had joined the Conferedate forces. Frazer, *Forts of the West*, 166.

38. Utley, *Frontiersmen in Blue*, 105, 175–210. Most of these forts were established in the mid-1850s, although the Cayuse War, an outgrowth of the Whitman massacre, had spanned the 1847–50 period, and had been pursued by local volunteers. Additional major confrontations included the Rogue River War of 1853 and again, in even more serious fashion, in 1855–56, and finally, the 1858 Indian War.

39. S. Cooper to John B. Floyd, Nov. 20, 1860, in *Report of the Secretary of War*, 1860, 190–91; Frazer, *Forts of the West*, 92.

40. The calculation, of course, incorporates all western arenas and not only those clashes arising from the protection of overland emigrants on the South Pass routes. Lowe, *Five Years a Dragoon*, vii–viii.

41. June 13, 14, 1849, entries, in Stansbury, *Exploration and Survey*, 26–27; letter of "Pawnee," June 10, 1849, in St. Louis *Missouri Republican*, July 6, 1849; St. Louis *Daily Missouri Republican*, Nov. 19, 24, 1849; Barry, *Beginning of the West*, 891–92.

42. Lowe, *Five Years a Dragoon*, 31–35. One Pawnee band had not initially responded to the summons to appear for talks, and Chilton sent troops out after them.

43. Letter of "Cheyenne," Apr. 9, 1850, in St. Louis *Daily Missouri Republican*, June 1, 1850.

44. St. Louis *Daily Missouri Republican*, Feb. 6, 1850; letter of "Cheyenne," July 8, 1850, in ibid., Aug. 9, 1850; Barry, *Beginning of the West*, 946. Dragoon Sergeant Percival Lowe indicated that he and the bugler made over $50 at or near Fort Kearny by selling emigrant "guides" based upon Captain Howard Stansbury's map and table of distances to inquiring overlanders. Lowe, *Five Years a Dragoon*, 35.

45. Barry, *Beginning of the West*, 980–82, 1000–1001, 1011–1012, 1033, 1045; Lowe, *Five Years a Dragoon*, 37. The various military companies, Indian officials, and others in attendance at the council returned to Leavenworth in mid-October.

46. May 19, 1852, entry, in Wayman, Journal and Letters (photocopies of MSS); May 24, 1852, entry of Richard Owen Hickman, in Phillips, ed., "'Dick's Works'" (1929), 245; New York *Daily Tribune*, July 8, 1852; June 12, 1852, entry, in Anable, Journal (MS).

47. Barry, *Beginning of the West*, 1108, 1113, 1126–27; Ferris, *The Mormons at Home* (1856), 54–55.

48. Hafen and Young, *Fort Laramie*, 209–10; June 16, 1853, entry, in *Diary of Basil Nelson Longsworth* (1927), 18; June 17, 18, 1853, entries, in "Journal of Henry Allyn" (1924), 401–2; June 15, 1853, entry, in McClure, Diary (reproduced), 27.

49. Barry, *Beginning of the West*, 1170–71. The Weston, Mo., *Reporter* of June 30, 1853, reported the mission, and the troops did return in mid-October.

50. Mantor, "Fort Kearny and the Westward Movement" (1948), 189–90; Mattes, *Great Platte River Road*, 225.

51. Barry, *Beginning of the West*, 1218–19; San Francisco *Daily Alta California*, Oct. 19, 1854. The journey to California was concluded the following spring.

52. The best treatment of this unhappy episode is McCann, "The Grattan Massacre" (1956), 1–25. See also Hafen and Young, *Fort Laramie*, 222–34. The St. Louis *Intelligencer* immediately bemoaned the stupidity of the officers' actions—"The whole affair was a horrible mistake, and the consequences hereafter will be grave." Quoted in San Francisco *Daily Alta California*, Nov. 8, 1854.

53. John E. Wool to Lt. Col. L. Thomas, Sept. 14, 1854, in "Papers Accompanying Report of the Secretary of War, of December 23, 1854," 33 Cong., 2 Sess., Sen. Ex. Doc. 16, Ser. 751 (1855), 104; Wool to Thomas, Oct. 31, 1854, including a copy of Major Haller's field return with a history of his operations, in ibid., 120–21; Peltier, "The Ward Massacre" (1965), 15–16.

464

54. June 23, July 5–9, 1855, entries of Capt. John B. S. Todd, in Mattison, ed., "The Harney Expedition against the Sioux" (1962), 103, 105, and Mattison's introductory note, 92.

55. Mattes, *Great Platte River Road*, 313.

56. Ibid., 311–31; "Report of General Harney, Commander of the Sioux Expedition," in *Report of the Secretary of War*, 1855, 34 Cong., 1 Sess., Sen. Ex. Doc. 1, Pt. 2, Ser. 811 (1855), 49–51; Utley, *Frontiersmen in Blue*, 111–12. With the army sometimes reprimanded for its increasing willingness in the 1850s to hold entire tribes accountable for the actions of a few, Harney was careful to point out in his report that his troops had found, on the warriors and in the camp, clear evidence that these Indians had been involved in the Grattan massacre, the mail party killings, and other depredations upon emigrants.

57. Bandel, *Frontier Life in the Army*, ed. Bieber (1932), 36–37; Mattison, ed., "The Harney Expedition against the Sioux," 130; Hoopes, "Thomas S. Twiss, Indian Agent" (1933), 358–59. Mattes, who absolves Harney's forces from wanton killing of women and children during the battle, contends that Harney's victory so stunned the Sioux nation that they remained "relatively peaceful" throughout the remainder of the 1850s. *Great Platte River Road*, 328.

58. Portland *Weekly Oregonian*, June 30, Aug. 25, 1855; John E. Wool to L. Thomas, Sept. 4, 1855, in U.S. War Dept., *Indian Disturbances in California* (1856), 11; Wool to Editors of Washington *National Intelligencer*, Apr. 2, 1856, in Portland *Weekly Oregonian*, June 21, 1856.

59. Portland *Weekly Oregonian*, Sept. 15, 1855.

60. Wool to Thomas, Sept. 4, 1855, in U.S. War Dept., *Indian Disturbances in California*, 11; Wool to Editors of Washington *National Intelligencer*, Apr. 2, 1856.

61. Hafen and Hafen, eds., *Relations with the Indians of the Plains* (1959), 15–18; Thomas S. Twiss to Commissioner of Indian Affairs, Sept. 12, 1856, in George W. Manypenny, *Report of the Commissioner of Indian Affairs*, Nov. 22, 1856, 34 Cong., 3 Sess., House Ex. Doc. 1, Ser. 893 (1857), 638.

62. Hafen and Young, *Fort Laramie*, 280–83; Hafen and Hafen, eds., *Relations with the Indians of the Plains*, 18–20; Sumner to Assistant Adjutant General, May 31, Aug. 9, 1857, in ibid., 24, 27–28.

63. Harney to L. Thomas, Aug. 22, 1857, in ibid., 146.

64. Portland *Weekly Oregonian*, May 16, 1857. Westbound travelers in 1858 happily discovered that the army had bridged several streams and rivers, among them the Bear and Weber rivers, and even had troops stationed at the Ham's Fork bridge. St. Louis *Daily Missouri Republican*, July 28, 1858; Aug. 22, 1858, entry, in Ackley, "Across the Plains in 1858" (1941), 207.

65. Bandel, *Frontier Life in the Army*, 50; St. Louis *Daily Missouri Republican*, July 9, 1858.

66. De Smet to "Reverend and Dear Father," Nov. 1, 1859, in Chittenden and Richardson, eds., *Life, Letters and Travels of Father Pierre-Jean De Smet* (1905), 2:723.

67. Bandel, *Frontier Life in the Army*, 55–56; A. S. Johnston to Irvin McDowell, Oct. 12, 1858, in *Report of the Secretary of War*, 1858, 35 Cong., 2 Sess., Sen. Ex. Doc. 1, Ser. 975 (1859), 158; McGregor to Editor, Sept. 3, 1858, in St. Louis *Daily Missouri Republican*, Oct. 2, 1858.

68. The following account of army protective activity on the California Trail in 1859 is based upon Maj. Isaac Lynde to F. J. Porter, Oct. 24, 1859, Porter to Lynde, June 5, 1859, Porter to 2nd Lt. E. Gay, Aug. 6, 1859, Porter's special orders of Aug. 14, 1859, Gay to Porter, Aug. 15, 1859, Lynde to Porter, Aug. 20, Sept. 10, 1859, all in *Report of the Secretary of War*, 1859, 36 Cong., 1 Sess., Sen. Ex. Doc. 2, Ser. 1024 (1860), 240–44, 189–90, 213–14, 218, 219–20, 236, 238–39.

69. See Chap. 5 above, p. 195, for additional details.

70. An account of the attack on the Nelson Miltimore train by what probably were "white Indians" is given in Chap. 5 above, pp. 195–96. The Mormon allegations are traced in Madsen, "Shoshoni-Bannock Marauders on the Oregon Trail" (1967), 6–10. Madsen, who recognizes that Mormons were not the most reliable sources when it came to discussing the U.S. Army, nonetheless feels there probably was truth to their charges.

71. Wallen to Capt. A. Pleasonton, Aug. 16, Oct. 1, 1859, in *Report of the Secretary of War*, 1859, 116, 120; Bancroft, *History of Oregon* (1886–88), 2:463–65. Minor Pawnee distur-

bances in what was now becoming settled area in Nebraska Territory during the summer of 1859 also resulted in a combined volunteer and army force overawing the offending band. Warner, "Indians Challenge the Nebraska Territorial Government" (1970), 54–55. Undermanned, Fort Kearny had been unable to supply the necessary troops to protect the threatened area near the Elkhorn River.

72. Captain Sturgis's command of 350 men suffered only two or three injuries in killing about twenty-five Indians on the Kansas River south of Fort Kearny in late July or early August. Burton, *City of the Saints*, 49; Portland *Weekly Oregonian*, Sept. 15, 1860.

73. S. Cooper to John B. Floyd, Nov. 20, 1860, in *Report of the Secretary of War*, 1860, 190–91; Mack, *Nevada: A History of the State* (1936), 299–311; Bancroft, *History of Nevada, Colorado, and Wyoming* (1890), 207–18; Morgan, *The Humboldt* (1943), 274–77. See also Miller, ed., "The Pyramid Lake Indian War of 1860" (Sept., Nov., 1957), 37–53, 98–113.

74. A. Cumming to Bvt. Col. C. F. Smith, Apr. 12, 1860, Lt. L. A. Williams to Weed, May 26, 1860, 1st Lt. D. D. Perkins to Williams, June 13, 1860, Weed to Williams, Aug. 12, 1860, Sgt. George L. Bishop to Perkins, Aug. 12, 1860, all in *Report of the Secretary of War*, 1860, 70, 77–78, 87–88, 94–95, 99–100, 205; Burton, *City of the Saints*, 516–17, 523, 526.

75. Williams to Howe, May 22, 1860, Howe to Acting Assistant Adjutant General, Aug. 22, 1860, Howe to 1st Lt. B. H. Robertson, Sept. 29, 1860, all in *Report of the Secretary of War*, 1860, 80–81, 100–101, 102–5. Howe, who had also been told to direct all emigrant parties to be well organized and constantly ready to defend themselves, was so piqued when one party left a man wounded by an Indian at Howe's depot hospital that he commented, "As usual, with ninety-nine one-hundredths of emigrants, their fire-arms, except revolvers, were in the wagons, some not loaded."

76. Knuth, "Alexander Piper's Reports and Journal" (1968), 223, 230–39; Piper to Maj. W. W. Mackall, Sept. 5, Oct. 3, 1860, in ibid., 251–55.

77. Col. G. Wright to Lt. Col. L. Thomas, Sept. 3, Oct. 10, 1860, in *Report of the Secretary of War*, 1860, 126, 141; Bancroft, *History of Oregon*, 2:465–69; Portland *Weekly Oregonian*, Oct. 27, 1860. The foreboding accounts of the Otter–Van Orman tragedy resulted in immediate demands by western congressmen for an accelerated program of federal protective aid to overlanders. From 1861 through 1864 Congress appropriated $145,000 for armed escorts of up to 100 men, who traveled to Oregon with the yearly emigration. See Fendall, "Medorem Crawford and the Protective Corps" (1971), 55–77, for an account of this activity.

78. For example, Charles Howard Crawford, an 1851 emigrant, recollected that "the emigration expected to have protection from the forts, but they were doomed to disappointment, and the savages did as they pleased," while an 1853 Oregon overlander specified four additional locations where forts were needed—Bear River, Fort Hall, Fort Boise or Grande Ronde, and Salmon Falls. Crawford, *Scenes of Earlier Days* (1898, 1962 reprint), 30; Dr. Thomas White to Samuel Porter Williams, Apr. 19, 1853, in Winther and Thornbrough, eds., *To Oregon in 1852* (1964), 30. See Chap. 2 above, pp. 85–87, for the West Coast newspaper demands.

79. Letter from "An Emigrant," Aug. 1, 1849, in New York *Daily Tribune*, Sept. 11, 1849; "Xenia" to the *Tribune*, Sept. 13, 1852, in ibid., Oct. 14, 1852; St. Louis *Daily Missouri Republican*, Apr. 20, 1849. Perhaps the most elaborate proposal was advanced by Henry O'Reilly, who wanted to line the trail with stockades twenty miles apart from Missouri to California. At each stockade twenty dragoons would be stationed, some of whom would ride daily between their outposts, thus providing a daily postal service, protection, and comfort for emigrants—and protection for O'Reilly's telegraph line, which was also to be part of the package. U.S. Congress, *Memorial of Henry O'Reilly* (1852), 1–34.

80. A good review of early frontier Indian policy is provided in Mattison, "The Indian Frontier on the Upper Missouri to 1865" (1958), 241–66. See also Guthrie and Gerald, "Upper Missouri Agency" (1941), 47–56; Schusky, "The Upper Missouri Indian Agency" (1971), 249–69.

81. Barry, *Beginning of the West*, 271–72, 797–98, 1015–16; W. Medill to W. L. Marcy, Nov. 30, 1846, in *Report of the Commissioner of Indian Affairs*, 1848, 30 Cong., 2 Sess., House Ex. Doc. 1, Ser. 537 (1848), 391–92; Trenholm and Carley, *The Shoshonis* (1964), 114–15.

82. Neil, "The Territorial Governor as Indian Superintendent" (1956), 213. Although Congress authorized the separation of the two offices in 1857, the practice ended only gradually, the last combination terminating in 1871.

83. Ibid., 236–37; Morgan, "The Administration of Indian Affairs in Utah" (1948), 383–409; Larson, "Brigham Young and the Indians," in Ferris, ed., *The American West* (1963), 176–87.

84. Lea to A. H. H. Stuart, Nov. 30, 1852, in *Report of the Commissioner of Indian Affairs, 1852*, 32 Cong., 2 Sess., House Ex. Doc. 1, Ser. 673 (1852), 293–94.

85. Twiss to A. B. Greenwood, Aug. 16, 1859, in *Report of the Commissioner of Indian Affairs, 1859*, 36 Cong., 1 Sess., Sen. Ex. Doc. 2, Pt. 1, Ser. 1023 (1860), 498–99.

86. Lea to Stuart, Nov. 30, 1852, in *Report of the Commissioner of Indian Affairs, 1852*, 294; Utley, *Frontiersmen in Blue*, 347; Munkres, "Indian-White Contact before 1870" (1971), 454–56. For a discussion of the differing understandings Indians and whites had of the function of annuity payments and "presents," see Schusky, "The Upper Missouri Indian Agency," 262.

87. See Chap. 5 above, pp. 167–70, for a consideration of Indian demands for compensation for the damage overland travel was inflicting upon their land and food supply during the 1840s. Interestingly enough, the 1840 petition that forty-four Indiana citizens sent to Congress seeking an improved federal road from the Missouri to Oregon and liberal land grants in Oregon also sought "the immediate appointment of agents to treat with the several tribes of Indians, through whose acknowledged territory said road may pass, for a quantity of land sufficient to construct, support, and keep in repair, a road from the west line of Missouri to Oregon, and to purchase of the Indians of the Oregon territory the lands designed to be settled, and to form treaties of peace, amity, and commerce with them." U.S. Congress, *Petition of a Number of Citizens of Indiana* (1840), 1–2.

88. Benton to Frémont, Mar. 20, 1843, in Jackson and Spence, eds., *The Expeditions of John Charles Frémont* (1970–73), 1:164–65.

89. Hafen, "Thomas Fitzpatrick and the First Indian Agency" (1928), 375–77; W. Medill to W. L. Marcy, Nov. 30, 1846 [1848], in *Report of the Commissioner of Indian Affairs, 1848*, 398–99; letter of T. J. T., Aug. 22, 1848, in St. Louis *Daily Missouri Republican*, Sept. 8, 1848. The 1848 treaty is conveniently reprinted in Kappler, ed., *Indian Treaties, 1778–1883* (1904, 1972 reprint), 571–72. For Lane's Oregon admonitions see Coan, "The First Stage of the Federal Indian Policy" (1921), 49–50. Prucha's summary account of "American Indian Policy in the 1840s," in Clark, ed., *The Frontier Challenge* (1971), 81–110, emphasizes that the main interest of government officials concerned with Indian affairs during the decade of the 1840s was in culturally transforming the Indians previously removed to the West. Prucha's review of the decade makes no mention of governmental acknowledgment of Indian concerns over the problems caused by the westbound emigrants.

90. Hafen, "Thomas Fitzpatrick and the First Indian Agency," 378–81; Hafen and Young, *Fort Laramie*, 177–96; Hill, "The Great Indian Treaty Council of 1851" (1966), 85–110; Barry, *Beginning of the West*, 1029–32; Kappler, ed., *Indian Treaties*, 594–96. Prior to ratification the Senate reduced the term from fifty to ten years, and evidently almost all the tribal leaders involved in the first signing were again contacted and agreed to the diminution. Anderson, "The Controversial Sioux Amendment to the Fort Laramie Treaty of 1851" (1956), 202–9, 219–20.

91. Luke Lea to A. H. H. Stuart, Nov. 30, 1852, and David D. Mitchell to Lea, Oct. 17, 1852, in *Report of the Commissioner of Indian Affairs, 1852*, 299, 357.

92. Lea to Stuart, Nov. 30, 1852, in ibid., 299–300; Holeman to Lea, Apr. 29, 1852, in Morgan, ed., "Washakie and the Shoshoni, Part II" (1954), 68–71; Holeman to Young, Sept. 25, 1852, in *Report of the Commissioner of Indian Affairs, 1852*, 439–44; Morgan, "The Administration of Indian Affairs in Utah," 387–91.

93. Holeman to Young, Sept. 30, 1853, in *Report of the Commissioner of Indian Affairs, 1853*, 33 Cong., 1 Sess., Sen. Ex. Doc. 1, Ser. 690 (1854), 443–45; Morgan, "The Administration of Indian Affairs in Utah," 392.

94. Palmer to George W. Manypenny, June 23, 1853, and Palmer to Joseph M. Garrison, June 22, 1853, in *Report of the Commissioner of Indian Affairs, 1853*, 447–48, 451–53.

Garrison's stock of presents included blankets (white, red, green, and blue in color), prints, shirts, butcher knives, camp kettles, and tobacco—and presumably similar goods were being distributed by Holeman and other agents.

95. Coan, "The Adoption of the Reservation Policy in Pacific Northwest" (1922), 14–15, indicates that the two Indian superintendents negotiated fifteen treaties between November, 1854, and January, 1856. Similar concessions to reservation status were being given in Nebraska Territory by Oto, Omaha, and Pawnee tribes in 1854 and 1857. See Warner, "Indians Challenge the Nebraska Territorial Government," 54. See Kappler, ed., *Indian Treaties, passim,* for the actual agreements.

96. John E. Wool to Lt. Col. L. Thomas, Sept. 4, 1855, in U.S. War Dept., *Indian Disturbances in California,* 11; Mack, *Nevada,* 294; Bancroft, *History of Utah* (1889), 477.

97. Hurt to Young, Sept., 1856, in *Report of the Commissioner of Indian Affairs,* Nov. 22, 1856, 34 Cong., 3 Sess., House Ex. Doc. 1, Ser. 893 (1857), 778–81; Morgan, "The Administration of Indian Affairs in Utah," 397–404.

98. William A. Hickman, Isaac Bullock, and Lewis Robinson to Young, Aug. 19, 1856, Young to George W. Manypenny, Aug. 30, Sept. 30, 1856, in Morgan, ed., "Washakie and the Shoshoni, Part III" (1954), 186–88.

99. Hoopes, "Thomas S. Twiss, Indian Agent," 353–64. Twiss was a firm believer in the importance of diplomacy and treaties when dealing with Indians, as he had evidenced in his earlier attempts to prevent Harney's 1855 punitive expedition. Indeed, on that occasion Twiss had advanced his beliefs so assiduously that Harney forbade the agent to participate in the treaty negotiations of early 1856 near Fort Pierre!

100. Bancroft, *History of Nevada, Colorado, and Wyoming,* 207; Morgan, ed., "Washakie and the Shoshoni, Part IV" (1955), 81–82; Moore, "Lander Cutoff" (1962), 50–51; Trenholm and Carley, *The Shoshonis,* 179–80. In 1859 Congress authorized Lander to distribute up to $5,000 in gifts to various Indians in the course of his operations for the purpose of insuring safe travel.

101. Mack, *Nevada,* 296–97; Forney to A. B. Greenwood, Sept. 29, 1859, Dodge to Forney, Jan. 4, 1859, Jarvis to Forney, Apr. 20, 1859, all in *Report of the Commissioner of Indian Affairs,* 1859, 733, 742, 745–46; Hafen and Hafen, eds., *Relations with the Indians of the Plains,* 176–82. Twiss had moved the Upper Platte headquarters from Fort Laramie approximately 100 miles west to Deer Creek in 1857. From 1857 until his 1861 resignation Twiss was embroiled in considerable controversy, much of it revolving around allegations that he, in collusion with nearby traders, was cheating the Indians of some of their annuity payments. See Hill, "Thomas S. Twiss, Indian Agent" (1967), 90–93.

102. Quoted in Madsen, "Shoshoni-Bannock Marauders on the Oregon Trail," 12.

103. Quoted in Utley, *Frontiersmen in Blue,* 55.

104. Ibid., 55–57.

105. May 29, 1849, entry, in "Diary of George Gibbs," 300–301.

106. June 12, 1845, entry, in Cooke, *Scenes and Adventures in the Army* (1859), 330. Army contingents on the trails supplied overlanders not only with advice concerning cutoffs and accurate figures on trail distances but also with information on the movements of potentially hostile Indian bands. See, e.g., the Aug. 30, 1849, entry, in Elisha B. Lewis, Diary (microfilm of typescript); June 12, Aug. 27, 1849, entries, in Sedgley, *Overland to California in 1849* (1877), 23, 53; June 12, 15, 1849, entries of Elisha Douglass Perkins, in Clark, ed., *Gold Rush Diary* (1967), 27, 32; July 17, 1860, entry, in Fish, Journal (MS and typescript), 13.

107. St. Joseph *Gazette,* May 3, 1850; Kanesville *Frontier Guardian,* May 15, 1850; Apr. 27, 1850, entry, in Jewett, Journal (typescript), 12. The only reason given for the anticipated lack of supplies was that expected shipments had not arrived and there was barely enough on hand for the resident troops.

108. Liberty, Mo., *Weekly Tribune,* July 6, 1849; May 29, 1849, entry, in "Diary of George Gibbs," 300–301; Mattes, "The Sutler's Store at Fort Laramie" (1946), 97. See also the remarks of Captain Charles Ruff on the free distribution of provisions to needy overlanders which Ruff felt prevented the deaths of some—quoted in Mantor, "Fort Kearny and the Westward Movement," 183–84.

109. See, e.g., the June 6, 1850, entry, in Keith, "Journal of Crossing the Plains"

([1961]), 3. For a helpful treatment of the sutler's or post trader's activities see Mattes, "The Sutler's Store at Fort Laramie," 93–138. Since the sutler was a businessman seeking profits and not organically related to the army, his role as an emigration assistant will be more carefully considered in conjunction with operators of other trading posts in Chaps. 7 and 8 below.

110. St. Joseph *Gazette,* July 10, 1850; Mattes, "The Sutler's Store at Fort Laramie," 99; advertisement, St. Joseph *Gazette,* Mar. 2, 1853, and subsequent issues.

111. Daniel P. Woodbury to Joseph G. Totten, June 2, 1849, in "Military Correspondence—War Department" (1930), 259; Mantor, "Fort Kearny and the Westward Movement," 189. Hugh A. Skinner, however, passing Fort Kearny in the spring of 1850, found the hospital still "in course of erection." May 28, 1850, entry, in Skinner, Diary (MS). For Fort Laramie see Dr. Caleb N. Ormsby to Mrs. Ormsby, June 30, 1849, in Ann Arbor *Michigan Argus,* Sept. 5, 1849, reprinted in Bidlack, *Letters Home* (1960), 22–23; J. H. McDonald to his father, May 26, 27, 1852 (MS); Hafen and Young, *Fort Laramie,* 274. In 1856 the old adobe building became uninhabitable and was torn down, being supplanted, at least for a time, by tents.

112. Bernard J. Reid was one forty-niner who took advantage of the offer and purchased at cost two holster pistols, an army rifle, and ammunition—to complement the belt revolver he had acquired earlier! The War Department offer was based upon 1849 congressional authorization. The Diary of Bernard J. Reid, Esq. (typescript), 3; Liberty *Weekly Tribune,* Mar. 23, 1849.

113. Mattes, *Great Platte River Road,* 187; letter of "Joaquin," July 21, 1849, in St. Louis *Daily Missouri Republican,* Aug. 29, 1849. At Fort Kearny, a Dr. Hammond was evidently in charge from 1849 to at least 1852; in 1854 a Dr. Alexander was stationed there. See letter of "Pawnee," June 23, 1849, in St. Louis *Daily Missouri Republican,* Aug. 6, 1849; W. N. to Editor, Aug. 2, 1852, in Salt Lake City *Deseret News,* Aug. 7, 1852; letter of "White Bear," May 20, 1854, in St. Joseph *Gazette,* June 7, 1854.

114. Erwin, comp., "Statistical Reports on the Sickness and Mortality of the Army" (1943), 317–21.

115. St. Louis *Sunday Republican,* Oct. 6, 1850; June 12, 1852, entry of John Hawkins Clark, in Barry, ed., "Overland to the Gold Fields of California" (1942), 251; New York *Daily Tribune,* July 8, 1852.

116. June 3, 1850, entry, in King, Journal (MS), 4; W. N. to Editor, Aug. 2, 1852, in Salt Lake City *Deseret News,* Aug. 7, 1852.

117. Ibid.

118. Colonel Joseph Mansfield inspected western military installations during 1853 and 1854. Concerning the Fort Dalles hospital, which also administered to its fair share of sick and injured overlanders, he wrote, "The hospital is miserable." Frazer, ed., *Mansfield on the Condition of the Western Forts* (1963), 176; Knuth, " 'Picturesque' Frontier," 300.

119. June 8, 1850, entry, in McDiarmid, Journal and Letters (microfilm of MSS and typescripts); June 22, 1850, entry, in Booth, Diary (MS and typescript); June 10, 1852, entry, in Anable, Journal (MS and copy); W. N. to Editor, Aug. 2, 1852, in Salt Lake City *Deseret News,* Aug. 7, 1852; Mattes, *Great Platte River Road,* 185, 205, 514; Hafen and Young, *Fort Laramie,* 165–66.

120. Reuben Knox to Eliza Knox, June 1, 1850, in Turner, ed., "Reuben Knox Letters, Part II" (1960), 250–51; letter of "Pawnee," June 6, 1849, in St. Louis *Missouri Republican,* June 25, 1849; Barry, *Beginning of the West,* 1081; May 24, 1852, entry, in Thomson, *Crossing the Plains* (1896), 38.

121. Bender, "The Soldier in the Far West," 175–76; Utley, *Frontiersmen in Blue,* 40–41; July 26, 1850, entry, in Coke, *A Ride over the Rocky Mountains* (1852), 156; letter of J. B. Colton, July 17, 1849, in Oquawka, Ill., *Spectator,* Oct. 3, 1849 (copy kindly made available to me by Dale Morgan of the Bancroft Library); Aug. 3, 1849, entry, in Mann, Diary, 34; July 25, 26, 29, 1849, entries, in Taggart, ed., "The Journal of David Jackson Staples" (1943), 137–38; July 24, 25, 29, 1849, entries, in Gould, Diary (typescript), 34, 36.

122. June 19, 1849, entry, in Stackpole, Journal (MS); June 21, 1849, entry, in Steck, Diary (MS).

123. May 23, 1849, entry of Elisha Douglass Perkins, in Clark, ed., *Gold Rush Diary,* 7;

St. Louis *Missouri Republican,* June 8, 12, 1849; Cincinnati *Morning Chronicle,* June 19, 1849; D. to Editor, June 15, 1849, in ibid., June 25, 1849. Apparently as early as 1845 the army was also called upon to retrieve individuals who had begun to emigrate westward without having settled all their bills. See St. Louis *Daily Missouri Republican,* Apr. 8, 1845.

124. Hale, *California as It Is,* ed. Hunter and Wellington (1851, 1954 reprint), 16; June 7, 1850, entry, in Grow, Journal (MS).

125. Letter of "Sioux," Oct. 23, 1849, in St. Louis *Daily Missouri Republican,* Jan. 1, 1850; letter of "Cheyenne," Apr. 9, 1850, in ibid., June 1, 1850; Robert Campbell to Editor, July 7, 1850, in Kanesville *Frontier Guardian,* July 24, 1850.

126. Dale Morgan's Introduction to Platt and Slater, *Travelers' Guide across the Plains* (1852, 1963 reprint), viii–ix; Knuth, " 'Picturesque' Frontier," 297–98, 300; Portland *Weekly Oregonian,* Aug. 9, 1856; June 15, 1859, entry, in Wilson, A Trip across the Plains (MS), 35–36.

127. June 16, 1852, entry, in Laird, Book (MS and typescript).

128. May 21, 1850, entry, in Payne, Saint Louis to San Francisco (typescript), 27; St. Joseph *Gazette,* Aug. 3, 1853; letter of J. W. B. Reynolds, June 14, 1856, in St. Louis *Sunday Morning Republican,* July 20, 1856. The belief that some prominent military officials wanted to abandon the trailside forts had some currency on the frontier, and one Missourian protested to his congressman in early 1852, arguing that Forts Kearny and Laramie had provided "instant relief" to "hundreds" of overlanders every year, and noting "what … would have been the situation of such unlucky pilgrims without the aid of these posts, you can imagine." Quoted in Hafen and Young, *Fort Laramie,* 174.

129. Since several important studies are available on this subject, only a summary survey will be offered in the following pages. See Jackson, *Wagon Roads West* (1952, 1964 reprint), Goetzmann, *Army Exploration in the American West* (1959), and Goetzmann, *Exploration and Empire* (1966), all of which have stressed the crucial importance of the federal government to western transportation.

130. In 1842 there was no contact; in 1843 Frémont reported seeing many emigrants as far as the Kansas River ford, where his party pushed westward to Fort St. Vrain instead of northwest to the Platte River. In late August the explorer's party intersected the emigrant trail in the Green River Valley region, and finally after lengthy investigations in the Salt Lake Valley they followed the usual trail to Fort Vancouver. In October Frémont met two Irish emigrants returning to Fort Boise following the disappearance of their horses and provided the men with provisions. Emigrants were also seen at Whitman's mission and Fort Walla Walla, but in no way can even the 1843 expedition be portrayed as having provided either guide, escort, or support services to the emigrants of that year. Frémont, *"Report* of the First Expedition, 1843," in Jackson and Spence, eds., *Expeditions of John Charles Frémont,* 1:168–337.

131. Goetzmann, *Army Exploration,* 75–77; Goetzmann, *Exploration and Empire,* 240–41; July 4, 22, Sept. 18, 1842, entries, in Frémont, *"Report* of the First Expedition, 1843," 192, 233, 283, and Sept. 14, 22, 1843, entries, in "A Report of the Exploring Expedition to Oregon and North California in the Years 1843–44," in Jackson and Spence, eds., *Expeditions of John Charles Frémont,* 1:516, 520–21.

132. Goetzmann, *Army Exploration,* 104–6, 108; Goetzmann, *Exploration and Empire,* 243–44, 247–48.

133. Goetzmann, *Army Exploration,* 112; Carleton, *Prairie Logbooks,* 32, 37, 53, 175, 178.

134. Stansbury, *Exploration and Survey,* 13–14; Goetzmann, *Army Exploration,* 219–24; Jackson, *Wagon Roads West,* 29–34.

135. Barry, *Beginning of the West,* 886–87; Sept. 15, 1849, entry, in Foster, Diary (typescript), 78; Hoffman, Journal, 26; Goetzmann, *Army Exploration,* 250–53.

136. Barry, *Beginning of the West,* 908–9; letter of J. W. Denver, July 18, 1850, in Liberty *Weekly Tribune,* Aug. 23, 1850.

137. Goetzmann, *Army Exploration,* 262–66, 277, 283; Harstad, "The Lander Trail" (1968), 15.

138. Jackson, *Wagon Roads West,* 75, 89–96.

139. Goetzmann, *Army Exploration,* 285–86; Jackson, *Wagon Roads West,* 140–45. Evi-

dently some work was done on the southern military road, since a few contracts were let to Utah workmen.

140. Goetzmann, *Army Exploration,* 294–95.

141. Jackson, *Wagon Roads West,* 121–31.

142. Captain Beckwith had assumed command of the enterprise in 1857 and the work was concluded in 1858. Ibid., 121, 131–35; Jackson, "The Army Engineers as Road Surveyors and Builders" (1949), 51–57.

143. Jackson, *Wagon Roads West,* 96–98, 101.

144. The following account of the Fort Kearny, South Pass, and Honey Lake Wagon Road is based, unless otherwise noted, on these sources: Harstad, "The Lander Trail," 14–28; Jackson, *Wagon Roads West,* 173–76, 191–217; U.S. Interior, *Report upon the Pacific Wagon Roads* (1859), 1–125; Branch, "Frederick West Lander, Road-Builder" (1929), 172–87.

145. Due to the fact that the Corps of Topographical Engineers had lost favor, Congress directed the Secretary of the Interior to oversee the work on the several territorial roads. The hope evidently was that practical and energetic men would be appointed who would produce immediate results. Political patronage, however, was the all too frequent outcome.

146. Meanwhile, the Interior Department demanded an accounting of funds from Magraw, who in turn fulminated at Lander for alleged misrepresentations. During the winter of 1858 and again in 1859 Lander and Magraw fought furiously in Washington following accidental meetings. There is little evidence that Lander misrepresented anything in the entire dispute.

147. Horace Greeley reported in 1859 that "a great majority of the California, with all the Oregon emigration" were taking Lander's route. Dispatch of July 6, 1859, in Greeley, *Overland Journey,* 160.

148. He had made a preliminary, partial survey late in the fall of 1858 which convinced him of the route's practicability, and he so informed mail contractor George Chorpenning, who used a variant trail throughout the winter, erecting a few mail stations at principal points. For a fuller treatment of Simpson's road-building activities in 1858 and 1859, see Jackson, *Wagon Roads West,* 147–55; Goetzmann, *Army Exploration,* 397–403; Alexander and Arrington, "Camp in the Sagebrush," 10.

149. Simpson's trail was also south of the notorious Hastings Cutoff, over which the ill-fated Donner party had struggled in 1846.

150. John B. Floyd to the President, Dec. 1, 1859, Simpson to Maj. F. J. Porter, June 10, 1859, Col. A. S. Johnston to Col. Samuel Cooper, Aug. 26, 1859, all in *Report of the Secretary of War,* 1859, 15, 194–95, 202–4, 221.

151. Capt. A. Pleasonton to Wallen, Apr. 28, 1859, Wallen to Pleasonton, Aug. 16, Oct. 1, 1859, in ibid., 97, 116, 119–20; Jackson, *Wagon Roads West,* 84–88; Goetzmann, *Army Exploration,* 356–57.

152. See, e.g., Edwin G. Hall to his father, May 11, 1849, in Hall, Letters (typescripts), 6; Apr. 14, 19, 21, 24, 1849, entries, in Shombre, Diary (MS and typescript), 13, 15, 16, 17.

153. There was good money to be made in selling a place at the head of the line to a man starved for news from home. Lines in front of the Sacramento post office were sometimes up to two blocks long. See letter of O. W. Nixon, Sept. 7, 1850, in Wilmington, Ohio, *Clinton Republican,* Nov. 1, 1850; unidentified letter of Aug. 31, 1852, in St. Joseph *Adventure,* Nov. 5, 1852, reprinted in Wyman, ed., *California Emigrant Letters* (1952), 172; Hafen, *The Overland Mail, 1849–1869* (1926), 45–46.

154. Henry Page to Mary A. Page, May 13, 1849, in Page, *Wagons West* (1930), 123.

155. David Dewolf to Matilda Dewolf, Dec. 12, 1849, Jan. 20, May 31, 1850, in Cox, ed., "Diary of the Overland Trail" (1925), 217, 219.

156. Bushnell, Autobiography (reproduced), 1, 18–28.

157. Pacific Mail Steamship Company steamers operated between Panama, California, and Oregon throughout the 1850s. Brought to Panama from the East Coast by boat and transported across the Isthmus by railroad, letters generally reached the West Coast in approximately four weeks. The sea mail began to function consistently in June, 1849. In 1858 over two million letters and nearly four million newspapers were conveyed in such

471

manner. See Hafen, *Overland Mail*, 38–42, 46, 48; Kemble, "The Genesis of the Pacific Mail Steamship Company" (1934), 240–54, 386–406. A consideration of the attempts by private entrepreneurs to profit by the desires for effective communication is found in Chaps. 7 and 8 below. The military mailmen were either eastbound troop detachments, army couriers who traveled with some regularity, particularly between Forts Kearny and Leavenworth, or special expresses irregularly dispatched. One such express from Fort Laramie in late June, 1849, carried emigrant letters for two cents apiece, and within one week at the fort, officers collected over $300. June 4, 22, 1849, entries, in Jagger, Diary (microfilm of MS); June 4, Aug. 2, 1849, entries of J. Goldsborough Bruff, in Read and Gaines, eds., *Gold Rush* (1944), 1:16, 67; June 14, 1849, entry, in Churchill, Diary (microfilm of typescript), 25; June 7, 1849, entry of Elisha Douglass Perkins, in Clark, ed., *Gold Rush Diary*, 22; June 25, 1849, entry, in "Diary of George Gibbs," 327. There is also evidence that in 1849 private entrepreneurs carried letters back to the states from Fort Laramie for anywhere from ten to twenty-five cents per letter. See, e.g., the July 2, 1849, entry, in Churchill, Diary, 35; June 2, 1849, entry, in Giffen, ed., *The Diaries of Peter Decker* (1966), 86; Epaphroditus Wells to Emma B. Wells, June 16, 1849, in Wells, Letters (typescripts); Hafen and Young, *Fort Laramie*, 153.

158. At that time Almon W. Babbitt was authorized—evidently at his own expense—to carry the mail between Salt Lake and Council Bluffs every other month, although one forty-niner indicated that the mail carrier left the Mormon capital only four times a year. Overlanders traveling via Salt Lake, or who chanced to meet Babbitt on the trail, sent letters back with him. C. G. Hinman explained that their traveling company gave the carrier $1.50 to wait thirty minutes while they hastily scribbled letters to their wives, and John Benson reported a thirty-five-cent postage fee per letter. Hafen, *Overland Mail*, 56–57; Kanesville *Frontier Guardian*, Apr. 4, 1849; Amos P. Josselyn to his wife, July 15, 1849, in Josselyn, Letters (MSS and typescripts); Chauncey Swan to Mary Swan, July 27, 1849, in Throne, ed., "Letters of a Forty-Niner" (1949), 69; June 7, 1849, entry, in Hinman, Diary (MS); July 15, 1849, entry, in Benson, Diary (typescript), 34.

159. Prior to the late summer implementation of the monthly service, postal activity on the plains continued in the 1849 patterns. There again were westbound departures from Salt Lake City (only two per year according to Jerome Dutton's June 13, 1850, letter to his brother LeRoy from Fort Laramie, in Dutton, "Across the Plains in 1850" [1910], 464), which Franklin Langworthy termed the "U.S. Mail" when he met the "conductors" at Pacific Springs on June 29 (*Scenery of the Plains, Mountains and Mines*, ed. Phillips [1932], 62). Postage fees of fifty cents per letter were reported by Henry Bloom on July 26, 1850, in Bloom, Diary (typescript). In 1850 postmasters were reported at both Forts Kearny and Laramie (James "Oneal" at Kearny and John S. Tutt at Laramie), and postage fees of five cents per letter at Kearny and ten cents at Laramie. Another overlander explained that letters placed in the government office at Laramie had to await an army train, and presumably the same situation obtained at the La Bonte River sixty-four miles west of Fort Laramie, where letters in a special box were transported to the frontier by government trains free of charge. May 11, 1850, entry, in Shields, Journal (MS and typescript); Fine, "Fort Laramie and the Historic Postal Markings of the West" (1961), 53; May 28, 1850, entry, in Skinner, Diary; May 23, 1850, entry, in Lewelling, Journal (typescript), 7; Finley McDiarmid to his wife, June 26, 1850, in McDiarmid, Journal and Letters.

160. Barry, *Beginning of the West*, 956–57, 971–72.

161. Hafen, *Overland Mail*, 58, 63–64. A bimonthly exchange service with Fort Dalles was also reported in the Nov. 15, 1851, Salt Lake City *Deseret News*.

162. Hafen, *Overland Mail*, 59, 64–65.

163. Barry, *Beginning of the West*, 1207–8; Salt Lake City *Deseret News*, Sept. 12, Nov. 7, 28, 1855.

164. Furniss, *The Mormon Conflict*, 51–53; Hafen, *Overland Mail*, 60–63; Arrington, *Great Basin Kingdom* (1958), 162–70.

165. Hafen, *Overland Mail*, 64–67; Bancroft, *History of Nevada, Colorado, and Wyoming*, 226.

166. See, e.g., Lem. Newell Doty to Editor, June 29, 1852, in New York *Daily Tribune*, Oct. 14, 1852; June 20, 1852, entry, in Sharp, Diary (MS). John Welch, westbound in 1854,

wrote a letter to his mother which he placed in a notched stick beside the trail along the Platte River in hopes that the mail carrier would stop for the letter, which he did. Welch, *An Overland Trip from Iowa to California* (1920), 55–56.

167. See Chap. 8 below for a further discussion of the number and location of these stations and their relationship to the overland emigrations.

168. Hafen, *Overland Mail*, 109–11. As noted above, Chorpenning began in the winter of 1858 to follow a shorter route west from Camp Floyd, quite similar to the trail surveyed the next summer by Captain James H. Simpson.

169. Nettels, "The Overland Mail Issue during the Fifties" (1924), 524–30; Hafen, *Overland Mail*, 87–90, 99. The congressional authorization had directed that the selection of the route be up to the contractor—and none of the bidders had anticipated operating on the route favored by the postmaster general from Tennessee, Aaron V. Brown.

170. The new postmaster general, Joseph Holt, found that the several mail routes servicing the Pacific Coast, including that via Panama, cost $2,184,697 per year and returned a mere $339,747.34. The result was a departmental deficit of more than $1,750,000. Hafen, *Overland Mail*, 134–36.

171. Ibid., 167–69, 187; Root and Hickman, "Pike's Peak Express Companies: Part III" (1945), 486–94; Settle, "The Role of Russell, Majors & Waddell in Western Overland Transportation," in Ferris, ed., *The American West* (1963), 85–87.

172. Maria Norton noted in 1859 that members of her traveling company had received "quite a number of letters" at Fort Laramie (July 14, 1859, entry, in Norton, Diary, 32), and Harriet Griswold, also in 1859, received a letter at Salt Lake City (Aug. 15, 1859, diary entry, in Griswold, Papers [MSS]).

173. For an example of the emerging debate over the significance of the military role in the westward movement and national development, see Nichols, "The Army and the Indians, 1800–1830" (1972), 151–52, 167–68.

CHAPTER SEVEN: Private Entrepreneurs, 1840–49

1. Hafen and Young, *Fort Laramie and the Pageant of the West* (1938), 24–30; Galbraith, *The Hudson's Bay Company as an Imperial Factor* (1957), 79; Beidleman, "Nathaniel Wyeth's Fort Hall" (1957), 197–214; Cannon, "Fort Hall on the Saptin River" (1916), 230; "Fort Boise: From Imperial Outpost to Historic Site" (1962), 33–34. Fort Hall had not become a Hudson's Bay Company post until 1837, when it was purchased from Nathaniel Wyeth, who had initially built it three years earlier to dispose of the trade goods he was unable to use at the Green River rendezvous when William Sublette reached the site first. Fort Vancouver, founded during the winter of 1824–25 where the Columbia and Willamette rivers joined, was another of the Hudson's Bay Company's posts of considerable importance to overlanders despite its location at the end of the trail. See Beidleman, "Nathaniel Wyeth's Fort Hall," 243–49; Galbraith, *Hudson's Bay Company,* 182. In 1840 the westbound missionaries and the Joel Walker emigrant family, who had traveled to the Green River Valley rendezvous with the American Fur Company trading caravan, engaged mountain man Robert Newell to pilot them to Fort Hall. Hafen, "Robert Newell," in Hafen, ed., *The Mountain Men and the Fur Trade* (1965–72), 8:271–72.

2. Hafen, "Lancaster P. Lupton," in ibid., 2:212. For the Fort Platte *vs.* Fort William squabbles over whiskey see also Jones, "Those Wild Reshaw Boys," in Taunton, ed., *Sidelights of the Sioux Wars* (1967), 5–6; McDermott, "John Baptiste Richard," in Hafen, ed., *The Mountain Men and the Fur Trade,* 2:290–94. Whiskey was still flowing freely at Fort Platte in 1843 when, at an evening dance, overlander John Boardman concisely commented that "some of the company got gay." July 14, 1843, entry, in "The Journal of John Boardman" (1929), 103. Rufus Sage described the fort in 1841 as having walls four feet thick and twenty feet high enclosing an area 250 feet long by 200 feet wide which contained twelve different buildings. Hafen and Hafen, eds., *Rufus B. Sage: His Letters and Papers* (1956), 4:220.

3. Fort John cost $10,000 according to one American Fur Company officer. Hafen and Young, *Fort Laramie,* 69–70. In 1842 John C. Frémont described the fort, which he already called Laramie, as a "quadrangular structure, built of clay. . . . The walls are about fifteen feet high, surmounted with a wooden palisade, and form a portion of ranges for houses, which entirely surround a yard of about one hundred and thirty feet square. Every apartment has its door and window, all, of course, opening on the inside. There are two entrances. . . . Over the great entrance is a square tower, with loopholes; and, like the rest of the work, built of earth. At two of the angles, and diagonally opposite each other, are large square bastions, so arranged as to sweep the four faces of the walls." July 16, 1842, entry, in *Report of the First Expedition, 1843,"* in Jackson and Spence, eds., *The Expeditions of John Charles Frémont* (1970–73), 1:218.

4. Bridger to P. Chouteau & Company, Dec. 10, 1843, quoted in Alter, *Jim Bridger* (1962), 209–10.

5. Walker, "Joseph R. Walker," in Hafen, ed., *The Mountain Men and the Fur Trade,* 5:372–73.

6. Aug. 22, 1841, entry, in Bidwell, *A Journey to California* (1842, 1937 reprint), 16–17; Williams, "Narrative of a Tour," in Hafen and Hafen, eds., *To the Rockies and Oregon* (1955), 237; Partoll, ed., "Mengarini's Narrative of the Rockies" (1938), 196; Munnick, "The Ermatinger Brothers," in Hafen, ed., *The Mountain Men and the Fur Trade,* 8:164–66.

7. Supplies were virtually nonexistent, however, and the information was vague and general, even from experienced mountaineers. Joseph Walker, who would have been able to provide more specific information, was not at the fort as the emigrants had hoped. See Aug. 11, 22, 1841, entries, in Bidwell, *Journey to California,* 14, 16–17; Stewart, *The California Trail* (1962), 20–21.

8. Jones, "Those Wild Reshaw Boys," 5; Hafen and Young, *Fort Laramie,* 99; Hastings, *The Emigrants' Guide to Oregon and California,* ed. Carey (1932), 9; Allen, comp., *Ten Years in Oregon* (1850), 154. Medorum Crawford later recalled that in 1842 between twenty-five and thirty men were employed at Fort Laramie, while fifteen to twenty were engaged at Fort Platte, mainly trading for buffalo robes with Indians. James Bordeaux was the principal official at Fort Laramie throughout the 1840s. Crawford, "Occasional Address" (1882), 12; McDermott, "James Bordeaux," in Hafen, ed., *The Mountain Men and the Fur Trade,* 5:68–69.

9. The 1842 emigrants were extremely commendatory of the assistance accorded them by the kindly proprietors of Forts Laramie, Hall, and Boise. See Hastings, *Emigrants' Guide*, 9, 20; Allen, comp., *Ten Years in Oregon*, 154, 164; Crawford, "Occasional Address," 14. In 1842, as in the year previous and in subsequent years, the overlanders were also much aided by the several Oregon missionary stations situated near the end of the trail. A full treatment of their role in facilitating overland emigration is provided in Chap. 10 below.

10. The extravagant sum was charged to the government. See Hastings, *Emigrants' Guide*, xxiv, 9, 19; Barry, *The Beginning of the West* (1972), 448. In addition to the many mountaineers met somewhere along the trails and hired by overland emigrants for guide service who are noted in this chapter, a great many former mountaineers were employed in the jumping-off towns to guide emigrant companies the entire length of the overland journey. See Chap. 3 above, pp. 108–11, for a summary of their significance in the emigration experience.

11. McDermott, "Joseph Bissonette," in Hafen, ed., *The Mountain Men and the Fur Trade*, 4:50.

12. The Papin boat—a platform placed on three dugout canoes spaced four feet apart—sank on May 28, jeopardizing the lives of several emigrant passengers. See Field, *Prairie and Mountain Sketches*, ed. Gregg and McDermott (1957), 35; May 29, 1843, entry, in Dale, ed., "A Fragmentary Journal of William L. Sublette" (1919), 107–8, n. 36; Barry, *Beginning of the West*, 476. The Papins apparently had established their ferry sometime in 1842. Root, "Ferries in Kansas: Part II" (Nov., 1933), 364.

13. July 13, 1843, entry, in Johnson and Winter, *Route across the Rocky Mountains*, ed. Cannon (1932), 14; July 14, 15, 1843, entries, in Bekeart, ed., "Journal of Pierson Barton Reading" (1930), 165–66.

14. Letter of M. M. M'Carver, July 13, 1843, reprinted from other newspapers in Wooster, Ohio, *Democrat*, Dec. 7, 1843; Sept. 12, 30, 1843, entries, in "Journal of John Boardman," 111, 113; Boardman to J. Wells, July 17, 1844, in Weston, Mo., *Journal*, Jan. 4, 1845, reprinted in "Documents" (1903), 275; Stewart, *The California Trail*, 45. For scarcity of supplies see also July 13, Aug. 27, Oct. 2, 1843, entries, in Bekeart, ed., "Journal of Pierson Barton Reading," 165, 175, 181. Despite their understandable concern with the paucity of supplies, most 1843 travelers spoke favorably of the kindness of post traders, especially François Payette at Fort Boise and Grant at Fort Hall. See Aug. 27, Oct. 2, 1843, entries, in ibid., 175, 181; Aug. 27, Sept. 20, 1843, entries, in Burnett, " 'Recollections and Opinions of an Old Pioneer' " (1904), 76, 81; Sept. 19, 1843, entry, in Nesmith, "Diary of the Emigration of 1843" (1906), 352.

15. See Jesse Looney to Maj. John C. Bond, Oct. 27, 1843, in Looney, "From the Far West" (1929), 355. Johnson and Winter, likewise 1843 overlanders, in their *Route across the Rocky Mountains*, which by 1846 was serving as a guidebook for overland travel, warned, "Nothing can be obtained at the trading establishments, except at an enormous price" (p. 177). J. M. Shively, whose travel guide of 1846 reflected his trail experiences of 1843, wrote with respect to Fort Bridger, "There is no use in going that way; they have no provisions, nor anything else that you want." At Fort Hall, however, Shively indicated it would be different: "Here you will have an opportunity of buying provisions, swapping cattle for horses, and will receive many acts of kindness from Captain Grant, the superintendent of the Fort." "The Shively Guide," in Morgan, ed., *Overland in 1846* (1963), 2:738–39. The obvious explanation for these differing experiences is that the slower travelers and later starters had to take what, if anything, was left at the several posts.

16. Aug. 20, 1843, entry, in Preuss, *Exploring with Frémont*, trans. and ed. Gudde and Gudde (1958), 85.

17. Indeed, the cryptic wording of Whitman's letter—"The present party is supposed to have expended no less than $2000 at Laramie's and Bridger's Forts, and as much more at Fort Hall and Fort Boise"—can even be interpreted as meaning that $2,000 was spent at each post, or a total of $8,000. Whitman to James M. Porter, n.d., rec'd by the Secretary of War June 22, 1844, in Nixon, *How Marcus Whitman Saved Oregon* (1895), 317.

18. Lenox, *Overland to Oregon*, ed. Whitaker (1904), 49; Burnett, " 'Recollections and Opinions of an Old Pioneer,' " 77; Oliphant, ed., "Passing of an Immigrant of 1843" (1924),

207. Grant read to the 1844 emigrants the route instructions Peter Burnett sent back to him to share with the oncoming overlanders. But that he did so by pouring "barrels of cold water" on the words of instruction and encouragement caused Washington Gilliam ever after to regard Grant "as a bad-hearted man." "Reminiscences of Washington Smith Gilliam" (1904), 205–6.

19. Oct. 11, 1843, entry, in Bekeart, ed., "Journal of Pierson Barton Reading," 183.

20. Walker forged much of the future California Trail along the Humboldt River on this important trip, while Chiles and a small party of packers laboriously worked their way into California via unexplored northern routes from Fort Boise, where Payette again provided helpful information. Stewart, ed., *The Opening of the California Trail* (1953), 41–47; Bekeart, ed., "Journal of Pierson Barton Reading," *passim*.

21. St. Louis *Daily Missouri Republican*, Oct. 31, 1844; July 25, 1845, entry, in Palmer, *Journal of Travels over the Rocky Mountains*, ed. Thwaites (1906), 74.

22. The founding date of Smith's post is not known. Its specific location apparently fluctuated, though remaining in the confines of the Bear Lake Valley. Stewart, ed., *Opening of the California Trail*, 62–63; Humphreys, "Peg Leg Smith" (1966), 29–32; Humphreys, "Thomas L. (Peg-leg) Smith," in Hafen, ed., *The Mountain Men and the Fur Trade*, 4:329; "Diary of Nicholas Carriger," in Morgan, ed., *Overland in 1846*, 1:384, n. 30.

23. Walker, "Joseph R. Walker," 374; Gregson and Gregson, "The Gregson Memoirs" (1940), 131; Carter, "Caleb Greenwood," in Hafen, ed., *The Mountain Men and the Fur Trade*, 9:190–91; Stewart, *The California Trail*, 90–93.

24. This attempt to cross the plains and mountains so late in the year was foolhardy, but luck held and Hastings's band reached Sutter's Fort on Christmas Day. Morgan, ed., *Overland in 1846*, 1:29–33; Barry, *Beginning of the West*, 560–61.

25. Case gave no indication that there was any smallpox among the emigrants at all; in fact, he spoke of Bissonette contriving "some plan to send the Indians off." Lyman, "Reminiscences of Wm. M. Case" (1900), 273–75; McDermott, "Joseph Bissonette," 50. A similar ruse was perpetrated on Crow Indians in 1849 by mountain traders along the Sweetwater River. But the forty-niners suspected the intent was to keep the Indians and emigrants apart for selfish and not humanitarian reasons—the mountain men recognizing that the emigrants would satisfy their needs more cheaply by trading with Indians than with mountaineers. June 17, 1849, entry, in Dr. T., Diary (copy of MS).

26. St. Louis *Daily Missouri Republican*, Sept. 16, 1844; Aug. 8, 1845, entry, in Palmer, *Journal of Travels*, 87.

27. Joel Palmer (Sept. 2, 1845, entry [at Fort Boise], in *Journal of Travels*, 99), James W. Nesmith (Aug. 28, 1843, entry [at Fort Hall], in "Diary of the Emigration of 1843," 350), James Clyman (Aug. 2, 1844, entry [at Fort Laramie], in Camp, ed., *James Clyman, Frontiersman* [1960], 90), and J. E. Lyle (June 25, 1845, letter from Fort Laramie, in St. Louis *Missouri Reporter*, Sept. 12, 1845, in Morgan, The Mormons and the Far West [typescripts]) all used the pejorative term, and other overlanders complained of generally high prices and the difficulty of concluding acceptable bargains. Edward Evans Parrish, for example, noted that one 1844 overlander received "a coarse hat" in exchange for a lame ox at Fort Bridger. Aug. 31, 1844, entry, in Parrish, "Crossing the Plains in 1844" (1889), 104–5. The statistics for this and subsequent tables in Chaps. 7 and 8 are derived from the diaries, letters, and newspaper accounts cited in the chapters. Since all emigrants did not quote prices for similar quantities, an attempt has been made to translate all prices into a single common denominator so that a more uniform impression can be given.

28. McDermott, "Joseph Bissonette," 51–53; Hafen and Young, *Fort Laramie*, 92–93, 118–19; McDermott, "John Baptiste Richard," 293–94; Jones, "Those Wild Reshaw Boys," 6–9. Francis Parkman, who witnessed some of the emigrant stopovers at Forts Bernard and Laramie in 1846, noted that many emigrants drank almost as energetically as they reoutfitted at Fort Bernard, which was obviously continuing Fort Platte's alcoholic tradition. Parkman observed one prominent emigrant train leader "drunk as a pigeon." June 28, 1846, entry, in Wade, ed., *The Journals of Francis Parkman* (1947), 2:447; Parkman to his father, June 28, 1846, in Jacobs, ed., *Letters of Francis Parkman* (1960), 1:45.

29. The possibility, of course, is that someone from Fort Laramie had a hand in the conflagration, but this remains only an unproven suspicion. However, Parkman had also commented that one of the reasons the American Fur Company was "exceedingly disliked

in this country" was because it "suppresses all opposition." June 16, 1846, entry, in Wade, ed., *Journals of Francis Parkman*, 2:440; Hafen and Young, *Fort Laramie*, 122–23.

30. Parkman to his mother, June 19, 1846, in Jacobs, ed., *Letters of Francis Parkman*, 1:44; Parkman, *The Oregon Trail*, ed. Feltskog (1969), 530, n. 19. Feltskog notes that for some unknown reason Parkman deleted the quoted comments from later editions of his book.

31. June 23, July 17, 1846, entries, in Bryant, *What I Saw in California* (1849), 107, 143; July 25, 1846, entry, in Lienhard, *From St. Louis to Sutter's Fort*, trans. and ed. Gudde and Gudde (1961), 95; Lavender, *Bent's Fort* (1954), 274.

32. McBride, "Reminiscences," quoted in Morgan, ed., *Overland in 1846*, 1:98.

33. Many overlanders had also suspected vested interest lurking beneath the assertions of Richard Grant and others at Fort Hall that it was impossible to take wagons to Oregon, assuming that the Hudson's Bay Company was deliberately misleading emigrants in the hope they would all go to California. Those charges will be treated in Chap. 10 below in the context of the conflicts between Oregon and California to secure the majority of oncoming overlanders.

34. In this letter of July 31, 1846, written at Fort Bridger just prior to the Donner party's departure from that point—printed in the Sangamo, Ill., *Journal*, Nov. 5, 1846, reprinted in Korns, "West from Fort Bridger" (1951), 192–94—Reed also castigated the "independent trappers" who swarmed about the emigrants for purposes of trade, terming them "as great a set of sharks as ever disgraced humanity, with few exceptions." Reed's later statement is quoted in Alter, *Jim Bridger*, 221. See also Stewart, *The California Trail*, 57, 60–61, 164–65, 167; Andrews, "Lansford W. Hastings and the Promotion of the Salt Lake Desert Cutoff" (1973), 148–50.

35. Barry, *Beginning of the West*, 583–85; Root, "Ferries in Kansas: Part II" (Nov., 1933), 364–65; Root, "Ferries in Kansas: Part II" (Aug., 1933), 266–67; "Diary of George McKinstry," in Morgan, ed., *Overland in 1846*, 1:204, 401–2, n. 12.

36. Among others, 1846 overlanders chose between a ferry in St. Joseph, the Evan Parrot ferry four miles above St. Joseph, the William Banks ferry approximately fifty-five miles upriver at Iowa Point (near Oregon, Mo.), the Thompson and Hayman ferry at or near Iowa Point, and the John Boulware ferry near Old Fort Kearny, perhaps ninety to a hundred miles upriver from Iowa Point. See Barry, *Beginning of the West*, 572, 575–78, 1052–53; Mattes, *The Great Platte River Road* (1969), 117 and maps following 140.

37. His exchange rate was doubtless similar to that prevailing at Fort Laramie, where Ralph Geer recalled that in 1847 it required two and even three lame animals to purchase a sound one. Geer, "Occasional Address" (1880), 35. This account of the origins of Goodyear's post has been drawn from Morgan, "Miles Goodyear and the Founding of Ogden" (1935), 209–15.

38. Morgan, "Miles Goodyear and the Founding of Ogden, II" (1953), 311–18. Under Mormon control Buenaventura continued as Brownsville, and after January, 1850, as Ogden.

39. Because their Salt Lake settlement was of such importance to overland travel, a separate chapter is devoted to Mormon-emigrant interaction; this chapter deals at length only with Mormon ferrying and trading-post activity beyond the Salt Lake perimeter.

40. Morgan, ed., "The Mormon Ferry on the North Platte" (1949), 111–67; Barry, *Beginning of the West*, 684.

41. The boat consisted of two dugout canoes twenty-three feet long held six feet apart by cross timbers. Oarsmen rowed it across the Platte. Morgan, ed., "The Mormon Ferry on the North Platte," 152, n. 53; June 17, 1847, entry, in "Journey to Zion: From the Journal of Erastus Snow, Part II" (1948), 266. In addition to Grover, the other appointed ferrymen were John S. Higbee, William A. Empey, Appleton M. Harmon, Edmund Ellsworth, Luke Johnson, Francis M. Pomeroy, James Davenport, and Benjamin F. Stewart.

42. Morgan, ed., "The Mormon Ferry on the North Platte," *passim*.

43. Apparently only four Mormons (among whom were Edmund Ellsworth and Levi Hancock) manned the 1848 boat, which, if not the same one used the previous year, was constructed in an identical manner. July 6, 1848, entry, in May, journal (MS); Morgan, ed., "The Mormon Ferry on the North Platte," 112.

44. Miller, "Early Oregon Scenes" (1930), 60; Morgan, "The Ferries of the Forty-

Niners, Part III—Section 1" (1960), 52; Stegner, *The Gathering of Zion* (1964), 202; May 22, 1848, entry, in Brooks, ed., *On the Mormon Frontier* (1964), 1:312; Mattes, "The Jumping-off Places on the Overland Trail," in McDermott, ed., *The Frontier Re-examined* (1967), 36–38.

45. The Papin ferry across the Kansas River was also back in business in 1848. John Calvin McCoy operated the Missouri River ferry at Kansas City in 1848, and Libeus T. Coon apparently began his ferry service at Plattsmouth, approximately thirty miles north of Old Fort Kearny, in the same year. Barry, *Beginning of the West,* 739–40; Wearin, "Plattsmouth Ferry" (1960); Root, "Ferries in Kansas: Part II" (Nov., 1933), 365.

46. It seems to have been in business when the 1848 overlanders passed, however, since a small eastbound party of Oregonians spent a day at "Robidoux Fort" on their way to St. Joseph, where they arrived May 11. Ebbert, "George Wood Ebbert" (1918), 266; Barry, *Beginning of the West,* 479; Mattes, "Robidoux's Trading Post at 'Scott's Bluffs' " (1949), 108; Mattes, *Great Platte River Road,* 438–41, 447–50.

47. Camp, ed., "William Alexander Trubody and the Overland Pioneers of 1847" (1937), 125–26.

48. June 3–7, 1848, entries, in Root, *Journal of Travels from St. Josephs to Oregon* (1850), 19; June 23, 24, 1848, entries, in May, Journal.

49. July 13, 1848, entry, in Pettijohn, Diary (MS). Pettijohn gave further evidence of the lucrative trades post operators made on July 1 at Fort Bridger, "where we sold one of our waggons for fifty cents in cash and bought another for fifteen dollars." Overlanders often tried to sell surplus supplies at the posts, perhaps in response to newspaper accounts urging them to take along considerable quantities of sugar and coffee because any surplus "can be disposed of at an excellent price at the different trading posts . . . on the route." See St. Louis *Daily Union,* Feb. 27, 1847, in Morgan, The Mormons and the Far West.

50. Ingersoll to Editor, Aug. 19, 1847, in Ingersoll, *Overland to California in 1847,* ed. McMurtrie (1937), 35; Aug. 28, 1847, entry, in "Diary of Mrs. Elizabeth Dixon Smith Geer" (1908), 163.

51. July 23, Aug. 8, 1848, entries, in May, Journal.

52. A contemporary report specified eleven different Missouri River ferries between St. Joseph and Council Bluffs in 1849, and alluded to yet others at "intermediate points." New Orleans *Daily Picayune,* May 26, 1849. See also Mattes, *Great Platte River Road,* 115–17; May 7, 1849, entry, in Burbank, Diary (microfilm of MS), 15; May 2, 1849, entry of John Edwin Banks, in Scamehorn, ed., *The Buckeye Rovers in the Gold Rush* (1965), 4; Barry, *Beginning of the West,* 849.

53. May 7, 1849, entry, in Read and Gaines, eds., *Gold Rush* (1944), 1:7; *Autobiography of Isaac Jones Wistar* (1937), 57.

54. By May 18 the Beaubien amd Ogee ferry had already crossed 700 wagons. St. Louis *Daily Missouri Republican,* June 3, 1849; May 7, 1849, entry, in Morgan, ed., *The Overland Diary of James A. Pritchard* (1949), 57, 145, n. 13; Barry, *Beginning of the West,* 795–96; Mattes, *Great Platte River Road,* 139; May 2–3, 1849, entries, in Johnston, *Overland to California* (1948), 35–39.

55. It is possible that the same boat was used for both endeavors. When the fur company post became an official government fort that summer, army personnel assumed control of the ferrying operations. Charges remained stable at $1 and $1.50 throughout the summer. Morgan, "The Ferries of the Forty-Niners, Part II" (1959), 186.

56. Morgan, "The Ferries of the Forty-Niners," 14–15, 25, 29–31; Mar. 4, Aug. 5, 1849, entries of John D. Lee, in Cleland and Brooks, eds., *A Mormon Chronicle* (1955), 1:99, 112. Obviously the operators had taken many of their returns in provisions and supplies, which they consumed during the summer. P. C. Tiffany's journal entry of June 6 (MS and typescript) noted that travelers knew the Mormons accepted provisions in lieu of ferriage fees, and Tiffany's company refrained from dumping all their surplus supplies at Fort Laramie because they wanted to retain enough to pay for their ferriage over the North Platte. Thus the total Mormon income must have been considerably higher than the $6,465 which the ten ferrymen divided equally at the end of the summer.

57. See, e.g., the June 22, 1849, entry, in Prichet, Diary (microfilm of typescript), 41–42; June 28, 1849, entry, in Caldwell, "Notes of a Journey to California by Fort Hall Route," in Read and Gaines, eds., *Gold Rush,* 2:1255; July 6, 1849, entry, in Hamelin, Jr.,

Journals (MSS and typescripts). Since most of the emigrant ferries were short-lived, conducted for no more than several weeks at the most, few names have survived. Bruff mentioned three Iowa emigrants conducting the ferry his company utilized; Isaac Foster named George R. Codding of Illinois as proprietor of one North Platte ferry; David Staples patronized a ferry operated by a party from Illinois; H. B. Frans of Illinois purchased a boat for $50 and operated it for a week; Alonzo Delano reported on a New Orleans overlander, Mr. Henderson, who had stopped for a short and profitable interlude; and toward the end of the ferrying season one Charles Dallas purchased a boat and operated it for a time. Morgan, "The Ferries of the Forty-Niners, Part II," 185–87; July 15, 1849, entry, in Taggart, ed., "The Journal of David Jackson Staples" (1943), 135; H. B. Frans to his parents, July 21, 1849, in Oquawka, Ill., *Spectator*, Oct. 10, 1849 (typescript included with the Cephas Arms Diary, which Dale Morgan was editing for publication and which he generously permitted me to use at the Bancroft Library in 1965); June 1, 1849, entry, in Delano, *Across the Plains and among the Diggings* (1853, 1936 reprint), 34.

58. Henry Tappan on June 19 indicated that 1,000 teams were waiting to cross between Deer Creek and the Mormon ferry, and Israel Hale indicated on June 21 that 800 wagons were waiting to be crossed at the Mormon ferry. June 19, 1849, entry, in Walters and Strother, eds., "The Gold Rush Diary of Henry Tappan" (1953), 126; June 21, 1849, entry, in Hale, "Diary of a Trip to California" (1925), 83. See also Morgan, "The Ferries of the Forty-Niners, Part II," 152, 186–87. Charges at these speculative endeavors ranged from $2 to $5 per vehicle. According to J. Goldsborough Bruff, there were also some attempts to drum up business by boosting certain ferries, but apparently the press of numbers was so great that advertising was not needed to insure more than enough customers. July 16, 1849, journal entry of Bruff, in Read and Gaines, eds., *Gold Rush*, 1:46.

59. For examples see the June 26, 1849, entry, in Everts, Journal (MS and typescript); July 3, 1849, entry, in Searls, *The Diary of a Pioneer* (1940), 42; Morgan's excellent compilation, "The Ferries of the Forty-Niners, Part II," 188.

60. Louis Vasquez of Fort Bridger may have had a hand in this endeavor. See Hafen, "Louis Vasquez," in Hafen, ed., *The Mountain Men and the Fur Trade*, 2:335; Vasquez, "Experiences at Fort Bridger" (1931), 107.

61. Morgan, "The Ferries of the Forty-Niners, Part III—Section 1," 52–54, 62, 65; Morgan, "The Ferries of the Forty-Niners, Part III—Section 2" (1960), 185, 199–201; July 11, 1849, entry, in Benson, Diary (typescript), 33; July 15, 1849, entry, in Murphy, Diary (MS); July 4, 1849, entry, in Gillespie, Diary (typescript), 7. Emigrant entrepreneurs on the cutoff who paid $500 for a Mormon boat proceeded to collect, by one account, $200 a day. At the Mormon ferry on the cutoff, Amos Steck, who paid $4 to have his wagon set across the river, learned that 2,000 wagons had been crossed prior to those of his company. July 17, 1849, entry, in Steck, Diary (MS and typescript). Morgan has estimated that 65 percent of the forty-niners traveled on the cutoff. The Mormon ferry on the Salt Lake road alone crossed approximately 1,500 wagons at an average fee of $4 a wagon. With the profits piling up, it was little wonder that Ezra Banks remarked after paying his $7, "While others are chasing wealth they are catching it, no dream." July 11, 1849, entry, in Scamehorn, ed., *The Buckeye Rovers in the Gold Rush*, 39. Among the identifiable emigrants who operated Green River ferries for a time were a man from Maine and Dr. M. B. Angel of Niles, Mich. July 4, 1849, entry, in Chamberlain, Diary (typescript), 16; July 3, 1849, entry, in Delano, *Across the Plains and among the Diggings*, 52.

62. June 26, 28, 1849, entries, in Johnston, *Overland to California*, 128–29; Paden, *The Wake of the Prairie Schooner* (1943), 301–2; July 31, 1849, entry, in *Journal of Samuel Rutherford Dundass* (1857), 43; Aug. 2, 1849, entry, in Tolles, Diary (typescript), 33.

63. Aug. 2, 1849, entry, in Doyle, Diaries and Letters (MSS and typescripts). Perhaps one reason no ford had earlier been established was the rumor among the emigrants that the canny Mormons had dug deep pits in the river to prevent fording attempts. Paden, *Wake of the Prairie Schooner*, 302. See also Chap. 8 below, p. 285.

64. June 30, 1849, entry, in Breyfogle, Diary (mimeographed copy), 14.

65. Barry, *Beginning of the West*, 737–38, 795–96; May 30, 1849, entry, in Taggert, ed., "The Journal of David Jackson Staples," 125; Kelly, *An Excursion to California* (1851), 1:59.

66. Bidlack, *Letters Home* (1960), 27; June 10, 1849, entry, in Morgan, ed., *Overland*

Diary of James A. Pritchard, 88; Morgan, "The Ferries of the Forty-Niners," 200–224; Morgan, "The Ferries of the Forty-Niners, Part II," 163, 169, 174; July 15, 1849, entry, in Clark, ed., *Gold Rush Diary* (1967), 64. William Kelly found the Mormon headquarters at the Platte impressive for such a temporary post—" . . . we found at the crossing a body of Mormons strongly entrenched in a heavy timber palisading, for their own protection and the security of their animals." Kelly, *An Excursion to California,* 1:174. E. A. Spooner reported Robidoux charged fees of $12 for shoeing a yoke of oxen, while Vincent Geiger merely indicated, "For goods of every description he charges the most exorbitant prices, & for work, truly extortionate." Nonetheless, as Jasper Hixson noted, "a land office business" was being done. June 11, 1849, entry, in Spooner, Diary (microfilm of MS); June 12, 1849, entry of Geiger, in Potter, ed., *Trail to California* (1945), 105; June 1, 1849, entry, in Hixson, Diary (photocopy of typescript), 14; Kelly, *An Excursion to California,* 1:205; Aug. 11, 1849, entry, in Stansbury, *Exploration and Survey of the Valley of the Great Salt Lake* (1853), 74.

67. July 25, 1849, entry, in Lord, Diary (MS and clippings); July 23, 1849, entry, in The Diary of Bernard J. Reid, Esq. (typescript), 43; July 12, 1849, entry of Banks, in Scamehorn, ed., *The Buckeye Rovers in the Gold Rush,* 39; July 25, 1849, entry, in Searls, *Diary of a Pioneer,* 55; June 27, 1849, entry, in Tiffany, Journal.

68. Less than half the overlanders passed Fort Bridger in 1849, and after the Hudspeth Cutoff was opened July 19, almost nobody except Oregon-bound overlanders went via Fort Hall. Morgan, ed., *Overland Diary of James A. Pritchard,* 160, n. 59.

69. June 9, 1849, entry, in Breyfogle, Diary, 11; July 1–2, 1849, entries, in Mann, Diary (typescript), 8, 10; June 19, 1849, entry, in Roseboom, ed., "Charles Tinker's Journal" (1952), 78; June 15, 1849, entry, in Giffen, ed., *The Diaries of Peter Decker* (1966), 97–98, 275, n. 91.

70. Aug. 6, 7, 9, 1849, entries of Bruss, in Read and Gaines, eds., *Gold Rush,* 1:73–78, 82, 521–22, n. 281; July 18, 1849, entry, in Howell, Diary (MS), 25; July 25, 1849, entry, in Murphy, Diary; July 24, 1849, entry, in Brown, "Memoirs of an American Gold Seeker" (1908), 147; July 6, 1849, entry, in Burbank, Diary, 65; Lavender, *Bent's Fort,* 341.

71. June 10, July 2, 1849, entries, in Johnston, *Overland to California,* 94, 132; Kelly, *An Excursion to California,* 1:193–94.

72. Churchill had been soured when a trapper's report that water and grass would be found twelve miles ahead proved untrue. Aug. 5, 1849, entry, in Churchill, Diary (microfilm of typescript), 42; Kelly, *An Excursion to California,* 1:159, 206; July 14, 1849, entry, in McCall, *The Great California Trail* (1882), 51; July 7, 1849, entry, in Delano, *Across the Plains and among the Diggings,* 54; Allen T. Ward to his parents, July 8, 1849, in Barnes, ed., "Letters of Allen T. Ward" (1967), 365.

73. Delano's company gave up quarters and half-dollars on several occasions to such "entrepreneurs," apparently always without subsequent successful delivery, and believed the traders to be perpetrating deliberate frauds upon the emigrants. June 12, 28, 1849, entries, in Delano, *Across the Plains and among the Diggings,* 29, 45; June 28, 1849, entry of Wakeman Bryarly, in Potter, ed., *Trail to California,* 123; June 30, 1849, entry, in Mann, Diary, 7.

74. "Old Boone" to Col. W. F. Switzler, May 17, 1849, in *Missouri Statesman,* June 8, 1849, reprinted in Wyman, ed., *California Emigrant Letters* (1952), 99.

75. See Mattes, *Great Platte River Road,* 463–68, for an unraveling of the complex geographical evidence for the several site locations. T. L. Green's two articles—"A Forgotten Fur Trading Post in Scotts Bluff County" (1934), 38–46, and " 'Scotts Bluffs, Fort John' " (1938), 175–89—had earlier called attention to the second Fort John. C. G. Coutant suggested that Bruce Husband and other fur company traders at Fort John remained at least indirectly helpful to emigrants by using their considerable influence to prevent Indians from attacking passing overland caravans. Coutant, *The History of Wyoming* (1899), 317. For the Robidoux quotation see Mattes, "Joseph Robidoux," in Hafen, ed., *The Mountain Men and the Fur Trade,* 8:307–8.

76. A Fort Laramie correspondent of the St. Louis *Daily Missouri Republican* wrote on Aug. 27, 1849, "Nearly all the parties remain here a few days to reset wagon tires, exchange and purchase cattle, mail letters for the States, and replenish their supply of provisions

from the Commissary, who is permitted to 'sell to those *actually* in want.'" The letter was printed in the Oct. 16, 1849, issue.

77. Since most overlanders had already passed when Laramie became an army post, sutler John S. Tutt's impact was scarcely felt in 1849. At Kearny, however, Lewis Bissell Dougherty prospered, telling Elisha Perkins that "if he had had on hand all the articles Californians enquired for he could have made more money than by going to the Gold region itself." Perkins added, "I could see in the short time I was in, that few merchants in the states do better than those appointed Sutlers." June 14, 1849, entry, in Clark, ed., *Gold Rush Diary*, 29–30. For further background on the sutler see Mattes, "The Sutler's Store at Fort Laramie" (1946), 94–99; "Post Sutlers at Fort Laramie" (1926), 318; Withers, ed., "Experiences of Lewis Bissell Dougherty" (1930), 359–61; Davis, "The Sutler at Fort Bridger" (1971), 37–38; Spear, "The Sutler in the Union Army" (1970), 121–22.

78. Hafen and Young, *Fort Laramie*, 131; June 19, 1849, entry, in Burbank, Diary, 48–49. A few emigrants traveling via Fort Hall were able to sell surplus bacon and flour at that post, which was undersupplied until a shipment from Oregon arrived in late July. July 18, 1849, entry, in Delano, *Across the Plains and among the Diggings*, 60.

79. May 21, 1849, entry, in Hixson, Diary, 11; J. M. Hixson to Robert H. Miller, May 20, 1849, in Liberty, Mo., *Weekly Tribune*, June 8, 1849. One emigrant estimated that the Fort Laramie traders sold items at four times their worth, and when they purchased from overlanders gave one-tenth value. June 3, 1849, entry, in Dr. T., Diary. Those who succeeded in selling some of their surplus, no matter what the price, considered themselves fortunate with so many having to abandon perfectly good merchandise. May 28, 1849, entry, in Breyfogle, Diary, 8. The chief trader at Fort Laramie told Joseph Berrien on May 30 that he had had 20,000 pounds of bacon abandoned by preceding companies which he would sell at one cent a pound, and that hundreds of pounds lay outside the fort that he was not even bothering to appropriate. May 30, 1849, entry, in Hinckley and Hinckley, eds., "Overland from St. Louis to the California Gold Field" (1960), 310.

80. Alexander Culbertson to P. Chouteau, Jr., & Company, Aug. 2, 1849, and Honore Picotte to P. Chouteau, Jr., & Company, July 20, 1850, quoted in Green, " 'Scotts Bluffs, Fort John,'" 179, 181.

81. For purposes of comparison, prices at Lassen's and Johnson's ranches in California have been included as well, these being the first locations in California reached by most overlanders in 1849.

82. June 24, 1849, entry, in Giffen, ed., *Diaries of Peter Decker*, 106; June 27, 1849, entry, in Morgan, ed., *Overland Diary of James A. Pritchard*, 101; July 23, 1849, entry, in Howell, Diary, 27; July 23, 1849, entry, in Burbank, Diary, 80.

83. June 16, 1849, entry, in Gould, Diary (typescript), 20; Thaddeus Levi Loomis to his parents, Aug. 12, 1849, in Anderson, "Grandfather Was a Forty-Niner" (1967), 42; June 29, 1849, diary entry of Charles Elisha Boyle, in Columbus, Ohio, *Evening Dispatch*, Nov. 2, 1849; June 30, 1849, entry, in Hixson, Diary, 27; St. Louis *Daily Missouri Republican*, Nov. 24, Dec. 4, 1849; Ursula B. Hascall to her sister, Feb. 14, 1850, in "Letters of a Proselyte" (1957), 255–56.

84. July 16, 1849, entry, in Prichet, Diary, 53–54.

85. In 1849 these were located east of Johnson's Ranch, the first settlement reached by forty-niners arriving via the Truckee River route, and east of Lassen's Ranch, the first settlement on the Lassen Cutoff. See, e.g., the Sept. 14, 1849, entry, in McCall, *The Great California Trail*, 83; Aug. 29, 1849, entry, in Jagger, Diary (microfilm of MS); Sept. 15, 17, 1849, entries, in Benson, Diary, 66–67.

86. July 17, Aug. 6, 1849, entries of J. Goldsborough Bruff, in Read and Gaines, eds., *Gold Rush*, 1:47, 73; John H. Peoples to Maj. D. H. Rucker, Oct. 24, 1849, in U.S. President, *Gen. Smith's Correspondence, California* (1850), 129.

87. May 10, 1849, entry, in Giffen, ed., *Diaries of Peter Decker*, 70; May 17, 1849, entry, in Johnston, *Overland to California*, 60.

CHAPTER EIGHT: PRIVATE ENTREPRENEURS, 1850–60

1. St. Louis *Daily Missouri Republican,* Feb. 14, 1850. A few of the 1850 backpackers, however, were forced to return when they found insufficient supplies at the first posts. Apr. 29, May 1, 1850, entries, in Blood, Diary (typescript), 4, 6–7.

2. Kanesville *Frontier Guardian,* May 1, 1850.

3. May 23, 1850, entry, in Booth, Diary (MS and typescript); Apr. 24, 1850, entry, in Shields, Journal (MS and typescript).

4. Ross, "The Old Shawnee Mission" (1928), 421; "Early Military Posts, Missions and Camps" (1881), 266; June 17, 1853, entry, in Falbo, trans. and ed., *California and Overland Diaries of Count Leonetto Cipriani* (1962), 76.

5. May 20, 21, 1850, entries, in Paden, ed., *The Journal of Madison Berryman Moorman* (1948), 11–12; Barry, *The Beginning of the West* (1972), 800–801.

6. The great Nemaha Indian subagency was also situated at the Presbyterian mission on the St. Joseph route. "Early Military Posts, Missions and Camps," 268; Meyer, "The Iowa Indians, 1836–1885" (1962), 281; May 31, 1850, entry, in "Diary Kept by William Edmundson" (1908), 518; May 7, 1850, entry, in Clapp, *A Journal of Travels to and from California* (1851), 15; Mattes, *The Great Platte River Road* (1969), 125.

7. Although Sarpy, Martin, and Gingry, of Kanesville, advertised their ferry operations at the Elkhorn and Loup Fork, the only specific name any emigrant associated with those ferries was that of Dr. M. H. Clark of the Clark, Townsend, Wheeling, and Company enterprise, also of Kanesville. Kanesville *Frontier Guardian,* Feb. 20, 1850; Langworthy, *Scenery of the Plains, Mountains and Mines,* ed. Phillips (1932), 15, n. 16; May 20, 21, 1850, entries, in McKinstry, Diary (microfilm of typescript), 21–22; Apr. 23, 1850, entry, in Stimson, "Overland Journey to California" (1922), 408.

8. Apr. 27, 1850, entry of James M. Slagle in his letter to his brother, May 15, 1850, in Forrest, "Forty Niners from Washington County, Pennsylvania" (1945), 7; May 2, 1850, entry, in Christy, Journal (MS); June 6, 1850, entry, in "Diary Kept by William Edmundson," 519; May 22, 1850, entry, in Udell, *Incidents of Travel to California* (1856), 14; May 24, 28, 29, 1850, entries, in Hinds, Diary (photocopy of typescript), 19, 25, 28. It cost from $1.25 to $2.50 to ferry a wagon over the Elkhorn River and from $1.25 to $3.50 to have a wagon set across the Loup Fork.

9. Root, "Ferries in Kansas: Part III" (May, 1934), 136–37; May 26, 1850, entry, in Frush, Diary (MS and typescript), 2; May 27, 1850, entry, in Dowell, Journal (copy of MS), 4; May 31, 1850, entry of Calvin Taylor, in Williams, ed., "Overland to the Gold Fields of California" (1969), 129.

10. Mattes, ed., "Capt. L. C. Easton's Report" (1953), 412; John F. Snyder to W. F. Snyder, May 22, 1850 (photocopy of MS); James M. Woods to Mrs. M. C. Woods, May 6–22, 1850, in Woods, Letters (typescripts); June 2, 1850, entry, in Littleton, Diary (typescript), 4. The Kansas River crossings most frequently utilized by overlanders were the Delaware crossing (Moses Grinter, ferryman) eight miles west of the Missouri border; the Indian Toley's ferry two miles west; the Papin or Topeka ferry crossing; the Beaubien and Ogee ferry at the Upper or Uniontown crossing; and Lucius Darling's "National Ferry" a short distance west of Uniontown. Barry, *Beginning of the West,* 903, 929–32, 952; Root, "Ferries in Kansas: Part II" (Nov., 1933), 363–65, and (Feb., 1934), 20.

11. See, e.g., June 4, 5, 1850, entries, in Littleton, Diary, 4; William Renfro Rothwell to his parents, May 10, 1850, in Rothwell, Journal and Letters (MSS and typescripts), 45. Consult Chap. 5 above, pp. 167–73, for further information on the Indian as entrepreneur.

12. May 31, 1850, entry, in Paden, ed., *Journal of Madison Berryman Moorman,* 16; May 11, 1850, entry, in Shields, Journal.

13. Drips cleared $3,500 during the 1850 season at his post, but apparently most of his profits accrued from the Indian trade. Mattes, *Great Platte River Road,* 463–67. Seth Lewelling (May 19, 1850, entry, in Lewelling, Journal [typescript], 7), Hugh A. Skinner (June 11, 1850, entry, in Skinner, Diary [MS]), and John Nevin King (June 15, 1850, entry, in King, Journal [MS], 6) were a few of the overlanders who made the slight detour to "Major" Drips's post.

14. May 26, 1850, entry, in Thomasson, Diary (typescript), 11; June 12, 1850, entry, in

Skinner, Diary; June 11, 1850, entry, in Hardy, Journal (MSS and typescripts); Mattes, "Joseph Robidoux," in Hafen, ed., *The Mountain Men and the Fur Trade* (1965–72), 8:309. Benjamin Dowell, on June 23 and presumably at Robidoux's, reported a fee of $8 for shoeing one horse. Dowell, Journal, 13.

15. [Henry?] Chatillon was evidently involved with Richard at Ash Point, where the principal activity seems to have been swapping or purchasing horses. July 16–17, 1850, entries, in Coke, *A Ride over the Rocky Mountains* (1852), 145, 148–49; May 29, 1850, entry, in Shields, Journal; May 29, 1850, entry, in Smith, *Journal of a Trip to California,* ed. Vail (n.d.), 41; May 21, 1850, entry, in Lewelling, Journal, 7; McDermott, "John Baptiste Richard," in Hafen, ed., *The Mountain Men and the Fur Trade,* 2:296.

16. Tompkins, Narrative (photocopy of MS), 71–72; McDermott, "Joseph Bissonette," in Hafen, ed., *The Mountain Men and the Fur Trade,* 4:53.

17. One emigrant was told that at least some of the proceeds would be used to furnish the garrison with a library. May 7, 1850, entry, in Ingalls, *Journal of a Trip to California* (1852), 24.

18. June 20, 1850, entry, in Booth, Diary; Jerome Dutton to LeRoy Dutton, June 13, 1850, in Dutton, "Across the Plains in 1850" (1910), 462; June 20–21, 1850, entries, in "Journal of A. W. Harlan" (1913), 43; June 21, 1850, entry, in McKinstry, Diary, 44.

19. June 22, 1850, entry, in Hinds, Diary, 52.

20. Joseph Price to Elizabeth Price, May 6, June 11, 1850, note at Fort Laramie, in Marshall, ed., "The Road to California" (1924), 252; June 16, 1850, entry, in Rothwell, Journal and Letters, 113.

21. June 21–22, 1850, entries, in McKinstry, Diary, 44–46. See also the June 13, 1850, entry, in Langworthy, *Scenery of the Plains,* 47.

22. June 29, 1850, entry, in McKinstry, Diary, 51–53; June 30, 1850, entry, in Hinds, Diary, 56. A. W. Harlan, whose company crossed the Platte twice, raged: ". . . we have been swindled in the most rascally manner and . . . the officers of the garrison at Laramie are concerned. . . . we have all agreed to write to others comeing not to cross the Platte at all hereafter." June 30, 1850, entry, in "Journal of A. W. Harlan," 45. Some, like Franklin Langworthy, who also recognized that lies had been told, preferred to blame agents of the North Platte ferry owners stationed at the fort rather than Uncle Sam's finest. June 21, 1850, entry, in Langworthy, *Scenery of the Plains,* 56.

23. Morgan, ed., "The Mormon Ferry on the North Platte" (1949), 114–15; Robert Campbell to Editor, July 7, 1850, in Kanesville *Frontier Guardian,* July 24, 1850; June 20, 1850, entry, in Hardy, Journal. The St. Joseph *Gazette* in its March 29 issue had apprised readers of the intent of Hickman and his Boone County compatriots to establish a "Ferry Across North Platte." Hickman's endeavor merits mention as the first season-long non-Mormon or non-mountaineer ferry operation west of Fort Kearny. Hickman's was also the concern in which Fort Laramie officers were financially interested, or so some overlanders believed. See the June 29, 1850, entry, in McKinstry, Diary, 51.

24. June 11, 1850, entry, in Shepherd, *Journal of Travel across the Plains* (1851, 1945 reprint), 12; Albert S. Holmes to his wife, June 24, 1850, in Milgram, "Estill & Co. Express" (1961), 328; June 21, 1850, entry, in Udell, *Incidents of Travel to California,* 19–20; June 20–23, 1850, entries, in Skinner, Diary; June 29, 1850, entry, in Paden, ed., *Journal of Madison Berryman Moorman,* 33. A large box for emigrant letters was again a welcome facet of the Mormon outpost. June 7, 1850, entry, in Shields, Journal. The Upper Ferry boats were attached to ropes strung across the river, and crossings were made in as little as five or ten minutes. June 20, 1850, entry, in Hardy, Journal.

25. The lower figure was not an unreasonable guess. In addition to the charges for wagons, fees of from 25 cents to $1 were assessed for transporting horses and mules across the river, while the cost for oxen ranged up to $2. Most animals, of course, were swum across, and many emigrants, because of lack of money, long waiting lines at the ferries, or, later in summer, low water levels, forded the river. Nonetheless, the business at the principal ferries was fantastic. Up to June 6, 1,600 wagons had already crossed at one ferry and the main segment of the migration had yet to arrive. During the high tide the Hickman ferry crossed an average of 300 wagons a day—$1,500—plus the not inconsiderable additional sums received for crossing animals. As of June 21 Franklin Langworthy stated

that 7,000 "teams"—i.e., wagons—had been crossed at the Upper Ferry. At least two men still remained operating one ferryboat on August 9. June 21, 1850, entry, in Langworthy, *Scenery of the Plains,* 56; John H. McBride to his wife, June 23, 1850, in McBride, Letters (typescripts); June 17, 1850, entry, in Rothwell, Journal and Letters, 113–14; June 6, 1850, entry, in Clapp, *Journal of Travels,* 25; June 29, 1850, entry, in Paden, ed., *Journal of Madison Berryman Moorman,* 33; Aug. 8, 9, 1850, entries, in Coke, *Ride over the Rocky Mountains,* 164–65.

26. Carson's trail stature was such that when he suggested to William Frush that due to the immense emigration it would be wiser to go to California by way of Oregon, Frush went to Oregon. May 15, June 18, Sept. 13, 1850, entries, in Frush, Diary; John S. Tutt to John Dougherty, July 1, 1850, quoted in Hafen and Young, *Fort Laramie and the Pageant of the West* (1938), 166; Quaife, ed., *Kit Carson's Autobiography* (1935), 138; letter of "Cheyenne," June 5, 1850, in St. Louis *Daily Missouri Republican,* July 20, 1850; May 5, 1850, entry, in Millington, Diary (microfilm of MS); F. T. Russell to W. F. Switzler, May 29, 1850, in Wyman, ed., *California Emigrant Letters* (1952), 107. Henry Coke, who met two mountaineers with cattle and horses to trade on a branch of the Green River, learned that after twelve years they had given up trapping in favor of the more lucrative emigrant trade. Aug. 27, 1850, entry, in Coke, *Ride over the Rocky Mountains,* 202–3.

27. May 26–27, 1850, entry, in Millington, Diary; June 1, 1850, entry, in Blood, Diary, 21; June 16, 1850, entry, in "The Memoirs of Lemuel Clarke McKeeby" (1924), 54; June 28, 1850, entry, in Keith, "Journal of Crossing the Plains" ([1961]), 5.

28. Huddleston traveled in A. P. Ankeny's company, and it is possible that Ankeny and not Huddleston was the major proprietor. See the June 24, 1850, entry, in Payne, Saint Louis to San Francisco (typescript), 55; July 9, 1850, entry, in Wolcott, Journal (MS); "James Huddleston, of Eugene, Or." (1890), 103–4. On the other Sublette ferry endeavors see the June 10, 1850, entry, in Sawyer, *Way Sketches,* ed. Eberstadt (1926), 50–51; July 19–22, 1850, entries, in Steele, *Across the Plains in 1850,* ed. Schafer (1930), 111–14, 119; July 4, 1850, entry, in King, Journal, 9; June 16, 1850, entry, in "Diary of Thomas Woodward" (1934), 437; July 3, 1850, entry, in Hardy, Journal; July 14, 1850, entry, in McKinstry, Diary, 67.

29. June 15, 20, July 3–4, 1850, entries of William H. Kilgore, in Muench, ed., *The Kilgore Journal* (1949), 31, 34, 39–40; May 28, June 10, 1850, entries, in Millington, Diary; June 7, 12, 13, 1850, entries, in Blood, Diary, 24, 27; July 20, 1850, entry, in Newcomb, Journal (photocopy of MS); June 23–26, July 4, 7, 1850, entries, in Shields, Journal; June 24, 1850, entry, in Cagwin, Diary (typescript), 37. There apparently was no ferry over the Bear River crossing prior to reaching Salt Lake in 1850, although in late June, Shields's emigrant party divided a tidy profit from one busy day's work with their extemporized ferry. The operators of these ferries carried on some trading with the passing emigrants, and of course Fort Bridger was also a stop on the trip to Salt Lake City.

30. One of the sutlers was at Loring, where he was identified by an emigrant as "Mr. Ritchie"; his two partners were at the Soda Springs branch location. Another overlander explained that an American enterprise, Owens, Rich, and Company, was trading at Fort Loring, which, together with the reference to "Owens Trading Post," suggests that sometime sutler John Owen was involved. Owen in 1850 also purchased the Catholic mission of St. Mary's in Montana and turned it into a trading post known as Fort Owen. See the July 23, 28, 1850, entries, in McKinstry, Diary, 76, 86–87; July 11, 1850, entry, in King, Journal, 10; July 26, 1850, entry, in Frush, Diary, 35; July 2, 1850, entry, in Ingalls, *Journal of a Trip to California,* 30; Lavender, *The Rockies* (1968), 98–99. For background on Cantonment Loring see Chap. 6 above, p. 208, and for additional mountain traders see the July 22, 1850, entry, in Krill, Diary (MS); Aug. 1, 1850, entry, in Dowell, Journal, 23; July 14, 1850, entry, in Dutton, "Across the Plains in 1850," 469; July 1, 2, 1850, entries, in "Diary of Orange Gaylord to California and Oregon" (1920), 411. "Peg-leg" Smith also operated his post in 1850, but in fall could no longer resist the golden fever and moved to California. Humphreys, "Peg Leg Smith" (1966), 32.

31. May 4, 15, June 1, 1850, entries, in Keller, *A Trip across the Plains* (1851, 1955 reprint), 7, 10, 14; July 12, 1850, entry, in Frink, *Journal of the Adventures of a Party of California Gold-Seekers* (1897), 73. At the fort John Williams discovered chickens for sale at $5 apiece. July 25, 1859, entry, in "Journal of John T. Williams" (1936), 403. C. W. Smith, on

June 28 at Soda Springs, "saw an old man who called himself Captain Grant" (*Journal of a Trip to California,* 64). If this was Richard Grant, he may have been associated with Loring's sutler faction, for according to Smith he was likewise urging travel on the Fort Hall road and contending that all cattle were sure to die on the Hudspeth Cutoff.

32. Letter of "Cheyenne," May 14, 1850, in St. Louis *Daily Missouri Republican,* June 9, 1850, reprinted in Wyman, *California Emigrant Letters,* 112–13.

33. Sept. 2, 7, 1850, entries, in McKinstry, Diary, 132, 137; Sept. 19, 1850, entry, in Jones, Diary (photocopy of MS). If the emigrants did not have money they reacted as James Williams did. Explaining his initial feelings upon learning the prices demanded for food, he wrote: "Then I began to get scared." Williams to his wife, Aug. 20, 1850, in Williams, Papers (MSS and typescripts). As Madison Moorman discovered, sometimes even having money could be problematical: "Our money was in Louisiana Bank Bills—and although it was worth as much as gold it was a hard matter to make the narrow-souled Missourians believe it." Aug. 28, 1850, entry, in Paden, ed., *Journal of Madison Berryman Moorman,* 77.

34. July 30, 1850, entry, in Christy, Journal. C., writing from Sacramento on Sept. 22, 1850, after completing an overland trip, stated that "there were hundreds of trading posts on Carson River." St. Louis *Daily Missouri Republican,* Nov. 18, 1850.

35. There were some unscrupulous traders. Samuel R. Thurston, veteran of an 1847 overland trip, wrote a letter printed in the Dec. 12, 1850, issue of the Washington *National Intelligencer* that emigrants should carefully avoid the "*sharpers*" who would meet them at the end of the trail to try to secure their possessions "for a song." At the other extreme, Fort Boise commander James Craigie earned plaudits from an 1850 passerby for his conscientious care of a destitute emigrant. The overlander had been wounded in a gunshot accident and Craigie was attending him at the post, washing and bandaging the wound twice daily. Sept. 24, 1850, entry, in Coke, *Ride over the Rocky Mountains,* 271–72.

36. Letter of J. W. B. Reynolds, Dec. 1, 1850, in St. Louis *Daily Missouri Republican,* Mar. 20, 1851; Aug. 31, 1850, entry, in McKinstry, Diary, 125. A comparison of the price ranges at trading posts in 1849 and 1850 (Table 6, Chap. 7, and Table 7, Chap. 8, below) reveals the decided increase in 1850.

37. An August 29 recapitulation of California prices for the merchandise and animals traders were accumulating for mere pittances indicated wagons were worth $100 to $150, harnesses $30 to $50 per set, horses and mules from $20 to $80 per head, and oxen $75 per yoke. St. Louis *Daily Missouri Republican,* Oct. 23, 1850; Aug. 31, 1850, entry, in "Journal of A. W. Harlan," 58; Aug. 8, 1850, entry, in Christy, Journal; Aug. 11, 1850, entry, in Rothwell, Journal and Letters, 188; Oct. 19, 1850, entry, in Langworthy, *Scenery of the Plains,* 150; R. J. Roylan to Joliet *Signal,* n.d., reprinted in St. Joseph *Gazette,* Oct. 16, 1850; New York *Herald,* Oct. 6, 1850; Sept. 14, 1850, entry, in Steele, *Across the Plains in 1850,* 208. See also San Francisco *Daily Alta California,* Sept. 19, 1850.

38. Wilson to his wife, Nov. 24, 1850, and to his father, Dec. 26, 1850, in Wilson, Letters and Day Book (MSS and typescripts).

39. Oct. 19, 1850, entry, in Langworthy, *Scenery of the Plains,* 150; Sept. 4, 1850, entry, in *Journal of John Wood* (1852), 66; Aug. 3, 1850, entry, in Diary of Trip to California, Henry Wellenkamp (typescript), 10; Aug. 7, 1850, entry, in Ingalls, *Journal of a Trip to California,* 42; Aug. 31, 1850, entry, in McKinstry, Diary, 125–26; Aug. 3, 1850, entry, in Christy, Journal.

40. New York *Daily Tribune,* Oct. 19, 1850; Oct. 11, 1850, entry, in Langworthy, *Scenery of the Plains,* 136. On August 21, in the Carson Valley, Hugh Skinner (Diary) passed a post operated by James Harnet and Alex Chauvin.

41. Two Wisconsin brothers named Hulburt had already been in business for three weeks when J. S. Shepherd passed their post on August 12 near Tragedy Springs on the Carson River route into California (*Journal of Travel,* 37), and Henry Davis and a man named Hays of an Ohio company had stopped at Humboldt Meadows, where they were doing "a good business." Two other men of that company had gone into business selling hay to the emigrants in the same area and were also doing well. There were even emigrant-operated ferries providing crossing services over the Humboldt River at $3 per wagon. Aug. 5, 9, 11, 12, 1850, entries, in Hardy, Journal; July 29, 1850, entry, in Evans, Journal (MS), 139.

42. July 29, 1850, entry, in "The Shoemaker Diary of 1850" ([1961]), 18; Aug. 7, 1850,

entry, in Shields, Journal; Aug. 24, 1850, entry, in Skinner, Diary; Aug. 22, 1850, entry, in Montgomery, Diary (MS), 65.

43. San Francisco *Daily Alta California*, July 23, 1850; Aug. 10, 1850, entry, in Abbey, *A Trip across the Plains* (1850), 56. D. A. Shaw viewed Ragtown in similar light: "It was the best place for catching suckers that I have ever seen." Shaw, *Eldorado, or California as Seen by a Pioneer* (1900), 117–18. For more background on Mormon Station's founders, and commentary on the reasons its founding date has so often been rendered as 1849, see Morgan, *The Humboldt* (1943), 199–201; Brooks, "The Mormons in Carson County" (1965), 8–11; Elliott, "Nevada's First Trading Post" (1970), 3–10. Emigrant mention of post construction is found in the July 5, 1850, entry, in Fawkes, ed., *The Journal of Walter Griffith Pigman* (1942), 31; July 14, 1850, entry, in Jewett, Journal (typescript), 37; July 16, 1850, entry, in Ellis, Diary (photocopy of MS). See also R. Wilson to Editor of *Alta California*, Sept. 21, 1850, reprinted in New York *Daily Tribune*, Nov. 22, 1850.

44. May 19, 1850, entry, in Ingalls, *Journal of a Trip to California*, 17; May 22, 1850, entry, in Rothwell, Journal and Letters, 63; St. Joseph *Gazette*, June 7, 1850.

45. During the weeks the Estill wagons were encamped at Pacific Springs, the Continental Divide became a temporary trading station where brandy and cigars were sold. Indeed, on July 10 Estill even promoted a cultural attraction: for a dollar emigrants could attend a concert by a "great violinist," Mr. Kelly. July 1, 1850, entry, in King, Journal, 9; July 10, 1850, entry, in McKinstry, Diary, 62.

46. St. Louis *Daily Missouri Republican*, Apr. 30, 1850; Liberty, Mo., *Weekly Tribune*, May 3, 1850; Barry, *Beginning of the West*, 937–39; St. Joseph *Gazette*, Aug. 21, 1850. One of Estill's major problems was that returnees seeking funds claimed to be Express Mail Line agents, thereby securing considerable sums of money from unsuspecting emigrants. It is not known whether the letters thus fraudulently received were ever posted. See St. Louis *Daily Missouri Republican*, Aug. 22, 1850.

47. Milgram, "Estill & Co. Express," 328–30.

48. Thissell, *Crossing the Plains in '49* (1903), 34–35.

49. St. Louis *Daily Missouri Republican*, Apr. 23, 1851; St. Joseph *Gazette*, May 14, 1851; Barry, *Beginning of the West*, 998.

50. Letter of "An Emigrant Captive," July 12, 1851, in St. Louis *Daily Missouri Republican*, Aug. 23, 1851; letter of Asa C. Call, Sept. 20, 1850, in New York *Daily Tribune*, Jan. 30, 1851.

51. The sparse emigration probably contributed to the lowering of prices at the Platte ferries. Susan Cranston reported fees of $3 at the lower and $2.50 at the upper crossing. June 16, 1851, entry, in Cranston, Journal (MS and typescript), 7. For the other 1851 enterprises see Morgan, ed., *The Overland Diary of James A. Pritchard* (1959), 153, n. 40; June 22, 1851, entry, in "Robert Robe's Diary while Crossing the Plains" (1928), 57; Jones, "Those Wild Reshaw Boys," in Taunton, ed., *Sidelights of the Sioux Wars* (1967), 11.

52. June 23, Aug. 11, 1851, entries, in Johnson, Diary (MS), 56, 91; July 2, 1851, entry, in "Robert Robe's Diary," 58; Aug. 10, Sept. 4, 1851, entries, in Crawford, "Journal of a Trip across the Plains" (1924), 159, 166; Aug. 23, 1851, entry, in Cranston, Journal, 16.

53. Jones, "Those Wild Reshaw Boys," 11; June 11, July 1, 1851, entries, in Johnson, Diary, 48, 61; June 22, July 1, 1851, entry, in "Robert Robe's Diary," 57; July 12, Aug. 9, 1851, entries, in "Diary of John S. Zeiber" (1923), 317, 321; July 9, 1851, entry, in Crawford, "Journal of a Trip across the Plains," 150; July 6, 11, 1851, entries, in Cranston, Journal, 10. Richard's partners in the bridge business were Langdon, Steele, Miller, and Randall. At Laramie their charge for crossing one wagon on the new bridge fluctuated between $2.50 and $3; at the Platte crossing the fee went unreported. McDermott, "Fort Laramie's Iron Bridge"(1962), 137. An 1852 overlander reported that the Laramie bridge alone had cost $2,400. June 14, 1852, entry, in Sharp, Diary (MS).

54. Kanesville *Frontier Guardian*, Mar. 21, 1851.

55. St. Joseph *Gazette*, Dec. 25, 1850, Feb. 28, 1851, and subsequent issues. Richard's name was frequently rendered as "Reshaw" or some such variant by contemporaries.

56. Mattes, "Seth E. Ward," in Hafen, ed., *The Mountain Men and the Fur Trade*, 3:363–64; McDermott, "James Bordeaux," in ibid., 5:71; McDermott, "Joseph Bissonette," 53; Richmond, "Developments along the Overland Trail" (1952), 174.

486

57. July 9, Aug. 27, 28, Sept. 6, 1851, entries, in Crawford, "Journal of a Trip across the Plains," 150, 164, 166; Aug. 9, 12, Sept. 22, 23, 25, Oct. 3, 1851, entries, in "Diary of John S. Zeiber," 321, 330–33; Elliott, "Richard ('Captain Johnny') Grant" (1935), 6; Wells, "Richard Grant," in Hafen, ed., *The Mountain Men and the Fur Trade,* 9:183–84; July 6, Aug. 17, 1851, entries, in Cranston, Journal, 10, 15; July 7, 1851, entry, in "Robert Robe's Diary," 58; Aug. 15, 1851, entry, in Johnson, Diary, 93. For mention of continued 1851 entrepreneurial activity at Soda Springs see Munkres, "Soda Springs: Curiosity of the Trail" (1971), 233–34.

58. Sept. 20, 1851, entry, in Bowen, Diary (microfilm of copy).

59. San Francisco *Daily Alta California,* Apr. 4, 1852.

60. Morgan, *The Humboldt,* 202–3; Bancroft, *History of Nevada, Colorado, and Wyoming* (1890), 69, 71; Brooks, "The Mormons in Carson County," 11–13; Mack, *Nevada: A History of the State* (1936), 149–53, 178; letter of L. Dow, Nov. 25, 1851, in New York *Daily Tribune,* Feb. 17, 1852.

61. For good measure, 1852 was also the year 10,000 Latter-Day Saints traveled to the Salt Lake Valley, similarly the largest Mormon migration of the antebellum period.

62. Barry, *Beginning of the West,* 1067–70; June 20, July 7, 11, 14, Sept. 5, 17, 1852, entries, in Verdenal, Journal (typescript), 17, 23–24, 37, 39; July 1, Aug. 24, 26, 1852, entries, in Hampton, Diary (typescript), bk. 2:1, bk. 3:1; July 10, 13, Aug. 25, 26, 1852, entries, in Anable, Journal (MS and copy); July 4, 6, 1852, entries, in Wayman, Journal and Letters (photocopies of MSS); June 24, July 19, 1852, entries, in Byers, Journal (MS), 39, 63; San Francisco *Daily Alta California,* Nov. 2, 1851. Ward and Guerrier left their Ash Point location in 1852 for Sand Point, nine miles west of Fort Laramie. Mattes, "Seth E. Ward," 364–65. Enoch W. Conyers, at Devil's Gate on July 2 ("Diary of E. W. Conyers" [1906], 455–56), identified the trader building a timber post there as "a Frenchman by the name of Schambau, who . . . was with Colonel Fremont during his notable trip through this country in the '40s." The St. Joseph *Gazette* in its Apr. 28, 1852, issue termed the post "Archambault's Fort." The entrepreneur in question was Auguste Archambeault. Frémont, "A Report of the Exploring Expedition to Oregon and North California," in Jackson and Spence, eds., *The Expeditions of John Charles Frémont* (1970–73), 1:383, 706. At one of the Soda Springs posts French traders had accumulated from 800 to 1,000 horses and mules for the emigrant trade. June 29, 1852, entry, in Lewis, Memorandum or Notes (MSS and typescripts).

63. Aug. 3, 1852, entry, in Sawyer, Journal (typescript), 26; Aug. 4, 5, 1852, entries, in Wayman, Journal and Letters, 157, 160; July 21, 1852, entry, in Snodgrass, Journal (MS and typescript).

64. San Francisco *Daily Alta California,* June 20, 1852; Sept. 1, 1852, entry, in Sharp, Diary. In the spring of 1852 the Carson Valley population alone was estimated at 4,000, and one overlander commented that Mormon Station was the first place that seemed like home since leaving the Missouri frontier. San Francisco *Daily Alta California,* May 8, 1852; Sept. 18, 1852, entry, in Gee, Journal (MS and typescript).

65. July 28, 1852, entry, in Paxson, ed., "T. Turnbull's Travels" (1914), 206; Sept. 9, 1852, entry, in Hampton, Diary, bk. 3:2; Aug. 8, 1852, entry, in Sharp, Diary.

66. Sept. 24, Oct. 1, 3, 8, 12, 1852, entries, in John N. Lewis, Diary (MS); Sept. 14, 15, 23, 1852, entries, in "Diary of E. W. Conyers," 500–501, 506–7; Oct. 2, 13, 23, 1852, entries, in Adams, "Crossing the Plains in 1852" (1905), 321, 324, 327; A. to T. J. Dryer, Aug. 21, 1852, in Portland *Oregonian,* Sept. 4, 1852; Crawford, *Scenes of Earlier Days* (1898, 1962 reprint), 64–65; "Diary of Mr. Davis" (1910), 380. The vegetables, fruit, and salmon available at these establishments were much appreciated by trail-weary travelers.

67. Sept. 17, 28, 30, 1852, entries, in Adams, "Crossing the Plains in 1852," 317, 320–21; Grant to Julia Dent Grant, Oct. 26, 1852, in Simon, ed., *The Papers of Ulysses S. Grant, I* (1967), 270.

68. Phillips, ed., " 'Dick's Works' " (1929), 258; July 11, 12, 24, 1852, entries, in Keen, Journal (typescript), 32, 70, 73, 86–87; J. H. McDonald to his father, May 26–27, 1852 (MS); Lobenstine, ed., *Extracts from the Diary of William C. Lobenstine* (1920), 31. Yet it would be erroneous to assume that overlanders could count on finding even necessary supplies at every post at any time during the 1850s. While it was rare for an overlander to report that standard provisions were not to be had at a major post—as Charles Stevens wrote about

Fort Hall in 1852—it did occur, although far less often than in the 1840s. Stevens to his brother and sister, Oct. 31, 1852, in Rockwood, ed., "Letters of Charles Stevens" (1936), 143.

69. Sept. 1, 1852, entry, in Anable, Journal; Aug. 15, 1852, entry, in Crane, Journal (MS); June 7 [6?], 1852, entry, in Keen, Journal, 42–43.

70. June 30, July 2, 27, 1842, entries, in Egbert, Diary (photocopy of typescript), 29, 32; June 13, 1852, entry, in Sharp, Diary; Aug. 17, 1852, entry, in Wayman, Journal and Letters, 172.

71. Long, A True Story ([1915]), 11; A. to T. J. Dryer, Aug. 16, 1852, in Portland Oregonian, Sept. 4, 1852; Meeker, The Busy Life of Eighty-five Years (1916), 48; Aug. 22, 1852, entry, in "Diary of E. W. Conyers," 487–88.

72. Cole, In the Early Days along the Overland Trail, comp. Hardy (1905), 65; Sept. 15, 1852, entry, in "Diary of E. W. Conyers," 501.

73. Overlanders reported crossing facilities at the following locations in 1852, including, in most cases, price per wagon: Elkhorn River, $2; Loup Fork River, $2.50 to $3; Kansas River; Big Blue River, $3; Laramie River, $1 to $3; Platte River at Fort Laramie, $2 to $8; North Platte River at Deer Creek and above, $2 to $8; Sweetwater River, 40¢ to $3; Green River, $3 to $16; Black's Fork; Weber River (before Salt Lake City), $2; Weber River (beyond Salt Lake City), $1 to $3; Bear River (beyond Salt Lake City), $3 to $5; Malad Creek, 50¢; Ham's fork, $1; Smith's Fork, 50¢ to $1; Thomas' Fork, $1 to $1.50; Carson River, $1; Portneuf Creek, 25¢; Portneuf River, $1 to $7; Snake River at Salmon Falls; Snake River near Bannock Creek; Snake River at Fort Boise, $2.50 to $3; Deschutes River, $2.50 to $5; the Cascades. At the Cascades there was also a short mule-drawn "railroad" which transported goods at the rate of seventy-five cents per 100 pounds from the boat landing on The Dalles side of the falls to the boat landing on the Portland side. The 1852 fare on the steamer to Portland from the Cascades was $6 per passenger. This range of ferry and bridge crossing fees has been drawn from the letters and diaries kept by 1852 overlanders. At many of these ferries and bridges overlanders were assessed additional fees for crossing draft animals and passengers, and some of the ferrymen met emigrants on the trail in efforts to direct them to the proper ferry. July 2, 1852, entry, in Barry, ed., "Overland to the Gold Fields of California" (1942), 267. A few of the new ferry operators of the year can be identified: Sidney Smith at the Kansas River approximately six miles below Uniontown; Frank J. Marshall at the Big Blue crossing (Barry, Beginning of the West, 1087–88, 1067–70); P. L. McLaughlin and Reuben Middleton at the Elkhorn and Loup Fork rivers (Kanesville Frontier Guardian and Iowa Sentinel, May 13, 1852; Kanesville Western Bugle, June 16, 1852); Clark, Townsend, Wheeling, and Company at the Elkhorn River (June 1, 1852, entry, in "Diary of Rev. John McAllister" [1925], 474); "Hawley's ferry" at the Loup Fork (June 5, 1852, entry, in ibid., 475); two mountain men at the Platte River crossing at Fort Laramie (letter of G. W. H., June 9, 1852, in St. Joseph Gazette, July 28, 1852); "Brusters ferry" at the North Platte crossing, where Mormons held forth again at the Upper Ferry, an Illinois emigrant ferry was mentioned, and an overlander indicated that at the Upper Ferry "6 scows were kept there by French and Negroes" (July 5, 1852, entry, in Gee, Journal; June 19, 1852, entry, in Clark, The California Guide [MS and typescript]; June 1, 1852, entry, in Keen, Journal, 36; June 14, 1852, entry, in Paxson, ed., "T. Turnbull's Travels," 174); Churby Wheettock and a man named Bently at the Green River, where at least two ferries were also maintained on the new Kinney Cutoff route, Mormons operated a ferry on the Salt Lake route, and one emigrant endorsed "Brigers ferry" at the Green River, presumably meaning the eminent mountaineer Jim Bridger, who also operated a ferry at Black's Fork (Aug. 20, 1858, entry, in Ackley, "Across the Plains in 1858" [1941], 206; June 25–26, 1852, entry, in Andrews, Journal [MS and typescript]; July 1, 1852, entry, in Clark, California Guide; June 29, 1852, entry, in Hayden, Diary [MS and typescript]; June 15, 1852, entry, in Snodgrass, Journal); Edward J. Allen, an 1852 overlander, established an emigrant ferry over the Snake River at Fort Boise in which overlander Ezra Meeker was also involved (Mahlberg, "Edward J. Allen, Pioneer and Roadbuilder" [1953], 157–58; Meeker, Busy Life, 49); an emigrant, "Mr. McCoy," was identified as the ferryman at the "upper ferry" on the Deschutes River, Mr. Olney operating the main ferry and resenting the emigrant competition to such a degree that he ultimately purchased their extemporized ferry for $1,000,

thereafter charging $5 per wagon, whereas the enterprising emigrants had only exacted a 3-dollar toll per wagon (Aug. 5, 1852, entry, in Fox, Memorandum [microfilm of diary typescript], 40; Sept. 13, 1852, entry, in "Diary of E. W. Conyers," 499–500; A. to T. J. Dryer, Aug. 16, 21, 1852, in Portland *Oregonian*, Sept. 4, 1852). For the Cascades "railroad" see Oct. 24–26, 1852, entries, in Adams, "Crossing the Plains in 1852," 328–29.

74. Silas V. Miller to his brother, Nov. 24, 1852 (photocopy of MS); Cartwright, *Natural History of Western Wild Animals,* ed. Bailey (1875), 200; June 5, 1852, entry, in Gage, Diary (typescript), 8; June 19, 1852, entry, in Clark, California Guide; Aug. 20, 1858, entry, in Ackley, "Across the Plains in 1858," 206.

75. Meeker, *Busy Life,* 27–28; June 29, July 1, 2, 1852, entries, in Bradley, Journal (MS), 75–76, 78, 80–81; July 24, 1852, entry, in Barry, ed., "Overland to the Gold Fields of California," 276.

76. Algeline Jackson Ashley had reported that there was a good bridge over the river on June 3; eight days later Solomon Kingery indicated it had been chopped down. June 3, 1852, entry, in Ashley, Diary (typescript), 3; June 11, 1852, entry, in Kingery, Letters (MSS and typescripts). The Fort Laramie bridge survived the traveling season.

77. One steamboat was in operation at St. Joseph, two at Kanesville/Council Bluffs. Caleb and Alice Richey to Lafayette and Hannah Richey, June 20, 1852, in "Richey Family Record" (1915), 590; Barry, *Beginning of the West,* 1087; Carpenter, I Crossed the Plains in the 50's (microfilm of MS); Phillips, ed., *Forty Years on the Frontier* (1925, 1957), 41.

78. May 20, 1852, entry, in Sawyer, Journal, 5; May 7–19, 1852, entries, in Kerns, "Journal of Crossing the Plains to Oregon" (1917), 157.

79. Brooks, *A Pioneer Mother of California* (1922), 19–20.

80. May 31, 1852, entry, in Crane, Journal.

81. White to Samuel Porter Williams, Apr. 19, 1853, in Winther and Thornbrough, eds., *To Oregon in 1852* (1964), 29.

82. Kanesville *Frontier Guardian and Iowa Sentinel,* May 6, 13, 20, 1852.

83. A. to T. J. Dryer, Aug. 16, 1852, in Portland *Oregonian,* Sept. 4, Oct. 30, 1852; Norton, "My Overland Trip to California in 1852" (Oct., 1934), 11; July 18, 1852, entry, in Keen, Journal, 77–78.

84. Morgan, "The State of Deseret" (1940), 99; Sept. 30, 1851, Jan. 12, 14, 17, 19–23, Mar. 2, 1852, entries of Hosea Stout, in Brooks, ed., *On the Mormon Frontier* (1964), 2:406, 413–19, 429; Salt Lake City *Deseret News,* June 26, 1852.

85. Morgan, "The Administration of Indian Affairs in Utah" (1948), 391–92; Arrington, *Great Basin Kingdom* (1958), 105–6; Holeman to Luke Lea, Nov. 3, 1852, in Morgan, ed., "Washakie and the Shoshoni, Part III" (1954), 141–45; H. B. Fleming to George W. Manypenny, Aug. 15, 1854, in ibid., 158–59.

86. Salt Lake City *Deseret News,* June 26, 1852.

87. June 14, 1852, entry, in Riker, *Journal of a Trip to California* ([1855?]), 14. See the June 14, 1852, entry, in Snodgrass, Journal, for a similar account of the same incident.

88. June 24, 1852, entry, in ibid.; June 19, 1852, entry, in Bradley, Journal, 60.

89. Later advertisements indicated additional stations had been established at Forts Kearny and Laramie, the North Fork of the Platte, and Salt Lake City. St. Joseph *Gazette,* Apr. 28, May 5, 1852; June 8, 1852, entry of James C. David, in Urbanek, "1852 on the Oregon Trail" (1962), 56; June 3, 1852, entry, in Fox, Memorandum, 15; June 6, 21, 1852, entries, in Crane, Journal; Barry, *Beginning of the West,* 1080–81. Jared Fox also thought the Blodget Express might be a hoax, but dispatched several letters anyway.

90. The road builders hired passing overlanders at the rate of $2 per day to assist with the project. July 15–18, 24, 29, 1852, entries, in Egbert, Diary, 35, 37–38; July 23–24, 1852, entries, in Hampton, Diary, bk. 2:4; May 17, 1852, entry, in Keen, Journal, 24.

91. Cooke, *Crossing the Plains in 1852* (1923), 14–15; Carpenter, I Crossed the Plains in the 50's.

92. Taylor to "Friend Hadley," July 17, 31, 1853, in Watertown, Wis., *Chronicle,* Nov. 2, 1853, reprinted in "Letters of S. H. Taylor to the Watertown Chronicle" (1921), 148; Sept. 3, 1853, entry, in "Diary of Mrs. Amelia Stewart Knight" (1933), 51; July 6, 7, 1853, entries, in Kaiser and Knuth, eds., "From Ithaca to Clatsop Plains" (1961), 341, 344 ff.

93. Taylor to "Friend Hadley," 138; J. H. Holeman to Brigham Young, Sept. 30, 1853,

in *Report of the Commissioner of Indian Affairs,* 1853, 33 Cong., 1 Sess., Sen. Ex. Doc. 1, Ser. 690 (1854), 446–47; Sept. 14, 1853, entry, in "Diary of Celinda E. Hines" (1921), 120. One of the prospering twenty-five posts in the Laramie region was that of Geminien P. Beauvais, begun in 1853 five miles east of Fort Laramie. Hanson, Jr., "Geminien P. Beauvais," in Hafen, ed., *The Mountain Men and the Fur Trade,* 7:38–39. In 1853 several posts were reported in the Soda Springs vicinity. Munkres, "Soda Springs," 233.

94. Miller to his brother, Nov. 24, 1852, 22.

95. San Francisco *Daily Alta California,* July 6, 1853; Grant, "Fort Hall under the Hudson's Bay Company" (1940), 39; Aug. 3, 1853, entry, in Kaiser and Knuth, eds., "From Ithaca to Clatsop Plains," 371.

96. The sutler advertisement is quoted in Barry, *Beginning of the West,* 1140, and the report on the St. Louis fire is found in the St. Joseph *Gazette,* Aug. 3, 1853.

97. Grant, "Fort Hall under the Hudson's Bay Company," 39; Aug. 2, 1853, entry, in Stuart and Stuart, eds., "Calvin B. West of the Umpqua" (1960), 93. One group of incoming overlanders reported that in the Carson Valley, "Speculators and traders were plenty . . . and nearly desperate for victims." San Francisco *Daily Herald,* Aug. 3, 1853, in Cohen, Scrapbooks (typescripts), 168–69.

98. The bridge was much more substantial than its 1851 predecessor, the twelve cedar arches being grounded on huge tree trunks filled with stone and gravel. July 26, 1853, entry, in Falbo, trans. and ed., *California and Overland Diaries of Count Leonetto Cipriani,* 89; June 26, 1853, entry, in McClure, Diary (reproduced), 34; San Francisco *Daily Alta California,* Aug. 7, 1854. On the proprietors and their rumored costs and profit, see the July 29, 1853, entry, in "Diary of Dr. Thomas Flint" (1923), 90; June 28, 1853, entry, in "Journal of Henry Allyn" (1924), 406; July 1, 2, 1853, entries, in Smith, Diary (MS); "Autobiography of William K. Sloan" (1926), 245–46; Barry, *Beginning of the West,* 1148–49.

99. Ward and Guerrier also operated a North Platte ferry in 1853 nine miles above the fort—at their Sand Point trading post. Barry, *Beginning of the West,* 1148–49; June 13, 1853, entry, in Newton, Diary (MS); Mattes, "Seth E. Ward," 365–66; Jones, "Seth E. Ward" (1927), 9; Jones, "Those Wild Reshaw Boys," 11; McDermott, "John Baptiste Richard," 297. In the absence of the bridge, a ferry was maintained over the Laramie River through the emigration period. These Laramie and Platte River ferries even operated at night, but Andrew McClure wanted no part of that: "Ferrying tonight and, from the noise, the ferrymen are all drunk. This is bad policy, swift stream; poor boat; dark night; and a drunken crew, too much risk." June 14, 1853, entry, in McClure, Diary, 25–26.

100. June 15, 1853, entry, in "Diary of Mrs. Amelia Stewart Knight," 44; June 30, 1853, entry, in McClure, Diary, 38. Prior to the rickety bridge's demise, emigrants paid from $1 to $3 to avoid fording the Sweetwater. Presumably this was Louis Ganard's bridge. See below, p. 299.

101. "Van Ogle's Memory of Pioneer Days" (1922), 271; July 13, 1853, entry, in Belshaw, Diary (typescript), 13; July 24, 1853, entry, in Kaiser and Knuth, eds., "From Ithaca to Clatsop Plains," 358. See also Haas, "Pioneer Autobiography" (Oct., 1938), 9. Thomas Flint estimated fifty residents at the Green River outpost on the Salt Lake road. Aug. 19, 1853, entry, in "Diary of Dr. Thomas Flint," 95.

102. May 14, 1853, entry, in Pengra, Diary (reproduced), 18; Haas, "Pioneer Autobiography," 9–10; Sept. 3, 1853, entry, in Newton, Diary; July 6, 1853, entry, in Ward, Diary (MS), 56; Aug. 5, 6, 9, 1853, entries, in "Journal of Henry Allyn," 425, 427.

103. John M. Hockaday to George W. Manypenny, June 17, 1854, in Morgan, ed., "Washakie and the Shoshoni, Part III," 159–60; Anderson, *Desert Saints* (1942), 96; Salt Lake City *Deseret News,* Feb. 19, Mar. 5, June 18, 1853.

104. Vasquez had apparently been involved in that same 1853 ferry operation. May 18, 1854, entry of Hosea Stout, in Brooks, ed., *On the Mormon Frontier,* 2:517; Alter, *Jim Bridger* (1962), 250–57; Aug. 27, 1853, entry, in "Diary of Dr. Thomas Flint," 97; Morgan, ed., "Washakie and the Shoshoni, Part III," 149–50, n. 69; Anderson, *Desert Saints,* 96; Gowans, "Fort Bridger and the Mormons" (1974), 49–67. Cohen, "James Bridger's Claims" (1940), 228–40, traces Bridger's long struggle to secure compensation from the U.S. government for the army's use of what he claimed was still his establishment. As Gowan's article makes clear, however, it was not.

105. "First Records of Carson Valley" (1966); Bancroft, *History of Nevada, Colorado, and Wyoming*, 72–73.

106. Ibid.; Marysville, Cal., *Daily Evening Herald*, Sept. 9, 1853.

107. By 1858 Father De Smet estimated that Dalles City had over 100 houses, many built of stone, and predicted a "fine future" for it. Its 1859 population has been estimated at 1,000. Chittenden and Richardson, eds., *Life, Letters and Travels of Father Pierre-Jean De Smet* (1905), 2:742; Knuth, " 'Picturesque' Frontier: the Army's Fort Dalles, Part Two" (1967), 24. One emigrant observed about Cascade Falls, "It appears to be quite a business place." Sept. 15, 18, 1853, entries, in Ellison, ed., "Diary of Maria Parsons Belshaw" (1932), 327–28; Sept. 16, 1853, entry, in Handsaker, Diary (reproduced), 32.

108. The Wood River "hospital," run by Dr. Clark, adjoined a grocery, mail station, and toll bridge. May 13, 1854, entry, in Burrel, Diary and Letter (MSS and typescripts), 8; May 28, June 11, 13, 16, 1854, entries, in Ebey, Diary (MS), 35, 48, 53, 57; May 31, June 3, 4, 9, 1854, entries, in McCowen, Diary (typescript), 18–19, 22–25. Richmond, "Developments along the Overland Trail," 246–47; June 11, 26, Sept. 12, 1854, entries, in The Diary of an Unknown Scout (typescript), 5, 7, 13; San Francisco *Daily Alta California*, Aug. 2, Nov. 10, 1854.

109. In 1853 and 1854 at least eight different steamboats were engaged temporarily or full-time in setting overlanders across the Missouri River. The *General Gaines,* operated by Wright Williamson and Company at St. Joseph in 1854, could transport twelve wagons and 200 head of cattle on one five-minute crossing. Barry, *Beginning of the West*, 144–45, 1205–6; May 5, 1853, entry, in "Diary of Mrs. Amelia Stewart Knight," 39; May 16, 1853, entry, in "Journal of Henry Allyn," 387; St. Joseph *Gazette*, Jan. 18, 1854; Wickman, "Peter A. Sarpy," in Hafen, ed., *The Mountain Men and the Fur Trade*, 4:294; Root, "Ferries in Kansas: Part I" (Feb., 1933), 23–24.

110. Barry, *Beginning of the West*, 1124–25; Baydo, "Overland from Missouri to Washington Territory in 1854" (1971), 79; June 6, 11, 1854, entries of Hosea Stout, in Brooks, ed., *On the Mormon Frontier*, 2:519; Aug. 19, 1854, entry, in Burrel, Diary and Letter, 36–37; Sept. 12, 1854, entry, in Diary of an Unknown Scout, 13; William A. Cornwall to Editor, San Francisco *Daily Alta California*, Oct. 27, 1854; Salt Lake City *Deseret News*, Aug. 10, 1854. Some of the new post and ferry proprietors identified in the 1854 trail literature include: John L. Ogee, who had contracted with Indian agent J. W. Whitfield to operate two ferries over the Kansas River near Uniontown, for which he received an annual salary of $580 (Barry, *Beginning of the West*, 1191, 1228–29); "Chouteas Trading Post" or the "Gratiot Houses," where chief trader J. P. B. Gratiot represented the Chouteau interest a few miles east of Fort Laramie (June 22, 1854, entry, in Murphy, Across the Plains [typescript], 4; McCann, "The Grattan Massacre" [1956], 5, n. 6); Joseph Bissonette's outpost, moved twice in 1854, the second time to get closer to Fort Laramie for protection from rampaging Indians, but remaining west of the fort (McDermott, "Joseph Bissonette," 55); mountain man Tim Goodale's ferry on the Green River, as well as similar enterprises conducted by mountaineers Kinney, Sublette, Robinson, and Baker—one overlander even asserting that there were forty-four ferryboats at the Green River in 1854 (Carter, "Tim Goodale," in Hafen, ed., *The Mountain Men and the Fur Trade*, 7:149–50; Baydo, "Overland from Missouri to Washington Territory in 1854," 79); A. P. Hawes's trading post near the Humboldt headwaters (San Francisco *Daily Alta California*, Nov. 15, 1854); Henry D. Isaacs's Snake River ferry at Fort Boise (Isaacs to Editor, Oct. 19, 1854, in Portland *Weekly Oregonian*, Oct. 28, 1854); and "Bakey's hotel" at Ragtown (Sept. 15, 1854, entry, in Murphy, Across the Plains, 11).

111. Wesley Tonner in a letter to "Dear Friends," Sept. 11, 1854, observed that *all* French roadside traders were worse thieves than the Indians (in Burrel, Diary and Letter, 44). See also the June 11, 1854, entry, in Ebey, Diary, 48–49; Baydo, "Overland from Missouri to Washington Territory in 1854," 74; June 29, 1854, entry, in Diary of an Unknown Scout, 7; Calvin Rohrer to "Dear Holly," Feb. 22, 1854, in St. Joseph *Gazette*, Apr. 19, 1854; St. Joseph *Gazette*, June 7, 1854; June 12, 1854, entry, in McCowen, Diary, 27; June 15–18, 21, 1854, entries of Hosea Stout, in Brooks, ed., *On the Mormon Frontier*, 2:520–21.

112. July 6, 1854, entry, in Myrick, Diary (photocopy of MS), 50; William Jedediah

Jones to Peter Jones, May 26, 1854, in Smith-Jones Family Papers (MSS); July 3, 1854, entry, in McCowen, Diary, 39. W. Scott Ebey evidenced a similar hint of frustration when he reported on John Richard's monopoly of the Sweetwater River posts in addition to his flourishing Platte bridge, through which "he had grown rich on the plains." Baydo, "Overland from Missouri to Washington Territory in 1854," 70.

113. Young, "Emigration," in Salt Lake City *Deseret News*, July 13, 1854.

114. William Keil to "Dear Brothers and Sisters," June [July] 12, 1855, in "From Bethel, Missouri, to Aurora, Oregon," trans. Bek (1953), 30; June 19, 20, 22, July 11, Sept. 17, 1856, entries, in Brown, *Journal of a Trip across the Plains* (1860), 37–39, 58, 100; Aug. 14, 1855, entry, in Remy and Brenchley, *A Journey to Great-Salt-Lake City* (1861), 1:53–54; "Fort Boise: From Imperial Outpost to Historic Site" (1962), 37–38; "Fort Hall, 1834–1856" (1968), 31. Some trail entrepreneurs who remained made the wrong decision. Jules Remy and Julius Brenchley, on August 8 just west of the Carson Valley, came upon an empty hut with fresh bloodstains on the floor, stark evidence of the fate which befell two post proprietors who had persevered there for two years. There was no indication of who the murderers had been, the only clue being that the men had been killed for their reputed savings of $300. Remy and Brenchley also described the murder of another Humboldt proprietor that year, presumably by Indians. *Journey to Great-Salt-Lake City*, 1:27, 92–93.

115. Council Bluffs *Weekly Bugle*, Mar. 24, 1858.

116. Salt Lake City *Deseret News*, July 11, 1855; Thomas S. Twiss to George W. Manypenny, Oct. 1, 1855, quoted in Hoopes, "Thomas S. Twiss, Indian Agent" (1933), 356; June 22, July 5, 10, 18, 1856, entries, in Brown, *Journal of a Trip*, 39–40, 51, 57, 62; July 22, 1857, entry, in Lowe, *Five Years a Dragoon*, ed. Russell (1965), 204; Oct. 21, 31, Nov. 2, 1857, entries, in "Diary of Judge William A. Carter" (1939), 94, 100, 101; Jones, "Those Wild Reshaw Boys," 14. The more clearly identifiable post and ferry operators of this four-year period include, in 1855: the "Leots Bluffs" post located four or five days' travel east of Fort Laramie (June 1, 1855, entry, in Bardin, Diary [photocopy of typescript], 4); "Dr. Winter's" post and "Perrin's station" along the Carson River, "Brown's" post and one kept by a Pole at Ragtown, "Captain Jones'" grogshop and "Peter Haws'" posts along the Humboldt—Haws apparently also maintaining a bridge over the Humboldt (Aug. 11, 14, 23, Sept. 3, 1855, entries, in Remy and Brenchley, *Journey to Great-Salt-Lake City*, 1:43, 51, 53–54, 88–93, 122–23, 137–38; Garland Hurt to Brigham Young, Sept., 1856, in *Report of the Commissioner of Indian Affairs*, Nov. 22, 1856, 34 Cong., 3 Sess., House Ex. Doc. 1, Ser. 893 [1857], 778–79); James Brown's bridges across the Weber and Ogden rivers (Dec. 13, 14, 18, 27, 1854, entries of Hosea Stout, in Brooks, ed., *On the Mormon Frontier*, 2:533–35, 537); in 1856: Tom Doolittle and Dan Patterson's newly built "ranch" at the Big Sandy a few days' travel west of Francis Marshall's Blue River post and ferry, "Bingham's" blacksmith shop at Pacific Springs, a man named Yates and Charley Connelly, westbound travelers that year, who established a trading enterprise at the Green River where "Baptiste Louisant" operated a ferry and post, "Black's Trading Post" at the Humboldt Sink, and Nixon's store at Mormon Station (May 24, July 19, 25, 28, Sept. 15, 22, 1856, entries, in Brown, *Journal of a Trip*, 17, 63, 66, 67, 99, 103; Maxwell, *Crossing the Plains* [1915], 145–46); Isaac Bullock and Lewis Robinson kept Mormon ferries at the Green River and Brigham and Joseph Young held the rights to the Bear River ferry and Malad bridge (Dec. 19–22, 31, 1855, entries of Hosea Stout, in Brooks, ed., *On the Mormon Frontier*, 2:573–75, 579); in 1857: G. H. Hollenberg's post at the Cottonwood Creek crossing in Kansas (Barry, ed. "Overland to the Gold Fields of California," 238, n. 17); Andrew Drips's trading post on the Platte River approximately twenty miles east of Fort Laramie (July 22, 1857, entry, in Lowe, *Five Years a Dragoon*, 204; Carter, "Andrew Drips," in Hafen, ed., *The Mountain Men and the Fur Trade*, 8:155); "Gilbert's station" in South Pass (Branch, "Frederick West Lander, Road-Builder" [1929], 183); "Jake Meek," an itinerant trader formerly associated with the Hudson's Bay Company, near City of the Rocks (Phillips, ed., *Forty Years on the Frontier*, 119); and in 1858: G. P. Beauvais's post five miles below Fort Laramie (St. Louis *Daily Missouri Republican*, Sept. 24, 1858, in *Publications of the Nebraska State Historical Society* [1922], 314; Kirk Anderson to Editor of *Missouri Republican*, Aug. 28, 1858, in Wells, "Kirk Anderson's Trip to Utah, 1858" [1961], 1); "Pete Mayette's" post along the Sweetwater (Aug. 20, 1858, entry, in Ackley, "Across the Plains in 1858," 206); "Jack Robinson's" post at Smith's Fork (Sept. 27, 1858, entry, in Lowe, *Five Years a Dragoon*, 256); and Jim Baker's post and ferry at the Green River

on the Salt Lake road (Mumey, "James Baker," in Hafen, ed., *The Mountain Men and the Fur Trade*, 3:44; Coutant, *The History of Wyoming* [1899], 369).

117. Bissonette achieved his monopoly over trade at the Upper Platte agency by dealing in illicit liquor. Jones, "Those Wild Reshaw Boys," 14; McDermott, "Joseph Bissonette," 56–57; July 5, 18, 1856, entries, in Brown, *Journal of a Trip*, 52, 62.

118. Mormon way stations had also been established at the Wood River, Pawnee Springs, the Big Sandy, Deer Creek, Devil's Gate, Pacific Creek, and Fort Supply. Stegner, *The Gathering of Zion* (1964), 273, 280; Arrington, *Great Basin Kingdom*, 162–70; Henry James Hudson to Editor of *The Mormon*, July 1, 1857, and Hudson, "Genoa and Its Progress," in Burke, ed., "Henry James Hudson and the Genoa Settlement" (1960), 223, 228–35; Aitchison, "The Mormon Settlements in the Missouri Valley" (1907), 288–89. Regarding the Fort Bridger situation, see the Aug. 2, 1856, entry of J. Robert Brown (*Journal of a Trip*, 69) for the statement that the Mormons had "bought him [Bridger] out, and now keep a store and post here. They persecuted him, and tried to cheat him out of his pay. They bought the fort and section of land for $8,000, and owe $4,000 of it yet." See also Alex Chambers to H. H. Bancroft, Jan. 4, 1885, in Chambers, "Fort Bridger" (1927–28), 91–95. For background information and 1857 population statistics on the Carson and neighboring valleys consult Brooks, "The Mormons in Carson County," 19–22, and Bancroft, *History of Nevada, Colorado, and Wyoming*, 75–83, esp. 80, n. 37. On the bitter Mormon-Gentile strife see Richards, "Washoe Territory" (1969), 215–19.

119. June 6, 7, 1857, entries, in "Arthur M. Menefee's Travels across the Plains" (1966), 7–8; Clark, "A Trip across the Plains in 1857" (1922), 170–72; July 21–24, 26, 28, 30, 1857, entries, in "Diary of Captain Phelps," in Hafen and Hafen, eds., *The Utah Expedition, 1857–1858* (1958), 95–96, 99–100; Oct. 3, 1857, entry, in "Diary of Judge William A. Carter," 79; M. H. W. to Editor, Aug. 22, 1858, in St. Louis *Daily Missouri Republican*, Sept. 1, 1858; Council Bluffs *Weekly Bugle*, Nov. 24, 1858.

120. Council Bluffs *Chronotype*, May 2, 1855, Apr. 30, July 2, 1856; Council Bluffs *Bugle*, Mar. 10, 1857.

121. Whenever possible, of course, posts already operating were pressed into service as way stations.

122. A listing of all the towns, farms, posts, and river-crossing facilities is an almost prohibitive task. For tabulations of way stations on certain segments of the route see Burton, *The City of the Saints*, ed. Brodie (1963), *passim*, esp. App. 1, 555–80; July 13, 16, 20, 1860, entries, in Fish, Journal (MS and typescript), 15–16; Council Bluffs *Weekly Bugle*, Apr. 11, 1860; Root and Hickman, "Pike's Peak Express Companies: Part III" (1945), 485–526, and "Pike's Peak Express Companies: Part IV" (1946), 36–92; Mattes and Henderson, "The Pony Express" (1960), 83–122; Mattes, *Great Platte River Road*, 150, 152, 270–80, 471–73.

123. May 24, 1859, entry, in Cramer, Journal (MS and typescript); Aug. 8, 16, 19, 1860, entries, in Burton, *City of the Saints*, 35, 154, 171.

124. July 7, 1859, entry, in Cramer, Journal; July 22, 1860, entry, in Fish, Journal, 17.

125. Albert D. Richardson to Editors of Lawrence, Kan., *Republican*, May 22, 1860, in Barry, ed., "Albert D. Richardson's Letters on the Pike's Peak Gold Region" (1943), 18.

126. Aug. 11, 1860, entry, in Burton, *City of the Saints*, 60.

127. In 1859 Horace Greeley reported that "R. D." owned 600 to 800 head of cattle while "J. R.'s" herd was enumerated at about 50 horses and 300 to 400 cattle and was valued at $75,000. Dispatch of July 8, 1859, in Greeley, *An Overland Journey from New York to San Francisco*, ed. Duncan (1964), 164. See also Chap. 11 below for an assessment of the relationship between the overland migrations and the range cattle industry.

128. Richard Burton indicated that Ganard spent $40,000 on his bridge, although early Wyoming historian C. G. Coutant maintained that the total cost of Ganard's bridge was $60,000—$30,000 initially and the second $30,000 for repairs in subsequent years. June 11, 1859, entry, in Wilson, A Trip across the Plains (MS), 34; June 23, 1859, entry, in Powell, Diary (typescript), 14; July 1, 1859, entry, in Mathews, *Crossing the Plains* ([1930]), 54–55; July 3, 1859, entry, in Cramer, Journal; July 6, 8, 1860, entries, in Fish, Journal, 13–14; July 6, 8, 1860, entries, in Fish, Diary (typescript), 10–11; Aug. 16, 1860, entry, in Burton, *City of the Saints*, 155–56; Coutant, *History of Wyoming*, 365, 367–68; Federal Writers' Project, *The Oregon Trail* (1939), 182.

129. Coutant, *History of Wyoming*, 366–67.

130. Aug. 20, 1859, entry, in Wilson, *Trip across the Plains*, 65; May 24, July 5, 1859, entries, in Cramer, *Journal*; Root, "Ferries in Kansas: Part III," 139–40. There were other problems: David Spain's company had stayed at the Elkhorn Hotel but for some reason refused to pay the full charges. The hotel proprietor followed them, demanding payment and threatening to call Indians down upon their traveling group. Finally, according to Spain, the "Land Lord . . . then proposed a compromise, begged off and we paid him three Dollars, gave him a cussing & left." Charles Tuttle, also in 1859, mentioned that the day before he reached the Weber River a Mexican had been shot in a quarrel at a post there, but he provided insufficient detail to indicate the nature of the altercation. Apr. 3, 5, 6, 1859, entries, in Morrison, ed., "The Diary of David F. Spain" (1958), 16; July 27, 1859, entry, in "California Diary of Charles M. Tuttle" (1931), 228.

131. F. W. Lander to A. B. Greenwood, Feb. 18, 1860, in U.S. President, *Massacre at Mountain Meadows* (1860), 128–30; Harstad, "The Lander Trail," 26. To counter the arguments of area entrepreneurs Lander then stationed a former soldier at Gilbert's trading post and a blacksmith at South Pass.

132. Apr. 18, 1859, entry, in Wilson, *Trip across the Plains*, 5; May 9, 1859, entry, in Millsap, ed., "Documents: Romanzo Kingman's Pike's Peak Journal" (1950), 68; June 1, 1860, entry, in Guill, *Diary* (typescript), 3. In the Carson Valley, at the other end of the trail, newspapers were also available, and had been for several years. See Bancroft, *History of Nevada, Colorado, and Wyoming*, 169; Sept. 12, 1859, entry, in Cramer, *Journal*.

133. May 27, 29, 31, June 4, 5, 1859, entries, in Cummings, *Journal* (MS and typescript); June 15, July 24, 1859, entries, in Norton, *Diary* (photocopy of typescript), 15, 37; May 13, 14, 16, 18, 23, 1859, entries, in Millsap, ed., "Romanzo Kingman's Pike's Peak Journal," 69–73; Mar. 27, 1860, entry of Edward J. Lewis, in Pratt, ed., "Diary of a Pike's Peak Gold Seeker in 1860" (1937), 208; Aug. 8, 1860, entry, in Burton, *City of the Saints*, 26; June 23, 1860, entry, in Guill, *Diary*, 5; Watkins, "History of Fort Kearny" (1911), 254–55; Albert D. Richardson to Editors of Lawrence *Republican*, June 5, 1860, in Barry, ed., "Richardson's Letters on the Pike's Peak Gold Region," 21; Sept. 1, 1859, entry, in Powell, *Diary*, 32; Sept. 19, 1859, entry, in Hall, "The Diary of a Trip from Ione to Nevada" (1938), 76. Statistics from the 1860 census also reveal the impressive non-Indian populations already residing in Nebraska (28,841), Utah (41,273), and Nevada (6,857) territories. *Population of the United States in 1860* (1864), 558, 564, 576.

CHAPTER NINE: THE MORMON "HALFWAY HOUSE"

1. Wilford Woodruff, quoted in Camp, ed., "William Alexander Trubody and the Overland Pioneers of 1847" (1937), 141, n. 10. Relationships between Saint and Gentile traveling groups on the trails continued to be peaceful throughout the emigration era. The difficulties which did develop occurred in the Salt Lake Valley.

2. Furniss, *The Mormon Conflict, 1850–1859* (1960) is the standard work on the causes and consequences of the Mormon War. Yet Furniss inexplicably pays no attention whatever to the significant interaction between the Saints and Gentile emigrants passing through the Salt Lake Valley. Without an awareness of the reactions of the tens of thousands of overlanders who trailed through the Mormon dominions prior to 1857—reactions widely communicated by letter, diary accounts, pamphlets, books, press reports, and by word of mouth on the Pacific Coast as well as in the eastern states—no treatment of the background of the Mormon War is complete. Lee, in "The Effect of Public Opinion on the Mormon Scheme of Self-Government" (1959), is more cognizant of the interrelationship between the emigrant passage through the Salt Lake Valley and national attitudes toward the Latter-Day Saints.

3. Campbell, "Brigham Young's Outer Cordon" (1973), 222; Arrington, *Great Basin Kingdom* (1958), 84–88; O'Dea, *The Mormons* (1957), 84; Nash, "The Salmon River Mission of 1885" (1967), 22–31; Hunter, "Brigham Young, Colonizer" (1937), 341–60; Hunter, "The Mormon Corridor" (1939), 179–200. Campbell ("Brigham Young's Outer Cordon," *passim*) questions the validity of the concept of the "outer cordon" outposts as a carefully executed design of defense for the Great Basin empire. While acknowledging that Brigham Young and other Church leaders had such dreams, Campbell argues persuasively that the actual reasons for beginning most of the "outer cordon" settlements as well as the timing of their establishment, the ineffective official support they received, and their early termination all fail to substantiate that the dreams ever became reality.

4. *The Seventh Census of the United States: 1850* (1853), 993, 998; *Population of the United States in 1860* (1864), 575–77; Aug. 1, 5, 1860, entries, in Fish, Diary (typescript), 25–26. Bancroft, in *History of Utah* (1889), 484, n. 9, noted that, census returns notwithstanding, the Mormons claimed an exaggerated population of 90,000 to 100,000 in 1860.

5. The multitudes of forty-niners traveling via Salt Lake City were doubtless influenced in their choice of route by the widely reprinted advices of former overlanders in stateside newspapers. William Gilpin's traveling instructions, for example, recommended "the large and prosperous settlement of the Mormons at Salt Lake . . . a central point to rest and recruit." Washington *National Intelligencer*, Feb. 17, 1849.

6. Arrington, *Great Basin Kingdom*, 64, 66–69; Arrington, "Coin and Currency in Early Utah" (1952), 59; Bancroft, *History of Utah*, 297–301; Morgan, "The Ferries of the Forty-Niners, Part III—Section 2" (1960), 199; Aug. 17, 1849, entry of John D. Lee, in Cleland and Brooks, eds., *A Mormon Chronicle* (1955), 1:114.

7. July 17–Aug. 17, 1849, entries, in ibid., 111–14; July 15, 1856, entry, in Brown, *Journal of a Trip across the Plains* (1860), 60; Brown, *Testimonies for the Truth* (1853), quoted in Arrington, *Great Basin Kingdom*, 67–68; Aug. 6, 1849, entry, in Stansbury, *Exploration and Survey of the Valley of the Great Salt Lake* (1853), 71; Babbitt to Editor of St. Louis *Union*, n.d., reprinted in St. Joseph *Gazette*, Oct. 19, 1849.

8. Aug. 14, Sept. 3, 1849, entries, in Webster, *The Gold Seekers of '49* (1917), 71–72, 78; Pearson, *Overland in 1849*, ed. Goodman (1961), 16, 18–19; July 29, 1849, entry, in McCall, *The Great California Trail* (1882), 62; Hafen, "Elijah Barney Ward," in Hafen, ed., *The Mountain Men and the Fur Trade* (1965–72), 7:347; Sept. 9, 1849, entry of Bruff, in Read and Gaines, eds., *Gold Rush* (1944), 1:169, 559, n. 25; July 26–28, 1849, entries, in Tolles, Diary (typescript), 31–32.

9. Evidence that the Church hierarchy was not as anxious for the overland trade in 1849 as most emigrants assumed is contained in the Mormon newspaper published in Kanesville, the *Frontier Guardian*, which on April 4, 1849, advised departing travelers not to depend on the Salt Lake Valley for provisions because little would be available there until after the fall harvest. Overlanders were advised to take all they would need with them from the Missouri River outfitting posts.

10. Young's 1847 statement is quoted in Stegner, *The Gathering of Zion* (1964), 170, and Young's sermon of July 14, 1850, is printed in the Salt Lake City *Deseret News*, July 20, 1850.

11. Ibid.; also issues of Aug. 10, 1850, July 10, Aug. 21, 1852, Jan. 8, 1853.

12. Aug. 11, 1850, entry, in Stine, Letters and Journal (typescripts); Brigham Young, Heber C. Kimball, and Willard Richards, "Fifth General Epistle of the Presidency of the Church of Jesus Christ of Latter Day Saints," Apr. 7, 1851, in Salt Lake City *Deseret News*, Mar. 22, 1851; Young, "Emigration," in ibid., July 13, 1854; Powers, "A Woman's Overland Journal to California" (Nov., 1950), 6.

13. Letter of L., Mar. 30, 1852, in New York *Daily Times*, May 18, 1852; Young, Kimball, and Richards, "Eighth General Epistle," Oct. 1, 1852, in Salt Lake City *Deseret News*, Oct. 16, 1852; Salt Lake City *Deseret News*, Jan. 8, 1853.

14. Letter of Brigham Young, Mar. 9, 1853, in New York *Daily Times*, May 31, 1853; Powers, "A Woman's Overland Journal" (Dec., 1950), 11. See also the *Deseret News* editorial of Nov. 6, 1852, and the unsigned letter dated at Independence, Mo., on May 1, 1852, in New York *Daily Tribune*, May 18, 1852, for evidence of Mormon desires for overland traffic through the Salt Lake Valley.

15. Young's July 14, 1850, sermon in Salt Lake City *Deseret News*, July 20, 1850; Salt Lake City *Deseret News*, June 26, July 10, 1852, July 30, 1853; Young, Kimball, and Richards, "Fourth General Epistle," Nov. 27, 1850, in ibid., Sept. 28, 1850; Young, Kimball, and Richards, "Fifth General Epistle." An interesting account of how one New England forty-niner detoured via Salt Lake City, became enamored with Mormonism, and joined the Church is found in Thurber, Journal (typescript).

16. Cooke, *Crossing the Plains in 1852* (1923), 43; Salt Lake City *Deseret News*, June 15, 1850; Morgan, ed., "Letters by Forty-Niners" (1949), 98; Fleming and Standing, "The Road to 'Fortune'" (1965), 260.

17. June 6, 1850, entry, in Keith, "Journal of Crossing the Plains" ([1961]), 3; Robert Campbell to Editor, July 7, 1850, in Kanesville *Frontier Guardian*, Aug. 24, 1850.

18. June 18, 1852, entry of Hosea Stout, in Brooks, ed., *On the Mormon Frontier* (1964), 2:439; Ferris, *Utah and the Mormons* (1854), 38; Aug. 6–13, 1850, entries of Taylor, in Williams, ed., "Overland to California in 1850" (1970), 327.

19. St. Joseph *Gazette*, Sept. 18, 1850; Salt Lake City *Deseret News*, June 15–Aug. 17, 1850.

20. Letter of "Gold Mines," Oct. 18, 1849, in St. Louis *Missouri Republican*, Jan. 18, 1850, reprinted in Morgan, ed., "Letters by Forty-Niners," 114–15; Brooks, ed., *On the Mormon Frontier*, 2:379, n. 45; Salt Lake City *Deseret News*, Aug. 24, 1850; St. Joseph *Gazette*, Dec. 24, 1851; Arrington, *Great Basin Kingdom*, 81–83. For evidence that not all stateside traders and merchants profited on their Salt Lake speculations see Barry, *The Beginning of the West* (1972), 988.

21. St. Joseph *Gazette*, Mar. 31, 1852.

22. For the Lamareaux advertisement see Salt Lake City *Deseret News*, July 6, 1850.

23. For the United States Hotel and Mrs. C. Reed's "Straw Bonnit and Hat Manufactory" advertisements see ibid., July 10[9], 1853. It is probable that at least one hotel was in operation by 1851, for on August 11, 1850, Henry Atkinson Stine recorded in his journal that although no hotels were then available, a very impressive one was under construction.

24. Foy, ed., "By Ox Team from Salt Lake to Los Angeles, 1850" (1930), 273; July 20, 21, 1849, entries, in McCall, *The Great California Trail*, 55, 57; July 7–16, 1849, entries of Edwin Hillyer, in Holzhueter, ed., "From Waupun to Sacramento in 1849" (1966), 238; Aug. 7, 8, 16, 18, 1849, entries, in Gould, Diary (typescript), 38–40; June 28, 1850, entry, in "The Memoirs of Lemuel Clarke McKeeby" (1924), 58; Aug. 11, 1850, entry, in Stine, Letters and Journal; July 28–Aug. 2, 1852, entries, in Udell, *Incidents of Travel to California* (1856), 67–68; letter of Michael Conner, July 4, 1852 (MS).

25. Sept. 2–5, 1849, entries, in Hutchings, Diary (microfilm of MS).

26. New York *Daily Times*, Sept. 21, 1852; Josselyn to his wife, July 15, 1849, in Josselyn, Letters (MSS and typescripts); July 18, 1849, entry, in John F. Lewis, Diary (MS and typescript); letter of John B. Hazlip, July 8, 1849, in Palmyra *Missouri Whig*, Oct. 4, 1849, reprinted in Morgan, ed., "Letters by Forty-Niners," 100; Aug. 7, 1849, entry, in Caldwell,

"Notes of a Journey to California by Fort Hall Route," in Read and Gaines, eds., *Gold Rush,* 2:1260; July 15, 1852, entry of John Hawkins Clark, in Barry, ed., "Overland to the Gold Fields of California" (1942), 273; Arrington, *Great Basin Kingdom,* 68–69.

27. See, e.g., the June 24, 1849, entry of Hosea Stout, in Brooks, ed., *On the Mormon Frontier,* 2:354; July 1, 1849, entry of John D. Lee, in Cleland and Brooks, eds., *A Mormon Chronicle,* 1:110–11; Beeson Townsend to Benjamin Franklin Townsend, Aug. 7, 1849, in Morgan, ed., "Letters by Forty-Niners," 112; William Wilson to Lovina Wilson, July 29, 1850, in Wilson, Letters and Day Books (MSS and typescripts); letter of Adonijah Strong Welch, Aug. 30, 1849, in Hermann, ed., "Document: Three Gold Rush Letters" (1959), 63–64; Aug. 7, 1849, entry, in Caldwell, "Notes of a Journey to California," 1260. The price of sugar and coffee remained uniform at 50 cents per pound throughout 1849 and 1850, beef generally sold at 12 cents per pound in the latter years, while bacon in 1849 sold for $12 per 100 pounds and ranged between 50 and 75 cents per pound the following year. When compared with the 1849 and 1850 rates in the tables in Chaps. 7 and 8 above, the slightly cheaper prices prevailing in Salt Lake City at the height of the gold rush are evident.

28. July 1, 1850, entry, in "Diary of Thomas Woodward" (1934), 442; July 2, 1850, entry, in Gorgas, Diary and Letters (MSS); Kiefer, ed., "Over Barren Plains and Rock-bound Mountains" (1972), 24; Dr. Horace Belknap to Abram McClary, Feb. 2, 1851, in Westholm, ed., "An Iowan in California, 1850" (1962), 463; Lagerberg, "The Bishop Hill Colonists in the Gold Rush" (1955), 467; Carpenter, I Crossed the Plains in the 50's (microfilm of MS).

29. Kelly, *An Excursion to California* (1851), 1:174; July 21, 1849, entry of Banks, in Scamehorn, ed., *The Buckeye Rovers in the Gold Rush* (1965), 47; letter of "Gold Mines," Oct. 18, 1849, in St. Louis *Missouri Republican,* Jan. 18, 1850, reprinted in Morgan, ed., "Letters by Forty-Niners," 116; M. M. to Chambers and Knapp, Jan. 24, 1850, in St. Louis *Missouri Republican,* Mar. 22, 1850, reprinted in Wyman, ed., *California Emigrant Letters* (1952), 93–94; July 23, 1853, entry, in Handsaker, Diary (reproduced), 20; St. Joseph *Gazette,* Mar. 8, 1854.

30. July 25, 1852, entry, in Barry, ed., "Overland to the Gold Fields of California," 277.

31. Stansbury, *Exploration and Survey,* 130–31; Gunnison, *The Mormons* (1856), 65. Although legal actions between emigrants seem to have been treated judiciously in Mormon courts, considerable controversy prevails pertaining to the outcome of cases between emigrants and Mormons, particularly during the winter. For a fuller treatment of these legal actions see pp. 325–29 below.

32. Although litigation pertaining to the overland journey continued to be heard in Salt Lake City courts, by 1852 and 1853 the editor of the *Deseret News* was pointing out how infrequently overland emigrants were resorting to legal action as compared with earlier years. Salt Lake City *Deseret News,* July 24, 1852, July 10 [9], 1853.

33. June 21, 28, July 5, 29, Aug. 2, 1850, June 29, 1852, entries, in Brooks, ed., *On the Mormon Frontier,* 2:371–73, 375–76, 440.

34. See, e.g., June 22, July 5, 8, 15, 25, Aug. 2, 1850, entries of Stout, in ibid., 2:371–76; Salt Lake City *Deseret News,* Aug. 24, 1850; Stansbury, *Exploration and Survey,* 131. See also Chap. 3 above, p. 105.

35. July 1, 1849, June 10, 25, July 6, 13, 30, Aug. 14, 1850, July 3, 6, 1852, entries of Stout, in Brooks, ed., *On the Mormon Frontier,* 2:354, 371–73, 376–77, 440–41; Salt Lake City *Deseret News,* July 6, 1850; Aug. 28, 1849, entry, in Hamelin, Journals (MSS and typescripts).

36. May 12, 1849, entry of John D. Lee, in Cleland and Brooks, eds., *A Mormon Chronicle,* 1:107–8; Salt Lake City *Deseret News,* July 13, 1850, Aug. 21, 1852; July 9, Aug. 12, 1850, entries of Stout, in Brooks, ed., *On the Mormon Frontier,* 2:373–74, 377; July 20, 1849, entry, in Hinman, Diary (MS); Foy, ed., "By Ox Team from Salt Lake to Los Angeles," 274; July 15, 1859, entry, in Wilson, A Trip across the Plains (MS), 53.

37. May 17, 1852, entry of Stout, in Brooks, ed., *On the Mormon Frontier,* 2:437–38; July 13, 1852, entry of John Hawkins Clark, in Barry, ed., "Overland to the Gold Fields of California in 1852," 271.

38. Brigham Young's statement is quoted in Brooks, "Indian Relations on the Mormon Frontier" (1944), 4. See also Morgan, "The Administration of Indian Affairs in Utah" (1948), 383–409; Gunnison, *The Mormons,* 165.

39. Stegner, *Gathering of Zion*, 158, 183, 192.

40. Ibid., 132–34, 187–91; St. Joseph *Gazette,* Feb. 8, 1850; John W. Jones to Editors, Jan. 31, 1851, in St. Louis *Daily Missouri Republican,* Mar. 21, 1851.

41. Paden, ed., "The Ira J. Willis Guide to the Gold Mines" (1953), 193–207; Royce, *A Frontier Lady,* ed. Gabriel (1932), 34; Aug. 29, 1849, entry of J. Goldsborough Bruff, in Read and Gaines, eds., *Gold Rush,* 1:157; Aug. 15, 1849, entry, in Castleman, Diary (microfilm of typescript), 62.

42. I am indebted to Prof. Thomas F. Andrews of Azusa Pacific College for a copy of the Young and Eagar *Emigrant's Guide,* which he is editing for publication. Silas Newcomb, who purchased a copy of this guidebook in Salt Lake City on July 17, 1850, was unimpressed with its validity and within two weeks had pronounced it "a poor thing." See entries of July 17, 31, in Newcomb, Journal (photocopy of MS), 123, 137. For information on the Cain and Brower guidebook see Korns, "West from Fort Bridger" (1951), 234; Salt Lake City *Deseret News,* Jan. 25, Feb. 22, 1851, July 10, 1852.

43. Korns, "West from Fort Bridger," 224–36; July 13, 15, 1850, entries, in Skinner, Diary (MS); Aug. 1, 1850, entry, in "Diary Kept by William Edmundson" (1908), 526.

44. Stewart, *The California Trail* (1962), 197–200, 205–6.

45. Ibid., 201–5; Korns, "West from Fort Bridger," 248–54, 264–68. See also Fleming and Standing, "The Road to 'Fortune,'" 248–71. Two or three companies of forty-niners also traveled over the Hastings Cutoff, enduring considerable suffering. Kelly, in "Gold Seekers on the Hastings Cutoff" (1952), 3–30 (a useful compendium), does not specifically estimate how many gold seekers traveled over the Hastings Cutoff in 1850 but does suggest that from July 20 to August 22 "an almost continuous stream of packers or wagon trains" traversed the much-maligned route.

46. Hafen and Hafen, eds., *Journals of Forty-Niners* (1954), 27–28; Foy, ed., "By Ox Team from Salt Lake to Los Angeles," 273–74. David Cheesman, who remained in Salt Lake City fifty-four days, until his child was born and his wife was again able to travel, reported plenty of work available in the city. He made money while waiting to travel the southwestern route by cutting hay and hauling it to the city for sale at from $10 to $12 per ton, and by hauling adobes for the Mormons.

47. Hafen and Hafen, eds., *Journals of Forty-Niners,* 28; Caughey, "Southwest from Salt Lake in 1849" (1937), 146–47; Caughey, ed., "The Jacob Y. Stover Narrative" (1937), 170; White, "An Autobiography" (1927), 207.

48. Caughey, "Southwest from Salt Lake," 147; Caughey, ed., "The Jacob Y. Stover Narrative," 170–71.

49. Hafen and Hafen, eds., *Journals of Forty-Niners,* 28–34; Hafen and Hafen, eds., *The Far West and Rockies: General Analytical Index* (1961), 15, 28; Caughey, "Southwest from Salt Lake," 147.

50. Hafen, "Elijah Barney Ward," 346–48; Caughey, "Southwest from Salt Lake," 148–63; Hafen and Hafen, eds., *Journals of Forty-Niners,* 35–42; Hafen and Hafen, eds., *The Far West and Rockies: General Analytical Index,* 120. There is, of course, a vast literature on the Death Valley forty-niners. In addition to Caughey's "Southwest from Salt Lake," two convenient summary accounts are Serven, "The Ill-Fated '49er Wagon Train" (1960), 29–40, and Wheat, "The Forty-Niners in Death Valley" (1939), 102–17.

51. Hafen and Hafen, eds., *Journals of Forty-Niners,* 43–44, 307; Hafen and Hafen, eds., *The Far West and Rockies: General Analytical Index,* 103.

52. Hafen and Hafen, eds., *Journals of Forty-Niners,* 44; Caughey, "Southwest from Salt Lake," 157, 163.

53. Ibid., 163–64; Salt Lake City *Deseret News,* Sept. 7, 14, 1850; Foy, ed., "By Ox Team from Salt Lake to Los Angeles," 273–74, 283–84; Hafen, "Elijah Barney Ward," 346.

54. Rice, "Early Freighting on the Salt Lake–San Bernardino Trail" (1942), 74–75; Remy and Brenchley, *A Journey to Great-Salt-Lake City* (1861), 1:306–454.

55. Lucius Fairchild to J. C. Fairchild, Apr. 24, 1849, in Schafer, ed., *California Letters of Lucius Fairchild* (1931), 13; St. Joseph *Gazette,* June 15, 1849; Aug. 3, 1849, entry of Lee, in Cleland and Brooks, eds., *A Mormon Chronicle,* 1:112.

56. Kanesville *Frontier Guardian,* Sept. 5, 1849; unidentified letters, Oct., 1849, in

Hannibal *Missouri Courier*, Jan. 10, 1850, reprinted in Morgan, ed., "Letters by Forty-Niners," 113; Liberty, Mo., *Weekly Tribune*, Aug. 23, 1850; St. Joseph *Gazette*, Mar. 17, 1852; Portland *Weekly Oregonian*, July 15, 1854; San Francisco *Daily Alta California*, June 14, 1855. Contemporaries may have employed a subtle distinction in discussing wintering overlanders, John B. Haas recalling that "Winter Mormons" were Gentiles forced by circumstances to winter in the valley while Mormon Hosea Stout identified "Winter Saints" as "those Emegrants who stop here, join the Church & marry wives and go to the mines in the Spring &c." Since few overlanders either married or joined the Church while in the Salt Lake Valley, perhaps "Winter Mormons" is the more appropriate appellation. Haas, "Pioneer Autobiography" (Dec., 1938), 6; Jan. 19, 1851, entry of Stout, in Brooks, ed., *On the Mormon Frontier*, 2:388.

57. Platt and Slater, *Travelers' Guide across the Plains* (1852, 1963 reprint), vii–viii, x; Goodell, "The Mormons, Nos. 1–9," Portland *Oregonian*, Apr. 10–June 26, 1852. Examples of emigrant and press references to Slater and Goodell's charges include Langworthy, *Scenery of the Plains, Mountains and Mines*, ed. Phillips (1932), 81–83; St. Joseph *Gazette*, Aug. 27, 1851; Liberty *Weekly Tribune*, Sept. 5, 1851; San Francisco *Daily Alta California*, July 14, 1852; New York *Daily Times*, Aug. 16, 1852. The Winter Mormons of 1850–51 were already complaining bitterly about their treatment in the Salt Lake Valley on their arrival in Oregon in May and June, 1851. The substance of their dissatisfactions had been made public long before Goodell penned his series of letters the following spring. See Portland *Oregonian*, June 7, 1851; Anson Dart to T. J. Dryer, May 31, 1851, in ibid., June 21, 1851.

58. Slater, *Fruits of Mormonism*, 1–2, 89–94; Goodell, "The Mormons," Portland *Oregonian*, Apr. 10, and "The Mormons, No. 6," ibid., May 22, 1852. Goodell's card requesting the depositions was first printed on June 26, 1852, and was repeated the following week in the July 3 issue of the *Oregonian*.

59. Portland *Oregonian*, May 29, July 3, 1852, July 15, 1854; letter of X., May 20, 1852, in St. Joseph *Gazette*, Aug. 4, 1852.

60. Unidentified letter, Oct., 1849, in Morgan, ed., "Letters by Forty-Niners," 113; Aug. 29, 1850, entry, in Langworthy, *Scenery of the Plains*, 96–97; Slater, *Fruits of Mormonism*, 9–10; Sacramento *Union*, June 28, 1851, reprinted in ibid., 87.

61. Aug. 29, 1850, entry, in Langworthy, *Scenery of the Plains*, 96; St. Joseph *Gazette*, Mar. 17, 1852; Slater, *Fruits of Mormonism*, 5–8. Some emigrants contended that the Saints particularly advised against traveling the southern route—a somewhat dubious assertion considering the advertisements by Mormon guides in the *Deseret News*, Willard Richard's editorial praising the route, and Brigham Young's strong advocacy of the southern trail—because only on the Salt Lake Cutoff did the Saints operate ferries which supplied Mormon coffers with impressive amounts of Gentile money.

62. Goodell, "The Mormons, No. 2," Portland *Oregonian*, May 1, 1852; Ferris, *The Mormons at Home* (1856), 122–23; Slater, *Fruits of Mormonism*, 5–7; St. Joseph *Gazette*, Mar. 17, 1852; James and McLarty, eds., "Three Generations in the Span of a Continent, Part II" (1954), 347.

63. Slater, *Fruits of Mormonism*, 80, 87; Aug. 20, 1856, entry, in Brown, *Journal of a Trip*, 80; Goodell, "The Mormons, Nos. 1, 5, 6," Portland *Oregonian*, Apr. 10, May 13, 22, 1852; Cooke, *Crossing the Plains in 1852*, 38–39; St. Joseph *Gazette*, Mar. 17, 1852.

64. Goodell, "The Mormons, Nos. 4, 5, 9," Portland *Oregonian*, Apr. 3, May 13, June 26, 1852; Holeman to Luke Lea, Mar. 29, 1852, in Morgan, ed., "Washakie and the Shoshoni, Part I" (1953), 183–86; Slater, *Fruits of Mormonism*, 87; letter of X., May 20, 1852, in St. Joseph *Gazette*, Aug. 4, 1852; New York *Daily Times*, Sept. 21, 1852.

65. The 2 percent tax prevailed at least during the 1849–50 and 1850–51 winters. According to one overlander, the tax was raised to 5 or 6 percent in the winter of 1851–52, and collected twice. Slater, *Fruits of Mormonism*, 81; letter of X., May 20, 1852, in St. Joseph *Gazette*, Aug. 4, 1852.

66. Slater, *Fruits of Mormonism*, 81; Goodell, "The Mormons, Nos. 6, 7," Portland *Oregonian*, May 22, June 12, 1852.

67. Slater, *Fruits of Mormonism*, 11–12, 32–34, 36–40; St. Joseph *Gazette*, Mar. 17, 1852; William B. Yates to Reuben Campbell, n.d., in ibid., Dec. 10, 1851.

68. Slater, *Fruits of Mormonism,* 12–13, 16–18; July 4, 1854, entry, in The Diary of an Unknown Scout (typescript), 8; Goodell, "The Mormons, Nos. 5, 6," Portland *Oregonian,* May 13, 22, 1852; St. Joseph *Gazette,* Mar. 17, 1852.

69. James and McLarty, eds., "Three Generations in the Span of a Continent," 347; Goodell, "The Mormons, No. 8," Portland *Oregonian,* June 26, 1852.

70. Slater, *Fruits of Mormonism,* 12–39, 53–54, 67–73, 76–79; Haas, "Pioneer Autobiography" (Dec., 1938), 6; Goodell, "The Mormons, Nos. 5, 6, 8," Portland *Oregonian,* May 13, 22, June 26, 1852.

71. Witnessing the incendiary terminology of the Mormon hierarchy was by no means confined to Winter Mormons. Slater, *Fruits of Mormonism,* 74–75, 80, 82–83, 88; Goodell, "The Mormons, Nos. 3, 5, 9," Portland *Oregonian,* May 8, 13, June 26, 1852; St. Joseph *Gazette,* Mar. 17, 1852. For an interpretive assessment of non-emigrant literature attacking alleged Mormon subversion, see Davis, "Some Themes of Counter-Subversion" (1960), 205–24.

72. Stansbury, *Exploration and Survey,* 134; Gunnison, *The Mormons,* 64–66.

73. Ferris, *Utah and the Mormons,* 192–93, 196.

74. Goodell, "The Mormons, No. 6," Portland *Oregonian,* May 22, 1852; Slater, *Fruits of Mormonism,* 22–24, 37–38.

75. July 28–Aug. 2, 1852, entries, in Udell, *Incidents of Travel to California,* 67–68.

76. Slater, *Fruits of Mormonism,* 15–16, 88; Goodell, "The Mormons, No. 5," Portland *Oregonian,* May 13, 1852; Sept. 16, Oct. 3, 1850, Feb. 15, Mar. 17, 1851, entries of Stout, in Brooks, ed., *On the Mormon Frontier,* 2:380–81, 393, 396; William B. Yates to Reuben Campbell, n.d., in St. Joseph *Gazette,* Dec. 10, 1851.

77. Edwin Bryant, a traveler of that year, wrote that "it is probable that some who have started will turn back in consequence of these apprehensions." May 7, 1846, entry, in Bryant, *What I Saw in California* (1849), 26. See also pp. 15–16 in ibid.; Morgan, ed., *Overland in 1846* (1963), 1:89; Phebe Stanton to her brothers and sisters, May 9, 1847, in Stanton, "On the Plains" (1915), 622–23.

78. Miller, "Early Oregon Scenes" (1930), 60; July 19, 1850, entry, in Dowell, Journal (copy of MS), 20; *The Autobiography of Theodore Edgar Potter* (1913), 70–72; S. H. Taylor to Editor, Dec. 17, 1853, in Watertown, Wis., *Chronicle,* Mar. 29, 1854, reprinted in "Letters of S. H. Taylor to the Watertown Chronicle" (1921), 155–56; Aug. 4, 1859, entry, in Cramer, Journal (MS and typescript).

79. George C. M'Cune to Editor, Aug. 2, 1852, in Salt Lake City *Deseret News,* Aug. 7, 1852; ibid., June 26, 1852; Ashel T. Barrett to his brother, July 3, 1853, in Kanesville *Western Bugle,* Sept. 21, 1853; July 24, 1852, entry of Clark, in Barry, ed., "Overland to the Gold Fields of California in 1852," 276–77; letter of "Radnor," Apr. 30, 1855, in Salt Lake City *Deseret News,* Aug. 1, 1855.

80. See, e.g., Morgan, ed., "Letters by Forty-Niners," 98–116; July 17, 1849, entry, in Holzhueter, ed., "From Waupun to Sacramento in 1849," 239; Washington *National Intelligencer,* Nov. 9, 1850; letter of J. H. K., July 28, 1849, in *Supplement* to New York *Daily Tribune,* Sept. 14, 1849; letter of S. B. F. Clark, July 19, 1849, in New York *Herald,* Oct. 8, 1849; Kanesville *Frontier Guardian,* Dec. 26, 1849; letter of John Udell, July 31, 1852, in Salt Lake City *Deseret News,* Aug. 7, 1852; July 24, 1849, entry, in Benson, Diary (typescript), 38–41; Salt Lake City *Deseret News,* July 24, 1852; Aug. 6–13, 1850, entries, in Williams, ed., "Overland to California in 1850," 328–29.

81. See, e.g., the June 23, 1849, entry, in Johnston, *Overland to California* (1948), 119; Aug. 3, 1859, entry, in Cramer, Journal. In 1852 one emigrant reported that Young had seventy-three wives, while another noted that he reputedly had fifty-two children under two and a half years of age. As for the rumored qualifications for acquiring additional wives, David Dewolf indicated that "constitutional strength" was a prerequisite for plural wives, while William Warner indicated that for every $1,000 net worth a Saint was permitted another wife. July 29, 1852, entry, in Bailey, Journal (MS and typescript); Harriet Steele to her sister, Mar. 29, 1853, in Steele, "Gold Rush Letters" (1964), 47; Aug. 17, 1849, entry, in Cox, ed., "Diary of the Overland Trail" (1925), 205; William Warner to his mother, Sept. 23, 1853, in Overland to California" (1926), 568.

82. Again, for examples, see the July 22, 1849, entry, in McCall, *The Great California*

Trail, 58; July 22, 1849, entry, in *Journal of Samuel Rutherford Dundass* (1857), 40; Aug. 12, 1849, entry, in Hamelin, Journals; Aug. 20 or 27, 1849, entry, in Hall, Diary (typescript), 14; July 21, 1850, entry, in Paden, ed., *The Journal of Madison Berryman Moorman* (1948), 50; July 11, 1852, entry, in Crane, Journal (MS). After listening to one of Brigham Young's sermons, 1850 overlander Adam Mercer Brown wrote in his diary that "his discourses would better grace a butcher's block than a pulpit." Quoted from Brown's 1850 diary by Kiefer, ed., "Over Barren Plains and Rock-bound Mountains," 24.

83. William B. Yates to Reuben Campbell, n.d., in St. Joseph *Gazette,* Dec. 10, 1851; Slater, *Fruits of Mormonism,* 34–35.

84. Slater, *Fruits of Mormonism,* 19–21; Aug. 6–13, 1850, entries, in Williams, ed., "Overland to California in 1850," 329; San Francisco *Daily Alta California,* July 14, 1852; Howard to Editor Beman Gates, Feb. 12, 1850, in Marietta, Ohio, *Intelligencer,* Apr. 18, 1850, reprinted in Clark, ed., *Gold Rush Diary* (1967), 178.

85. St. Joseph *Gazette,* Mar. 17, 1852; recollection of David Jackson Staples, quoted in Hannon, *The Boston-Newton Company Venture* (1969), 163; July 11, 14, 17, 1852, entries, in "Diary of E. W. Conyers" (1906), 462–66. On the other hand, the Saints could be equally persistent if they were searching for a particular company which had performed kindnesses to Mormon travelers while en route to Salt Lake City, as Thomas Flint's traveling group discovered in 1853, when they experienced special treatment in the valley because of earlier assistance they had accorded Mormon travelers. Sept. 7, 8, Oct. 25, 1853, entries, in Westergaard, ed., "Diary of Dr. Thomas Flint" (1923), 100, 110.

86. San Francisco *Daily Herald,* Apr. 8, 1855; Aug. 14, 1854, entry, in Brooks, ed., *On the Mormon Frontier,* 2:525. John D. Lee, who became the scapegoat for the Mountain Meadows massacre, offered additional corroboration of other murders of passing overlanders by valley Mormons. See Brooks, *John Doyle Lee* (1972), 366; Lee, "The Effect of Public Opinion on the Mormon Scheme of Self-Government," 93–97.

87. July 6, 1849, entry, in McCall, *The Great California Trail,* 48; letter of C. D., Aug. 21, 1852, in New York *Daily Times,* Oct. 16, 1852.

88. July 14, 1849, entry, in Gray, Diary (MS), 81; Kenderdine, *A California Tramp* (1888), 117; June 26, 1850, entry, in McBride, Journal (MS), 86.

89. "Report of Messrs. Brandebury, Brocchus, and Harris, to the President of the United States," Dec. 19, 1851, in *Congressional Globe,* 32 Cong., 1 Sess., App., 86–90 (Jan. 9, 1852).

90. See, e.g., New York *Daily Times,* Apr. 21, May 11, 1857.

91. *Congressional Globe,* 35 Cong., 1 Sess., 451, 1084–86 (Jan. 27, Mar. 11, 1858).

92. The foregoing account of the Mountain Meadows massacre is based upon Brooks's authoritative history of the tragedy, *The Mountain Meadows Massacre* (1962), *passim,* and on her biography, *John Doyle Lee,* 201–17, 357–67, 372.

CHAPTER TEN: WEST COAST ASSISTANCE

1. For a California example of the systematic approach to countering detractors in the public press, see John Marsh to Thomas O. Larkin, Aug. 12, 1845, in Hammond, ed., *The Larkin Papers* (1952–64), 3:309–10.

2. Carey, in his introduction to a reprint of Hastings's famous *Emigrants' Guide to Oregon and California* (1932), xiv, contends that Sutter had already sent a California booster to Fort Hall in 1844 to divert Oregon emigrants to California.

3. For a concise summary of the debate concerning Greenwood's relationship to Sutter, see Andrews, "The Ambitions of Lansford W. Hastings" (1970), 483–84.

4. Aug. 8, 1845, entry, in Palmer, *Journal of Travels over the Rocky Mountains*, ed. Thwaites (1906), 87–88.

5. Ibid., 88–89; Lockley, ed., "Recollections of Benjamin Franklin Bonney" (1923), 38–40; Robertson, *Fort Hall: Gateway to the Oregon Country* (1963), 231–34; Bancroft, *History of Oregon* (1886–88), 2:511; statement of Truman Bonney, James Bonney, and Abner Frazer, June 17, 1846, in Morgan, ed., *Overland in 1846* (1963), 2:568; Sept. 30, Oct. 1, 1845, entries, in *New Helvetia Diary* (1939), 4.

6. Wells, "Richard Grant," in Hafen, ed., *The Mountain Men and the Fur Trade* (1965–72), 9:175–76; A. H. Thompson to Editor, n.d., in Burlington *Iowa Territorial Gazette and Advertiser*, Dec. 20, 1845, in Morgan, The Mormons and the Far West (typescripts). The same letter was widely reprinted. See Albany, N.Y., *Atlas*, Dec. 23, 1845. Robertson (*Fort Hall*, 44, 192, 231, 240) has stressed the circumstantial evidence that Sutter and John McLoughlin of the Hudson's Bay Company had made a deal in which McLoughlin agreed to help divert emigrants to California, a policy which would be to the advantage of both Sutter, who wanted American settlers, and the British company, which did not. See below, pp. 357–60, for a further consideration of the Hudson's Bay Company's relationship to the overland emigrants.

7. Oregon City *Oregon Spectator*, June 25, 1846, in Morgan, ed., *Overland in 1846*, 2:567–71, 749–50, n. 61; Hastings, *Emigrants' Guide*, xiv–xx.

8. Jesse Applegate to "Future Emigrants to Oregon," Aug. 10, 1846, in Springfield, Ill., *Sangamo Journal*, Oct. 29, 1846, reprinted in Morgan, ed., *Overland in 1846*, 2:637; Bancroft, *History of Oregon*, 1:542–52; July 2, 1846, entry, in Bryant, *What I Saw in California* (1849), 118.

9. Stewart, *The California Trail* (1962), 142–44, 155–57; John R. McBride's 1846 reminiscenses quoted in Morgan, ed., *Overland in 1846*, 1:93–94, 99; Charles F. Putnam to Joseph Putnam, July 11, 1846, in ibid., 2:604; July 10, 16, 18, 1846, entries, in Bryant, *What I Saw in California*, 127, 142, 144.

10. Comprehensive summaries of the experiences of the 1846 emigrants on the Hastings Cutoff are contained in Korns, "West from Fort Bridger" (1951), 1–223, and Morgan, ed., *Overland in 1846*. See also Creer, "Lansford W. Hastings and the Discovery of the Old Mormon Trail" (1949), 175–86.

11. Andrews, in "The Controversial Hastings Overland Guide" (1968), 21–34, "Lansford W. Hastings and the Promotion of the Salt Lake Desert Cutoff" (1973), 133–50, and "The Ambitions of Lansford W. Hastings," 473–91, has begun the needed task of re-examining Hastings's role in the events of the tumultuous travel year of 1846. Despite the damaged reputation of the cutoff, several hundred gold rushers did attempt it in subsequent years. See Kelly, "Gold Seekers on the Hastings Cutoff" (1952), 3–30, for a summary account.

12. San Francisco *California Star*, Feb. 27, Sept. 4, 11, Dec. 4, 1847; Morgan, ed., *Overland in 1846*, 2:750, n. 61.

13. San Francisco *California Star*, Sept. 4, 1847; San Francisco *Daily Alta California*, Aug. 14, 1851.

14. Winther, "The Development of Transportation in Oregon, 1843–49" (1939), 316–18.

15. Oct. 27–Nov. 30, 1847, entries, in "Diary of Mrs. Elizabeth Dixon Smith Geer" (1908), 169–73.

16. On August 23, 1851, from his post at The Dalles, W. B. G. informed the *Oregonian*

editor that a recent drowning victim was the seventh of the season in the Columbia River (Portland *Oregonian*, Sept. 20, 1851), while in 1853 Henry Allyn's journal revealed that he had consumed two frustrating weeks in passing from The Dalles to his destination on The Dalles side of Portland (Aug. 25–Sept. 6, 1853, entries, in "Journal of Henry Allyn" [1924], 431–35). For a brief summary of some of the developments on the river see Johansen, "The Oregon Steam Navigation Company" (1941), 179–88.

17. Portland *Oregonian*, Jan. 1, 1853.

18. Paden, *Prairie Schooner Detours* (1949), 140.

19. Bancroft, *History of Oregon*, 1:484, 511–12; Clark and Tiller, *Terrible Trail* (1967), 16–17, 34–44; Smith, ed., *The Narrative of Samuel Hancock* (1927), 27; Barlow, "Reminiscences of Seventy Years" (1912), 254. Meek's group numbered approximately 150 wagons.

20. Clark and Tiller, *Terrible Trail, passim;* Bancroft, *History of Oregon*, 1:513–16; St. Louis *Daily Missouri Republican*, July 17, 1846.

21. Although many review articles have been written on Barlow's road, this reconstruction of the development of this important route, unless otherwise indicated, is based on the following sources: Bancroft, *History of Oregon*, 1:517–22; Bailey, "The Barlow Road" (1912), 287–92; Barlow, "History of the Barlow Road" (1902), 71–80; Wilkins, "Samuel Kimbrough Barlow" (1925), 211–20.

22. Wooley, "Mt. Hood or Bust" (1959), 7; Oregon City *Oregon Spectator*, Oct. 29, 1846, in Morgan, ed., *Overland in 1846*, 2:662–63; Sept. 3, 1848, entry, in Root, *Journal of Travels from St. Josephs to Oregon* (1850), 36.

23. Aug. 31, 1847, entry, in Pettijohn, Diary (MS); Portland *Oregonian*, Nov. 20, 1852. The 1852 proprietors, Sylvester and John B. Hall, probably discovered, as had Samuel Barlow, that if you did not demand cash from travelers but instead took notes and promises to pay "soon," you rarely collected a cent. The Halls reported having collected $2,950.35 in cash and having $701.50 outstanding in notes. For Barlow's frustrating experiences in endeavoring to collect his outstanding notes see Barlow, "Reminiscences of Seventy Years," 268.

24. Bancroft, *History of Oregon*, 1:531–32. The legislature, responding to Governor George Abernethy's urgent request, also appointed a committee to evaluate the merits of the respective routes and to memorialize the U.S. Congress for monies to finance the construction of a wagon road across the Blue and Cascade mountains. Abernethy's Address to Legislature, Dec. 2, 1845, in Hammond, ed., *Larkin Papers*, 5:22–26.

25. Bancroft, *History of Oregon*, 1:542–58; Applegate, "Notes and Reminiscences" (1921), 14–39; Helfrich, "The Applegate Trail" (1971), 1–6; Aug. 8, 1846, entry, in Thornton, *Oregon and California in 1848* (1849), 1:161–62; Burcham, "Scott's and Applegate's Old South Road" (1940), 411–12; Winther, "The Development of Transportation in Oregon," 321. For a short sketch of the intrepid mountaineer Moses Harris see Peltier, "Moses 'Black' Harris," in Hafen, ed., *The Mountain Men and the Fur Trade*, 4:103–17.

26. Bancroft, *History of Oregon*, 1:558–65; Applegate, "Notes and Reminiscences," 39–41; Stone, "Southern Route into Oregon" (1946), 140–44; Burcham, "Scott's and Applegate's Old South Road," 412–16; Dec. 29, 1846, entry, in Carey, ed., "Diary of Reverend George Gary—III" (1923), 332–33; Tabitha Brown to her brother and sister, Aug., 1854, in "A Brimfield Heroine" (1904), 200; Aug. 8, Nov. 14, 1846, entries, in Thornton, *Oregon and California in 1848*, 1:161–62, 175, 234; Thornton, "Occasional Address" (1879), 54–55. Thornton also charged that Jesse Applegate sold some of the relief provisions brought out to suffering emigrants: "He first reduced us to the verge of starvation, that he might thus be enabled to gather up the last dollar that remained to us."

27. Applegate, "Notes and Reminiscences," 40–41; Jesse Applegate to "Future Emigrants to Oregon," Aug. 10, 1846, in Morgan, ed., *Overland in 1846*, 2:637; Helfrich, "The Applegate Trail," 8–9; Stone, "Southern Route into Oregon," 146–47. The waybill was eventually completed, since the Oregon City *Oregon Spectator* printed a "Way Bill from Fort Hall to Willamette Valley" signed by Jesse Applegate in its Apr. 6, 1848, issue. Paden, *Prairie Schooner Detours*, 218.

28. Bancroft, *History of Oregon*, 1:565–66; Stone, "Southern Route into Oregon," 144–46; Thornton to Editor, Feb. 13, 1847, in Oregon City *Oregon Spectator*, Mar. 4, 1847, and David Goff to Editor, Apr. 3, 1847, in ibid., Apr. 29, 1847, both reprinted in Morgan,

ed., *Overland in 1846*, 2:670–82, 778, n. 160, 788–89, n. 167; June 3, 7, 1847, entries, in Carey, ed., "Diary of Reverend George Gary—IV" (1923), 401–3.

29. Bancroft, *History of Oregon*, 1:565–66, 623–24; Jesse Applegate to his brother, Oct. 11, 1847, partially reprinted in Burcham, "Scott's and Applegate's Old South Road," 416; Applegate, "Notes and Reminiscences," 41–42. Bancroft contended that in exchange for his efforts in denouncing the southern route, Thornton was appointed "supreme judge" of Oregon Territory.

30. Bancroft, *History of Oregon*, 1:623–24; Dorris, "The Oregon Trail" (1918), 522.

31. Stone, "Southern Route into Oregon," 148–51; Bancroft, *History of Oregon*, 1:567.

32. Helfrich, "The Applegate Trail," 9–16; Burcham, "Scott's and Applegate's Old South Road," 419–23.

33. Bancroft, *History of Oregon*, 2:305, n. 19; Clark, "Harney Basin Exploration, 1826–60" (1932), 108–10; Portland *Oregonian*, Oct. 16, 1852, Mar. 12, 19, May 28, Oct. 15, 1853; Sprague, "Willamette Highway" (1940), 244.

34. Bancroft, *History of Washington, Idaho, and Montana* (1890), 63–65; Mahlberg, "Edward J. Allen, Pioneer and Roadbuilder" (1953), 157–60; Baydo, "Overland from Missouri to Washington Territory in 1854" (1971), 80.

35. Stewart, *The California Trail*, 67–74, 137–41, 197–200, 203–6, 268, 324; Goodwin, "Development of the Emigrant Routes of Northern Nevada" (1965), 29–30.

36. Swartzlow, "Peter Lassen, Northern California's Trail-Blazer" (1939), 291–301; Burnett, " 'Recollections and Opinions of an Old Pioneer' " (1904), 381–87; Stewart, *The California Trail*, 196–97, 201, 207–15; Helfrich, "The Applegate Trail," 9; Liberty, Mo., *Weekly Tribune*, July 6, 1849; Barry, *The Beginning of the West* (1972), 722, 748–49. Stewart asserts that Lassen did not travel to Missouri in 1847 but that he merely went east on the trail in 1848 to meet the emigrants that he intended to lead to his ranch.

37. Stewart, *The California Trail*, 215; Oct. 7, 1849, entry, in Stuart, *My Roving Life* (1895), 1:73; Evans, Memorandum Book across the Plains (microfilm of MS); Haun, A Woman's Trip across the Plains in 1849 (MS), 38; Hale, *California as It Is*, ed. Hunter and Wellington (1851, 1954 reprint), 24. Paden, in *Prairie Schooner Detours*, 218–19, summarizes some of the evidence suggesting that Lassen had not deliberately falsified the mileage figures but may have been mistakenly relying on Jesse Applegate's 1848 waybill (see n. 27 above).

38. Stewart, *The California Trail*, 215, 268–72, 292. There is ample testimony in emigrant diaries about the influential nature of the Myers and Hudspeth action, and also about considerable emigrant unhappiness with Myers and Hudspeth when the cutoff turned into the long way around. See, e.g., Aug. 23, 24, 1849, entries, in Howell, Diary (MS), 50–52; Sept. 11, 12, 1849, entries, in Mattes and Kirk, eds., "From Ohio to California in 1849" (1950), 417–19.

39. Rebecca Reeve to Mary W. Ely, Dec. 30, 1849, in Winther, "From Tennessee to California in 1849" (1948), 66, 43, n. 3; M. M. to Editors, Jan. 24, 1850, in St. Louis *Missouri Republican*, Mar. 22, 1850, reprinted in Wyman, ed., *California Emigrant Letters* (1952), 94; Helfrich, "The Applegate Trail," 10; Stewart, *The California Trail*, 297; Oct. 7, 1849, entry, in Stuart, *My Roving Life*, 1:73; Kelly, *An Excursion to California* (1851), 2:91–92; Jonathan Clark to his brother, n.d., in Dubuque *Miners' Express*, Feb. 13, 1850, quoted in Lorch, "Iowa and the California Gold Rush of 1849" (1932), 362. That Lassen profited greatly from the sale of foodstuffs and other materials to the forty-niners is clear from the letter of John Wilson to Thomas S. Schackleford, Apr. 12, 1850, at San Francisco (Culmer, ed., "California Letter to John Wilson" [1930], 200–205). Wilson, who had traveled over the Lassen route in 1849, wrote, "Last year 20 000$ worth of potatoes turnips & cabbage & pumpkins could have been sold there, besides shoes boots, clothes, *beef* to more than 3 times that much if they had been there to be sold." Indeed, Wilson had been so impressed with the profit potential of Lassen's enterprise that he and an Oregonian purchased two-thirds of Lassen's holdings, agreeing to pay $15,000 each within five years.

40. Oct. 21, 22, 1849, entries, in Read and Gaines, eds., *Gold Rush* (1944), 1:234, 603, n. 155. Bruff particularly stressed the way these scoundrels, whose names he indicated he could supply, assured weary overlanders that the remaining road was "the most rugged and difficult road ever travelled by Christians" so that the emigrants would leave their wagons and stock and trudge ahead on foot.

41. Oct. 14, 1849, entry, in Doyle, Diaries and Letters (MSS and typescripts). See also Jerome B. Howard to Beman Gates, Feb. 16, 1850, in Marietta, Ohio, *Intelligencer,* Apr. 25, 1850, reprinted in Clark, ed., *Gold Rush Diary* (1967), 180.

42. Reed to Mary C. Keyes, May 16, 1847, in "The Miller-Reed Diary," in Morgan, ed., *Overland in 1846,* 1:287; Paden, *Prairie Schooner Detours,* 137. Ware's *Emigrants' Guide to California* (ed. Caughey [1932], 31), the most popular guidebook among the gold rushers, reminded overlanders of the fate of the Donner party as justification for the advice that travelers "oppose any experiments in your party, in leaving the regular route of travel to try roads said to be shorter."

43. Oswald, "James P. Beckwourth," in Hafen, ed., *The Mountain Men and the Fur Trade,* 6:55–57; Mack, *Nevada: A History of the State* (1936), 120–21; Marysville, Cal., *Herald,* June 3, 1851; James P. Beckwourth to Editors, July 27, 1853, in Marysville *Daily Evening Herald,* Aug. 13, 1853. In his autobiography Beckwourth indicated that the only compensation he ever received for his important route discovery was $200 from some Marysville residents, even though he had expended $1,600 of his own funds in improving the trail. Oswald, ed., *The Life and Adventures of James P. Beckwourth* (1972), 516–19.

44. Stewart, *The California Trail,* 300, 305; Marysville *Herald,* Nov. 13, 1855.

45. Stewart, *The California Trail,* 300, 305; San Francisco *Daily Alta California,* Aug. 6, 22, 1852, July 8, 1854.

46. Stewart, *The California Trail,* 305–6; San Francisco *Daily Alta California,* Aug. 23, 1852. Sonora residents also outfitted a major relief expedition in behalf of overlanders utilizing the new route the following year. Ibid., Oct. 3, 1853; Ryan, "Sonora Trail and Sonora Pass of 1853" (Jan., 1956), 11–12, (Feb., 1956), 10.

47. Stewart, *The California Trail,* 300, 305; Goodwin, "Development of the Emigrant Routes of Northern Nevada," 39; Helfrich, "The Applegate Trail," 12; San Francisco *Daily Alta California,* June 29, 1852; Aug. 15, 22, 1852, entries, in Kingery, Letters (MSS and typescripts).

48. Stewart, *The California Trail,* 300, 310, 314; Marysville *Herald,* June 12, July 10, 1851; San Francisco *Daily Alta California,* Aug. 22, 1852; R. S. McIntosh to St. Louis *Intelligencer,* Feb. 23, 1854, reprinted in St. Joseph *Gazette,* Mar. 8, 1854.

49. For a discussion of the role of community newspapers in this, see Chap. 2 above, pp. 86–88, and for an overall summary of the California wagon road crusades see White, "Surmounting the Sierras" (1928), 3–19.

50. See, e.g., R. S. McIntosh to St. Louis *Intelligencer,* Feb. 23, 1854, and extract from S. M. Bowman letter to St. Louis *Republican,* also printed in St. Joseph *Gazette,* Mar. 8, 1854; St. Joseph *Gazette,* Nov. 3, 1852; Phillips, ed., *Forty Years on the Frontier* (1925, 1957), 1:53–54; Aug. 10, 1849, entry of Wakeman Bryarly, in Potter, ed., *Trail to California* (1945), 186; San Francisco *Daily Herald,* Aug. 4, 1853, in Cohen, Scrapbooks (typescripts), 168–69; San Francisco *Daily Alta California,* Aug. 6, 1852.

51. John McLoughlin to Hudson's Bay Company, Dec. 4, 1843, in Rich, ed., *The Letters of John McLoughlin, 1839–44* (1943), 190–91; McLoughlin to Hudson's Bay Company, Nov. 20, 1845, in Judson, ed., "Dr. John McLoughlin's Last Letter to the Hudson's Bay Company" (1915), 125; Merk, "The Oregon Pioneers and the Boundary" (1924), 693; Husband, "Senator Lewis F. Linn and the Oregon Question" (1971), 14. In a speech on January 9, 1843, Linn told his senatorial colleagues that the Hudson's Bay Company, by the hand of its employees or through its control over area Indians, had murdered over 500 men *before* 1829, and that "the yearly slaughter has gone on ever since, ranging between fifteen and twenty men during the year 1842." *Congressional Globe,* 27 Cong., 3 Sess., App., 79 (Jan. 9, 1843).

52. William Peel to Capt. John Gordon, Sept. 27, 1845, in Scott, ed., "Report of Lieutenant Peel on Oregon" (1928), 62–63; letter of S. M. Gilmore, Nov. 11, 1843, in *Western Journal,* Mar. 15, 1845, reprinted in "Documents" (1903), 281; letter of unnamed emigrant, in Towanda, Pa., *Bradford Reporter,* Dec. 4, 1844, quoted in Holmes, "John McLoughlin," in Hafen, ed., *The Mountain Men and the Fur Trade,* 8:244–45; Hastings, *Emigrants' Guide,* 22, 51, 58; "The Shively Guide," in Morgan, ed., *Overland in 1846,* 2:740; Watt, "Recollections of Dr. John McLoughlin" (1887), 24.

53. Letter of S. M. Gilmore, Nov. 11, 1843, 281; Nov. 3, 1843, entry, in "The Journal of John Boardman" (1929), 118; Montreal *Gazette,* Oct. 14, 1845; Hastings, *Emigrants' Guide,*

22, 58; Watt, "Recollections of Dr. John McCloughlin," 24–25; Bancroft, *History of Oregon*, 1:409, 456, 503; W. Kaye Lamb, Introduction, in Rich, ed., *The Letters of John McLoughlin, 1844–46* (1944), lii; Leader, "McLoughlin's Answer to Warre Report" (1932), 215, 214–29 *passim*.

54. McLoughlin to Hudson's Bay Company, Dec. 4, 1843, in Rich, ed., *Letters of John McLoughlin, 1839–44*, 190; McLoughlin, "Copy of a Document" (1881), 52–53; Leader, "McLoughlin's Answer to Warre Report," 215; Murray, "The Role of the Hudson's Bay Company in Pacific Northwest History" (1961), 25–26; Robertson, *Fort Hall*, 45.

55. Lamb, Introduction, lii; Galbraith, *The Hudson's Bay Company as an Imperial Factor* (1957), 226–27, 238–41; Leader, "McLoughlin's Answer to Warre Report," 214–29.

56. In addition to Leader, "McLoughlin's Answer to Warre Report," 214–29, see McLoughlin, "Copy of a Document," 52–55; McLoughlin to Hudson's Bay Company, July 1, 1846, in Rich, ed., *Letters of John McLoughlin, 1844–46*, 160; McLoughlin to Hudson's Bay Company, Nov. 20, 1845, in Judson, ed., "Dr. John McLoughlin's Last Letter," 124–25; McLoughlin to Hudson's Bay Company, Dec. 4, 1843, in Rich, ed., *Letters of John McLoughlin, 1839–44*, 190–91, for further defenses of his policies.

57. In the spring of 1843 McLoughlin did extend credit to dissatisfied Oregonians, enabling them to follow Lansford Hastings to California—credit which, in the main, the company never recovered. Leader, "McLoughlin's Answer to Warre Report," 215, 220–21; McLoughlin, "Copy of a Document," 54; "Letter of Dr. John McLoughlin to Oregon Statesman" (1907), 294–99; Murray, "The Role of the Hudson's Bay Company in Pacific Northwest History," 29–30; Galbraith, *Hudson's Bay Company*, 227; Holmes, "John McLoughlin," 245.

58. Hudson's Bay Company directors had specifically warned McLoughlin not to assist the American missionaries, who began arriving in the late 1830s, assuming that the missionaries' main intention was the founding of a U.S. settlement. McLoughlin, however, sold the churchmen all the supplies they needed to begin their mission stations, and extended the Hudson's Bay Company's protective umbrella to the little outposts situated among potentially hostile Indians. See Murray, "The Role of the Hudson's Bay Company in Pacific Northwest History," 29; McLoughlin to the Hudson's Bay Company, Dec. 4, 1843, in Rich, ed., *Letters of John McLoughlin, 1839–44*, 191.

59. A second Presbyterian outpost, supervised by Henry Spalding at Lapwai, and located considerably farther from the main trail than even the Whitman station, also apparently provided minimal assistance to westbound overlanders. H. H. Spalding to Joel Palmer, Apr. 7, 1846, in Washington *National Intelligencer*, Sept. 8, 1846; Dorris, "The Oregon Trail," 513.

60. Ibid., 513; Coonc, "Reminiscences of a Pioneer Woman," ed. Lewis (1917), 15.

61. Bancroft, *History of Oregon*, 1:515, 452, n. 17; Sept. 30, 1845, entry, in Palmer, *Journal of Travels*, 121–24; Peltier, "Moses 'Black' Harris," 113–14.

62. Robertson, "Reminiscences of Alanson Hinman" (1901), 268–69.

63. Oct. 10, 1843, entry, in Winton, ed., "William T. Newby's Diary" (1939), 237–38; Burnett, "'Recollections and Opinions of an Old Pioneer'" (1904), 82–83; H. H. Spalding to Joel Palmer, Apr. 7, 1846, in Washington *National Intelligencer*, Sept. 8, 1846. Due to the request by neighboring missionaries for his medical skills, Whitman was absent when most of the 1843 overlanders passed through Waiilatpu. Some of the famished passersby took advantage of the opportunity to break into the Waiilatpu storehouse and take what they desired. Lavender, *Westward Vision* (1963), 380.

64. Robertson, "Reminiscences of Alanson Hinman," 269; Narcissa Whitman to Clarissa Prentiss, Nov. 3, 1846, and to Clarissa P. Kinny, May 20, 1844, in "Mrs. Whitman's Letters" (1894), 91, 180; letter of Marcus Whitman, Apr. 1, 1847, quoted in Morgan, ed., *Overland in 1846*, 2:790, n. 173.

65. To provide winter employment for tarrying overlanders Whitman had them build and operate a mill some twenty miles from the mission. Robertson, "Reminiscences of Alanson Hinman," 269.

66. Narcissa Whitman to Clarissa P. Kinny, May 20, 1844, and to Clarissa Prentiss, Nov. 3, 1846, in "Mrs. Whitman's Letters," 180, 91; letter of Marcus Whitman, Apr. 1, 1847, in Morgan, ed., *Overland in 1846*, 2:790, n. 173; Gregg, *A History of the Oregon Trail, Santa Fe*

Trail, and Other Trails (1955), 193, 243–45; Bancroft, *History of Oregon*, 1:647–61, 666, 686–97. The causes of the brutal attack on the Whitmans were many, the most immediate of which concerned Whitman's inability to cure most Indians who had contracted measles from passing emigrants, a failure which led to Indian rumors that Whitman must be poisoning the Indians, since white children with measles were not dying.

67. For the Shortess relief effort utilizing materials contributed by valley settlers, see Bancroft, *History of Oregon*, 1:409–10; Lavender, *Westward Vision*, 382.

68. See Oct. 6–Nov. 1, 1845, entries, in Palmer, *Journal of Travels*, 128–57; Bancroft, *History of Oregon*, 1:520–22.

69. Prefatory remarks and Dec. 8, 10, 1845, entries, in "Journal of Thomas Holt," in Morgan, ed., *Overland in 1846*, 1:191–93, 397, n. 2.

70. Dec. 3, 1846–Jan. 21, 1847, entries, in ibid., 1:190–99; Oregon City *Oregon Spectator*, Mar. 18, 1847, in ibid., 2:676; Thornton, "Occasional Address," 68.

71. San Francisco *California Star*, Nov. 13, 1847, Feb. 12, 1848; William R. Allen to Washington Franklin Allen, May 4, 1851 (typescript); Bancroft, *History of Oregon*, 2:174–75; Portland *Oregonian*, May 24, 1851; Sept. 15, 1851, entry, in Crawford, "Journal of a Trip across the Plains" (1924), 168.

72. A. to Thomas J. Dryer, Aug. 16, 1852, in Portland *Oregonian*, Sept. 4, 1852; B. E. Stewart to Dryer, Sept. 13, 1852, in ibid., Oct. 2, 1852; ibid., Oct. 9, 1852; Lot Whitcomb to Dryer, Nov. 1, 1852, in ibid., Nov. 6, 1852.

73. Portland *Oregonian*, Sept. 18, Oct. 2, 9, Nov. 6, 20, 1852; San Francisco *Daily Alta California*, Oct. 13, 14, 1852.

74. "An Immigrant" to Thomas J. Dryer, Oct. 21, 1852, in Portland *Oregonian*, Oct. 23, 1852; Lot Whitcomb to Dryer, Oct. 5, Nov. 1, 1852, in ibid., Oct. 9, Nov. 6, 1852; ibid., Nov. 6, 1852.

75. Whitcomb to Dryer, Nov. 1, 1852, in ibid., Nov. 6, 1852; ibid., Oct. 9, Dec. 4, 1852; Oct. 15, 1852, entry, in Adams, "Crossing the Plains in 1852" (1905), 325.

76. See pp. 350–51 above; San Francisco *Daily Alta California*, Nov. 21, 1853; S. H. Taylor to Editor, Dec. 17, 1853, in Watertown, Wis., *Chronicle*, Mar. 29, 1854, reprinted in "Letters of S. H. Taylor to the Watertown Chronicle" (1921), 150; Sept. 28, 1853, entry, in Williams, "Diary of a Trip across the Plains" (1922), 225.

77. Bancroft, *History of Oregon*, 1:749–51; John E. Ross to George L. Curry, Nov. 10, 1854, "Statement of W. T. Kershaw," Nov. 21, 1857, Joel Palmer to B. F. Dowell, Dec. 17, 1857, all in U.S. Congress, *Protection Afforded by Volunteers of Oregon and Washington Territories* (1859), 15, 41–43, 55.

78. John E. Ross to Jesse Walker, Aug. 8, 1854, Walker to Ross, Nov. 6, 1854, "Memorial Asking Congress to Pay Certain Soldiers and Other Persons for Services Rendered and Supplies Furnished in the Rogue River War of 1854," "Statement of D. R. Calhoon," Nov. 13, 1857, "Statement of E. W. Conner," Nov. 18, 1857, all in ibid., 8–9, 12–13, 29, 36–38; "Volunteer" to Thomas J. Dryer, Sept. 5, 1855, in Portland *Weekly Oregonian*, Sept. 29, 1855. The Oregon territorial legislature later petitioned the U.S. Congress for funds to reimburse the volunteers for their expenses. Charity for needy overlanders continued through to the end of the decade. In 1860 the Salem, Oregon, citizenry contributed $650 for one of the families involved in the Otter–Van Orman massacre by Indians. Ibid., Dec. 1, 1860.

79. Stewart, *Ordeal by Hunger* (1960), 54–55.

80. Quoted from Sutter's *Reminiscences* by H. B. Van Sicklen in his Introduction to *New Helvetia Diary*, xix. See also ibid., xii–xix; "General Sutter's Diary—IV" (reproduced); letter of Thomas O. Larkin, Apr. 20, 1846, in Hammond, ed., *Larkin Papers*, 4:333; Zollinger, *Sutter: The Man and His Empire* (1939), 112–13, 208.

81. Stewart, ed., *The Opening of the California Trail* (1953), 81–84; Lockley, ed., "Recollections of Benjamin Franklin Bonney," 39, 44.

82. Stewart, *Ordeal by Hunger*, 77, 95–103.

83. Ibid., *passim*, esp. 103–4, 148–78, 283–84; John Sinclair to William A. Bartlett, Jan. 29, 1847, in Washington *National Intelligencer*, Sept. 16, 1847; Monterey *Californian*, Mar. 27, 1847, reprinted in Morgan, ed., *Overland in 1846*, 2:713; San Francisco *California Star*, Feb. 6, 1847; Bryant, *What I Saw in California*, 250–51. The daily wage finally paid to members of the rescue teams ranged between $1.50 and $3 depending on the type of

service performed. It is possible that some received $5 per day for their efforts in the heaviest snow.

84. Stewart, *Ordeal by Hunger, passim.* There were also bad luck, perfidy, and ineptitude. Some of the "rescuers" proved to be more interested in the valuables possessed by the Donner emigrants than in saving lives. Further, Selim E. Woodworth, a U.S. naval officer on leave who assumed leadership of much of the rescue effort, proved unable to support his rescue teams. Stewart, in his excellent account of this entire affair, intimates that had Woodworth been braver and more forceful, many more lives might have been saved. Ibid., 237, 254, 284–85.

85. Ibid., 271. The quotation is from 191.

86. D. H. Rucker to Persifer F. Smith, Dec. 20, 1849, in U.S. President, *Gen. Smith's Correspondence, California* (1850), 135. For examples of reports by early-arriving overlanders predicting great suffering for those yet to come, see San Francisco *Alta California*, Aug. 13, 1849, and letter of "Traveller," Aug. 30, 1849, in Windsor *Vermont Chronicle*, Oct. 24, 1849.

87. Rucker to Smith, Dec. 20, 1849, Rucker to John H. Peoplis [*sic*], Sept. 14, 1849, Rucker to John Chandler, Sept. 18, 1849, all in U.S. President, *Gen. Smith's Correspondence, California*, 134–40, 96–97; San Francisco *Alta California*, Dec. 15, 1849; Groh, *Gold Fever* (1966), 152. Forty-niner Elisha Douglass Perkins, on meeting the first of the government relief parties and learning of the 100,000-dollar governmental appropriation, commented approvingly: "Pity but the Government treasures could always be appropriated to a good purpose, in relieving misery instead of causing it." Sept. 26, 1849, entry, in Clark, ed., *Gold Rush Diary*, 138.

88. Rucker to Smith, Dec. 20, 1849, Chandler to Rucker, Nov. 14, 1849, Hunt to Rucker, Nov. 8, 1849, Foreman to Rucker, Nov. 7, 1847 [*sic*], Kilburn to Rucker, Oct. 22, 1849, all in U.S. President, *Gen. Smith's Correspondence, California*, 135, 109–17.

89. Peoples to Rucker, Sept. 22, Dec. 12, 1849, Rucker to Smith, Dec. 20, 1849, in ibid., 127–28, 117–22, 135, 140.

90. Oct. 14, 1849, entry of Bruff, in Read and Gaines, eds., *Gold Rush*, 1:221. See also Grosh, *Gold Fever*, 154–55; Rucker to Smith, Dec. 20, 1849, and Oct. 5–12, 1849, entries in Rucker's Journal, in U.S. President, *Gen. Smith's Correspondence, California*, 137–38, 144–47.

91. Hunt to Rucker, Nov. 8, 1849, in ibid., 113.

92. Hale, *California as It Is*, 28–29.

93. Rucker to Peoples, Sept. 14, 1849, Rucker to Foreman, Sept. 26, 1849, Foreman to Rucker, Nov. 7, 1847 [*sic*], Rucker to Smith, Dec. 20, 1849, all in U.S. President, *Gen. Smith's Correspondence, California*, 96, 99, 115, 137.

94. Peoples to Rucker, Dec. 12, 1849, Rucker to Peoples, Nov. 13, 1849, in ibid., 122, 104.

95. Peoples to Rucker, Dec. 12, 1849, in ibid., 118–19.

96. See, e.g., Foreman to Rucker, Nov. 7, 1847 [*sic*], Kilburn to Rucker, Oct. 22, 1849, Peoples to Rucker, Dec. 12, 1849, Rucker to Smith, Dec. 20, 1849, all in ibid., 115, 116, 122, 139–40. See also St. Joseph *Gazette*, July 31, 1850.

97. Aug. 7, 1850, entry, in *Journal of John Wood* (1852), 46; San Francisco *Daily Alta California*, July 24, 31, Aug. 29, 1850. Trail-littering began early in 1850, with Henry Wellenkamp noting that at every campground west of Fort Laramie they found abandoned wagons and other materials. June 20, 1850, entry, in Diary of Trip to California, Henry Wellenkamp (typescript), 4. Adam Mercer Brown, who found the stench "awful" when his company made the desert crossing to the Carson River in late August, indicated that "dead and dying animals literally covered the trail, and we were compelled to seek a new route to avoid them." Aug. 27, 1850, entry, in Kiefer, ed., "Over Barren Plains and Rock-bound Mountains" (1972), 27.

98. Letter of E. H. N. Patterson, in *Placer Times*, July 31, 1850, reprinted in San Francisco *Daily Alta California*, Aug. 2, 1850; James L. Demier to friend, Aug. 2, 1850, in St. Louis *Daily Missouri Republican*, Nov. 6, 1850; San Francisco *Daily Alta California*, Sept. 6, Oct. 5, 1850; Sept. 10, 11, 1850, entries, in Jones, Diary (photocopy of MS); July 30, Aug. 4, 1850, entries, in Diary of Trip to California, Henry Wellenkamp, 9–110.

99. Henry Page to his wife, Sept. 29, 1850, in Page, *Wagons West* (1930), 293; July 24,

1850, entry, in Jewett, Journal (typescript), 41; San Francisco *Daily Alta California*, July 26, 27, Aug. 22, Sept. 26, 1850. Waldo's letter (of Sept. 15, at the Truckee River station) was also printed in the Sept. 29, 1850, Sacramento *Transcript*, the Nov. 29, 1850, St. Joseph *Adventure* (Wyman, ed., *California Emigrant Letters*, 116), and the Aug. 26, 1853, Marysville *Daily Evening Herald*.

100. Mack, *Nevada*, 139; Henry Page to his wife, Sept. 29, 1850, in Page, *Wagons West*, 293.

101. J. Neely Johnson to Relief Committee, Aug. 19, 1850, in San Francisco *Daily Alta California*, Aug. 22, 1850; New York *Herald*, Oct. 7, 1850; San Francisco *Daily Alta California*, Aug. 18, 1850; Aug. 26, 1850, entry, in Paden, ed., *The Journal of Madison Berryman Moorman* (1948), 74, 125, n. 164; St. Louis *Daily Missouri Republican*, Dec. 23, 1850; letters of William Waldo, Sept. 15, 1850, in Marysville *Daily Evening Herald*, Aug. 26, 1853, and Sept. 28, 1850, in Liberty *Weekly Tribune*, Dec. 27, 1850.

102. Johnson to Relief Committee, Aug. 19, 1850, in San Francisco *Daily Alta California*, Aug. 22, 1850; Ralston to Sacramento Relief Committee, Sept. 6, 1850, in ibid., Sept. 13, 1850; U.S. Congress, *Resolution of the Legislature of California, for . . . Waldo, Hall, and Petrie* (1852), 1; letter of Waldo, Sept. 15, 1850, in Marysville *Daily Evening Herald*, Aug. 26, 1853.

103. Hartman, "The California and Oregon Trail" (1924), 19; Johnson to F. Foreman, Aug. 9, 1850, in Marysville *Herald*, Aug. 20, 1850; Johnson to Relief Committee, Aug. 19, 1850, in San Francisco *Daily Alta California*, Aug. 22, 1850.

104. Waldo to F. Foreman, Sept. 12, 15, 1850, in Marysville *Daily Evening Herald*, Aug. 26, 1853; letter of Waldo, Sept. 28, 1850, in Liberty *Weekly Tribune*, Dec. 27, 1850. For the 1850 suicides see Delano, *Across the Plains and among the Diggings* (1853, 1936 reprint), 104; James W. Evans to Ellis G. Evans, Oct. 27, 1850, in Evans, ed., "A Missouri Forty-Niner's Trip across the Plains" (1948), 41; June 20, 1850, entry, in Payne, *Saint Louis to San Francisco* (typescript), 50; July 16, 1850, entry, in Thomasson, Diary (typescript), 34; St. Louis *Daily Missouri Republican*, Sept. 21, 1850.

105. New York *Herald*, Oct. 7, 1850; San Francisco *Daily Alta California*, Aug. 18, 1850.

106. U.S. Congress, *Resolutions of the Legislature of California, Recommending the Payment of a Debt* (1852), 1; S. B. Bright to Sacramento Relief Committee, Sept. 22, 1850, in Marysville *Herald*, Oct. 8, 1850; U.S. Congress, *Resolution of the Legislature of California, for Waldo, Hall, and Petrie*, 1; Bryan, "From Marthasville to Marysville in 1850" (1963), 125.

107. San Francisco *Daily Alta California*, June 26, July 19, 1852. Among those identified as playing a supervisory role in 1852, either at a relief station or in charge of supply trains, were John Bodley, General James Estel, General Rains, General Price, and General J. W. Denver (the term "general" may have been an honorific one in some of these instances). See San Francisco *Daily Alta California*, Aug. 10, Oct. 22, 1852; Norton, "My Overland Trip to California in 1852" (Sept., 1934), 10.

108. Aug. 22, 1852, entry, in Sharp, Diary (MS); San Francisco *Daily Alta California*, Aug. 8–10, 1852; Mack, *Nevada*, 139–40.

109. San Francisco *Daily Alta California*, Aug. 8, 10, 1852; Sept. 3, 4, 1852, entries, in Egbert, Diary (photocopy of typescript), 49.

110. July 16 [15], 1852, entry, in Keen, Journal (typescript), 75a.

111. For two bitter emigrant accusations against Bodley and his son, who kept an expensive water station on the desert crossing to the Truckee River, see the Aug. 9, 1852, entry of Richard Owen Hickman, in Phillips, ed., " 'Dick's Works' " (1929), 258; St. Joseph *Gazette*, Nov. 3, 1852. Overlander R. H. P. Snodgrass characterized the government relief operation as "one grand humbug good business for those engaged in it." July 20, 1852, entry, in Snodgrass, Journal (MS and typescript). For a sampling of the press coverage of the Bodley affair, see San Francisco *Daily Alta California*, Oct. 22, 28, 1852.

112. Ibid., June 26, Oct. 22, 28, 1852; Aug. 9, 1852, entry, in Phillips, ed., " 'Dick's Works,' " 258.

113. Sanford, A Trip across the Plains (typescript), 10.

114. See, e.g., "Reminiscences of Experiences on the Oregon Trail" (1901), 223, 227; Miller, "Early Oregon Scenes" (1930), 170–71; Aug. 23, 1850, entry, in Skinner, Diary (MS); July 21, 1852, entry, in Paxson, ed., "T. Turnbull's Travels" (1914), 198.

CHAPTER ELEVEN: THE OVERLANDERS IN HISTORICAL PERSPECTIVE

1. Mattes, "New Horizons on the Old Oregon Trail," in Billington, ed., *People of the Plains and Mountains* (1973), 46.

2. Morgan, ed., *Overland in 1846* (1963), 1:115. Morgan was describing the 1846 travel year, which he found "in some respects representative of all overland migrations, but the terrible climax in the Sierra Nevada also makes it unique."

3. May 9–July 7, 1844, entries, in Parrish, "Crossing the Plains in 1844" (1889), 84–92; "Reminiscences of Honorable John Minto" (1901), 145; Ben F. Headen to Mr. and Mrs. Winchester Payne, Sept. 16, 1853 (typescript).

4. Examples and illustrations for the interpretations in this concluding chapter have frequently been derived from previous chapters. Where this occurs, as in the present instance, the sources will not again be identified.

5. Statistics derived from the Fort Kearny and Fort Laramie emigrant registers convincingly portray the rapidly changing male/female ratios. In 1850 a late summer Fort Laramie report revealed that a mere 7 percent of the 42,530 passing emigrants were women and children; by 1852 the Fort Kearny totals revealed a substantial increase to 33 percent women and children; and in 1853 a slight rise to 35 percent was indicated. Letter of "Laramie," Aug. 26, 1850, in St. Louis *Daily Missouri Republican*, Oct. 3, 1850; June 4, 1852, entry, in Hampton, Diary (typescript); St. Joseph *Gazette*, Aug. 3, 1853.

6. May 30, 1849, entry, in The Diary of Bernard J. Reid, Esq. (typescript), 13–14. The anticipated grave was not needed, however, since the overlander recovered.

7. T. J. S. to Editor, May 25, 1852, in New York *Herald*, June 23, 1852.

8. Several astute newspaper editors early foresaw the stimulating impact the overland emigrations would have upon western settlement. See St. Louis *Weekly Reveille*, Apr. 26, 1847, quoted by Joost, "Reveille in the West," in McDermott, ed., *Travelers on the Western Frontier* (1970), 231–32; St. Louis *Daily Missouri Republican*, Apr. 23, 1851. See also Danker, "The Influence of Transportation upon Nebraska Territory" (1966), 194–95.

9. Forty-niner Augustus Burbank estimated the mileage from St. Joseph to Johnson's Ranch in California at 1,900 miles and wrote, "This is the distance from Civilization to Civilization on this overland route." Sept. 21, 1849, entry, in Burbank, Diary (microfilm of MS), 137.

10. Atkinson, "Occasional Address" (1881), 33; Brooks, "The Plains Across" (1902), 803.

11. Rees, "Quotations from the Journal and Register" (1875), 7.

12. "Constitution of the Oregon Pioneer Association" (1875), 4. Although the organization was not limited to Oregon residents who had come overland, the association was always most concerned with those who had made the overland journey.

13. "Third Annual Reunion" (1876), 12; "Seventh Annual Reunion" (1880), 11–12.

14. "The Annual Business Meeting" (1892), 17–21.

15. Ibid., 18–19.

16. Ibid., 23–24.

17. Himes, "Twenty-second Annual Reunion" (1895), 7–8. Presumably, similar debates were heard at the annual meetings of the Society of California Pioneers, which was organized in August, 1850. Initially, the California society established two categories of membership: all those who were California residents prior to January 1, 1849, qualified as senior members; all those who resided in California before January 1, 1850, were regarded as junior members. When all the senior members had died, all distinctions were ended and membership was thrown open to all male descendants of California residents, male and female, before January 1, 1850. "The Society of California Pioneers" (1942), 25–26.

18. July 15, 1849, entry, in Diary of Bernard J. Reid, 39.

19. For the use of saleratus see the July 22, 1849, entry, in Stuart, *My Roving Life* (1895), 1:39; Troxel, "Food of the Overland Emigrants" (1955), 18. Foster's remarks appear in the June 13, 1849, entry of his Diary (typescript), 35; Steele's in the June 11, 1850, entry of *Across the Plains in 1850*, ed. Schafer (1930), 60. In contrast, Brigham Young sternly lectured his westbound Mormon caravan in 1847 on the evils of needlessly killing and

wounding so many buffalo, birds, and other game. May 18, 1847, entry of William A. Empey, in Morgan, ed., "The Mormon Ferry on the North Platte" (1949), 126.

20. July 11, 1849, entry, in Clark, ed., *Gold Rush Diary* (1967), 61.

21. Forty-niner Alexander Ramsay heard a host of different ministers on Sundays during his pilgrimage across the continent. Among the different denominations they represented he listed Methodist, Episcopal, Presbyterian, and Baptist. May 20, 27, July 1, 1849, entries, in Mattes, ed., "Alexander Ramsay's Gold Rush Diary" (1949), 444–46, 451.

22. David Dewolf to Matilda Dewolf, June 17, 1849, between Forts Kearny and Laramie, in Cox, ed., "Diary of the Overland Trail" (1925), 191.

23. July 15, Aug. 23, Oct. 18, 1843, entries, in Nesmith, "Diary of the Emigration of 1843" (1906), 341, 349, 358; June 3, 6, 15, 19, July 4, 8, Aug. 7, 1849, entries, in Chamberlain, Diary (typescript), 6, 9, 11, 16, 18, 30; May 7, 1850, entry, in Langworthy, *Scenery of the Plains, Mountains and Mines,* ed. Phillips (1932), 13; letter of "Cheyenne," June 2, 1850, in St. Louis *Daily Missouri Republican,* July 16, 1850; Carpenter, I Crossed the Plains in the 50's (microfilm of MS).

24. St. Louis *Missouri Republican,* May 15, 1846, in Morgan, ed., *Overland in 1846,* 2:530; Thornton, "Occasional Address" (1879), 34; June 8, 1849, entry, in Delano, *Across the Plains and among the Diggings* (1853, 1936 reprint), 27; Apr. 28, 1849, entry, in Stackpole, Journal (MS); June 10, 1849, entry of John Edwin Banks, in Scamehorn, ed., *The Buckeye Rovers in the Gold Rush* (1965), 18; Diary of Bernard J. Reid, 6; May 11, 1849, entry, in Hamelin, Journals (MSS and typescripts); Aug. 14, 20, 1849, entries, in Howell, Diary (MS), 40, 47; June 26, 1850, entry, in Paden, ed., *The Journal of Madison Berryman Moorman* (1948), 32; May 11, 1850, diary entry of H., in San Francisco *Daily Alta California,* Sept. 21, 1850; June 16, 1851, entry, in Johnson, Diary (MS), 50; Quincy A. Brooks to "Dear Ruter," Nov. 7, 1851, in "Letter of Quincy Adams Brooks" (1914), 213; May 25, Aug. 23, 1852, entries, in "Diary of E. W. Conyers" (1906), 434, 490; June 22, 1852, entry, in Owen, Journal (MS); Hunt, *By Ox-Team to California* (n.d.), 10.

25. Inman, "My Arrival in Washington in 1852" (1927), 254; May 19, 1850, entry, in A Chapter from the Diary of the Late Judge James B. Persinger (typescript), 7.

26. See, e.g., John A. Sutter to Thomas O. Larkin, Oct. 8, 1845, in Hammond, ed., *The Larkin Papers* (1952–64), 4:10: "A good Many of this Emigrants have Cash more or less. Some of them have several thousand Dollars in Gold. Not one Company has arrived before in this Country, which looked so respectable as this." Further, a member of Colonel Stephen W. Kearny's 1845 expedition described many Oregon emigrants as "rich," and many forty-niners were particularly well endowed. One study of the Michigan argonauts estimates that the average Michigan forty-niner took $400 with him, all of which had as depressing an impact on the Michigan economy as it had a stimulating impact in California. Albany, N.Y., *Atlas,* July 22, 1845; Bidlack, *Letters Home* (1960), 12–13. See also Roske, "The World Impact of the California Gold Rush" (1963), 187–232.

27. See Merk, "The Oregon Pioneers and the Boundary" (1924), 681–99, for a careful analysis of the impact of the Oregon emigrations upon the settlement of the Anglo-American disupte.

28. Ellison, "The Beginnings of the Apple Industry in Oregon" (1937), 326–27; McClintock, "Henderson Luelling, Seth Lewelling" (1967), 155–59; C. Lancaster to Elisha Whittlesey, Dec. 9, 1850 (MS); July 11, 1847, entry of William A. Empey, in Morgan, ed., "The Mormon Ferry on the North Platte," 138–39, 162, n. 98.

29. Barlow, "Reminiscences of Seventy Years" (1912), 276–78; Williamson, "Dr. James R. Cardwell" (1927), 14. More than one overlander saw his visions of success and security dashed by the exigencies of the overland journey. An 1846 Missourian who endeavored to take two hives of honeybees overland to Oregon also almost succeeded, only to have the onset of cold wintry weather kill his bees just before he reached the settlements. "Report of Lieutenant Neil M. Howison on Oregon" (1913), 53–54.

30. For references to an 1852 trail drive of approximately 1,500 turkeys, purchased for fifty cents each in the States and for which the Illinois drover was offered $8 apiece in California, see Barry, *The Beginning of the West* (1972), 1084–85; San Francisco *Daily Alta California,* Aug. 1, 1852. In 1853 the Fort Kearny registry book listed forty-two goats as having passed that location; in both 1852 and 1853 one hog was also reported having

passed Fort Kearny. Oregon City *Oregon Spectator,* Oct. 20, 1853, in Kaiser and Knuth, eds., "From Ithaca to Clatsop Plains" (1961), 241, n. 6; letter of F. Longfield, Aug. 6, 1852, in Salt Lake City *Deseret News,* Dec. 11, 1852; St. Joseph *Gazette,* Aug. 3, 1853.

31. In 1854, for example, it was reported that 40,000 head of livestock were wintering in the Carson Valley. San Francisco *Daily Alta California,* Nov. 9, 1854. See Gard, *The Chisholm Trail* (1954), for the standard treatment of this most famous of all cattle trails. Gard indicates that a great many Texas cattle were trailed north, east, and west during the 1840s and 1850s. Skaggs, "Northward across the Plains" (1972), 52–68, surveys the post-1866 trails out of Texas, estimating that between five and twelve million head of Texas cattle were trailed to market between 1866 and 1885.

32. Applegate, "A Day with the Cow Column in 1843 (1900), 371–72; letter of M. M. McCarver, June 3, 1843, in "Documents" (1903), 177; May 31, June 1, 1843, entries, in Bekeart, ed., "Journal of Pierson Barton Reading" (1930), 151.

33. Burnett estimated that $300 spent on "young heifers" in Missouri would bring the overlander a return of $4,000 in Oregon, and he rhapsodized that Oregon was "the finest country for raising cattle you ever saw." St. Louis *Daily Missouri Republican,* Sept. 17, 1844. Prior to the California gold rush most non-draft animals were trailed to Oregon, the first sheep being taken across the Oregon Trail in 1844. By 1850 it is estimated that at least 10,000 cows and breeding stock and between 500 and 1,000 sheep had been trailed into Oregon. Kingston, "Introduction of Cattle into the Pacific Northwest" (1923), 181–83; Minto, "Sheep Husbandry in Oregon" (1902), 222; Barry, *Beginning of the West,* 677; Lomax, "History of Pioneer Sheep Husbandry in Oregon" (1928), 126–31.

34. Barry, *Beginning of the West,* 785; Hafen and Hafen, eds., *Journals of Forty-Niners* (1954), 27; Campbell, "Miles Morris Goodyear," in Hafen, ed., *The Mountain Men and the Fur Trade* (1965–72), 2:187–89.

35. For example, J. Watt Gibson, a Missouri forty-niner frustrated by gold-mining, moved east on the trail in 1851 seeking to purchase cattle from oncoming overlanders to fatten and sell in California at premium prices. Having little success, he traveled overland to Missouri in 1851 and returned in 1852 with a drove of nearly 600 head, while a brother brought an equal-sized herd. In 1853 another brother trailed approximately 1,000 cattle to California. The brothers Gibson returned by sea, some bringing at least 600 more cattle across the plains in 1854, and two more trailing a drove of some 800 to California in 1855. They continued in the California cattle business through 1859. Gibson, *Recollections of a Pioneer* (1912), *passim;* Aug. 16, 1855, entry, in Remy and Brenchley, *A Journey to Great-Salt-Lake City* (1861), 1:58. For the quotation see Amos Mecartney to his father, Oct. 7, 1852 (photocopy of MS).

36. Fuller, Journals (typescripts).

37. For contemporary estimates of trail herd losses see S. H. Taylor to "Friend Hadley," July 17, 31, 1853, in Watertown, Wis., *Chronicle,* Nov. 2, 1853, reprinted in "Letters of S. H. Taylor to the Watertown Chronicle" (1921), 148; Marysville, Cal., *Daily Evening Herald,* Aug. 30, 1853; San Francisco *Daily Alta California,* Sept. 1, 1853.

38. Marysville *Daily Evening Herald,* Oct. 24, 1853; Barry, *Beginning of the West,* 1096; Mecartney to his father, Oct. 7, 1852. Of course with the extremely heavy demand, livestock prices in Missouri also skyrocketed, William Stark noting in 1853 that prices were higher than he had ever known them (typescript letter).

39. "Diary of Dr. Thomas Flint" (1923), *passim.* Not all droves crossed as cheaply as did Flint's outfit, one Californian estimating that it cost approximately $5 per head for ferry and bridge tolls and feed during an overland trail stock drive. Headen to Payne, Sept. 16, 1853. To lessen the likelihood of Indian harassment, some drovers presented the natives with the bull calves born en route. See Newcombe, "Alson J. Streeter—an Agrarian Liberal" (1945), 421–22.

40. St. Joseph *Gazette,* Sept. 8, 1852; June 30, 1853, entry, in "Journal of Henry Allyn" (1924), 407; May 27, 1854, entry, in Burrel, Diary and Letter (MSS and typescripts), 12; June 6, 1854, entry, in Doyle, Diaries and Letters (MSS and typescripts).

41. Barry, *Beginning of the West,* 1158; Salt Lake City *Deseret News,* July 10 [9], 1853; San Francisco *Daily Alta California,* July 26, 1853; Portland *Oregonian,* Apr. 16, 1853; Cureton,

"The Cattle Trail to California" (1953), 100; Georgetta, "Sheep in Nevada" (1965), 25; Oliphant, *On the Cattle Ranges of the Oregon Country* (1968), 32.

42. Letter of "Cheyenne," Apr. 9, 1850, in St. Louis *Daily Missouri Republican,* June 1, 1850; Powers and Younger, "Cholera on the Overland Trails" (1973), 38–39.

43. Ferguson, *The Experiences of a Forty-Niner,* ed. Wallace (1888), 104–5.

44. Frederick W. Barnard to his sister, Apr. 1, 1849, in Barnard, Letters (MSS). For an analysis of the fur traders' attitudes toward the natives see Saum, *The Fur Trader and the Indian* (1965), esp. 55–59.

45. John Wilson to Thomas S. Shackleford, Apr. 12, 1850, in Culmer, ed., "California Letter of John Wilson" (1930), 213; June 22, 1852, entry, in Crane, Journal (MS).

46. For examples see the June 5, 1851, entry, in Bidwell, *A Journey to California* (1842, 1937 reprint), 5; Johnson and Winter, *Route across the Rocky Mountains,* ed. Cannon (1932), 9–10; July 16, 1843, entry, in Bekeart, ed., "Journal of Pierson Barton Reading," 167; Sept. 12, 1844, entry, in Parrish, "Crossing the Plains in 1844," 108; Charles T. Stanton to Sidney Stanton, July 12, 1846, in New York *Herald,* Nov. 4, 1846, reprinted in Morgan, ed., *Overland in 1846,* 2:612; May 6, 21, 25, 27, June 21, 1846, entries, in Bryant, *What I Saw in California* (1849), 24, 49, 58, 61–62, 103; June 14, 1849, entry of Bennett C. Clark, in Bieber, ed., "Diary of a Journey from Missouri to California" (1928), 21; May 31, 1849, entry, in Tiffany, Journal (MS and typescript); June 29, 1849, entry, in Mann, Diary (typescript), 6; May 23, 1850, entry, in Becker, ed., *Thomas Christy's Road across the Plains* (1969); June 13, 1850, entry, in Wolcott, Journal (MS); Dr. George W. Davis to Walters [*sic*] Watkins, Dec. 6, 1850 (MS and typescript); Aug. 26, 1852, entry, in Owen, Journal; July 18, 1852, entry of Richard Owen Hickman, in Phillips, ed., "'Dick's Works'" (1929), 255; July 22, Sept. 1, 1852, entries, in Kerns, "Journal of Crossing the Plains to Oregon" (1917), 173, 181.

47. See, e.g., June 30, July 8, 1849, entries, in Sedgley, *Overland to California in 1849* (1877), 32, 35; July 24, 1849, entry, in Hinckley and Hinckley, eds., "Overland from St. Louis to the California Gold Field" (1960), 339; letter of R. H. D., June 25, 1850, in St. Louis *Daily Missouri Republican,* Aug. 28, 1850; Aug. 16, 1850, entry, in Wolcott, Journal; Aug. 21, 1853, entry, in Graham, Journal (MS and typescript), 19; June 9, 1852, entry of James C. David, in Urbanek, "1852 on the Oregon Trail" (1962), 56. Sedgley wrote that the dust was so suffocating that they were forced to stop "and we remained seven hours, lying flat on the ground." Regarding "that cussed insect," Wolcott noted the plains variety made all previous encounters with mosquitoes seem like heaven, and John Prichet advanced the intriguing theory that the plains mosquitoes were so "blood thirsty" because they lived "principally on the blood of buffaloes and savage Indians." June 8, 1849, entry, in Prichet, Diary (microfilm of typescript), 34.

48. Postscript 1852 entry, in Lewis, Diary (MS).

49. The "Journal of A. W. Harlan" (1913) is particularly filled with references to the intriguing flora and fauna of the West. See also John H. McBride to his wife, June 9, 1850, in McBride, Letters (typescripts); Shombre, Diary (MS and typescript), inside back cover; Aug. 21, 1849, entry, in Tiffany, Journal; May 29, 1849, entry, in Hinckley and Hinckley, eds., "Overland from St. Louis to the California Gold Field," 308. For snowballing and ice deposits see the July 6, 1849, entry of Wakeman Bryarly, in Potter, ed., *Trail to California* (1945), 137; July 16, 1849, entry, in Castleman, Diary (microfilm of typescript), 43. Mattes, in "Chimney Rock on the Oregon Trail" (1955), 1–26, contends that Chimney Rock was clearly the most remarked-upon natural landmark en route. The carving or painting of names and initials on the several trail landmarks was so common that most diarists make reference to the activity.

50. May 29, 1853, entry, in Kaiser and Knuth, eds., "From Ithaca to Clatsop Plains," 260; Aug. 25, 1846, entry, in Bryant, *What I Saw in California,* 228. E. S. Ingalls in his July 5, 1850, journal entry suggested another possible result for those undertaking an overland trip to California—"see the country and recover their manhood." *Journal of a Trip to California* (1852), 31. But probably the most exaggerated description of western beauty was offered by Dr. T. in his June 6, 1849, diary entry where he suggested that if men were always surrounded by such beautiful natural scenery they would not even think evil thoughts, let alone commit sins.

51. Sept. 14, 1844, entry, in Parrish, "Crossing the Plains in 1844," 108; Thomas White to Samuel Porter Williams, Apr. 19, 1853, in Winther and Thornbrough, eds., *To Oregon in 1852* (1964), 17; Thornton, *Oregon and California in 1848* (1849), 1:159; Charles Tuttle to Maria Tuttle, May 16, 1849, in Tuttle, Letters (MSS and typescripts); May 24, June 1, 1846, entries, in Bryant, *What I Saw in California,* 55–56, 67.

52. See, e.g., the Oct. 6, 1847, entry, in "Diary of Mrs. Elizabeth Dixon Smith Geer" (1908), 167; July 21, 1853, entry, in *Diary of Basil Nelson Longsworth* (1927), 23; July 13, 1850, entry, in Sawyer, *Way Sketches,* ed. Eberstadt (1926), 94; July 9, 1850, entry, in Evans, Journal (MS), 120; June 4, 1849, entry, in Batchelder, Journal (MS), 15; May 23, 1846, entry, in "Diary of Virgil Pringle," in Morgan, ed., *Overland in 1846,* 1:168; June 16, 1849, entry of Elisha Douglass Perkins, in Clark, ed., *Gold Rush Diary,* 33; June 17, 1849, entry, in Dr. T., Diary; July 21, 1850, entry, in Diary of Trip to California, Henry Wellenkamp (typescript), 7.

53. Although "Great American Desert" terminology was infrequently used, a sizable number of emigrants were willing for the native nomads of the plains to retain what Amos Steck described as a "God forsaken Country." May 29, 1849, entry, in Steck, Diary (MS and typescript); May 7, July 3, 1849, entries, in Hixson, Diary (photocopy of typescript), 4, 29.

54. While there is a vast secondary literature concerning the "Great American Desert" concept, perhaps the most incisive recent analysis is Bowden, "The Great American Desert and the American Frontier," in Hareven, ed., *Anonymous Americans* (1971), 48–79. See also Parker, "Wading to California" (1964), 35–43. For examples of emigrant restriction of the "Great American Desert" to relatively small areas, see the July 24, 1850, entry, in "The Memoirs of Lemuel Clarke McKeeby" (1924), 67; July 25, 1850, entry of William H. Kilgore, in Muench, ed., *The Kilgore Journal* (1949), 51; Aug. 1, 2, 1850, entries, in Shields, Journal (MS and typescript); July 20, 21, 1852, entries, in Gage, Diary (typescript), 15; Crane, "An Overland Trip to California" (1901), 383. Others in addition to overland travelers were of importance in breaking down the "Great American Desert" ideology. One such was urban promoter William Gilpin. For a concise treatment of Gilpin's career see Schnell, "William Gilpin and the Destruction of the Desert Myth" (1969), 131–44.

55. For background data see Cotterill, "Early Agitation for a Pacific Railroad" (1919), 396–414; Russel, "The Pacific Railway Issue in Politics" (1925), 187–201. Overlanders were, of course, much interested in the possibilities of a railroad to the Pacific, discussing the topic often. They were divided over the logistic feasibility of the enterprise, some calling it visionary and impracticable, particularly after seeing the mountains, others speaking confidently of tunnels and easy passes. See, e.g., July 13, Sept. 8, 1849, entries, in McCall, *The Great California Trail* (1882), 50, 81; Jasper M. Hixson, Jr., to Robert H. Miller, Aug. 17, 1849, in Liberty, Mo., *Weekly Tribune,* Oct. 26, 1849; Udell, *Incidents of Travel to California* (1856), 108–9.

56. "The Map of T. H. Jefferson," in Morgan, ed. *Overland in 1846,* 1:244; Aug. 18, 1850, entry in Whitman, Diary (MS).

57. These statistical estimates are based upon Appendix C, "Passenger Arrivals and Departures by Sea, San Francisco, 1849–1870," in Wright, "The Making of Cosmopolitan California" (1940), 341; Appendix B, "Passengers by the Isthmian Routes, 1848–1869," in Folkman, *The Nicaragua Route* (1972), 163; Kemble, "The Gold Rush by Panama" (1949), 45–46; Bieber, "The Southwestern Trails to California in 1849" (1925), 375; Egan, *The Eldorado Trail* (1970), 280.

58. Pomfret, ed., *California Gold Rush Voyages* (1954), 3, 8; Kemble, "Pacific Mail Service between Panama and San Francisco" (1933), 412–13; Kemble, "The Gold Rush by Panama," 53–55; Perez-Venero, "The 'Forty-Niners through Panama" (1972), 460–69.

59. Goodman, "California Fleet 1849" (1963), 45–46; Pomfret, ed., *California Gold Rush Voyages,* 8; Howe, *Argonauts of '49* (1923), 172–73.

60. For example, two Knoxville, Tennessee, residents traveling to San Francisco by way of Panama in 1850 expended $552.42 for the venture, or approximately $275 apiece. Anderson, "By Sea to the California Gold Fields" (1968), 7. See also Rydell, "The Cape Horn Route to California, 1849" (1941), 154; Howe, *Argonauts of '49,* 175; Kemble, "The Gold Rush by Panama," 56; Kemble, "The Panama Route to the Pacific Coast" (1938), 9; Kemble, *Panama Route, 1848–1869* (1943), 148.

61. These statistics are derived from a comparative study of 258 Oregon-California Trail diarists who indicated with reasonable precision when they crossed the Missouri River (or launched out on serious travel from one of the jumping-off points west of the river) and when they reached a commonly identifiable destination point in California and Oregon (usually Placerville or Oregon City). While some minor adjustments had to be made, particularly regarding destinations, no attempt was made to eliminate diarists who sojourned for uncommonly long periods in Salt Lake City or at similar trail locations. This because the need or desire to recruit and recuperate was an important part of the overland journey. Unfortunately, many gold rush diarists could not be incorporated in this survey because they eagerly plunged into mining activities shortly after crossing the Sierra summit. Even so, the important comparisons between 1849 and 1850 journey time are each based upon sixty-nine diarists, almost all California-bound. In computing the number of days consumed, both the day of crossing the Missouri River (which for most emigrants marked the inception of the trip) and the day of arrival in the Pacific Coast settlements were counted as a travel day.

62. See, e.g., Stewart, ed., *The Opening of the California Trail* (1953), *passim;* Sawyer, *Way Sketches, passim.*

63. See the June 17, 1846, entry, in Wade, ed., *The Journals of Francis Parkman* (1947), 2:442; letter of "Joaquin," July 21, 1849, in St. Louis *Daily Missouri Republican,* Aug. 29, 1849; June 10, 1849, entry, in Webster, *The Gold Seekers of '49* (1917), 45, 104; June 7, 14, 1850, entries, in Williams, ed., "Overland to the Gold Fields of California" (1969), 132, 137; May 1, 1850, entry, in Smith, *Journal of a Trip to California,* ed. Vail (n.d.), 22; Washington *National Intelligencer,* July 27, 1850; Aug. 9, 1850, entry of Adam Mercer Brown, in Kiefer, ed., "Over Barren Plains and Rock-bound Mountains" (1972), 25. A favorite topic of speculation was *why* so many Missourians died en route. Two of the more creative, if unscientific, hypotheses were that Missourians had neglected to outfit adequately with medicines for the trip and that Missourians had "peculiar habits."

64. Read and Gaines, eds., *Gold Rush* (1944), 1: *passim;* Littleton, Diary (typescript), *passim;* St. Louis *Sunday Republican,* Oct. 6, 1850; Sylvester Hall and John B. Hall to the public, Nov. 25, 1852, in Portland *Oregonian,* Dec. 11, 1852; San Francisco *Daily Alta California,* Oct. 11, 1852. One 1852 traveler's tabulation of 105 fresh graves up to the Sweetwater River, however, found Missourians with only 15 percent of the deaths compared with 24 percent for Wisconsin residents and 20 percent for both Illinoisans and Iowans. St. Joseph *Gazette,* Sept. 8, 1852.

65. This ordering of states contributing the majority of Kanesville departures is based upon tabulations of lists published in the 1849, 1850, 1851, and 1852 Kanesville *Frontier Guardian* and *Frontier Guardian and Iowa Sentinel.* An emigrant paid ten cents to have his name and home address printed in the paper. See also St. Louis *Daily Missouri Republican,* June 10, 1844.

66. "The Missouri Heritage of the West" (1938), 80; *The Seventh Census of the United States: 1850* (1853), xxxvi; *Population of the United States in 1860* (1864), 34, 405; Appendix A, "The Native-Born Population of California, Distributed According to Place of Birth," in Wright, "The Making of Cosmopolitan California," 339; Douglas, "Origins of the Population of Oregon in 1850" (1950), 105–8.

67. Wright, "The Making of Cosmopolitan California, Part II" (1941), 73. Bruff, Littleton, and the Fort Laramie emigrant registrar also recorded the ages of deceased overlanders whenever the grave markers provided such information, and a tabulation of this data is also useful for an analysis of the average ages of the gold rushers. In 1849 the youngest to die was three years and four months and the oldest seventy-three years, but the vast majority (42 percent) were in their twenties, with the next most populous segment of 20 percent composed of overlanders in their thirties. In 1850 Littleton reported that the youngest to die was a seven-month-old infant and the oldest a seventy-four-year-old traveler, but again 43 percent were in their twenties and 20 percent in their thirties. The Laramie register data revealed 37 percent of the deceased to be in their twenties and 22 percent in their thirties, and, as rather conclusive testimony to the allure of gold, noted that an eighty-year-old Missouri man and an eighty-seven-year-old Illinois traveler had suc-

515

cumbed to the cholera. John H. Hays's 1852 death tabulation between Independence and Fort Laramie identified 41 percent in their twenties. San Francisco *Daily Alta California*, Oct. 11, 1852.

68. See, e.g., Lorch, "Iowa and the California Gold Rush of 1849" (1932), 344, 368, 367, n. 134; Webster, *Gold Seekers of '49*, 20; Potter, ed., *Trail to California*, 8; Dutton, "Across the Plains in 1850" (1910), 448; Shaffer, "The Management of Organized Wagon Trains" (1961), 358–59; Ware, *The Emigrants' Guide to California*, ed. Caughey (1932), 1, 6–8; Cincinnati *Morning Chronicle*, Feb. 13, 1849.

69. For examples of this attitude see Hastings, *The Emigrants' Guide to Oregon and California*, ed. Carey (1932), 142; Lucius Fairchild to J. C. Fairchild, Apr. 23, 1849, in Schafer, ed., *California Letters of Lucius Fairchild* (1931), 11.

70. See, e.g., Crawford, *Scenes of Earlier Days* (1898, 1962 reprint), 51–52; Sept. 3, 1853, entry, in "Diary of Mrs. Amelia Stewart Knight" (1933), 51; *The Overland Journey of Joseph Francl* (1968), 33; July 24, 1850, entry, in "Memoirs of Lemuel Clarke McKeeby," 68; Shepherd, *Journal of Travel across the Plains* (1851, 1945 reprint), 44; Thomas White to Samuel Porter Williams, Apr. 19, 1853, in Winther and Thornbrough, eds., *To Oregon in 1852*, 29; Snodgrass, Journal (MS and typescript), Appendix; Lafayette Spencer to William Spencer, Dec. 27, 1852, in Spencer, "Journal of the Oregon Trail" (1908), 305; May 10, 1853, entry, in Pengra, Diary (reproduced), 16.

71. "The Diary of Jacob R. Snyder" (1931), 260; Jagger, Diary (microfilm of MS); opening statement and Apr. 27, 1850, entry, in Rothwell, Journal and Letters (MSS and typescripts), 23; Pomroy, Diary and Account Book (photocopy of MS).

72. Lewis to his wife, Aug. 29, 1852, in Lewis, Memorandum or Notes (MSS and typescripts); Grindell, Overland Narrative (typescript); Wayman, Journal and Letters (photocopies of MSS); Tompkins, Narrative (photocopy of MS), 24–26; Bagley, "Crossing the Plains" (1922), 165.

73. Smith, Diary (MS), *passim*. DeVoto, in *The Year of Decision: 1846* (1943), 144, suggested that the value of a family traveling outfit ranged between $700 and $1,500.

74. In Federal Writers' Project, *The Oregon Trail* (1939), 32, an average annual death rate of 500 in 20,000, or 2½ percent, is suggested had the overlanders stayed at home.

75. Compared with Sarah Wisner's guess of 30,000 deaths between 1842 and 1859 (quoted in Mattes, *The Great Platte River Road* [1969], 82), D'Arcy's estimate ("Historical Review, Champoeg" [1928], 224) of 25,000 to 30,000 between 1830 and 1859 for the Oregon Trail alone, and Ellenbecker's assertion ("Graves along the Oregon Trail" [1936], 9) of five graves per mile along the 4,000 miles of trail and cutoff, Mattes's estimate (*Great Platte River Road*, 82) of approximately 15,000 for the California Trail prior to 1860 is somewhat more moderate. Variations within given years are equally disparate. For the much-studied year of 1849 Bancroft asserted (*History of California* [1886–90], 6:149) that 5,000 was not too small a figure, while Stewart's thorough evaluations (*The California Trail* [1962], 227–28, 292–93) led him to conclude that rumors notwithstanding, 750 emigrant deaths was a far more accurate estimate. More recently Groh (*Gold Fever* [1966], 87) had suggested 1,000 as an appropriate figure for 1849, while Mattes (*Great Platte River Road*, 84) apparently believes that at least 2,000 emigrants died on the trails that year. Powers and Younger ("Cholera on the Overland Trails," 38) largely adopt Mattes's calculations, although noting that cholera in 1849 and other years wreaked its considerable havoc on southwestern trails as well. My own reading of emigrant counts of fresh graves, statistics reported by trailside observers, and estimates by overlanders themselves lead me to conclude that Mattes's 6 percent figure is probably somewhat high, and that while Stewart may have been overly cautious in accepting emigrant evaluations of deaths within their midst, his conservative mortality estimates are not far wrong.

76. Adams, "Crossing the Plains in 1852" (1905), 288–329; Aug. 20, 1852, entry, in Clark, The California Guide (MS and typescript).

77. Mattes, *Great Platte River Road*, 82–88; Powers and Younger, "Cholera on the Overland Trails," 32–49; Meeker, *The Ox Team or the Old Oregon Trail* (1906), 81; McLear, "The St. Louis Cholera Epidemic of 1849" (1969), 171–81; John H. McBride to his wife, June 9, 1850, in McBride, Letters (typescripts).

78. Read, "Diseases, Drugs and Doctors on the Oregon-California Trail" (1944),

260–76; Groh, *Gold Fever*, 7–11, 93, 109, 115–19. The Mormon Trail was generally regarded as the most disease-free segment of the overland route, as Stegner points out in *The Gathering of Zion* (1964), 206, 209–10.

79. These estimates are based upon an analysis of emigrant diaries for the antebellum era. Particularly useful for the 1849 year is the series of articles by Morgan, "The Ferries of the Forty-Niners" (1959–60).

80. For examples of the various types of drowning disasters see the June 22, 1850, entry, in Kelly, ed., "The Journal of Robert Chalmers" (1952), 43; June 6, 14, 1849, entries, in Tiffany, Journal; Geer, "Occasional Address" (1880), 36; June 17, 1849, entry, in Doyle, Diaries and Letters; June 30, 1852, entry, in "Jonathan L. Moore Book" (1966), 27; June 2, 3, 1853, entries, in "Journal of Henry Allyn," 395–96; James M. Woods to his wife, Aug. 4, 1850, in Woods, Letters (typescripts).

81. June 24, 1850, entry, in "Diary of Orange Gaylord to California and Oregon" (1920), 409; Sept. 7, 1847, entry, in "Diary of Mrs. Elizabeth Dixon Smith Geer," 164.

82. Perhaps as many as fifty emigrants were accidental victims of fatal shootings during the antebellum years. The heavy loss of life was not, of course, due completely to carelessness. The embryonic status of weaponry safety precautions doubtless was responsible for some of the mishaps, as accidental shootings were also extremely common in the U.S. Army at that time. See Carleton, *The Prairie Logbooks*, ed. Pelzer (1943), 113, 255.

83. "Diary of Jacob R. Snyder," 260; Thornton, "Occasional Address," 34; Kelly, *An Excursion to California* (1851), 1:44. Potter, in his Introduction to the 1849 journals of Vincent Geiger and Wakeman Bryarly (*Trail to California*, 58), wrote: "Perhaps there was never, at any other time, so great a number of firearms per capita among a civilian population, as was to be found on the overland trail."

84. Letter of "Pawnee," May 18, 1849, in St. Louis *Missouri Republican*, June 4, 1849.

85. Gregg, "Missourians in the Gold Rush" (1945), 150–51; *Congressional Globe*, 30 Cong., 2 Sess., Sen., 580 (Feb. 22, 1849); St. Louis *Sunday Morning Republican*, Mar. 25, 1849; St. Louis *Daily Missouri Republican*, Mar. 14, 1850.

86. Hastings maintained that fatalities from the accidental discharge of emigrant guns were far more common than deaths from Indian attacks. Ware, *Emigrants' Guide to California*, 13; Hastings, *Emigrants' Guide*, 9–10, 149–50; Wheat, "The Jayhawkers at the Missouri" (1940), 105; June 13, 1841, entry, in Bidwell, *Journey to California*, 6–7; Hafen and Young, *Fort Laramie and the Pageant of the West* (1938), 97.

87. Kelly, *An Excursion to California*, 1:38; letter of "California," Apr. 19, 1849, in St. Louis *Daily Missouri Republican*, Apr. 25, 1849.

88. Kelly, *An Excursion to California*, 1:76; May 29, June 28, 1849, entries, in Orvis, Journal (MS and typescript); June 26, 1849, entry, in Brown, "Memoirs of an American Gold Seeker" (1908), 140; May 26, 1849, entry, in McCall, *The Great California Trail*, 25; letter of "Pawnee," June 23, 1849, in St. Louis *Daily Missouri Republican*, Aug. 6, 1849; letter of "Joaquin," July 21, 1849, in ibid., Aug. 29, 1849.

89. June 28, July 22, 1849, entries, in Delano, *Across the Plains and among the Diggings*, 46, 62.

90. See, e.g., July 18, 19, 1843, entries, in Winton, ed., "William T. Newby's Diary" (1939), 226; "Sketch of Mrs. Susan P. Angell" (1933), 55; June 17, 1849, entry, in Diary of Bernard J. Reid, 24.

91. May 26, 1851, entry, in The Diary of T. M. Barber (typescript), 5; Clarissa E. Taylor to "Dear Mrs. Hadley," July 6, 1853, in "Letters of S. H. Taylor to the Watertown Chronicle," 137; Waters, "Account of a Trip across the Plains in 1855" (1929), 63; Marysville *Daily Herald*, Aug. 21, 1856; Oct. 31, 1849, entry of J. Goldsborough Bruff, in Read and Gaines, eds., *Gold Rush*, 1:349–50; "Memories of Jane D. Kellogg" (1916), 90; May 10, 1850, entry, in Becker, ed., *Thomas Christy's Road across the Plains;* Henderson, "Young Adventure," ed. Strong (1973), 89–90; Marysville *Daily Evening Herald*, Aug. 13, 1853.

92. June 22, 1849, entry, in Delano, *Across the Plains and among the Diggings*, 22; letter of John Swigart, William Price, and Ebenezer Price, July 25, 1850, in St. Louis *Daily Missouri Republican*, Oct. 23, 1850; Bancroft, *History of Nevada, Colorado, and Wyoming* (1890), 695, n. 2; Manring, "Recollections of a Pioneer of 1859" (1910), 163. For an account of one who was temporarily lost on the plains see Neilson, "On the Plains in 1852" (1928), 209–10.

93. Quincy A. Brooks to "Dear Ruter," Nov. 7, 1851, in "Letter of Quincy Adams Brooks," 213; Sept. 7, 1843, entry, in Winton, ed., "William T. Newby's Diary," 233; Mattes, *Great Platte River Road,* 92–93, 187; Lyman, ed., "Reminiscences of Hugh Cosgrove" (1900), 263; Kelly, *An Excursion to California,* 1:83; Hoffman, Journal (MS and typescript translation); "Diary of Judge William A. Carter" (1939), 78–79.

94. Howe, *Argonauts of '49,* 178–81; June 6, 1852, entry, in Adams, "Crossing the Plains in 1852," 289. In his Apr. 8, 11, 1852, entries, Moore rendered "traveled" as "travaild." "Jonathan L. Moore Book," 23.

95. St. Joseph *Gazette,* Oct. 27, 1852.

96. Wells to his wife, July 23, 1849, in Wells, Letters (typescripts); James W. Evans to Ellis G. Evans, Oct. 27, 1850, in Evans, ed., "A Missouri Forty-Niner's Trip across the Plains" (1948), 39. J. B. Newbrough, in an Aug. 25, 1849, letter from near Sacramento, asserted that most arriving emigrants would never repeat the plains crossing, and that "if I was in the States I would not cross the plains for fifty thousand miles of solid gold." Wooster, Ohio, *Democrat,* Dec. 20, 1849.

97. George H. Hall to his mother, Dec. 16, 1849, in Hall, Letters (MSS).

98. Cyrus Hurd, Jr., to his father, Mar. 6, 1849, in Dart, "Letters of a Yankee Forty-Niner" (1947), 645–46; Samuel E. Cross to Beman Gates, Oct. 6, 1849, in Marietta, Ohio, *Intelligencer,* Dec. 20, 1849, reprinted in Clark, ed., *Gold Rush Diary,* 165.

99. A. A. Skinner to John N. Skinner, Feb. 21, 1846, in Wooster, Ohio, *Democrat,* Aug. 6, 1846; Hiram G. Ferris to J. A. Barnett, Dec. 29, 1850, and Ferris to S. H. Tyler, Jr., Mar. 5, 1854, in Ferris, ed., "Hiram Gano Ferris of Illinois and California" (1947), 296, 301. James E. Squire, in a letter of July 18, 1849, expressed similar convictions: "My constitution is robust and vigorous, and I have an appetite like a shark, but I can assure you that it has been obtained by great hardship and fatigue." In Morgan, ed., "Letters by Forty-Niners" (1949), 106. See also the letter of William B. Royall, Mar. 25, 1850, in Wyman, ed., *California Emigrant Letters* (1952), 155, and in Howe, *Argonauts of '49,* 181.

Bibliography

Abbey, James. *A Trip across the Plains*. New Albany, Ind., 1850.

Ables, T. J. Letter, 1857, typescript. Henry E. Huntington Library, San Marino, Cal.

Ackley, Richard Thomas. "Across the Plains in 1858." *Utah Historical Quarterly*, 9 (July–Oct. 1941): 190–228.

Adams, Cecelia Emily McMillen. "Crossing the Plains in 1852." *Transactions of the Thirty-second Annual Reunion of the Oregon Pioneer Association for 1904*. Portland, 1905, pp. 228–329.

Aitchison, Clyde B. "The Mormon Settlements in the Missouri Valley." *Quarterly of the Oregon Historical Society*, 8 (Sept., 1907): 276–89.

Albany, N.Y., *Atlas*, Mar. 1, 1844–Feb. 23, 1849.

Alexander, Thomas G., and Leonard J. Arrington. "Camp in the Sagebrush: Camp Floyd, Utah, 1858–1861." *Utah Historical Quarterly*, 34 (Winter, 1966): 3–21.

Allen, A. J., comp. *Ten Years in Oregon: Travels and Adventures of Doctor E. White and Lady, West of the Rocky Mountains*. Ithaca, N.Y., 1850.

Allen, Dr. William R. Letter, 1851, typescript. Western Historical Manuscripts Collection, University of Missouri, Columbia.

Alter, J. Cecil. *Jim Bridger*. Norman, 1962.

Altrocchi, Julia Cooley. *The Old California Trail: Traces in Folklore and Furrow*. Caldwell, Idaho, 1945.

Ambler, Charles H. "The Oregon Country, 1810–1830: A Chapter in Territorial Expansion." *Mississippi Valley Historical Review*, 30 (June, 1943): 3–24.

———. "West Virginia Forty-Niners." *West Virginia History*, 3 (Oct., 1941): 59–75.

American Agriculturist, 2 (Nov., 1843): 273.

Anable, Henry Sheldon. Journal, 1852–54, MS and longhand copy. Bancroft Library, University of California, Berkeley.

Anderson, George L. "By Sea to the California Gold Fields, 1850–1851." *Trail Guide*, 13 (Mar., 1968): 1–23.

Anderson, Harry. "The Controversial Sioux Amendment to the Fort Laramie Treaty of 1851." *Nebraska History*, 37 (Sept., 1956): 201–20.

Anderson, Nels. *Desert Saints: The Mormon Frontier in Utah*. Chicago, 1942.

Anderson, Niles. "Grandfather Was a Forty-Niner." *Western Pennsylvania Historical Magazine*, 50 (Jan., 1967): 33–50.

Andrews, D. B. Journal, 1852, MS and typescript. Beinecke Rare Book and Manuscript Library, Yale University, New Haven.

Andrews, Thomas F. "The Ambitions of Lansford W. Hastings: A Study in Western Myth-Making." *Pacific Historical Review*, 39 (Nov., 1970): 473–91.

———. "The Controversial Hastings Overland Guide: A Reassessment." *Pacific Historical Review*, 37 (Feb., 1968): 21–34.

———. "Lansford W. Hastings and the Promotion of the Salt Lake Desert Cutoff: A Reappraisal." *Western Historical Quarterly*, 4 (Apr., 1973): 133–50.

———. "Satire and the Overland Guide: John B. Hall's Fanciful Advice to Gold Rush Emigrants." *California Historical Society Quarterly*, 48 (June, 1969): 99–111.

"The Annual Business Meeting." *Transactions of the Eighteenth Annual Reunion of the Oregon Pioneer Association for 1890*. Portland, 1892, pp. 13–25.

Applegate, Jesse. "A Day with the Cow Column in 1843." *Quarterly of the Oregon Historical Society*, 1 (Dec., 1900): 371–83.

Applegate, Lindsay. "Notes and Reminiscences of Laying Out and Establishing the Old Emigrant Road into Southern Oregon in the Year 1846." *Quarterly of the Oregon Historical Society*, 22 (Mar., 1921): 12–45.

Arms, Cephas. Diary, 1849–50, printed as letters in Knoxville, Ill., *Journal*, Oct. 17, 1849–June 12, 1850. Typescript copies made available to me by Dale L. Morgan of the Bancroft Library, University of California, Berkeley, in 1966.

Arrington, Joseph Earl. "Skirving's Moving Panorama: Colonel Fremont's Western Expeditions Pictorialized." *Oregon Historical Quarterly*, 65 (June, 1964): 133–72.

Arrington, Leonard J. "Coin and Currency in Early Utah." *Utah Historical Quarterly*, 20 (Jan., 1952): 56–76.

———. *Great Basin Kingdom: An Economic History of the Latter-Day Saints, 1830–1900*. Cambridge, Mass., 1958.

"Arthur M. Menefee's Travels across the Plains, 1857." *Nevada Historical Society Quarterly*, 9 (Spring, 1966): 3–29.

"Art. I—Annals of California." *Edinburgh Review*, 107 (Apr., 1858): 295–321.

"Art. IV." *Edinburgh Review*, 86 (Oct., 1847): 367–96.

"Art. VI." *Edinburgh Review*, 78 (July, 1843): 157–92.

"Art. VI—The Northern Pacific: California, Oregon and the Oregon Question."

Southern Quarterly Review, 8 (July, 1845): 191–243.

"Art. VIII. Adventures on the Prairies." *North American Review*, 69 (July, 1849): 175–96.

"Art. VIII—North American Boundary. . . ." *Westminister Review*, 39 (Feb., 1843): 160–205.

"Art. VIII. The Oregon Question." *Edinburgh Review*, 82 (July, 1845): 238–65.

"Art. VIII. The Oregon Territory." *Foreign Quarterly Review*, 35 (July, 1845): 489–517.

"Art. IX—Oregon and the Territory of Washington on the Pacific." *De Bow's Review*, 14 (June, 1853): 599–605.

"Article X. Critical Notices." *American Biblical Repository*, 12 (July, 1838): 250–51.

Ashley, Algeline Jackson. Diary, 1852, typescript. Henry E. Huntington Library, San Marino, Cal.

"Associations of Emigrants to Oregon." *Oregonian, and Indian's Advocate*, 1 (Aug., 1839): 349.

Atkinson, G. H. "Occasional Address." *Transactions of the Eighth Annual Re-union of the Oregon Pioneer Association; for 1880.* Salem, 1881, pp. 28–38.

Augusta *Maine Farmer and Mechanic's Advocate*, Jan. 1, 1843–Dec. 31, 1848.

Austin, Henry. Diary, 1849, typescript. Bancroft Library, University of California, Berkeley.

Austin, Judith. "Joseph Thing." In LeRoy R. Hafen, ed., *The Mountain Men and the Fur Trade of the Far West*. 10 vols. Glendale, Cal., 1965–72, 9:365–77.

Autobiography of Isaac Jones Wistar, 1827–1905. Philadelphia, 1937.

The Autobiography of Theodore Edgar Potter. Concord, N.H., 1913.

"Autobiography of William K. Sloan, Western Pioneer." *Annals of Wyoming*, 4 (July, 1926): 235–64.

Bagley, Clarence B. "Crossing the Plains." *Washington Historical Quarterly*, 13 (July, 1922): 163–80.

Bailey, Mary Stuart. Journal, 1852, MS and typescript. Henry E. Huntington Library, San Marino, Cal.

Bailey, Thomas A. *The American Pageant: A History of the Republic*, 4th ed. 2 vols. Lexington, Mass., 1971.

Bailey, Walter. "The Barlow Road." *Quarterly of the Oregon Historical Society*, 13 (Sept., 1912): 287–96.

Bancroft, Hubert Howe. *California Inter Pocula*. San Francisco, 1888.

———. *History of California*. 7 vols. San Francisco, 1886–90.

———. *History of Nevada, Colorado, and Wyoming, 1540–1888*. San Francisco, 1890.

———. *History of Oregon*. 2 vols. San Francisco, 1886–88.

———. *History of Utah*. San Francisco, 1889.

———. *History of Washington, Idaho, and Montana*. San Francisco, 1890.

Bandel, Eugene. *Frontier Life in the Army, 1854–1861*, edited by Ralph P. Bieber. Glendale, Cal., 1932.

Bardin, James. Diary, 1855, photocopy of typescript. Bancroft Library, University of California, Berkeley.

Baritz, Loren. "The Idea of the West." *American Historical Review*, 66 (Apr., 1961): 618–40.

Barlow, Mary S. "History of the Barlow Road." *Quarterly of the Oregon Historical Society*, 3 (Mar., 1902): 71–81.

Barlow, William. "Reminiscences of Seventy Years." *Quarterly of the Oregon Historical Society*, 13 (Sept., 1912): 240–86.

Barnard, Frederick W. Letters, 1849, 1852, MSS. Beinecke Rare Book and Manuscript Library, Yale University, New Haven.

Barnes, Lela, ed. "Letters of Allen T. Ward, 1842–1851, from the Shawnee and Kaw (Methodist) Missions." *Kansas Historical Quarterly*, 33 (Autumn, 1967): 321–76.

Barry, J. Neilson. "The Murals in the State Capitol." *Oregon Historical Quarterly*, 40 (June, 1939): 149–60.

Barry, Louise. *The Beginning of the West: Annals of the Kansas Gateway to the American West, 1540–1854*. Topeka, 1972.

———. "Charles Robinson—Yankee '49er: His Journey to California." *Kansas Historical Quarterly*, 34 (Summer, 1968): 179–88.

———, ed. "Albert D. Richardson's Letters on the Pike's Peak Gold Region." *Kansas Historical Quarterly*, 12 (Feb., 1943): 14–57.

———, ed. "Overland to the Gold Fields of California in 1852: The Journal of John Hawkins Clark, Expanded and Revised from Notes Made during the Journey." *Kansas Historical Quarterly*, 11 (Aug., 1942): 227–96.

Batchelder, Amos. Journal, 1849–50, MS.

Bancroft Library, University of California, Berkeley.

Baur, John E. "The Health Seeker in the Westward Movement, 1830–1900." *Mississippi Valley Historical Review,* 46 (June, 1959): 91–110.

Baydo, Gerald. "Overland from Missouri to Washington Territory in 1854." *Nebraska History,* 52 (Spring, 1971): 65–87.

Beard, Charles A., and Mary R. Beard. *The Rise of American Civilization.* 2 vols. New York, 1929.

Becker, Robert H. "Diseños." *American West,* 4 (Feb., 1967): 55–64, 92–95.

———, ed. *Thomas Christy's Road across the Plains.* Denver, 1969.

Beers, Henry Putney. "The Army and the Oregon Trail in 1846." *Pacific Northwest Quarterly,* 28 (Oct., 1937): 339–62.

Beidleman, Richard G. "Nathaniel Wyeth's Fort Hall." *Oregon Historical Quarterly,* 58 (Sept., 1957): 197–250.

Bekeart, Philip B., ed. "Journal of Pierson Barton Reading." *Quarterly of the Society of California Pioneers,* 7 (Sept., 1930): 148–98.

Bell, James Christy, Jr. *Opening a Highway to the Pacific: 1838–1846,* vol. 96 of *Columbia University Studies in History, Economics and Public Law.* New York, 1921.

Belshaw, George. Diary, 1853, typescript. Henry E. Huntington Library, San Marino, Cal.

Bender, A. B. "The Soldier in the Far West, 1848–1860." *Pacific Historical Review,* 8 (June, 1939): 159–78.

Bennett, James. *Overland Journey to California.* New Harmony, Ind., 1906.

Benson, John H. Diary, 1849, typescript. Archives and Manuscripts Division, Nebraska State Historical Society, Lincoln.

Benton, Thomas Hart. *Thirty Years' View.* 2 vols. New York, 1856.

Berry, William, and Thomas Berry. Contract, duplicate copy of original. Berry-Thomson-Walker Family Papers, 1830–93, Western Historical Manuscripts Collection, University of Missouri, Columbia.

Bidlack, Russell E. *Letters Home: The Story of Ann Arbor's Forty-Niners.* Ann Arbor, Mich., 1960.

Bidwell, John. *A Journey to California.* San Francisco, 1937; reprint of 1842 ed.

Bieber, Ralph P. "California Gold Mania."

Mississippi Valley Historical Review, 35 (June, 1948): 3–28.

———. "The Gold Rush and Its Historians." *Yale Review,* 39 (Dec., 1949): 370–74.

———. "The Southwestern Trails to California in 1849." *Mississippi Valley Historical Review,* 12 (Dec., 1925): 342–75.

———, ed. "Diary of a Journey from Missouri to California in 1849." *Missouri Historical Review,* 23 (Oct., 1928): 3–43.

Billington, Ray Allen. *America's Frontier Heritage.* New York, 1966.

———. "Books That Won the West: The Guidebooks of the Forty-Niners & Fifty-Niners." *American West,* 4 (Aug., 1967): 25–32, 72–75.

———. *The Far Western Frontier, 1830–1860.* New York, 1956.

———. *Westward Expansion: A History of the American Frontier,* 3d ed. New York, 1967.

———. *Words That Won the West: 1830–1850.* N.p., 1964.

Blood, James A. Diary, 1850, typescript. California Section, California State Library, Sacramento.

Bloom, Henry Sterling. Diary, 1850–52, typescript as it appeared in Kankakee, Ill., *Daily Republic,* May 27–June 3, 1931. Bancroft Library, University of California, Berkeley.

Blue, George Vern. "France and the Oregon Question." *Oregon Historical Quarterly,* 34 (Mar., 1933): 39–59.

———. "The Oregon Question—1818–1828." *Quarterly of the Oregon Historical Society,* 23 (Sept., 1922): 193–219.

Blum, John M., Edmund S. Morgan, Willie Lee Rose, Arthur M. Schlesinger, Jr., Kenneth M. Stampp, and C. Vann Woodward. *The National Experience: A History of the United States,* 3d ed. New York, 1973.

Boorstin, Daniel J. *The Americans: The National Experience.* New York, 1965.

Booth, Caleb. Diary, 1850, MS and typescript. Beinecke Rare Book and Manuscript Library, Yale University, New Haven.

Boston *Daily Journal* (formerly *Evening Mercantile Journal*), Jan. 3, 1837–Dec. 30, 1845.

Bourne, Edward Gaylord. "The Legend of Marcus Whitman." *American Historical Review,* 6 (Jan., 1901): 276–300.

Bowden, Martyn J. "The Great American Desert and the American Frontier, 1800–1882: Popular Images of the

Plains." In Tamara K. Hareven, ed., *Anonymous Americans: Explorations in Nineteenth-Century Social History*. Englewood Cliffs, N.J., 1971, pp. 48–79.

Bowen, James Edgar. Diary, 1851, microfilm of copy. Bancroft Library, University of California, Berkeley.

Boyle, Charles Elisha. Diary, 1849, serialized in Columbus, Ohio, *Dispatch*, Oct. 2–Nov. 11, 1949.

"Boy's Funeral Followed Oregon Trail." *Missouri Historical Review*, 25 (Oct., 1930): 194–95.

Bradley, Henry. Journal, 1852, MS. Beinecke Rare Book and Manuscript Library, Yale University, New Haven.

Branch, E. Douglas. "Frederick West Lander, Road-Builder." *Mississippi Valley Historical Review*, 16 (Sept., 1929): 172–87.

———. *Westward: The Romance of the American Frontier*. New York, 1930.

Brayer, Herbert O. "Insurance against the Hazards of Western Life." *Mississippi Valley Historical Review*, 34 (Sept., 1947): 221–36.

Breyfogle, Joshua D., Sr. Diary, mimeographed copy in Section III, Genealogical Pamphlets, vol. 5. Archives and Manuscripts Division, Kansas State Historical Society, Topeka.

Bright, Verne. "The Folklore and History of the 'Oregon Fever.'" *Oregon Historical Quarterly*, 52 (Dec., 1951): 241–53.

"A Brimfield Heroine—Mrs. Tabitha Brown." *Quarterly of the Oregon Historical Society*, 5 (June, 1904): 199–205.

Bristow, Elijah. Letters, 1845. Eugene, Ore., 1961, reproduced by Lane County Pioneer-Historical Society. Bancroft Library, University of California, Berkeley.

Brooks, Elisha. *A Pioneer Mother of California*. San Francisco, 1922.

Brooks, Juanita. "Indian Relations on the Mormon Frontier." *Utah Historical Quarterly*, 12 (Jan.-Apr., 1944): 1–48.

———. *John Doyle Lee: Zealot–Pioneer Builder–Scapegoat*. Glendale, Cal., 1972.

———. "The Mormons in Carson County, Utah Territory." *Nevada Historical Society Quarterly*, 8 (Spring, 1965): 5–23.

———. *The Mountain Meadows Massacre*. Norman, 1962.

———, ed. *On the Mormon Frontier: The Diary of Hosea Stout, 1844–1861*. 2 vols. Salt Lake City, 1964.

Brooks, Noah. "The Plains Across." *Century Magazine*, 63 (Apr., 1902): 803–20.

Brown, Benjamin. *Testimonies for the Truth: A Record of Manifestations of the Power of God, Miraculous and Providential*. Liverpool, 1853.

Brown, J. Robert. *Journal of a Trip across the Plains of the U.S. from Missouri to California, in the Year 1856*. Columbus, Ohio, 1860.

Brown, John Evans. "Memoirs of an American Gold Seeker." *Journal of American History*, 2 (Jan.-Mar., 1908): 129–54.

Bryan, Charles W., Jr. "From Marthasville to Marysville in 1850." *Bulletin of the Missouri Historical Society*, 19 (Jan., 1963): 115–26.

Bryant, Edwin. *What I Saw in California*, 4th ed. New York, 1849.

Burbank, Augustus Ripley. Diary, 1849–51, microfilm of MS. Bancroft Library, University of California, Berkeley.

Burcham, Mildred Baker. "Scott's and Applegate's Old South Road." *Oregon Historical Quarterly*, 41 (Dec., 1940): 405–23.

Burke, James M., S.J., ed. "Early Years at St. Mary's Pottawatomie Mission: From the Diary of Father Maurice Gailland, S.J." *Kansas Historical Quarterly*, 20 (Aug., 1953): 501–29.

Burke, Marguerette R., ed. "Henry James Hudson and the Genoa Settlement." *Nebraska History*, 41 (Sept., 1960): 201–35.

Burnett, Peter H. "'Recollections and Opinions of an Old Pioneer.'" *Quarterly of the Oregon Historical Society*, 5 (Mar., 1904): 64–99, (Dec., 1904): 370–401.

Burrel, Mary. Diary and Letter, 1854, MSS and typescripts. Beinecke Rare Book and Manuscript Library, Yale University, New Haven.

Burton, Richard F. *The City of the Saints and across the Rocky Mountains to California*, edited by Fawn M. Brodie. New York, 1963.

Bushnell, James Addison. Autobiography, 1852. Eugene, Ore., 1959, reproduced by Lane County Pioneer-Historical Society. Bancroft Library, University of California, Berkeley.

Byers, William Newton. Journal, 1852, MS. Western History Department, Denver Public Library.

Cagwin, N. A. Diary, 1850, typescript. California Section, California State Library, Sacramento.

Caldwell, Dr. [T. G.?]. "Notes of a Journey to

California by Fort Hall Route, June to Oct[r], 1849—Found in Mountains." In George Willis Read and Ruth Gaines, eds., *Gold Rush: The Journals, Drawings, and Other Papers of J. Goldsborough Bruff.* 2 vols. New York, 1944, 2:1247–69.

"California." *American Review,* 3 (Apr., 1849): 331–38.

"California." *United States Magazine, and Democratic Review,* 23 (Aug., 1848): 169–76.

"California Diary of Charles M. Tuttle, 1859." *Wisconsin Magazine of History,* 15 (Sept., 1931): 69–85, (Dec., 1931): 219–33.

California Gold Rush Letters, 1849–59, collection of MSS and typescripts. Bancroft Library, University of California, Berkeley.

"The California Wagon Road." *De Bow's Review,* 21 (July, 1856): 58–63.

Camp, Charles L., ed. *James Clyman, Frontiersman.* Portland, 1960.

———, ed. "William Alexander Trubody and the Overland Pioneers of 1847." *California Historical Society Quarterly,* 16 (June, 1937): 122–43.

Campbell, Eugene E. "Brigham Young's Outer Cordon—a Reappraisal." *Utah Historical Quarterly,* 41 (Summer, 1973): 220–53.

———. "Miles Morris Goodyear." In LeRoy R. Hafen, ed., *The Mountain Men and the Fur Trade of the Far West.* 10 vols. Glendale, Cal., 1965–72, 2:179–88.

Campbell, Mrs. Paul. "Benoni Morgan Hudspeth." *Idaho Yesterdays,* 12 (Fall, 1968): 9–13.

Cannon, Miles. "Fort Hall on the Saptin River." *Washington Historical Quarterly,* 7 (July, 1916): 217–32.

Carey, Charles H., ed. "Diary of Rev. George Gary." *Quarterly of the Oregon Historical Society,* 24 (Mar., 1923): 68–105; "Diary of Reverend George H. Gary—II" (June, 1923): 153–85; "Diary of Reverend George Gary—III" (Sept., 1923): 269–333; "Diary of Reverend George Gary—IV" (Dec., 1923): 386–433.

———, intro. "British Side of Oregon Question, 1846." *Oregon Historical Quarterly,* 36 (Sept., 1935): 263–94.

Carleton, James Henry. *The Prairie Logbooks: Dragoon Campaigns to the Pawnee Villages in 1844, and to the Rocky Mountains in 1845,* edited by Louis Pelzer. Chicago, 1943.

Carmen, Harry J., Harold C. Syrett, and Bernard W. Wishy. *A History of the American People,* 3d ed. 2 vols. New York, 1967.

Carpenter, Helen McCowen. Diary, 1856, typescript. Henry E. Huntington Library, San Marino, Cal.

Carpenter, James C. I Crossed the Plains in the 50's, microfilm of narrative MS recollections. Archives and Manuscripts Division, Kansas State Historical Society, Topeka.

Carter, Harvey L. "Andrew Drips." In LeRoy R. Hafen, ed., *The Mountain Men and the Fur Trade of the Far West.* 10 vols. Glendale, Cal., 1965–72, 8:143–56.

———. "Caleb Greenwood." In LeRoy R. Hafen, ed., *The Mountain Men and the Fur Trade of the Far West.* 10 vols. Glendale, Cal., 1965–72, 9:187–92.

———. "John Gantt." In LeRoy R. Hafen, ed., *The Mountain Men and the Fur Trade of the Far West.* 10 vols. Glendale, Cal., 1965–72, 5:101–15.

———. "Tim Goodale." In LeRoy R. Hafen, ed., *The Mountain Men and the Fur Trade of the Far West.* 10 vols. Glendale, Cal., 1965–72, 7:147–53.

Cartwright, David W. *Natural History of Western Wild Animals and Guide for Hunters, Trappers, and Sportsmen,* edited by Mary F. Bailey, 2d ed. Toledo, Ohio, 1875.

Casler, Melyer. *A Journal Giving the Incidents of a Journey to California in the Summer of 1859, by the Overland Route.* Fairfield, Wash., 1969; reprint of 1863 ed.

Castleman, P. F. Diary, 1849–51, microfilm of typescript. Bancroft Library, University of California, Berkeley.

Caughey, John Walton. "Southwest from Salt Lake in 1849." *Pacific Historical Review,* 6 (June, 1937): 143–64.

———. "The Transit of the Forty-Niners or Why, Oh Why, Did They Ever Leave Wyoming." In Roger Daniels, ed., *Essays in Western History in Honor of Professor T. A. Larson,* vol. 37 of University of Wyoming Publications. [Laramie], 1971, pp. 17–27.

———, ed. "The Jacob Y. Stover Narrative." *Pacific Historical Review,* 6 (June, 1937): 165–81.

Chamberlain, William E. Diary, 1849, typescript. Bancroft Library, University of California, Berkeley.

Chambers, Alex. "Fort Bridger." *Annals of Wyoming,* 5 (Oct., 1927–Jan., 1928): 91–95.

Chandless, William. *A Visit to Salt Lake; Being a Journey across the Plains and a Residence in the Mormon Settlements at Utah.* London, 1857.

Channing, Edward. *A History of the United States.* 6 vols. New York, 1925.

A Chapter from the Diary of the Late Judge James B. Persinger, 1850, typescript. Typescript Collection, State Historical Society of Missouri, Columbia.

Chenoweth, F. A. "Occasional Address." *Transactions of the Tenth Annual Re-union of the Oregon Pioneer Association for 1882.* Salem, 1883, pp. 28–35.

Child, Andrew. *Overland Route to California,* Introduction by Lyle H. Wright. Los Angeles, 1946; reprint of 1852 ed.

Chittenden, Hiram Martin, and Alfred Talbot Richardson, eds. *Life, Letters and Travels of Father Pierre-Jean De Smet, S.J., 1801–1873.* 4 vols. New York, 1905.

Christy, Thomas. Journal, 1850, MS. Bancroft Library, University of California, Berkeley.

Churchill, Stillman. Diary, 1849, microfilm of typescript. Bancroft Library, University of California, Berkeley.

Cincinnati *Cist's Advertiser,* Jan. 8, 1845–June 24, 1846, Jan. 3–Dec. 26, 1849.

Cincinnati *Daily Gazette,* Jan. 1–Dec. 3, 1849.

Cincinnati *Morning Chronicle,* Jan. 26–June 30, 1849.

Clapp, John T. *A Journal of Travels to and from California.* Kalamazoo, Mich., 1851.

Clark, Dan Elbert. *The West in American History.* New York, 1937.

Clark, Eva Turner, ed. *California Letters of William Gill.* New York, 1922.

Clark, John. The California Guide, 1852–56, MS and typescript journal. Beinecke Rare Book and Manuscript Library, Yale University, New Haven.

Clark, Keith, and Lowell Tiller. *Terrible Trail: The Meek Cutoff, 1845.* Caldwell, Idaho, 1967.

Clark, Robert Carlton. "Harney Basin Exploration, 1826–60." *Oregon Historical Quarterly,* 33 (June, 1932): 101–14.

Clark, Thomas D. "Edwin Bryant and the Opening of the Road to California." In Roger Daniels, ed., *Essays in Western History in Honor of Professor T. A. Larson,* vol. 37 of University of Wyoming *Publications.* [Laramie], 1971, pp. 29–43.

———. *Frontier America: The Story of the Westward Movement,* 2d ed. New York, 1969.

———, ed. *Gold Rush Diary: Being the Journal of Elisha Douglass Perkins on the Overland Trail in the Spring and Summer of 1849.* Lexington, Ky., 1967.

Clark, William. "A Trip across the Plains in 1857." *Iowa Journal of History and Politics,* 20 (Apr., 1922): 163–223.

Cleland, Robert Glass, and Juanita Brooks, eds. *A Mormon Chronicle: The Diaries of John D. Lee, 1848–1876.* 2 vols. San Marino, Cal., 1955.

Coan, C. F. "The Adoption of the Reservation Policy in Pacific Northwest, 1853–1855." *Quarterly of the Oregon Historical Society,* 23 (Mar., 1922): 1–38.

———. "The First Stage of the Federal Indian Policy in the Pacific Northwest, 1849–1852." *Quarterly of the Oregon Historical Society,* 22 (Mar., 1921): 46–89.

Cohen, Victor H. "James Bridger's Claims." *Annals of Wyoming,* 12 (July, 1940): 228–40.

Cohen, William Gibbons. Scrapbooks, typescripts of misc. California newspaper articles, 1853–56. Henry E. Huntington Library, San Marino, Cal.

Coke, Henry John. *A Ride over the Rocky Mountains to Oregon and California.* London, 1852.

Cole, Gilbert L. *In the Early Days along the Overland Trail in Nebraska Territory, in 1852,* compiled by Mrs. A. Hardy. Kansas City, Mo., 1905.

Coleman, John, Thomas J. Hayter, and Washington L. Hayter. Coleman-Hayter Letters, 1840–1900, MSS and typescripts. Western Historical Manuscripts Collection, University of Missouri, Columbia.

Condon, Thomas. "The Process of Selection in Oregon Pioneer Settlement." *Quarterly of the Oregon Historical Society,* 1 (Mar., 1900): 60–65.

Connelley, William Elsey. "National Aspects of the Old Oregon Trail." *Collections of the Kansas State Historical Society, 1913–1914,* 13 (1915): 415–23.

Conner, Michael. Letter, 1852, MS. Beinecke Rare Book and Manuscript Library, Yale University, New Haven.

"Constitution of the Oregon Pioneer Association." *Constitution and Quotations from the Register of the Oregon Pioneer Association.* Salem, 1875, pp. 3–6.

Cooke, Lucy Rutledge. *Crossing the Plains in 1852.* Modesto, Cal., 1923.

Cooke, Philip St. George. *Scenes and Adventures in the Army; or, Romance of Military Life.* Philadelphia, 1859.

Coonc, Elizabeth Ann. "Reminiscences of a

Pioneer Woman," edited by William S. Lewis. *Washington Historical Quarterly*, 8 (Jan., 1917): 14–21.

Coons, Frederica B. *The Trail to Oregon.* Portland, 1954.

Cotterill, Robert S. "Early Agitation for a Pacific Railroad, 1845–1850." *Mississippi Valley Historical Review*, 5 (Mar., 1919): 396–414.

Council Bluffs *Bugle*, Jan. 2, 1855–Apr. 8, 1856, Mar. 3, 1857–July 25, 1860.

Council Bluffs *Chronotype*, Dec. 13, 1854–Dec. 24, 1856.

Coutant, C. G. *The History of Wyoming from the Earliest Known Discoveries.* Laramie, 1899.

Cox, Edwin E., ed. "Diary of the Overland Trail and Letters of Captain David Dewolf." *Transactions of the Illinois State Historical Society for the Year 1925*, Pub. 32 of the Illinois State Historical Library. [Springfield, 1925], pp. 183–222.

Coy, Owen Cochran. *The Great Trek.* San Francisco, 1931.

Cramer, Richard S. "British Magazines and the Oregon Question." *Pacific Historical Review*, 32 (Nov., 1963): 369–82.

Cramer, Thomas J. B. Journal, 1859, MS and typescript. Beinecke Rare Book and Manuscript Library, Yale University, New Haven.

Cramer, William E. "The March of Our Republic—Is It Unfavorable to Progress and Improvements?" *Merchant's Magazine*, 13 (Dec., 1845): 546–50.

Crane, Addison Moses. Journal, 1852, MS. Henry E. Huntington Library, San Marino, Cal.

Crane, Ellery Bicknell. "An Overland Trip to California in the Year 1860." *Proceedings of the Worcester Society of Antiquity*, 17 (1901): 367–87.

Cranston, Susan Marsh. Journal, 1851, MS and typescript. Bancroft Library, University of California, Berkeley.

Crawford, Charles Howard. *Scenes of Earlier Days.* Chicago, 1962; reprint of 1898 ed.

Crawford, Medorum. "Occasional Address." *Transactions of the Ninth Annual Re-union of the Oregon Pioneer Association; for 1881.* Salem, 1882, pp. 9–19.

Crawford, P. V. "Journal of a Trip across the Plains, 1851." *Quarterly of the Oregon Historical Society*, 25 (June, 1924): 136–69.

Creer, Leland H. "Lansford W. Hastings and the Discovery of the Old Mormon Trail." *Western Humanities Review*, 3 (July, 1949): 175–86.

Crow, Norma Lee. "A Comparison of Stereotypes of Pioneer Travel on the Oregon Trail with Pioneer Diaries and Reminiscences." M.A. thesis, Washington State University, Pullman, 1967.

Culmer, Frederic A., ed. "California Letter of John Wilson, 1850." *Missouri Historical Review*, 24 (Jan., 1930): 200–213.

Cummings, Charles J. Journal, 1859, MS and typescript. Beinecke Rare Book and Manuscript Library, Yale University, New Haven.

Cummins, Sarah J. *Autobiography and Reminiscences.* N.p., 1914.

Cureton, Gilbert. "The Cattle Trail to California, 1840–1860." *Historical Society of Southern California Quarterly*, 35 (June, 1953): 99–109.

Current, Richard N., T. Harry Williams, and Frank Freidel. *American History: A Survey*, 3d ed. New York, 1971.

Currey, George B. "Occasional Address." *Transactions of the Fifteenth Annual Reunion of the Oregon Pioneer Association for 1887.* Portland, 1887, pp. 32–47.

Dale, Edward Everett, ed. *The Journal of James Akin Jr.,* University of Oklahoma Bulletin, University Studies No. 9. Norman, 1919.

Dale, Harrison C. "The Organization of the Oregon Emigrating Companies." *Quarterly of the Oregon Historical Society*, 16 (Sept., 1915): 205–27.

———, ed. "A Fragmentary Journal of William L. Sublette." *Mississippi Valley Historical Review*, 6 (June, 1919): 99–110.

Danker, Donald F. "The Influence of Transportation upon Nebraska Territory." *Nebraska History*, 47 (June, 1966): 187–208.

D'Arcy, Peter H. "Historical Review, Champoeg, the Plymouth Rock of the Northwest." *Oregon Historical Quarterly*, 29 (Sept., 1928): 217–24.

Dart, Margaret S. "Letters of a Yankee Forty-Niner." *Yale Review*, 36 (June, 1947): 643–66.

Davis, A. I. Letter, 1853, MS and typescript. Beinecke Rare Book and Manuscript Library, Yale University, New Haven.

Davis, David Brion. "Some Themes of Counter-Subversion: An Analysis of Anti-Masonic, Anti-Catholic, and Anti-Mormon Literature." *Mississippi Valley Historical Review*, 47 (Sept., 1960): 205–24.

Davis, Dr. George W. Letter, 1850, MS and typescript. Beinecke Rare Book and Manuscript Library, Yale University, New Haven.

Davis, W. N., Jr. "The Sutler at Fort Bridger." *Western Historical Quarterly,* 2 (Jan., 1971): 37–54.

———. "Will the West Survive as a Field in American History? A Survey Report." *Mississippi Valley Historical Review,* 50 (Mar., 1964): 672–85.

Delano, Alonzo. *Across the Plains and among the Diggings.* New York, 1936; reprint of 1853 ed.

DeVoto, Bernard. *The Year of Decision: 1846.* Boston, 1943.

DeWitt, Ward G., and Florence Stark DeWitt, eds. *Prairie Schooner Lady: The Journal of Harriet Sherrill Ward, 1853.* Los Angeles, 1959.

"Diary Kept by William Edmundson, of Oskaloosa, while Crossing the Western Plains in 1850." *Annals of Iowa,* 8 (Oct., 1908): 516–35.

"Diary of an Emigrant of 1845." *Washington Historical Quarterly,* 1 (Apr., 1907): 138–58.

The Diary of an Unknown Scout, 1852, typescript found by Mrs. J. McGurk and thus sometimes also called the McGurk Diary. Archives and Manuscripts Division, California State Historical Society, San Francisco.

Diary of Basil Nelson Longsworth. Denver, 1927.

The Diary of Bernard J. Reid, Esq., Written by Him during His Journey Overland to California in '49, typescript. Historical Society of Western Pennsylvania, Pittsburgh.

"Diary of Captain Phelps." In LeRoy R. Hafen and Ann W. Hafen, eds., *The Utah Expedition, 1857–1858,* vol. 8 of *The Far West and the Rockies Historical Series.* Glendale, Cal., 1958, pp. 89–138.

"Diary of Celinda E. Hines." *Transactions of the Forty-sixth Annual Reunion of the Oregon Pioneer Association, Portland, June 20, 1918.* Portland, 1921, pp. 69–125.

"The Diary of Dr. Jonathan Clark." *Argonaut,* 97 (Aug. 1, 8, 15, 22, 1925), p. 3 in each issue.

"Diary of Dr. Thomas Flint: California to Maine and Return, 1851–1855." *Annual Publications of Historical Society of Southern California,* 12 (1923): 53–127.

"Diary of E. W. Conyers, a Pioneer of 1852." *Transactions of the Thirty-third Annual Re-union of the Oregon Pioneer Association, June 15, 1905.* Portland, 1906, pp. 423–512.

"The Diary of George Gibbs." In Raymond W. Settle, ed., *The March of the Mounted Riflemen.* Glendale, Cal., 1940, pp. 273–327.

"Diary of George McKinstry: With a Letter to P. B. Reading." In Dale L. Morgan, ed., *Overland in 1846: Diaries and Letters of the California Trail.* 2 vols. Georgetown, Cal., 1963, 1:199–218.

"The Diary of Jacob R. Snyder." *Quarterly of the Society of California Pioneers,* 8 (Dec., 1931): 224–60.

Diary of Jay Green, Pub. no. 5 of the San Joaquin Pioneer and Historical Society. Stockton, Cal., 1955.

"Diary of Jesse Harritt, 1845." *Transactions of the 39th Annual Reunion of the Oregon Pioneer Association, Portland, June 21, 1911.* Portland, 1914, pp. 506–26.

"Diary of John S. Zeiber, 1851." *Transactions of the Forty-eighth Annual Reunion of the Oregon Pioneer Association, Portland, July 1, 1920.* Portland, 1923, pp. 301–35.

"Diary of Judge William A. Carter: Describes Life on the Trail in 1857." *Annals of Wyoming,* 11 (Apr., 1939): 75–110.

"Diary of Mr. Davis, 1852." *Transactions of the 37th Annual Reunion of the Oregon Pioneer Association, Portland, June 11th, 1909.* Portland, 1910, pp. 355–81.

"Diary of Mrs. Amelia Stewart Knight: An Oregon Pioneer of 1853." *Transactions of the Fifty-sixth Annual Reunion of the Oregon Pioneer Association for 1928.* Portland, 1933, pp. 38–54.

"Diary of Mrs. Elizabeth Dixon Smith Geer." *Transactions of the 35th Annual Reunion of the Oregon Pioneer Association, Portland, June 19th, 1907.* Portland, 1908, pp. 153–79.

"Diary of Nicholas Carriger." In Dale L. Morgan, ed., *Overland in 1846: Diaries and Letters of the California Trail.* 2 vols. Georgetown, Cal., 1963, 1:143–58.

"Diary of Orange Gaylord to California and Oregon in 1850, a Second Trip to Oregon in 1853, Including Gaylord Family History." *Transactions of the Forty-fifth Annual Reunion of the Oregon Pioneer Association, Portland, July 19, 1917.* Portland, 1920, pp. 394–439.

"Diary of Rev. John McAllister: A Pioneer of 1852." *Transactions of the Fiftieth Annual*

Reunion of the Oregon Pioneer Association, Portland, June 15, 1922. Portland, 1925, pp. 471–508.

"Diary of S. M. Jamison, 1850." *Nevada Historical Society Quarterly,* 10 (Winter, 1967): 3–27.

The Diary of T. M. Barber, 1851, typescript. Archives and Manuscripts Division, Nebraska State Historical Society, Lincoln.

"Diary of Thomas Woodward while Crossing the Plains of California in 1850." *Wisconsin Magazine of History,* 17 (Mar., 1934): 345–60, (June, 1934): 433–46.

Diary of Trip to California, Henry Wellenkamp, 1850, typescript. Typescript Collection, State Historical Society of Missouri, Columbia.

"Diary of Virgil Pringle." In Dale L. Morgan, ed., *Overland in 1846: Diaries and Letters of the California Trail.* 2 vols. Georgetown, Cal., 1963, 1:159–88.

"Difficulties of Emigration to Oregon." *Oregonian, and Indian's Advocate,* 1 (Jan., 1839): 123–25.

"Disposition of the Hudson's Bay Company." *Oregonian, and Indian's Advocate,* 1 (July, 1839): 314–15.

"Document." *Quarterly of the Oregon Historical Society,* 1 (Dec., 1900): 398–402.

"Documentary." *Quarterly of the Oregon Historical Society,* 2 (June, 1901): 187–203.

"Documents." *Quarterly of the Oregon Historical Society,* 4 (June, 1903): 177, (Sept., 1903): 270–86, (Dec., 1903): 395–409.

Dorris, Jonathan Truman. "Federal Aid to Oregon Trail prior to 1850." *Oregon Historical Quarterly,* 30 (Dec., 1929): 305–25.

———. "The Oregon Trail." *Journal of the Illinois State Historical Society,* 10 (Jan., 1918): 473–547.

Douglas, Jesse S. "Origins of the Population of Oregon in 1850." *Pacific Northwest Quarterly,* 41 (Apr., 1950): 95–108, with four accompanying tables.

Dowell, Benjamin Franklin. Journal, 1850, ink copy of MS. Bancroft Library, University of California, Berkeley.

Doyle, Simon. Diaries and Letters, 1849–54, MSS and typescripts. Beinecke Rare Book and Manuscript Library, Yale University, New Haven.

Drago, Harry Sinclair. *Roads to Empire: The Dramatic Conquest of the American West.* New York, 1968.

Driver, I. D. "Annual Address." *Transactions of the Fifteenth Annual Reunion of the Oregon Pioneer Association for 1887.* Portland, 1887, pp. 21–31.

Drury, Clifford M. "The Oregonian and Indian's Advocate." *Pacific Northwest Quarterly,* 56 (Oct., 1965): 159–67.

Dunlop, Richard. *Great Trails of the West.* Nashville, Tenn., 1971.

Dutton, Jerome. "Across the Plains in 1850." *Annals of Iowa,* 9 (July–Oct., 1910): 447–83.

Dyck, Cornelius J. "In the California Gold Rush." *Mennonite Life,* 11 (Jan., 1956): 25–28.

"Early Military Posts, Missions and Camps." *Transactions of the Kansas State Historical Society,* 2 (1881): 263–70.

Eastham, E. L. "The Occasional Address." *Transactions of the Thirteenth Annual Reunion of the Oregon Pioneer Association for 1885.* Salem, 1886, pp. 7–11.

Ebbert, George Wood. "George Wood Ebbert." *Quarterly of the Oregon Historical Society,* 19 (Sept., 1918): 263–67.

Ebey, W. Scott. Diary, 1854, MS. Bancroft Library, University of California, Berkeley.

"Editorial." *Oregonian, and Indian's Advocate,* 1 (June, 1839): 286–88.

"Editorial." *Oregonian, and Indian's Advocate,* 1 (July, 1839): 313–14.

"Editorial. Our Society, and Emigration to Oregon." *Oregonian, and Indian's Advocate,* 1 (Aug., 1839): 346–49.

Egan, Ferol. *The El Dorado Trail: The Story of the Gold Rush Routes across Mexico.* New York, 1970.

Egbert, Eliza Ann. Diary, 1852, photocopy of typescript. Bancroft Library, University of California, Berkeley.

Ellenbecker, J. G. "Graves along the Oregon Trail." *Pony Express Courier,* 3 (Nov., 1936): 9.

Elliott, Russell R. "Nevada's First Trading Post: A Study in Historiography." *Nevada Historical Society Quarterly,* 13 (Winter, 1970): 3–10.

Elliott, T. C. "The Earliest Travelers on the Oregon Trail." *Quarterly of the Oregon Historical Society,* 13 (Mar., 1912): 71–84.

———. "Richard ('Captain Johnny') Grant." *Oregon Historical Quarterly,* 36 (Mar., 1935): 1–13.

Ellis, John W. Diary, 1850–51, photocopy of MS. California Section, California State Library, Sacramento.

Ellison, Joseph W. "The Beginnings of the

Apple Industry in Oregon." *Agricultural History*, 11 (Oct., 1937): 322–44.

———. "The Covered Wagon Centennial: March of the Empire Builders over the Oregon Trail." *Washington Historical Quarterly*, 21 (July, 1930): 163–78.

———, ed. "Diary of Maria Parsons Belshaw, 1853." *Oregon Historical Quarterly*, 33 (Dec., 1932): 318–33.

"The Emigrants." *Niles' National Register*, 68 (Aug. 2, 1845): 341–42.

"Emigrants for California." *Niles' National Register*, 69 (Sept. 6, 1845): 7.

Epstein, Daniel M. "The California Gold Rush as Reported by the Marshall Statesman." *Michigan History*, 34 (Mar., 1950): 19–28.

Erwin, Marie H., comp. "Statistical Reports on the Sickness and Mortality of the Army of the United States, 1819–1860." *Annals of Wyoming*, 15 (Oct., 1943): 315–75.

Evans, Burrell Whalen. Memorandum Book across the Plains, 1849, microfilm of MS journal. Bancroft Library, University of California, Berkeley.

Evans, James B., ed. "A Missouri Forty-Niner's Trip across the Plains." *Missouri Historical Review*, 43 (Oct., 1948): 38–47.

Evans, James William. Journal, 1850, MS. Bancroft Library, University of California, Berkeley.

Eversole, Mildred, ed. "Richard J. Oglesby: Forty-Niner, His Own Narrative." *Papers in Illinois History and Transactions for the Year 1938*. Springfield, 1939, pp. 158–71.

Everts, F. D. Journal, 1849, MS and typescript. Beinecke Rare Book and Manuscript Library, Yale University, New Haven.

"The Expedition of Major Clifton Wharton in 1844." *Collections of the Kansas State Historical Society, 1923–1925*, 16 (1925): 272–305.

Falbo, Ernest, trans. and ed. *California and Overland Diaries of Count Leonetto Cipriani from 1853 through 1871*. Portland, 1962.

Faris, John T. *On the Trail of the Pioneers: Romance, Tragedy and Triumph of the Path of Empire*. New York, 1920.

Favour, John. Diary, 1859, MS. Bancroft Library, University of California, Berkeley.

Fawkes, Ulla Staley, ed. *The Journal of Walter Griffith Pigman*. Mexico, Mo., 1942.

Fayette *Missouri Democrat*, Apr. 2–Dec. 17, 1845.

Federal Writers' Project. *The Oregon Trail*. New York, 1939.

Fendall, Lon W. "Medorem Crawford and the Protective Corps." *Oregon Historical Quarterly*, 72 (Mar., 1971): 55–77.

Ferguson, Charles D. *The Experiences of a Forty-Niner during Thirty-four Years' Residence in California and Australia*, edited by Frederick T. Wallace. Cleveland, 1888.

Ferris, Benjamin G. *Utah and the Mormons*. New York, 1854.

Ferris, Mrs. Benjamin G. *The Mormons at Home; with Some Incidents of Travel from Missouri to California, 1852–3, in a Series of Letters*. New York, 1856.

Ferris, Joel E., ed. "Hiram Gano Ferris of Illinois and California." *California Historical Society Quarterly*, 26 (Dec., 1947): 289–307.

Field, Matthew C. *Prairie and Mountain Sketches*, edited by Kate L. Gregg and John Francis McDermott. Norman, 1957.

Fine, Harry L. "Fort Laramie and the Historic Postal Markings of the West." *Montana, the Magazine of Western History*, 11 (July, 1961): 53–55.

"First Records of Carson Valley, Utah Territory, 1851." *Nevada Historical Society Quarterly*, 9 (Summer-Fall, 1966): n.p.

Fish, Carl Russell. *The Rise of the Common Man, 1830–1850*, vol. 6 of *A History of American Life*. New York, 1937.

Fish, Lafayette. Diary, 1860, typescript. Bancroft Library, University of California, Berkeley.

Fish, Mary C. Journal, 1860, MS and typescript. Bancroft Library, University of California, Berkeley.

Fleming, L. A., and A. R. Standing. "The Road to 'Fortune': The Salt Lake Cutoff." *Utah Historical Quarterly*, 33 (Summer, 1965): 248–71.

Folkman, David I., Jr. *The Nicaragua Route*. Salt Lake City, 1972.

Forrest, Earle R. "Forty Niners from Washington County, Pennsylvania." *Pony Express*, 12 (Sept., 1945): 6–8.

"Fort Boise: From Imperial Outpost to Historic Site." *Idaho Yesterdays*, 6 (Spring, 1962): 14–16, 33–39.

"Fort Hall, 1834–1856." *Idaho Yesterdays*, 12 (Summer, 1968): 28–31.

Foster, Isaac. Diary, 1849–50, typescript. Henry E. Huntington Library, San Marino, Cal.

Fowler, Nolan. "Territorial Expansion—a Threat to the Republic?" *Pacific Northwest Quarterly*, 53 (Jan., 1962): 34–42.

Fox, Jared. Memorandum, 1852–54, microfilm of diary typescript. Bancroft Library, University of California, Berkeley.

Foy, Mary E., ed. "By Ox Team from Salt Lake to Los Angeles, 1850: A Memoir by David W. Cheesman," *Historical Society of Southern California, Annual Publications*, 14 (1930): 271–337.

Francis, Samuel Dexter. Diary, 1841–62, MS and typescript. Beinecke Rare Book and Manuscript Library, Yale University, New Haven.

Frazer, Robert W. *Forts of the West: Military Forts and Presidios and Posts Commonly Called Forts West of the Mississippi River to 1898*. Norman, 1965.

———, ed. *Mansfield on the Condition of the Western Forts, 1853–54*. Norman, 1963.

"Fremont's Expeditions." *United States Magazine, and Democratic Review*, 17 (July, Aug., 1845): 68–77.

Fresh, John H. Letter, 1851, MS. Western Historical Manuscripts Collection, University of Missouri, Columbia.

Frink, Margaret Ann Alsip. *Journal of the Adventures of a Party of California Gold-Seekers*. Oakland, 1897.

Frizzell, Mrs. Lodisa. *Across the Plains to California in 1852*, edited by Victor Hugo Paltsits. New York, 1915; reprinted from New York Public Library *Bulletin* of Apr., 1915.

"From Bethel, Missouri, to Aurora, Oregon: Letters of William Keil, 1855–1870, Part I," translated by William G. Bek. *Missouri Historical Review*, 48 (Oct., 1953): 23–41; "Part II" (Jan., 1954): 141–53.

"From California." *Niles' National Register*, 72 (July 24, 1847): 330.

Frost, Mary Perry. "Experience of a Pioneer." *Washington Historical Quarterly*, 7 (Apr., 1916): 123–25.

Frush, William H. Diary, 1850, MS and typescript. Beinecke Rare Book and Manuscript Library, Yale University, New Haven.

Fuller, Randall. Journals, 1849–54, typescripts. Archives and Manuscripts Division, Nebraska State Historical Society, Lincoln.

Furniss, Norman F. *The Mormon Conflict, 1850–1859*. New Haven, 1960.

Gage, Stephen T. Diary, 1852, typescript. California Section, California State Library, Sacramento.

Galbraith, John S. *The Hudson's Bay Company as an Imperial Factor, 1821–1869*. Berkeley, 1957.

Galbreath, C. B. "Ezra Meeker: Ohio's Illustrious Pioneer." *Ohio Archaeological and Historical Quarterly*, 36 (Jan., 1927): 3–47.

Gara, Larry. "Gold Fever in Wisconsin." *Wisconsin Magazine of History*, 38 (Winter, 1954–55): 106–8.

Gard, Wayne. *The Chisholm Trail*. Norman, 1954.

Garraty, John A. *The American Nation*, 2d ed. 2 vols. New York, 1971.

Gee, Perry. Journal, 1852–53, MS and typescript. Beinecke Rare Book and Manuscript Library, Yale University, New Haven.

Geer, Ralph C. "Occasional Address." *Transactions of the Seventh Annual Re-union of the Oregon Pioneer Association; for 1879*. Salem, 1880, pp. 32–42.

"General Sutter's Diary—IV." *Argonaut*, Feb. 16, 1878, reproduction. California Section, California State Library, Sacramento.

Georgetta, Clel. "Sheep in Nevada." *Nevada Historical Society Quarterly*, 8 (Summer, 1965): 17–38.

Ghent, W. J. *The Road to Oregon: A Chronicle of the Great Emigrant Trail*. New York, 1934.

Gibson, J. Watt. *Recollections of a Pioneer*. St. Joseph, Mo., 1912.

Giffen, Helen S., ed. *The Diaries of Peter Decker: Overland to California in 1849 and Life in the Mines, 1850–1851*. Georgetown, Cal., 1966.

Gillespie, Robert. Diary, 1849, typescript. Typescript Collection, State Historical Society of Missouri, Columbia.

Gilman, Rhoda R. "Pioneer Aeronaut: William Markoe and His Balloon." *Minnesota History*, 38 (Dec., 1962): 166–76.

Goetzmann, William H. *Army Exploration in the American West, 1803–1863*. New Haven, 1959; paperbound ed., 1965.

———. *Exploration and Empire: The Explorer and the Scientist in the Winning of the American West*. New York, 1966.

Goldsmith, Oliver. *Overland in Forty-Nine*. Detroit, 1896.

Goodman, John B., III. "California Fleet 1849." *The Westerners Brand Book, Book Ten, Los Angeles Corral, 1963*. Los Angeles, 1963, pp. 35–50.

Goodwin, Cardinal. *The Trans-Mississippi West (1803–53): A History of Its Acquisition and Settlement*. New York, 1922.

Goodwin, Victor O. "Development of the Emigrant Routes of Northern Nevada." *Nevada Historical Society Quarterly*, 8 (Fall-Winter, 1965): 27–41.

Gordon, Leon M., II. "The Influence of River Transportation on St. Joseph and Elkhart Counties, 1830–1860." *Indiana Magazine of History*, 46 (Sept., 1950): 283–96.

Gorgas, Solomon A. Diary and Letters, 1850–51, MSS. Henry E. Huntington Library, San Marino, Cal.

Gould, Charles. Diary, 1849, typescript. Bancroft Library, University of California, Berkeley.

Gowans, Fred R. "Fort Bridger and the Mormons." *Utah Historical Quarterly*, 42 (Winter, 1974): 49–67.

Graebner, Norman A. "American Interest in California, 1845." *Pacific Historical Review*, 22 (Feb., 1953): 13–27.

———, Gilbert C. Fite, and Philip L. White. *A History of the United States*. 2 vols. New York, 1970.

Graham, Calvin Heron. Journal, 1853, MS and typescript. Archives and Manuscripts Division, Kansas State Historical Society, Topeka.

Grant, Louis S. "Fort Hall under the Hudson's Bay Company, 1837–1856." *Oregon Historical Quarterly*, 41 (Mar., 1940): 34–39.

[Granville Overland Company, Ohio]. Journal, 1849, MS and typescript. Beinecke Rare Book and Manuscript Library, Yale University, New Haven.

Gray, Charles G. Diary, 1849, MS. Henry E. Huntington Library, San Marino, Cal.

Greeley, Horace. *An Overland Journey from New York to San Francisco in the Summer of 1859*, edited by Charles T. Duncan. New York, 1964.

Green, T. L. "A Forgotten Fur Trading Post in Scotts Bluff County." *Nebraska History Magazine*, 15 (Jan.-Mar., 1934): 38–46.

———. "'Scotts Bluffs, Fort John.'" *Nebraska History*, 19 (July-Sept., 1938): 175–89.

Greenhow, Robert. *The History of Oregon and California*, 3d ed. New York, 1845.

———. *Memoir, Historical and Political, on the Northwest Coast of North America, and the Adjacent Territories*. New York, 1840.

Gregg, Jacob R. *A History of the Oregon Trail, Santa Fe Trail, and Other Trails*. Portland, 1955.

Gregg, Kate L. "Boonslickers in the Gold Rush to California." *Missouri Historical Review*, 41 (July, 1947): 345–60.

———. "Missourians in the Gold Rush." *Missouri Historical Review*, 39 (Jan., 1945): 137–54.

Gregson, James Marshall, and Eliza Marshall Gregson. "The Gregson Memoirs." *California Historical Society Quarterly*, 19 (June, 1940): 113–43.

Gressley, Gene M., ed. *The American West: A Reorientation*, vol. 32 of University of Wyoming *Publications*. [Laramie], 1966.

Grindell, John. Overland Narrative, 1850, typescript journal. Beinecke Rare Book and Manuscript Library, Yale University, New Haven.

Griswold, Harriet Booth. Papers, including 1859 diary, MS. Archives and Manuscripts Division, California State Historical Society, San Francisco.

Groh, George W. *Gold Fever: Being a True Account, Both Horrifying and Hilarious, of the Art of Healing (so-called) during the California Gold Rush*. New York, 1966.

Grow, Dr. S. L. Journal, 1850, MS. Beinecke Rare Book and Manuscript Library, Yale University, New Haven.

Guill, Mary Jane. Diary, 1860, typescript. California Section, California State Library, Sacramento.

Gunnison, John W. *The Mormons, or, Latter-Day Saints, in the Valley of the Great Salt Lake*. Philadelphia, 1856.

Guthrie, A. B., Jr. *The Way West*. Boston, 1949.

Guthrie, Chester L., and Leo L. Gerald. "Upper Missouri Agency: An Account of Indian Administration on the Frontier." *Pacific Historical Review*, 10 (Mar., 1941): 47–56.

H. Journal, 1850, serialized in San Francisco *Daily Alta California*, Sept. 21–Oct. 6, 1850.

Haas, John B. "Pioneer Autobiography." *Pony Express Courier*, 5 (June, 1938): 7–10, and succeeding issues to (Jan., 1939): 7–10. [Narrative recollections of 1853–54 overland journey.]

Hafen, Ann W. "Lancaster P. Lupton." In LeRoy R. Hafen, ed., *The Mountain Men and the Fur Trade of the Far West*. 10 vols. Glendale, Cal., 1965–72, 2:207–16.

Hafen, LeRoy R. "Elijah Barney Ward." In LeRoy R. Hafen, ed., *The Mountain Men and the Fur Trade of the Far West*. 10 vols. Glendale, Cal., 1965–72, 7:343–51.

———. "Louis Vasquez." In LeRoy R. Hafen, ed., *The Mountain Men and the Fur Trade of the Far West*. 10 vols. Glendale, Cal., 1965–72, 2:321–38.

———. *The Overland Mail, 1849–1869*. Cleveland, 1926.

———. "Robert Newell." In LeRoy R. Hafen, ed., *The Mountain Men and the Fur Trade of the Far West*. 10 vols. Glendale, Cal., 1965–72, 8:251–76.

———. "Thomas Fitzpatrick and the First Indian Agency of the Upper Platte and Arkansas." *Mississippi Valley Historical Review*, 15 (Dec., 1928): 374–84.

———, ed. *The Mountain Men and the Fur Trade of the Far West*. 10 vols. Glendale, Cal., 1965–72.

———, and Ann W. Hafen, eds. *The Far West and Rockies: General Analytical Index . . . Supplement to the Journals of Forty-Niners, Salt Lake to Los Angeles*, vol. 15 of *The Far West and the Rockies Historical Series*. Glendale, Cal., 1961.

——— and ———, eds. *Handcarts to Zion: The Story of a Unique Western Migration, 1856–1860*, vol. 14 of *The Far West and the Rockies Historical Series*. Glendale, Cal., 1960.

——— and ———, eds. *Journals of Forty-Niners: Salt Lake to Los Angeles*, vol. 2 of *The Far West and the Rockies Historical Series*. Glendale, Cal., 1954.

——— and ———, eds. *Relations with the Indians of the Plains, 1857–1861*, vol. 9 of *The Far West and the Rockies Historical Series*. Glendale, Cal., 1959.

——— and ———, eds. *Rufus B. Sage: His Letters and Papers, 1836–1847*, vols. 4 and 5 of *The Far West and the Rockies Historical Series*. Glendale, Cal., 1956.

——— and ———, eds. *To the Rockies and Oregon: 1839–1842*, vol. 3 of *The Far West and the Rockies Historical Series*. Glendale, Cal., 1965.

——— and ———, eds. *The Utah Expedition, 1857–1858*, vol. 8 of *The Far West and the Rockies Historical Series*. Glendale, Cal., 1958.

———, and Francis Marion Young. *Fort Laramie and the Pageant of the West, 1834–1890*. Glendale, Cal., 1938.

———, W. Eugene Hollon, and Carl Coke Rister. *Western America*, 3d ed. Englewood Cliffs, N.J., 1970.

Haines, Francis, Sr. "Goldilocks on the Oregon Trail." *Idaho Yesterdays*, 9 (Winter, 1965–66): 26–30.

———. "Pioneer Portrait: Robert Newell." *Idaho Yesterdays*, 9 (Spring, 1965): 2–9.

Haines, Robert W. "Baker's Covered Wagon Centennial." *Oregon Historical Quarterly*, 53 (Sept., 1952): 209–13.

Hale, Israel F. "Diary of a Trip to California in 1849." *Quarterly of the Society of California Pioneers*, 2 (June 30, 1925): 61–130.

Hale, John. *California as It Is*, edited by Thomas B. Hunter, Jr., and Richard L. Wellington. N.p., 1954; reprint of 1851 ed.

Hall, Edwin G. Letters, 1849, typescripts. California Section, California State Library, Sacramento.

Hall, George H. Letters, 1849–50, MSS. Beinecke Rare Book and Manuscript Library, Yale University, New Haven.

Hall, Mark W. "Journalism in California: The Pioneer Period, 1831–1849." *Journal of the West*, 10 (Oct., 1971): 624–36.

Hall, O. J. Diary, 1849, typescript. Bancroft Library, University of California, Berkeley.

Hall, Susan Mitchell. "The Diary of a Trip from Ione to Nevada in 1859." *California Historical Society Quarterly*, 17 (Mar., 1938): 75–80.

Ham, Edward B., ed. "Journey into Southern Oregon: Diary of a Pennsylvania Dutchman." *Oregon Historical Quarterly*, 60 (Sept., 1959): 375–407.

Hamelin, Joseph P., Jr. Journals, 1849–50, 1856, MSS and typescripts. Beinecke Rare Book and Manuscript Library, Yale University, New Haven.

Hammond, George P., ed. *The Larkin Papers*. 10 vols. Berkeley, 1952–64.

Hampton, William Perry. Diary, 1852–59, typescript. California Section, California State Library, Sacramento.

Handlin, Oscar. *America: A History*. New York, 1968.

———. *The History of the United States*. 2 vols. New York, 1967.

Handsaker, Samuel. Diary, 1853. Eugene, Ore., 1965, reproduced by Lane County Pioneer-Historical Society. Bancroft Library, University of California, Berkeley.

Hanna, Esther Belle. Journal, 1852, typescript. Bancroft Library, University of California, Berkeley.

Hannon, Jessie Gould. *The Boston-Newton Company Venture: From Massachusetts to California in 1849*. Lincoln, Neb., 1969.

Hansen, William A. "Thomas Hart Benton and the Oregon Question." *Missouri Historical Review*, 63 (July, 1969): 489–97.

Hanson, Charles E., Jr. "Geminien P. Beauvais." In LeRoy R. Hafen, ed., *The Mountain Men and the Fur Trade of the Far West*. 10 vols. Glendale, Cal., 1965–72, 7:35–43.

Hardy, Francis A. Journal, 1850, MS and typescript. Beinecke Rare Book and Manuscript Library, Yale University, New Haven.

Harrington, Dan. "Pioneer Reminiscences." *Pony Express Courier,* 3 (Oct., 1936): 13.

Harstad, Peter T. "The Lander Trail." *Idaho Yesterdays,* 12 (Fall, 1968): 14–28.

Hart, Jim A. "James Redpath, Missouri Correspondent." *Missouri Historical Review,* 57 (Oct., 1962): 70–78.

Hart, Newell. "Rescue of a Frontier Boy." *Utah Historical Quarterly,* 33 (Winter, 1965): 51–54.

Hartford, Conn., *Courant,* Jan. 1, 1841–Dec. 31, 1844, Jan. 1, 1848–Dec. 31, 1849.

Hartman, Amos William. "The California and Oregon Trail, 1849–1860." *Quarterly of the Oregon Historical Society,* 25 (Mar., 1924): 1–35.

Hastings, Lansford W. *The Emigrants' Guide to Oregon and California,* edited by Charles Henry Carey. Princeton, 1932.

Hastings, Loren B. Journal, 1847, typescript. Beinecke Rare Book and Manuscript Library, Yale University, New Haven.

Haun, Catherine Margaret. A Woman's Trip across the Plains in 1849, MS narrative recollections. Henry E. Huntington Library, San Marino, Cal.

Hawgood, John A. *America's Western Frontiers: The Exploration and Settlement of the Trans-Mississippi West.* New York, 1967.

Hawkins, Albert. "Centennial of the Covered Wagon." *Oregon Historical Quarterly,* 31 (June, 1930): 115–24.

Hayden, Charles W. Diary, 1852–53, MS and typescript. Beinecke Rare Book and Manuscript Library, Yale University, New Haven.

Hays, Arthur Homer, ed. "Diary of Taylor N. Snow, Hoosier Fifty-Niner." *Indiana Magazine of History,* 28 (Sept., 1932): 193–208.

Headen, Ben F. Letter, 1853, typescript. Western Historical Manuscripts Collection, University of Missouri, Columbia.

Heaton, P. S. "The Old Lone Tree." *Nebraska History,* 31 (June, 1950): 147–52.

Helfrich, Devere. "The Applegate Trail." *Klamath Echoes,* no. 9 (1971): 1–106.

Henderson, Lucy Ann. "Young Adventure," edited by Ronald Thomas Strong. *Nevada Historical Society Quarterly,* 16 (Summer, 1973): 67–99.

Henderson, Paul C. *Landmarks on the Oregon Trail.* New York, 1953.

Henderson, Sarah Fisher, Nellie Edith

Latourette, and Kenneth Scott Latourette, eds. "Correspondence of the Reverend Ezra Fisher." *Quarterly of the Oregon Historical Society,* 16 (Mar., 1915): 65–104.

Hentz, Charles. Letters, 1849–50, photocopies of typescripts. Bancroft Library, University of California, Berkeley.

Hermann, William H., ed. "Document: Three Gold Rush Letters of Adonijah Strong Welch." *Iowa Journal of History,* 57 (Jan., 1959): 61–73.

Hicks, John D., George E. Mowry, and Robert E. Burke. *A History of American Democracy,* 3d ed. Boston, 1966.

Hill, Burton S. "The Great Indian Treaty Council of 1851." *Nebraska History,* 47 (Mar., 1966): 85–110.

———. "Thomas S. Twiss, Indian Agent." *Great Plains Journal,* 6 (Spring, 1967): 85–96.

Himes, George H. "Annual Address." *Transactions of the 35th Annual Reunion of the Oregon Pioneer Association, Portland, June 19th, 1907.* Portland, 1908, pp. 134–52.

———. "Twenty-second Annual Reunion." *Transactions of the Twenty-second Annual Reunion of the Oregon Pioneer Association for 1894.* Portland, 1895, pp. 5–11.

Hinckley, Ted, and Caryl Hinckley, eds. "Overland from St. Louis to the California Gold Field in 1849: The Diary of Joseph Waring Berrien." *Indiana Magazine of History,* 56 (Dec., 1960): 273–352.

Hinds, T. W. Diary, 1850, photocopy of typescript. Bancroft Library, University of California, Berkeley.

Hine, Robert V. *The American West: An Interpretive History.* Boston, 1973.

———, and Edwin R. Bingham, eds. *The American Frontier: Readings and Documents.* Boston, 1972.

Hinman, C. G. Diary, 1849–50, MS. Western History Department, Denver Public Library.

"A Historic Document: A Contract for Transportation across the Plains to California." *Quarterly of the California Historical Society,* 11 (Mar., 1932): 34.

Hixson, Jasper Morris. Diary, 1849, photocopy of typescript. Bancroft Library, University of California, Berkeley.

Hockett, W. A. Experiences along the Oregon Trail in 1847, MS and typescript recollections. Archives and Manuscripts Division, Nebraska State Historical Society, Lincoln.

Hoffman, Wilhelm. Journal, 1849–50, MS

and typescript translation. Beinecke Rare Book and Manuscript Library, Yale University, New Haven.

Holliday, Jaquelin Smith. "The California Gold Rush in Myth and Reality." Ph.D dissertation, University of California, Berkeley, 1959.

———. "The California Gold Rush Reconsidered." In K. Ross Toole, John Alexander Carroll, Robert M. Utley, and A. R. Mortensen, eds., *Probing the American West: Papers from the Santa Fe Conference.* Santa Fe, 1962, pp. 35–41.

———. "Some Notable Views of the Elephant." *American West Review,* 1 (Sept. 15, 1967): 12–13, 29.

Holmes, Kenneth L. "John McLoughlin." In LeRoy R. Hafen, ed., *The Mountain Men and the Fur Trade of the Far West.* 10 vols. Glendale, Cal., 1965–72, 8:235–45.

Holtz, Milton E. "Old Fort Kearny—1846–1848: Symbol of a Changing Frontier." *Montana, the Magazine of Western History,* 22 (Autumn, 1972): 44–55.

Holzhueter, John O., ed. "From Waupun to Sacramento in 1849: The Gold Rush Journal of Edwin Hillyer." *Wisconsin Magazine of History,* 49 (Spring, 1966): 210–44.

Hoopes, Alban W. "Thomas S. Twiss, Indian Agent on the Upper Platte, 1855–1861." *Mississippi Valley Historical Review,* 20 (Dec., 1933): 353–64.

Hopkins, Sarah Winnemucca. *Life among the Paiutes: Their Wrongs and Claims,* edited by Mrs. Horace Mann. Boston, 1883.

Hough, Emerson. *The Covered Wagon.* New York, 1922.

———. *The Passing of the Frontier: A Chronicle of the Old West,* vol. 26 of *The Chronicles of America.* New Haven, 1921.

Howe, Octavius Thorndike. *Argonauts of '49: History and Adventures of the Emigrant Companies from Massachusetts, 1849–1850.* Cambridge, Mass., 1923.

Howell, Elijah Preston. Diary, 1849, MS. State Historical Society of Missouri Manuscripts, Columbia.

Hughes, Willis B. "The First Dragoons on the Western Frontier, 1834–1846." *Arizona and the West,* 12 (Summer, 1970): 115–38.

Hulbert, Archer Butler. *Forty-Niners: The Chronicle of the California Trail.* Boston, 1931.

———, ed. *The Call of the Columbia: Iron Men and Saints Take the Oregon Trail,* vol. 4 of *Overland to the Pacific.* Denver, 1934.

Humphreys, Alfred Glenn. "Peg Leg Smith." *Idaho Yesterdays,* 10 (Summer, 1966): 28–32.

———. "Thomas L. (Peg-leg) Smith." In LeRoy R. Hafen, ed., *The Mountain Men and the Fur Trade of the Far West.* Glendale, Cal., 1966, 4:311–30.

Hunt, Nancy A. *By Ox-Team to California.* N.p., n.d. [Recollections of 1854 overland journey.]

Hunter, Milton R. "Brigham Young, Colonizer." *Pacific Historical Review,* 6 (Dec., 1937): 341–60.

———. "The Mormon Corridor." *Pacific Historical Review,* 8 (June, 1939): 179–200.

Husband, Michael B. "Senator Lewis F. Linn and the Oregon Question." *Missouri Historical Review,* 66 (Oct., 1971): 1–19.

———. "To Oregon in 1843: The 'Great Migration.' " *Kansas Quarterly,* 5 (Spring, 1973): 7–16.

———. "William I. Marshall and the Legend of Marcus Whitman." *Pacific Northwest Quarterly,* 64 (Apr., 1973): 57–69.

Hutchings, James Mason. Diary, 1849, microfilm of MS. Bancroft Library, University of California, Berkeley.

Iman, Margaret Windsor. "My Arrival in Washington in 1852." *Washington Historical Quarterly,* 18 (Oct., 1927): 254–60.

Ingalls, Eleazar Stillman. *Journal of a Trip to California.* Waukegan, Ill., 1852.

Ingersoll, Chester. *Overland to California in 1847; Letters Written en route to California, West from Independence, Missouri, to the Editor of the Joliet Signal,* edited by Douglas C. McMurtrie. Chicago, 1937.

Inman, Henry, and William F. Cody. *The Great Salt Lake Trail.* Topeka, 1910.

Jackman, E. R., ed. "After the Covered Wagons: Recollections of Russell C. and Ellis S. Dement." *Oregon Historical Quarterly,* 63 (Mar., 1962): 5–40.

Jackson, Donald, and Mary Lee Spence, eds. *The Expeditions of John Charles Frémont.* 2 vols., supplement, map portfolio. Urbana, Ill., 1970–73.

Jackson, W. Turrentine. "The Army Engineers as Road Surveyors and Builders in Kansas and Nebraska, 1854–1858." *Kansas Historical Quarterly,* 17 (Feb., 1949): 37–59.

———. *Wagon Roads West: A Study of Federal Road Surveys and Construction in the*

Trans-Mississippi West, 1846–1869. New Haven, 1964; reprint of 1952 ed.

Jacobs, Melvin Clay. *Winning Oregon: A Study of an Expansionist Movement.* Caldwell, Idaho, 1938.

Jacobs, Wilbur R., ed. *The Historical World of Frederick Jackson Turner: With Selections from His Correspondence.* New Haven, 1968.

————, ed. *Letters of Francis Parkman.* 2 vols. Norman, 1960.

Jagger, D. Diary, 1849–50, microfilm of MS. Bancroft Library, University of California, Berkeley.

James, Eugenia Learned, and Vivian K. Mc-Larty, eds. "Three Generations in the Span of a Continent: The Zumwalt Family, Part I." *Missouri Historical Review,* 48 (Apr., 1954): 249–63; "Part II" (July, 1954): 341–51.

"James Huddleston, of Eugene, Or." *Transactions of the Seventeenth Annual Reunion of the Oregon Pioneer Association for 1889.* Portland, 1890, pp. 103–4.

Jewett, Mendall. Journal, 1850–51, typescript. Western History Department, Denver Public Library.

Johansen, Dorothy O. "The Oregon Steam Navigation Company: An Example of Capitalism on the Frontier." *Pacific Historical Review,* 10 (June, 1941): 179–88.

————. "A Working Hypothesis for the Study of Migrations." *Pacific Historical Review,* 36 (Feb., 1967): 1–12.

"John T. Milner's Trip to California: Letters to the Family." *Alabama Historical Quarterly,* 20 (Fall, 1958): 523–63.

Johnson, John A. Letters, 1849, printed in *Pioneering on the Plains.* Kaukauna, Wis., 1924.

Johnson, John Lawrence. Diary, 1851, MS. Beinecke Rare Book and Manuscript Library, Yale University, New Haven.

Johnson, Overton, and William H. Winter. *Route across the Rocky Mountains,* edited by Carl L. Cannon. Princeton, 1932.

Johnston, John Franklin. A Trip to the Gold Fields of California in 1852, photocopy of typescript. Archives and Manuscripts Division, Ohio State Historical Society, Columbus.

Johnston, William G. *Overland to California.* Oakland, 1948.

"Jonathan L. Moore Book." *Lane County Historian,* 11 (Summer, 1966): 23–34.

Jones, Brian. "Those Wild Reshaw Boys." In Francis B. Taunton, ed., *Sidelights of the Sioux Wars,* English Westerners' Spec. Pub. no. 2. London, 1967, pp. 5–46.

Jones, Carlton. Diary, 1850, photocopy of MS. Carlton Jones Papers, 1820–50, Western Historical Manuscripts Collection, University of Missouri, Columbia.

Jones, Hoyle. "Seth E. Ward." *Annals of Wyoming,* 5 (July, 1927): 5–18.

Joost, Nicholas. "Reveille in the West: Western Travelers in the St. Louis *Weekly Reveille,* 1844–50." In John Francis McDermott, ed., *Travelers on the Western Frontier.* Urbana, Ill., 1970, pp. 203–40.

Josephy, Alvin M., Jr. "Indians in History: The White Man's Books Speak with Forked Tongue." *Atlantic,* 225 (June, 1970): 70–71.

Josselyn, Amos Piatt. Diary, 1849, microfilm of typescript. Bancroft Library, University of California, Berkeley.

————. Letters, 1849–50, MSS and typescripts. California Section, California State Library, Sacramento.

"Journal of A. W. Harlan while Crossing the Plains in 1850." *Annals of Iowa,* 11 (Apr., 1913): 32–62.

"Journal of Henry Allyn, 1853." *Transactions of the Forty-ninth Annual Reunion of the Oregon Pioneer Association, Portland, June 16, 1921.* Portland, 1924, pp. 372–435.

"The Journal of John Boardman: An Overland Journey from Kansas to Oregon in 1843." *Utah Historical Quarterly,* 2 (Oct., 1929): 99–121.

"Journal of John T. Williams, 1850." *Indiana Magazine of History,* 32 (Dec., 1936): 393–409.

Journal of John Wood. Chillicothe, Ohio, 1852.

"The Journal of Major Osborne Cross." In Raymond W. Settle, ed., *The March of the Mounted Riflemen.* Glendale, Cal., 1940, pp. 31–272.

Journal of Samuel Rutherford Dundass. Steubenville, Ohio, 1857.

"Journal of Thomas Holt." In Dale L. Morgan, ed., *Overland in 1846: Diaries and Letters of the California Trail.* 2 vols. Georgetown, Cal., 1963, 1:189–98.

"Journey to Zion: From the Journal of Erastus Snow." *Utah Humanities Review,* 2 (Apr., 1948): 107–28; "Part II" (July, 1948): 264–84.

Judson, Katharine B., ed. "Dr. John McLoughlin's Last Letter to the Hudson's Bay Company, as Chief Factor, in

Charge at Fort Vancouver, 1845." *American Historical Review*, 21 (Oct., 1915): 104–34.

Kaiser, Leo M., and Priscilla Knuth, eds. "From Ithaca to Clatsop Plains: Miss Ketcham's Journal of Travel." *Oregon Historical Quarterly*, 62 (Sept., 1961): 237–87; "Part II" (Dec., 1961): 337–402.

Kanesville, Iowa, *Frontier Guardian*, Feb. 7, 1849–June 18, 1852. Titled *Frontier Guardian and Iowa Sentinel* after Mar. 4, 1852.

Kanesville, Iowa, *Western Bugle*, scattered issues, 1852–53.

Kappler, Charles J., ed. *Indian Treaties, 1778–1883*. New York, 1972; reprint of 1904 ed.

Keen, Richard. Journal, 1852, typescript. California Section, California State Library, Sacramento.

Keith, F. F. "Journal of Crossing the Plains in 1850." In *Two Argonauts on the Oregon Trail*. [Menlo Park, Cal., 1961.]

Keithley, George. *The Donner Party*. New York, 1972.

Keller, George. *A Trip across the Plains and Life in California*. Oakland, 1955; reprint of 1851 ed.

Kelly, Charles. "Gold Seekers on the Hastings Cutoff." *Utah Historical Quarterly*, 20 (Jan., 1952): 3–30.

———. "The Hastings Cutoff." *Utah Historical Quarterly*, 3 (July, 1930): 67–82.

———. "The Salt Desert Trail." *Utah Historical Quarterly*, 3 (Apr., 1930): 35–52.

———, ed. "The Journal of Robert Chalmers: April 17–September 1, 1850." *Utah Historical Quarterly*, 20 (Jan., 1952): 31–55.

Kelly, William. *An Excursion to California*. 2 vols. London, 1851.

Kemble, John Haskell. "The Genesis of the Pacific Mail Steamship Company." *California Historical Society Quarterly*, 13 (Sept., 1934): 240–54, (Dec., 1934): 386–406.

———. "The Gold Rush by Panama, 1848–1851." *Pacific Historical Review*, 18 (Feb., 1949): 45–56.

———. "Pacific Mail Service between Panama and San Francisco, 1849–1851." *Pacific Historical Review*, 2 (Dec., 1933): 405–17.

———. *Panama Route, 1848–1869*. Berkeley, 1943.

———. "The Panama Route to the Pacific Coast, 1848–1869." *Pacific Historical Review*, 7 (Mar., 1938): 1–13.

Kenderdine, Thaddeus S. *A California Tramp and Later Footprints*. Newton, Pa., 1888.

Kerns, John T. "Journal of Crossing the Plains to Oregon in 1852." *Transactions of the Forty-second Annual Reunion of the Oregon Pioneer Association, Portland, June 25, 1914*. Portland, 1917, pp. 148–93.

Kiefer, David M., ed. "Over Barren Plains and Rock-bound Mountains [1850 journal of Adam Mercer Brown]." *Montana, the Magazine of Western History*, 22 (Autumn, 1972): 16–29.

Kihn, Phyllis. "Connecticut and the California Gold Rush: The Connecticut Mining and Trading Company." *Connecticut Historical Society Bulletin*, 28 (Jan., 1963): 1–13.

King, John Nevin. Journal, 1850, MS. Beinecke Rare Book and Manuscript Library, Yale University, New Haven.

Kingery, Solomon. Letters, 1852–53, containing continuous journal entries, MSS and typescripts. Beinecke Rare Book and Manuscript Library, Yale University, New Haven.

Kingston, C. S. "Introduction of Cattle into the Pacific Northwest." *Washington Historical Quarterly*, 14 (July, 1923): 163–85.

Kirkpatrick, Charles Alexander. Journal, 1849–50, ink copy of MS. Bancroft Library, University of California, Berkeley.

Knuth, Priscilla. "Alexander Piper's Reports and Journal." *Oregon Historical Quarterly*, 69 (Sept., 1968): 223–68.

———. "'Picturesque' Frontier: The Army's Fort Dalles." *Oregon Historical Quarterly*, 67 (Dec., 1966): 293–346; "Part Two," 68 (Mar., 1967): 5–52.

———, and Charles M. Gates, eds. "Oregon Territory in 1849–1850." *Pacific Northwest Quarterly*, 40 (Jan., 1949): 3–23.

Korns, J. Roderic. "West from Fort Bridger: The Pioneering of the Immigrant Trails across Utah, 1846–1850." *Utah Historical Quarterly*, 19 (Jan.-Oct., 1951): 1–297.

Krill, Abram. Diary, 1850, MS. Beinecke Rare Book and Manuscript Library, Yale University, New Haven.

Kroll, Helen B. "The Books That Enlightened the Emigrants." *Oregon Historical Quarterly*, 45 (June, 1944): 103–23.

Lagerberg, Matt. "The Bishop Hill Colonists in the Gold Rush." *Journal of the Illinois State Historical Society*, 48 (Winter, 1955): 466–69.

Laird, Moses F. Book, 1852–55, MS and typescript journal. Beinecke Rare Book and

Manuscript Library, Yale University, New Haven.

Lamar, Howard R. *The Far Southwest, 1846–1912: A Territorial History.* New Haven, 1966.

Lancaster, C. Letter, 1850, MS. Warner M. Bateman Papers, Western Reserve Historical Society, Cleveland.

Lane, S. A. Diary, 1850, photocopy of MS. Bancroft Library, University of California, Berkeley.

Langworthy, Franklin. *Scenery of the Plains, Mountains and Mines,* edited by Paul C. Phillips. Princeton, 1932.

Larson, Gustive O. "Brigham Young and the Indians." In Robert G. Ferris, ed., *The American West: An Appraisal.* Santa Fe, 1963, pp. 176–87.

Laut, Agnes C. *The Overland Trail: The Epic Path of the Pioneers to Oregon.* New York, 1929.

Lavender, David. *Bent's Fort.* Garden City, N.Y., 1954 (paperbound ed.).

———. *The Rockies.* New York, 1968.

———. *Westward Vision: The Story of the Oregon Trail.* New York, 1963.

Leader, Herman A. "McLoughlin's Answer to Warre Report." *Oregon Historical Quarterly,* 33 (Sept., 1932): 214–29.

Lee, George Robert. "The Effect of Public Opinion on the Mormon Scheme of Self-Government." M.A. thesis, University of Oklahoma, Norman, 1959.

Leeds *Mercury,* Jan. 1, 1842–July 25, 1846.

Lenox, Edward Henry. *Overland to Oregon: In the Tracks of Lewis and Clarke,* edited by Robert Whitaker. Oakland, 1904.

"Letter and Circular of Information for Prospective Emigrants to Oregon." *Quarterly of the Oregon Historical Society,* 11 (Sept., 1910): 307–12.

"Letter Describing a March to Utah in 1859." *Annals of Iowa,* 13 (Apr., 1923): 611–18.

"Letter of Dr. John McLoughlin to Oregon Statesman, June 8, 1852." *Quarterly of the Oregon Historical Society,* 8 (Sept., 1907): 294–99.

"Letter of Quincy Adams Brooks." *Quarterly of the Oregon Historical Society,* 15 (Sept., 1914): 210–15.

"Letters of a Proselyte: The Hascall-Pomeroy Correspondence." *Utah Historical Quarterly,* 25 (July, 1957): 237–57.

"Letters of S. H. Taylor to the Watertown [Wis.] Chronicle." *Quarterly of the Oregon Historical Society,* 22 (June, 1921): 117–60.

Lewelling, Seth. Journal, 1850–52, typescript. California Section, California State Library, Sacramento.

Lewis, Elisha B. Diary, 1849, microfilm of typescript. Bancroft Library, University of California, Berkeley.

Lewis, John F. Diary, 1849, 1852–54, MS and typescript. Beinecke Rare Book and Manuscript Library, Yale University, New Haven.

Lewis, John N. Diary, 1851–55, MS. Bancroft Library, University of California, Berkeley.

Lewis, Thomas C. Memorandum or Notes, 1852–53, MSS and typescripts of journal and letters. Beinecke Rare Book and Manuscript Library, Yale University, New Haven.

Liberty, Mo., *Weekly Tribune,* Apr. 4, 1846–Apr. 9, 1852.

Lienhard, Heinrich. *From St. Louis to Sutter's Fort, 1846,* translated and edited by Erwin G. Gudde and Elisabeth K. Gudde. Norman, 1961.

"Lieut. Fremont's Expedition to Oregon and California." *Niles' National Register,* 67 (Feb. 1, 1845): 339.

Littell's Living Age, 4 (Feb. 1, 1845): 284.

Littleton, Micajah. Diary, 1850, typescript. California Section, California State Library, Sacramento.

Lobenstine, Belle W., ed. *Extracts from the Diary of William C. Lobenstine, December 31, 1851–1858.* N.p., 1920.

Lockley, Fred. *Captain Sol. Tetherow, Wagon Train Master.* Portland, n.d.

———, ed. "Recollections of Benjamin Franklin Bonney." *Quarterly of the Oregon Historical Society,* 24 (Mar., 1923): 36–55.

———, ed. "Reminiscences of William H. Packwood." *Quarterly of the Oregon Historical Society,* 16 (Mar., 1915): 33–54.

Lomax, Alfred L. "History of Pioneer Sheep Husbandry in Oregon." *Oregon Historical Quarterly,* 29 (June, 1928): 99–143.

London *Times,* Jan. 1, 1842–Dec. 31, 1848, with the aid of Palmer's index.

Long, Margaret. *The Oregon Trail: Following the Old Historic Pioneer Trails on the Modern Highways.* Denver, 1954.

Long, Mrs. Mary Jane. *A True Story: Crossing the Plains in the Year of 1852 with Ox Teams.* [McMinnville, Ore., 1915.]

Loomis, Leander V. *A Journal of the Birmingham Emigrating Company,* edited by Edgar M. Ledyard. Salt Lake City, 1928.

Looney, Jesse. "From the Far West." *Journal of*

the *Illinois State Historical Society,* 22 (July, 1929): 354–56.

Lorch, Fred W. "Iowa and the California Gold Rush of 1849." *Iowa Journal of History and Politics,* 30 (July, 1932): 307–76.

Lord, Isaac S. P. Diary, 1849–51, MS and clippings from the Elgin, Ill., *Western Christian.* Henry E. Huntington Library, San Marino, Cal.

Lorton, William B. Diary and Letters, 1848–50, microfilm of typescripts. Bancroft Library, University of California, Berkeley.

Louisville *Examiner,* June 19, 1847–Dec. 8, 1849.

Lowe, Percival G. *Five Years a Dragoon ('49 to '54) and Other Adventures on the Great Plains,* edited by Don Russell. Norman, 1965.

Lyman, H. S., ed. "Reminiscences of F. X. Matthieu." *Quarterly of the Oregon Historical Society,* 1 (Mar., 1900): 73–104.

———, ed. "Reminiscences of Hugh Cosgrove." *Quarterly of the Oregon Historical Society,* 1 (Sept., 1900), 253–69.

———, ed. "Reminiscences of Wm. M. Case." *Quarterly of the Oregon Historical Society,* 1 (Sept., 1900): 269–95.

Lyne, James. Letters, 1849–50, MSS and typescripts. Beinecke Rare Book and Manuscript Library, Yale University, New Haven.

McBride, John H. Letters, 1850, typescripts. Archives and Manuscripts Division, Nebraska State Historical Society, Lincoln.

McBride, John R. Reminiscences, 1846, quoted in Dale L. Morgan, ed., *Overland in 1846: Diaries and Letters of the California-Oregon Trail.* 2 vols. Georgetown, Cal., 1963, 1:90–100.

McBride, W. S. Journal, 1850, MS. Henry E. Huntington Library, San Marino, Cal.

McCall, Ansel James. *The Great California Trail in 1849.* Bath, N.Y., 1882.

McCann, Lloyd E. "The Grattan Massacre." *Nebraska History,* 37 (Mar., 1956): 1–25.

McClintock, Thomas C. "Henderson Luelling, Seth Lewelling and the Birth of the Pacific Coast Fruit Industry." *Oregon Historical Quarterly,* 68 (June, 1967): 153–74.

McClure, Andrew S. Diary, 1853. Eugene, Ore., n.d., reproduced by Lane County Pioneer-Historical Society. Bancroft Library, University of California, Berkeley.

McCollum, William. *California as I Saw It,* edited by Dale L. Morgan. Los Gatos, Cal., 1960.

McCowen, George. Diary, 1854–61, typescript. Henry E. Huntington Library, San Marino, Cal.

McCoy, Samuel Finley. Diary, 1849, printed in *Pioneering on the Plains.* Kaukauna, Wis., 1924.

McDermott, John Dishon. "Fort Laramie's Iron Bridge." *Annals of Wyoming,* 34 (Oct., 1962): 137–44.

———. "James Bordeaux." In LeRoy R. Hafen, ed., *The Mountain Men and the Fur Trade of the Far West.* 10 vols. Glendale, Cal., 1965–72, 5:65–80.

———. "John Baptiste Richard." In LeRoy R. Hafen, ed., *The Mountain Men and the Fur Trade of the Far West,* 10 vols. Glendale, Cal., 1965–72, 2:289–303.

———. "Joseph Bissonette." In LeRoy R. Hafen, ed., *The Mountain Men and the Fur Trade of the Far West.* 10 vols. Glendale, Cal., 1965–72, 4:49–60.

McDermott, John Francis, ed. *An Artist on the Overland Trail: The 1849 Diary and Sketches of James F. Wilkins,* San Marino, Cal., 1968.

———. "Gold Rush Movies." *California Historical Society Quarterly,* 33 (Mar., 1954): 29–38.

McDiarmid, Finley. Journal and Letters, 1850, microfilm of MSS and typescripts. Bancroft Library, University of California, Berkeley.

McDonald, J. H. Letter, 1852, MS. Archives and Manuscripts Division, Ohio State Historical Society, Columbus.

McIlhany, Edward Washington. *Recollections of a '49er.* Kansas City, Mo., 1908.

Mack, Effie Mona. *Nevada: A History of the State from the Earliest Times through the Civil War.* Glendale, Cal., 1936.

McKinstry, Byron Nathan. Diary, 1850–52, microfilm of typescript. Bancroft Library, University of California, Berkeley.

McLear, Patrick E. "The St. Louis Cholera Epidemic of 1849." *Missouri Historical Review,* 63 (Jan., 1969): 171–81.

McLoughlin, John. "Copy of a Document." *Transactions of the Eighth Annual Re-union of the Oregon Pioneer Association; for 1880.* Salem, 1881, pp. 46–55.

McMaster, John Bach. *A History of the People of the United States, from the Revolution to the Civil War.* 8 vols. New York, 1929.

McNary, Lawrence A. "Route of Meek Cutoff, 1845." *Oregon Historical Quarterly,* 35 (Mar., 1934): 1–9.

Madsen, Brigham D. *The Bannock of Idaho.* Caldwell, Idaho, 1958.

———. "Shoshoni-Bannock Marauders on the Oregon Trail, 1859–1863." *Utah Historical Quarterly,* 35 (Winter, 1967): 3–30.

Mahlberg, Blanche Billings. "Edward J. Allen, Pioneer and Roadbuilder." *Pacific Northwest Quarterly,* 44 (Oct., 1953): 157–60.

Malone, Dumas, and Basil Rauch. *Crisis of the Union, 1841–1877.* New York, 1960.

Manchester *Guardian,* Jan. 1, 1842–Dec. 31, 1848.

Mann, Henry R. Diary, 1849, typescript. Bancroft Library, University of California, Berkeley.

Manning, James W. "Literacy on the Oregon Trail: Books across the Plains." *Oregon Historical Quarterly,* 41 (June, 1940): 189–94.

Manring, B. F. "Recollections of a Pioneer of 1859: Lawson Stockman." *Quarterly of the Oregon Historical Society,* 11 (June, 1910): 162–76.

Mantor, Lyle E. "Fort Kearny and the Westward Movement." *Nebraska History,* 29 (Sept., 1948): 175–207.

"The Map of T. H. Jefferson." In Dale L. Morgan, ed., *Overland in 1846: Diaries and Letters of the California Trail.* 2 vols. Georgetown, Cal., 1963, 1:237–44.

Marcy, Randolph B. *The Prairie Traveler: A Hand-book for Overland Expeditions.* New York, 1859.

Marshall, Philip C. "New Jersey Expeditions to California in 1849." *Proceedings of the New Jersey Historical Society,* 70 (Jan., 1952): 17–36.

———. "The Newark Overland Company." *Proceedings of the New Jersey Historical Society,* 70 (July, 1952): 173–87.

Marshall, Thomas M., ed. "The Road to California: Letters of Joseph Price." *Mississippi Valley Historical Review,* 11 (Sept., 1924): 237–57.

Marysville, Cal., *Herald,* Aug. 6, 1850–July 10, 1856, Dec. 17, 1856.

Masters, Joseph. Papers, pertaining to Oregon Trail research. Archives and Manuscripts Division, Kansas State Historical Society, Topeka.

Mathews, Edward James. *Crossing the Plains.* [New York, 1930.]

Mattes, Merrill J. "Chimney Rock on the Oregon Trail." *Nebraska History,* 36 (Mar., 1955): 1–26.

———. "Fort Laramie, Guardian of the Oregon Trail." *Annals of Wyoming,* 17 (Jan., 1945): 3–20.

———. *The Great Platte River Road: The Covered Wagon Mainline via Fort Kearny to Fort Laramie,* vol. 25 of Nebraska State Historical Society *Publications.* [Lincoln], 1969.

———. "Joseph Robidoux." In LeRoy R. Hafen, ed., *The Mountain Men and the Fur Trade of the Far West.* 10 vols. Glendale, Cal., 1965–72, 8:287–314.

———. "The Jumping-off Places on the Overland Trail." In John Francis McDermott, ed., *The Frontier Reexamined.* Urbana, Ill., 1967, pp. 27–39.

———. "New Horizons on the Old Oregon Trail." In Ray Allen Billington, ed., *People of the Plains and Mountains: Essays in the History of the West Dedicated to Everett Dick.* Westport, Conn., 1973, pp. 45–62.

———. "Robidoux's Trading Post at 'Scott's Bluffs,' and the California Gold Rush." *Nebraska History,* 30 (June, 1949): 95–138.

———. "Seth E. Ward." In LeRoy R. Hafen, ed., *The Mountain Men and the Fur Trade of the Far West.* 10 vols. Glendale, Cal., 1965–72, 3:357–84.

———. "The Sutler's Store at Fort Laramie." *Annals of Wyoming,* 18 (July, 1946): 93–138.

———, ed. "Alexander Ramsay's Gold Rush Diary of 1849." *Pacific Historical Review,* 18 (Nov., 1949): 437–68.

———, ed. "Capt. L. C. Easton's Report: Fort Laramie to Fort Leavenworth via Republican River in 1849." *Kansas Historical Quarterly,* 20 (May, 1953): 392–416.

———, and Paul Henderson. "The Pony Express: Across Nebraska from St. Joseph to Fort Laramie." *Nebraska History,* 41 (June, 1960): 83–122.

———, and Elsey J. Kirk, eds. "From Ohio to California in 1849: The Gold Rush Journal of Elijah Bryan Farnham." *Indiana Magazine of History,* 46 (Sept., 1950): 297–318, (Dec., 1950): 403–20.

Mattison, Ray H., ed. "The Harney Expedition against the Sioux: The Journal of Capt. John B. S. Todd." *Nebraska History,* 43 (June, 1962): 89–130.

———. "The Indian Frontier on the Upper Missouri to 1865." *Nebraska History,* 39 (Sept., 1958): 241–66.

———. "The Upper Missouri Fur Trade: Its Methods of Operation." *Nebraska History,* 42 (Mar., 1961): 1–28.

Maxwell, William Audley. *Crossing the Plains,*

Days of '57: A Narrative of Early Emigrant Travel to California by the Ox-Team Method. San Francisco, 1915.

May, Richard Martin. Journal, 1848, with subsequent narrative entries in 1849 and the 1850s, MS. Bancroft Library, University of California, Berkeley.

Meacham, Walter E. *Old Oregon Trail: Roadway of American Home Builders.* Manchester, N.H., 1948.

Mecartney, Amos. Letter, 1852, photocopy of MS. In possession of John M. Mecartney, Bluffton, Ohio.

Meeker, Ezra. *The Busy Life of Eighty-five Years: Ventures and Adventures.* Seattle, 1916.

———. *The Ox Team or the Old Oregon Trail, 1852–1906,* 3d ed. Omaha, 1906.

Meinig, D. W. *The Great Columbia Plain: A Historical Geography, 1805–1910.* Seattle, 1968.

"The Memoirs of Lemuel Clarke McKeeby." *California Historical Society Quarterly,* 3 (Apr., 1924): 45–72, (July, 1924): 126–70.

"Memories of Jane D. Kellogg." *Transactions of the Forty-first Annual Reunion of the Oregon Pioneer Association, Portland, June 19, 1913.* Portland, 1916, pp. 86–94.

Merk, Frederick. *Manifest Destiny and Mission in American History: A Reinterpretation.* New York, 1963.

———. "The Oregon Pioneers and the Boundary." *American Historical Review,* 29 (July, 1924): 681–99.

———. "The Oregon Question in the Webster-Ashburton Negotiations." *Mississippi Valley Historical Review,* 43 (Dec., 1956): 379–404.

Merrill, H. Journal, 1849, typescript. In possession of J. S. Holliday, Lafayette, Cal.

Meyer, Roy W. "The Iowa Indians, 1836–1885." *Kansas Historical Quarterly,* 28 (Autumn, 1962): 273–300.

Milgram, James W. "Estill & Co. Express." *Utah Historical Quarterly,* 29 (Oct., 1961): 326–30.

"Military Correspondence—War Department Relating to Fort Kearny." *Publications of the Nebraska State Historical Society,* 21 (1930): 250–68.

Miller, Charles S., and Natalie Joy Ward. *History of America: Challenge and Crisis.* New York, 1971.

Miller, David E. "The Parting of the Ways on the Oregon Trail—the East Terminal of the Sublette Cutoff." *Annals of Wyoming,* 45 (Spring, 1973): 47–52.

Miller, James D. "Early Oregon Scenes: A Pioneer Narrative." *Oregon Historical Quarterly,* 31 (Mar., 1930): 55–68.

Miller, Joel. Journal, 1853, MS. Bancroft Library, University of California, Berkeley.

Miller, Silas V. Letter, 1852, photocopy of MS. Bancroft Library, University of California, Berkeley.

Miller, William C., ed. "The Pyramid Lake Indian War of 1860." *Nevada Historical Society Quarterly,* 1 (Sept., 1957): 37–53; "Part 2" (Nov., 1957): 98–113.

"The Miller-Reed Diary, with Letters by J. F. Reed and Virginia Reed." In Dale L. Morgan, ed., *Overland in 1846: Diaries and Letters of the California Trail.* 2 vols. Georgetown, Cal., 1963, 1:245–305.

Millington, D. A. Diary, 1850–51, microfilm of MS. Bancroft Library, University of California, Berkeley.

Millsap, Kenneth F., ed. "Documents: Romanzo Kingman's Pike's Peak Journal, 1859." *Iowa Journal of History,* 48 (Jan., 1950): 55–85.

Minto, John. "Sheep Husbandry in Oregon." *Quarterly of the Oregon Historical Society,* 3 (Sept., 1902): 219–47.

"The Missouri Heritage of the West." *Missouri Historical Review,* 33 (Oct., 1938): 79–92.

"Missouri History Not Found in Textbooks." *Missouri Historical Review,* 55 (Oct., 1960): 92–98.

Monaghan, Jay. *The Overland Trail.* Indianapolis, 1947.

Montgomery, William. Diary, 1850, MS. Henry E. Huntington Library, San Marino, Cal.

Montreal *Gazette,* Jan. 14, 1843–June 30, 1846.

Moody, Ralph. *The Old Trails West.* New York, 1963.

Moore, J. K., Jr. "Lander Cutoff." *Annals of Wyoming,* 34 (Apr., 1962): 50–51.

Moores, Charles B. "Annual Address." *Transactions of the Thirty-second Annual Reunion of the Oregon Pioneer Association for 1904.* Portland, 1905, pp. 262–88.

Morgan, Dale L. "The Administration of Indian Affairs in Utah, 1851–1858." *Pacific Historical Review,* 17 (Nov., 1948): 383–409.

———. "The Ferries of the Forty-Niners." *Annals of Wyoming,* 31 (Apr., 1959): 5–31; "Part II" (Oct., 1959): 145–89; "Part III—Section 1," 32 (Apr., 1960): 51–69; "Part III—Section 2" (Oct., 1960): 167–203.

————. *The Humboldt: Highroad of the West.* New York, 1943.

————. "Miles Goodyear and the Founding of Ogden." *Utah Historical Quarterly,* 21 (July, 1953): 195–218; "II" (Oct., 1953): 307–29.

————, ed. "The Mormon Ferry on the North Platte: The Journal of William A. Empey, May 7–August 4, 1847." *Annals of Wyoming,* 21 (July-Oct., 1949): 111–67.

————. The Mormons and the Far West, collection of typescripts of newspaper articles. Henry E. Huntington Library, San Marino, Cal.

————. "The Significance and Value of the Overland Journal." In K. Ross Toole, John Alexander Carroll, Robert M. Utley, and A. R. Mortensen, eds., *Probing the American West.* Santa Fe, 1962, pp. 26–34.

————. "The State of Deseret." *Utah Historical Quarterly,* 8 (Apr.-Oct., 1940): 65–251.

————, ed. "Letters by Forty-Niners: Written from Great Salt Lake City in 1849." *Western Humanities Review,* 3 (Apr., 1949): 98–116.

————, ed. *The Overland Diary of James A. Pritchard from Kentucky to California in 1849.* Denver, 1959.

————, ed. *Overland in 1846: Diaries and Letters of the California-Oregon Trail.* 2 vols. Georgetown, Cal., 1963.

————, ed. "Washakie and the Shoshoni: A Selection of Documents from the Records of the Utah Superintendency of Indian Affairs; Part I, 1849–1852." *Annals of Wyoming,* 25 (July, 1953): 141–89; "Part II—1852," 26 (Jan., 1954): 65–80; "Part III—1852–1857" (July, 1954): 141–90; "Part IV—1857–1859," 27 (Apr., 1955): 61–88; "Part V—1860–1862" (Oct., 1955): 198–220.

————, ed. *The West of William H. Ashley: The International Struggle for the Fur Trade of the Missouri, the Rocky Mountains, and the Columbia, with Explorations beyond the Continental Divide, Recorded in the Diaries and Letters of William H. Ashley and His Contemporaries, 1822–1838.* Denver, 1964.

Morison, Samuel Eliot. *The Oxford History of the American People.* New York, 1965.

Morris, Ralph C. "The Notion of a Great American Desert East of the Rockies." *Mississippi Valley Historical Review,* 13 (Sept., 1926): 190–200.

Morris, Richard B., and William Greenleaf. *U.S.A.: The History of a Nation.* 2 vols. Chicago, 1969.

Morrison, John D., ed. "The Diary of David F. Spain." *Colorado Magazine,* 35 (Jan., 1958): 11–34, (Apr., 1958): 81–112.

"Mrs. Whitman's Letters." *Transactions of the Twenty-first Annual Reunion of the Oregon Pioneer Association for 1893.* Portland, 1894, pp. 53–219.

Muench, Joyce Rockwood, ed. *The Kilgore Journal.* New York, 1949.

Mumey, Nolie. "James Baker." In LeRoy R. Hafen, ed., *The Mountain Men and the Fur Trade of the Far West.* 10 vols. Glendale, Cal., 1965–72, 3:39–47.

Munkres, Robert L. "Ash Hollow: Gateway to the High Plains." *Annals of Wyoming,* 42 (Apr., 1970): 5–43.

————. "Independence Rock and Devil's Gate." *Annals of Wyoming,* 40 (Apr., 1968): 23–40.

————. "Indian-White Contact before 1870: Cultural Factors in Conflict." *Journal of the West,* 10 (July, 1971): 439–73.

————. "The Plains Indian Threat on the Oregon Trail before 1860." *Annals of Wyoming,* 40 (Oct., 1968): 193–221.

————. "Soda Springs: Curiosity of the Trail." *Annals of Wyoming,* 43 (Fall, 1971): 215–35.

————. "Wives, Mothers, Daughters: Women's Life on the Road West." *Annals of Wyoming,* 42 (Oct., 1970): 191–224.

Munnick, Harriet D. "The Ermatinger Brothers: Edward and Francis." In LeRoy R. Hafen, ed., *The Mountain Men and the Fur Trade of the Far West.* 10 vols. Glendale, Cal., 1965–72, 8:157–73.

Murphy, Andrew Lopp. Diary, 1849, MS. Spencer Research Library, University of Kansas, Lawrence.

Murphy, Patrick H. Across the Plains, 1854 diary, typescript. Bancroft Library, University of California, Berkeley.

Murray, Keith A. "The Role of the Hudson's Bay Company in Pacific Northwest History." *Pacific Northwest Quarterly,* 52 (Jan., 1961): 24–31.

Myrick, Elizabeth T. Rankin. Diary, 1854, photocopy of MS. Bancroft Library, University of California, Berkeley.

"Narrative of James Longmire, a Pioneer of 1853." *Washington Historical Quarterly,* 23 (Jan., 1932): 47–60, (Apr., 1932): 138–50.

Nasatir, Abraham P., ed. *A French Journalist in the California Gold Rush: The Letters of Etienne Derbec.* Georgetown, Cal., 1964.

Nash, John D. "The Salmon River Mission of 1855." *Idaho Yesterdays*, 11 (Spring, 1967): 22–31.

Neil, William M. "The Territorial Governor as Indian Superintendent in the Trans-Mississippi West." *Mississippi Valley Historical Review*, 43 (Sept., 1956): 213–37.

Neilson, J. Barry. "On the Plains in 1852." *Oregon Historical Quarterly*, 29 (June, 1928): 209–10.

Nelson, John. Letters, 1851, 1853, photocopies of MSS. Archives and Manuscripts Division, Nebraska State Historical Society, Lincoln.

Nesmith, James W. "Diary of the Emigration of 1843." *Quarterly of the Oregon Historical Society*, 7 (Dec., 1906): 329–59.

———. "The Occasional Address." *Transactions of the Third Annual Re-union of the Oregon Pioneer Association*. Salem, 1876, pp. 42–62.

Nettels, Curtis. "The Overland Mail Issue during the Fifties." *Missouri Historical Review*, 18 (July, 1924): 521–34.

New Helvetia Diary: A Record of Events Kept by John A. Sutter and His Clerks at New Helvetia, California, from September 9, 1845, to May 25, 1848. San Francisco, 1939.

New Orleans *Daily Picayune*, Jan. 1, 1842–June 12, 1849.

New York *Daily Tribune*, Apr. 10, 1841–Dec. 31, 1853.

New York *Herald*, Jan. 1, 1842–Dec. 31, 1852.

New York *Times*, Sept. 18, 1851–Dec. 31, 1860, and scattered issues in 1930, with the aid of the *Times* index.

New York *Working Man's Advocate*, Jan. 1, 1841–Dec. 31, 1846. Titled *Young America!* after Mar. 29, 1845.

Newcomb, Silas. Journal, 1850–51, photocopy of MS. Henry E. Huntington Library, San Marino, Cal.

Newcombe, Alfred W. "Alson J. Streeter—an Agrarian Liberal." *Journal of the Illinois State Historical Society*, 38 (Dec., 1945): 414–45.

Newport, R.I., *Herald of the Times*, Jan. 5, 1843–Dec. 27, 1849.

Newton, Jotham. Diary, 1853, MS. Bancroft Library, University of California, Berkeley.

Nichols, Roger L. "The Army and the Indians, 1800–1830—a Reappraisal: The Missouri Valley Example." *Pacific Historical Review*, 41 (May, 1972): 151–68.

Niles' National Register, vols. 57–65, 1839–49.

Nixon, Oliver W. *How Marcus Whitman Saved Oregon*, 2d ed. Chicago, 1895.

Norton, L. A. "My Overland Trip to California in 1852." *Pony Express Courier*, 1 (Sept., 1934): 10–11, (Oct., 1934): 10–11.

Norton, Maria J. Diary, 1859, photocopy of typescript. Bancroft Library, University of California, Berkeley.

Nunis, Doyce B., Jr. "The Enigma of the Sublette Overland Party, 1845." *Pacific Historical Review*, 28 (Nov., 1959): 331–49.

———, ed. *Josiah Belden: California Overland Pioneer, His Memoir and Early Letters*. Georgetown, Cal., 1962.

Nusbaumer, Louis. Diary, 1849–50, typescript translation. Bancroft Library, University of California, Berkeley.

Oakley, Francile B. "Arkansas' Golden Army of '49." *Arkansas Historical Quarterly*, 6 (Spring, 1947): 1–85.

O'Dea, Thomas F. *The Mormons*. Chicago, 1957.

Oliphant, J. Orin. *On the Cattle Ranges of the Oregon Country*. Seattle, 1968.

———, ed. "Passing of an Immigrant of 1843." *Washington Historical Quarterly*, 15 (July, 1924): 205–10.

Olson, James C., ed. "The Diary of James Mason, Ohio to California, 1850." *Nebraska History*, 33 (June, 1952): 103–21.

"The Oregon." *American Agriculturist*, 3 (Oct., 1844): 325–26.

"Oregon." *Chambers' Edinburgh Journal*, 12 (Mar. 11, 1843): 61–62.

"Oregon." *Niles' National Register*, 65 (Oct. 28, 1843): 138–39.

"Oregon." *Niles' National Register*, 68 (June 14, 1845): 228–29.

"Oregon." *Niles' National Register*, 68 (June 14, 1845): [240].

"Oregon." *Spectator*, 18 (Nov. 22, 1845): 1116.

"Oregon and California." *Niles' National Register*, 70 (July 4, 1846): 281.

"The Oregon Dispute—the Last News from America." *Economist*, 3 (May 17, 1845): 453.

"Oregon Emigrants." *Niles' National Register*, 68 (June 21, 1845): 246.

"The Oregon Fever." *Niles' National Register*, 68 (May 31, 1845): 203.

Oregon Legislative Assembly Council. *Report of the Committee on Military Affairs*, Feb. 3, 1858, with *Supplementary Report*, Jan. 14, 1859.

"The Oregon Question." Reprinted from the

Examiner, n.d., in *Littell's Living Age,* 5 (June 14, 1845): 495–98.

"The Oregon Question." *North American Review,* 62 (Jan., 1846): 214–52.

"The Oregon Territory." *Eclectic Magazine of Foreign Literature, Science, and Art,* 1 (Apr., 1844): 458–69.

"The Oregon Territory." *Economist,* 4 (June 6, 1846): 733–35.

Orvis, Andrew M. Journal, 1849–50, MS and typescript. Beinecke Rare Book and Manuscript Library, Yale University, New Haven.

Oswald, Delmont R. "James P. Beckwourth." In LeRoy R. Hafen, ed., *The Mountain Men and the Fur Trade of the Far West.* 10 vols. Glendale, Cal., 1965–72, 6:37–60.

———, ed. *The Life and Adventures of James P. Beckwourth as Told to Thomas D. Bonner.* Lincoln, Neb., 1972.

"Our City is No Speculative Bubble." *Missouri Historical Review,* 37 (Oct., 1942): 115–16.

"Overland to California." *Ohio Archaeological and Historical Quarterly,* 35 (July, 1926): 567–71.

The Overland Journey of Joseph Francl. San Francisco, 1968.

Owen, East S. Journal, 1852–54, MS. Beinecke Rare Book and Manuscript Library, Yale University, New Haven.

Paden, Irene D. *Prairie Schooner Detours.* New York, 1949.

———. *The Wake of the Prairie Schooner.* New York, 1943.

———, ed. "The Ira J. Willis Guide to the Gold Mines." *California Historical Society Quarterly,* 32 (Sept., 1953): 193–207.

———, ed. *The Journal of Madison Berryman Moorman, 1850–1851.* San Francisco, 1948.

Page, Elizabeth. *Wagons West: A Story of the Oregon Trail.* New York, 1930.

Painesville, Ohio, *Telegraph,* Mar. 1, 1843–Mar. 25, 1846.

Palmer, Joel. *Journal of Travels over the Rocky Mountains; to the Mouth of the Columbia River, Made during the Years 1845 and 1846,* edited by Reuben Gold Thwaites as vol. 30 of *Early Western Travels, 1748–1846.* Cleveland, 1906.

Park, Edmund Botsford Calvin. Letters, 1849, typescripts. Bancroft Library, University of California, Berkeley.

Parker, Inez Eugenia Adams. "Early Recollections of Oregon Pioneer Life." *Transactions of the Fifty-sixth Annual Reunion of the Oregon Pioneer Association for 1928.* Portland, 1933, pp. 17–36.

Parker, Watson. "The Causes of American Gold Rushes." *North Dakota History,* 36 (Fall, 1969): 337–45.

———. "Wading to California: The Influence of the Forty-Niners on the Notion of a Great American Desert." *Great Plains Journal,* 3 (Spring, 1964): 35–43.

Parkes, Henry Bamford. *The United States of America: A History,* 3d ed. New York, 1968.

Parkman, Francis. *The Oregon Trail,* edited by E. N. Feltskog. Madison, Wis., 1969.

Parrish, Edward Evans. "Crossing the Plains in 1844." *Transactions of the Sixteenth Annual Reunion of the Oregon Pioneer Association for 1888.* Portland, 1889, 82–122.

Partoll, Albert J., ed. "Mengarini's Narrative of the Rockies." *Frontier and Midland,* 18 (Spring, 1938): 193–202.

Paul, Rodman W. "An Interpretation of California's Golden Era." *The Westerners Brand Book, Los Angeles Corral, 1948.* Los Angeles, 1949, pp. 27–31.

———. "The Mormons as a Theme in Western Historical Writing." *Journal of American History,* 54 (Dec., 1967): 511–23.

Paxson, Frederic L. *History of the American Frontier, 1763–1893.* Boston, 1924.

———, ed. "T. Turnbull's Travels from the United States across the Plains to California." *Proceedings of the State Historical Society of Wisconsin at Its Sixty-first Annual Meeting, 1913.* Madison, 1914, pp. 151–225.

Payne, James A. Saint Louis to San Francisco: Being an Account of a Journey across the Plains in 1850, Together with My Experience in Steamboating on the California Rivers until the Fall of 1853, typescript diary. Archives and Manuscripts Division, Ohio State Historical Society, Columbus.

Pearson, Gustavus C. *Overland in 1849,* edited by Jessie H. Goodman. Los Angeles, 1961.

Pease, David E. Diary, 1849–50, typescript. Archives and Manuscripts Division, Nebraska State Historical Society, Lincoln.

Peltier, Jerome. "Moses 'Black' Harris." In LeRoy R. Hafen, ed., *The Mountain Men and the Fur Trade of the Far West.* 10 vols. Glendale, Cal., 1965–72, 4:103–17.

———. "The Ward Massacre." *Pacific Northwesterner,* Spokane Corral, 9 (Winter, 1965): 12–16.

Pengra, Charlotte Emily Stearns. Diary, 1853. Eugene, Ore., n.d., reproduced by Lane County Pioneer-Historical Society. Bancroft Library, University of California, Berkeley.

Penrose, S. B. L. "The Wagon Train of 1843—Its Dual Significance." *Oregon Historical Quarterly,* 44 (Dec., 1943): 361–69.

Perez-Venero, Alejandro. "The 'Forty-Niners through Panama." *Journal of the West,* 11 (July, 1972): 460–69.

Perkins, Dexter, and Glyndon G. Van Deusen. *The United States of America: A History,* 2d ed. 2 vols. New York, 1968.

Pettijohn, Isaac. Diary, 1847, MS. Bancroft Library, University of California, Berkeley.

Philadelphia *United States Gazette,* scattered issues, 1842–47.

Phillips, Paul C., ed. "'Dick's Works,' an Overland Journey to California in 1852: The Journal of Richard Owen Hickman." *Frontier,* 9 (Mar., 1929): 242–60.

———, ed. *Forty Years on the Frontier, as Seen in the Journals and Reminiscences of Granville Stuart; Gold-Miner, Trader, Merchant, Rancher and Politician.* 2 vols. Cleveland, 1925; Glendale, Cal., 1957.

Piercy, Frederick Hawkins. *Route from Liverpool to Great Salt Lake Valley,* edited by Fawn M. Brodie. Cambridge, Mass., 1962.

Pipes, Nellie Bowden, trans. "Extract from Exploration of the Oregon Territory, the Californias, and the Gulf of California, Undertaken during the Years 1840, 1841 and 1842, by Eugene Duflot de Mofras." *Quarterly of the Oregon Historical Society,* 26 (June, 1925): 151–90.

Platt, Philip L., and Nelson Slater. *Travelers' Guide across the Plains upon the Overland Route to California.* San Francisco, 1963; reprint of 1852 ed.

Pomeroy, Earl. *The Pacific Slope: A History of California, Oregon, Washington, Idaho, Utah, and Nevada.* New York, 1965.

———. "Toward a Reorientation of Western History: Continuity and Environment." *Mississippi Valley Historical Review,* 41 (Mar., 1955): 579–600.

Pomfret, John E., ed. *California Gold Rush Voyages, 1848–1849: Three Original Narratives.* San Marino, Cal., 1954.

Pomroy, Horace Barton. Diary and Account Book, 1850, photocopy of MS. Bancroft Library, University of California, Berkeley.

Population of the United States in 1860; Compiled from the Original Returns of the Eighth Census, under the Direction of the Secretary of the Interior, by Joseph C. G. Kennedy, Superintendent of Census. Washington, 1864.

Portland *Oregonian,* Dec. 4, 1850–Dec. 29, 1860.

"Post Sutlers at Fort Laramie Nebraska Territory." *Annals of Wyoming,* 4 (Oct., 1926): 318.

Potter, David Morris, ed. *Trail to California: The Overland Journal of Vincent Geiger and Wakeman Bryarly.* New Haven, 1945.

Powell, Fred Wilbur, ed. *Hall J. Kelley on Oregon.* Princeton, 1932.

Powell, John W. Diary, 1859, typescript. Bancroft Library, University of California, Berkeley.

Powers, Mary Rockwood. "A Woman's Overland Journal to California." *Amateur Book Collector,* 1 (Sept., 1950): 1–2, (Oct., 1950): 1–2, (Nov., 1950): 6, (Dec., 1950): 11–12, (Jan., 1951): 5–6.

Powers, Ramon, and Gene Younger. "Cholera on the Overland Trails, 1832–1869." *Kansas Quarterly,* 5 (Spring, 1973): 32–49.

Pratt, Harry E., ed. "Diary of a Pike's Peak Gold Seeker in 1860." *Colorado Magazine,* 14 (Nov., 1937): 201–19.

Preuss, Charles. *Exploring with Frémont: The Private Diaries of Charles Preuss, Cartographer for John C. Frémont on His First, Second, and Fourth Expeditions to the Far West,* translated and edited by Erwin G. Gudde and Elisabeth K. Gudde. Norman, 1958.

Price, Glenn, ed. "From Hannibal to the Gold Fields in 1849: The Reminiscences of Charles C. Brady." *Pacific Historian,* 4 (Nov., 1960): 145–52; "Part II," 5 (Feb., 1961): 5–14; "Part III" (May, 1961): 77–83.

Prichet, John. Diary, 1849–51, microfilm of typescript. Bancroft Library, University of California, Berkeley.

Prosch, Thomas W., ed. "Diary of Dr. David S. Maynard while Crossing the Plains in 1850." *Washington Historical Quarterly,* 1 (Oct., 1906): 50–62.

Prucha, Francis Paul. "American Indian Policy in the 1840s: Visions of Reform." In John G. Clark, ed., *The Frontier Challenge:*

Responses to the Trans-Mississippi West. Lawrence, Kan., 1971, pp. 81–110.

———. *The Sword of the Republic: The United States Army on the Frontier, 1783–1846.* New York, 1969.

Publications of the Nebraska State Historical Society, 20 (Lincoln, 1922): entire volume.

Quaife, Milo Milton, ed. *The Diary of James K. Polk during His Presidency, 1845 to 1849.* 4 vols. Chicago, 1910.

———, ed. *Kit Carson's Autobiography.* Chicago, 1935.

Ramsdell, T. M. "Reminiscences." *Transactions of the Twenty-fourth Annual Reunion of the Oregon Pioneer Association for 1896.* Portland, 1897, pp. 108–12.

Rawling, Gerald. "The Oregon Trail." *History Today,* 11 (Nov., 1961): 743–52.

Rea, J. "Seeing the Elephant." *Western Folklore,* 28 (Jan., 1969): 21–26.

Read, Georgia Willis. "Diseases, Drugs, and Doctors on the Oregon-California Trail in the Gold-Rush Years." *Missouri Historical Review,* 38 (Apr., 1944): 260–76.

———. "Women and Children on the Oregon-California Trail in the Gold-Rush Years." *Missouri Historical Review,* 39 (Oct., 1944): 1–23.

———, ed. *A Pioneer of 1850: George Willis Read, 1819–1880.* Boston, 1927.

———, and Ruth Gaines, eds. *Gold Rush: The Journals, Drawings, and Other Papers of J. Goldsborough Bruff.* 2 vols. New York, 1944.

"A Record Trip from California to Missouri." *Missouri Historical Review,* 24 (July, 1930): 608.

Rees, Willard H. "Quotations from the Journal and Register." *Constitution and Quotations from the Register of the Oregon Pioneer Association.* Salem, 1875, pp. 7–14.

"Reminiscences of Honorable John Minto, Pioneer of 1844." *Quarterly of the Oregon Historical Society,* 2 (June, 1901): 119–67; "Reminiscences of Experiences on the Oregon Trail in 1844—II" (Sept., 1901): 209–54.

"Reminiscences of Washington Smith Gilliam." *Transactions of the Thirty-first Annual Reunion of the Oregon Pioneer Association for 1903.* Portland, 1904, pp. 202–20.

Remy, Jules, and Julius Brenchley. *A Journey to Great-Salt-Lake City.* 2 vols. London, 1861.

"Report of Lieutenant Neil M. Howison on Oregon, 1846." *Quarterly of the Oregon Historical Society,* 14 (Mar., 1913): 1–60.

Review of Josiah T. Marshall, *The Farmer and Emigrant's Hand Book. American Review,* 2 (Sept., 1845): 326.

Reynolds, Sidney O. "The Redskin Who Saved the White Man's Hide." *American Heritage,* 11 (Feb., 1960): 50–55, 108–11.

Rhodes, James Ford. *History of the United States from the Compromise of 1850 to the McKinley-Bryan Campaign of 1896,* new ed. 8 vols. New York, 1920.

Rhodes, Richard. *The Ungodly: A Novel of the Donner Party.* New York, 1973.

Rice, William B. "Early Freighting on the Salt Lake–San Bernardino Trail." *Pacific Historical Review,* 11 (Mar., 1942): 73–80.

Rich, E. E., ed. *The Letters of John McLoughlin from Fort Vancouver to the Governor and the Committee: Second Series, 1839–44.* Toronto, 1943.

———, ed. *The Letters of John McLoughlin from Fort Vancouver to the Governor and the Committee: Third Series, 1844–46.* Toronto, 1944.

Richards, Kent D. "Washoe Territory: Rudimentary Government in Nevada." *Arizona and the West,* 11 (Autumn, 1969): 213–32.

Richardson, Caroline. Journal, 1852, MS. Bancroft Library, University of California, Berkeley.

Richardson, James D., comp. *A Compilation of the Messages and Papers of the Presidents, 1789–1902.* 10 vols. Washington, 1903.

Richardson, William H. "The Argonauts of Jersey City." *Proceedings of the New Jersey Historical Society,* 11 (Apr., 1926): 170–86, (July, 1926): 369–77, (Oct., 1926): 525–31.

"Richey Family Record: 1707–1907." *Transactions of the 40th Annual Reunion of the Oregon Pioneer Association, Portland, June 20, 1912.* Portland, 1915, pp. 586–622.

Richmond, Robert W. "Development along the Overland Trail from the Missouri River to Fort Laramie, before 1854." *Nebraska History,* 33 (Sept., 1952): 154–79; "II, The Mormon Trail" (Dec., 1952): 237–47.

———, and Robert W. Mardock. *A Nation Moving West: Readings in the History of the American Frontier.* Lincoln, 1966.

Ridge, Martin, and Ray Allen Billington, eds. *America's Frontier Story: A Documentary History of Westward Expansion.* New York, 1969.

Riegel, Robert E., and Robert G. Athearn. *America Moves West*, 5th ed. New York, 1971.

Riker, John F. *Journal of a Trip to California by the Overland Route.* [Urbana, Ohio, 1855?]

"Robert Robe's Diary while Crossing the Plains in 1851." *Washington Historical Quarterly*, 19 (Jan., 1928): 52–63.

Robertson, Frank C. *Fort Hall: Gateway to the Oregon Country.* New York, 1963.

Robertson, James R. "Reminiscences of Alanson Hinman." *Quarterly of the Oregon Historical Society*, 2 (Sept., 1901): 266–86.

Rockwood, E. Ruth, ed. "Letters of Charles Stevens." *Oregon Historical Quarterly*, 37 (June, 1936): 137–59.

Root, George A. "Ferries in Kansas: Part I—Missouri River." *Kansas Historical Quarterly*, 2 (Feb., 1933): 3–28; "Part I—Missouri River—Continued" (May, 1933): 115–38; "Part II—Kansas River" (Aug., 1933): 251–93; "Part II—Kansas River—Continued" (Nov., 1933): 343–76; "Part II—Kansas River—Concluded," 3 (Feb., 1934): 15–42; "Part III—Blue River" (May, 1934): 115–44; "Part XII—Marmaton River, Part XIII—Wakarusa Creek, Part XIV—Turkey Creek," 6 (Feb., 1937): 14–20.

———, and Russell K. Hickman. "Pike's Peak Express Companies: Part III—The Platte Route." *Kansas Historical Quarterly*, 13 (Nov., 1945): 485–526; "Part IV—The Platte Route—Concluded," 14 (Feb., 1946): 36–92.

Root, Riley. *Journal of Travels from St. Josephs to Oregon.* Galesburg, Ill., 1850.

Roseboom, Eugene H., ed. "Charles Tinker's Journal: A Trip to California in 1849." *Ohio State Archaeological and Historical Quarterly*, 61 (Jan., 1952): 64–85.

Roske, Ralph J. "The World Impact of the California Gold Rush, 1849–1857." *Arizona and the West*, 5 (Autumn, 1963): 187–232.

Ross, Earle D. "Horace Greeley and the West." *Mississippi Valley Historical Review*, 20 (June, 1933): 63–74.

Ross, Edith Connelley. "The Old Shawnee Mission." *Collections of the Kansas State Historical Society*, *1926–1928*, 17 (1928): 417–35.

Rothwell, William Renfro. Journal and Letters, 1850, MSS and typescripts. Beinecke Rare Book and Manuscript Library, Yale University, New Haven.

Rounds, Glen. *The Prairie Schooners.* New York, 1968.

"The Route to California." *American Review*, 2 (Aug., 1848): 204–12.

Royce, Sarah Eleanor Bayliss. *A Frontier Lady: Recollections of the Gold Rush and Early California,* edited by Ralph Henry Gabriel. New Haven, 1932.

Rucker, Maude Applegate. *The Oregon Trail and Some of Its Blazers.* New York, 1930.

Russel, Robert R. "The Pacific Railway Issue in Politics prior to the Civil War." *Mississippi Valley Historical Review*, 12 (Sept., 1925): 187–201.

Russell, Don. "How Many Indians Were Killed? White Man versus Red Man: The Facts and the Legend." *American West*, 10 (July, 1973): 42–47, 61–63.

Ryan, John P. "Sonora Trail and Sonora Pass of 1853." *Pony Express*, 22 (Jan., 1956): 11–12, (Feb., 1956): 10–12.

Rydell, Raymond A. "The Cape Horn Route to California, 1849." *Pacific Historical Review*, 17 (May, 1941): 149–63.

St. Joseph *Gazette*, Apr. 25, 1845–Oct. 4, 1854.

St. Louis *Missouri Republican*, Jan. 1, 1840–Dec. 31, 1851, Jan. 1–Dec. 31, 1855, scattered issues in 1856, June 1–Dec. 31, 1858.

Salt Lake City *Deseret News*, June 15, 1850–June 25, 1856.

San Francisco *Alta California*, Jan. 4, 1849–Dec. 13, 1855.

San Francisco *California Star*, Jan. 9, 1847–Dec. 23, 1848. Titled *California Star and Californian* after Nov. 18, 1848; originally published in Yerba Buena.

San Francisco *Daily Herald*, scattered issues in 1855.

Sanford, Mary Fetter Hite. A Trip across the Plains, 1853, typescript recollections. California Section, California State Library, Sacramento.

Santee, J. F., ed. "Letters of John R. Tice." *Oregon Historical Quarterly*, 37 (Mar., 1936): 24–44.

Saum, Lewis O. *The Fur Trader and the Indian.* Seattle, 1965.

Sawyer, Lorenzo. *Way Sketches: Containing Incidents of Travel across the Plains,* edited by Edward Eberstadt. New York, 1926.

Sawyer, Mrs. Francis H. Journal, 1852, typescript. Bancroft Library, University of California, Berkeley.

Scamehorn, Howard L., ed. *The Buckeye Rovers in the Gold Rush.* Athens, Ohio, 1965.

Schafer, Joseph. "Notes on the Colonization of Oregon." *Quarterly of the Oregon Historical Society*, 6 (Dec., 1905): 379–90.

———, ed. *California Letters of Lucius Fairchild*, vol. 31 of Wisconsin Historical Publications *Collections*. Madison, 1931.

Schnell, J. Christopher. "William Gilpin and the Destruction of the Desert Myth." *Colorado Magazine*, 46 (Spring, 1969): 131–44.

Schouler, James. *History of the United States of America, under the Constitution*, rev. ed. 7 vols. New York, 1904.

Schroeder, John H. "Rep. John Floyd, 1817–1829: Harbinger of Oregon Territory." *Oregon Historical Quarterly*, 70 (Dec., 1969): 333–46.

Schusky, Ernest L. "The Upper Missouri Indian Agency, 1819–1868." *Missouri Historical Review*, 65 (Apr., 1971): 249–69.

Scott, Leslie M. "Influence of American Settlement upon the Oregon Boundary Treaty of 1846." *Oregon Historical Quarterly*, 29 (Mar., 1928): 1–19.

———, ed. "Report of Lieutenant Peel on Oregon in 1845–46." *Oregon Historical Quarterly*, 29 (Mar., 1928): 51–76.

Searls, Niles. *The Diary of a Pioneer and Other Papers*. San Francisco, 1940.

Sedgley, Joseph. *Overland to California in 1849*. Oakland, 1877.

Senter, Riley. *Crossing the Continent to California Gold Fields*. Exeter, Cal., 1938.

Serven, James Edsall. "The Ill-Fated '49er Wagon Train." *Historical Society of Southern California Quarterly*, 42 (Mar., 1960): 29–40.

Settle, Raymond W. The Role of Russell, Majors & Waddell in Western Overland Transportation." In Robert G. Ferris, ed., *The American West: An Appraisal*. Santa Fe, 1963, pp. 81–88.

———, ed. *The March of the Mounted Riflemen*. Glendale, Cal., 1940.

"Settlement of the Oregon Controversy by Arbitration." *Spectator*, 19 (Jan. 10, 1846): 35.

"Seventh Annual Reunion." *Transactions of the Seventh Annual Re-union of the Oregon Pioneer Association; for 1879*. Salem, 1880, pp. 7–14.

The Seventh Census of the United States: 1850. An Appendix, Embracing Notes upon the Tables of Each of the States, etc. J. D. B. De Bow, Superintendent of the United States Census. Washington, 1853.

Shafer, Gladys. "Eastward Ho! Ezra Meeker Memorializes the Oregon Trail, 1905–1910." *American West*, 5 (Nov., 1968): 42–49.

Shaffer, Leslie L. D. "The Management of Organized Wagon Trains on the Overland Trail." *Missouri Historical Review*, 55 (July, 1961): 355–65.

Sharp, Robert L. Agreement and Diary, 1852, MSS. Archives and Manuscripts Division, Ohio State Historical Society, Columbus.

Shaw, D. A. *Eldorado, or California as Seen by a Pioneer, 1850–1900*. Los Angeles, 1900.

Shaw, Reuben Cole. *Across the Plains in Forty-Nine*, edited by Milo Milton Quaife. Chicago, 1948; reprint of 1896 ed.

Shepherd, J. S. *Journal of Travel across the Plains to California and Guide to the Future Emigrant*. N.p., 1945; reprint of 1851 ed.

Sherman, Henry. "The Oregon Territory." *Hunt's Merchants' Magazine*, 6 (Apr., 1842): 306–19.

Shields, James G. Journal, 1850, MS and typescript. Beinecke Rare Book and Manuscript Library, Yale University, New Haven.

"The Shively Guide." In Dale L. Morgan, ed., *Overland in 1846: Diaries and Letters of the California-Oregon Trail*. 2 vols. Georgetown, Cal., 1963, 2:734–42.

"The Shoemaker Diary of 1850." *Two Argonauts on the Oregon Trail*. [Menlo Park, Cal., 1961?]

Shombre, Henry J. Diary, 1849, MS and typescript. Archives and Manuscripts Division, Kansas State Historical Society, Topeka.

Shortess, Robert. "First Emigrants to Oregon." *Transactions of the Twenty-fourth Annual Reunion of the Oregon Pioneer Association for 1896*. Portland, 1897, pp. 92–107.

Simon, John E. "Wilhelm Keil and Communist Colonies." *Oregon Historical Quarterly*, 36 (June, 1935): 119–53.

Simon, John Y., ed. *The Papers of Ulysses S. Grant, Volume I: 1837–1861*. Carbondale, Ill., 1967.

Skaggs, Jimmy M. "Northward across the Plains: The Western Cattle Trail." *Great Plains Journal*, 12 (Fall, 1972): 52–68.

"Sketch of Mrs. Susan P. Angell, a Pioneer of 1852." *Transactions of the Fifty-sixth Annual Reunion of the Oregon Pioneer Association for 1928*. Portland, 1933, pp. 55–56.

Skinner, Hugh Alexander. Diary, 1850–51, MS. Spencer Research Library, University of Kansas, Lawrence.

Slater, Nelson. *Fruits of Mormonism; or A Fair and Candid Statement of Facts Illustrative of Mormon Principles, Mormon Policy, and Mormon Character, by More than Forty Eye-witnesses.* Coloma, Cal., 1851 (photocopy reprint).

Smith, Arthur D. Howden, ed. *The Narrative of Samuel Hancock, 1845–1860.* New York, 1927.

Smith, Charles W. *Journal of a Trip to California,* edited by R. W. G. Vail. New York, n.d.

Smith, Duane Allen. "The Army and Western Transportation, 1824–1851." *1959 Brand Book of the Denver Posse of The Westerners.* Boulder, 1960, pp. 279–308.

Smith, Henry Nash. *Virgin Land: The American West as Symbol and Myth.* New York, 1950.

Smith, Jedediah, and William Jedediah Jones. Letters, 1854–56, MSS. Smith-Jones Family Papers, Bancroft Library, University of California, Berkeley.

Smith, John. Diary, 1853, MS. Henry E. Huntington Library, San Marino, Cal.

Snelling, W. J. "Oregon Territory." *New England Magazine,* 2 (Feb., 1832); reprinted in Archer Butler Hulbert, ed., *The Call of the Columbia: Iron Men and Saints Take the Oregon Trail,* vol. 4 of *Overland to the Pacific.* Denver, 1934.

Snodgrass, R. H. P. Journal, 1852, MS and typescript. Beinecke Rare Book and Manuscript Library, Yale University, New Haven.

Snyder, John F. Letter, 1850, photocopy of MS. Archives and Manuscripts Division, Kansas State Historical Society, Topeka.

"The Society of California Pioneers: A Brief Resume of Its History and Purpose." *Publication of the Society of California Pioneers for 1942.* San Francisco, 1942, pp. 25–27.

Spear, Donald P. "The Sutler in the Union Army." *Civil War History,* 16 (June, 1970): 121–38.

Spence, Clark C., ed. *The American West: A Source Book.* New York, 1966.

Spencer, Lafayette. "Journal of the Oregon Trail." *Annals of Iowa,* 8 (Jan., 1908): 304–10.

Spooner, E. A. Diary, 1849–50, microfilm of MS. Archives and Manuscripts Division, Kansas State Historical Society, Topeka.

Sprague, Charles A. "Willamette Highway—the Seventh across the High Cascades." *Oregon Historical Quarterly,* 41 (Sept., 1940): 243–49.

Springfield, Mo., *Advertiser,* May 21, 1844–Feb. 28, 1846.

Staats, Stephen. "The Occasional Address." *Transactions of the Fifth Annual Re-union of the Oregon Pioneer Association; for 1877.* Salem, 1878, pp. 46–59.

Stackpole, William T. Journal, 1849, MS. Beinecke Rare Book and Manuscript Library, Yale University, New Haven.

Stansbury, Howard. *Exploration and Survey of the Valley of the Great Salt Lake of Utah.* Washington, 1853.

Stanton, Phebe. "On the Plains." *Transactions of the 40th Annual Reunion of the Oregon Pioneer Association, Portland, June 20, 1912.* Portland, 1915, pp. 622–25.

Stark, William. Letter, 1853, typescript. Typescript Collection, State Historical Society of Missouri, Columbia.

Starr, Franklin. Diary, 1849, microfilm of MS. Bancroft Library, University of California, Berkeley.

Starr, Kevin. *Americans and the California Dream, 1850–1915.* New York, 1973.

The Statutes at Large and Treaties of the United States of America, vol. 9. Boston, 1851.

Steck, Amos. Diary, 1849, MS and typescript. Archives and Manuscripts Division, Colorado State Historical Society, Denver.

Steckmesser, Kent Ladd. *The Westward Movement: A Short History.* New York, 1969.

Steele, Harriet. "Gold Rush Letters." *Pacific Historian,* 8 (Feb., 1964): 43–52.

Steele, John. *Across the Plains in 1850,* edited by Joseph Schafer. Chicago, 1930.

Stegner, Wallace. *The Gathering of Zion: The Story of the Mormon Trail.* New York, 1964.

Stewart, Agnes. Diary, 1853. Eugene, Ore., 1959, reproduced by Lane County Pioneer-Historical Society. Bancroft Library, University of California, Berkeley.

Stewart, George R. *The California Trail: An Epic with Many Heroes.* New York, 1962.

———. *Ordeal by Hunger: The Story of the Donner Party,* new ed. Boston, 1960.

———. "The Prairie Schooner Got Them There." *American Heritage,* 13 (Feb., 1962): 4–17, 98–102.

———, ed. *The Opening of the California Trail.* Berkeley, 1953.

Stewart, Helen. Diary, 1853. Eugene, Ore., 1961, reproduced by Lane County Pioneer-Historical Society. Bancroft Library, University of California, Berkeley.

Stimson, Fancher. "Overland Journey to California by Platte River Route and

South Pass in 1850." *Annals of Iowa,* 13 (Oct., 1922): 403–40.

Stine, Henry Atkinson. Letters and Journal, 1850, typescripts. California Section, California State Library, Sacramento.

Stitzel, Jacob. Diary, 1849, microfilm of MS. Bancroft Library, University of California, Berkeley.

Stone, Buena Cobb. "Southern Route into Oregon: Notes and a New Map." *Oregon Historical Quarterly,* 47 (June, 1946): 135–54.

Stuart, Joseph Alonzo. *My Roving Life.* 2 vols. Auburn, Cal., 1895.

Stuart, Reginald R., and Grace D. Stuart, eds. "Calvin B. West of the Umpqua." *Pacific Historian,* 4 (May, 1960): 48–57, (Aug., 1960): 87–96, 112.

Swartzlow, Ruby Johnson. "Peter Lassen, Northern California's Trail-Blazer." *California Historical Society Quarterly,* 18 (Dec., 1939): 291–314.

T., Dr. Diary, 1849, ink copy of MS. Bancroft Library, University of California, Berkeley.

Taggart, Harold F., ed. "The Journal of David Jackson Staples." *California Historical Society Quarterly,* 20 (June, 1943): 119–50.

Tamony, Peter. " 'To See the Elephant.' " *Pacific Historian,* 12 (Winter, 1968): 23–29.

"Third Annual Reunion." *Transactions of the Third Annual Re-union of the Oregon Pioneer Association.* Salem, 1876, pp. 7–13.

Thissell, G. W. *Crossing the Plains in '49.* Oakland, 1903.

Thomas, Robert. "Buckeye Argonauts." *Ohio State Archaeological and Historical Quarterly,* 59 (July, 1950): 256–69.

Thomasson, A. H. Diary, 1850, typescript. California Section, California State Library, Sacramento.

Thomson, Origen. *Crossing the Plains, Narrative of the Scenes, Incidents and Adventures Attending the Overland Journey.* Greensburg, Ind., 1896.

Thoreau, Henry D. *The Works of Henry D. Thoreau.* 5 vols. New York, 1908–13.

Thornton, Jessy Quinn. "Occasional Address." *Transactions of the Sixth Annual Re-union of the Oregon Pioneer Association for 1878.* Salem, 1879, pp. 29–71.

———. *Oregon and California in 1848.* 2 vols. New York, 1849.

Throne, Mildred, ed. "Letters of a Forty-

Niner." *Iowa Journal of History,* 47 (Jan., 1949): 63–77.

Thurber, Albert King. Journal, 1849, typescript. Bancroft Library, University of California, Berkeley.

Tiffany, P. C. Journal, 1849–51, MS and typescript. Beinecke Rare Book and Manuscript Library, Yale University, New Haven, Conn.

Tobie, Harvey E. "From the Missouri to the Columbia, 1841." *Oregon Historical Quarterly,* 38 (June, 1937): 135–59.

———. "George Wood Ebbert." In LeRoy R. Hafen, ed., *The Mountain Men and the Fur Trade of the Far West.* 10 vols. Glendale, Cal., 1965–72, 4:83–96.

———. "Joseph L. Meek." In LeRoy R. Hafen, ed., *The Mountain Men and the Fur Trade of the Far West.* 10 vols. Glendale, Cal., 1965–72, 1:313–35.

———. "Stephen Hall Meek." In LeRoy R. Hafen, ed., *The Mountain Men and the Fur Trade of the Far West.* 10 vols. Glendale, Cal., 1965–72, 2:225–40.

Tolles, James S. Diary, 1849–50, typescript. California Section, California State Library, Sacramento.

Tompkins, Edward Alexander. Narrative, 1850, photocopy of diary MS. Henry E. Huntington Library, San Marino, Cal.

Trenholm, Virginia Cole, and Maurine Carley. *The Shoshonis: Sentinels of the Rockies.* Norman, 1964.

Troxel, Kathryn. "Food of the Overland Emigrants." *Oregon Historical Quarterly,* 56 (Mar., 1955): 12–26.

Turner, Charles W., ed. "Reuben Knox Letters, 1849–1851." *North Carolina Historical Review,* 37 (Jan., 1960): 66–93; "Part II" (Apr., 1960): 243–70; [Concluded] (July, 1960): 397–418.

Tuttle, Charles Albion. Letters, 1849, MSS and typescripts. Bancroft Library, University of California, Berkeley.

Twiss, Travers. *The Oregon Question Examined.* London, 1846.

Udell, John. *Incidents of Travel to California, across the Great Plains.* Jefferson, Ohio, 1856.

U.S. Congress. *Annals of Congress.* 16 Cong., 1 Sess.–17 Cong., 2 Sess., 1820–23.

———. *Congressional Globe.* 26 Cong., 2 Sess.–32 Cong., 1 Sess., 1840–52; 35 Cong., 1 Sess., 1858.

———. *Memorial of Henry O'Reilly.* Senate

Misc. Doc. 67, Ser. 629, 32 Cong., 1 Sess. Washington, 1852.

———. *Petition of a Number of Citizens of Indiana, Praying the Occupation and Settlement of the Oregon Territory, and the Construction of a Road Thereto; and Remonstrating against the Construction of the Proposed Ship-Canal across the Isthmus of Darien.* Senate Pub. Doc. 244, Ser. 358, 26 Cong., 1 Sess. Washington, 1840.

———. *Petition of a Number of Citizens of Kentucky, Praying the Adoption of Measures to Promote the Settlement of the Oregon Territory.* Senate Pub. Doc. 172, Ser. 357, 26 Cong., 1 Sess. Washington, 1840.

———. *Petition of a Number of the Citizens of the State of Missouri, Praying a Donation of Land to Settlers in the Oregon Territory.* Senate Pub. Doc. 40, Ser. 355, 26 Cong., 1 Sess. Washington, 1840.

———. *Protection Afforded by Volunteers of Oregon and Washington Territories to Overland Immigrants in 1854.* House Misc. Doc. 47, Ser. 1016, 35 Cong., 2 Sess. Washington, 1859.

———. *Resolution of the Legislature of California, for the Relief of Captain William Waldo, Charles N. Hall, and J. J. Petrie.* Senate Misc. Doc. 21, Ser. 629, 32 Cong., 1 Sess. Washington, 1852.

———. *Resolutions of the Legislature of California, Recommending the Payment of a Debt Incurred by the City of Sacramento, in Providing for the Sick and the Burial of Deceased Emigrants to That City.* Senate Misc. Doc. 23, Ser. 629, 32 Cong., 1 Sess. Washington, 1852.

———, Committee on Military Affairs. *Military Posts on the Route to Oregon, Dec. 31, 1845.* House Report 13, Ser. 488, 29 Cong., 1 Sess., 1858.

U.S. Department of the Interior. *Depredations and Massacre by the Snake River Indians.* House Ex. Doc. 46, Ser. 1099, 36 Cong., 2 Sess. Washington, 1861.

———. *Indian Councils.* Senate Ex. Doc. 35, Ser. 1031, 36 Cong., 1 Sess. Washington, 1860.

———. *Report of the Chief Engineer.* House Ex. Doc. 5, Ser. 569, 31 Cong., 1 Sess. Washington, 1849.

———. *Report upon the Pacific Wagon Roads.* Senate Ex. Doc. 36, Ser. 984, 35 Cong., 2 Sess. Washington, 1859.

———. *Reports of the Commissioner of Indian Affairs, 1849–60, 1863.* 31 Cong., 1 Sess.–36 Cong., 2 Sess., 38 Cong., 1 Sess.

U.S. Department of War. *Report from the Secretary of War, in Compliance with a Resolution of the Senate, in Relation to the Establishment of a Line of Military Posts from the Missouri to the Oregon or Columbia River.* Senate Doc. 231, Ser. 358, 26 Cong., 1 Sess. Washington, 1840.

———. *Indian Depredations in Oregon and Washington.* House Ex. Doc. 29, Ser. 1097, 36 Cong., 2 Sess. Washington, 1861.

———. *Reports of the Commissioner of Indian Affairs, 1840–48.* 26 Cong., 1 Sess.–30 Cong., 2 Sess.

———. *Reports of the Secretary of War, 1840–60.* 26 Cong., 1 Sess.–36 Cong., 2 Sess.

U.S. President. *Gen Smith's Correspondence, California.* Senate Ex. Doc. 52, Ser. 561, 31 Cong., 1 Sess. Washington, 1850.

———. *Indian Disturbances in California.* Senate Ex. Doc. 26, Ser. 819, 34 Cong., 1 Sess. Washington, 1856.

———. *Massacre at Mountain Meadows.* Senate Ex. Doc. 42, Ser. 1033, 36 Cong., 1 Sess. Washington, 1860.

———. *Message from the President of the United States, in Answer to a Resolution of the Senate Relative to the British Establishments on the Columbia, and the State of the Fur Trade, &c.* Pub. Doc. 39, Ser. 203, 21 Cong., 2 Sess. Washington, 1831.

———. *Message from the President of the United States to the Two Houses of Congress, Dec. 2, 1845.* House Ex. Doc. 2, Ser. 480, 29 Cong., 1 Sess. Washington, 1845.

Urbanek, Mae. "1852 on the Oregon Trail." *Annals of Wyoming,* 34 (Apr., 1962): 52–59.

Utley, Robert M. *Frontiersmen in Blue: The United States Army and the Indian, 1848–1865.* New York, 1967.

Vail, R. W. G. "Gold Fever: A Catalogue of the California Gold Rush Centennial Exhibition." *New York Historical Society Quarterly,* 33 (Oct., 1949): 237–71.

Van Every, Dale. *The Final Challenge: The American Frontier, 1804–1845.* New York, 1964.

"Van Ogle's Memory of Pioneer Days." *Washington Historical Quarterly,* 13 (Oct., 1922): 269–81.

Van Trump, James D., and Alfred D. Reid, Jr., eds. "A California Gold Rush Letter from Bernard J. Reid." *Western Pennsylvania Historical Magazine,* 44 (Sept., 1961): 217–35.

Vasquez, Hiram. "Experiences at Fort

Bridger, with the Shoshones and in Early Colorado." *Colorado Magazine*, 8 (May, 1931): 106–8.

Verdenal, John M. Journal, 1852, typescript. Bancroft Library, University of California, Berkeley.

Victor, Frances Fuller. "The First Oregon Cavalry." *Quarterly of the Oregon Historical Society*, 3 (June, 1902): 123–63.

Wade, Mason, ed. *The Journals of Francis Parkman*. 2 vols. New York, 1947.

Walker, Ardis M. "Joseph R. Walker." In LeRoy R. Hafen, ed., *The Mountain Men and the Fur Trade of the Far West*. 10 vols. Glendale, Cal., 1965–72, 5:361–80.

Walker, Henry Pickering. *The Wagonmasters: High Plains Freighting from the Earliest Days of the Santa Fe Trail to 1880*. Norman, 1966.

Walters, Everett, and George B. Strother, eds. "The Gold Rush Diary of Henry Tappan." *Annals of Wyoming*, 25 (July, 1953): 113–39.

The War of the Rebellion: A Compilation of the Official Records of the Union and Confederate Armies, Series I, Vol. L, Part I. Washington, 1897.

Ward, Harriet S. Diary, 1853, MS. Henry E. Huntington Library, San Marino, Cal.

Wardell, M. L. "Oregon Immigration prior to 1846." *Quarterly of the Oregon Historical Society*, 27 (Mar., 1926): 41–64.

Ware, Joseph E. *The Emigrants' Guide to California*, edited by John Caughey. Princeton, 1932.

Warner, Mildred. "Indians Challenge the Nebraska Territorial Government: I." *Great Plains Journal*, 9 (Spring, 1970): 53–58.

Washington, D.C., *Daily Union*, scattered issues, 1845–53.

Washington, D.C., *National Intelligencer*, Nov. 1, 1843–Dec. 31, 1850.

Waters, Lydia Milner. "Account of a Trip across the Plains in 1855." *Quarterly of the Society of California Pioneers*, 6 (June, 1929): 59–79.

Watkins, Albert. "History of Fort Kearny." *Collections of the Nebraska State Historical Society*, 16 (1911): 227–67.

Watkins, T. H. "The Revoloidal Spindle and the Wondrous Avitor." *American West*, 4 (Feb., 1967): 24–27, 69–70.

Watson, William J. *Journal of an Overland Journey to Oregon, Made in the Year 1849*. Jacksonville, Ill., 1851.

Watt, Joseph. "Recollections of Dr. John McLoughlin." *Transactions of the Fourteenth Annual Reunion of the Oregon Pioneer Association for 1886*. Portland, 1887, pp. 24–27.

Wayman, John Hudson. Journal and Letters, 1852, photocopies of MSS owned by Fred A. Rosenstock. Bancroft Library, University of California, Berkeley.

Wearin, Otha D. "Plattsmouth Ferry." *Branding Iron*, Los Angeles Westerners Corral No. 53 (June, 1960): n.p.

Webb, Todd. *The Gold Rush Trail and the Road to Oregon*. Garden City, N.Y., 1963.

Webb, W. L. "Independence, Missouri, a Century Old." *Missouri Historical Review*, 22 (Oct., 1927): 30–50.

Webb, Walter Prescott. *The Great Plains*. Boston, 1931.

Webster, Kimball. *The Gold Seekers of '49*. Manchester, N.H., 1917.

"The Wedding in the Gate of the Rocky Mountains." *United States Magazine, and Democratic Review*, 24 (Feb., 1849): 123–28.

Weisel, George F., ed. "Dodson's Death: The Diary of John F. Dodson; His Journey from Illinois to His Death at Fort Owen in 1852." *Montana, Magazine of History*, 3 (Spring, 1953): 24–33.

Welch, John Allen. *An Overland Trip from Iowa to California in 1854*. Hutchinson, Kan., 1920.

Wells, Epaphroditus. Letters, 1849, typescripts. Bancroft Library, University of California, Berkeley.

Wells, Eugene T. "The Growth of Independence, Missouri, 1827–1850." *Bulletin of the Missouri Historical Society*, 16 (Oct., 1959): 33–46.

———. "Kirk Anderson's Trip to Utah, 1858." *Bulletin of the Missouri Historical Society*, 18 (Oct., 1961): 3–19.

Wells, Merle. "Richard Grant." In LeRoy R. Hafen, ed., *The Mountain Men and the Fur Trade of the Far West*. 10 vols. Glendale, Cal., 1965–72, 9:165–86.

Wells, William. Letters, 1849, typescripts. California Section, California State Library, Sacramento.

Westergaard, Waldemar, ed. "Diary of Dr. Thomas Flint." *Annual Publications of Historical Society of Southern California*, 12 (1923): 53–127.

Westholm, Woodrow, ed. "An Iowan in California, 1850." *Annals of Iowa*, 36 (Fall, 1962): 462–65.

Wheat, Carl I. "The Forty-Niners in Death Valley." *Historical Society of Southern California Quarterly,* 21 (Dec., 1939): 102–17.

———. "The Jayhawkers at the Missouri: A Remarkable Discovery." *Historical Society of Southern California Quarterly,* 22 (Sept., 1940): 103–8.

Wheeler, George Nelson. Diary, 1850–51, MS. Henry E. Huntington Library, San Marino, Cal.

White, Chester Lee. "Surmounting the Sierras: The Campaign for a Wagon Road." *Quarterly of the California Historical Society,* 7 (Mar., 1928): 3–19.

White, Stewart Edward. *The Forty-Niners: A Chronicle of the California Trail and El Dorado,* vol. 25 of *The Chronicles of America.* New Haven, 1921.

White, William Wellington. "An Autobiography." *Quarterly of the Society of California Pioneers,* 4 (Dec. 31, 1927): 202–16.

Whitman, Abial. Diary, 1850, MS. Beinecke Rare Book and Manuscript Library, Yale University, New Haven.

Wickman, John E. "Peter A. Sarpy." In LeRoy R. Hafen, ed., *The Mountain Men and the Fur Trade of the Far West.* 10 vols. Glendale, Cal., 1965–72, 4:283–96.

Wilkes, George. *The History of Oregon, Geographical and Political.* New York, 1845; reprinted in *Washington Historical Quarterly,* vols. 1–5.

Wilkins, Mary Barlow. "Samuel Kimbrough Barlow: A Pioneer Road Builder of Oregon." *Quarterly of the Oregon Historical Society,* 26 (Sept., 1925): 209–24.

Willard, James F. "Sidelights on the Pike's Peak Gold Rush, 1858–59." *Colorado Magazine,* 12 (Jan., 1935): 3–13.

Williams, Burton J., ed. "Overland to California in 1850: The Journal of Calvin Taylor." *Utah Historical Quarterly,* 38 (Fall, 1970): 312–49.

———, ed. "Overland to the Gold Fields of California in 1850: The Journal of Calvin Taylor." *Nebraska History,* 50 (Summer, 1969): 125–49.

Williams, James. Papers, 1850, MSS and typescripts of letters. Archives and Manuscripts Division, Ohio State Historical Society, Columbus.

Williams, Joseph. "Narrative of a Tour from the State of Indiana to the Oregon Territory in the Years 1841–2." In LeRoy R. Hafen and Ann W. Hafen, eds., *To the*

Rockies and Oregon, 1839–1842, vol. 3 of *The Far West and the Rockies Historical Series.* Glendale, Cal., 1955, pp. 199–287.

Williams, T. Harry, Richard N. Current, and Frank Freidel. *A History of the United States to 1877,* 3d ed. New York, 1969.

Williams, Velina A. "Diary of a Trip across the Plains in 1853." *Transactions of the Forty-seventh Annual Reunion of the Oregon Pioneer Association, Portland, June 19, 1919.* Portland, 1922, pp. 178–226.

Williamson, H. M. "Dr. James R. Cardwell." *Transactions of the Fifty-second Annual Reunion of the Oregon Pioneer Association; Portland, June 19, 1924.* Portland, 1927, pp. 14–15.

Willis, Edward J. Journal, 1849, MS and typescript. Beinecke Rare Book and Manuscript Library, Yale University, New Haven.

Wilmington, Ohio, *Clinton Republican,* Aug. 1, 1850–Apr. 18, 1855.

Wilson, John S. A Trip across the Plains, 1859–60 MS journal. Beinecke Rare Book and Manuscript Library, Yale University, New Haven.

Wilson, William. Letters and Day Books, 1850–51, 1853, MSS and typescripts. Beinecke Rare Book and Manuscript Library, Yale University, New Haven.

Wilson, Woodrow. *A History of the American People.* 5 vols. New York, 1902.

Windsor *Vermont Chronicle,* Jan. 4, 1843–Dec. 31, 1850.

Winther, Oscar Osburn. "The Development of Transportation in Oregon, 1843–49." *Oregon Historical Quarterly,* 40 (Dec., 1939): 315–26.

———. "From Tennessee to California in 1849: Letters of the Reeve Family of Medford, New Jersey." *Journal of the Rutgers University Library,* 11 (June, 1948): 33–84.

———. "Immigrant Trains." *RQ,* 8 (Spring, 1969): 163–73.

———, and Gayle Thornbrough, eds. *To Oregon in 1852: Letters of Dr. Thomas White, La Grange County, Indiana, Emigrant,* vol. 23 of Indiana Historical Society *Publications.* Indianapolis, 1964.

Winton, Harry N. M., ed. "William T. Newby's Diary of the Emigration of 1843." *Oregon Historical Quarterly,* 40 (Sept., 1939): 219–42.

Withers, Ethel Massie, ed. "Experiences of Lewis Bissell Dougherty on the Oregon

Trail." *Missouri Historical Review,* 24 (Apr., 1930): 359–78, (July, 1930): 550–67, 25 (Oct., 1930): 102–15, (Jan., 1931): 306–21, (Apr., 1931): 474–89.

Wolcott, Lucian McClenathan. Journal, 1850–51, MS. Henry E. Huntington Library, San Marino, Cal.

Wood, Elizabeth. "Journal of a Trip to Oregon 1851." *Quarterly of the Oregon Historical Society,* 27 (Mar., 1926): 192–203.

Wood, Joseph Warren. Diary, 1849–53, MS. Henry E. Huntington Library, San Marino, Cal.

Woods, James M. Letters, 1850. Typescript Collection, State Historical Society of Missouri, Columbia.

Wooley, Ivan M. "Mt. Hood or Bust: The Old Road." *Oregon Historical Quarterly,* 60 (Mar., 1959): 5–88.

Wooster, Ohio, *Democrat,* Jan. 5, 1843–Jan. 31, 1850.

Wright, Doris Marion. "The Making of Cosmopolitan California: An Analysis of Immigration, 1848–1870." *California Historical Society Quarterly,* 19 (Dec., 1940): 323–43; "Part II," 20 (Mar., 1941): 65–79.

Wright, Muriel H., ed. "The Journal of John Lowery Brown, of the Cherokee Nation en Route to California in 1850." *Chronicles of Oklahoma,* 12 (June, 1934): 177–213.

Wyman, Walker D. "Atchison, a Great Frontier Depot." *Kansas Historical Quarterly,* 11 (Aug., 1942): 297–308.

———. "Council Bluffs and the Westward Movement." *Iowa Journal of History,* 47 (Apr., 1949): 99–118.

———. "Omaha: Frontier Depot and Prodigy of Council Bluffs." *Nebraska History Magazine,* 17 (July-Sept., 1936): 143–55.

———. "The Outfitting Posts." *Pacific Historical Review,* 18 (Feb., 1949): 14–23.

———, ed. *California Emigrant Letters.* New York, 1952.

Young, F. G. "The Oregon Trail." *Quarterly of the Oregon Historical Society,* 1 (Dec., 1900): 339–70.

Young, Sheldon. Diary, 1849–50, typescript. Henry E. Huntington Library, San Marino, Cal.

Zenor, B. J. "By Covered Wagon to the Promised Land." *American West,* 11 (July, 1974): 30–41.

Zollinger, James Peter. *Sutter: The Man and His Empire.* New York, 1939.

Index

Abandoned persons: and emigrant cooperation, 148
Abbey, James, 166
Abbott, Henry L., 235
Abernethy, Gov. George, 341, 503
Abundancy and deficiency motivation, 434
Accidents: and danger, 409–13
Adams, Cecelia, 162, 181, 408, 413
Adams, T. M., 110
Agriculture: overlanders' contribution to, 391
"Air Line to California," 100–101
Albany (N.Y.) *Atlas,* 42
Alcohol, 147; and Indians, 166; at trading posts, 1853, 291
Alexander and Hall, 104, 105
Allen, Edward J., 351
Allen, W. R., 139, 140
Allyn, Henry, 194, 291–93, 395
Altrocchi, Julia Cooley, 16–17
America Moves West, 26
American Agriculturist, 54
American Biblical Repository, 29
American Fur Co., 110, 245, 263, 264, 476–77
The American Nation series, 24
American Pioneer Trails Association, 15
American Review, 50
American Trails series, 18
The American West: An Interpretive History, 26
American Western Frontiers, 26
Anderson, George L., xv

Andrews, Maj. George P., 221
Andrews, Thomas F., 8
Animals, draft, 107–8, 152–53, 438, 457; and emigrant cooperation, 143–45; and Indians, 182–83, 370; and traders, 1840s, 261
Applegate, Jesse, 10, 340, 392, 421, 503; "Cow Column," 5, 17, 25, 26; and new route to Oregon, 348–50
Applegate, Lindsay, 348, 349
Applegate company, 158
Applegate family, 7
Applegate party: and relief, 362
Applegate Trail, 349–50, 356, 364, 365; and Indians, 185
Arapaho Indians, 213, 223, 225, 226
Archambeault, Auguste, 297
Archambeault, R., and Co., 289
Arkansas: and gold rush, 8
Arms, Cephas, 162
Army: forts (map), 212; protection, 201–21; and information, 227; medical services of, 229–30; and justice, 231; and wintering overlanders, 231–32; 1857 march on Mormons, 303
Army Corps of Topographical Engineers, 232, 233
Ash Hollow, 8; Battle of, 209
Ashburton, Lord, 31
Ashley, William, 29
Atchison, David R., 50
Atchison, Kan., 73
Athearn, Robert G., 26

Attitudes and impressions: of overlanders, 396, 400
Augusta (Me.) *Age,* 41

Babbitt, Almon W., 216, 305, 306, 322, 472
Backpackers, 274–75
Bagley, Clarence, 407
Baker, Edward D., 51
Baker, Jim, 274
Bancroft, Herbert Howe, 23
Banks, John Edwin, 124, 134, 163, 260, 312
Baptists: mission school, 268
Barlow, Samuel K., 347
Barlow, William, 391
Barlow-Palmer party, 362
Barlow Road, 349, 350
Beard, Charles, 24–25
Beard, Mary, 24–25
Beaubien, Charles, 257
Beauvais, Geminien P., 490
Beckwith, Edward G., 235
Beckwourth, Jim, 355
"Begging papers," 170
Bell, James Christy, 12
Belshaw, George, 291
Bennett, James Gordon, 51, 147, 166
Benson, Ezra, 327, 328
Benson, John, 135, 333
Bent, William, 273
Benton, Thomas Hart, 44, 50, 65, 91, 176, 223, 232, 357
Berrien, Joseph, 150
Best Guide to the Gold Mines, 317
Bible: and emigration boosters, 46
Biddle, B. R., 208

Bidwell-Bartleson party, 24, 110, 118, 157, 245
Big Trees Road, 356
Bigler, Gov. John, 86, 375, 377
Billington, Ray Allen, 24, 25–26, 91
Bingham, Edwin R., 26
Bissonette, Joseph, 250, 279, 297, 298
"Bissonnette, Kenceleur & Co.," 290
Blacksmiths, 230, 260
Blodget, George E., 287
Blodgett and Co., 106
Blood, James, 163
Bloom, Henry, 149
Blue Bucket gold mine, 345
Boardman, John, 248, 474
Bodley, John, 377
Boggs, Lilburn W., 57
Bonney, Benjamin Franklin, 28, 31
Bonney, Wales, 126, 128, 130
Boone, Daniel, 45, 46
"Boonslick" region, Mo., 8
Boorstin, Daniel, 27
Bordeaux, James, 270, 279, 297
Boston *Daily Journal,* 45
Boston-Newton Joint Stock Company of Massachusetts, 8
Bowen, James, 154
Bowlin, James B., 48, 51
Boyce, William W., 336
Boyle, Charles, 96, 164, 166
Bradley, Henry, 285
Branch, E. Douglas, 25
Branderbury, Lemuel G., 336
Brenchley, Julius, 321, 492
Bridger, Jim, 14, 210, 245, 248–50, 252, 253; as trader, 261; and Mormons, 294; suits against, 314
Bridges: maps, 246, 258, 269; in 1851, 278–79; in 1850s, 289–91; in 1859–60, 299
Bristow, Elijah, 110
Britain: treaty of 1846, 43, 61
British: public opinion, 1840s, 31–36; in Oregon, 43; and Indians, 47
British and Foreign Review, 32
Brocchus, Perry E., 336
Brookmire, Mr. (Pa.), 107
Brooks, Elisha, 285
Brooks, Quincy Adams, 162
Brower, Arieh C., 317, 318
Brown, James, 240, 285, 286, 293, 437
Bruff, J. Goldsborough, 132, 141, 153, 305; and trading of persons, 167; on ferries,

256–57, 479; and trading, 261; on Lassen, 354; and relief, 369; and statistics, 405
Bryant, Edwin, 8, 57, 74, 127, 141, 252, 399; guidebook of, 75; and Indians, 179
Buchanan, President James, 236
"Buckeye Rovers," 8
Buffalo, 386, 454
Bulkley, Spencer, 126
Burbank, Augusta, 264
Burlington (Iowa) *Hawkeye,* 58
Burnett, Peter, 26, 53, 57, 157, 165, 392
Burns, Mr.: and Indian robbery, 181–82
Burns, Hugh, 110–11
Burns, W. P., 335
Burrel, Mary, 165, 395
Burton, Richard, 107, 298, 299
Busby, Joseph, 293, 294
Bushnell, James, 239–40
Business ethics: of outfitters, 112–14; and ferrymen, 1852, 286
Butterfield, John, 242

Cabanne, John, 247, 250
Cagwin, N. A., 274
Caine, Joseph, 317, 318, 321
Calhoun, John C., 47, 51
California: efforts to get emigrants, 339–42; route improvements, 351–56; and relief, 365–77
California gold rush. *See* Gold rush
"The California Relief Train," 377
California Star, 50, 57, 342
"California trail," 10
The California Trail . . . , 19
California Wagon Road Act, 1855, 88
Camels, 437
Camp Floyd, 210, 217
Campbell, James, 147
Canadian-Gila overland trail, 430
Cantonment Loring, 274
Cardwell, James R., 391
Carpenter, Helen, 132
Carpenter, James, 173, 288
Carson, Kit, 14, 273; and North Platte route, 272
Carson Trail, 88, 351, 369–70, 373
Case, William, 250
Cash: and overland trip, 1850s, 288–89
Catholics: mission schools of, 268

Cayuse Indians, 159, 179
Chamberlain, William, 389
Chambers' Edinburgh Journal, 32
Chandler, John H., 369
Chandless, William, 134
Channing, Edward, 24
Chapen, M. L., 130
Charlestown (Va.) Mining Co., 8
Cheesman, David, 498
Cheyenne Indians, 183, 188; and Army, 216–17; and Twiss, 225, 226
Child, Andrew, 107
Chiles, Joseph, 111, 351
Chilton, Robert H., 207, 213, 227–29
Chimney Rock, 8
Chinook Indians, 158
Cholera, 124
Chorpenning, George, 240, 242
Chouteau, Pierre, Jr., and Co., 264, 270
Christian settlers: and emigration to Oregon, 43
Christy, Thomas, 268, 275
Chronicles of America series, 24
Churchill, Stillman, 263
Cincinnati *American,* 29
Cincinnati *Atlas,* 47
Cincinnati *Chronicle,* 36, 44; and heroism, 58
Clapp, John, 153
Clark, Bennett C., 119
Clark, Dan Elbert, 25
Clark, John, 110, 132, 152, 171, 333, 408
Clark, John Hawkins, 26, 108, 179, 312
Clark, Thomas D., 25
Clayton, William, 317, 318
Clinton, Dr. Jerter, 315
Coates, James, 110
Codding, George R., 479
Cogswell, O. H., 310
Coke, Henry, 108, 153, 179
Cole, Gilbert, 284
Communities: on trails, 1854, 295
Community: and overlanders, 385, 387–89
Connecticut Mining and Trading Co., 8
Conyers, Enoch, 127, 284
Cooke, Lucy, 288
Cooke, Philip St. George, 215, 227
Coons, Frederica B., 17
Cooper, Chandler, 363
Cooperation: and overlanders, 141–49, 385, 387–89; and

Cooperation (cont.)
food, 145–48; and abandoned persons, 148
Corby, John, 278
Costs: of overland trip, 405–8
Council Bluffs: as starting point, 98; size of, 115. See also Kanesville, Iowa
Council Bluffs Weekly Bugle, 73
The Covered Wagon, 14
Covered Wagon Centennial Celebration, 422
Covered wagons: as symbol, 3; in 1850s, 107–8
"Cow Column," 17, 25, 26, 392, 419, 421
Coy, Owen C., 13
Craigie, James, 485
Cramer, Molly, 167
Cramer, Thomas, 167, 300
Cramer, William E., 55
Crane, Addison, 148, 283, 334, 396; quoted, 288
Cranston, Susan, 486
Crawford, Charles Howard, 466
Crawford, Medorum, 90
Crawford, P. V., 163, 281
Cross, Osborne, 123, 163, 170, 207
Cummins, Sarah, 158
Currey, George B., 4, 132, 179
Currey, Gov. George L., 86

Daily Missouri Republican. See St. Louis Daily Missouri Republican
Dallas, Charles, 479
Dana, Richard Henry, 92
Dangers, 408–14
Dante's Inferno, 16
Davenport (Iowa) Gazette, 66
Davis, George W., 139
Davis, Jefferson, 51
Davis, W. N., Jr., xvi
Dawson, Nicholas, 183
"A Day with the Cow Column in 1843," 5. See also "Cow Column"
Death Valley, 320, 321
Deaths: number of, 516
DeBow's Review, 66
Decker, Peter, 264
Delano, Alonzo, 133, 136, 145, 166, 182, 263, 413
Dent, Capt. F. T., 192, 221
Department of Indian Affairs, 221, 223
Derbec, Etienne, 64–65
Derby, George H., 235
Deseret News, 163, 195, 296, 307, 308, 329; and mail, 241; advertisements in, 310, 319,

321; and prices, 312; and guidebooks, 317; and Hambleton, 332
Desert myths, 55
De Smet, Father Pierre-Jean, 15, 118, 156; and Harney, 217; on Dalles City, 491
Detroit Advertiser, 41, 78
Devil's Gate, 8
DeVoto, Bernard, 5–7
Dewolf, David, 239, 389
Diaries and journals, 4–5
Dickerson, John H., 235
Digger Indians, 160, 165; and theft, 183; and massacres, 185
Disease, 380; and Indians, 395; and dangers, 408–9
Dixon (Ill.) Telegraph, 176
Dodge, A. C., 45
Dodge, Frederick, 226
Dodge, Henry, 202
Doniphan massacre, 176
Donner, George, 131
Donner, Mrs. George, 49
Donner, Tamsen, 15
Donner Cutoff, 17
Donner party, 7, 8, 17, 25, 26, 79, 80, 184, 341, 351, 354, 367; and Derbec, 65
Donner tragedy, 190, 252, 267, 319, 338, 370, 378, 420; use of by press, 49–50
Dorris, Jonathan, 9
Dougherty, Lewis B., 229
Douglass, James, 360
Doyle, Simon, 259–60; on Lassen, 354
Drago, Harry Sinclair, 16
Drake, Dr. Daniel, 92
Drips, Andrew, 270
Drownings, 410
Dryer, T. J., 83, 85–86; and massacres, 190, 192; and government, 201; on Haller, 216
Dundass, Samuel, 259
Dunlop, Richard, 17
Dunn, John, 33, 34
Dutton, Jerome, 114
Dyck, Johannes, 127

Eagar, J., 317, 318
Eastbound overlanders, 124–31; time for trip, 130; and relief, 377–78
Eastern Snake Indians. See Snake Indians
Eastham, E. L.: quoted, 10–11
Easton, Langdon C., 233
Economist, 33, 35
Edinburgh Review, 32, 35, 425
Edwards, Philip L., 118

Egan, Howard, 321
El Dorado route, 88
Ellenborough, Lord, 31
Elliot, George R., 374
Elliott, Elijah, 350–51, 364
Elliott, T. C., 11
Emigrant-Indian interaction, 156–200
Emigrant interaction, 118–55; and turn-arounds, 122–24; and eastbound overlanders, 124–31; and trail rumors, 135–37; and physicians, 137–40
Emigrant's Guide, 317
Empey, William, 286, 293
Ermatinger, Francis, 245
Estill, James M., 277
Evans, George Henry, 54
Evans, James, 133, 159, 414
Exploration: and federal government, 232–39

Faine, J. C., and Co., 104
Fairchild, Lucius, 114, 208
The Far Western Frontier . . . , 24
Faris, John T., 12
Farnham, Elijah, 163; and trading of persons, 167; and Indians, 183
Farnham, Thomas J., 39, 54, 92, 108
Farr, Aaron F., 313
Favour, John, 155
Fayette Missouri Democrat, 57
Fears: of overland journey, 28, 29–30
Federal government, 9, 201–43; aid and newspapers, 57–58; and protection from Indians, 47–48; aid and Pacific Coast press, 84–87; and military protection, 201–21; treaties with Indians, 221–27; and supplying information, 227; and exploration, 232–39; and roads, 233–39; and mail, 239–43. See also Army
Federal Writers' Project, 11
Ferguson, Charles D.: on Indians, 396
Ferries, 477, 478–79, 490; of the forty-niners, 8; maps, 246, 258, 269; 1840–49, 247; in 1840s, 252–60; and Mormons, 253–54, 257–59, 273, 274, 285, 286–87, 289–90, 293–94; 1850–60, 267–74; cost of, 1850, 274; in 1851, 278; in 1852, 284–87; chartering of, 1852, 286–87; in 1854, 295; in 1859–60,

Ferries (cont.)
299–300; fees, 1852, 488; in
1854, 491
Ferris, Benjamin, 178, 308,
336; and Mormons, 329–30
Ferris, Mrs. Benjamin, 127
Ficklin, Orlando B., 46
Firearms: and accidents,
410–13
Fish, Charles, 252
Fisher, Ezra, 42, 61
Fitzpatrick, Thomas, 110, 183,
223–24, 226; and Indians,
169
Fleming, Hugh B., 214
Flint, Thomas, 394
Florence Bridge Co., 297
Floyd, John, 28, 91
Food: and emigrant coopera-
tion, 145–48; and trading
with Indians, 165–66; at
trading posts, 1850, 275; sell-
ing of by Mormons, 306–7;
prices of, 497
Foote, Lt. Rennselaer W., 213
Ford, Nathaniel, 110
Foreign Quarterly Review, 34
Foreman, Ferris, 369
Forney, Jacob, 226
Fort Bernard, 270
Fort Bridger, 209, 245
Fort Buenaventura, 253
Fort Dalles, 208
Fort Deposit, 347
Fort Grattan, 209
Fort Hall, 165, 208, 474; and
propaganda, 339, 341
Fort John, 270
Fort Kearny, 8, 20, 98, 102,
205–6, 270
Fort Laramie, 8, 9, 12, 20, 26,
185; reconstructed emigrant
register, 1850, 122; Treaty,
1851, 198; Treaty Council,
1851, 223–24; as trading
post, 245; in 1850, 272
Fort Payne, 209
Fort Vancouver, 208, 474
The Forty-Niners, 24
Forty-Niners: The Chronicle of the
California Trail, 13
Foster, Isaac, 386
Fox, Dixon Ryan, 24
Fox Indians, 169
Francher, Charles, 336
Francis, Samuel, 165
Francl, Joseph, 188
Frans, H. B., 479
Frémont, John Charles, 15, 44,
54, 69, 248; and Benton,
223; as explorer, 232, 233;
on Fort Laramie, 474
French, 425

Frink, Margaret, 177
Frizzell, Lodisa, 132
Fruits of Mormonism . . . , 323,
324, 327, 329
Fuller, Randy, 394
Fulmer, David, 286, 293
Fur trade: end of era of, 118;
decline of, 244–45

Gage, Stephen, 284
Gaines, John P., 364
Gambling: in 1840s, 260–61; in
1853, 291
Ganard, Louis, 299
Gantt, John, 110
Garnett, Richard, 214, 291
Garrett, Augustus O., 104
Garrison, Joseph, 225
The Gathering of Zion . . . , 18
Gatton, Benjamin, 162
Gay, Lt. E., 218
Gaylord, Orange, 410
Geary, John W., 79
Geer, Elizabeth, 182, 256; and
The Dalles, 342–44
Genoa community, 297
Gentry, Meredith P., 47
Ghent, W. J., 14
Gill, William, 111
Gilliam, Cornelius, 110
Gilmore, Charles, 362
Gilmore, Matthew, 362
Gilpin, William, 69, 74
Glenn and Co., 105
Goff, David, 348
Goff, Scott, 348
Goheen, S. M. E., 105
Gold rush, 4–5, 62–64; influ-
ence of, 7–9; press coverage
of, 77–78; and military pro-
tection, 206–7
The Gold Rush Trail and the Road
to Oregon, 17
Gold rushers: letters from, 74;
character of, 77–78; motiva-
tion of, 94–97; and Indians
and smallpox, 456; ages of,
515
Goldsmith, Oliver, 147
Goodale, Tim, 273
Goodell, Rev. J. W., 323, 324,
325, 326, 327, 328, 329, 330,
334, 335, 337
Goodwin, Cardinal, 25
Goodyear, Miles, 69, 252–53,
392
Gordon, Lt. G. A., 218
Government. See Army; Federal government
Grant, George, 334
Grant, Richard, 247, 248, 250,
252, 256, 265, 281; and efforts to get emigrants, 340

Grant, Ulysses S.: quoted, 282
Grattan, Lt. John L., 214–15
Grattan massacre, 214–15
Gray, Charles, 153, 335
Gray, W. H., 118
"Great American Desert," 30,
35, 399, 409, 514
Great Britain. See Britain;
British
The Great Platte River Road, 20
Great Salt Lake Trail, 421
Great Trails of the West, 17
The Great Trek, 13
Greeley, Horace, 94, 155; and
Oregon, 36–40; and
heroism, 53
Green, Jay, 171
Greenhow, Robert, 45–46
Greenwood, Caleb, 14, 110,
187, 248, 339, 340
Gregg, Jacob R., 15
Gressley, Gene, xvi
Grier, Maj., 221
Griffin, John S., 118
Grindell, John, 407
Grover, Thomas, 254
Grow, Dr. S. L., 231
Gruwell-Derr company, 320
Guerrier, William, 290, 291,
297
Guidebooks: 1849–60, 75; by
Mormons, 317–18
Guides: employment of and
press, 57; in 1850s, 108–11
Guill, Mary, 180, 300
Gunnison, John, 235, 313, 315,
329
Guthrie, A. B., 13–14

Haas, John B., 166–67
Hafen, LeRoy R., 25
Hall, Edwin G., 112
Hall, George, 414
Hall, O. J., 132
Hall, Willard P., 50, 69
Haller, Granville O., 215–16,
225
Hambleton, M. D., 332
Hambleton, Mrs. M. D., 332
Handsaker, Samuel, 294
Hannegan, Edward A., 50
Hansford and Peacock, 101
Harlan, A. W., 181, 483
Harney, Gen. William S., 209,
215, 216–17
Harris, B. D., 336
Harris, Moses, 57, 69, 102,
348; as guide, 110; and re-
lief, 361
Hart, Albert Bushnell, 24
Hartford (Conn.) Daily Courant,
41
Hartman, Amos William, 9–10

Harvey, Thomas H., 169
Hastings, Lansford, 8, 25, 59, 93, 107, 110, 123, 160, 178, 248–50, 252, 353; and Indians, 183; and California's virtues, 340–41; on McLoughlin, 357; and costs, 406; and firearms, 412
Hastings, Loren, 129, 183
Hastings Cutoff, 16, 50, 354; and water, 149
Haun, Catherine, 162
Hawgood, John A., 26
Henderson, Paul C., 18
Henness Pass, 88
Hensley, Samuel J., 318–19
Hentz, Charles, 136
Heroism: and proponents of emigration, 50–55
Hickman, David H., 273
Hickman ferry, 483
Hickok, Wild Bill, 16
Hillyer, Edwin, 167, 333
Himes, George H., 11
Hinds, T. W., 272
Hine, Robert V., 26
Hines, Celinda E., 167
Historians: and overlanders, 3–27
History of American Life series, 24
The History of Oregon and California, 45
History of the Oregon Territory, 33
History of the Oregon Trail, Santa Fe Trail and Other Trails, 15
History of the People of the United States, 24
Hitchcock, Isaac, 252
Hixson, Jasper M., 146, 480; quoted, 399
Hockaday, John M., 242
Hoffman, Wilhelm, 117, 133
Holeman, Jacob H., 188, 193, 196, 224–25, 287, 326
Holladay, Benjamin, 310
Hollon, W. Eugene, 25
Holloway party massacre, 196–97
Holman, F. V.: quoted, 383
Holt, Thomas, 362–63
Hoover, President Herbert, 20
Hopkins, Sarah Winnemucca, 458
Hopper, Charles, 111
Horses, 108; trading of with Indians, 162–64; Indian stealing of, 181–82
Horticulture: overlanders' contribution to, 391
Hough, Emerson, 14, 24, 25
House Committee on Military Affairs, 22; report quoted, 48

Howard, Jerome, 334
Howe, Lt. Col. M. T., 178, 193, 220
Howell, Elijah, 182
Huddleston, James, 274
Hudson, Henry, 297
Hudson's Bay Co., 5, 33, 245, 301, 349; and Greeley, 40; and Indians, 47; and New York Herald, 53–54; Snake River operations, 340; and relief to overlanders, 357–60
Hudspeth, Benoni, 133, 353
Hudspeth Cutoff, 353
Huffaker, S. D., 321
Hulbert, Archer Butler, 13
Humboldt River: and massacres, 185; danger on trail, 196–97
Hunt, Jefferson, 319, 320
Hunt, Robert, 369–70
Hunt's Merchants' Magazine, 46
Huntsman's Echo, 300
Hurt, Garland, 182, 225, 226
Hutchings, James, 311
Hyde, Orson, 72, 77, 335

Illinoians: and Mormons, 334–35
Indentured servitude, 106
Independence, Mo.: as outfitting post, 68, 70–72, 98; size of, 115
Independence Expositor, 70
Independence Mission Expositor, 59
Independence Rock, 8
Independence Western Expositor, 58, 59
Indians: and overlanders, 9, 395–96; and G. R. Stewart, 19; and public opinion, 1840s, 39; and overland boosters, 46–47; and government protection from, 46–48; and Hudson's Bay Co., 47; advice on treatment of, 1850s, 75–77; and eastbound overlanders, 127–28; and roadside messages, 134; and trail rumors, 135–36; aid to emigrants, 156–60; emigrant interaction with, 156–200; as guides, 157; payment to, 157–58; and mail, 158–59; as traders, 160–67; and trading of food, 165–66; and alcohol, 166; and trading of persons, 166–67; and tribute, 167–70; and tolls, 170–73; map of depredations, 172; fictional massacres by, 175–76; and

robbery, 177, 180–84, 198; distrust of, 177; and danger, 178–80, 408; and travel discipline, 179–80; and real massacres, 184–86, 189–92; number killed by overlanders, 185; emigrant disregard for, 186–89; and federal government, 203; and Army, 213–17; treaties with, 221–27; missions for, 268; and Brigham Young, 315; and McLoughlin, 359; and draft animals, 370; and historical perspective, 386; and diseases, 395. See also White Indians; specific tribes
Ingersoll, Chester, 256; and Indians, 187
Iowa: and gold rush, 8
Iowa Capitol Recorder, 47–48
Iowa Indians: and fictional massacre, 175–76

Jackson, Andrew, 115
Jackson, Bill, 14
Jackson, David E., 29
Jarvis, Robert B., 226
Jefferson, T. H., 400
Jewett, Mendall, 373
Johansen, Dorothy O., 8; migration hypothesis of, 93–94
Johnson, J. Neely, 372, 374, 375
Johnson, John A., 136–37
Johnson, John L., 134, 170, 180
Johnson, Overton, 107, 129, 158, 186
Johnson Cutoff, 88, 355
Johnston, Col. Albert Sidney, 210, 217, 236
Johnston, William, 159, 261–62
Jones, Jane, 134
Jones, William, 295
Josselyn, Amos, 311
Journal des Débats, 64
Journal of an Exploring Tour beyond the Rocky Mountains, 29
Justice: and Army, 231; and Mormons, 313–15, 327–28

Kanesville, Iowa: as outfitting post, 68, 72–73. See also Council Bluffs
Kanesville Frontier Guardian, 65, 72–73, 74, 405; and Indians, 75–77; on gold rushers, 77–78
Kansas City, Mo., 73
Kansas State Historical Society, 11

Kearny, Col. Stephen W., 56, 69, 74, 223, 233; and military protection, 202, 203, 205
Keen, Richard, 127, 167, 283
Keil, William, 180
Keith, Jacob, 192
Keith, Joseph, 192
Kelley, Hall, 29, 30, 91, 357
Kelly, William, 162, 164, 312, 410, 412
Kerns, John T., 285
Ketcham, Rebecca: quoted, 288–89
Kickapoo Indians, 169
Kilburn, Charles L., 369
Kimball, Hiram, 241
King John: quoted, 44
Kingery, Solomon, 285
Kinkead, John H., 308–10
Kinney, Jim, 186–87
Kirk, John, 237
Knight, Amelia Stewart, 157, 288
Knox, Dr. Reuben, 104, 105, 120, 136; quoted, 139–40
Krill, Abram, 163

Lamareaux, A. L., 259, 310
Lancaster, C., 35–36
Lander, Frederick, 160, 226, 235, 236–37, 300
Landmarks (map), 212
Landmarks on the Oregon Trail, 18
Lane, Gov. Joseph, 223
Langdon, Steele and Co., 279
Langworthy, Franklin, 119, 153, 483
Lassen, Peter, 233, 353, 354, 355, 369
Lassen Cutoff, 16, 132, 353–54, 355, 356, 369, 370; and roadside messages, 133; and food shortage, 146
Latrine arrangements, 422
The Latter-Day Saints' Emigrants Guide, 317, 318
Laut, Agnes C., 12–13
Lavender, David, 18
Lea, Luke: quoted, 222, 223
Lee, Daniel, 118
Lee, Jason, 91, 118
Lee, John D., 154, 184, 305, 322, 337
Leeds *Mercury,* 35
Le Guerrier, William, 279
Lexington (Mo.) *Express,* 65
Lewis, John, 397
Lewis, Thomas, 407
Lewis and Clark, 30
Liberty, Mo., 73

Liberty *Weekly Tribune,* 66, 101
Lienhard, Heinrich: quoted, 159
Life insurance, 111, 439–40
Lincoln, Abraham, 119
Linn, Lewis F., 29, 44, 46, 357
Liquor. *See* Alcohol
Littering, 149–55, 508
Little Thunder, Chief, 215
Littleton, Micajah, 159, 405
Liverpool *Times,* 33
Livestock: and West Coast economy, 391–95, 512
Livingston, James M., 308–10
London *Exmainer,* 34
London *Morning Chronicle,* 33
London *Times,* 31, 32–33, 34, 35
Lone Tree, 8
Long, Margaret, 18
Long, Mary Jane, 158, 284
Long, Stephen H., 30
Longmire, James, 158
Lord, Isaac, 132, 137, 153, 170
Loring, William W., 206, 207, 208
Lorton, William, 112
Louisville *Courier,* 74
Louisville *Examiner:* and fictional massacre, quoted, 175–76
Louisville *Journal,* 58
Lovejoy, Mr., 183
Luelling, Eliza, 391
Luelling, Henderson, 391
Lupton, Lancaster P., 245
Lynde, Maj. Isaac, 178, 217
Lytle, Andrew, 273

McBride, John, 252, 409
McBride, W. S., 132, 162, 335–36
McCall, Ansel, 132, 156, 311; on Indians as traders, 162; and Indians, 187–88
McCollum, D. T., 103
McCowen, George, 295
McCutchen, William, 365, 367
McDiarmid, Finley, 162
McDonald, Mr., 274
McDonald, Archibald, 252
McDougal, Mr., 339
McDuffie, George, 44
McLaughlin and Middleton, 286
McLaws, Capt. L., 218
McLoughlin, Dr. John, 31, 33, 35–36, 365, 502; and relief, 357–60, 363; and Indians, 359
McKay, Thomas, 348

McKinstry, Byron, xvi, 147; on Indians, 177–78; on Indian robbery, 181; and North Platte route, 272; on traders and theft, 276
McMaster, John Bach, 24
McMillen, James, 203
McPike and Strother, 105, 106
Madison (Ind.) *Courier and Constitutional Advocate,* 56
Magraw, William M. F., 236, 241
Mail, 107, 472; and turn-arounds, 124; and eastbound overlanders, 126; and Indians, 158–59; and federal government, 239–43; service in 1850, 277; in 1852, 287–88; and Mormons, 326
Maine Farmer and Mechanic's Advocate, 38
Malheur River route, 345, 350, 364
Manchester *Guardian,* 31–32
Mann, Henry, 163, 263
Marcy, Randolph B., 107
Mardock, Robert W., 26
Marsh, John, 92
Marshall, Francis J., 269, 281
Martin, S., 72
Marysville, Cal., 355
Marysville *Daily Evening Herald,* 196; and relief, 81; and government aid, 86–88
Massachusetts: and gold rush, 8
Massacres: map, 172; mythical, 175–76, 455; real, 184–86, 189–92; by white Indians, 193–97
Mattes, Merrill, 8, 20, 379
May, Richard, 256
Mayer, Henry, 291
Maynard, David, 158
Meacham, Walter E., 15
Medical care: and Army, 229–30; and Mormons, 315
Meek, Joseph, 69, 130
Meek, Stephen H. L., 348, 353, 378; as guide, 110; and Malheur River route, 345, 350; and relief, 361
Meek, William, 391
Meeker, Ezra, 124, 285; and Oregon Trail, 20–22
Merchant's Magazine, 55
Merk, Frederick, 5
Metcalfe, Sir Charles, 31
"Methodist influence," 349
Methodists: mission schools of, 268; and relief, 360
Milk: and cooperation, 147–48
Miller, Silas, 160, 289

Milner, John T., 179
Miltimore, Nelson, 195, 196
Milwaukee *Sentinel and Herald*, 39, 326
Minto, John, 159
Miranda, Francisco, 38
Missing persons: and danger, 413
Missionaries, 118; in Oregon and relief, 360–61
Missions, 268; map, 269
Missouri: and gold rush, 8
Missouri Gazette, 28
Missouri River frontier (map), 99
Missourians: and Mormons, 334–35, 337; as overlanders, 403–5; death rate of, 515
Mitchell, D. D., 169, 223
Mofras, Eugene Duflot de, 425
Monaghan, Jay, 15
Montgomery, William, 277
Montreal *Gazette*, 33, 34
Moody, Ralph, 17
Moor, Thomas, 286, 314
Moore, Jonathan, 413
Moore, Thomas P., 169
Moores, Charles, 184
Moorman, Madison, 164, 175; and white Indians, 194
Morehead, Joseph C., 355–56
Morgan, Dale L., xvi, xviii, 4, 26, 379, 419; and gold rush, 7; and ferries, 8
"Mormon Corridor," 303
Mormon Station, 277, 281, 295
Mormon Trail, 10, 18, 72, 256; end of stations, 297
Mormon War, 1857–58, 209, 303, 313, 336, 391
Mormon Way-Bill, to the Gold Mines, 317
Mormons, 27, 69, 119; as overlanders, 18–19; and supplies, 75; and rumors, 136; and Indians, 182; and massacres, 184, 194; and military presence, 209–10; and Army, 217–18; and mail, 241, 326; and ferries, 1840s, 253–54, 257–59; as blacksmiths, 260; and ferries, 1850, 273, 274; and ferries, 1852, 285; and ferry charters, 286–87; integrity of and overlanders, 287; and ferries, 1853, 289–90; and ferry charters, 1853, 293–94; and Jim Bridger, 294; in 1855–58, 296; and overlanders, 302–37; map, 304; and collecting of debris, 305; and trading, 306–12;

prices charged by, 312; and justice, 313–15, 327–28, 497; and medical care, 315; guidebooks of, 317–18; and routes, 318–21; anti-Mormon writers, 323–24; and Winter Mormons, 323–26; and taxes, 326–27, 330; anti-emigrant rhetoric, 328–29; leaders of, 333–34; and Illinoians and Missourians, 334–35; economy of, 390; and disease, 409; and latrine arrangements, 422; and horse thieves, 460; ferries, 477, 478, 479, 480
Mosquitoes, 513
Motivation, 90–117; and public relations campaigns, 91–94; and gold rushers, 94–97
Mott, Israel, 294
"Mountain fever," 409
Mountain Meadows massacre, 184, 194, 337
Mountaineers: and route information, 261–63; as traders, 273, 274
Mounted Riflemen, 205, 206, 207–8, 209, 213, 214
"Moving Mirror of the Overland Trail," 96
Mules, 108
Munger, Asahel, 118
Munkres, Robert L., 9
Mussett, Rev. Alvin, 315
Myers, John J., 133, 353

Nesmith, James, 349, 389
The New American Nation series, 24
New Genesee Farmer, 55
New Jersey: and gold rush, 8
New Orleans *Daily Picayune*, 46, 55; and Donner tragedy, 49; and guides, 57; and gold rush, 66
New Orleans *Weekly Bulletin*, 46
New York *American*, 39
New York *Aurora*, 38
New York *Daily Times*, 336
New York *Daily Tribune*, 36–40; and Donner tragedy, 49; and heroism, 53; in 1850s, 64; and gold rush, 66
New York *Evening Mirror*, 45
New York *Gazette*, 58–59
New York *Herald*: and Donner tragedy, 49; and heroism, 51–53; in 1850's, 64; and railroad to Oregon, 428
New York *Journal of Commerce*, 41

New York *Morning News*, 55
Newark Overland Co., 8
Newby, William, 179
Newell, Robert, 110
Newport (R.I.) *Herald of the Times*, 41
Newspapers: in New York and emigration, 51–55; southern and heroism, 55–56; western and heroism, 56; and advice to overlanders, 74–77; coverage of gold rush, 78
Newton, Jotham, 140, 291
Niles, John M., 44
Niles' National Register, 50
Nixon, O. W., 140
Noble, Dr. J., 132
Noble Pass, 88
Nobles, William H., 356
Nobles Cutoff, 356
North American Review, 41, 66
Norton, L. A., 171–73
Norton, Maria, 209
Notre Dame University: and gold rush, 97
Nusbaumer, Louis, 157

Ogden, Edmund A., 233
Ogee, Louis, 257
Ogle, Charles H., 210
Ohio: and gold rush, 8
The Old California Trail..., 16–17
Old Oregon Trail, 15
The Old Trails West, 17
Olney, Nathan, 215
Olney, Nathaniel, 225; ferry, 286
On the Trail of the Pioneers, 12
Opening a Highway to the Pacific, 1838–1846, 12
Oregon: migration of 1843, 5; and Greeley, 36–40; arguments for emigration to, 1840s, 42–45; movement to and other U.S. western movements, 45; and 1852 relief movements, 81–83; and overlanders and Indian guides, 157; Indian wars in, 210; efforts to get emigrants, 339–42; routes and The Dalles, 342–44; route improvements, 344–51; and relief, 360–65
Oregon Argus, 176
Oregon Pioneer Association, 4, 10, 11, 184, 382, 385, 389
Oregon Provisional Emigration Society, 43, 91
Oregon Spectator, 57, 81, 363
Oregon Trail, 9, 10; Memorial Association, 20; and Meeker, 20–22; in 1852, 282

The Oregon Trail (Federal Writers' Project), 11
The Oregon Trail (Long), 18
The Oregon Trail (Parkman), 12
The Oregon Trail and Some of Its Blazers (Rucker), 13
Oregonian, and Indian's Advocate, 43, 92
Ormsby, Maj. William M., 220
Orvis, Andrew, 147, 412
Otter–Van Orman massacre, 184, 190–92, 221
Outfitting posts, 97–100, 111–17; in 1850s, 68–73; and business ethics, 112–14; size of towns, 115
Overland emigration: as cooperative experience, 27; arguments against, 1840s, 41; arguments for, 1840s, 42–45; those against, 1849–60, 64–66
Overland in 1846, 419
The Overland Trail (Laut), 12
The Overland Trail (Monaghan), 15
Overlanders: and historians, 3–27; categories of writings about, 4; and typical years, 4; and Indians, 9; and 1850s, 15–16; and heroism, 50; advice to 1850s, 74–77; and public relations campaigns, 91–94; and emigrant interaction, 118–55; number of, 1840–48, 119; number of, 1849–60, 120; and roadside messages, 133; and cooperation, 141–49; and littering, 149–55; aid from Indians, 156–60; distrust of Indians, 177; lack of concern for Indian danger, 178–80; and separating from companions, 183; number killed by Indians, 185; disregard for Indians, 186–89; reaction to army presence, 208; and private entrepreneurs, 1840–49, 244–66; and private entrepreneurs, 1850–60, 267–301; as merchants, 1850, 277–78; and Mormons, 302–37; West Coast assistance to, 338–78; and Hudson's Bay Co., 357–60; relief to, 357–78; and relief in Oregon, 360–65; and relief in California, 365–77; in historical perspective, 379–416; and cooperation and community, 385, 387–89; and West Coast economy, 390–95; attitudes and impressions of, 396–400; and future of West, 397–400; negative appraisals by, 414–16; number of deaths, 516. *See also* Eastbound overlanders
Owen, East, 173
Owen, John, 226, 279, 459, 484
Owen, Robert Dale, 44
"Owens Trading Post," 274
The Ox Team, 22
Oxen, 107–8; price of, 114

Pacific Coast press: and gold rush, 79; and government aid, 84–87
Pacific Mail Steamship Co., 471
Pacific Railroad Surveys, 233
Pacific Wagon Road Expedition, 160
Pacific Wagon Road Office, 232
Paden, Irene D., 16
Page, Henry, 164, 181, 239
Pageot, Alphonse Joseph Yves, 425
Paiute Indians, 156, 157, 458; war, 210
Palmer, Joel, 111, 129, 225, 340; and Indian horses, 164; and Indians, 179; on prices, 250; quoted, 339; and Oregon routes, 347
Panama route, 56, 66–68, 402
Papin, Joseph, 247
Papin, Louis, 247
Papin ferry, 252, 257, 475, 478
Paris (steamship), 396
Parkenham, Richard, 51
Parker, Samuel, 29, 118
Parkman, Francis, 7, 15, 26, 127; *The Oregon Trail*, 12; on emigrant-trader interaction, 250–51
Parkville, Mo., 73
Parrish, Edward, 476; and Indians, 179
The Passing of the Frontier, 24
Paul, Rodman, xvi
"Pawnee" (pseud.), 410–12
Pawnee Indians, 169, 207; and tolls, 171, 173; and robbery, 183–84; and massacres, 185; and Ogle, 210; and Chilton, 213; and Army, 214; 1848 treaty, 223
Paxson, Frederic L., 25
Payette, François, 248
Payne, Bob, 414
Payne, James, 108, 162, 181, 232
Pengra, Charlotte, 143
Peoples, John H., 369
Peoria party, 92
Perkins, Elisha, 96, 153, 260, 437; on cooperation, 387
Perry, Charles A., 105–6
Perry, Elias H., 106
Persinger, James B., 120
Phelps, William Wines, 313
Philadelphia *Ledger*, 47
Philadelphia *National Gazette*, 29
Philly, James, 277–78
Physicians, 446–47; and emigrant cooperation, 137–40; Army, 229–30
Pike, Zebulon, 30
Pike's Peak region, 119
Pilcher, Joshua, 29
Pilgrim's Progress, 16–17
Pioneer Line, 102, 105, 153; deaths on, 436
Piper, Alexander, 220–21
Platt, Philip L., 107, 178, 231
Poinsett, Joel R., 202
Polk, President James, 32, 47, 48, 94; and military protection, 202, 205
Pollock, James, 44
Polygamy, 326, 334, 336, 500
Pomeroy, Earl, xvi
Pomeroy company, 321
Pomroy, Horace, 407
Pony Express, 298
Porter, Rufus, 100–101
Portland *Weekly Oregonian*, 85, 217, 323, 324, 351; and relief, 81; and Ward massacre, 190; and federal government, 201
Post sutlers, 264
Potawatomi Indians, 260, 268
Powell, Ludwell E., 205
Powers, Mary, 179
"Prairie post offices," 132
Prairie Schooner Detours, 16
Pratt, Parley P., 318, 337
Pratt, Philip L., 323
Pratte, Bernard, 247, 250
Presbyterians: missions to Indians, 268, 269; and relief, 360–61
Preuss, Charles, 233, 248
Price, Joseph, 120
Price ranges at trading posts, 1841–48, 251; 1849, 265; 1850, 276; 1851, 1853–60, 290; 1852, 283
Pritchard, James, 4–5, 164
Private entrepreneurs: 1840–49, 244–66; in 1849, 264–65; 1850–60, 267–301; and stagecoaching, 298
Public opinion: 1840–48, 28–61; 1849–60, 62–89

Public relations campaigns, 91–94
Pyramid Lake Indian War, 210, 218–20, 237

Quakers: mission schools, 268

Radnor (Winter Mormon), 333
Ragtown, 277, 296, 374
Railroads, 400
Rains, Gen., 375
Ralston, Judge James A., 374
Rawling, Gerald, 9
Raymond, R. S., 287
Reading, Pierson, 167; and Indians, 179
Reed, James, 252, 367
Reed, Virginia, 179, 354
Reese, Enoch, 281
Reese, John, 281, 294
Reeside, John E., 241
Reid, Bernard J., 96–97, 102–3, 148, 260, 385–86
Relief: movement, 1850s, 79–83; to overlanders, 357–78; and California, 365–77; and eastbound emigrants, 377–78
Religion: and Winter Mormons, 325–26
Reminiscences, 4
Remy, Jules, 321, 492
Reynolds, Maj., 218
Reynolds, J. W. B., 232
Reynolds, John, 46
Rhodes, James Ford, 23–24
Richard, John, 250, 270, 285, 297, 299–300; and bridges, 278–79, 290, 291
Richards, Willard, 307
Richardson, Caroline, 175
Richmond, Robert W., 9, 26
Ridge, Martin, 26
Riegel, Robert E., 26
Riker, John: quoted, 287
Rise of American Civilization, 24–25
Rister, Carl Coke, 25
The Road to Oregon . . . , 14
Roads: and federal government, 233–39
Roads to Empire . . . , 16
"Roadside telegraph," 131–34
Robbery: and eastbound overlanders, 127; and Indians, 177, 180–84, 198; and white Indians, 194
Roberts, Benjamin S., 206
Robidoux: family, 256, 263–64, 270, 277; trading post, 260
Robinson, Lewis, 297
Rogers, Cornelius, 118

Roosevelt, President Theodore, 22
Root, George, 8
Root, John, 147
Root, Riley, 256
Ross, John E., 364
Rothwell, William, 406–7; quoted, 100; on outfitters, 112; and white Indians, 193
Routes, 400–402; to California and newspapers, 1850s, 66–68; and roadside messages, 133; information and traders, 1840s, 261–63; and Mormons, 318–21; improvements (maps), 238, 343
Royce, Sarah, 170
Rucker, Maj. D. H., 368, 370, 372
Rucker, Maude Applegate, 13
Ruff, Capt. Charles F., 206, 207
Rumors, trail: and emigrant interaction, 135–37; and route changes, 136
Rusk, Thomas S., 412
Russell, Majors and Waddell's Central Overland California and Pike's Peak Express Co., 242
Russell's Pony Express, 242
Ryan, Elisha, 291

Sac Indians, 169
Sacramento: as overland terminus, 87
Sacramento Placer Times, 81
Sacramento Transcript, 80, 81
Sacramento Union, 84
St. Joseph, Mo.: as outfitting post, 68–69; as starting point, 98, 100; size of, 115
St. Joseph Adventure, 70
St. Joseph Gazette, 69, 290, 310; and protection from Indians, 47; and Donner tragedy, 49; and heroism, 56, 57; and guides, 57; and gold rush, 62–64; in 1850s, 65; and Panama route, 67; and Weston, 73
St. Louis Beacon, 29
St. Louis Daily Missouri Republican, 41–42, 47, 57, 75, 77, 103, 104, 107, 405; and Donner tragedy, 49; and heroism, 56, 58, 61; and gold rush, 67; and trains, 101; and massacres, 175; and backpackers, 274–75
St. Louis Daily Union, 57, 65, 69
St. Louis Inquirer, 29
St. Louis New Era, 59

Salt Lake City Deseret News. See Deseret News
Salt Lake Cutoff, 318
Salt Lake Valley, 119
San Francisco Daily Alta California, 334, 377; on gold rushers, 78; and relief movement, 79–81; on relief, 1852, 83; and government action, 84; and Mormons, 330; and California-Oregon rivalry, 342
San Francisco Daily Herald: on gold rushers, 78; and relief, 81
Sanderson, Winslow F., 206, 207, 213, 272
Sands and Howes, 437
Sanford, Mary, 377
Santa Fe expedition, 38
Sawyer, Lorenzo, 146–47, 403
Sawyer, Mrs. Francis H., 282, 285
Schlesinger, Arthur M., 24
Schoekendick, W., 128
Schouler, James, 23
Scientific American, 100
Scott, Felix, 364
Scott, Levi, 348, 349, 350
Scroggins, Thomas D., 240
Sea routes, 401–2
Searls, Niles: quoted, 260–61
Semple, James, 50
Seymour, E. Sanford, 75
Sharp, Robert, 164, 282
Shaw, D. A., 170
Shaw, Reuben, 148, 159
Shawnee Indians, 268
Shell Creek: and tolls, 171
Shepard, Cyrus, 118
Shepherd, J. S., 112
Shepherd train, 195
Sherwood, Henry G., 313
Shields, James, 120
Shively, J. M., 111, 157, 160, 357, 475
Shortess, Robert, 362
Shoshoni Indians, 157, 160, 225, 226
Shotwell, James, 412
Shumway, Charles, 257
Simonson, Maj. John S., 206
Simpson, James H., 220, 237–39
Sims, Leonard H., 48
Sioux Indians, 157; as traders, 162, 164; and alcohol, 166; and tribute, 169; and Hastings, 183; and massacres, 185; and Battle of Ash Hollow, 209; and Army, 214–16; and Fitzpatrick, 223; and Twiss, 225, 226

Skinner, Hugh, 120, 145, 157, 378, 439–40
Slater, Nelson, 107, 178, 323, 324, 325, 326, 327, 328, 329, 330, 334, 335, 337
Slogans, 389–90
Smallpox, 456
Smith, Bensley and Co., 370
Smith, Capt. A. J., 221
Smith, Caleb B., 48
Smith, I. B., 364
Smith, Jedediah S., 29
Smith, John: and costs, 407–8
Smith, Joseph, 336
Smith, O. K., 320
Smith, "Peg-leg," 248, 264, 389
Smith, Persifer F., 368
Snake Indians, 179; as traders, 162, 163, 164; murder of, 187
Snake River: and massacres, 185
Snelling, W. J., 29–30, 38
Snodgrass, R. H. P., 282
Snooks family, 56
Snow, William, 313
Snyder, Jacob, 406, 410
Society of California Pioneers, 385, 389, 510
Soda Springs, 8
Soldiers: and ferries, 1850, 272
Sonora Trail, 355–56
South Pass route, 18, 48, 68, 87, 96, 119; and Frémont, 44; and New York Tribune, 66
Southern Quarterly Review, 56
Spalding, Eliza, 118
Spalding, Henry H., 118, 357
Spanish Trail route, 67
Spectator, 34, 35
Spence, Clark C., 26
Spencer, John C., 202
Springfield (Ill.) Journal, 59
Stackpole, William, 112
Stagecoaches, 107, 298
Stansbury, Howard F., 150, 233, 313, 329
Stanton, C. T., 365
Starkweather, David A., 45
Starvation, 39
Steamboats, 491; as ferries, 256, 285
Steck, Amos, 162–63
Steckmesser, Kent L., 26
Steele, John, 386
Steen, Maj. E., 221
Stegner, Wallace, 18
Steptoe, Edward J., 214, 235
Stevens, Charles, 165
Stevens, Isaac I., 225
Stevens-Murphy party, 17, 110, 156, 351, 365
Stewart, George R., 19, 20, 189

Stewart, Joseph, 220
Stewart, Peter G., 362
Stock speculation, 377; in 1850, 275–76; in 1851, 281; in 1852, 282, 284; in 1853, 289, 291–93
Stock trading, 260–61
Stockton, Cal., 356
Stockton, Robert F., 69
Stout, Hosea, 105, 313, 315, 332; quoted, 335
Strong, Curtis C.: quoted, 383
Stuart, Benjamin, 363
Suberr, Lorenzo, 196
Sublette, Andrew, 110
Sublette, William L., 20, 29, 474
Sublette route, 274
Sumner, Edwin V., 213, 216–17
Sutter, John, 92, 317, 339, 340, 351; and relief, 365–67, 368
Sybille, Adams and Co., 245

Tappan, Henry, 115
Taxes: and Mormons, 326–27, 330
Taylor, Calvin, 152, 308, 334
Taylor, John, 335
Taylor, S. H., 181, 288
Taylor, Zachary, 134
Thomas, Wind-Wagon, 100
Thomasson, A. H., 164
Thompson, Mr. (Kan.), 100
Thompson, Mr. (Mormon), 325
Thompson, Jacob, 44
Thompson, James, 44
Thompson, John, 336
Thompson, John A. "Snow-shoe," 241
Thomson, Origen, 163
Thoreau, Henry David, 90
Thornton, Jessy Quinn, 91, 112, 203–5, 348, 349, 410
Tice, John R., 180
Tiffany, P. C., 261
Time: average for overland journey, 403
Tinker, Charles, 261
"To the Oregon Emigrants," 341
Toley (Shawnee Indian), 252
Tolles, James, 259, 305
Tolls: and Indians, 170–73; in 1852, 286; in 1853, 291
Tompkins, E. A., 13, 407
Tooly, James, 197
Topic, 35
Tracy, F. B., 43
Traders: and theft, 276
Trading: with Indians, 160–67; of persons, 166–67; forts, 244–45; and Mormons, 306–12

Trading posts, 492; maps, 246, 258, 269; 1840–49, 248–52, 264–65; in 1850, 269, 270, 275–77; in 1851, 279–81, 290; in 1852, 281–83; 1853–60, 290; 1855–58, 296–97
Trail(s): and historians, 4, 10–13; books, 10–22; conges-tion, 120–22
Trail guides. See Guides
Trail to Oregon, 17
Trains, passenger: in 1850s, 101–6
Transportation: and American experience, xv; experiments, 100–108
Travel discipline: and Indians, 179–80
"Traveling community," 387–90
Travels in the Great Western Prairies, 39
Tribute: Indian demand for, 167–70
Tucker, Stephen S., 208
Tule Lake massacre, 185, 189
Turn-arounds, 122–24
Turnbull, Thomas, 154, 196
Turner, Frederick Jackson, 421
Turner and Allen, 101–4
Tutt, John S., 229
Tutt and Dougherty, 289
Twiss, Thomas, 225, 297; quoted, 222
Twiss, Travers, 35
Two Years before the Mast, 92
Tyler, President John, 48; and military protection, 202
"Typical-year" approach, 4, 379–81

Udell, John, 330
Uniontown, 260
United States. See Army; Fed-eral government
United States Magazine, and Democratic Review, 44–45; and Donner tragedy, 50; and gold rush, 64
Utah: Expedition, 209, 217–18; Indians, 235
Ute Indians: and Mormons, 294

Van Orman, Abigail, 192
Van Orman, Reuben, 192
Van Vliet, Stewart, 230
Vasquez, Louis, 245, 252, 294; as trader, 261; suits against, 314
Vaughan, Dr. J. M., 330, 336
Vaughan, William, 111

Vavasour, Mervin, 359
Vermont Chronicle, 41, 66

Wagons: abandoned, 153–54
Waiilatpu station, 360, 361
The Wake of the Prairie Schooner, 16
Waldo, William, 372, 373, 374, 375
Walk to California, 106–7
Walker, Courtney M., 118
Walker, Capt. Jesse, 365
Walker, Joel P., 108–10, 118, 119
Walker, Joseph, 245, 248
Walker War, 294
Walla Walla Indians, 162
Wallen, Henry D., 218, 239
Ward, Alexander, 184, 190
Ward, Anthony, 263
Ward, Barney, 321
Ward, Elijah Barney, 320
Ward, Harriet, 134, 291
Ward, Newton, 190
Ward, Mrs. Newton, 190
Ward, Seth, 279, 290, 291, 297
Ward, William, 190
Ward massacre, 85, 184, 189–90, 215, 216
Ware, Joseph, 67, 160, 412; guidebooks of, 75
Warner, Theodore F., 310
Warner, William, 235
Warre, Henry J., 359
Warren, H., 179
Washakie, Chief, 160, 225, 226
Washington *Daily National Intelligencer*, 29, 50, 55, 485
Washington *Union*, 45; and protection from Indians, 47
Washington Territory: route improvements, 351
Water wagons, 149
Watt, Joseph: quoted, 383
The Way West, 13–14
Wayman, John H., 137, 213, 407
Weather: and "typical year," 380
Webb, Todd, 17–18
Webster, Daniel, 31
Weed, Stephen H., 220
Weller, John, 87
Wells, Daniel H., 293
Wells, William, 158–59, 414

Wentworth, John, 48; quoted, 51
West: future of and overlanders, 397–400
West Coast: assistance, 338–78; economy and overlanders, 390–95
West Virginia: and gold rush, 8
Western Atlas, and Saturday Evening Gazette, 41
Western Journal, 46
Weston, Mo., 73; size of, 115
Weston *Journal*, 47
Westport–Kansas City: size of, 115
The Westward Movement, 26
Westward Vision . . ., 18
Wharton, Maj. Clifton, 202–3, 205
Wharton, Capt. Henry, 209, 213, 232, 233
What I Saw in California, 57, 74
Wheelbarrow men, 106–7
Wheeling, Clark and Co., 279
Whitcomby, Lot, 364
White, Dr. Elijah, 110, 126, 128, 247, 345
White, Stewart Edward, 24
White, Dr. Thomas, 171, 286
White Indians: map of depredations, 172; and robbery, 194; and massacres, 193–97
Whitman, Abial, 135, 400
Whitman, Dr. Marcus, 118, 419, 475, 506; as guide, 110, 248; eastbound trip of, 130; as physician, 137; and Indians, 157, 177; and white Indians, 193; and relief, 360
Whitman, Narcissa, 118, 361
Whitman massacre, 18, 69, 210, 362, 364, 507
Wiggins, John, 176
Wiggins, William, 111
Wilkes, George, 45
Wilkins, James, 96, 133, 160–62
Willamette Valley, 7
Williams, John T., 112
Williams, Joseph, 28, 31
Williams, Gen. L. A., 193
Williamson, Robert S., 235
Willis, Edward J., 145
Willis, Ira J., 317, 318
Wilson, John, 206, 300, 396
Wilson, William, 276

Wilson, Woodrow, 24
Windsor, Margaret, 390
Winter, William, 107, 129, 158, 186
Winter crossings, 130
Winter Mormons, 323–26, 499
Winthrop, Robert C., 44, 50
Wisconsin: and gold rush, 8
Wistar, Isaac, 257
Wolf Creek: and tolls, 171
Women: and historians of overlanders, 24, 25; in 1850 trains, 105; and eastbound travel, 129; as overlanders, 444
Wood, Mr. and Mrs. (Eng.), 197
Wood, Elizabeth, 157, 167
Wood, John, 123, 147, 188, 276, 372
Woodbury, Daniel P., 205
Woodson, Samuel H., 240
Woodward, Absolom, 240, 241
Wooster (Ohio) *Democrat*, 66
Working Man's Advocate, 54
Wright, Ben, 189, 364
Wyeth, Nathaniel, 474
Wyman, Walker D., 8

Yates, William, 334
"The Year of Decision," 5–7
Young, B. H., 317, 318
Young, Brigham, 128, 131, 176, 277, 302; on Indians, 188; on white Indians, 195; and Indians, 222, 225, 315; and Holeman, 224; and mail, 241; and ferries, 253–54, 287, 293; quoted, 296; and supportive settlements, 297; Express and Carrying Co., 297; plans for Mormon settlements, 303; and travelers in Salt Lake City, 306; and trade with overlanders, 306–10; and routes, 319, 321; and Vaughan murder, 332; wives of, 500
Young, F. G., 10
Young, John, 286, 293
Young, Joseph, 286, 293
Young, Phineas, 293
Young America!, 54

Zeiber, John, 159, 171

IN MEMORIAM

John D. Unruh, Jr., died on January 18, 1976, following surgery for a brain tumor. He was thirty-eight years old, and had taken his doctorate with honors the previous October. His death has saddened and impoverished all of us. The Department of History has lost one of its chief claims to graduate distinction; the world of intellect and scholarship has lost a superb researcher, writer and creative artist; the students at Bluffton College, where John had taught for over a decade, have lost a teacher of unsurpassed ability; and I have lost one of the dearest friends I have had or shall have. John was a combination of everything good. In him compassion was allied with wisdom, personal radiance with a mind of absolutely the first rank, a perfect moral sense with a perfect historical sense, humor with humanity, scholarship with social action, God with joy. It is characteristic of John that his doctoral dissertation, "The Plains Across: The Overland Emigrants and the Trans-Mississippi West, 1840–1860," has been judged by a major university press to be worthy of publication without major revision. It is sorrowful beyond expression that this book must stand as a posthumous memorial to him, rather than as the beginning of an outstanding professional career. And beyond that, at the outermost extreme of grief, lies our knowledge that we can no longer receive from him the blessings that he so generously gave, and that we—spiritually, intellectually, and morally undernourished beings that we are—so desperately need. This was a man.

University of Kansas   CLIFFORD S. GRIFFIN
Lawrence, 1976